Dr John Fahey worked at Defence Signals Directorate and served in regimental and intelligence postings in the British and Australian armies. He is an Honorary Fellow of the Department of Security Studies and Criminology at Macquarie University and the author of *Australia's First Spies*.

Praise for *Australia's First Spies*

'Based on extensive research in Australian, British and American archives … vigorous and lucid writing'
—Peter Edwards, *The Australian*

'lays bare both brilliance and the incompetence in the first 45 years of Australian intelligence'
—Tim Coyle, *The Australian Naval Institute*

'It is a meticulously researched investigation full of well-grounded assessments, but it is also a well-crafted narrative, all the more appealing because its stories and characters are real.'
—Peter Monteath, *Journal of Pacific History*

'a fascinating exploration of a largely uncharted domain of Australian history in the formative years of the first half of the twentieth century'
—John Blaxland, *Honest History*

'an important book dealing with … a remarkable story'
—Rhys Crawley, *Australian Historical Studies*

TRAITORS AND SPIES

ESPIONAGE AND CORRUPTION IN HIGH PLACES IN AUSTRALIA, 1901–50

JOHN FAHEY

ALLEN&UNWIN
SYDNEY · MELBOURNE · AUCKLAND · LONDON

To the men and women who keep Antenora full

First published in 2020

Copyright © John Fahey 2020

Allen & Unwin
83 Alexander Street
Crows Nest NSW 2065
Australia
Phone: (61 2) 8425 0100
Email: info@allenandunwin.com
Web: www.allenandunwin.com

 A catalogue record for this book is available from the National Library of Australia

ISBN 978 1 76087 770 5

Index by Garry Cousins
Set in 11/15 pt Minion by Midland Typesetters, Australia
Printed and bound in Australia by SOS Print + Media

10 9 8 7 6 5 4 3 2

 The paper in this book is FSC® certified. FSC® promotes environmentally responsible, socially beneficial and economically viable management of the world's forests.

The gates of hell are open night and day;
Smooth the descent, and easy is the way:
But to return, and view the cheerful skies,
In this the task and mighty labour lies.

Virgil, *The Aeneid*, Book 6

CONTENTS

LIST OF FIGURES

TRAITORS AND SPIES

PREFACE

Traitors and Spies is about spies and spying in Australia in the first half of
the last century, and what the actors involved got right and wrong. It is a
'warts and all' story, as all good history should endeavour to be, because there
is no point in delusion. All bad history—history that strays from what can be
derived from the available evidence—is delusion.

As a work of history, *Traitors and Spies* is written for the serious reader
but it is also a book written for the reader who likes a good yarn, and to
these I apologise for the trappings of a hidden world: the frequent notations
up the back, the list of abbreviations, the bi-graphs and tri-graphs; and the
unfamiliar terms, like HUMINT for human intelligence and CIC for counter-
intelligence corps. I hope the Abbreviations and Glossary will help with these
mysterious technicalities.

In dealing with the acronyms, some are very hard to follow, especially those
used for the KGB, or Komitet Gosudarstvennoy Bezopasnosti (Committee for
State Security).[1] This organisation has been called by a multitude of names
over the years, so for sanity's sake we will use NKGB for the civilian agency
and GRU for Russian military intelligence throughout *Traitors and Spies*.

As a history, this book deals with the reality of the time and it therefore
draws heavily upon the files and documents held within the national archives
of Australia, the United Kingdom and the United States. The value of these
files lies in their contemporaneity. They were written by busy bureaucrats
who thought their words would ever remain secret, and only read by even
busier bureaucrats across a range of agencies. This imposes a level of honesty

that is higher than in a memoir or a history, where authors have much more time to reflect upon and choose what they will say, and worry about how their words will be received. I prefer to spend my time among the faceless bureaucrats, because I know that, even though they are faceless, they are committed servants of their governments. They are real people whose story deserves to be told as truthfully as possible.

John Fahey

INTRODUCTION

SECURITY INTELLIGENCE IN AUSTRALIA, 1901–50

As well as being a history of espionage and counterespionage in Australia, this book is also a history of the long and difficult struggle to create an ethical, professional and well-managed counterespionage organisation in Australia. This may sound like a straightforward task for a government, but not for Australian governments, as we will see. The formation of such an organisation was attempted a number of times between Federation in 1901 and the formation of the Australian Security Intelligence Organisation (ASIO) in 1949. Even then, it took another two years for ASIO to rid itself of the corruption and criminality of previous years.

The formation and work of ASIO is one of the most glaring examples in Australian history of myth being portrayed as truth, and this was not a myth perpetuated by mistake. The creation of ASIO was essential if the Australian government was going to fulfil its first duty, to defend the nation and its people from external attack. By 1949 Australia had been under sustained attack from external threats since 1908 and had consistently failed to effectively address them. Rather, it chose to create organisations in which individuals and groups were left unchecked to pursue their own vendettas against those they deemed threatening. The result was the development of an extraordinary level of corruption and, as circumstantial evidence suggests,

1

fraud, deceit, illegal arrests and assaults were carried out by Australian officials against Australian citizens.

Allegations of impropriety, amateurism and partisan partiality often levelled against ASIO are true of the organisations and the people that ASIO replaced. The allegations against ASIO, once it passed its initial teething period, are no more than poorly researched partisan mythology. The problem caused by this preponderance of partisan myth is that it detracts from the true story of the real oppression and callous disregard of the law that did occur. The targets of these terrible actions were not only communists or foreigners, but Australian citizens who held what were, at the time, unpopular religious or political views.

Today, we have numerous books and articles exposing the historic injustices perpetrated against communists, socialists, trade unionists and even the Australian Labor Party (ALP). Between 1916 and 1949, there is some truth to these allegations, but many of the books and articles written fail to identify other individual Australians and groups that were systematically hounded by Australia's security services and even illegally deprived of their freedom and property by Australian governments. These individuals and groups were not communists, socialists, unionists or Labor members, but the devout and the odd. It was not the experienced, well-organised and highly competent communists who were most at risk; it was the easily identified and vulnerable who were the prey of the pre-1949 security services. That this was the case is unsurprising.

Unlike foreign intelligence work directed against foreign governments, security intelligence is far more morally and ethically problematic and thus far harder to objectively write about. The problem is that security intelligence work involves citizens spying upon fellow citizens, neighbours upon neighbours, friends upon friends, even family members upon family members. The viciousness and spite that lies under the surface of everyday social intercourse will always influence security intelligence as people try to damage one another by reporting them to the authorities. As Anna Funder's *Stasiland* and the works of Aleksandr Solzhenitsyn show, security intelligence services require careful supervision and people of the highest moral character to serve as their functionaries if they are to avoid being drawn into a sordid world of anonymous revenge and punishment. In December 1943, in his evidence at the judicial inquiry into the behaviour of Lieutenant Colonel Robert

Frederick Bird Wake—the then Director of the wartime Security Service in Queensland—one of Australia's most experienced and successful intelligence officers, Rupert Basil Michel Long, the Director of Naval Intelligence, made this clear when he testified:

> Security work is dirty work, very dirty, and it is only the very clean people who can come out of that dirt uncontaminated ... It is playing around with people's private lives ... any weakness in anybody's character in the Security Service is a thing which must not be allowed to persist ...[1]

The risk of allowing anyone with a flawed character to serve in the Security Service was that the opportunities to blackmail others were so great that, according to Long, it knocked police force members into 'a cocked hat'—their work 'was child's play compared to the opportunities a Security Officer would have'.[2] Long's concerns were well founded. His evaluation of Wake as a dangerous man, because he held a 'childlike outlook' on the need for highly principled behaviour, would prove prescient. As time went on, it became obvious that 'degeneracy brought about by his powerful position in the Security Service' was Wake's contribution to Australia's history.[3] The damage done by the childish outlook inherent in the wartime Security Service would lead to events that Paul Hasluck, the official historian who wrote the political and social volumes of the Second World War, called 'the grossest infringement of civil liberty made during the war'.[4] This was not the only infringement though, and perhaps not even, as we will see, the worst.

Yet there were good things happening too, as those working within the wartime intelligence system identified the weaknesses and dangers of security intelligence work. Men like Long and the Assistant Director of Military Intelligence, Lieutenant Colonel R.A. Little, were willing to speak out and take action to limit the freedom of the Security Service where they could. The bad news, and this is being very charitable, was that Australian governments at all levels naively left the wartime Security Service to do what it thought it should do without effective oversight. A less charitable view is that politicians of all stripes left the Security Service alone providing it harassed their opponents and those groups they opposed. Indeed, it is striking that many of the failures and crimes that the post-war organisation, ASIO, is accused of are the crimes

3

of the wartime Security Service working under both conservative and ALP governments.

Security intelligence entails watching citizens live their everyday lives in order to identify those among the community who would destroy the body politic, society and others in turn for whatever reason they have decided is worth the price. Security intelligence is the frank admission that society harbours dark forces and we cannot completely trust one another. It is a necessary sign of failure as a society that we need spies to keep us safe during the night. As such, it carries a stigma that makes it far more distasteful to the average citizen than foreign intelligence activities. There is good reason for this stigma and there is good reason for careful oversight of our security intelligence apparatus.

Despite these concerns, no mature society can secure itself without having a security intelligence system. The reality of life is that individuals, groups and nations will seek to benefit through theft and intimidation if they can get away with it. Highly focused and well-directed professional espionage is a reality we have to address today, just as it was a reality when the nation of Australia was formed in 1901. Where did this threat come from? Surprisingly it did not just come from other nation states like Germany or Russia, it also came from political activists, like Alexander Mikhailovich Zuzenko, who fled repression in Russia and arrived in Australia in 1905.[5] Following the failure of the 1905 uprising in Russia many anarchists, socialists and communists fleeing the crackdown gravitated to Australia via the sparsely populated regions of Siberia and China.

Their means of travel was often via clandestine networks of likeminded exiles expelled by Tsarist authorities. They moved east through Siberia, then crossed the border to Harbin in China or travelled from Vladivostok to Japan and from there to Australia. The reason that so many ended up in Brisbane and Queensland most likely reflected the ease with which newly arrived non-English-speaking Russians could find unskilled work in that state's workshops and cane fields. When Zuzenko arrived in Brisbane, the number of Russians there and in wider Queensland was sizeable enough for him to disappear. By 1917, the Russian population in Queensland had grown to somewhere around 5000 people.[6]

Support from the large Russian refugee community enabled activists like Zuzenko to attempt to export Russian anarchist and socialist revolution to the working masses of Australia. Much to their chagrin, they found the average Australian worker to be even less interested in such things than their apathetic British counterparts.[7] To his disdainful dismay, Zuzenko discovered Australia's workers only cared about wages and working conditions and lacked any enthusiasm for revolution. In the Russian community and among intellectuals and the free spirited, however, Zuzenko would find sufficient eager recruits.[8] Zuzenko was laying the foundations of the future Communist Party of Australia (CP-A), including the clandestine capability that would later be put to use by the Russian intelligence services (RIS) in the service of the Soviet Union.

From within the relatively large Russian communities in Brisbane and, to a lesser extent, Melbourne, Russian communist agitators like Zuzenko had a safe haven from which to agitate. Given the majority of Russians were leftist political refugees, it was logical they would adopt the new Soviet government as their own and provide a safe base for that government's intelligence, agitation and propaganda operations. Within this small community lay the expertise necessary for clandestine activity and for the open activism promoting the utopian appeal of Bolshevik communism.

This mixing of utopians and professional intelligence officers was to prove very effective in developing contacts and turning them into intelligence sources working against Australian society. The actions of these groups and networks, the support provided to them by supportive fellow travellers and the lethargic, self-satisfied societies they sought to overthrow, would in time lead to the penetration of Australian institutions, universities, government departments and political parties on a scale never before achieved by any foreign power.

All of this—the massive espionage effort of the Bolsheviks and their adherents, the small intelligence activities of foreign spies in Australia, and the illegality, abuses and failures of Australia's security intelligence system in the face of these threats—is the story of this book. As Virgil tells us, the gates to hell are always open, the path down is easy and smooth and, just as Virgil emphasises, getting back out of hell is the hard part.

CHAPTER 1

KEEPING AUSTRALIA WHITE

The need to establish an effective security intelligence system in Australia arose from the need to police the *Immigration Restriction Act 1901*, the White Australia policy, which was part of the price demanded by the protectionists and unions for supporting Federation. Following the founding of the new Commonwealth, the first federal election in March 1901 saw all contending parties support the immediate creation of an immigration restriction Act that would effectively ban all non-whites from entering the country. The White Australia policy was an essential objective of the Protectionist Party and the Australian labour movement.

The strongest opposition to White Australia came from London, where the official position was that all citizens of the Empire, regardless of colour or race, constituted a single body politic. Having permitted Australia's colonies to form a dominion under a parliamentary democracy, however, London had little effective say. It was also opposed by Japan, but on the grounds that it was an insult for Australia to include the Japanese among 'Asians'.[1]

For the first Australian government, that of Edmund Barton, the problem was not passing the *Immigration Restriction Act 1901*, it was enforcing it. The new government faced opposition from primary producers in the north of Australia, ranging from pearlers to sugar growers. It was always likely that such industries would connive to undermine the act, particularly in Queensland, where Pacific Islanders were relied upon for cheap labour on the cane fields. The legal and illegal entry of all people coming to Australia now had to be monitored, yet this was not the only problem. More difficult was how to deal with the existing non-white population of Australia. Who were they, and how could the Commonwealth authorities identify them and, if necessary, remove them?

The man charged with enforcing the Act was Edmund Barton's long-time assistant and now private secretary, Atlee Arthur Hunt. Hunt was born at Baroonda Station on the Fitzroy River, Queensland, on 7 November 1864 to local graziers, Arthur, who had come to Australia from England, and Elizabeth Sheriff Hunt from Adelaide.[2] The family later moved from Baroonda to Darling Street, Balmain, in Sydney, where Arthur Hunt established a footwear factory and from where Atlee Hunt attended Balmain Primary School and Sydney Grammar School. This history suggests that Atlee came from a hard-working, entrepreneurial and relatively successful middle-class family. In 1879, he obtained a position in the NSW Lands Department as a junior clerk and worked as a private tutor for individuals studying for university exams while he studied for the Bar.[3] On 21 March 1892, Hunt was admitted as a member of the NSW Bar.[4]

As his career progressed, Hunt was introduced to prominent lawyers, including Arthur Bruce Smith, QC, and Edmund Barton. This association led him to be selected as junior council to Smith when representing NSW railway commissioners in a case heard by Barton, who was sitting as arbitrator. Hunt became a close associate of Barton and was a strong proponent of Federation, serving as Secretary of the NSW Federal Association and General Secretary of the Federal League, the latter being the organisation that oversaw the NSW referendum on Federation.

Following the successful referenda around the country and the formation of the Commonwealth of Australia in January 1901, Hunt remained Barton's private secretary, and with the election of the minority Barton government in May of that year, he was appointed as Secretary and Permanent Head of the Department of External Affairs, later Home Affairs, within which lay the Prime Minister's Office.[5] Effectively, Atlee Hunt was the head of the nascent Australian public service and as close a confidant of the first prime minister as it was possible to be.

Despite Hunt's strong connections with Barton, he owed his appointment to External Affairs to another lawyer turned politician. The Attorney-General, Alfred Deakin, supported Hunt against the abrasive Tasmanian public servant, George Charles Steward, who had to take second best as Hunt's deputy.[6] Hunt won the position because he could work with people, something Steward could not do.

Hunt quickly got down to business. The prime consideration within the security establishment of the time was the enforcement of the provisions of the Immigration Restriction Act and its regulatory regime. The enforcement of the Act was perhaps the most important task assigned to Hunt and his department and one he took very seriously indeed.

The Immigration Restriction Act passed through its readings in Parliament and received Royal Assent on 23 December 1901, and by the time it received that assent Atlee Hunt had begun to create an intelligence system that would enable his department to more and more closely monitor and screen individuals entering Australia and to identify and validate the status of individuals already in Australia in order to remove, as the Australian electorate wished, as many as possible.

The task was a significant one. The Commonwealth census of 1901, which excluded Aboriginal inhabitants, numbered the population of Australia at 3,773,801 of which 2,908,303 were native born, 679,159 were from the United Kingdom and 25,788 from New Zealand, resulting in the Australian population being almost 96 per cent British and white.[7] As for the rest, 38,352 were Germans, 29,907 Chinese, 16,144 Scandinavian, 12,507 from the Americas (including 7448 United States citizens), 10,363 Pacific Islanders, 7637 Indian, 5678 Italian and 3593 Japanese.[8] Another 23,245 other residents were from the rest of the world, 5203 were born at sea and 7922 had not specified a place of birth.[9] Even excluding the 67,622 white Europeans from Europe and the United States, this left 69,684 Asians, Indians and individuals born at sea or who had not specified their birthplaces who had to be investigated and managed in accordance with the requirements of the Immigration Restriction Act. This required the creation of an extensive intelligence apparatus.

On top of this, Hunt had to deal with the continual movement of people to and from Australia. In 1902, the number of new immigrants was 45,501, of whom 41,751 (91.75 per cent) were British or white.[10] Of the remaining 3750, some 686 individuals who were not entering Australia under an approved

8

contractual arrangement or family reunion scheme were subjected to the dictation test, which up until 1908 was never used on any European.[11] Of this group only 33 (4.8 per cent) passed the test and were admitted to Australia. The rest were sent back to where they had come from.

Despite the best efforts of the Australian electorate and its political leadership the newly created Commonwealth could not entirely prevent the entry of non-whites into Australia. The reality was that, excluding Aboriginal Australians, Australia had a non-white immigrant population of 1.8 per cent and a significant number of these people had been born in Australia, thereby complicating matters for those desiring a purely white population. In 1902, non-whites could still enter Australia under the sponsorship of employers and as part of a family reunion scheme allowed by the Act. As a result, 3750 non-white individuals entered Australia that year, of whom 1336 were Chinese, 1176 were Pacific Islanders and 513 were Japanese. By 1907, the total number of non-whites entering Australia had dropped by 454 individuals to 3263, but compared with 1902, this represented a 55.5 per cent decline in the portion of non-white immigrants entering Australia, with this group declining from 8.16 per cent of all immigrants in 1902 to only 4.53 per cent of all immigrants in 1907.[12]

Despite the effectiveness of the Act and, most importantly for our story, its implementation by the bureaucracy, the number of Chinese immigrants to Australia increased from 1336 in 1902 to 1424 in 1907. The number of Japanese entering Australia remained remarkably consistent, with 513 entering in 1902 and 521 in 1907. The group most successfully excluded was Pacific Islanders, with a decline of 89.8 per cent from 1176 in 1902 to 121 in 1907.[13] Stopping people at ports of entry using the services of customs officials, harbour masters and other local officials was obviously effective.

It is therefore no surprise to find in the files maintained by Hunt and the Department of External Affairs numerous communications with officials at ports and harbours all around Australia and in Papua, Thursday Island and other territories administered by Australia. On top of this, there is correspondence dealing with matters relating to the application of the Act to local non-whites addressed to state police commissioners, police officers, postmasters, municipal officials and, most importantly, employers of specialised non-white labour.

The immigration restrictions placed on non-whites caused problems in those industries that needed specialised non-white labour. Right from its beginnings, the Immigration Restriction Act led to real difficulties in industries including sugar, pearling and maritime, all of which relied upon non-white labour and expertise, and their demand for skilled workers was a significant 'pull' factor in Australian businesses undermining the Act if they could get away with it.[14] In fact, one of the more aggressive of these businesses, the Wanetta Pearling Company of Thursday Island, would later work closely with Hunt in extending Australia's intelligence system overseas.[15]

The company in question was operated by Reginald (Reg) Hockings and his nephew. Hockings aggressively approached the Department of External Affairs about the problems he faced in managing his specialist Japanese pearl divers and the Indonesian and Malay crews on his luggers. From this early correspondence in 1903 a close relationship developed between Hockings and Hunt.[16] The pearling industry had been a major opponent of the Immigration Restriction Act and in 1905, objecting to the imposition of the Act, the pearlers of Thursday Island, including Hockings, departed for the Aru Islands in the Netherlands East Indies (NEI), only returning in 1908.[17]

The return of the pearling fleet saw Hockings back on Thursday Island, where he had a home, offices, store and slipway, and now he equipped the company with wireless communications between his luggers and his offices. By 1910, Hunt was actively but informally assisting Hockings in dealing with the Consulate General of His Imperial Japanese Majesty, via Mr Edward W. Foxall a Japanese linguist who worked for the Consulate, in recruiting and managing Japanese pearl divers and crews.[18] It comes as no surprise that during World War I, Hockings and two of his trusted employees, Tommy Labuan and Batcho Mingo, supported by the Wanetta Company's radio network, would become Australia's most effective human intelligence (HUMINT) organisation.[19]

The approach Hunt took in building an intelligence service is clearly shown in his pragmatic management of the relationship with the pearlers of Thursday Island and the Imperial Japanese Government. Hunt was good with people; this was the very reason that Alfred Deakin had championed him as Secretary of External Affairs over George Steward in 1901. This faculty enabled Hunt to keep people close and to turn them into long-term confidants and supporters, even when they disagreed with him or Australia.

Hunt successfully smoothed the very difficult relationship with an aggrieved Japan over the provisions of the Immigration Restriction Act.

In a 'private' letter dated 3 December 1908 to the Consul-General, translated by Edward Foxall, Hunt takes great pains to 'speak a little more freely than I could in an official communication', explaining how the Act, and specifically the rescinded section 3 allowing family reunion, operated.[20] This was a sticky subject as the rescinded section had allowed Japanese wives and children to join their husbands and fathers in Australia. Hunt knew the approach of the Consul-General asking for Japanese citizens to be exempted had not 'the slightest chance' and that this entailed a loss of face for the Japanese.[21] Hunt warns the Consul-General not to pursue the matter as the real targets of the change were the Chinese, not the Japanese. The letter further mollifies the Consul-General by emphasising there is no 'want of good feeling in Australia towards the Japanese. We admire them and want to be at peace with them and to trade with them.'[22]

This letter worked, and Hunt received a reply from Foxall dated 11 December telling him that he had read Hunt's 'exceedingly valuable' letter and had not understood the Chinese aspect of the problem and 'the much larger concessions' that would be involved if the provision was changed back.[23] Hunt had frankly and politely laid down the reality of Australia's White Australia policy, thus preventing Japanese embarrassment if a formal approach had been made and rejected.

At the same time as he was politely fending off the Japanese, Hunt was maintaining a correspondence with Australia's first foreign spy, Wilson Le Couteur, who, with the support of Barton and Hunt, had conducted Australia's first intelligence operation spying on the French and British condominium in the New Hebrides in 1901.[24] In 1906 Le Couteur was back on Jersey in the Channel Islands and involving himself in matters relating to the New Hebrides at the Colonial Office. He was also reporting open source, or publicly available information, and other intelligence on the British government's negotiations with France over the islands to the Australian government. Hunt was also obtaining information from yet another agent, Hastings D'Oyly, who was reporting secretly on the internal British government discussions he participated in at the Colonial Office in London.[25]

The personal approach that Hunt took with Le Couteur, D'Oyly, Hockings and the Japanese extended to Colonel Sir James Burns, and the many executives of his shipping company, Burns Philp and Co., and to state officials and individuals all around Australia. Hunt encountered them through the normal business of government, and maintained relationships with many of these people. They provided him with intelligence on any activities that were of interest to his department, and top of this list until 1914 was non-white immigration and the status of non-white residents.

The way in which this system developed was dictated by the realities of low budgets, few resources and no manpower. 'Doing favours' oiled the wheels of the system as it still does today. Money leaves a trail but a verbal agreement between two individuals to do something that is not overheard, and which is later done, is hard to identify, and pure gold in the world of the spy. Hunt's personal papers abound in hints of this: 'I am treating your letter as entirely unofficial'; 'I do not propose to put it in the official file'; 'I have no recollection of Mr Steel'; and 'I am giving you a letter of introduction for Mr. Whitford … at one time connected with this Department … of course his visit is entirely a private one but I should be glad if you could show him a little courtesy during his stay in Vila.'[26]

All of this was lubrication for the engine of information flows. Obtaining information sufficient to identify the race and rights of an individual to reside in Australia created a highly effective system for identifying people who could pose a threat. When war was declared in August 1914, Australia had a well-developed security system ready to focus on threats from Germans as well as non-whites.

········

During this early period the only other organisation with an interest in security intelligence was the intelligence branch of the General Staff and, later, the Australian Intelligence Corps (AIC), and even here there was a close connection with Hunt and his department.

One of the frequent reports that Hunt received from members of the public related to the actions of suspicious Japanese, a matter of some concern to many in the overtly racist environment that then existed in Australia. One such letter, written by a James Johnston on 4 June 1909, raises suspicions about the Japanese cook at the Sea Breeze Hotel at Nelson Bay in New South Wales. This letter was passed by Hunt to the Secretary of the Department of Defence who passed it to the Commandant of the AIC who ordered a clandestine investigation. This investigation was subsequently undertaken by Captain J.T. Wilson, Officer Commanding the AIC in New South Wales, who discovered that the population of Nelson Bay regarded Johnston as a 'busybody' who wrote to the authorities 'in order to damage other people'.[27] The local doctor thought Johnston was 'demented' and there the matter rested.[28]

This is one of the first occasions we find of the Australian Army investigating civil matters in Australia. Unfortunately, it would not be the last. The AIC had been formed on 5 December 1907 by Colonel William Bridges, who had taken the opportunity to establish it during the absence of Major General Charles Hoad in London.[29] Hoad was no supporter of an intelligence corps and proved a fixed enemy of the new organisation when he returned.

Hoad dismissed intelligence as something any officer could do provided he had access to a nation's budget estimates, gazettes and newspapers, and in 1909 he killed off an early attempt to form a foreign intelligence service to spy on Japan.[30] Hoad also loathed Bridges and did his best to damage Bridges' career by attacking any initiative of Bridges, including the AIC and the need for intelligence training.[31]

Bridges took a deep interest in intelligence and had personally completed two or three intelligence operations in the Pacific on behalf of the War Office in London.[32] The creation of the AIC now upset the brittle relationships among the officer corps of the new Australian Army. This was made worse by the need to deprive existing units of money and resources so the AIC could carry out its functions under its first commander, the well-connected Lieutenant Colonel J.W. McCay from Victoria.[33]

The root of the army's problems in the early 1900s lay in its formation— the expedient merging of various state militia forces. In retrospect, it would have been easier and perhaps healthier to have formed a completely new army and forced individuals serving in the now defunct state militias to apply for positions in competition with serving soldiers from the states, Britain and the rest of the Empire. This would have been more expensive and time-consuming, but it would have lessened the intense rivalry for positions and status by politically well-connected part-time militia officers. The result was that the merging of the militias into a new army led to some profound structural difficulties that would not be addressed until after 1945.

The early AIC does not appear to have been much interested in security intelligence. At the first school of instruction for AIC officers in January 1909, there was not a single presentation on security intelligence and the only mention of enemy spies in Australia occurred in an exercise presented by

McCay, describing a theoretical German invasion of Victoria in 1913, which was preceded by the destruction of the railway bridge and attached telephone lines at the Werribee River on the Melbourne to Geelong line, and at Moorabool on the Ballarat line, by explosives planted by German workers there in 1912. Strangely, McCay doesn't address the problem of how these spies were to be neutralised.[34]

Yet in 1909, the AIC was involving itself in investigating Japanese spies on the New South Wales coast, and by 1912 it was officially investigating Australian citizens and residents for the first time, at the behest of the civilian authorities. The AIC began listing the names of the owners of motor vehicles that the army might need to commandeer, and it was investigating and listing the names and details of foreign subjects living in Australia and of individuals holding wireless licences or involved with homing pigeons.[35]

· · · · · · · · ·

As war approached in 1914, the fear of espionage, Zeppelins and submarines caught hold of the public imagination in Britain and, to a lesser extent, in Australia. Germany—the most likely potential enemy—was not very good at espionage. Like many countries, Germany had left intelligence collection to the army and navy. This resulted in an intelligence effort that was narrowly focused and run by operations staffs along military lines. Germany's intelligence system was therefore inefficient, poorly tasked and poorly resourced. In Australia, the German intelligence effort comprised the occasional tour by Walter de Haas, the German Trade Commissioner in Sydney, and visits from German businessmen from time to time.[36] All of which was normal commercial activity.

The people most interested in de Haas's activities were the management of Burns Philp and Co., Australia's leading shipping and trading company in the Pacific and the commercial rival of all foreign businesses, including German businesses, in the Pacific.[37] Burns Philp no doubt passed its concerns about de Haas's trip around Australia to Hunt, in the hope that by insinuating German spying, Australian officials would limit de Haas's ability to develop German trade links in what they saw as Burns Philp's exclusive marketplace. It appears that Burns Philp was the commercial equivalent of Nelson Bay's James Johnson.

Other than providing economic and commercial intelligence—one of the accepted tasks of a trade commissioner—Walter de Haas never demonstrated any behaviour that could even remotely be called espionage. Besides, in 1915, as a trade commissioner under diplomatic cover, he was quickly interned and deported to Germany after war broke out, hardly a useful position in which to place an effective spy.

We do know that one German spy did enter Australia, in January 1911. This man was Karl Paul Gustav Hentschel, a German language teacher who had resided at Sheerness and Chatham in Kent in order to spy on the Royal Navy dockyards there on behalf of the German Navy's intelligence organisation, the Nachrichten-Abteilung. Hentschel's main problem was that, like most of the agents employed by the German military forces, he was a man capable of substantial immorality. This character flaw led him to encourage his English wife, Patricia, to have an affair with his leading agent, the Chief Gunner on HMS *Agamemnon*, George Parrott.[38] Despite his dubious morality, it appears that Hentschel wanted to escape from the world of espionage, and perhaps, to save his marriage at the same time, by migrating to Australia.

On his arrival in Australia, Hentschel appears to have liked what he found and he returned to Britain to bring out his wife and family.[39] Unfortunately for him, his travels to Australia and his letters to his wife led to his identification as a German spy when the new British Secret Service Bureau, headed by Captain Vernon Kell, opened his letters on their arrival in Britain.[40]

When Hentschel arrived back in Britain he found Kell's men waiting for him and he was taken into custody. The British did not want to arrest Hentschel for spying; they wanted to turn him into a double agent spying for them on his masters at the Nachrichten-Abteilung. A good indication that poor old Hentschel had had enough of spying was that as soon as the Secret Service Bureau let him go, he turned himself in to the police at Chatham. Unfortunately for Hentschel, Chatham's police were uninterested. He was forced to find a more sophisticated police force and he took himself off to the City of London Police at Old Jewry Station. The City of London Police accepted his admission of spying for Germany and he was arrested and charged. The subsequent court case continued the farcical character of events, when Hentschel threatened to publicly expose the Secret Service Bureau's attempts to bribe him into becoming a British spy if he was taken to trial.[41] Hentschel was released without further action but was left in no doubt about what would happen if he broke confidence again.

The only other foreign power suspected of conducting intelligence operations in Australia was of course Japan and there is ample circumstantial evidence that officers of both the Imperial Japanese Navy (IJN) and Imperial Japanese Army (IJA), supported by civilians, were conducting intelligence collection operations in Australia.

In 1909, a Naval Reserve officer, Lieutenant John Gillette Fearnley, identified the problem associated with the suspected Japanese espionage. Fearnley's assessment of this activity was quite sophisticated for the time, in that he held that Australia did not understand the context for the Japanese activity, and that it could either be just routine intelligence gathering or something more dangerous. What made Fearnley's assessment sophisticated was that he pointed out that Australia simply did not know what the Japanese were doing and why. His conclusion was that Australia needed a secret intelligence organisation to spy on Japan.[42]

The reasons for Japan's interest would remain opaque but suspicion of travelling Japanese would remain high and, even though the IJN provided the naval escorts for Australian troop convoys, there was an ever-increasing level of unsubstantiated suspicion that would eventually break up the Anglo-Japanese alliance and help alienate Japan from the West.

•••••••••

Prior to 1914, the security intelligence network created by Hunt and worked by his Department of External Affairs, later Home Affairs, was focused on identifying and removing non-white migrants or residents. This task involved identifying, monitoring and cataloguing at least 2 per cent of the entire population, if we take into account those individuals caught up in the process who would eventually be deemed 'acceptable'. Added to this work was that of the AIC; it was more focused on military intelligence, with some crossover into civilian activities driven by military need. In 1909, the two very quickly came together when Hunt, a master of co-opting other people to conduct his activities for him, was beset by resourcing issues and so passed the reports of Japanese spies at Nelson Bay to Defence for action. All of this security intelligence work was directed at foreigners and non-white residents or immigrants. Xenophobic and racist all of this may be, but anti-socialist and anti-communist it was not.

The claims that Australia's security intelligence establishment was created simply to suppress socialism or political dissenters are wrong. Political dissent was still the province of state police forces and state judicial systems and it would not become a matter of national concern until the chaos of World War I and the mismanagement of the Australian body politic in 1916 and 1917 by William Morris Hughes.

……… …… ……

Hunt's capacity resulted in him remaining in or controlling his position until 1908, when Andrew Fisher's government came to power. Concerned about the closeness of Hunt to his political opponents, Fisher moved to create a separate department in 1911–12.[43] No longer part of Home Affairs, the Prime Minister's Office was renamed the Prime Minister's Department and headed by another professional public servant, Malcolm Shepherd, who was quite understandably, more politically acceptable to the ALP and Prime Minister Fisher than Hunt, the close friend of Edmund Barton and Alfred Deakin. The fact that Hunt remained head of External Affairs suggests that Fisher retained confidence in Hunt, although not enough to keep him in charge of the Prime Minister's Department.

Hunt served successive governments equally as well as he had served the earlier ones. He was a professional public servant with an excellent record and, most importantly, experienced in enforcing the Immigration Restriction Act and running Australia's security intelligence and foreign intelligence networks.

During his extended service, Hunt served five prime ministers as private secretary and Secretary of External Affairs. After the changes of 1911, he served as Secretary of External Affairs and Home Affairs under the governments of Andrew Fisher, Joseph Cook and William Morris Hughes—eleven administrations led by seven very different personalities.[44] Eleven governments over 21 years meant an average life of under two years per government and this helped create the strong culture of ownership over national policy within the nascent Commonwealth public service.

The decision of Andrew Fisher's government to retain Atlee Hunt as Secretary of the Department of External Affairs would, within four years, prove fortuitous as Australia entered the war of 1914. Australia at war was faced with a need to quickly create an effective foreign intelligence system as well as an internal security intelligence system that would meet the needs of war. Having kept Atlee Hunt in a position from which he continued to run his intelligence system, Australia was well placed to create the intelligence networks it needed. The success of Hunt's system now needs to be considered within the context of the war, which is the subject of the next chapter.

CHAPTER 2

WAR, SECURITY, POLITICAL SUBTERFUGE AND CORRUPTION

It is ironic that the first Australian casualty in the war of 1914 was the AIC, which was disbanded and its officers posted to the newly created Australian Imperial Force (AIF), intended to serve alongside the British Army in the Middle East. Though the aim was to redeploy officers to ensure no wasted effort, organisationally it was short-sighted. The dissolution of the AIC ensured the subordination of the intelligence function to the operations staffs of the AIF and the home military forces. This meant that Australia's military was left to bumble its way along the path to developing and managing the intelligence function so necessary for effective operations. Just how ineffectually this intelligence function was carried out is clearly demonstrated by the contrast between the army's focus on reading people's mail and chasing down non-existent spy rings compared with the successes the Australian Commonwealth Naval Board (ACNB) accumulated in foreign HUMINT and signals intelligence (SIGINT) operations throughout the Pacific and Indian ocean region.

The first step towards ensuring Australia's wartime security was the passing of the *War Precautions Act 1914*, under which operations such as censorship that were implemented in Britain could be legally imposed in Australia. The provisions of the Act provided the Commonwealth with the power to try civilians by court martial if they were deemed to have obtained information for communication to the enemy, or for any purpose that jeopardised the operations of His Majesty's armed forces.[1] It also subjected civilians to court martial if they endangered the safety and security of lines of communications, including ship departures and arrivals, dockyards, railways, railway schedules, harbours or public works, or if they spread false reports designed to cause alarm.[2]

The War Precautions Act also enabled the government, through orders published by the Governor-General, to deport and intern aliens and, where deemed necessary, Australian citizens. It imposed a legal obligation on individuals to report information covered by a government order issued under the Act, such as reporting any suspicious behaviour to the police or authorities. Contravention of the Act was a criminal offence punishable by fines and prison of up to six months. By any measure, this was draconian legislation.

One of the first intelligence measures undertaken by Australia in mid-1914 was easy to implement: the reading of people's mail. The impetus for this came from the British, who had developed the plan for postal censorship by the end of 1913.[3] Australian government authorities simply copied this plan and implemented it in its entirety.[4] The objective was simple: to hinder the transmission by post of intelligence to an actual or prospective enemy and to hinder the transmission by post of instructions from that prospective enemy to its agents in Australia.[5]

Postal censorship was to begin as soon as a 'precautionary period' was established, but to minimise public anxiety at home and irritation abroad the censorship would be carried out in strict secrecy against identified individuals. With the declaration of war, a partial or complete censorship would be imposed on all mail going to specified countries. The purpose was not to stop all correspondence, not even to the enemy country, but to ensure no sensitive information was passed.[6]

Australia imposed censorship of all communications from 5.00 p.m. on 3 August 1914—the afternoon before war was officially declared—and appointed Lieutenant Colonel McCay, the ex-commander of the AIC, as the Deputy Chief Censor (Australia), on the same day.[7] The Deputy Chief Censor was based in Melbourne, then the centre of Commonwealth administration, and therefore close to the Postmaster-General's department. The Deputy Chief Censor was subordinate to the Censor in London and it was to that office, and the Australian military and naval forces, that the Deputy Censor reported. By November 1914, intelligence reports from the 1st Military District (Queensland) show that the Australian system was running smoothly and that all letters passing through Brisbane destined for countries abroad, including those going to the United Kingdom, were being opened and read.[8]

The significance of the military control of censorship was that it brought the surveillance of civilian communications into the orbit of the military bureaucracy. The danger with this was that, as we will see, once the military became involved in this single aspect of civilian intelligence collection, it provided a smooth and easy way for the military to become more and more involved in civilian life through the exercise of the security intelligence function. In Britain, this risk had been averted by keeping the actual work of censorship strictly within His Majesty's General Post Office.[9]

In Australia, the inherent risk of allowing the military to become involved in controlling civilian activity was aptly demonstrated on 28 February 1918 when Lieutenant C.A. Lempriere of Military Intelligence, accompanied by a police detective, executed a search warrant signed by the commander of the 3rd Military District, Brigadier R.E. Williams, on the Clerk-Assistant of the House of Representatives. Unsurprisingly, the Clerk-Assistant provided no assistance to these intruders on the sovereignty of the Commonwealth Parliament. This did not stop Lieutenant Lempriere and his helper. They made their way to the offices of ALP members and searched them, seizing printed pamphlets found in the room of J.H. Catts, an ALP Member of the House of Representatives.[10] If Australia's military authorities would so blatantly search the Parliament, what else had they been doing?

Aside from initiating the wartime postal and wireless censorship systems, the initial focus of the security intelligence system operating within the Royal Australian Navy (RAN), the army and External Affairs, was the arrest of all German and Austrian officers and reservists in Australia in accordance with instructions issued by the Secretary of State for the Colonies on 9 August 1914.[11] This action was not as simple as it sounded as it potentially involved the arrest of individuals aboard vessels of other nations. This was particularly problematic when the vessels were from the United States.

The problem of searching US ships was one that the Australian government was alert to and when the Admiralty issued its instructions, Hunt, hoping to avoid an argument with the Americans, responded by pointing out that the instructions would be 'contrary to custom' and suggested that having

21

enemy citizens provide a form of parole in which they promised not to fight against British forces might suffice.[12] Hunt's idea was most likely developed after the US Consul-General raised the issue of the '30 or more Germans' sailing as passengers on the American steamer *Ventura*.[13] Hunt proposed these passengers sign a written undertaking not to fight against British forces or be refused permission to leave Australia prior to their embarkation on the *Ventura*.[14] Given the lack of comment in the newspapers of the day, it is likely that the episode passed without upsetting Washington.

The irony of this affair was that detaining German nationals on neutral vessels did not cause Australia the heartache that detaining and interning German crews did. German passengers were invariably white, but the crews of their merchant vessels were not. When Australia interned the crews of seven German ships—*Germania, Stolzenfels, Turul, Prinz Sigismund, Signal, Scharzfels* and *Widenfels*—at the outbreak of war, 320 crew members were non-white. The mix was eclectic: there were 166 Indians, who were actually British subjects, 109 Chinese, who appear not to have been British subjects, 27 Malays, again British subjects, twelve Marshall Islanders, five Arabs and one Afghan.[15]

The Australian government squirmed as it faced the possibility of breaching the Immigration Restriction Act itself by bringing the non-white crewmen into internment camps in Australia. The intention was to send them straight back to their countries of origin but, as the master of the *Germania* pointed out, due to the war, neither he nor the other masters could access money to pay their wages and discharge them lawfully. The lawyers acting for the ship owners and the seamen, the wonderfully named Sly and Russell of George Street, Sydney, suggested imprisoning the non-British Chinese seamen aboard the *Germania* until the matter was finalised.[16] This enabled Sly and Russell to stall the deportation of the Chinese crewmen for two weeks until the lawyers Feez, Ruthning and Baynes of Brisbane, acting on behalf of the master and owners of the *Prinz Sigismund*, could join the fun. To top it off, the Prize Court refused to authorise the deportation of the non-white crews, who, along with the white crew members of the *Germania* and *Stolzenfels*, were now under its jurisdiction.

As if this was not complicated enough, the Chinese sailors aboard the ships had contacted the Acting Consul-General for China, who was now complaining about their food, outstanding wages and the Australian authorities' failure to return them to their home port of Hong Kong. In the end, in order to keep Australia white, the Department of External Affairs had to pay £4000 for the seamen's steamer tickets back home, proving that in 1914, even in a war where coloured imperial troops would fight and die alongside their Australian comrades, keeping Australia white came first.[17]

All of this activity fell within the purview of External Affairs and its management of the White Australia policy. The surveillance system that Hunt had put together for this purpose comprised the various offices of the Department of Trade and Customs, supported by state police forces and other official bodies. The additional threats now posed by enemy aliens and prisoners of war could not be met by this ad hoc system, as the cost of housing, feeding and caring for these detainees was well beyond the budgets of the departments and organisations involved. The only organisation with the budget to guard prisoners of war and enemy aliens was the army. As the RAN did not see this as their role, it was more than happy to pass it off onto the army.

Thus, the Australian Army became the de facto security intelligence organisation and operator of detention camps in Australia. A single camp was established at Liverpool, just outside of Sydney, and all of the internees held in the smaller state camps were concentrated there. A total of 6739 men, 84 women and 67 children were interned. Of these, approximately 1000 had come from other parts of the British Empire, such as Hong Kong, Singapore and India, and were therefore, as far as the war regulations were concerned, being held illegally by Australian military authorities.

Of the 6890 individuals interned, at the end of the war 5276 were repatriated back to Germany and Austria, 1124 were liberated back into the Australian population, 202 had died, mainly due to Spanish influenza, 58 had escaped, 50 had been declared insane and 46 Slavs and Czechs had been repatriated to Serbia to fight Austria, and 134 released.[18] Given that the 1911 census counted 32,990 German-born residents and 2774 Austrian, the 5890 individuals interned in Australia represented around 16.5 per cent of the Germans and Austrians living in Australia. In all of this activity, not one enemy spy was detected and for the very good reason that there weren't any, not even the unfortunate Walter de Haas.

Despite the enthusiasm of Military Intelligence in rounding up and imprisoning enemy aliens and the occasional non-white British citizen, they missed some enemy aliens. Among those overlooked were two Turks, Mullah Abdullah and Badsha Mohammed Gool. Unfortunately, these two decided that, as good Muslims and Turks, they should attack Australia by shooting at the Silverton Tramway train on 1 January 1915. Three people were killed and six wounded. They then killed a man at a cottage they came upon before they were both killed by police, some Indian workmen and others who were not interested in either taking them alive or in burying them.[19] No newspaper of the time drew any attention to this very real failure of Australia's security intelligence system.

········

As the incident at Silverton showed, the security intelligence system operating in Australia in 1914 was decidedly ad hoc and was to remain so until the demands of war forced the British government to extend the reach of Vernon Kell's service. The problem facing Kell's organisation was simply that the number of spies uncovered in Britain was so remarkably low that either the German spy rings were exceptionally professional, or they did not exist.

The first move to formalising Australia's security intelligence system took place on 5 August 1915 when a memorandum was sent from London asking the Australian government to select a suitable officer to communicate directly with the Central Counter Espionage Bureau (CCEB) at Adelphi Court, London.[20] Andrew Fisher mislaid this memorandum and the lack of a reply led the Secretary of State for the Colonies to send an enciphered cable to the Australian government on 26 November 1915 via the Governor-General's office. As a result, the Governor-General's Official Secretary, Major George Steward, who was responsible for decoding such cables, was alerted to the initiative and was able to insinuate himself into the world of espionage.[21] By 29 November 1915, the Australian government had, somewhat surprisingly, nominated Steward as Vernon Kell's man in Melbourne.[22]

If the selection of Steward for this position was above board, then it was a mistake. Steward was not an easy man to work for or with. Described as arrogant and bullying, he was, according to Hunt, lacking in people skills and only able to get people to work for him by 'driving' them.[23] If, however, the selection of Steward was a manoeuvre by the new prime minister, William Morris Hughes, to set up an extra-legal organisation that would spy on Hughes' behalf, then Steward was the right man for the job.

On 14 January 1916, having finally obtained a copy of the lost memorandum, Steward wrote to Hughes recommending that a circular be sent by the Commonwealth to all state governments asking them to empower Steward to communicate directly with the commissioners of police.[24] He also asked that Hughes instruct the Minister of Defence to allow Steward to communicate directly with the service intelligence sections. At the same time, Steward communicated with Kell asking for details on how the CCEB in London operated so that the organisation could be replicated in Australia.[25]

Steward controlled all communications between Australia and the CCEB, as he not only held the ciphers for the secret telegrams but also the Colonial Office bag through which all written correspondence for the CCEB was sent.[26] On 14 January 1916, Steward, still holding his appointment as the Official Secretary to the Governor-General of Australia, was formally appointed by Hughes as the Officer-in-Charge of the Commonwealth Counter Espionage Bureau (CEB) and directed to work in cooperation with the British equivalent.[27]

On the same day, a form letter was sent to all state premiers telling them of Steward's appointment and asking for their police commissioners to cooperate with the new bureau. A similar letter was sent to the Minister of Defence, Senator George Pearce, asking him to authorise the same cooperation from naval and military intelligence and to the Attorney-General asking for the cooperation of his department.[28]

It appears that Steward was champing at the bit to start his career as a spy—by 17 January 1916 he was writing to Hughes asking to be informed as soon as the permissions from ministers and premiers were received.[29]

Hunt at External Affairs received his letter detailing Steward's new position on 18 January 1916 and sent a bland reply.[30] There is no indication in the files of how happy Hunt or the Attorney-General's Department were about Steward, the Official Secretary to the Governor-General, holding the post of Officer-in-Charge of the CEB. But little or no help would be given by Commonwealth departments to the CEB. At the Attorney-General's Department, the move to appoint Steward attracted the attention of the Secretary, Sir Robert Garran, and George Knowles, his right-hand man. On 11 February Garran recommended to the Attorney-General—a role Hughes held concurrently with the position of prime minister—the establishment of an intelligence branch within the department.[31] No further action was taken on this recommendation, but Garran and Knowles were now attempting to take control of civil security intelligence themselves.

Steward's bureau upset a lot of people within the military and navy, and the departments of the Attorney-General and External Affairs. In time, Steward's abrasive and arrogant behaviour alienated others, while his bureau, which had no resources of its own, alienated state governments as their police were diverted to undertake unfunded work for the Commonwealth. This was never going to work.

The most mystifying aspect of this whole affair was the attitude of the Governor-General Sir Ronald Mungo Ferguson in allowing Steward to take the job in the first place. This question is especially relevant because the Governor-General appears to have regarded the whole thing as a rather distasteful joke. He even took to calling Steward 'Pickle the Spy' after Alastair Ruadh MacDonnell, a Scot who reputedly used the covername 'Pickle' when he spied on Bonny Prince Charlie for the British Crown.

The joke soon wore off as Steward became more and more distracted by his spying and—as Government House in Melbourne was his headquarters—more and more disreputable individuals began hanging around at all hours of the day and night.

It appears as though Ferguson may have originally thought that spying was the sort of gentleman's adventure detailed by Erskine Childers in his 1903 book *The Riddle of the Sands*.[32] The reality was very different and even more concerning to the Governor-General who now found out that Steward, under the malign influence of Prime Minister Hughes, was conducting secret investigations into the lives of members of parliament and other notables Hughes deemed his enemies.[33]

The other player in this story was, of course, the prime minister, a man whose political machinations would cause a litany of damage throughout this period of Australian history. Hughes had taken over the leadership of the ALP-led government from Andrew Fisher when Fisher resigned due to ill health. Compared to Fisher, though, Hughes held few ethical concerns about destroying his political enemies. He epitomised what we would now call the 'whatever it takes' philosophy and his management of the conscription referenda shows that he did not shy away from causing extensive social and political unrest if it served his interest.

The evidence that Hughes appointed Steward to serve Hughes rather than

Australia is circumstantial, but extensive. In a memorandum to Hughes dated 2 February 1917, a year after the bureau was supposedly founded, Steward clearly states that it was written 'in accordance with your verbal instructions', before offering what appears to be a plea for forgiveness for having passed reports to Pearce, the Minister of Defence.[34] Steward then makes it clear to Hughes that he 'understood that in future I shall look to you for direction—as was indicated when the organisation was first established'.[35] Hughes was bringing his dog to heel and he showed his displeasure by ignoring Steward's pleas for staff and resources.

'Not to be circulated' is scrawled in red pencil across the top of the first page of Steward's memorandum. Hughes presumably wrote this and then underlined in the same red pencil on Steward's covering letter that there were two copies of this memorandum. It's highly likely both copies were soon in Hughes' safekeeping.

The purpose of Steward's memorandum was to get Hughes to authorise some staff and resources for the CEB, as he was working alone and using the resources of his office as Official Secretary. In fact, his memorandum makes it clear that the CEB barely existed—consisting of Steward and a petty cash float of £100 to pay informers. This was so inadequate that Steward had paid out £120 over the twelve months, leaving him '£20 out of pocket'.[36]

All of this suggests that Hughes established Steward in the role because, as the Governor-General's Official Secretary, Steward lay outside Cabinet oversight, and this enabled his bureau to operate on Hughes' behalf free of the constraints of departmental advice from the likes of Hunt, Garran or Knowles. It also allowed Hughes to control the flow of intelligence and information to the Australian government by having Steward pass all communications to Hughes before anyone else in government saw it. It appears that Hughes established the CEB as a political tool for his own use and this established the tradition of political interference in Australian security intelligence that was to plague it until the 1950s.

As if all of this was not bad enough, later, on 12 February 1917, most likely due to prompting from the Governor-General, Steward raised the problem of the bureau's constitutionality with Hughes. While the government authorised the CEB in January 1916, the decision had not gone before the Governor-General's Executive Council for approval. There can be no doubt that the Governor-General understood the significance of this failure and that he had raised the matter with Steward, most likely because he was tired of the bureau's activities and the impact on Government House. Effectively, the CEB had no legal authority to receive or expend Commonwealth funds and no official standing to investigate or take action against citizens. It was, as Steward informed Hughes on 12 February 1917, an extra-legal entity working for Hughes and beyond the province of law as it had not been authorised by the Executive Council.[37]

Despite Steward again drawing this to Hughes' attention by sending a desperate telegram from the Warrigal Club in Sydney on 24 February, it appears that Hughes was not overly receptive to Steward's recommendations.[38]

Looking at the story of the CEB from today's vantage point, it is difficult to see how it could be described as the first security intelligence organisation in Australia. It was created as the result of a covert approach from Steward to Hughes who agreed, seemingly on the basis that it would work exclusively for Hughes. From the beginning Steward worked for Hughes and, as the Official Secretary to the Governor-General, he was outside the control of the Australian government. The bureau had no personnel and, other than the cash float of £100—a sum for which there is no provenance showing it actually came from Commonwealth funds—it had no resources. Finally, it was an illegal entity that had never been ratified by the Executive Council. To call this bureau Australia's first security intelligence agency is a stretch.

Despite all of these complications, Steward threw himself into the work, issuing Circular No. 1—1916 on 1 February 1916 to Commonwealth departments, the intelligence branches of the armed forces and, presumably, to all state police forces and governments. According to Circular No. 1, the CEB was charged 'to undertake the widest possible interchange with the British Government of confidential intelligence ... in both peace and war'.[39] As a result, and to enable this:

> the Bureau will have access to all sources of intelligence throughout the Commonwealth as to bring to common focus all the intelligence services of the country. Officers and others concerned are required to make available to the Bureau without delay particulars of any suspicious cases, which may come under their notice, of activity on the part of hostile secret service agents, or suspected enemy activities directed to the capture of British trade, and to seditious purposes.[40]

As an opening gambit, this was pretty breathtaking and it did nothing to build relationships with existing organisations, such as the ACNB and the Naval Staff, which would have bridled at the reference to enemy activity directed at the capture of British trade.

The reaction was swift. On 11 February 1916, Robert Garran, the Secretary of the Attorney-General's Department, minuted Attorney-General Hughes recommending that an intelligence branch be established within the department. This branch was to be staffed by Mr Synan, Mr F.W.E. Gabriel, Mr A.J. Furmedge and Detective Clugston of the Victoria Police, who were to be supported by a clerical assistant competent in shorthand and typing.[41] This is the first indication of an attempt to establish a security intelligence organisation within an established department. There is a marginal note in Garran's hand recommending that this minute should be raised again at the end of the month.[42] Garran's recommendations were ignored by Hughes but, as we will see, this was a battle that would continue for a long time.

Despite the machinations of Steward and Prime Minister Hughes, there were changes implemented as both the military authorities and the Attorney-General's Department under Robert Garran began to sideline Steward by creating a Commonwealth police organisation.[43] This did not mean that Steward was going to go quietly, and on 4 September 1917 he was advising Hughes, in his position of Attorney-General, that the CEB now had permanent representatives in both Brisbane and Sydney and in other capitals around Australia.[44] Given the CEB's lack of resources, it appears that Steward was relying on the voluntary work of his associates and other officials around Australia.

Within months, Steward became involved in yet another bitter dispute, this time with Commander John Latham, an Honorary (unpaid) RAN legal officer briefly attached to naval intelligence from mid-1917 to early 1918.[45] This dispute became so bitter that Steward's complaints to Hughes and numerous other worthies began to raise eyebrows. Among those Steward tried to involve was Malcolm Shepherd, the Secretary of the Prime Minister's Department. Finally, the dispute annoyed the grown-ups enough that Shepherd ordered Steward and Latham to work together, although Shepherd pointedly addressed his letter to Steward under his title as 'Official Secretary to the Governor-General' and not as the head of the CEB.[46] This was a carefully administered bureaucratic slap in the face.

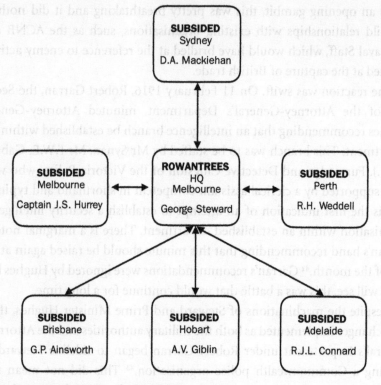

Figure 2.1: Organisation of the CEB in 1917

Note: ROWANTREES was the telegraphic address of Steward's office and SUBSIDED the telegraphic address of his organisation's representatives in each state.

Source: List of Officers, 29 November 1917, A400, 1, Commonwealth Investigation Service Historical—Miscellaneous Matters Queensland, BC65724, NAA, CP46/2, 24 Commonwealth Counter Espionage Bureau, BC246073, NAA and A432, 1955/4429, Commonwealth Police Establishment of CIS, BC1110736, NAA.

Despite the animosity that had arisen between Steward and Latham, Steward's real enemy within the RAN was the Director of the Naval Staff, Captain Walter Thring. As Director of the Naval Staff, Thring was also the effective head of naval intelligence. Thring was the real deal. He was a master of organisation and the intelligence system he had built up within the Naval Staff between May 1913, when he arrived in Australia, and the outbreak of war in August 1914, was the most extensive and efficient of Australia's intelligence organisations, but it only focused on activity on the seas and in foreign countries. Other than securing naval dockyards and protecting shipping, the ACNB intelligence system left security intelligence to Hunt and the military.

Steward's intrusion into the ACNB's business had led to the outbreak of infighting between him and Latham. Thring subsequently excluded Steward's bureau from any involvement in naval security matters, effectively banning Steward from all ports, shipyards and maritime activity, leading Steward to complain to Admiral Cresswell, the Chief of the Australian Naval Staff, who dutifully ignored Steward and left Thring to manage the Naval Staff, the Navy and Australia's maritime security.[47]

The ACNB was not alone in opposing Steward's CEB. Other organisations and individuals were hostile towards Steward, particularly Edmund Piesse, the Director of Military Intelligence (DMI), and Malcolm Shepherd at the Prime Minister's Department. Shepherd cleverly undermined Steward by diligently complaining on the CEB's behalf about the lack of support from state governments, most likely knowing that the complaints would lead to all support being cut off. This worked, and support for Steward's investigations was withdrawn in a number of jurisdictions.[48] The bureaucracy was fighting back against Steward and Hughes.

Steward even upset the Commonwealth Meteorologist, H.A. Hunt, who had lost his assistant, G.F. Ainsworth, to Steward's organisation. The correspondence on Ainsworth went from November 1915 to March 1919 as the obviously angry Commonwealth Meteorologist demanded his assistant returned from whatever work he was doing for the CEB. Unfortunately, the absent weather forecaster was lost to meteorology.[49]

The Attorney-General's Department began the process of winding back Steward's CEB and the involvement of military intelligence in civilian affairs through the establishment of the Commonwealth Police Force on 12 December 1917. John Williams, an ex-inspector of the NSW Police, was appointed commissioner of the new force of 50 personnel. The function of the new force was the enforcement of Commonwealth laws across the nation and the conducting of 'confidential enquiries independently of the State Police'.[50]

In February 1918, the Steward situation became so bad a conference was arranged at Melbourne's Victoria Barracks to work out how the Commonwealth and states would manage security matters.[51] The problem was money. The states were unwilling to continue performing functions that were the responsibility of the Commonwealth without the Commonwealth paying for their services. The states had a point, as the work caused by Commonwealth departments, including the military and the CEB, asking for support from state police had become onerous and expensive.[52]

H.B. Lefroy, the premier of Western Australia, held the view that the only proper channel of communication between his state and the Commonwealth was via prime minister to premier and vice versa; no exceptions.[53] Of course, if the Commonwealth was willing to pay Western Australia £5000 per annum, then the state, led by its premier, would be only too pleased to assist in setting up a more workable system.[54] Hunt advised William Watt, the acting prime minister, not to accept this claim.[55]

The West Australians were not alone. In 1914, New South Wales had, like other states, responded quickly to the establishment of a close working relationship between the CEB and the state police force, but the length of the war, as well as the growing cost to the budget, had dimmed patriotic fervour. By 1918, this arrangement was coming apart and James Mitchell, the Inspector-General of the NSW Police, wrote a report pointing out the vastly increasing levels of Commonwealth tasking that NSW Police now had to manage. The answer New South Wales proposed was quite simple and fair: Commonwealth bodies could task the CEB with investigations, which it could carry out itself or hand over to the state police.[56] W.A. Holman, the premier of New South Wales, supported his Inspector-General's recommendations, but the proposals were all filed away and forgotten.[57]

At this conference, the idea of a Special Intelligence Bureau (SIB), which had been floated previously, was further discussed and agreed to. The SIB was 'to be regarded as an agency which may be used, and which in all ordinary cases ... should be used, as the channel of inquiries about matters within its scope'. The problem for the SIB though was that the Secretaries of the executive departments ensured the SIB could not interfere in their affairs by insisting that, 'in exceptional cases', they could keep the matters in their own hands and away from the SIB.[58]

By 10 October 1918, the game was up for Steward and the CEB. It was his real boss, the Governor-General, Munro Ferguson, who dealt the blow. On this day, in reply to an earlier letter from the acting prime minister, William Watt, the Governor-General wrote a personal reply, saying:

it had occurred to me that you might like me to ask the Secretary of State to supply a copy of a special Cypher to be handed over to the officer whom you propose to appoint to take over the secret duties now discharged by the Official Secretary, so as to enable the former to communicate secretly and direct with the Central Bureau in London ...[59]

With Hughes away in Britain, a group of leading politicians and bureaucrats, including his deputy, William Watt, the Minister for Defence, George Pearce, Edmund Piesse of the newly created Pacific Branch, and no doubt Sir Robert Garran and George Knowles, with the apparent connivance of the Governor-General, moved to close down the CEB by having Steward replaced as Kell's representative in Australia.

The official end of the CEB occurred on 6 November 1918 when Watt authorised the closure and handing over of its functions to the Defence Department, where 'it could be most effectually carried out' under the control of Major Piesse.[60] In February 1919, Cabinet agreed that the functions of the CEB, along with those security intelligence activities undertaken by Piesse's section within the Prime Minister's Department, be transferred to the newly formed SIB within the Attorney-General's Department, something that they were sure Hughes would accept as he had always held the post of Attorney-General and this would keep the security intelligence apparatus under his personal control.[61] This new branch, the SIB, would eventually become the Commonwealth Investigation Service (CIS) before being renamed the Commonwealth Investigation Bureau (CIB).[62] The CIB was funded by the simple act of disbanding the Commonwealth Police, whose role it also took over.[63]

Hughes didn't like it and by early 1919, in accordance with the directions of the prime minister,[64] CIB staff numbers were down to ten, with two of these—one in Rockhampton and one in Brisbane—having just been given notice of termination.[65] Unsurprisingly, Williams had resigned and Major Harold Edward Jones was appointed to temporarily lead the much-diminished force.[66]

This was not the end of the matter, and behind the scenes Pearce was meeting with his colleague, Littleton Groom, Minister for Works and Railways and Vice-President of the Executive Council, and writing to Watt recommending his own man, Edmund Piesse, for the position as head of the CIB.[67]

On 12 February 1919, Steward tendered his resignation to Watt who, the very same day, dictated a letter of reply accepting the resignation while expressing 'cordial thanks' for the work, 'which was entirely novel in Australia'.[68]

Senator Pearce's recommendation of Edmund Piesse for the position of head of the CIB is odd. Edmund Piesse had been the DMI during the war and was being positioned as the head of the new Pacific Branch, effectively the Australian foreign intelligence assessment agency, an initiative close to Pearce's heart. It may be that Pearce was signalling his agreement to Watt's earlier recommendation of Piesse for the CIB job in November 1918, while keeping back his ambitions for the Pacific Branch. All of this placed Piesse, along with Pearce, Hunt and others, among the most bitter of Hughes' opponents. As Pearce makes clear in his letter to Watt, he was actively lobbying other ministers to support Piesse in the position. Among those he lobbied was Groom, who was acting in the post of Attorney-General during Hughes' absence overseas.[69]

An indication of the careful thought that was put into pushing Piesse for the position was Pearce's inclusion of a summary of Piesse's military record to provide Watt with ammunition if he had to deal with complaints from M.P. Pimentel, the Secretary of the Soldier's National Party, who was an assiduous campaigner for government jobs being kept for returned servicemen, something Piesse was not.

The planned functions of the CIB were to investigate certain non-technical matters on behalf of the army and navy, to identify and investigate passports, aliens and undesirable immigrants, to conduct inquiries for departments and deal with matters affecting the administration of Commonwealth laws.[70]

All of this toing and froing shows a real political struggle was taking place within the government for control of Australia's security intelligence system. The growth of military and naval intelligence sections during the war had been significant and so had the extent of civil matters they involved themselves in. The same had been true for the CEB, Customs and other departments, including Works and Railways. The ad hoc nature of these organisations led to them becoming involved in aspects of Australian life in which they had little business or authority. This, added to their reliance on state police forces, led to the need for the Commonwealth to address the states' complaints of carrying the cost of Commonwealth investigations into matters that seemed to be of little merit.[71]

Early in 1919, the formation of the CIB was finally justified by the need to resource the Commonwealth's security intelligence system so it could operate independently of the states. Underlying this was a desire by civilian officials to keep the military out of civilian affairs.[72] In one of these official's words:

The experience gained since the war has proved that it is desirable that matters affecting the civilian side of the Community should be dealt with by a purely civilian organisation composed of officers whose civil training specially fits them for investigating duties, whilst on the other hand, the activities of Naval and Military Officers should be limited to matters affecting the technical side of their respective branches of the service.[73]

Piesse did not get the job of heading the CIB. The machinations of Watt, Pearce and their supporters were well known to Hughes, who ensured Piesse was kept well away from the CIB. Hughes also made sure the new CIB, if not his creature, would be small and ineffective. The job of heading it went instead to Steward's old protégé Harold Jones.

Harold Edward Jones was born at Beveridge, Victoria, on 22 August 1878 to George and Margaret Jones. His father, an English immigrant from Liverpool, was a platelayer for the Victorian Railways and in 1896 Harold Jones joined the Victorian Railways engineering department. In 1904, he transferred to the Crown Solicitors Office before moving to the Federal Taxation Department in 1911.[74] Jones also served in the militia, first as a soldier in the Corps of Engineers, and then as a lieutenant in the new Australian Intelligence Corps under John Monash, the soon to be legendary Australian general, who had been the head of the Australian Intelligence Corps in Victoria prior to joining the AIF.[75]

In 1914, Jones was posted to the position of head of the Intelligence Section, General Staff, working on security intelligence within the Attorney-General's Department. From here he made his way to the post of deputy to Steward in the CEB. With Steward's demise, the job of decoding the British Security Services (known as MI5) telegrams fell to Jones, and he would hold this function until 1943. In 1919, following Steward's fall, Jones was promoted to the position of Director of the CIB, a position he held until 1 January 1944.

Jones was a conscientious and hardworking officer, if somewhat pedestrian and perhaps a little abrasive.[76] Under his leadership, the CIB did not obtain the resources it needed and it remained so bereft of money and people that it is erroneous to call it an agency independent of the states or the army, upon whose good graces it depended.[77] Jones worked well, however, with the two secretaries of the Attorney-General's Department—Garran and later, to a lesser extent, Knowles, who presided over his later career.

The new organisation headed by Jones had 45 personnel, of whom eight were inspectors.[78] Jones took up his appointment on 1 March 1919 and the Governor-General in Council approved this on 25 June 1919.[79] The budget was £10,325 of which £9005 was for salaries.[80] On 30 May 1919, Jones was appointed Director of the CIB.[81] He was also appointed as the officer to which Kell's organisation, now widely known as MI5, would entrust its ciphers and through whom it would communicate with the Australian government.[82]

Instead of creating a security intelligence organisation, the Cabinet created a mishmash organisation, with the CIB now operating within the Attorney-General's Department. It was not a central security service like MI5, but more a coordinating body intended to centralise and rationalise the activities of investigation staff in other Commonwealth departments 'so as to bring about a more efficient and economical working'.[83] How this was to happen in a bureaucracy riven by personal animosities and ambitions was left to the imagination of everyone concerned. In fact, it is safe to say that the decision of the Australian Cabinet appears to have been an attempt to satisfy British demands for a security service while ensuring the CIB was stillborn.

Of more importance to the Cabinet was the need for an organisation to investigate frauds upon the Commonwealth which, in the immediate aftermath of 1914–18 and the indiscriminate dishing out of money and other benefits to returned soldiers, had become widespread and costly. The CIB was to undertake all such investigations and, as an aside, would also take control of records created during the war relating to persons, firms and companies, including all records of aliens entering, living in or leaving Australia.[84] The Australian government had left the internal security prerogatives assumed by Military Intelligence, state police forces and other organisations, uncovered and unfunded. This left Australian security intelligence in the hands of the dilettante and, soon enough, the procedurally corrupt.

The machinations surrounding Steward and the CEB in 1918 may have been part of the reason for the subsequent falling-out between Watt and Hughes. This falling-out saw the end of Watt's political career and the submission of Pearce to Hughes' leadership. It also saw the end of Piesse's career at the Pacific Branch of the Prime Minister's Department, Pearce's creation, which was closed down by Hughes. Atlee Hunt's career in the front-line administration of the nation also ended when he was moved to the position of Public Service Arbitrator, from where he revenged himself on the politicians by limiting pay rises and making independent decisions that were not well received.

Australia's internal security intelligence entered the period of armistice following November 1918 in much the same state as it entered war in 1914. Responsibility was divided up between the intelligence organisations of the RAN and the General Staff, state police forces, Customs, Immigration, the Department of External Affairs and, after its formation on 1 November 1919, the CIB. It was not a system that would endure and, as we will see, it was most definitely not a system that could meet the threats posed by professional intelligence organisations.

CHAPTER 3

UTOPIA AND ITS AGENTS

With the end of the war in November 1918 the security intelligence authorities in Australia, such as they were, began refocusing their attention on the threat posed by socialism and, more frighteningly, Bolshevik communism. From this distance, it is easy to underestimate the fear of Bolshevism that prevailed at this time or to overemphasise the hysterical component of this fear. In 1919, the world faced the problems inherent in suddenly releasing populations from the restrictions imposed by wartime necessity. There were also employment and social challenges as returning soldiers, many of them wounded, looked for employment and tried to reintegrate into their former lives. Today, we recognise this is no easy transition and, in 1919, the numbers of soldiers returning were very large indeed.

These returning soldiers were re-entering societies, Australia's included, where division and disruption were great and radicals of all hues were trying to build a future that conformed to their vision of how a society should operate. In Russia, the government had fallen into the hands of a highly radical and repressive regime that had no hesitation in using murder and terror as political tools. In Germany, the world saw the potential expansion of the new Soviet system as radical socialists battled the forces of reaction and democracy. In Australia, Britain and the United States, labour unrest and political agitation dramatically increased as these societies released the pent-up energy of years of wartime restraint. It is little wonder that many political and bureaucratic leaders saw revolution as a daily possibility.

The violent utterances and radical plans spelt out by some groups did not help this situation, and it was the radical socialists, particularly those thought to be Bolsheviks, who attracted the most fear and thus the most attention.

In Australia, concern was mostly directed at the socialists and anarchists who had coalesced around the anti-conscription campaigns. These groups were seen by many Australians of the time as unpatriotic saboteurs rather than citizens proffering a legitimate but different point of view. The organisation that quickly came to be viewed as potentially the most dangerous was, ironically, the International Workers of the World (IWW), an American labour organisation formed in Chicago in 1905.

The IWW espoused socialist revolution using emotive language that inflamed passions and fears, and it popped up in Australia soon after it was formed. Its arrival was not welcomed by anyone, even those in the ALP and union movement who came closest to sharing its vision. After all, Australia's union movement had organised itself very effectively at a very early stage in the development of the colonies and it had even formed its own political wing in the form of the ALP. This political party, previously led by Hughes, favoured winning workers' rights at the ballot box rather than at the barricades.[1] Its response to the IWW was one of careful cooperation, which, as time passed, turned to hostility.

The IWW's numerous calls for general strikes and other revolutionary actions were not acceptable to the majority of Australians. In Australia, trouble seemed to foment itself in any industrial action where the IWW had a presence. Whether this trouble was caused by the IWW or not, it was quickly ascribed to them by everyone else, including the unions and the ALP.

For example, in 1909, strikers at Broken Hill assaulted and stoned police and intimidated many people in the streets as well as threatening businesses, and the IWW was held responsible.[2] A year later, on 8 February 1910, 500 IWW members paraded through Sydney under a red flag to protest the arrest of the leaders of a drawn-out coal strike, including one who had been taken to Goulburn Gaol in leg irons. The demonstration arrived outside the Central Criminal Court, where the cases against the arrested leaders were being heard, after having stopped off at Parliament House to groan at Premier

Charles Wade.[3] However, the NSW Police moved in, captured the red flag and arrested six men, including three wharf workers and a coal lumper, and noted the names of a number of others.[4]

From a conservative political perspective, the harsh response to the IWW agitation and demonstrations was counterproductive and the ALP, led by Fisher, defeated Alfred Deakin's protectionist and conservative government in the federal election of April 1910, and New South Wales elected its first ALP government under James McGowen, the son of a boilermaker. Despite this, the violence of the language used by the IWW and the willingness of its members to use physical threats and to fight with police ensured that the organisation and other socialist groups were seen as a rising threat.

With the outbreak of war in 1914, official concern regarding socialist agitation became more pronounced as these groups invariably undermined the arguments of the Australian government's support of the war. The idea that it was a rich man's war fought by poor men had some merit in the minds of many workers and their families. However, with the military contribution of Australia being restricted to those who volunteered to fight, the socialist position did not gain many adherents. All of this changed in 1916 due to three developments.

The first development that damaged the public's willingness to accept the government's position on the war occurred in faraway Dublin when the British military savagely suppressed the Easter Rising of Irish Nationalists, popularly called Fenians. The suppression of the rising was one thing, but the summary execution of its leaders alienated Irish opinion and nowhere more so than in Ireland, the United States and Australia. The security intelligence apparatus of Australia added Fenians to its list of subversive individuals and organisations.

The second development was the massive casualty rates produced by industrialised warfare. Humanity had never experienced slaughter of such an extent and duration as on the Western Front. Millions of men were being killed and maimed in a small corner of Europe, and Australia's volunteer force, who had already suffered 26,111 casualties, of whom 8141 were killed, in the eight months of Gallipoli, were now being fed into this meat grinder. The Australian casualties in the Battle of the Somme—23,000, of whom 6800 were killed—were truly horrendous because they were inflicted in a mere seven weeks.[5]

The third development was the Australian government's initiative to impose conscription in order to meet the butcher's bill in France, a bill that volunteerism could no longer fill. Now the socialists' catch-call that poor men would be sacrificed on the battlefield for the benefit of the rich carried real weight. The role of the socialists in organising labour unrest through the unions and their outspoken opposition to the war effort marked them out to many of their fellow Australians as being disloyal, if not treasonous. The effectiveness of the anti-conscription campaign, which resulted in the defeat of the government's efforts to introduce universal military training, fanned further the flames of suspicion.

The opposition of pacifists and socialists to the war effort in Australia was irritating to the government but, in the main, it lay within the spectrum of behaviour seen in such circles overseas. As such, it could be railed against and petty restrictions could be placed on speeches and printed material; however, the opposition was legal and thus tolerated unless it in anyway involved cooperation with the enemy.[6]

From mid-1916 to the end of the war the Australian government was in a difficult predicament. On the one hand it was faced with the political need to give all of its support to the soldiers fighting overseas and their families and friends at home while facing a nation that, despite all of the propaganda, was in no way directly threatened by the war and knew it. Perhaps this explains why the conscription referendum of 1916 was so bitterly prosecuted by the government and why, having failed once, it tried again and lost in 1917 as well.

The bitterness of the political battles over conscription contaminated Australian politics and government for the next 50 years and that included the way in which the government, particularly Prime Minister Hughes, now began to operate unconstitutionally.

The semi-truce between the Hughes-led wartime government and the working class remained more or less in place until the Bolshevik coup d'état of October 1917 in St Petersburg. This event alarmed the governments of France, Britain, the United States and their allies, including Australia, and it greatly pleased the German military, who had engineered the return of Lenin and the Bolsheviks in the expectation that they would undermine Russia's war effort. The October 1917 revolution now led to the Bolshevik dictatorship, which immediately withdrew Russia from the war, leaving Germany free to turn on Russia's Western allies. The Bolsheviks were now not only seen as illegitimate, but as an enemy. This suited Prime Minister Hughes who saw nothing wrong with personally leading soldiers to seize the *Hansard* of the Queensland Parliament from the Queensland Government Printing Office on 26 November 1917 on the grounds that speeches made by members of that parliament contained banned material under the *War Precautions Act 1914*. The privilege of a sovereign Australian parliament did not stand for much with William Hughes and neither did using Charles Steward's CEB to conduct a covert harassment of his ideological enemies, among whom the IWW and many unionists stood tall.[7] Luckily, unlike in Russia, in Australia this sort of government action was constrained and reversed by the courts.

The Bolsheviks signed the Treaty of Brest-Litovsk with Germany and the Central Powers in March 1918. This action had major ramifications through-out the world. Lenin and Trotsky avoided signing the Treaty of Brest-Litovsk themselves, but if this was intended to distance them from the action, it failed dismally. The release of the large German armies in the East and their rede-ployment for service in France was devastating for Britain and its allies, but on top of that, the Bolsheviks renounced all of Russia's international agree-ments and its substantial foreign debts, which affected Britain more than any other nation. The subsequent murder of the Romanovs in July 1918 added to the horror and presaged the even greater horrors that were to come.

The standing of socialists everywhere was tainted by these actions. Now, being a socialist was to be a supporter of a regime that had positioned itself as the sworn enemy of all non-socialist forms of government and which was collaborating in a very real sense with the German enemy. In Australia, social-ists—both local and Russian emigres—and their Bolshevik allies confronted an existing workers' party, the ALP, and a mature union movement. Austra-lian workers did not need the leadership of socialists; they were quite capable of organising and looking after their own interests.

The creation of the ALP and the union movement in Australia lacked the Marxist perspective on the importance of theory and on the need for a socialist elite to foment the struggle of the workers against the oppression of the capitalist classes. The spontaneous creation of Australia's workers' party and unions also meant that a variety of political and cultural perspectives were brought within the new structures. Foremost among these cultural perspectives was the workers' adherence to their religious viewpoints. Thus, Australian workers were more likely to be divided along the sectarian lines of Protestant and Catholic rather than along theoretical lines such as those

42

between the Menshevik, Bolshevik, Decembrist and Social Revolutionary factions.

This ensured that the Australian working-class organisations could be forceful proponents of working-class rights, wages and conditions, but they would remain socially and culturally conservative. In Australia, ideology consisted of getting better wages and conditions and improving the social standing of working families. The ideological framework of European socialists and their never-ending debates was far too theoretical and nebulous to be of much use to the practical and realistic Australian working class.

In 1918 and 1919, when socialist and Bolshevik agitators attempted to spread communism to Australia, the most resolute and violent reactionaries they encountered were working-class ex-servicemen. The returning servicemen had fought long and hard for their country and they had done so as volunteers, who had witnessed two referenda defeated by the arguments of socialists, unions and working-class leaders. Effectively, the message was that the volunteers serving in the Australian services were fools at best and class traitors at worst. It is hard to imagine a better example of how to alienate a group and convince it that there was indeed a 'them and us' in Australian society; it is unsurprising that this feeling was high among returning servicemen and the families of the fallen and maimed.

The revolution in Russia added a new level of urgency to the fears of governments towards radical socialists and anyone close to them. The success of the Bolshevik gamble was never assured and in fact seemed highly improbable. Yet, the divisions among the Russian political parties and their inability to compromise left the way open for a strongly directed, ruthless organisation to grab power, and this is exactly who Lenin and the Bolshevik faction were and what they did.

For Lenin and the Bolsheviks, the immediate objectives were peace at any price, the destruction of their internal enemies and consolidation of their position. As Kaiser Wilhelm II put it, the Bolsheviks cynically surrendered the western part of Tsarist Russia to the Germans at Brest-Litovsk and accepted the peace conditions imposed at the point of a German sword.[8] This was the action of a strong and well-directed organisation with no compunction about the impact of their actions on others. The next step was to terrorise all opponents and the entire population to reduce the willingness of individuals to support another coup d'état, this time against the Bolsheviks.

There was a delay in the plan to terrorise Russia into submission due to the unexpectedness of the Bolshevik success and the confusion and chaos of formulating and running a new government in the face of many opponents who, luckily for the Bolsheviks, could not put aside their differences long enough to destroy the new regime. This delay did not impress Lenin, although it took him until early August 1918 to begin demanding that the Bolsheviks in Penza and elsewhere organise public executions that would make the people 'tremble' for 'hundreds of kilometres around'.[9] Lenin wanted a terror and he wanted one immediately.

It was around three weeks later, on 30 August 1918, that the Bolsheviks got the excuse they wanted for imposing a regime of terror on Russia. On that day, two unconnected events occurred. In Moscow, a young Socialist Revolutionary, Fanya Kaplan, shot and seriously wounded Lenin, and in St Petersburg in an entirely unrelated attack, a Worker's Popular Socialist Party member, Leonid Kannegiser, murdered the head of the St Petersburg Cheka. Following these events, the Bolsheviks reinstated the death penalty they had abolished in October 1917 and unleashed Felix Dzerzhinsky and his Cheka (soon to be renamed the NKGB) against all the opponents of the Bolsheviks and anyone else the Bolsheviks deemed worthy of a firing squad.

Dzerzhinsky had an asset in his back pocket for such an eventuality. This was Colonel Eduard Berzin, the commander of the Latvian Regiment guarding the Kremlin, a man well placed to promote the idea of a coup d'état against the Bolshevik leadership. The operation, later called the Envoys' Plot by the Soviets, targeted the Russian opponents of the Bolsheviks and the intelligence officers of Britain and France. The plot involved a 'coat dragging' operation—an operation in which a loyal agent deliberately seeks to be recruited by an opposing intelligence organisation in order to capture their operatives. The operation involved a NKGB officer, Yan Buikis, known as Shmidkhen, convincing Sidney Reilly, a rather bizarre British Secret Intelligence Service officer, that Colonel Berzin was willing to mount a coup. Reilly then involved Robert Bruce Lockhart, a junior British diplomat, and Joseph Fernand Grénard, the French Consul-General, and all three started cultivating Berzin. This cultivation involved Reilly paying Berzin 1,200,000 roubles, money the latter immediately deposited into the NKGB's bank account.[10]

After the two unconnected attacks of 30 August, all Dzerzhinsky had to do was connect Kaplan, Kannegiser and the foreign spies represented by Reilly,

and launch a publicity blitz about counter-revolutionaries and foreign capitalist governments conspiring to bring down the regime. The Red Terror was
triggered, and Dzerzhinsky and the NKGB began the systematic murder of
everyone they thought could better serve the revolution as a corpse than as
an active citizen. The resulting terror did nothing to soothe concerns abroad.

The standing of the Bolsheviks among Western governments was also
eroded by their loud insistence on the illegitimacy of all existing forms of
government and their willingness to foster workers' revolutions in other
states. The Bolsheviks inspired and supported revolution in Finland using the
NKGB; however, anti-Bolshevik forces led by the ex-Tsarist officer General
Carl Mannerheim, with the support of German troops, very quickly killed
this socialist revolution off.[11] Berlin's tolerance only went so far.

The British Cabinet kept a close eye on reports of Bolshevik cooperation
with Germany and the spread of revolutionary fervour among the socialist groupings around the world and, most particularly, around the Empire.
Soviet Russia was now seen as hostile and enjoying extensive support from
socialists within Britain and the Empire, although—oddly—there was not
the same level of concern over the Bolsheviks and their supporters as there
was over the IWW, who were now banned in many countries around the
world, including Australia.[12]

In Britain, the first action taken was to counter Soviet propaganda using
dependable British newspaper owners. On 14 November 1918, Cabinet
decided the Foreign Office would actively collect what intelligence on the
Bolsheviks it could and pass it to the newspapers of Sir George Riddell and
Lord Burnham for publication.[13] Of course, what was published in London
was quickly picked up and re-published in Australia and the rest of the
Empire. The importance given by the British government to propaganda is
shown in the way the *Monthly Report* of the Political Intelligence Department
of the Foreign Office was distributed via the Empire Parliamentary Association to all of the individual members of colonial legislatures.[14]

The Western allies also began sending financial and logistical aid to the
anti-Bolshevik factions in Russia. In November, with the collapse of Germany,
troops could now be sent to Russia as well.

The decision to intervene in Russia faced significant challenges. First, the
anti-Bolshevik groups in Russia would not cooperate or compromise with one
another. This fatally split the anti-Bolshevik forces, resulting in an inability

to set up a responsible government that could be formally recognised on the international stage. Second, Russia was a long way from Western Europe or the United States, so sending and supplying military expeditionary forces there was going to be very difficult. Third, the people of the democratic countries that had formed the Allied powers during the war were weary—they had just finished fighting for four years and now they were faced with the possibility of another war in Russia. Given all of this, as well as the need to reduce defence expenditures, the resulting failure of the Allied expedition to Murmansk and Archangel should have been easily foreseen.

....

Britain's concern with Bolshevism was fully appreciated in Australia, where, as we have already discussed, there was a widespread dislike for the industrial disruption caused by socialist unions during the war. High-profile strikes, particularly those affecting coal, ports and shipping led to growing public and official concerns that disputes over wages and conditions were being used to disrupt the war effort.[15] These local concerns were augmented by the reports of Bolshevik activity that London was sending to Melbourne.[16]

The reaction of the Australian government towards the growing influence of socialists was to increase the surveillance of communists and socialists, their organisations and groups.[17] This initial response was somewhat restrained, with Military Intelligence, the SIB and special branches of state police forces continuing a more or less systematic surveillance of pacifists, Irish Nationalists and communists. These surveillance operations relied heavily on the censorship of mail, which was quite extensive, and only sometimes on penetration agents who attended meetings and internal discussions of the various groups.

The argument for maintaining surveillance was greatly assisted by the tendency of the various radical groups to indulge in boasting. Calling small groups of social malcontents the 'Central Executive Council' and 'Group 31'—as the IWW was prone to do—may have been impressive when winning over youthful converts to the cause and in the internecine battles between divergent interpretations of the dogma, but it also frightened security bureaucrats and their ministers.[18] It was also useful in justifying the need for the various security intelligence organisations and the jobs of the people working in them.

The major error made by the dreamers and schemers for socialist revolution was to extrapolate the likelihood of revolution in Australia from the Bolshevik coup d'état of October 1917. What they missed in that march of history was that the Bolsheviks had enjoyed a massive stroke of luck in the disorganisation of their opponents and, even then, they only survived by the skin of their teeth.

In Australia, the shenanigans of the divided, argumentative and constantly changing groups of socialist and communist revolutionaries were conducted within a society where the legal and political processes were well established, completely stable and where the art of compromise was widely understood and practised. This capacity for compromise even extended across class divides, with members of the Australian working class occupying positions of both prestige and authority. It is also notable that so many members of the working-class aristocracy, men like George Pearce, William Watt and William Morris Hughes, could so easily move from the ALP to the parties of the liberals and conservatives who opposed them.

Yet, there were socialist, communist and anarchist groups promoting Bolshevik ideology in Australia and they were strongest in Brisbane. The existence of a Russian community there containing a large number of exiled socialists escaping the Okhrana, the Tsarist secret police, meant Brisbane had a number of experienced Bolshevik agitators, and they soon took control of the Russian community's organisations and turned them towards the work of radicalising both Russian migrants and Queenslanders.

The main organisation used for this purpose was the Russian Workers Association, 'the Russian Group' led by Peter Simonoff, the self-declared representative of the Bolshevik regime,[19] and Alexander Zuzenko.[20] Given the infatuation of the Australian government with immigrants, Simonoff and Zuzenko soon attracted attention.

The authorities identified the threat posed by the Russian Workers Association through the censor intercepting and reading Simonoff's letters.[21] By August 1918, Simonoff's letters were being routinely intercepted and his intention to travel back to Russia via the Philippines and China were discovered. This information appears to have been provided to the US Consul-General in Australia, who subsequently issued a point-blank refusal to provide Simonoff with a visa to land in the Philippines in order to connect with a ship to China. His only other option was to sail via Japan, but the obliging nature of the

Japanese Consul-General frightened him off this course of action. As a result, he decided it was sensible to remain in Brisbane and continue his revolutionary work in the relative safety of that city.[22]

Simonoff was an effective publicist, speaker and writer, and made full use of these abilities in promoting the Soviet Union as a workers' paradise, and in attacking the standing of capitalism and democracy in Australia and anywhere else these things existed until his departure for Russia in June 1921.[23] Before he left, he became one of the founders of the Communist Party of Australia (CP-A), formed in October 1920.

A man who would become even more interesting than Simonoff to the authorities in Australia and Britain was his sometime associate, Alexander Mikhailovich Zuzenko. Born in Riga, Latvia, on 29 April 1884, Zuzenko spent his schooldays there before joining the merchant marine.[24] He appears to have developed a dislike of religion and a liking for socialism, anarchism and violent revolution. These interests invariably brought him the attention of the Okhrana. Around 1905, it appears that Zuzenko became a member of the Socialist Revolutionary Party Combat Organisation which conducted acts of terrorism including assassination of government officials.[25] By 1906, the situation in Russia had become too difficult for Zuzenko and he decided to sign on to a Norwegian ship and found himself in Australia.

Other than his political activism, Zuzenko seems to have settled into Australia quite well, although he found the local brand of worker to be seriously lacking in revolutionary fervour. After assuming a leadership role in the Russian community and agitating among his workmates, little is known about him until he began his career as a clandestine agent of the Communist International (Comintern), the front organisation founded by Lenin on 2 March 1919 to bring Communist parties from around the world under Bolshevik control. It is also likely that he was recruited as an NKGB agent around this time. This is unsurprising as we know Zuzenko was a close associate of Yakov Peters, Deputy Chief of the NKGB under Dzerzhinsky, and, later, Leonid Mikhailovich Zakovsky, also known as Štubis, a senior Main Directorate of State Security (NKVD) officer (Commissar 1st Class of State Security).[26]

The available evidence suggests Zuzenko first entered Australia somewhere between early 1904 and late 1911, with the later date being the more likely. How Zuzenko got into Australia is unknown, but it is assumed he arrived as part of a ship's crew and simply deserted, as there is no indication in the files of his entry. Given that Zuzenko was a qualified and experienced seaman, the idea that he slipped into Australia from a ship is plausible. The absence of any file dealing with his jumping ship is not surprising as Australian authorities took action only where the ship's deserter was not European. Where the deserter was European, as in the case of R. Jensen who deserted the SS *Gulf of Bothnia* in May 1903, no action was taken because the 'Master took every precaution' and the deserter 'was not a prohibited immigrant'.[27] Of the 79 files looked at, only those dealing with non-Europeans were aggressively followed up. However, it is also possible that Zuzenko used another alias as he appears to have had plenty during his career. They included the names Soosenko, Nazarenko, Tuzenko, Matulishenko, Toni Tollagsen Tjorn, Suzenko, Klauchenko, Sanee Mamin, Mamon and Mammon. It is hard to say how many of these were covernames and how many were the result of the well-established inability of Australian bureaucrats to correctly and consistently spell a foreign name.[28]

The first official record of an Alexander Zuzenko in Australia is dated 3 November 1916. This file deals with the issue of Alien Registration Certificate 36, to Mr Alexander Michael Soosenko, at Mourilyan, just outside of Innisfail in Queensland.[29] This file appears to be the source of the information used by the Australian authorities when Zuzenko was first deported. However, given his background, little weight can be given to the information he supplied in his application.

Zuzenko most likely lived in Australia from around 1911 and operated in Queensland, particularly around Innisfail (then called Geraldton), and in Brisbane until he was deported to Odessa on 25 March 1919 following the breaking up of the Russian Workers Association in the aftermath of the Brisbane Red Flag Riots.[30] At the time of Zuzenko's deportation, Australian authorities did not appreciate his importance. As far as they were concerned, he was just another undesirable alien; however, Zuzenko was most likely an agent of the Leninist faction of the Communist Party and an operative for the IWW before becoming an agent of the Comintern following its foundation by Lenin in 1915.

Following his deportation, Zuzenko went back to the Soviet Union and disappeared for a while. It appears that he, like many Russian extremists, had a bit of a love–hate relationship with the Australian working class. The cause of this was the apparent lack of enthusiasm of Australian workers for revolutionary struggle.[31] Yet in 1920, Zuzenko wrote a number of articles on the possibility of a successful workers' revolution in Australia, which he held to be the weak link in the British Empire because, he later argued, 'British workers pay close attention to events in "the freest of democracies", Australia'.[32]

These writings attracted the attention of Feodor Andreevich Sergeeff who arranged for Zuzenko to meet with Vladimir Ilyich Lenin. This meeting did take place and Zuzenko spent over an hour at the Kremlin talking with Lenin. Following this, Lenin recommended to Grigory Yevseyevich Zinoviev, the Chairman of the Comintern and Politburo member, that Zuzenko prepare a report for the Comintern on Australia's potential as revolutionary prospect.[33]

Australia's revolution was to be accomplished, according to Zuzenko, by the creation of an Australian communist party controlled by a central committee controlled in turn by the Comintern's Third International Congress.[34] Zuzenko's subsequent report was well received and he was employed by the Comintern to travel clandestinely to Australia and form a communist party there.[35]

Zuzenko was selected for this work over another Australian communist and IWW activist, an American citizen called Paul Freeman, because, according to the American communist John Reed, Freeman was ill-suited to clandestine work, as he had 'no idea of illegal work at all'.[36] Local communist activists had already begun to create a unified Australian communist party willing to subordinate itself to Lenin's Bolsheviks before Zuzenko arrived, but it suffered the usual divisiveness of mutually hostile factions riven by personal and doctrinal conflicts. By 1922, communist groups in Australia had degenerated into internal warfare; this situation needed to be addressed and the groups brought together. The Comintern, at the direction of Lenin, saw Zuzenko as the best man for the job.[37]

The plan was for Zuzenko to introduce Bolshevik discipline and the mix of open activism and clandestine 'illegal work' necessary to suborn the political and social systems of the target country.[38] The problem was getting Zuzenko past Hunt's surveillance system.

In order to do this, Zuzenko turned up in Vancouver and used the communist network there to help him create a legend—a cover identity and history—good enough to get him past the customs officers in Australia. It was for this reason that passport number 30397, originally held by Norwegian Toni Tollagsen Tjorn, was obtained and altered. Zuzenko and his comrades displayed a high degree of sophistication and organisation in this operation spoilt only by the presence of William Bennett, a Royal Canadian Mounted Police (RCMP) agent.[39] The activities of the Russian émigrés and Canadian communists in Vancouver had attracted the attention of the RCMP and they had planted Bennett in the clandestine communist organisation. Zuzenko was thus identified as an agent. Bennett also identified the alias, that of Toni Tollagsen Tjorn, that Zuzenko would be using to enter Australia, as well as some previous aliases and the route via New Zealand that he would use to get into Australia. Most importantly, Bennett also learned that the local communists in Vancouver believed Zuzenko was an official agent acting under the direct control of the 'Executive' in Moscow.[40] All of this was reported to the Australian authorities and MI5 by the RCMP.[41]

During his time in Canada, Zuzenko is reported to have told Bennett and the other members of the Canadian group that he was an agent of the Comintern, and he left no doubt that he was working under an alias and on secret orders. The reason he spent so much time in Vancouver appears to have been caused by difficulties in obtaining a seaman's position on a ship sailing for Australia. He may also have had other tasks to carry out while in Canada, but if so, there is no evidence of what these tasks were.[42]

According to the RCMP, the operation undertaken in Australia by Zuzenko upon his arrival there was successful; however, the exact objectives and nature of Zuzenko's operation remained unknown. This evaluation was most likely based upon secret reporting by the RCMP's clandestine agents working within the Canadian Bolshevik groups. It appears that the arrest of Zuzenko within a month of his arrival in Australia did not prevent him carrying out his tasking.[43]

A further attempt by Zuzenko to re-enter Australia under the name Nazarenko in the company of a man called Michael Rosenberg[44] was detected in December 1924.[45] The fact that Zuzenko made repeated attempts to enter Australia indicates that whatever else he did, he was seen as the Australian specialist within the Comintern. This makes Zuzenko quite significant because it suggests he established the cells that would later enable the main military intelligence directorate of the general staff of the Soviet Army (GRU), NKVD and CP-A to successfully penetrate the Australian government and institutions in the 1940s. Zuzenko's reward for all of his effort was similar to that of many other dedicated Soviet intelligence operatives: he was arrested and executed in the Stalinist purge of 1938 after he was ironically charged with being a British spy, a normal practice of the Soviet regime.[46]

In Australia, much of the reporting on the Russians living in Brisbane was being generated by the agents of Military Intelligence led by Captain C. Woods of the 1st Military District Headquarters (HQ) in Brisbane. Official interest in the Russians extended well beyond 1st Military District to the Commonwealth Cabinet, particularly Acting Prime Minister Watt, who frequently made marginal notes on the official reports. The main source for these reports was an army agent, covername 77, who appears to have penetrated to the heart of the Russian Workers Association (RWA).[47] Agent 77 was so well embedded that he could detail the efforts of the association to shield one member named Resanoff, also known as Bykoff, from deportation.[48]

Other reports provided by Agent 77 were mundane and simply described activities such as an RWA picnic at Dutton Park. This event was attended by 40 Russians, 20 socialists and all the members of the IWW. Although all of this could have been reported by any informed observer, Agent 77 had the advantage of being privy to the actual conversations of the attendees.[49]

Agent 77 was not the only intelligence agent working directly against the RWA in Brisbane. The CIB was running another three covert inquiry agents: Alex King, A.B. Dungey and L.C. McCallum. For reasons of secrecy, these men were not sworn members of the CIB, but inquiry agents being paid a per diem rate under 'special arrangements'.[50] Despite their effectiveness in surveilling the everyday activity of the radicals, they all failed to identify Zuzenko and his activities.

On the surface, the activities of the various socialist and workers' groups were simple political and industrial agitation for better conditions and pay, and this was indeed the case. However, these groups also attracted individuals whose unhappiness with society was more profound and offered a pool of talent that would be hard for any revolutionary to resist. They also provided the security intelligence operatives with a selection of people whose essentially negative outlook on the world would soon turn them against their revolutionary comrades and make them perfect candidates for work as double agents.

Organised by Zuzenko, the RWA's numbers and influence grew within radical circles; however, the invariable arguments and splits soon began to break up much of Zuzenko's work and the groups dissolved into divisiveness.

Rather than being a thorn in capitalism's side, Australian Bolsheviks and socialists were a motley collection of angry and discordant individuals.[51]

Another factor in the demise of the RWA was the enmity it attracted from returned soldiers who had not forgiven left wing radicals and pacifists for their part in defeating the conscription referendum. This hostility led to returned servicemen forming anti-Bolshevik groups, which was a dangerous development as many of these men had been frontline soldiers inured to violence by years of experience in war. For many frontline infantry soldiers, a violent brawl with civilians or police was of little consequence. They soon showed their capacity for violence on William Street in Brisbane when, on 23 March 1919, they attacked a procession of the RWA headed by men carrying red flags, the so-called Red Flag Riots.

There is no doubt that scuffles broke out and punches were exchanged, but the reports of shots being fired are highly questionable. The CIB in Brisbane dismissed Queensland Police reports that the Russians were armed and 'ready for action' and identified returned soldiers as the main offenders, which indeed they were.[52]

The real problem for the authorities was the backlash. The returned servicemen had the support, or at least acquiescence, of much of the population. After all, they were returned heroes who had shown their willingness to die for their country—and without the wholehearted support of that country, if the conscription referenda were anything to go by. The moral weight of that bore heavily on the Australian community, but the sacrifice of the families of the dead and wounded bore down upon the community even more heavily than the service of the soldiers. Given a choice between supporting Russian communists and the families of the fallen and their returned comrades, it was no contest.

The groundswell of public support, justified or not, was shown by the size of the anti-Bolshevik assemblies that then took place. On 24 March, over 5000 people gathered, of whom approximately 3000 broke away from the meeting at North Quay, Queen and William streets, and marched across Victoria Bridge to the RWA hall in Merivale Street. It was here that the Queensland Police, under the command of Commissioner Frederic Urquhart, were waiting for them with rifles and fixed bayonets. To recently returned soldiers, many of whom were, as we have already mentioned, infantry with experience of hand-to-hand fighting, the appearance of police with fixed bayonets would have been like a red rag to an anti-communist.

A small part of the crowd, around 50 or so men, attacked the police with fence palings, missiles and anything they could lay their hands on. Predictably, some of the returned soldiers were armed with weapons brought back from France and they opened fire, shooting two mounted police officers.[53] The best report of the battle of Merivale Street is that provided by Richard James, the CIB Inquiry Agent present at the demonstration.

James describes the initial demonstration as boisterous but relatively orderly, with some calling for no violence or damage to property. When the crowd arrived in Merivale Street, they found it blocked by a double row of police, so they stopped and milled about. At this point, around nine mounted police charged down the road from the rear of the crowd, trampling some of them and trapping the rest between the foot police and the mounted charge. The crowd then turned 'very angry' and the fence palings were ripped up and used as clubs and missiles against the mounted police. As this occurred, gunshots were heard. The report goes on to say that there was some surprise at the way the returned soldiers were handled compared to the Bolshevik demonstration.[54]

James is perhaps being a little disingenuous here as the difference in the behaviour of the Bolsheviks and the returned soldiers was substantial. The latter group were men returned from war who, as they demonstrated to the Queensland Police Mounted Branch, could handle themselves in a tight spot. They were also the only group that included armed individuals and who ignored the legal restrictions placed by the authorities on their march. There was also the massive difference in numbers, with approximately 300 socialists and communists facing off against about 3000 returned soldiers and their supporters.

That said, it has to be asked who in their right mind would have ordered an attack by mounted police on such a crowd from the rear, when the crowd could not move away except through lines of police armed with rifles and fixed bayonets. One report said that around a hundred men received bayonet wounds, but verifying this is impossible.

The action of the Queensland Police produced three outcomes. The first was a widespread belief, one firmly held by the Commonwealth government and many of its officials, that the Queensland Police actively supported communism. The second was an intensification of community resentment towards the Russians and their communist and socialist sympathisers. The third was that it gave impetus to the conservative side of politics to begin organising to protect the country if state governments did not.

On 25 March, at a meeting of returned soldiers and concerned citizens at Albert Square, there were sustained verbal attacks on 'dirty, greasy Russians and other Aliens'. [55] The meeting, chaired by the president of the Returned Sailors and Soldiers Imperial League, Major H.B. Taylor, passed a resolution:

That the gathering of returned soldiers and sympathisers have assembled for the purpose of voicing their determination that the fruits
of victory shall not be wasted in the interests of the Bolshevists and
other extremists. We pledge ourselves to unity and action and urge
the Authorities to intern and deport all Bolshevic [sic] Russians and
their sympathisers. We demand that the State Government cease their
toleration. We further solemnly and sincerely declare that further lack
of courage by our Public men will surely provoke drastic action by
Returned Soldiers. [56]

The motion was seconded by Brigadier-General Spenser Brown and passed unanimously. The crowd then moved to the offices of the ALP-affiliated *Daily Standard*, which had called them 'Riotous Soldiers' for their behaviour on Monday 24 March, while declaring the Bolshevik meeting of Sunday 23 March 'A Victory for the Bolsheviks'. The *Daily Standard* was lucky there was a large contingent of police present. Other than a few broken windows, the establishment survived. [57]

The official Commonwealth files of the time show that the Common-wealth and state authorities were not just blindly anti-socialist or opposed to left-wing groups, they were concerned about the right-wing element as well. As we have seen, however, the right had greater community support in 1919.

For the Russian émigrés in Brisbane, the Red Flag Riots came as a shock. The RWA was now under surveillance and its members, indeed any Russian, was regarded as anti-Australian. Still, life moves on and in London, a decision had been taken by the Lloyd George government to try to normalise relations with the new Soviet Union. The decision led to the Copenhagen Conference of 1919–20 between British representative James O'Grady, MP, and his Soviet counterpart, Maxim Litvinov, which covered the exchange of prisoners between Great Britain and Soviet Russia. The resulting agreement was signed on 12 February 1920, and its provisions for the repatriation of soldiers and citizens being held prisoner would cause problems for Australia. [58]

Australia had not been involved in the negotiation of the agreement but was now expected by both London and Moscow to conform to it. As a result, by November 1920, Simonoff was claiming that roughly 4000 Russians were 'anxious to return to Russia', but none of them could afford to pay the passage.[59] This placed the Australian government in a bit of a predicament. The agreement provided for the return of soldiers and civilians at the cost of the country from which they were leaving. This meant that Britain paid for the facilities and fares of all of the Russians being repatriated to the Soviet Union and likewise the Soviets paid for the British returning home. The Australian government, however, charged each returning Russian £75 for their ticket to Shanghai, and now Simonoff, on behalf of the Soviet government, was claiming that this breached the terms of the Copenhagen Agreement.[60]

Worse, according to Simonoff, was that the returning Russians were being sent via Japan, which placed them in the hands of the Japanese. Simonoff took matters further and started advising those Russian citizens wishing to return to the Soviet Union not to pay the £75 demanded by the Australian government.[61] Simonoff's actions added to the growing view that the sole objective of the Soviet Union and its supporters was agitation and disruption.

Annoyance grew within the Australian government and Hunt, the official charged with removing unwanted foreigners from Australia, rejected Simonoff's claims, advising the Secretary of the Prime Minister's Department that he did not propose to reply 'in view of the terms employed by the writers.'[62] As far as the Australian government was concerned, the terms of the Copenhagen Agreement had nothing to do with Australia, it was a British agreement with the Soviet Union and Australia was not 'prepared to supply means of transport or to incur any expense on their account'.[63]

The Australian government's decision was not another outbreak of colonial bloody-mindedness. It was far more complex than that. The £75 charged to recoup costs in the repatriation of Russian citizens covered both the passage to Shanghai and the demands of the British colony of Hong Kong, which required all travellers to have sufficient funds to sustain themselves in Hong Kong while waiting for steamers to other places.[64] The British negotiators in Copenhagen had gotten Britain into a bit of a fix by promising to pick up the costs of repatriations without understanding the ramifications across the Empire.

Within Australia, the activities of the RWA and its leadership, particularly Simonoff, were now drawing attention from not only the authorities but from the outraged self-appointed guardians of public safety and proper behaviour. Government files on the matter contain the usual number of denunciations and calls to stronger action that fill such files worldwide. Part of the problem was that Simonoff was in the business of proselytising, meaning propaganda and sermons, and these attracted growing hostility.

The vehicle for this activity was the newspaper *Soviet Russia*, in the pages of which Simonoff and other fellow travellers joyfully described the workers' paradise, while leaving out the butchery of the Red Terror. It also did not help that the subtitle of *Soviet Russia* was *Official Organ of the Russian Soviet Government Bureau*.[65] Being a newspaper, *Soviet Russia* was subject to postal censorship and had to be registered with a supreme court to be sent by post, which, in those days of the monopoly of government postal services, meant that without that registration, *Soviet Russia* could not be distributed, and the government could at any time remove the registration.

Soviet Russia attracted its fair share of adverse commentary. One particularly adverse editorial appeared in *The Sun* of 19 April 1920 and seems to have generated action by Captain E.E. Longfield Lloyd of the Intelligence Section of the General Staff in the 2nd Military District in Sydney. Lloyd will become very prominent in the history of security intelligence that follows.[66]

As was usual with Australia's Military Intelligence and other agencies of the time, newspaper reporting garnered their attention. In this case, Lloyd deemed *Soviet Russia* an illegal publication, as it had not been registered with the Supreme Court of New South Wales before being distributed, and he recommended to the DMI in Melbourne that action be taken before the War Precautions Regulations were rescinded.[67] In a flagrant example of the Australian Army's willingness to intervene in civilian matters—the type of gratuitous interference that the solicitor-general, Sir Robert Garran, and his deputy, George Knowles, were trying to stop—Lloyd wrote to the Director of Military Intelligence that 'all of the persons connected with the paper [*Soviet Russia*] are well known Extremists, and have in the past been constantly under notice'.[68] Not only was Lloyd recommending action by the army but, as his letter makes clear, he had already been speaking to the NSW Police Force about Simonoff, and they had agreed on taking prompt action.[69]

In this routine letter of April 1920 we clearly see the activities that concerned Knowles and Garran: the readiness of the army to involve itself in a civilian matter in peacetime; the use of wartime regulations to damage a civilian organisation before those regulations were rescinded; and the close and unhealthy relationship between a civilian police force and the army in conniving to take action against an organisation of which they were suspicious. Lloyd betrays the real significance of this action when he tells the DMI that the NSW Police had placed the matter of *Soviet Russia* before the NSW government, which had declined to take action. Having failed to get their political masters to do their bidding, the NSW Police were now clandestinely circumventing the government's decision by taking the matter to the army for further action.[70]

Lloyd's superiors did not reject his recommendation; but thankfully, they sought a legal opinion from the Attorney-General's Department.[71] The initial advice provided was measured. As far as the Attorney-General's Department was concerned, Simonoff was a public advocate of Bolshevism in Russia and although he fostered a 'mirage which shows Soviet Russia as an Idealistic State', he had not yet advocated Bolshevism in Australia. In fact, the assessment of Simonoff's propaganda was that it was mainly harmless. The author of the minute could only say that 'it is doubtful if his propaganda can be said to be sufficiently dangerous to warrant the use of such regulations at this stage'.[72] Though it was also suggested that the use of the words 'Official Organ of the Russian Soviet Government Bureau' might be challenged,[73] as far as the Attorney-General's Department was concerned, Simonoff's actions were legal.

Another example of the military's tendency to involve itself in civilian matters was an earlier action, in March 1919, of Major-General L. Lee, the Commandant of 2nd Military District, Sydney, who wanted the NSW Police to stop a march by Sydney Bolsheviks and others if they displayed a red flag.[74] His reason for this was that he believed if the march went ahead 'conflict with returned soldiers [was] probable'.[75]

The matter was put before the Commonwealth Cabinet and Acting Prime Minister Watt, then the ALP premier of New South Wales, William Holman, was asked to take action. Following this, Major-General Lee spoke to the Inspector General of Police and, using the War Precautions Regulations, issued search warrants to enable NSW Police to search the books and records of the Social Democratic League and Industrial Labour Party, whom he deemed the 'two most dangerous organisations in the State'.[76] No one seems to have worried about this intrusion by the military into civil freedoms.

Another concern for Australia's authorities was the continuing trouble in Ireland as a result of the Easter Rebellion of 1916. This action automatically brought to a head the entire underlying sectarian concerns of Protestant Australians and those emigrants of staunchly Protestant stock who had migrated from Britain to Australia. The questionable loyalty of the Catholic population was always of concern to a segment of the Australian community and the files dealing with disloyalty are full of demands from Orange Orders and loyalist Protestant associations all over Australia for the government to deal harshly with the Catholic Church and its wayward followers.[77]

It did not help matters that Irish loyalists produced poetry of a nature that would draw the ire of the patriotic and the attention of the authorities when it was sent from the former to the latter. One example in the files is a poor copy of a poem, 'Is this the Hour?' by Father James E. Coyle of Birmingham, Alabama, published in the *Birmingham Age-Herald* of 17 March 1915:

> To-day, our hated over-lord
> Is grappling with the Teuton foe;
> O strengthen, Lord, the Kaiser's sword
> To smite the worker of our woe;
> To England smite who ne'er did spare,
> No, never through the long, long years,
> For Irish griefs, for Ireland's tears.[78]

According to the American writer, Joseph Schrantz, who would later write a book, The Reverend's Revenge, about Father Coyle's subsequent murder on the steps of his own church, this poem did not win Father Coyle any friends among the many English antecedents living in Birmingham, Alabama, named after Birmingham, England.[79] Coyle was shot dead by E.R. Stephenson, a Southern Methodist Episcopal minister and member of the Ku Klux Klan, in front of a multitude of witnesses after a service. Despite this, and in the good traditions of Alabama, Stephenson was found not guilty because of temporary insanity caused by his daughter having just been married by Coyle to a Puerto Rican man called Pedro Gussman.[80]

In Australia, although the military authorities kept up a regular stream of reporting on the activities of Irish Catholics, their opposition to Britain and their passive support of Germany, the impact on the higher levels of government remained limited until 1920, when hostilities between the British and the Irish Nationalists broke out in open warfare. Even then, calls by various loyalist organisations for action to be taken against Irish Nationalists activities were rejected, particularly when the activities of the Irish Nationalists were legal and there appeared to be little interest among Australians of Irish extraction to do anything more than send money home, speak disparagingly of England and raise their families in Australia.[81]

Going back to Australia's homegrown socialists, the bulk of official interest was focused on the activities of the pacifists, individuals and groups who had formed the coalition that so narrowly defeated the conscription referenda. One notable case was the prosecution of the printers Robert Fraser and Frederick Jenkinson, who operated the left-leaning printing company Fraser and Jenkinson from 343–345 Queen Street, Melbourne. Prior to 1916, the firm printed books, pamphlets, plays and assorted other materials. However, in 1916, the company became a mainstay for the printing of publicity material for the NO vote. This brought them into conflict with the government and the military censor, and on 13 January 1916, H.E. Jones, then a captain in the Intelligence Section of the General Staff (Military Intelligence), and Detective Sainsbury of the Victoria Police, visited the firm in relation to the printing of anti-conscription circulars for the Socialist Party.[82] The following day, Jones, on behalf of the Defence Minister with whom he had discussed the matter, directed Fraser and Jenkinson to print no further circulars for the No-Conscription Fellowship without first submitting the material for the approval of the minister.[83]

Interestingly, Military Intelligence, encouraged by army commanders and government ministers, dealt with anti-conscription groups in the same way they would have dealt with groups carrying out actual sabotage or espionage. The result was that many future notables, including the future prime minister, John (Jack) Curtin, and the future three-time premier of Victoria, John Cain, were reported on, and Cain lost his position at Defence as a result.[84] Curtin is quoted in the files as simply saying 'I would rather see the British Empire fall down than to see conscription introduced into this country'.[85] In the file on Cain, the one thing underlined was not his membership of the Socialist Party but the fact his parents were Irish.[86]

More disconcerting still was that Military Intelligence was dealing with a solicitor, Ernest Bateman of 352 Collins Street, who was attending meetings of the No-Conscription Fellowship and passing information back to Military Intelligence via Brigadier General Williams, the Commandant of 3rd Military

60

District. On 10 January 1916, in a letter to Brigadier Williams, Bateman made it clear he was assembling a group of friends to attend a meeting of the fellowship 'next Friday and break it up'.[87] Although the press did not describe any meeting occurring in Footscray, it did report that the meeting of the fellowship at the Richmond Town Hall on 13 January 1916 was disrupted by a group of aggressive and noisy soldiers.[88] The official file contains no comment on Bateman's intentions, and no action to stop him disrupting the meeting was recorded.

The printers Fraser and Jenkinson were again caught up in part of the government's crackdown on what they saw as subversive groups, in an incident at Socialist Hall in which Captain Jones of Military Intelligence and Detective J.A. Howard of Victoria Police searched the hall and the home of Fred Holland at 86 Clarence Street, Fitzroy.[89] Robert S. Ross, one of the socialist leaders, was found not guilty of the charges laid as a result of these raids.[90]

This incident was just one of a number in which Fraser and Jenkinson were prosecuted and sometimes found guilty, sometimes innocent. Of course, as the printer of *The Socialist* and much of the anti-conscription material, they were going to find themselves in the government's crosshairs.[91] It wasn't until the printing of 7000 copies of a pamphlet entitled *The Republic* on behalf of the Irish National Association and the Young Irish Party, however, that the full weight of the law was brought to bear on the company.

The Republic was one of three publications brought to the attention of the government in November 1919 as being seditious and therefore illegal under Commonwealth law. The other two publications were *The Advocate*, printed and published by William Collins, and *Australia*, printed by J. Roy Stevens and published by G.R. Baldwin of Collins Street. In his opinion provided to the government, the Solicitor-General, Robert Garran, dismissed the case against *The Advocate* and *Australia* in one sentence as not being strong enough to warrant proceedings. He dedicated the other four pages of his report to *The Republic*, the printing and publication of which he found to be an offence under regulation 27A of the War Precautions Act, in that it advocated, incited and encouraged disloyalty and hostility to the British Empire and, additionally, it offended against regulation 28(1)(a), in that it was likely to cause disaffection to His Majesty.[92]

Garran went for the big guns and recommended prosecution for sedition under the Common Law, specifically for seditious libel, a charge that could be heard under state laws, given he was unsure if there was a Commonwealth law applicable to the offence.[93] The government accepted the Solicitor-General's advice and Fraser and Jenkinson, as well as their company, found themselves committed for trial on 16 February 1920 at a preliminary hearing on Thursday 11 December 1919.[94] At their trial the following February, both men were found not guilty.[95]

It would seem that being the printer of choice for radical socialists was not going to get you into as much trouble as being the printer for Irish Catholic Nationalists, and if this seems to be a ridiculous statement, then we need look no further than the case of Constable C.P. Stuart of Queensland.

Stuart was a long-serving constable of the Queensland Police Force based in Warwick. When war was declared, like many patriotic Australians, Stuart rushed to join the AIF and went overseas. He was then returned home because he had reached the mandatory retirement age of 46 years. From all accounts, Stuart remained adamant that if the age limit was raised, he would re-join his comrades in France. That not being the case, he restarted his 30-year-old career with Queensland Police where his superiors described him as 'loyal and intelligent', 'very cautious and tactful' and, prior to the war, 'always a staunch supporter of the Liberals'. He impressed his sergeant and the Mayor of Toowoomba, Job Stone, a staunch Protestant and loyalist, so much they recommended him for appointment to the Commonwealth Police. On 19 December 1917, seven days after it was gazetted,[96] he joined the force and, despite his stellar career and patriotism, Stuart's Catholicism caused alarm, and confidential documents were kept from him.[97] The Stuart case was not isolated and the surveillance of Irish Catholics continued.

In July 1920, the army and police were still watching the activities of dangerous Irish Catholics and particularly those of Archbishop Daniel Mannix.[98] It seems there was still one group seen as more dangerous than the Bolsheviks.

This situation suited the myriad Protestant and loyalist organisations, including the Orange Order, that were spread across Australia at the time. These organisations and their leaders besieged the government with wild accusations, demands for action and advice on how to keep the pernicious Catholics in their place.[99]

When the Commonwealth prevented Sir Osmond Thomas Grattan Esmonde, 12th Baronet Ballynastragh, the representative of the Irish

Nationalist leadership, from landing in Australia, various Protestant organisations were fulsome in their praise of the government and the relevant files are full of their votes of appreciation. Even the British Empire League of Canada sent a letter of support for the action.[100]

The legal mechanism used to prevent Esmonde, who was effectively a white British citizen, from landing was to demand that he swore the Oath of Allegiance to the Crown. This ploy worked as Esmonde could not swear such an oath and he was thus legally denied entry.[101]

Thus, as the war ended for Australia, a whole new set of problems appeared in which the future security of the nation was seen to be threatened by socialist revolutionaries and union activists, by pacifists, conscientious objectors and even by Irish Catholics. The difficulty the authorities now had was in separating the truly dangerous from the body of people who were simply exercising their democratic freedoms to complain and criticise government.

....

As Australia moved from war to peace in 1919, the country had endured a significant shock from the casualties suffered at Gallipoli and, more seriously, from the bloody conflict on the Western Front. This shock was exacerbated as the Australian government moved to make good these losses through conscription in 1916 and, having lost the referendum, again in 1917, an action that intensified the political schisms begun by the first referendum. It was these schisms that much of the ad hoc security intelligence system was directed against as the government of Hughes tried to impose its will on a reluctant electorate.

From the security intelligence perspective, the war had not produced acts of sabotage or espionage, as there were no active German or enemy spies, and the Japanese were allies. So, throughout this early period of Australia's history the targets for the nation's security intelligence systems remained constant, with non-white residents and immigrants being the main focus until socialists, anarchists and Irish Nationalists were also targeted. None of these groups posed an actual danger to Australia's security and only one group, the adherents of Lenin's Bolshevik faction, would go on to develop into such a threat.

CHAPTER 4

UNWANTED AND UNLOVED—SECURITY INTELLIGENCE, 1919–39

During 1919, as the Commonwealth reduced its outlays at the end of the war and began to focus on the problems of peace, it is no surprise that spending on defence was slashed and, along with this, spending on security intelligence. The efforts to build an Australian intelligence organisation now faltered and H.E. Jones' new CIB had its hands full as it tried to deal with subversive Irishmen and Bolsheviks and the growing number of investigations of fraud being perpetrated upon the Commonwealth by returned soldiers, contractors and others. In essence, the CIB had not been created as a security intelligence organisation but as a replacement for the now defunct Commonwealth Police, although a much smaller and cheaper one.

The minuscule capability left to the CIB meant that, just as Steward's CEB and Military Intelligence had had to rely on state police forces, it too would remain reliant on them and, increasingly, on Military Intelligence as well. With the end of the war, the patriotic imperative to provide support to the Commonwealth had evaporated and the complaints from state governments about the costs associated with providing law enforcement support to the Commonwealth agencies increased.

In security intelligence, now part of the CIB's remit, this lack of resources and money created an environment in which the armed services, customs, immigration and other departments were forced to create multiple informal channels to get things done. This led to a marked growth in the workload of police for which the Commonwealth provided no payment.[1] It also created a very strong culture of doing whatever it took to get the job done and, from there, the path descended into procedural corruption.

Except for Tasmania and the Northern Territory, Jones' CIB did get offices, each manned by an inspector and an inquiry agent. The inspector for New South Wales was E.E. Longfield Lloyd.[2] All of these officials were then appointed as responsible officers under the Immigration Restriction Act, an action which legally established their power over migrants and people in Australia on visas.

This record shows that not much happened in the CIB between 1919 and 1934, when it was expanded in November of that year by the recruitment of three new inquiry officers, Robert Frederick Bird Wake, William Barnwell and Jack Magnusson, to the Sydney office.[3] A further two clerks, Frederick Gallagher Galleghan—later famous as Black Jack Galleghan, the Commanding Officer of 3/30th Battalion, 2nd AIF—and Desmond Alfred Alexander, appear to have been appointed as additional Inquiry Officers in the Sydney office in September 1937. There was no further increase in frontline CIB personnel until two more inquiry officers were appointed in Brisbane and Adelaide on 11 October 1939, over a month after the war was declared.

Evidence appears to show Jones was not a very successful empire builder. A month after the start of World War II, Australia's counterespionage capability consisted of the part-time attention of seventeen inquiry officers, seven of whom were in Sydney, who conducted investigations into fraud and theft from the Commonwealth and migration issues; security intelligence matters were of little importance. Effectively, Australia had no counterespionage capability and as a result this job once again fell into the hands of a hotchpotch of amateur organisations ranging from departmental security sections to Military Intelligence to state police forces.

In New South Wales, as in other states, the police force had developed a large section dedicated to detecting and surveilling individuals or groups whose intentions or behaviours were regarded as seditious or disloyal. Of course, most of these individuals and groups were on the left of the political spectrum and some, particularly the various communist groups and the IWW, were closely watched. However, the interest of the authorities was

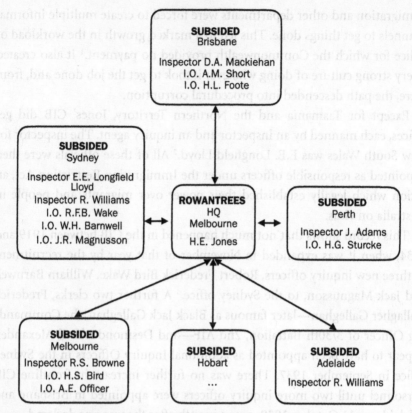

Figure 4.1: Organisation of the CIB in 1935

Note: ROWANTREES was the telegraphic address of Steward's office and SUBSIDED the telegraphic address of his organisation's representatives in each state.

Source: Memorandum to Secretary, 11 January 1935, Aliens, Registration of, BC209208, NAA, A433, 1942/2/2815.

not restricted just to the left. Right-wing groups such as the New Guard and newly rising fascist groups were also watched and, given the right's penchant for uniforms and official recognition, it is likely the police had little difficulty in obtaining intelligence on this side of politics.

The involvement of the police in this area soon led to the growth of a very close relationship with naval and Military Intelligence officials, as well as the small staff of the CEB in Sydney. Police tend to be very jealous of their prerogative as the sole upholders of the laws and their involvement in assisting Military Intelligence was simply part of a strategy of wresting control of Australia's security intelligence work from the relevant Commonwealth bodies.

One of the more capable and ambitious police officers to become involved in security intelligence was William John MacKay, a Scot, known within the NSW Police Force as 'Wee Wullie'. MacKay was one of the bigger characters in the NSW Police, being tall and well-built enough to pull the right-wing dissentient Francis de Groot off his horse at the opening of the Sydney Harbour Bridge in 1932, and ambitious and ruthless enough to subdue the razor gangs and criminal underworld of Sydney.

MacKay was a man of many talents, much drive and, unfortunately, a capacity to do whatever was necessary to get a result that satisfied his political masters and protected and promoted the NSW Police Force.[4]

Born in Glasgow on 28 November 1885, MacKay grew up in that tough city and joined the Glasgow Police Force in 1904.[5] MacKay's career there should have been assured, given his father, Murdoch MacKay, was an inspector. However, after a relatively rapid promotion to the rank of detective constable in 1906, something went astray. In December 1909, things were good enough for the new detective MacKay to marry Jennie Ross Drummond, but, somewhat surprisingly, the newlyweds immediately immigrated to Australia.[6]

The MacKays arrived in Sydney in 1910 and by 10 June MacKay was a probationary constable of the NSW Police Force.[7] MacKay served his time on the beat at a couple of Sydney stations before being posted to a position of chief clerk in the office of the metropolitan superintendent. This move placed MacKay close to the centre of power in the NSW Police. Cannily, he had learned how to take shorthand and type, skills that his peers ignored but which were in growing demand.[8]

His skill in taking shorthand notes led MacKay to be transferred to political surveillance, particularly of the IWW. His efforts in this area led to further advancement and by 1922, aged 32, he had risen to the rank of detective sergeant at Clarence Street Station. A year later, on 10 April 1923, he was appointed sergeant first class.[9] MacKay had risen quickly, but his career's trajectory was still within the usual timeframes in the police force's seniority-based system. It was following his promotion and transfer to the publicity-rich environment of Darlinghurst as the inspector-in-charge on 11 June 1927 that his career really took off.

Confronting MacKay at Darlinghurst was the job of dealing with the so-called razor gangs that were battling for control of the brothels and illegal drinking establishments in the area. Within a short period, his direct methods of policing—greatly assisted by the criminal consorting laws, which allowed criminals found in one another's company to be arrested and imprisoned if convicted—ended the lawlessness, at least in public. His reward was promotion as superintendent-in-charge of the Detective Branch on 20 January 1928.[10]

Superficially, MacKay's reputation was built upon three pillars. The first was his no-nonsense approach to criminality, something clearly demonstrated by his work in destroying Darlinghurst's razor gangs. The second was his openness to new ideas, evidenced by his learning of shorthand and typing and, later on, his willingness to introduce new scientific and technical systems, such as fingerprinting, photography and forensics from Britain, America and Europe, into the NSW Police. The third pillar of MacKay's reputation was his fearsome ruthlessness, something subordinates, the criminal gangs of Sydney and striking workers quickly learned to respect. MacKay did not play nicely or fairly.

MacKay's standing among the officers of the NSW Police makes it clear that he was seen as a copper's copper, an officer with a firm approach and a clear understanding of the needs and demands of policing New South Wales. This also made him a dangerous threat to the wider society, as his drive to achieve the desired result made him capable of significant procedural corruption. MacKay made sure that the government of the day got what it asked for from the NSW Police.

MacKay's approach to policing has been retrospectively painted as that of 'a bully boy for the haute bourgeoisie'.[11] In my view, this is a very superficial analysis of what drove MacKay and his behaviour. His first desire was to ensure the standing of the NSW Police as the unchallenged custodians of the law of New South Wales. It was in pursuit of this goal that he delivered results to his political masters regardless of their politics or class. As long as they left the NSW Police alone and ensured it received the money and men it wanted, MacKay was their faithful servant. Wee Wullie and his men had no time for bourgeois sensibilities. The truth is that he had two abiding ambitions: first, to become the commissioner of the NSW Police and second, to ensure the standing and the institutional power of the NSW Police Force. Once MacKay's ambitions are clearly understood, it is easy to see how he was able to so successfully serve both conservative and ALP governments in New South Wales and the Commonwealth.

One of the myths that damaged MacKay in the eyes of Australia's political left is the tale of his involvement in the Rothbury Incident of 16 December 1929. This incident involved an ill-disciplined contingent of NSW Police shooting at striking miners at Rothbury in the Hunter Valley. They killed Norman Brown, an innocent bystander, and wounded ten others.[12] The irony is, MacKay was in Sydney when the police opened fire; if he had been present, it would have been unlikely that any police officer would have fired a pistol.[13] It is illuminating that many historians and writers fall for this lie, oddly propagated by MacKay himself.[14] The officer who lost control of his men was Superintendent Beattie, not William MacKay.

Of course, the NSW Police publicly closed ranks around Beattie and his men, but privately MacKay assessed the causes of the incident as Beattie's weak leadership, the incompetence of the second-in-command, Inspector Boland, and the fact that many of the police present were second rate and some were known alcoholics.[15]

This incident, one of the more notable in the history of Australia's often troubled mining industry, resulted from the determination of the union leadership and the NSW Minister for Mines and Forests, Reginald Weaver, a noted anti-socialist, to draw the miners of Rothbury into a confrontation with police. Weaver, later a member of the New Guard, was at Rothbury on 15 December, the day before the police detachment opened fire on the striking miners, and he did his best to create the conditions necessary for a confrontation.[16]

What makes Rothbury interesting in the life of William J. MacKay is that he created the lie of his own involvement in what was a criminal act by NSW Police and one of the worst incidents in the history of Australian industrial conflict. Why would MacKay claim to be the leader of police who wantonly shot miners? Why would he want to make himself the bête noire of the left? In the absence of any explanation by MacKay, we can only guess at his motives, but promoting himself as a ruthless and dangerous man in order to cow others seems to be the only logical answer.[17]

Paradoxically, MacKay didn't need to do this. On his arrival later that day at Rothbury, MacKay took command and immediately ordered violent and unscrupulous action to be taken against the strikers and anyone supporting them. Motorised flying squads of police raided homes to break up meetings and savagely assaulted many locals. The miners struck back, particularly at Ashtonfields, where they assaulted and stripped several strike-breakers. MacKay responded in kind and his men violently broke up union marches at Abermain's No. 1 and 2 mines. By the end of January 1930, the Hunter coal-fields were once again quiet, but local feelings against the NSW Police would remain bitter for a long time afterwards.[18]

The methods employed by MacKay also included the egregious use of false accusations to tie union leaders up in court cases, the planting of evidence, the use of agent provocateurs and, as we have seen, when necessary, brute force and violence against individuals deemed to be dangerous or problem-atic.[19] This is reflected in his actions against Francis de Groot in 1932. After de Groot cut the ribbon that was to officially open the Sydney Harbour Bridge in an act of protest at the fact that the ALP Premier, Jack Lang, was opening the Bridge and not the Governor of NSW, MacKay had him sent to the Lunatic Reception House at Darlinghurst, where he was detained until the examining psychiatrist found him quite sane.

MacKay's disruption of unionists even included a raid on the NSW Trades Hall on 22 July 1929, in which union leaders were charged with conspir-acy to unlawfully molest, intimidate and assault non-union workers. The charges were subsequently thrown out of court when the unionists' lawyer, H.V. (Doc) Evatt, the future Attorney-General for whom MacKay would work as Director of Security, counter-alleged that the police involved, includ-ing MacKay, had concocted the case and falsified documents.[20] Despite this loss, the result would have been fine for MacKay, as the unionists had to pay Evatt for his services and were kept too busy by their own cases to be foment-ing more unrest.

This brings us to the conundrum of why there was no investigation of the police or action taken against MacKay when the Lang government was elected on 4 November 1930. Indeed, how did this enemy of the workers manage to be promoted to metropolitan superintendent on 30 March 1932 by the NSW Executive Council acting on the advice of the ALP premier, Jack Lang? Even more interestingly, for our story, why did the Curtin government appoint him as the first Director-General of the Security Service working under his old foe, the Commonwealth Attorney-General H.V. Evatt?

The truth is MacKay was no conservative lackey, he was much more dangerous than that. He was a clever, vain, ambitious and power-hungry man willing to do whatever it took to obtain and hold onto power and influence, both for himself and his force. As long as a government did not intrude on the prerogatives of the NSW Police, MacKay would uphold the legitimacy of that government. Lang and the NSW ALP were extremely familiar with this sort of beast. They knew how to work alongside MacKay very well.

Lang and the NSW ALP were not disappointed by MacKay. When the extreme right started to mobilise itself against Lang's government in New South Wales, the NSW Police treated them exactly as they had treated striking unionists. The difference was that the target—the right-wing New Guard, formed in early 1931 under the leadership of the solicitor Colonel Eric Campbell—was an easy mark compared to the unions.[21] The major weakness of the New Guard's leadership was their naivety in thinking that MacKay and the NSW Police would welcome their support in defence of NSW law.

The New Guard's offer to provide the NSW Police with an auxiliary force was never going to be welcomed. The police would not countenance the competition for both their institutional power and their status as the law enforcement agency in New South Wales. Instead, the New Guard was quickly and comprehensively infiltrated by 'friendly' policemen completely loyal to MacKay.[22] It was thus compromised right from its beginning and the risk it presented to the democracy of New South Wales identified and neutralised by the ruthless procedural corruption of William MacKay and the NSW Police.[23] Despite the self-serving claims made after the event by Colonel Campbell, the NSW Police never encouraged or assisted the New Guard. They destroyed it.

All of the techniques used against unionists—the laying of spurious but distracting charges, the planting of evidence, the use of agent provocateurs—were used anew. Campbell was charged with using 'insulting words', de Groot was charged with offensive behaviour and, on 1 April 1932, when a large crowd of New Guardsmen assembled in Liverpool Street outside the Central Police Court where de Groot was appearing, they were violently attacked by the police. The orders reputedly given to these police by MacKay were finished off with: 'whether you believe in the New Guard, the Labor Party or the Communist Party, go out there and belt their bloody heads off'.[24]

Much to the general disgust of many people in New South Wales, MacKay's police carried out their orders to the letter.[25] The action destroyed the New Guard's claims that they were acting with the approval of the police and it destroyed their leadership's hope of gaining police support. To rub the New Guard's nose in it, MacKay followed up the confrontation of Liverpool Street

71

with a show of force by parading every NSW police officer available through the centre of Sydney.

The overt use of force was supplemented by covert action, including what can only be described as a staged attack on the unionist Jock Garden at his home in Maroubra. This incident was most likely either police officers or agents provocateurs acting on behalf of MacKay and masquerading as New Guard.[26] The truth of the matter was lost in the public outrage generated by the attack on an unarmed man in his family's home. Garden and MacKay appear to have had their own private working arrangements for dealing with problems, including doing favours for one another when it suited their purposes. Thus, when MacKay needed a victim on the ALP side of politics, Garden was someone he could deal with. As for Garden, having MacKay deal with the more extreme members of the union movement was something that may have attracted him into such an arrangement.

What the New Guard and its leadership had not banked upon was the dedicated hostility of MacKay and the NSW Police in defence of the constitutional government or, more importantly, in defence of their own status as the sole guardians of law and order in New South Wales. They also did not recognise that MacKay was capable of generating a political assault on them in the form of the Garden attack, and was not above planting evidence—the ogre-like uniform ostensibly used by members of the 'inner "Fascist" group in the "New Guard"' discovered at the scene was, interestingly, the only such uniform ever found. Longfield Lloyd dismissed New Guard involvement in the assault on Garden, reporting that 'it is not considered by competent observers to have been ordered by the "New Guard" administration'.[27] Recent research by Richard Evans shows that the claims made in the NSW Parliament by M.W.D. Weaver, MLA, asserting that the assault on Garden was a police conspiracy, were most likely true.[28]

Even the 'Old Guard', supposedly a shadowy organisation of right-wing extremists rumoured to be senior military officers was, I believe, a fabrication of MacKay's fertile mind. With the New Guard neutralised by the stripping away of their standing in the community, MacKay needed a new threat, so he created the Old Guard. Otherwise it strikes me as amazing that in an organisation reputed to number thousands no actual members were ever identified. It is preposterous to believe even for a second that a right-wing organisation wedded to the preservation of the nation against communism could have kept its existence and the names of thousands of members absolutely quiet when the NSW Police identified the entire New Guard establishment and the identity of its members within weeks of taking on the task. The sole evidence for the existence of the Old Guard is that provided by William MacKay and the NSW Police, and this includes the ridiculous dark bedsheet uniforms that some of Australia's leading conservatives were supposed to have worn during their meetings. The fact that these uniforms were only worn for the taking of police photographs is, to my mind, highly suspicious.

The reward for MacKay's service was promotion to the top, as metropolitan superintendent, a post that assured him of being the next commissioner when Walter Childs retired. Following his promotion, MacKay moved to the post of superintendent-in-charge of the Detective Branch and took control of the NSW Police Force's growing capabilities in political surveillance. MacKay now oversaw the penetration of and reporting on political groups of all persuasions. This 'even-handedness' has led some to see MacKay's willingness to deal firmly with both the radical right and left as being somewhat dutiful to the people of New South Wales. The truth is that his even-handedness was a strategic necessity in maintaining his own power and the power of the NSW Police Force.[29]

Soon after his appointment as commissioner of the NSW Police in April 1936, MacKay left on one of the long study tours of England, Germany, Italy and the United States that Australia's bureaucrats and politicians make at regular intervals. In the United States, he met J. Edgar Hoover, the head of the Federal Bureau of Investigation (FBI) and a man of similar tendencies to his own, and was much impressed. Hoover had taken a little-known federal office and, in less than twenty years, turned it into a well-resourced national institution. During this tour, at least according to the historian Frank Cain, MacKay showed his fascist leanings in the way he responded to the discipline and organisation of a Hitlerjugend labour battalion he inspected. At first glance MacKay's desire to replicate a similar organisation in New South Wales under the control of the police appears to support such allegations.[30] However, MacKay's tendencies were, as we have seen, limited to serving his political masters, and at this time, these were within the ALP. Whatever his motivations, and however distasteful his techniques, he was a good constitutionalist.

The trip abroad provided MacKay with ideas that he implemented on his return. In most of these cases, MacKay acted as a professional police officer and most of his reforms were sensible and overdue in Australia. Among them were the introduction of the cadet-police system, the introduction of short-hand training for police officers and the creation of specialised squads. He also founded the scientific sections of the CIB, including the ballistics and criminal methods department, and he expanded the existing radio control system.

Due to the efforts of MacKay, both as a superintendent and later, as commissioner, the NSW government allowed the NSW Police Force to create the Subversive Organisations Bureau (SOB), the largest and most effective of the many security intelligence organisations operating in Australia at the time. In early 1939, on MacKay's recommendation, this unit was merged with the security intelligence section of the Army's 2nd Military District to form a unique organisation, the NSW Military Police Intelligence Section (MPIS). The MPIS would become the largest and most extensive security intelligence organisation in Australia.

CHAPTER 5

PERSONS OF INTEREST, 1919–39

hile William MacKay was building his legend in New South Wales, the CIB under H.E. Jones was battling away with poor resources, little money and little or no interest from governments of any persuasion. As far as Jones was concerned, the Security Section of the CIB was tasked with the 'protection' of Australia and the Empire from the acts of individuals and organisations openly advocating the seizure of power by unconstitutional means.[1] Basically, this meant keeping watch on the activities of communists, socialists and their supporters, but it also included right-wing extremists, foreign nationals and migrants from Italy, Serbia and, a little later, Germany as well. The CIB's Security Section, such as it was, also maintained its watch on communist organisations to keep the Australian government informed of developments within those groups. Jones claimed their influence had spread with the fall in economic conditions in Australia from 1929 to 1931.[2]

Regulating immigration remained the priority for the CIB, and Jones claimed that the organisation played a significant role in recommending the establishment of the *Aliens Registration Act 1920* to replace the wartime regulations requiring the registration of foreigners in Australia. The Aliens Registration Act had come into effect on 1 January 1921, but, as Jones told MI5, the CIB had such limited resources and state police forces had become so difficult to deal with on these matters, the CIB could not enforce the provisions of the Act. The exception to this was in the case of Asians, presumably because they were easy to spot among the predominantly white population, which remained antagonistic towards them.[3]

Among the arriving aliens, Jones singled out Italians for special mention.[4] Italians appear to have become a problem for the CIB during the years 1926–27, when there was an increase in European migration to Australia. Italians stood out because they brought 'customs, habits and thoughts foreign to the British race', and fascists and anti-fascist socialists and communists were included among their numbers. They also included members of organised crime groups. Of all the Italian groups that entered Australia during this period, it was the criminal associations and not the fascists and anti-fascists who would create the most problems for Australia's police and the CIB.

Jones found that the fascist groups, who were actively supported by the Italian consulates in Australia, were quick to establish social organisations and worked hard to extend their influence in Australia's Italian community.[5] Italians already in Australia often attempted to coerce new arrivals into joining these organisations. The number of Italian fascists landing in Australia was estimated by the CIB to have been greater than the number of anti-fascists due to the agreement between the Australian and Italian governments on nomination of immigrants and the capacity of the Italian government to limit the number of anti-fascists immigrating by withholding permits to travel and land.[6]

The largely white, British population of Australia, more specifically the population of North Queensland, began to become uneasy at the number of Italians settling in their towns and cities. The Italians didn't help matters by their willingness to work hard, eat odd foods and talk in an unintelligible language. Of all of these characteristics, the worst was working hard because this led to the accumulation of wealth and property, including farms.

The activities of the Italian fascist groups were now the major worry for the CIB, which devoted considerable time and resources to penetrating these organisations to identify the links they had to the Italian consulates in Australia. This work enabled the CIB to build up a detailed list of fascists, which included consular officials, and enabled them to identify the role of Italian diplomats as being central to the activities of the wider fascist organisations in Australia.[7]

The other problem the CIB identified was the arrival of Italian criminal organisations in Australia and their subsequent involvement in murder and arson in Queensland and New South Wales.[8] The state most affected was Queensland where the criminal activities of the various Italian criminal organisations were lumped together as the actions of a single organisation, the aptly misnamed Black Hand (Mano Nera in Italian).[9] Although the CIB were initially worried about the Neapolitan Camorra, the organisation most influential was the Calabrian 'ndrangheta, a word derived from the Greek, meaning, in the Calabrian version, 'manly virtue' or to 'engage in a defiant and valiant attitude'.[10] This organisation is most often called 'The Honoured Society'.

The violence within the newly arrived Italian communities suggests to me that recently arrived Italian gangsters were working out the rules of the road in their new country. Unfortunately, their preferred negotiating methods included indiscriminate violence, which attracted the attention of the authorities.

One notable instance was the murder of Guiseppina Bacchietta (misreported as Bacchiella in the newspapers), in a botched bombing aimed at a gangster staying in her house on 8 October 1934.[11] This attracted so much public outrage that the Italian gangsters involved decided that they could calm things down by murdering their own associates, including an Ingham farmer, Domenico Scarcella in June 1935, Francesco Guglielmo Femio in December 1936 and, one of the bosses, Vincenzo D'Agostino in 1938.[12] All of these crimes, as well as many more, remain unsolved, although with the death of D'Agostino in 1938, the violence abated somewhat.

In fact there was no Mano Nera organisation; the term simply described a form of extortion used by the Sicilian Cosa Nostra (translated literally as 'our thing'), commonly known as the Mafia, the Calabrian 'ndrangheta and the Camorra, all of whom appear to have been active competitors within the newly arrived Italian community in Australia. The murders, bombings and other criminal activities committed by Italians drew outrage from the Australian community, which wanted to rid itself of these new threats.

What this period tells us is that Australia's security and police organisations lacked the expertise to deal with even run-of-the-mill gangsters. In fact, it merely took the silence of the Italian community to make it impossible for either the police or the CIB to establish if Italian criminal organisations even existed in Australia.[13] Given this lack of basic intelligence capabilities, it is hardly surprising that there is no mention in any official documentation of the existence of a foreign intelligence agency operating in Australia.

· · · · · · · ·

It was at this time, November 1934, that Robert Frederick Bird Wake, one of the more flamboyant characters in the early history of Australian security intelligence, appeared on the scene as the CIB's inspector in Brisbane. The new inspector used the high profile of the Italian cases to establish his own public profile and used the independence of his position in Brisbane to create the personal networks of influence, particularly with politicians, police, public servants and newspapers, that he would later develop into a bureaucratic protection racket. Thus, it appears that the Italian gangsters of Queensland were crucial in enabling Wake to begin his campaign of social climbing, something he would prove adept at.

The attention of Wake and the CIB became firmly fixed on the problems created by Italian criminals, and the need for Queensland authorities to be seen to be acting firmly and decisively. The CIB's effectiveness in dealing with the problem did not come from their investigative capabilities or experience, it came from the appointment of CIB investigators as 'responsible persons' under the immigration laws. This meant that the CIB could quickly check the immigration status of Italian immigrants and, if anything was found amiss, they could arrange rapid deportation, thus moving the problem out of their jurisdiction.[14] Given the inability of the Queensland Police to contain the problem, obtain convictions or clean up the Italian community, it was decided that any Italian who attracted attention could be more effectively dealt with by deportation.

In 1937, Wake accompanied the Commissioner of the Queensland Police, Cecil Carroll, on a visit to North Queensland to oversee one such police and CIB operation, which was systematically checking the immigration status of Italian residents. Inspector Wake's arrival presaged the imminent deportation of anyone found or even alleged to be involved in illegal activity. As the Brisbane *Truth* trumpeted in June 1937, 'The Northern foreigner fears only one thing—deportation—and this is exactly what Inspector Wake's appearance seemed to foreshadow.'[15] It didn't work. The flaw in the approach was that the Italian criminals quickly worked out that if the CIB and police were moving in against them in Queensland, a quick trip to another state soon neutralised the threat.

The problems posed by Italian criminal organisations persisted right up until 1940. As war approached, the concerns over the Italian community grew and the efforts of the CIB in combatting what was seen as 'propaganda of a most insidious kind' led to the arrest of a number of individuals including, as Wake was keen to tell the press, a number of women.[16]

By December 1939, Wake was able to announce to the newspapers that 'there was no Black Hand in Queensland'. They were 'all gone' and 'broken up'.[17] Despite Wake's braggadocio, none of the perpetrators of any of these crimes were ever caught and the Italians who were frightened away from North Queensland simply went to other states and laid low until the authorities lost interest and they could return.[18] The outbreak of war meant that widespread internment of Italians temporarily broke up the activities of the organisations.

······ ······ ······

In the period between the wars it was the public activities of communists and socialists in challenging the political system that caused the most concern for the CIB. In the late 1920s and early 1930s, the growing influence of fascist organisations in the immigrant communities, particularly in the Italian community and later in the German community, also began to be of interest to the CIB. Macedonian, Serbian and Yugoslav immigrants also received attention from the authorities, as these communities were identified as bringing their cultural habits and national connections with them into Australia; however, the Macedonian Revolutionary Society, Comitadjis, which had fought against Turkish sovereignty for over a century, was the only organisation Jones mentions.[19]

The real interest for the CIB, however, continued to be in the home-grown groups, which, on the right of politics, consisted of what Jones called 'self-protection units'.[20] Jones listed these organisations as the New Guard in New South Wales, the League of National Safety in Victoria, the Citizen League in South Australia and the Black Shirts in Western Australia. Apart from their right-wing leanings and interest in fascism, these organisations had further endeared themselves to the CIB and Jones by complaining about the CIB's lack of action against their socialist and communist enemies. As a result, the CIB, like the NSW Police, was not particularly lenient when dealing with what they called 'ill-advised bodies'.[21] The result was that the

CIB, with the support of the bureaucratic and political establishment, soon limited the appeal and effectiveness of these organisations by cutting off or reducing sources of funding and, notably, by forcing 'the withdrawal of certain misguided army officers who were directly associated with them'.[22]

Despite Jones' claims, we need to be careful in accepting his viewpoint regarding the effectiveness of the CIB in dealing with these radical groups of both extremes, as the communists, particularly, were well led, reasonably well resourced and highly experienced in techniques of clandestine activity. On the other hand, the right-wing groups made the mistake of operating completely in the open in the expectation that the general populace and sympathetic government officials would actively support them. It was a classic mistake of the right, as the officials, even when personally supportive, tended to act in accordance with their duty to the state. This was hardly unsurprising because the most striking characteristic of conservatives is to conduct themselves in strict accordance with their duty.

More importantly though, the CIB and its Security Section did not have either the manpower or resources it needed to carry out even a small part of the necessary work. In his correspondence with MI5 in London, Jones was over-egging the pudding for his British readers.

The problems for the CIB appeared on both sides of the ledger and were caused by the dramatic depression that was now afflicting Australia. On one side of this ledger, the dire economic circumstances created the environment in which more and more people were searching for answers from the political extremes, thus growing the number of individuals and groups that the CIB needed to deal with. On the other side of the ledger, the financial predicament of the government caused by the decline in tax returns made expansion of the CIB virtually impossible, especially given the addiction of the governments of the time to the classical economic theory that government must live within its means.

··· ··· ···

As time passed and Germany witnessed the success of a far more radical form of right-wing socialism in the Nazi Party, there was an added need to not only watch home-grown adherents of this new ideology, but also watch their diplomatic representatives now operating in Australia. It was an additional burden, for which the CIB was poorly equipped.

In Australia, as in Britain, concern over Nazi influence grew as the new government of Adolf Hitler rapidly subjugated all resistance in Germany and began its propaganda war against democracy and its other opponents. One of Australia's leading Nazi provocateurs was Dr Johannes Heinrich Becker of Tanunda in South Australia. Fortunately for the CIB, he appears to have quickly alienated himself from the German establishment in Australia through his arrogance and lack of patience. Becker had immigrated to Australia in 1927 and joined the Nazi Party on 1 March 1932. Soon after Hitler's rise to the chancellorship of Germany, Becker was appointed a Landesvertrauensmann, the Nazi Party's 'state trustee', for Australia. Effectively, he was the Nazi Party's direct representative in Australia, given the task of fomenting political links between Australian Nazis and the German party, free of the restraints existing within the German foreign service's diplomatic corps.

As a result of his aggressiveness, Becker developed a very poor relationship with Dr Rudolf Asmis, who had been appointed as Germany's Consul-General in Sydney in 1932. His aggressive approach to promoting the new Nazi regime also alienated most of the leadership of Australia's German community. Asmis was not a Nazi appointment and was the sort of German that Becker loathed, but he would prove to be a hard-working and effective Consul-General.

One of Asmis's first acts, other than making contacts and networking with Australia's social and governmental elites, was to limit the activities of Becker and, eventually, to have him replaced as Landesvertrauensmann. Becker's inability to build smooth relationships with the representatives of the German Foreign Ministry was not unusual and reflected Hitler's penchant for creating competing centres of power within his regime. Asmis was the more effective operator of the two[23] and soon Becker was replaced by Johannes Frerck of Sydney.

One of Asmis's close associates, Lars Gustav Brundahl was a petty criminal, thief, bigamist and conman with an extensive reputation for lying and violence. He posed as a German and claimed to be American although he had been born at Westport, New Zealand, on 28 December 1885.[24] In other words, he was an entirely disreputable character that Asmis could put to good use carrying out the deniable dirty tasks for the consulate in Australia.[25] Longfield Lloyd's assessment of him was a 'man of pleasant disposition' who was 'liked by all who knew him'.[26] The only people who misread Brundahl more erroneously than Lloyd were the Nazi regime in Germany who, at the intervention of Asmis, appointed him to the honorary position of trade commissioner.

Although the position was unpaid, it was an important post for anyone willing to exact bribes from businesses attempting to trade between Germany and Australia, and it meant Brundahl owed Asmis a debt of gratitude. It also enabled Brundahl to identify businesses that he could loan money to at high interest from his private accounts. As a result, Asmis increased his power and influence and Brundahl made money and actively manipulated Australian–German trade in his own interests through his control of the German–Australian Chamber of Commerce.[27]

If Australia's internal security organisations were not particularly effective, neither were Nazi Germany's representatives in Australia. Brundahl's corruption in running trade between the two countries soon attracted the jealous eyes of a retired SS man, G. Hardt, with connections to SS Reichsführer Heinrich Himmler and Richard Walther Darré, the Reich Minister for Food. Despite these connections, Asmis warned Brundahl about Hardt's moves against him; Asmis preferred his own devil managing trade. In typical Nazi Party fashion, this dispute then involved the new Consul-General to New Zealand, Dr Walter Hellenthal, who was connected to Herman Göring. As all of this activity swirled around, the threat of war increased and the unfortunate Frerck's delicatessen shop in William Street was subjected to demonstrations by a crowd of around a thousand people led by the CP-A on Friday 9 December 1938—just one of many outside his shop.[28]

Asmis replaced Frerck with his personal choice for the position, Walter Ladendorff, as the Landeskreisleiter (District Leader) in New South Wales in 1936 and as the Landesvertrauensmann for Australia in 1937.[29] He ensured that Ladendorff remained more manageable than prior appointees by arranging for Brundahl to provide a loan of money to him that Ladendorff could not easily repay.[30]

By 1935, the CIB's Security Section faced two active ultranationalist foreign groups: Italy's Fascists and Germany's Nazis. Even at this early stage, the threat posed was appreciated, with Jones telling MI5 that both groupings presented 'a tinge of potential danger in the advent of war'.[31] This tinge of potential danger resulted in the CIB secretly starting investigations of Australians with German or Italian antecedents, fascist or Nazi leanings, or associations with either of these groups. Even with the increased attention given to the Nazi and Fascist threat, evidence of German and Italian espionage was hard to come by, although interception of the Italian Vice-Consul's communications indicated that he, Commander Vitali, was abusing his diplomatic privilege to undertake espionage activities. No evidence of this type of activity appears to have been found implicating the Germans; however, it was while trawling for information that the CIB first noticed the newly founded Australia First Movement (AFM).[32]

The AFM's main objective appears to have been a desire to foster among Australians a stronger spirit of nationalism. The prime movers of this organisation were the anti-conscriptionist activist, sometime socialist and anti-militarist W.J. Miles and Percy R. Stephensen, a 'man of letters' and the author and publisher of *The Foundations of Culture in Australia*.[33] Together both men published the periodical *The Publicist*, the first issue coming out in July 1936. *The Publicist* was stridently anti-British and anti-American and displayed a notable admiration for Japan. It also argued for a stronger and more self-interested form of Australian nationalism. It was, according to the official historian, Paul Hasluck, 'erratic and disorganised', 'opposed to so-called internationalism', 'monarchical', 'autarchic', 'anti-Semitic', 'anti-communist' and a 'soap box with the tatters of "literature" and "culture" hanging to it'.[34]

Miles and Stephensen also ran the Yabba Club, a discussion group that was open to anyone wishing to attend. Like the Yabba Club, the AFM was an informal network of rather odd people representing a mixture of the socialist, fascist and anarchic viewpoints sometimes found in anti-globalisation movements today.[35]

Other than keeping an eye on the members of the AFM and filing the odd report, the CIB did not take or recommend any action against it or its members. As we will see, this would change dramatically with the entry of Japan into the war in 1941.

One group that did not get a mention in Jones' reporting to MI5 on the state of Australia's security intelligence was the Japanese. This does not mean that the CIB or other Commonwealth and state agencies did not keep an eye on them. The Japanese community in Australia was most definitely kept under close scrutiny, but for the purpose of enforcing the Immigration Restriction Act rather than from fear of Japanese espionage.

It is somewhat ironic that the man responsible for Australia's security intelligence function in the interwar period overlooked the threat posed by

Japanese spying, as it was the fear of Japanese spying that led to the first calls for an Australian intelligence service.[36] The concerns of individuals were raised at government level but were soon lost in the politics of the armed services and the parsimony of the Commonwealth government. However, in March 1912, the actions of a Japanese staff officer, Major Asada Ryoitsu, provided a warning that the Japanese military was taking an interest in Australia. What that interest was, no one knew. This situation was not helped by the behaviour of Major Asada.

The Japanese had notified the Australian government of Major Asada's visit, but had not thought to provide the reasons for it. As there was no capability at the Commonwealth level, the task of watching Asada fell to state police forces and Military Intelligence, neither of which were equipped or trained for this type of work. Asada immediately realised he was being watched and took the opportunity to play silly games with the police and Military Intelligence personnel watching him. This led to increased suspicion and finally farce when the Western Australian Military Intelligence Section assessed that the real purpose of Asada's visit was to inspect Japanese spy networks in Australia.[37]

This assessment was ridiculous because a real intelligence officer would have avoided contact with officialdom and, if such contact was necessary, would have operated clandestinely to protect any networks that existed. The reality was that Asada was from the operations branch of the Imperial General Staff and had probably simply come to Australia to have a look around for himself, something operations officers of the Imperial Japanese Army (IJA) did on a regular basis and in similar ham-fisted ways.[38] The Asada visit did have one positive outcome for Australia: the Commonwealth finally had to formally do something about security and this led to the passing of the *Crimes Act 1914*.[39]

Asada had no concern for the impact of his visit on Australians, and he had even less for the damage he did to the relationship between Australia and Japan. His request to have Mr Ichikawa of the Mitsui Bussan Kaisha company post to him a package of maps and plans of Australian fortifications on his return to Japan caused further damage to an already ruptured relationship. The crudity of Asada's activity is indicative of an amateur playing a game rather than a professional conducting intelligence collection.

Back in 1912, the reality was that the Imperial Japanese Navy's (IJN) battle fleet was only six to seven days' steaming from Australia's capital cities, and the Admiralty and Australian Commonwealth Naval Board knew it. By the end of the 1914–18 war, Australia's security authorities had identified Japan as the country's major threat and had started the work of building some intelligence capability by underwriting a Japanese-language program led by Professor James Murdoch at the University of Sydney and the Military College, Duntroon.[40] All of this fell apart with the destruction of the Pacific Branch and the sidelining of Edmund Piesse, Atlee Hunt and William Watt by William Hughes in 1921. In 1921, the IJN's main battle fleet was still only six days' steaming from Australia's capital cities, and this was still the case in September 1939.

So, as the war approached, various groups in Australia supported fascism, Nazism and communism to greater or lesser degrees and a significant minority of Australians gravitated to the simplistic messages of these groups and individuals. At the centre of national political power, Australia's government remained locked in a malaise of inaction created by the conflicting personalities and philosophies of the governing parties. It was beyond the Cabinet of the day to sit down and start planning the expansion and organisation of anything associated with defence or to make preparations for war. Security intelligence remained a subject remote from the concerns of the decision-makers, other than the necessary functions of the registration and surveillance of aliens and the management of some perfunctory checking of personal details of public servants and military personnel.

As war broke out, the CIB had approximately fifteen officers to conduct all investigations into fraud and theft from the Commonwealth, migration and security intelligence matters.[41] Of these officers, only Lloyd could speak Japanese. Even with a population of just over seven million, this was a farcical state of affairs for which Australia's bureaucrats and politicians were responsible. Australia's ability to manage its own security intelligence was non-existent, but luckily so was the capacity of the German, Italian and Japanese intelligence services in Australia. Still, no one in Australia's government knew that, and it is little wonder that in late November 1938 Jones, the head of the CIB, was on sick leave with yet another bout of severe dyspepsia.[42]

CHAPTER 6

WHAT? AGAIN? 1939 AND WAR

The Australian government found it difficult to confront the coming of war at the political level. The government of Joe Lyons had supported if not pushed Neville Chamberlain's appeasement policies with both Italy and Germany, and, when Lyons died on 7 April 1939, this strategy was maintained under his successor, Robert Menzies. The rise of Menzies did not presage a new approach, particularly as Menzies did not enjoy the full support of Country Party leader Earle Page and many other members of the ruling parties. This was a personal grudge, as Page held Menzies responsible for the pressure that Page believed hastened the death of Lyons. As a result, Menzies and his supporters expended energy squaring off against Page and his supporters that would have been better used in thinking and talking about the coming war.

This lack of clear policy direction would result in Australia being highly reactive to events. Menzies' declaration of war on 3 September 1939, which is often portrayed as an act of blind loyalty, may not have been this at all. The political necessity of being seen to immediately aid Britain was met by this early declaration, but behind the scenes the imperative appears to have been to make sure Australia took no quick action.

On 13 September, New Zealand unconsciously ramped up the pressure on Australia by offering 6000 troops to take over garrison duties from British units in Asia and the Pacific by 13 November 1939 and then offering to increase this to 16,000 troops by May 1940.[1] In both Britain and Australia, New Zealand's action cut the ground out from under Menzies. The Australian government was caught between the trenchant opposition of the ALP and the unions, aided and abetted by the CP-A, to sending any Australian troops overseas, and an electorate that would punish the government if it did not. As if this was not enough, the government had to deal with the professional ambitions of the generals, who wanted to serve in a critical theatre rather than garrisoning imperial backwaters.[2]

Despite all of this, the Menzies government remained shy of committing the AIF overseas and took refuge in the agreed plan to train the AIF in Australia.[3] This fell apart on 28 November when the Australian government was forced to match New Zealand's decision to deploy troops overseas on 2 January 1940.[4] While Australia would send troops, it was not going to send artillery or other equipment or materials that could not be quickly replaced. Parsimony was still priority number one it seems.[5]

This parsimony also applied to the CIB and the security intelligence system in Australia despite the fact that senior ministers, including Menzies and the chiefs of staff, were concerned at the current state of affairs. The main worry was that there was no central Commonwealth authority to carry out security intelligence and that the current hotchpotch of many mutually hostile agencies was highly inefficient.

Yet, even the armed services were not united on the issue, with the ACNB staying aloof except on the subject of the security of dockyards and other naval facilities. As for the army and the Royal Australian Air Force (RAAF), they desired a single system overseen by Military Intelligence. Outside of the military, the only Commonwealth agency interested in security intelligence was the CIB at the Attorney-General's Department, now led by George Knowles, who was no supporter of military involvement in civilian affairs.[6] The scene was now set for one of those long-running bureaucratic wars that would last as long as World War II itself. As if this were not enough, other players were moving to get in on the action.

One of these players was William MacKay, now the commissioner of the NSW Police, who in early 1939 recommended to the premier of New South Wales, B.S.B. Stevens, that a national conference be held to coordinate the responsibilities for internal security between the states and the

Commonwealth.[7] This initiative smacks of opportunism. The canny MacKay, with his functioning MPIS in Sydney, was pitching for a leading role at the centre of national affairs. Despite his motives, MacKay was right.

The response to MacKay's suggestion was muted and defensive. The Commonwealth proposed that everybody had to be consulted, and this would, as fully intended, take enough time to enable Secretary for Defence Co-Ordination Frederick Shedden and other bureaucrats to mark out their territory.

Shedden had learned his craft from Lord Hankey, the long serving Cabinet Secretary in London, something of which he was inordinately proud. Shedden's objective was to ensure he maintained total control of Australia's security affairs. Unfortunately for Shedden's peace of mind, his obstructionism ran into opposition from the archetypical political trouble-maker, Attorney-General William Hughes, who strongly endorsed MacKay's recommendations.

On 1 March 1939, Hughes moved to outflank Shedden by making a direct approach to the Defence Minister, Geoffrey Street, to hold the conference. Despite this, with the need to coordinate the CIB, the intelligence sections of the navy, army and RAAF and the commissioners of the six state police forces, and with Shedden running interference, getting approval for MacKay's conference took until 12 May, just over three months after the first letter from New South Wales.[8]

In this exchange of views there can be little doubt that Hughes, most likely aided and abetted by his departmental head, Knowles, worked on Street to convince him of the need for a Commonwealth security service controlled by a civilian department and not by the military. This may explain the later attempt by Street and Robert Menzies to form a wartime security organisation.

In Sydney, where MacKay ruled the roost, things moved faster than in Melbourne or the paddocks of Canberra, which, since 1927, was the projected home of the Commonwealth government. MacKay had been successfully working for some time to establish a closer working relationship between his force, Military Intelligence and the CIB. With the outbreak of war, his objective was accomplished when the Security Branch of the Military Intelligence Section of the General Staff in 2nd Military District merged with the NSW Police Subversive Organisations Branch to form the MPIS housed at police headquarters in Sydney under MacKay's watchful eye. The resulting organisation was quickly tasked with watching communists and suspicious foreigners, particularly Japanese, Italians and Germans.[9]

One small initiative of this period serves to underline the amateurism that still bedevilled Australia's security intelligence system, if it could be called a system. This was the re-employment of Harry Freame, a soldier of Japanese-Australian descent who had served with Lloyd at Gallipoli, by Military Intelligence. He was to serve as a secret agent spying on the Japanese Consulate-General and the Japanese community in Sydney and New South Wales. Freame was down on his luck. His wife had died and his orchard at Kentucky outside of Armadale had, like so many Soldier's Settlement blocks, failed and been sold from under him. Finding himself in need of work, there can be little doubt that Freame reached out to his old comrade, Lloyd.[10] It would appear that Lloyd passed him on to Military Intelligence who, despite knowing that the Japanese community in NSW and Japan's consular officials were fully aware that Freame was an Australian spy, re-employed him in a clandestine role.

The employment of Freame and the expansion of Military Intelligence into civilian security intelligence was not resisted by H.E. Jones' CIB because, as already mentioned, it was in no position to undertake additional work and was swamped by the growing influx of refugees fleeing Nazism in Europe. Ironically, Jewish refugees were the group the CIB focused its attention on because someone, probably Jones, had decided that Jews lucky enough to escape Nazi Germany could only have done so because they had agreed to work for the Nazis.[11] Before we accuse Jones of anti-Semitism, however, we need to consider that this logic was applied to non-Jewish Germans who had also fled Nazi Germany. So, happily, Australia's CIB was not anti-Semitic, just not very bright.

What Jones did not know was that in 1939 the Nazi regime was more than happy to let Jews, and other groups it viewed as undesirable or impure, leave its territories as long as they handed over their property and wealth in return for the exit visa. It was a state-sponsored program of demanding money with menaces that would soon turn into armed robbery before descending into robbery and homicide on a gigantic scale.

Jones also did not appreciate that in 1939 the Nazi regime would never have used Jews as spies. This would have affronted the central tenet of Nazism that Jews had no redeeming features as human beings at all. It is likely that such an idea was so foreign to a man like Jones that he would never have consciously considered it.

The Australian government's failure to create its own well-resourced intelligence organisations had now left it blind. In stark contrast to the bureaucrats and politicians of 1914, the generation between 1920 and 1945 seemed to lack foresight and ambition in these matters. Jones and his officers were mediocre officials from the margins of the public service. Their effectiveness can be seen in their failure between 1921 and 1939 to win resources, money, status or effectiveness for the CIB or to rationalise the work it did and the way it did it. The CIB carried no weight in departmental struggles. Its work was seen as of little importance to government until the threat of war began to grow from around 1935 until 1939, by which time it was too late to reform or rebuild the CIB to be an effective security intelligence organisation. Perhaps its only accomplishment was getting the Adjutant-General to ban army officers from membership of secret organisations, other than the Masons, an organisation to which many military, police and other uniformed officers belonged.

Jones' behaviour as the sole gatekeeper for all communications between MI5 in London and Australia clearly demonstrated the smallness of his thinking. His doling out of infrequent morsels of intelligence to Australia's government agencies and political leaders and his overly optimistic reporting to London of affairs in Australia shows him and his organisation to be ineffectual and unimportant. It would take until 1945 and a number of disasters in the relationship between MI5 and the Australian government for the British to realise that the CIB and its security service successor were utterly inept and unprofessional, and by then the threat had become very, very serious.

By the end of 1939, outside the navy, Australia's intelligence services were chaotic, and politicians and bureaucrats began to realise that the informal system that underpinned Australia's security intelligence was unequal to its tasks. There was constant internecine warfare between departments, the military and the Commonwealth and the states. The most they were capable of was monitoring the movements and activities of aliens and British subjects of dubious loyalty. There was no serious possibility of identifying or dealing with organised espionage carried out by foreign agents or their handlers in Australia. There was even less capacity to manage the day-to-day security of sensitive activities, facilities and information, including that provided to Australia by its allies. This failure to protect sensitive allied information would be the catalyst for the formation of ASIO ten years later in 1949.

There had been earlier efforts by the Australian government to create a national security apparatus under one department, but these had little chance of surviving the vested interests within the bureaucracy. The one throw of the dice was made in late 1938, when the Lyons government finally started to think about doing something about Australia's security intelligence system. Like distracted governments everywhere, they opted for an interdepartmental committee to look into the system. The Inter-Departmental Committee on National Intelligence submitted its recommendations on 7 February 1939, and these were promptly filed and forgotten until June of 1940, when Robert Menzies resurrected them in his capacity as the Minister for Defence Co-ordination.[12]

With the declaration of war, the problem of inadequate and disorganised security intelligence once again led the chiefs of staff to agitate for a more coordinated system that actually met their needs. Jones tried ineffectually to promote the claims of the CIB and MacKay continued building his empire in New South Wales. Meanwhile, in the Attorney-General's Department, Knowles was working his way towards sidelining the CIB and Jones by creating a new civilian organisation to take control of all security intelligence matters under the auspices of his department.[13]

The need for action arose from the failure to institute the agreed processes for controlling internal security contained in Chapter 6 of Part 1 of the *War Book*, the detailed plan of action that was intended to be implemented by the Commonwealth government upon the declaration of war.[14] This outlined that as soon as a 'precautionary stage' was declared, the Attorney-General's Department would hand over to Military Intelligence its entire investigation service and records, all of which would be incorporated into the Intelligence Section of the General Staff. Knowles and Hughes had no intention of letting this happen, and it didn't.[15]

In mid-1939, Menzies, in true lawyerly fashion, had attempted to address the problem of creating a single security intelligence organisation by drawing upon the findings of the interdepartmental committee's report of February 1939.[16] The recommendations of the committee had aligned with the requirements of Chapter 6 of the *War Book*: that 'the Attorney-General's Department should prepare to hand over to the Intelligence Section of the General Staff at Army Headquarters the personnel and records of the Investigation Branch (the CIB) as pre-arranged'.[17]

Once again, Cabinet temporised by suggesting yet another interdepartmental committee be established to oversee intelligence and the creation of a security organisation in the Department of Defence.[18] This recommendation was not even accepted by the entire interdepartmental committee.[19] Some members, no doubt including Knowles' representative, objected to placing a security intelligence organisation under the auspices of Defence.[20] The Attorney-General's Department would have been hostile to the loss of the CIB, its personnel and files and to the intrusion of the military into civilian affairs. The ground was now set for a bureaucratic war between the departments of the Attorney-General and Defence, a war that would only cease with the formation of ASIO.[21]

The proposals Menzies put up in June of 1940 make fascinating reading. The starting point was the original list of recommendations provided in February 1939; however, Menzies took these further and recommended the establishment of a completely new civilian department for internal civil security with its own minister and a director to act as its permanent head. This new department would take over the CIB from the Attorney-General's Department and establish close liaison with the intelligence sections of the services. It would assume responsibility for prosecuting individuals breaching security regulations and would take over and run internment.[22]

Menzies even recommended the new department would take over all of the internal security functions currently held by state police forces and that it would seek direct access to their personnel and records as part of this. Lastly, it would create a new police force by amalgamating the 'ACT Police, Naval Police, Army Watchmen, Defence Establishments Guards and any other persons similarly employed' into one force.[23]

Effectively, Menzies was recommending the creation of an organisation in Australia with responsibilities for collecting intelligence on citizens and then for prosecuting and imprisoning them. This was an organisation closer to Stalin's NKGB than it was to Britain's MI5.

Like many dangerous ideas, Menzies' proposal was well intentioned. His analysis of the existing Australian system as divided, prone to unnecessary 'friction', and of suffering from 'a want of co-operation' and 'the absence of any incisive action' was completely true.[24] Menzies also needs to be given credit for attempting to keep the military out of civilian security affairs, something he makes clear in his telegrams to Stanley Bruce, the Australian High Commissioner in London.[25]

None of these recommendations had any chance of proceeding as they stepped on the toes of every vested interest within the existing security intelligence system. It took the CIB and peace officers from the Attorney-General's Department, the military police from army, naval police from navy, the RAAF police from the RAAF and the Defence Establishments Guard from defence. Worse, Menzies also stepped on the toes of the states and their overly precious police commissioners.[26]

The first riposte to this initiative came on 10 June 1940, before Menzies even tabled his agendum. W. Forgan Smith, the premier of Queensland, wrote making it clear that Queensland had little intention of agreeing to the proposals being mooted in Melbourne and Canberra. The creation of a 'Local Security Officers Force' would be, as far as Smith was concerned, 'an embarrassment to the State Commissioner of Police and his officers in maintaining peace and order in the community'.[27] As far as Queensland was concerned, the existing arrangement between the state police and the military authorities worked well. In Queensland, so Smith said, the police had it all under control: 'in co-operation with the MI Service, investigating subversive activities of aliens and disaffected persons and it has the whole of the alien population of Queensland under strict supervision'.[28] If the Commonwealth really wanted to assist, Smith helpfully suggested, it could take over the manpower-intensive work of providing guards for vulnerable points.

The sting was in the tail of Smith's letter, where it was pointed out 'that while the State Government is responsible for the preservation of order within the State, it can hardly be expected to agree to the Head of its Police Force being placed under the control of an officer in the service of another Government', that is the Commonwealth.[29] Queensland was simply the first state to reject the Commonwealth's initiative. New South Wales and Western Australia temporised rather than reject the initiatives, while South Australia offered to cooperate, as did Victoria. Tasmania said no.[30]

The coup de grâce was administered on 12 September 1940 by the 'assembled Commissioners of Police representing the States' who had met to consider 'fully and carefully' the National Security (Local Security Officers) Regulations, number 164 of 1940. The regulations were, as far as the commissioners were concerned, unworkable.[31] They argued that their state auxiliary and special police could 'meet any emergency which is likely to arise' and they could mobilise even more men 'at a moment's notice'.[32] Given this capability, the commissioners considered 'the formation of another body of auxiliary police . . . unnecessary'.[33] If, however, the Commonwealth proceeded with the formation of a new body, then the commissioners wanted it on a national basis and wanted it to take over their auxiliary police forces. The relevant state police commissioner would then command this new force in each state.[34] The Commonwealth would pick up the cost of state organisations that would effectively remain in the control of the states. These recommendations were 'submitted purely in a spirit of helpfulness towards the Commonwealth'.[35]

Of course, nobody then or now believed that the spirit of helpfulness of Australia's state governments extended beyond looking after their own self-interests. It was the typical ruse of getting the Commonwealth to carry the cost of state organisations in return for empty promises of help in times to come.

The proposed local security officers' force was declared dead by the War Cabinet on 18 February 1941. The decision to form a new Commonwealth Security Service and the formation of the RSL Volunteer Defence Corps apparently made such an organisation unnecessary. It even made the proposed National Security (Local Security Officers) Regulations unnecessary as well.[36]

It would be wrong to see Australia as unique in suffering from such internal self-interested machinations. At around the same time in Britain, a similar battle was going on between the armed services, MI5, MI6, the Ministry of Information, the Board of Trade and the Cabinet Office over the way in which Britain's intelligence and security systems would be organised. The difference between Britain and Australia was that in London Winston Churchill was far more powerful than Menzies was in Melbourne or Canberra. Churchill got his way by ruthlessly sacking anyone he decided was not trying hard enough, whereas Menzies could not even get his own Cabinet to work together or support him.

CHAPTER 7

1940—THE FIFTH COLUMN PANIC

Australia may have been at war, but little happened, and what did happen occurred slowly. The Commonwealth looked to expanding the navy and the army sufficiently to ensure, if Britain and its allies won, a seat at any post-war peace conferences. Having identified and resourced this objective, there was then nothing of substance done to reorganise finances, mobilise industry or prepare the nation for war. In the intelligence sphere, the navy activated its maritime surveillance and control system and integrated this into the Admiralty's worldwide system as it had done in 1914. The army focused on recruiting and manning a Second AIF and worked to ensure it went to the Middle East and France, where medals and military glory could be won, and not to the backwater of Malaya.[1]

All of this business as usual faffing around changed on 10 May 1940, when the Wehrmacht's panzer divisions burst out to blitzkrieg across Holland, France and Belgium, and in London a new prime minister, the bellicose, energetic and hard-driving Winston Churchill, launched blitzkrieg on the establishment. As Churchill took over government, Britain and Australia began to realise that the war in France was being lost, and over the next eight weeks, it was. This left the Wehrmacht's divisions dominating the entire coast of Europe across the channel. It was a disaster of monumental proportions and excuses needed to be found.

The speed and completeness of the German victories, and the seeming ease with which their combined arms operated, had to be explained to Churchill, parliament and the people, and the best excuse was that the Germans had cheated. This cheating was, of course, their superior use of special forces, spies and the infamous but non-existent 'fifth column', a term first coined during the Spanish Civil War by the Nationalist General Emilio Mola to describe Nationalist loyalists inside the Republican-held city of Madrid besieged by the four columns of Mola's army. This was how appalling leadership, strategic incompetence and poor unit performance was to be explained away.

The Wehrmacht did conduct some notable special operations—particularly the capture and destruction of Fort Eben-Emael in Belgium and the taking of a bridgehead in the centre of Rotterdam by Luftwaffe paratroopers—however, the gains from these operations were tactical. The strategic and operational success of the Wehrmacht was in reality due to excellent staff work, a commitment to training, and a highly disciplined combined arms approach using armoured formations, air support and mobile artillery.

The fifth column excuse was widely and quickly accepted, and the generals began to see, or rather create, fifth columns everywhere. The idea that a small and highly dedicated team could wreak havoc reinforced Churchill's predilection for small group operations. As the fifth column scare spread through Britain's official classes in 1940, one can detect the element of wishful thinking in many of the files dealing with the subject. The German fifth column had obviously been highly effective, and it was now vital that they should be effectively countered and emulated.

Overestimation of the effectiveness of German intelligence had begun earlier in the war. The problem facing Britain's MI5 was the lack of identifiable German intelligence networks. This conundrum presented MI5 with two possible answers. Either the German intelligence networks didn't exist or they were so good they hadn't been detected. MI5 erroneously chose to believe their German opponents were highly effective. Of course, from a bureaucratic perspective, this was the correct way to answer such a conundrum. As a result, a vast system was created to counter a threat that was nowhere near as dire as officialdom believed.

The idea of a highly efficient and widespread German spy network was hard to deal with sensibly because the failure to detect it did not mean it did not exist. In fact, it was MI5's own efficiency that made the matter worse, as the limited German intelligence activity in Britain was soon stopped by several key arrests, particularly that of Arthur Owens, which we will discuss below.

On 31 October 1939, the British Cabinet responded to concerns about German agents operating in Britain by appointing a Leakage of Information Committee—consisting of Lord Hankey, Minister without Portfolio, the Secretary of State for War, the Secretary of State for Dominion Affairs and the Secretary of State for Home Affairs—to examine whether information was being passed to the enemy, including via communication links between the United Kingdom, Northern Ireland and Eire, The Republic of Ireland[2]

Hankey was the right man for this particular job, having served as the Secretary of the Committee for Imperial Defence from 1912 until 1938 and Cabinet Secretary from 1916 until 1938.[3] This had put him at the heart of Britain's defence and intelligence operations for all but the first twelve years of the twentieth century. In a verbal report on 2 November 1939, Hankey recommended the tapping of all telephone calls between Eire, the United Kingdom and Northern Ireland and the re-routing of all telegraphic traffic through London, where it would be scrutinised. In addition, he recommended sending experts and equipment to Eire to allow the Irish government to establish its own intercept capability directed at clandestine German or Italian wireless networks.[4]

Hankey's committee found that sampling of telephone, telegraph and radio traffic produced no evidence of information being passed to the enemy via these means. It did not identify any large enemy spy networks or the existence of clandestine radio networks. The committee found no clandestine radio transmission had ever been detected in Britain. Of course, this was not seen as proof of non-existence but proof of a higher level of German sophistication, making the signals hard to find.

As a result, considerable resources, time and effort were used in creating a radio interception service dedicated to the detection and reporting of clandestine radio signals from within Britain itself.[5] This service found such a dearth of enemy clandestine radio communication it later added to its purview the bigger role of intercepting British and Allied transmissions to identify poor operator technique and error that could provide the enemy with the cribs that are so essential to breaking codes and ciphers.

The other aspect of the intelligence equation that the British government and its advisors needed to consider was that radio transmissions, telegrams and letters had to be created and sent by someone: who could these people be? The answer was superficially easy: it was the large number of enemy aliens now living in Britain. What to do about this was harder, and the British government and its advisors split into two camps. The first, comprising the military and MI5, argued for the simplistic approach of surveilling and interning all enemy aliens.[6] Ranged against this argument were the Home Office and the Home Secretary, Sir John Anderson, who strongly argued that aliens and anti-Nazi refugees posed no threat to the security of Britain. As far as the Home Secretary and Home Office were concerned, the surveillance and internment demanded by the chiefs of staff would 'inflict a good deal of hardship on aliens' and this would lead to criticism and questions in parliament.[7]

Hankey's committee supported Anderson and the Home Office but the argument had leaked from Cabinet and threatened to become a political controversy.[8] Prime Minister Chamberlain brokered a compromise, which saw the Home Office's reservations taken into account, but the preparations for internment were put in train.[9] In true British fashion, the decision was implemented slowly and the only hard action taken was the registration of all aliens and the preparation of internment facilities for those aliens deemed high risk.

Superficially, rounding up and interning tens of thousands of Germans, Austrians and Italians looked like a reasonable thing for the British government to do. It certainly addressed the public's demands for action against German and Austrian nationals living in Britain. However, the difficulty of sorting the dangerous from the unfortunate was more exacting, time-consuming and costly than many realised. On top of this, there was the need to house, clothe and feed these internees, many of whom detested the Nazi and fascist regimes. The reality was appreciated by the British government and its advisors and little action was taken to implement wholesale internment. In fact, the British government, particularly Churchill and Sir John Anderson, had accepted the Home Office view that the anti-Hitler refugees from Germany and Austria could provide Britain with substantial benefits in fighting the war. Events would prove Churchill, Sir John Anderson and the Home Office to be right.

In Australia, the situation regarding internments of enemy aliens appeared to be similar, but this similarity was more the product of government indecision and inaction than of informed discussion as to the best way forward. The other problem that would bedevil Australia was the greater deference the political leadership would give to the advice of the military establishment, particularly the General Staff.

The result of this was that, although Australia's various security bodies would harass foreign communities—especially the Italians of northern Queensland—and intern Japanese residents, the logistics and costs were so prohibitive that only 6780 Australian residents were interned in September 1942 at the height of the invasion panic generated by the Japanese successes in Asia.[10]

One practice Australia did not adopt from Britain was the security vetting of all applicants for government jobs, including those in scientific programs and the armed services. As a result, the CP-A and its associates in the Russian intelligence services (RIS) would extensively penetrate Australia's governmental, scientific and military institutions on a scale that no one in 1939 could have imagined. All of that lay in the not-too-distant future.

The decision not to introduce security vetting was not as silly as it later looked. The reality was that vetting all government, military and persons conducting sensitive work was a massive undertaking made many times worse by the rapid growth of government and military organisations due to the war. In Britain, security vetting of individuals holding sensitive positions began in 1938 and MI5 was charged with conducting these 'clearances' to work. This created a large workload which MI5 was not prepared for and, as preparations for war increased, MI5's capabilities were further tested to breaking point.

It is instructive to consider that in January 1939, MI5 was receiving an average of 2300 submissions for vetting every week, which by September had grown to 6800 and by June 1940 to 8000 a week.[11] Given this, and the fact that until cleared a new employee could not take up their post, it is clear why the Australian government shied away from this activity.

On top of this, there remained travel and border control to oversee and, as in Britain, there was the flood of denunciations from the spiteful, the dutiful and the just plain mad.[12]

In Britain, MI5 had 83 officers and 253 support staff, almost entirely women, organised into four branches—A, B, C and D.[13] A Branch was responsible for personnel, finance and administration, including the registry (the cross-referenced card index of individuals, names, covernames, events, clues, operations, organisations and any other piece of information deemed worthy of remembering); B Branch was the investigative arm of MI5, responsible for investigating all threats to security; C Branch undertook vetting duties; and D Branch provided security advice to government agencies and the munitions industry and oversaw border protection.[14] For such a small organisation, the tasks being imposed by the resumption of hostilities were well beyond its capabilities. Australia's security intelligence system was even smaller and split among a number of competing agencies and services.

When war broke out in September 1939, Germany's foreign intelligence organisation, the Amstgruppe Auslandsnachrichten und Abwehr (Abwehr), led by Admiral Canaris, had managed to plant only six active agents in Britain. The tradecraft involved in running these six agents, and the 30 or so espionage operations they conducted, was so poor that four were arrested as soon as war was declared. These arrested agents were so ill prepared that MI5 assessed them as 'unimportant'.[15]

Another agent, My Eriksson, a Swedish national who had been identified as a German agent in 1938, was left free until December 1939, most likely to allow MI5 to identify her network. When no progress was made in this, she was arrested for providing untrue information on an exit permit.[16]

The final agent, codename SNOW, was Arthur Owens, a Welsh electrical engineer who had been an agent of MI6 since 1936. Owens is acknowledged in the *Official History of British Intelligence in the Second World War* as a regular source for MI6 from 1936. This would mean that MI6 had penetrated the Abwehr's networks from an early date and that the rapid rounding up of the entire Abwehr network after the outbreak of war resulted from this.

In 1938, Owens reported to MI6 that he had been appointed by the Abwehr as the 'chief' agent in Britain and would be receiving a clandestine radio set. When his radio duly arrived, Owens turned it over to MI6. With the declaration of war, Owens was handed off by MI6 to MI5 after his wife and son exposed him as a German spy.[17] The problem with Owens was that he did not seem to know which side he should be working for. His efforts as an XX ('Double Cross') operative, that is an identified German agent successfully recruited to work for MI5, sending false intelligence via his German radio to the Abwehr seemed to engender enough trust for British authorities to permit him to travel to Portugal in the company of Walter Dickens, an

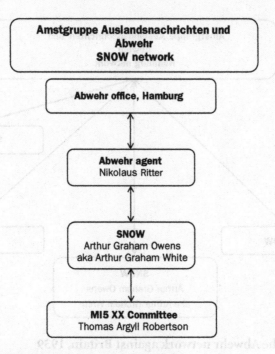

Figure 7.1: The SNOW Abwehr network, 1939

Source: Hinsley and Simkins, *Security and Counter-Intelligence*, pp. 41–2.

ex-Royal Naval Air Service officer with a criminal history for fraud who was now an MI5 operative. Owens' behaviour became so erratic, though, that his handlers, led by the Scottish MI5 agent Thomas Argyll Robertson, eventually viewed him as untrustworthy and dangerous and he was arrested.

Following his arrest, Owens was detained at Wandsworth and Dartmoor prisons from where he continued to operate as a double agent and was instrumental in setting up the XX system, which was to tear the heart out of Germany's HUMINT effort in Britain.[18] The problem was that it had been so easy, the British did not believe in their own success and kept looking for the real German spy networks.

One of the initiatives of the new Churchill administration was the creation on 27 May 1940 of a centralised, high-level internal security oversight body, the Security Executive, led by Conservative politician Lord Swinton, as the Director-General, and A.M. Wall, General Secretary of the London Society of Compositors and a member of the Trades Union Congress General Council, as his deputy. Isaac Foot, a Liberal MP, later joined the executive to ensure

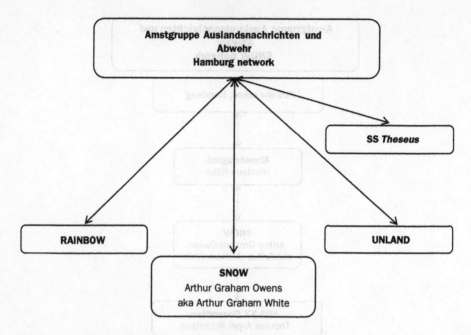

Figure 7.2: The Abwehr network against Britain, 1939

Source: Hinsley and Simkins, *Security and Counter-Intelligence*, pp. 44, 92, 102–3 and 123.

all three major political parties were represented.[19] Joseph Ball, an ex-MI5 officer whose credentials included a stint working in the Conservative Central Office, assisted Swinton and his fellow political overseers.[20] Swinton now had executive control over MI5 and MI6, overseeing all counterespionage activities in Great Britain and the British Isles including Eire.[21]

The other of Churchill's initiatives, and the one most relevant to the Australian story, was the creation of a new department for irregular warfare, the Special Operations Executive (SOE), authorised by Cabinet on 1 July 1940. It was placed under its own minister, Hugh Dalton. The British SOE was now about to be exported across the Commonwealth.

The SOE was not, strictly speaking, an intelligence organisation, as the collection of intelligence was a by-product of its irregular warfare activities. Its role was not to insert HUMINT operatives and then collect, collate and report their findings. Rather, SOE trained and infiltrated saboteurs into enemy-occupied areas to, as Churchill bluntly put it, set Europe ablaze. Unfortunately, starting fires in other people's backyards attracts a lot of hostile attention and hostile attention very quickly becomes hostile action, which, in the case of the Germans, was fast, indiscriminate and brutal, and, as a result, highly effective in destroying local support for British intelligence and sabotage operations.

One result of this increasingly hostile environment was that it became increasingly difficult to mount traditional intelligence operations and, as they did not operate in large armed parties, MI6 operatives were either lost to the Germans, stopped reporting or were withdrawn to safety. This left the intelligence collection field clear for SOE and it now took over many of the roles previously held by the War Office, MI6 and other agencies.

Churchill's initiative in setting up the SOE had little direct effect on MI5, but that did not stop him from quickly dispensing with its leadership and demanding an increased security intelligence effort by the organisation. Just over a month after Churchill became prime minister, on 11 June 1940, Major General Vernon Kell and his deputy, Sir Eric Holt-Wilson, were sacked.[22] Their crime was being too slow to respond to the threat posed by the fifth column and the large numbers of enemy aliens still walking free among the British population.

Over at MI6, the Chief, 'C', Sir Stewart Menzies, managed to survive. The reasons for this are largely unknown, but Menzies' adroit use of SIGINT derived from the operations of the Government Code and Cypher School (GC&CS), which came under the auspices of MI6, is often offered as the rationale.[23] Yet Menzies was more than just a conduit for SIGINT to Churchill and he had long been an adroit player of Whitehall's mandarin politics.

In Britain, the reservations over internment were swept away and between 26 June and 11 July 1940 there were 27,000 aliens, including 4000 Italians, and members of the British Union of Fascists (BUF) rounded up and interned. Excepting German or Italian members, the Communist Party of Great Britain (CP-GB) was exempted because it was feared that any repressive action against the members of the CP-GB would have unfortunate industrial repercussions;[24] however, the *Daily Worker*, the CP-GB's official paper, was suppressed and closed.

Swinton addressed the organisational problems within MI5 by devolving responsibility for certain activities to Regional Security Liaison Officers (RSLOs) based at Civil Defence Regional HQs. By doing this, Swinton was able to create a local network of MI5 representatives, police and military officials. This incorporated the police forces more fully into the security apparatus as well as ensuring that local military and service commands had a local point of contact. This new arrangement took an enormous amount of pressure off MI5's HQ as the vast amount of the reporting made by the public could be vetted locally. In this way, the desks and sections at MI5's HQ were freed up for work that was more important, while a wide-ranging surveillance was still maintained.

This reorganisation was welcome, but the other side of the coin was that Swinton, Wall and Foot were now competitors of MI5 in the day-to-day running of the organisation. This finally led to confrontation between the Security Executive and MI5 when the executive ordered MI5 to recruit lawyers and detectives from the police forces.[25] In November 1940, the British War Cabinet commissioned Sir David Petrie, a retired officer of the Indian Police who had also served as a member and chair of the Indian Public Service Commission, to undertake an inquiry into the organisation.

Despite substantial opposition, mostly from Sir Alexander Cadogan, the Permanent Under-Secretary for the Foreign Office, who considered the appointment of Petrie as a 'bad move', Petrie was appointed, and his report handed to the War Cabinet on 13 February 1941.[26] Petrie's findings were unsurprising. He found that the rapid expansion of MI5 from 33 officers and 119 support staff in September 1938 to 234 officers and 676 support staff in January 1941 had led to a serious dislocation in the recruitment, training and organisation of senior staff.[27] They were not experienced or well trained enough to do their jobs effectively. He also recommended that politicians should not interfere in the day-to-day operations of the organisation, whose affairs were rightly the concern of the Director of MI5 and should be left to that person.

The outcome was that Petrie was appointed as the Director of MI5 and he quickly came to an amicable agreement with Swinton in April 1941. As Director-General, Swinton would be responsible through the Security Executive to the Lord President for the affairs of MI5 and other agencies falling under his supervision, while Petrie would run the day-to-day operations of MI5.[28] This arrangement worked well, and Petrie remained in his position until he retired in 1946. This makes Petrie one of the principal players in the unsuccessful efforts to modernise and professionalise both Britain's and Australia's security services during the war.

Dominion representatives in London were kept informed about the progress of counterintelligence in Britain and they reported this back to their respective governments. In Australia, similar fears were held and similar discussions had been taking place, but nothing concrete had been done because of the administrative and political difficulties involved.[29] However, fresh impetus seems to have been created by the arrival in mid-1940 of a signal or letter from General Edmund Ironside, the Chief of the Imperial General Staff in London, to General Brudenell White, the Australian Chief of the General Staff, detailing the threats posed by German and Italian espionage and fifth columnists. Unfortunately, this communication came from the War Office, not MI5, so there is no way of knowing what it contained because it was never filed, and White kept its contents secret from his own staff.

At this stage of the war, Ironside's grasp on reality and his job was slipping. In another signal to all military commands in the United Kingdom, Ironside credulously detailed for his subordinates the threat posed by individuals 'preparing aerodromes in this country' for use by the Germans. This signal has been described as 'extraordinary' by historians working in the area and was most likely the basis of the later telegram he sent to White claiming the 'existence of a highly organised world-wide organisation of Italians and Germans for the prosecution [of] para-military and fifth column activities.'[30] The arrival of this signal was unfortunate, as it arrived in the middle of the debate on internal security in Australia.[31]

It was in this debate that Attorney-General Hughes, advised by George Knowles, recommended that the CIB, already part of the Attorney-General's Department, should form the basis of the new security intelligence organisation.[32] Hughes also made the very relevant point that by its very nature, internal security intelligence intruded upon the rights of the individual to such an extent that legal questions constantly arose, particularly where prosecution was being considered. For this reason, and most likely at the prompting of Knowles, Hughes argued for the closest relationship between any security intelligence organisation and the law department.

Despite the communications and discussions of mid-1940, by January 1941 little of significance had been achieved and Australia's security system remained relatively disorganised. As a result, the security of government information was completely compromised and, in a small town—which is all Canberra was—there was an even greater level of insecurity than there was in Melbourne.

The compact size of Australia's government in 1939–40 meant that everyone knew everyone else. Journalists, politicians, ministers and bureaucrats mixed with diplomats and foreign officials and anyone else who stayed at one of the few hotels or accommodation facilities that existed. It also meant that officials had to transfer sensitive documents up and down the rail lines between Melbourne (the original location for the government), Canberra and Sydney (the locus of the RAN and much of the army).

The result was that official information in Australia was highly vulnerable. Information and gossip, rumour and the telling of tales out of school energised social relationships, and the need to curry favour with journalists and other departments meant that information, secret or not, was readily available to anyone admitted to the inner sanctums of those hotels and accommodation blocks. The resulting familiarity made keeping secrets very difficult and, unsurprisingly, Canberra leaked like a sieve. Melbourne was little better.

All of this was understood and drove the services' strong desire for the formation of a security intelligence organisation, however the General Staff remained hostile towards any attempt to remove their responsibility for security in Australia, something that Knowles at the Attorney-General's Department was determined to do.

The effect of this inter-departmental conflict over the control of Australia's security intelligence was that it took from June 1940 until March 1941 for a temporary compromise to be reached. Driven by Attorney-General Hughes, the War Cabinet agreed to the formation of the Commonwealth Security Service (CSS), led by Lloyd, under the auspices of the Attorney-General's Department, to commence operations on 31 March 1941.[33] This compromise was driven by the Attorney-General's Department in an attempt to stop the formation of a Defence security intelligence organisation that Knowles feared would be controlled by the General Staff. The formation of the CSS under Lloyd circumvented the army's initiative for a security service controlled by Defence.[34]

The new head of this service would be Lloyd, who had recently been appointed Deputy Director of the CIB. Lloyd had served with the 1st Battalion on Gallipoli before he was returned to Australia suffering typhoid fever in 1916. On his recovery, Lloyd was posted to Military Intelligence in Sydney where he enrolled in Professor Murdoch's Japanese language program in which his old comrade, Harry Freame, was an instructor. In May 1921, following Prime Minister Hughes' destruction of the Pacific Branch and Atlee

Hunt's intelligence system—including the Japanese language program—Lloyd found a position in the new CIB.

Lloyd did well within the CIB, rising to senior positions under H.E. Jones. He served diligently and, because of his Japanese language training, he was hand-picked to undertake translation duties in legal cases involving Japanese fishermen and was seconded to John Latham's 1934 mission to the Netherlands East Indies and Japan. Lloyd appears to have enjoyed the diplomatic circuit, as one of his faults was, as far as Knowles was concerned, 'his manner of writing [which] is involved in the extreme . . . [and] his language is rather the language of the diplomat'. Knowles was not being complimentary, but was providing the reasons why he could not recommend Lloyd as the replacement for Jones.[35] Another contemporary intelligence commentator, Lieutenant Colonel John Mawhood, was even less complimentary, reporting to Knowles and the Attorney-General that Lloyd had 'neither the intelligence, personality or knowledge' to head a security service.[36]

Most likely at the insistence of Knowles, the CSS was to be based in Canberra, well away from General Headquarters (GHQ) at Victoria Barracks and the bulk of the government's departments in Melbourne.[37] Officially, the CSS was to take over all security matters previously dealt with by the armed services, but with some exceptions. The exceptions were actually substantial and included security intelligence as it affected the armed services, censorship and internment of civilians.[38]

Lloyd's CSS consisted of himself as Director, with the Australian Commonwealth Naval Board (ACNB) represented by Commander C.R. Little, the army by Major C.A.K. Cohen and the RAAF by Squadron Leader H.J. Hilary Taylor. The staff included a chief clerk plus another clerk, three typists and a switchboard operator. The army loaned three Military Intelligence officers and another clerk.[39] A further six personnel—two section chiefs, three more clerks and a messenger—were being moved from the public service to the CSS and each state was to have a section leader and other staff allocated to it.

Despite the compromise agreement, the army had no intention of turning over its files to the CSS or of allowing it to operate without being effectively controlled by the chiefs of staff, which effectively meant by the Chief of the General Staff because the ACNB didn't want to be involved and the Air Staff were not capable of fighting the General Staff on this issue. The result was that the CSS was not effective. It lacked money, men and resources.

It was not able to arrange the centralisation of its files, let alone obtain the transfer of the files held by the armed services to a central registry. In the main, the activities of the players were little affected by the formation of the CSS and it had absolutely no impact upon the security problems faced by Australia's government.

Indeed, it was soon after the formation of the CSS that, in April 1941, Australia experienced its first major security scare when highly sensitive signals intelligence (SIGINT) derived from decrypting Germany's or another country's high-level communications found its way from a 'Most Secret' document read by Robert Menzies in London to the *Sydney Morning Herald* of 23 April and then *The Times* of London after Menzies had copied the information into an official telegram to his deputy, Arthur Fadden, in Australia.[40]

The analysis of the communications that passed from Menzies to Fadden concerning this incident shows that Menzies sent the information to Fadden via Australia's communications channels without having consulted Churchill. The British did not miss the reporting in *The Times* or the by-line attributing it to the *Sydney Morning Herald*. There can be no doubt that Churchill raised this directly with Menzies, who on 26 April was urgently telegramming Fadden that he was 'amazed to note the close relation' of the *Sydney Morning Herald*'s summary of the situation in the Middle East to the text of the cables.[41]

It was during this period, June 1940 to March 1941, that Harry Freame was attached as an interpreter to the first Australian Legation to Tokyo, led by Sir John Latham. His appointment was disclosed in Australia's newspapers, as was Freame's work as a secret intelligence agent. It was known that the Kempeitai, the Military Police of the IJA, had destroyed the entirety of the British MI6 networks in Japan and murdered the MI6 station chief, James Cox. The Japanese prime minister, General Tojo Hideki, had announced that anyone caught spying on Japan would be harshly dealt with. It comes as no surprise that Freame later told his wife and other witnesses that he had been garotted on a Tokyo street, shortly before dying in Sydney, allegedly from the injuries he sustained.[42] That Australia's secret intelligence system sent Freame to Tokyo after he had been publicly identified as a secret agent is an indication of the amateurism that pervaded the system and its leadership and amounts to criminal negligence.

So, by early 1941 Australia had made little headway in reorganising its security intelligence system. The army was fighting off all attempts to exclude Military Intelligence from involving itself in civilian matters, the

Attorney-General's Department was working hard to undermine the army and the Cabinet was ineffectual. As if all of this was not enough, the British decided to impose upon the situation by sending across a representative, Lieutenant Colonel Mawhood, an ex-member of the 1st AIF and possibly a representative of MI5. Unfortunately, Mawhood's role is unclear because it appears to have been informally agreed between the Chief of the Imperial General Staff and Brudenell White, leaving no record of what the intentions behind Mawhood's mission actually were.

CHAPTER 8

THE MAWHOOD MYSTERY

John Mawhood is something of an enigma. He was born in November 1896 in Kirkee, modern-day Khadki, a cantonment in the city of Poona in the present-day state of Maharashtra in India. His father was John William Mawhood, an Officiating First Assistant in the Mechanical Branch of the Small Arms Factory at Kirkee.[1] Mawhood's father also served in the Poona Volunteer Rifles, rising to the rank of Colour Sergeant and gaining the Indian Volunteer Force Long Service Medal. The young Mawhood joined his father in this unit and left when the family moved to Melbourne in March 1914.[2]

The family took up residence at 9 Woods Parade, Ascot Vale, which was subsequently named Kirkee, after their home in India. This remained the family's address for some time and subsequent records of Mawhood's movements into and out of Australia give this address as his residence in Australia in 1920 and 1922.[3]

It appears that Mawhood and his brother went to Scotch College in Melbourne and, by early 1915, Mawhood became a student at Melbourne University's Dookie Agricultural College near Shepperton, where he subsequently enlisted in the 1st AIF.[4] The young Mawhood was posted as a gunner to the Artillery before he transferred to the Provost Corps where, by the end of 1917, he had risen to the rank of corporal.[5] In late 1917, as part of a group

110

of thirteen Australian volunteers, Mawhood discharged from the Australian Army to undertake officer training in the Indian Army.[6] He was later commissioned as a second lieutenant in the Indian Army and attached to the Guides Cavalry (Frontier Force) Regiment.[7]

The fact that Mawhood was attached and not posted strongly suggests from the beginning he was being groomed for an intelligence role in the Indian Army. From 23 February 1918 until August 1919 he was at the Quetta Cadet College before attending the Indian Army's Intelligence School.[8] Later that year, he was at Gullundar (Jullundur in the Punjab), where he most likely earned the clasps for service in Afghanistan and the North-West Frontier for 1919.[9]

During his service with this unit, Mawhood seems to have served in Northern Persia as part of NORPERFORCE, a British expeditionary force despatched to defend British interests in Persia from Bolshevik forces. It would seem that while he was in Northern Persia, he was the acting brigade major from November 1920 until December 1921 before becoming a brigade major in the Persian Army.[10] If this is true, then it is likely that Mawhood served directly under Major General Sir Edmund Ironside, the man who in 1940 would create Military Mission 104.[11] Mawhood's appointment as a brigade major in both the Indian and Persian armies means that he was a member of the small group of officers who, under Ironside, engineered the Reza Khan coup in Persia.[12]

Mawhood's qualifications for this work would have been his language skills, which would have included formal Urdu, Punjabi and Farsi as well as the vernacular he would have learned as a boy growing up in India. This potentially explains why as a junior officer he was appointed to fill the senior position of brigade major for a Persian Army unit.

Mawhood's history in India and Persia suggests that he was an effective officer and his subsequent appointment as a staff officer in the Military Intelligence Branch of General HQ in Delhi would support this. Whatever the success or otherwise of his military career, he departed India permanently in December 1922 to return to the United Kingdom via Australia and resigned his commission on 24 January 1923.[13]

In 1925, Mawhood became a trading station manager for Unilever in Nigeria.[14] On 11 August 1927, after a three-week engagement during a period of leave in London, he married C.M. Barber. He then returned to Lagos to finish the final eighteen months of his contract with Unilever.[15] From this time, Mawhood disappears, only to show up again in 1939.[16]

The lack of any profile or history during this period is suspicious. It is the sort of profile, dropping in and out of the record, that can be associated with someone working in intelligence, especially someone involved in overseas intelligence; however, there is no hard evidence of Mawhood having served in either MI5 or MI6. But then, you would expect that to be the case.

Mawhood next crops up in the record on 29 August 1939 when he was commissioned into the British Army as part of a group with Lieutenant Colonel H.W.S. Venn, Major J.T. Avison, Captain H.F. Magnus, Captain T.P. Spens and Captain A.H.P. West.[17] This group stands out because they were all appointed to the Territorial Army Special List in reasonably senior ranks— Venn as a lieutenant colonel, Avison as a major and Mawhood and the rest as captains.[18] Within a week, their initial ranks were rescinded and they were all re-gazetted as lieutenants.[19] This might not seem strange in the case of Mawhood, whose highest substantive rank had been lieutenant, but within a year, all of the members of the group held ranks ranging from major to lieutenant colonel, indicating some degree of confusion about their status. The way in which their commissioning was handled suggests the group consisted of civilian experts brought in together, with civilian salary levels that could only be matched by appointing them to very senior ranks.[20]

The contortions involving the commissioning of this group is suspicious. At the time the group was commissioned, MI5's recruitment process was chaotic, and in a desperate search for personnel each MI5 officer 'tore around' recruiting friends and acquaintances to fill positions. This led to an influx of retired officials, officers and people from other ministries.[21] It is possible that Mawhood and others in the group were being recruited into MI5's D Branch (protective security). This would explain why Mawhood was able to show senior Australian officials an official MI5 pass and why MI5 reportedly vouched for him to their Australian interlocutor, H.E. Jones of the CIB. It also suggests Mawhood was recruited into the Territorial Army and from there into protective security working under MI5's D Branch.[22] It strongly suggests that, despite later denials by MI5 officials, Mawhood worked within or for MI5, although not as an officer of MI5.

It is likely that few, including the later Director of MI5, Sir David Petrie, and his senior officers, knew what Mawhood's orders actually were. These may have been lost in the confusion of the time. Most certainly, officers like Lieutenant Colonel E.A. Airy were not privy to the real mission given to Mawhood and would have accepted or played to any disavowals of Mawhood's status they received from London.[23] Given all of this, and Petrie's later need to rebuild bridges with the Australian Security Service, the disavowal of Mawhood as an MI5 representative needs to be taken with a pinch of salt.[24]

The criticism that arose later about Mawhood and his work may possibly have been due to him not being MI5's man, but one of Hugh Dalton's from the newly formed SOE. After all, the agreement to send Military Mission 104 to Australia was made between the War Office in London and the Chief of the General Staff in Australia. Perhaps it was decided to task Mawhood with two missions. Indeed, given the dearth of experienced security intelligence officers in MI5 in 1940, it is probable that MI5 decided to piggyback on the War Office's mission. This might explain the conflicting evidence relating to his status as an MI5 representative.

MI5's own files show that Mawhood was tasked with providing the Australian Military Forces with advice on the establishment of a Military I(b) system similar to the War Office's I(b) system, which was charged with conducting offensive intelligence collection operations within the United Kingdom in association with MI5.[25] A signal sent by Sir John Dill, the Chief of the Imperial General Staff at the time, to Brudenell White at the end of June 1940 detailed the objectives of Military Mission 104 as being:

that a special branch be set up in the DOMINIONS:–
1. To initiate the defensive action against enemy fifth column and para-military activities,
2. To initiate offensive action by organising our own fifth column and allocate military activities in territories either likely to be occupied by the enemy or which are suspect [26]

This reads more like the setting up of a SOE-type organisation, but with the additional task of setting up a 'defensive' security intelligence organisation.[27]

Military Mission 104, like Mawhood, seems to have had two purposes. The documentary evidence shows that the mission was not an open-ended commitment to Australia. The mission was only to be operating in Australia until mid-1941, after which it redeployed to Singapore, Malaya and Burma, and, in July 1941, its members were indeed redeployed with one posted to the Bush Warfare School in Malaya and another to No. 104 Special Training School Singapore.[28]

Oddly, if he was in fact the commander of Military Mission 104, Mawhood remained in Australia; and this was not an afterthought, as his wife and two young children, John, aged eleven, and Cecilia, aged twenty months, had accompanied him to Australia. This is solid evidence that the authorities in Britain did not see Mawhood's appointment in Australia as a short-term affair, as his wife made quite clear in comments reported in the *Sydney Morning Herald*, confirming the family had come from Nottingham and would be in Sydney for the duration of the war.[29] This does not fit with the plans for Mission 104, which clearly stated that it would train commandos in New Zealand and Australia who would then undertake the training of further classes of commandos. Once the first school of commando graduates had been trained, Mission 104 was to move to Singapore and set up shop there. Yet, Mawhood and his family were in Australia and announcing they would be here for the duration of the war.

None of this makes any sense. Neither does Mawhood as the Commanding Officer of a commando training establishment. Mawhood was a 44-year-old newly recruited wartime Intelligence Corps officer. At that age, he was too old and out of date to be involved in training commandos and thus too old to be the commanding officer of a commando training unit. He had no recent frontline combat experience, no record of technical expertise in explosives, communications or living off the land or any other skill set relevant to commando operations.

This does not add up, and in Freddie Spencer Chapman's book *The Jungle is Neutral*, it is clear that, although the objectives of the mission were vague, it concerned SOE-type activity and, more darkly, intelligence agents and their activities.[30] If there was an intelligence role attached to Military Mission 104, and the evidence suggests there was, then this appears to have been where Mawhood came in.

From a military perspective, the most experienced officer on the mission was Captain James Michael Calvert of the Royal Engineers. Calvert was a regular officer who had served extensively in China and who spoke both Mandarin and Cantonese. In addition, he had spied on the IJA in China, specifically around Shanghai in late 1937 and early 1938, where he was captured and given the treatment by the Kempeitai during his interrogation.[31] Given that he was an engineer officer highly experienced in demolitions and had both languages and experience of China and the Japanese, he was ideal for this mission. Calvert would go on to become famous as one of Orde Wingate's senior commando officers, and served in Burma with Wingate's Chindits, raiding deep behind Japanese lines.

Captain Frederick Spencer Chapman of the Argyll and Sutherland Highlanders was perhaps not as well suited for the mission. His areas of expertise were survival and field craft, but he was a cold weather and mountain warfare expert, not an expert in jungle warfare. In fact, the main reason he accepted a posting to the mission was simply that he had never been to Australia and wished to visit.[32]

The last two members of the mission were technical experts, Warrant Officer Class II Frank Misselbrook, the communications expert, and Warrant Officer Class II Peter Stafford, the weapons instructor.[33] All of the technical expertise for training commandos lay with these four men, not with Mawhood.

In Australia, one man in particular took a distinct interest in Military Mission 104 and this was the long-time opponent of military interference in civil security intelligence affairs, Sir George Knowles, Secretary of the Attorney-General's Department.

Of all of the actors in the saga surrounding the creation of an Australian security intelligence organisation, Knowles was the most consistent and clear-sighted in attempting to address the needs of national security within the proper framework of a liberal democracy, which ensured the primacy of the legal standing of the individual citizen while also protecting the nation from attack.

Knowles' hostility towards military involvement in civil security intelligence was longstanding and in keeping with his strict adherence to the doctrines of Wesleyan Methodism, his particular brand of Christianity.

Knowles was born in Toowong, Brisbane, on 14 March 1882 to George Hopely Knowles, an English-born immigrant and now postmaster, and his wife Mary, a native-born Queenslander.[34] The young George attended Warwick West Boys' School and Toowoomba Grammar as a dayboy before seeking a position as a clerk in the Queensland public service in 1898. Knowles served as a clerk in the office of the chief inspector of Stock and Registrar of Brands while studying accountancy part-time at the Brisbane Central Technical College. This led Knowles to the Queensland Auditor-General's Department before he decided to join the new Commonwealth Audit Office in Melbourne on 1 September 1902.[35]

Knowles took up his new position and enrolled in night classes at the University of Melbourne in 1903 where his endeavours gained him a Bachelor of Law in 1907, a Master of Law in 1908, a Bachelor of Arts in 1910, a Master of Arts in 1912 and honours in the schools of logic, philosophy and law.[36] In 1907, Knowles was recruited by Sir Robert Garran into the Attorney-General's Department, in which he would serve until 1946. In 1908, he married his next-door neighbour, co-religionist and long-term fiancée, Mary Bennett, before raising three sons and a daughter.[37]

Intelligent, dedicated and loyal to his mentor Garran, Knowles advanced rapidly within the Attorney-General's Department, becoming the Assistant Parliamentary Draftsman and deputy to Garran in June 1913. For the next eighteen years, Knowles served Garran, acting in his boss's absences as the secretary of the department and solicitor-general before, in 1931, taking over the roles permanently. As a result of his success in his various roles, including as one of the leading champions of Canberra as the nation's capital, Knowles was knighted on 2 January 1939.

From 1939 until his retirement in 1946, Knowles continued the fight to create a truly civilian security intelligence organisation and to limit the impositions of the wartime governments on the civil rights of Australians, particularly under the erratic Attorney-General Doc Evatt, whom Knowles could not stand.[38]

Knowles was so adamantly opposed to the involvement of the military in civilian affairs, especially security intelligence, that he intended to wrest all responsibility for internal security out of the hands of the army. He was particularly incensed by the extra-legal activities of Major R.F.B. Wake's unauthorised and illegal Field Security Service (FSS) in Queensland.[39]

As the Australian government's most senior legal advisor, Knowles objected to uniformed soldiers investigating any matter of a civil nature outside areas in which military operations were occurring under a general mobilisation for home defence. In November 1941, no such areas existed in Queensland or any part of the Australian mainland and thus Knowles, as secretary of the Attorney-General's Department, was advising Evatt that Wake's FSS was illegal and was conducting illegal operations against Australian citizens in Queensland that were now drawing adverse public comment.[40]

The problems Knowles faced were fivefold. The first was the low calibre of people employed within the CIB, including its leaders, both of whom

Knowles—their boss—regarded as sub-par officials unsuitable for the job of director-general of any security service.[41]

The second problem was the influence of the militia officers who dominated the wartime Military Intelligence organisation. The well-connected officers were quite capable of going outside official channels to speak directly to their political masters, including ministers.

The third problem was the usefulness of an ethically malleable security intelligence system that, as we will see, could be and was used by ministers for partisan political interests, including tapping the telephones of members of parliament from both their own and the opposition parties.

This problem also betrayed the self-interested hypocrisy of Evatt who, in a parliamentary answer to a question from Arthur Calwell, the Federal Member for Melbourne, informed the House that it 'is a principle which I consider should be recognized' that 'no home should be entered except at the direction of the civil authority' before going on to say that 'I am anxious that the civil authorities and the military authorities shall have jurisdiction in their own spheres'.[42] Of course, Evatt did not mention his association with Wake or his posse of selected investigators who spied on anyone Evatt wanted to spy upon. It seems the only people aware of this were the people involved and, a little later, the NKGB.[43]

The fourth problem was the lack of money and resources in his department and, consequently, within the CIB and security services.

The fifth problem, and probably the worst, was the informal network of procedurally corrupt officials, military officers and police that would go on to dominate the wartime security intelligence system in Australia. This problem would lead to transgressions of such severity that visiting MI5 officials were aghast at the political manipulation and influence that permeated the wartime Australian security intelligence establishment.

If Mawhood made errors, then the worst was getting involved in the internecine bureaucratic warfare that was well established by the time he arrived. In becoming a partisan of Knowles, Mawhood committed a major error of judgement, especially as he was a British Army officer posted to assist the Australian Army, not the Attorney-General's Department.

Yet, MI5 and the War Office cannot wriggle out of their responsibility for the outcome either. It appears from the contemporaneous record in 1940 that Mawhood came to Australia with two missions: the primary one, to advise and support Australia's military authorities in establishing proper counter-intelligence and force protection capabilities and the second, which is detailed here in a quote of MI5's telegram to Jones used by Knowles in early 1942:

incidental to this work it was suggested that Mawhood might be able to help with the organisation of Security Intelligence Bureau on broader basis which has been under discussion. As we assume your Bureau (that is the Commonwealth Investigation Service) will be the basis of any expansion of security work we have explained fully to Mawhood your position and the relationship with us. Mawhood is most anxious to avoid any overlapping and proposes taking the earliest possible opportunity of calling upon you and discussing details.[44]

This telegram is very important in establishing Mawhood's credentials, particularly in light of the later disavowals by MI5, because it was sent by MI5 to Australia via Jones, the only person holding copies of MI5's codebooks in Australia. Thus, as Knowles says in his minute to Evatt, 'it seems clear there-fore that Lieutenant Colonel Mawhood came out with the full approval of the War Office and MI5'.[45] One cannot argue that it was otherwise and later claims that he was not an MI5 representative need to be read with a clear understanding that the title of MI5 officer, which later MI5 officers said Mawhood was not, does not exclude Mawhood from being MI5's represen-tative. It's a fine distinction, but it fits with the normal bureaucratic tactic of sending a junior officer to carry out a difficult task because later they can be disavowed and accused of going beyond the brief.

It was the existing state of affairs in Australia that doomed any British effort to influence the Australian government to create a professional security service. The competing interests of the army, the Attorney-General's Department, the CIB, state police forces and their partisans in politics and government. Indeed, there appears to have been a split on the subject within the Australian Army as White, the Chief of the General Staff, kept the details of Mission 104 from his own staff at Army HQ.[46] White appears not to have even told his minister about the mission.

It is interesting to consider, however, whether White spoke to Knowles about Military Mission 104. The reasons for suspecting that they may have discussed the matter lies in the secrecy surrounding the mission and the fact that Knowles knew about the mission and MI5's involvement from the very beginning. This idea is not beyond the realms of probability. Both men had an association going back to the early 1920s, when Knowles provided legal opinions to White who had been the chairman of the Commonwealth Public Service Board.[47] Both had served as long-time senior public servants and it is likely that White would have sought advice from Knowles about the best way to carry out civil security intelligence work. If so, it is also likely both men had come to an agreed modus vivendi about the mission and its objectives. The problem was they didn't tell anyone else, and perhaps White didn't tell Knowles all of the detail either.[48]

Fate struck with a vengeance on 13 August 1940 as the aircraft carrying Brigadier Geoffrey Street, Minister for the Army and Repatriation, James Fairbairn, Minister for Air and Civil Aviation, Sir Henry Gullett, Vice-President of the Executive Council and White—all 'close and loyal friends', according to White—crashed on approach to Canberra airport killing all on board.[49] This incident severely damaged the government and deeply affected Menzies, who called it 'the most devastating tragedy' he had experienced.[50] The impact of this incident cannot be overestimated. At the time, Menzies had few friends in Cabinet, even fewer in the party rooms, and none among his senior military advisors. Now, he had lost the services of his closest colleagues.

With the death of White, responsibility for Mission 104 passed to the new Chief of the General Staff, Lieutenant General Vernon Sturdee. He advised that the army should control the new commando troops, but that they should be called 'assault troops' rather than 'para troops' and that their role would be to 'initiate military and special activities against the enemy in any area occupied by him'.[51] Sturdee also recommended that the training organisation and facilities be approved. His minister, P.A. McBride, agreed and the Department of Defence Co-ordination was asked to begin the process of considering suitable sites.[52] They chose cold and wet Wilsons Promontory in Victoria, not the best training ground for troops who would end up fighting in the tropics or North Africa.

As all of this was happening in Australia, Mawhood was providing the New Zealand chiefs of staff with a series of recommendations for a separate security service and the outline of an organisational plan in a paper passed to the New Zealand prime minister entitled 'Security Intelligence Service'. This was tabled and approved by the New Zealand Cabinet on 27 November

1940.[53] The New Zealand Security Intelligence Bureau (NZSIB) was subsequently created on 10 February 1941 under the command of Major Kenneth Folkes and staffed by approximately 30 men.[54]

In Australia, if Mawhood contributed to the disaster that was impending, he did not do so alone. The utter bloody-minded intransigence of the General Staff and the weak malleability of the political leadership in the face of military opposition played their role too, as did the ignorance of London and its failure to provide effective support to Mawhood.

On balance, the evidence suggests that MI5's later repudiation and disavowal of Mawhood's work in Australia and New Zealand is unfair, as his efforts in New Zealand were successful.[55] The New Zealand government found him dependable and sensible and they implemented his recommendations without any issues arising. However, in New Zealand, as in Australia, there were those who did not want a stand-alone civilian security intelligence service and in New Zealand it was the Police Force that worked against one.

The NZSIB would later be brought down by a clever hoax worked out by two criminals, Sydney Gordon Ross, a self-confessed burglar, and Charles Remmers, an ex-policeman and career criminal, who developed an interest in national security while serving time together at Waikeria Prison. Once released, Ross, acting under Remmers' instruction, visited Robert Semple, the Minister of Public Works and National Service, on 28 March 1942 with a false story of a 'fifth column' of twenty individuals. He avoided involving the police by simply insisting that he would speak to no one other than Major Folkes. The next day, Semple arranged for Ross to have an interview with Prime Minister Peter Fraser, who then brought Major Folkes into the matter, and Folkes accepted the story as true.[56]

Ross fabricated evidence of Nazi infiltration that deluded Folkes. The New Zealand Police Force capitalised on the ensuing scandal surrounding the hoax by leaking the details to the New Zealand Truth, which then destroyed the credibility of the NZSIB by contrasting its efforts with those of 'quick-witted detectives'.[57] All of this reeked of a set-up, but none of it involved John Mawhood, to whom we now return.

Mawhood flew back to Sydney on Thursday 28 November 1940, well before the 'fifth column' plot arose. From Sydney, Mawhood flew to Melbourne.[58] A couple of days before his departure, the New Zealand prime minister telegraphed Australia to ask for details on the plans and likely dates for the first commando course.[59] In Australia, the General Staff were still ruminating and it took until 20 December, almost a month later, for a reply to be sent to New Zealand. This reply was not spontaneous; it was provoked by a second telegram from an annoyed New Zealand prime minister on 20 December telling the Australian government that New Zealand 'would be greatly obliged' by a reply.[60]

In Australia, the military authorities were procrastinating and the New Zealand prime minister was soon informed that Australia's military was still considering the 'objects of Lt. Colonel Mawhood's mission';[61] however, the Australian government finally agreed to the number of New Zealand officers and men to attend the proposed courses in February 1941.[62] It took almost two months from when the New Zealand government first asked for details of the commando courses for official approval of the courses and facilities in Australia to be signed off by Menzies on 21 January. It was a mere two days before Menzies departed for the Middle East and London, leaving Archie Fadden as acting prime minister.[63]

Menzies had limited the knowledge of the special training establishments and their activities to himself, Fadden and the Minister for the Army, Percy Spender. It was necessary for the Secretary for Defence Co-Ordination, Frederick Shedden, to be informed and for the Treasury Secretary to be informed on all matters of expenditure, but of nothing else.[64] No one from the Attorney-General's Department was included as this was strictly a military activity.

Until this time, Mawhood's mission ran smoothly. There are some suggestions he alienated Sturdee and other senior military officers from the beginning, but given the intensity of the hostility of the General Staff towards Mawhood and the lengths to which they went to harm him, the post-war allegations made by some of these officers have to be treated with considerable care. It also needs to be remembered that Australia's generals were a very bitter and defensive group of individuals quite prepared to sacrifice duty for institutional and personal status and gain.[65]

On 22 January 1941, the day before Menzies departed Australia for the UK, the Secretary of State for Dominion Affairs sent a cable to the British High Commission in Australia informing the High Commissioner, Sir Geoffrey Whiskard, that the Australian General Staff had sent a cable to the military liaison officer at Australia House saying there was a problem with Military Mission 104. This cable took five days to arrive at the British High Commission and it was immediately forwarded to Fadden.[66] The problem, according to the Australian General Staff, was that, 'whilst preparations are proceeding for the establishment of special units', the Australian government had not issued 'definite written instructions' about the matters arising from the mission.[67]

The timing of this exchange, so close to the final approval for the training of the special units and the impending departure of Menzies, strongly suggests that Australia's General Staff were making mischief. It was the first time in this affair that Australia's military leaders would behave unconstitutionally by going behind their government's back to the authorities in London, but it would not be the last.

The UK High Commissioner was ordered to placate Australia's military and official leadership, upset at the lack of information relating to Military Mission 104, while the British government arranged for a more clearly worded exposition of the objectives of the mission. This duly arrived on 27 January, in a telegram from the Secretary of State for the Dominions to the Australian government. According to this telegram, Lieutenant Colonel Mawhood and his team were charged with three distinct roles covering military and civilian activities including:

a) Steps to counter possible Fifth Column activities on the part of the enemy in Australia itself and to train personnel (including foreign nationals) in offensive action of this nature such as sabotage.

b) Constitution of independent companies, which would receive special training to fit them to take part in combined operations.

c) Formation of military missions which would be available to organise guerrilla operations in enemy territory in which large proportion of the population was hostile to enemy and friendly to us, e.g. Ethiopia or (in certain circumstances) Manchuria.[68]

If this cablegram did not worry the General Staff, a second, sent on 31 January, would have caused dismay by directly linking the Mawhood mission with the SOE. This cablegram invited the Australia authorities to send personnel to train at the proposed SOE HQ and training centre in Singapore.[69] As we already know, the Australian Army wanted nothing to do with the SOE and they made it quite clear that they were not interested. They declined the invitation because, as they argued, they had their own training centre and did not need to send personnel to Singapore.

122

Of course, the Australian training centre was not yet operational, but then neither was the SOE's in Singapore. As for Mawhood and his party, the Australian military authorities believed they needed to take direct control of the mission.[70] As an additional ploy, Australia's military moved to get rid of Mawhood by making him available for service in Singapore as early as April 1941, while retaining Mission 104 until September 1941, as agreed.[71] This was a cheeky move. Australia's military authorities were ridding themselves of the British officer in command of a British military mission, while they retained his command for their exclusive use, and they were doing so by going behind the War Office's back in dealing directly with the Singapore command.

Unsurprisingly, the offer to release Mawhood in April was not taken up by the British authorities in Singapore.[72] The General Staff could ask for his recall, but they could not pass him around and yet keep his team.[73] News of this development appears to have crossed the Tasman and, on 28 April, the acting New Zealand prime minister suggested that if Australia did not want Mawhood, then New Zealand did.[74] It appears that Mawhood only alienated senior military officers in Australia and this puts the lie to the subsequent condemnations of Mawhood in the extant MI5 files and the personal reminiscences of the Australian military officers involved in the affair.

If the New Zealand government was aware of the efforts to get rid of Mawhood, so too was the Australian government. On 20 May, Fadden sent Spender a memorandum asking for a secret report to be prepared on Mission 104.[75] The report from Spender, entitled 'Proposed Formation and Training Special Assault Troops (Para-Military Troops)', was completed by 6 June and covered all of the points raised by Fadden but one. The first two Australian companies had been raised and were undergoing training, which would be completed by September 1941 and suitable instructors for the next course would have been trained. As well, the twelve Special Intelligence Officers being trained by Mawhood were now qualified to work in the Special Operations Section and, along with special personnel in the companies, they would be available to cooperate with the new Security Service (Canberra) in countering any fifth column activities in Australia.[76]

Spender was unable to report on the work of Mawhood in Malaya, Burma and New Zealand. It appears that this information was not available to Australian authorities, as Mawhood rightly refused to discuss it with them. It would also seem that the New Zealand government and the colonial authorities in Burma and Malaya were not inclined to discuss these matters with Australia either.[77]

Spender followed Fadden's instructions and, wisely, kept his report secret from the General Staff. Indeed, the report was a poke in the eye for the General Staff as Spender ignored their demands to refer to the troops in question as 'assault troops'. Throughout the report Spender uses the term 'para-military troops' and, significantly for our story, Spender made it clear that Mission 104 was also tasked to provide advice to the Australian government on the reorganisation of the security intelligence system and was part of the SOE's Far East operations.[78]

In outlining this part of the role of the special companies, Spender is clear he was drawing on information he received directly from Mawhood. Spender was informed by Mawhood that the SOE was now responsible for all fifth column activities, with tasks of a political or economic nature being controlled by a civil head.[79] This is yet more evidence of Mawhood's connection to both SOE and MI5.

Despite being briefed by Mawhood, Spender was cautious enough to seek corroborating evidence of Britain's policy in this area and he recommended that until such confirmation had been received, and the Australian government had made a decision on what they would do, the special companies should be restricted to military activities only. He then went even further, suggesting that when such confirmation was received, the Australian government should consider following the UK model and place all economic and political activities under the control of a civilian head, perhaps the Director of the Security Service.

This decision may explain why Australia's generals dumped the first of these highly trained commando companies—1st Independent Company—in the islands to Australia's north to garrison a useless airstrip at Kavieng, New Ireland, and man outposts such as Namatanai in New Ireland, Vila in the New Hebrides, Tulagi on Guadalcanal, Buka Passage on Bougainville and Lorengau on Manus Island, all as far from any expected action as the generals could find.

In terms of Australia's security intelligence, the Australian Army was under significant pressure to surrender the prerogatives it had appropriated. The attack was led by the General Staff's bête noire, Knowles. The adherents within the Knowles camp included Spender and, most likely, Menzies, whose earlier efforts to reform Australia's security intelligence had been thwarted by the General Staff. These were powerful opponents and the positioning of the Menzies government behind Knowles helps explain the attacks Australia's generals and their supporters made on Menzies in 1941.

The Spender report was part of this struggle. Spender's recommendations that an augmented civilian-led security service be created and tasked with protecting national security caused more ructions in the relationship between the government and the military. The recommendation that the new organisation would report directly to either the prime minister or the Minister for Defence Co-ordination, both positions that were held by Menzies, effectively excluded the military from any operational role or oversight of security intelligence in Australia. As always, any such move was seen as an attack on the standing of the permanent officers and they were determined to fight it off.

Spender, now the Minister for the Army, attempted to allay the concerns of the military by leaving Lloyd in place and moving the service from the Attorney-General's Department to the Prime Minister's Department. This was not enough. The scene was set for an escalation in the fight over control of Australia's security intelligence system. It is here that Mawhood strayed from the path of being a representative of the British government and made the error of becoming a partisan of the civilian push for control of the security intelligence establishment.

A more sensible man would have taken cover, stayed away from the brawling and sent cablegrams to London informing them of the situation and asking for further instructions. It is not known if he did that. MI5's records do not show any evidence of him sending reports back to London during the war; however, this does not mean they were not sent. If, as we suspect, Mawhood was also working for SOE, then the absence of documentary evidence is understandable because SOE's greatest failing was in the maintenance of its own records. Another possibility is that Mawhood's telegrams are buried in War Office files.

Whatever happened, Mawhood set out on a path that damaged his mission and the standing of MI5 and SOE with Australia's military establishment and government and led to his efforts being called 'misguided' and he a man 'of unhappy memory'.[80]

To be fair to Mawhood, in late 1944 another British visitor, Lieutenant Colonel E.A. Airy, who was most definitely representing MI5, would find

Australia's Security Service so full of 'unhappy' officers and 'intrigue' that he admitted he had 'experienced a certain amount of difficulty in not becoming involved'.[81]

The first indication we have that Mawhood had become too involved in Australia's internal politics is a marginal note that Spender made for Menzies on a memorandum dated 10 June 1941. In this note, Spender advises Menzies to meet with Mawhood and hear what he had to say.[82] As Spender was writing this recommendation to Menzies, Mawhood was meeting with Knowles who was also recommending that it was 'in the interests of the Commonwealth for the prime minister, the Attorney-General and the Service Ministers' to grant Mawhood an interview.[83] This alignment of Menzies, Spender and Knowles behind Mawhood doomed his standing with the military establishment, who, unfortunately, were the people he actually worked for.

According to Knowles, Mawhood spent around two hours with each of these ministers and over an hour with Menzies and Knowles.[84] Now Attorney-General, Hughes interposed himself and had Knowles prepare a Cabinet memorandum recommending that Mawhood be appointed to conduct an investigation into the set-up of a security service. According to Knowles, this led to a dispute between Spender and Hughes over the terms of the inquiry and, as a result, Spender had the inquiry extended to include the activities of Military Intelligence.[85]

On 4 July, Hughes was recommending that the government make use of Mawhood's internal security expertise while he was in Australia. He could, recommended Hughes, carry out an inquiry into the Security Service, which would be used to inform the Cabinet.[86] The problem with Hughes' proposal was not just that he was arguing for an inquiry into part of his own department, but that it now included, at the Army Minister's request, a direction that Mawhood investigate Military Intelligence.[87]

Why Menzies would allow this proposal to go forward is hard to fathom given he was under threat from the malcontents within his own party and his coalition partners in government, and John Curtin and the ALP were just sitting back waiting for the government to implode around Menzies. It is even possible that the whole inquiry into the Security Service was being used to destabilise Menzies. The involvement of the ruthless manipulator Hughes in this affair should not be regarded as Billy doing his best for the country. The more likely reason he was pushing for the inquiry was because he knew it would destroy Menzies. Throughout his political life, Hughes proved himself willing to do almost anything that benefitted him politically. Helping to create a damaging confrontation between a weakened prime minister and his senior military advisors during a war would have been of no consequence to Hughes, a man Menzies would later describe as 'almost invariably destructive'.[88]

Spender was different. His main concern was the defence of Australia in Asia and he was a strong critic of the reliance Australia was placing on Britain's undertakings to send the Royal Navy to Singapore if Japan attacked. It is likely that Spender was honestly attempting to place Australia's system of security intelligence on a better footing but, in so doing, he got the politics wrong.

On 8 July, Secretary of the Department of Defence Co-ordination and Secretary to the Cabinet Shedden showed War Cabinet Agendum 238/1941 and Minute (1171) to Mawhood and instructed him to conduct an inquiry and report on the newly formed Security Service and, fatefully, on Army Intelligence.[89] Mawhood replied the same day that he would commence work immediately.[90]

In preparation for the work ahead Mawhood asked for the necessary office accommodation and staff and he expressed the view that the relevant authorities, presumably including those in London, be officially informed of his mission.[91] If Mawhood was only now informing London of the problems he was facing and the fact that he had involved himself in internal Australian political infighting, something anathema to MI5, then it explains why he was later so heavily criticised by senior MI5 officials. Mawhood was now to learn that in Australia it was one thing for the government to order something done and quite another thing to obtain the funding and resources for the work. This would become a significant problem, but not as much of a problem as that of being a British officer on attachment to the Australian Army who was now conducting investigations on that army's Military Intelligence branch for the Australian government.

The following day Shedden wrote to Spender on behalf of Mawhood asking for the services of Major Sexton, one of the Australian officers assigned to assist him, as well as typists, office space and fuel ration tickets, which Mawhood found impossible to obtain from the army.[92] Not only had the government launched what was perceived as a direct attack on the army, it appeared that they wanted the army to pay for it too.

The backlash against the War Cabinet's decision was immediate, forceful and unconstitutional. In an odd interpretation of the constitutional powers of the Australian government, Major General Sir John Northcott, the Deputy Chief of the General Staff, instructed Mawhood 'to consider the War Cabinet minute suspended until such time as he received directions from the Military Board'.[93] It would appear that, for the Australian Army, the Military Board outranked the elected government of the day.

Northcott moved quickly to neutralise the threat by ordering Mawhood to leave Melbourne on a tour of inspection. Northcott's justification for this action was that, as a serving officer, Mawhood was solely subject to the direct control of the Military Board. To some extent, this was true. Mawhood was a British officer on loan to the Australian government, ostensibly to the Australian Army, so Northcott was acting within his strict rights as the deputy.[94] As to Mawhood's secret status, the arrangements between the War Office in London, MI5 and White were irrelevant as his formal status now placed him in an impossible position.[95]

The constitutional issues did not stop with Northcott's dismissal of a Cabinet decision directing Mawhood to other work. The unconstitutionality now took a more sinister turn as General Sturdee, the Australian government's senior military advisor, went behind his government's back and secretly requested the War Office in London recall Mawhood immediately. Worse still, Sturdee did this after his deputy, Northcott, had unsuccessfully sought the permission of Spender, the Minister of the Army, to send the telegram to the War Office. Spender had specifically forbidden this and yet Australia's General Staff went ahead anyway.

The unconstitutional actions of the Australian General Staff were uncovered by their nemesis, Knowles, when Lloyd, now the head of the new Security Service, inadvertently told him of Sturdee's actions and of a War Office order for Mawhood to return home.[96]

Knowles wasted no time in alerting Menzies to the crisis and a telegram was immediately sent to Stanley Bruce, the Australian High Commissioner in London, alerting him to the army's actions.[97] This was followed the next day by another, warning Bruce not to be influenced by the views of the War Office as these would simply be the partisan views of Australia's generals being repeated back to him.[98]

On 12 July, Shedden informed Spender that Sturdee had gone behind his back to the War Office.[99] In a masterful understatement worthy of *Yes Minister*'s Sir Humphrey Appleby, Shedden called it 'a most perplexing matter'.[100] Despite the actions of Knowles and Menzies, the army won this first skirmish as, on 12 July, Shedden wrote to Mawhood asking him to defer commencing his investigations until further notice.[101] By 14 July, in compliance with the Australian Army's demands, a telegram from the War Office was sent to Australia ordering Mawhood's immediate return to the United Kingdom.[102]

This whole episode underlined Australia's reputation as a nation beset by internecine political warfare for pathetically small prizes in which unconstitutional behaviour was the norm. The British government's archives show officials, ranging from those in the Foreign Office to those in MI5 and MI6, were quite at ease writing into the official record their disgust at the unconstitutionality and corruption of Australia's political and governmental institutions.[103]

This view was further reinforced by the way in which Jones and then Lloyd used their position as the holder of MI5's codes in Australia to send their own personal reports back to MI5 criticising their perceived opponents and their political and bureaucratic masters.[104] Australia's generals were not alone in acting unconstitutionally.

The situation degenerated to farce as the government began to grasp the extent of the army's hostility towards Mawhood and the inquiry he was charged to conduct. As a result, the matter of the investigation into the Security Service and Military Intelligence was brought forward at a War Cabinet meeting in Sydney on 18 July 1941 and Minute (1227) drafted, outlining the history of the decision to mount the investigation. Hughes, as the Attorney-General, advised the Cabinet that he had learned Lloyd had been informed by somebody of the comments Northcott had made to Cabinet criticising Mawhood. It was left unsaid that Lloyd was the army's puppet and was being passed details on secret cabinet discussions by Northcott.[105] If Hughes is to be believed, and there is no reason not to, then Northcott had deliberately broken Cabinet confidentiality. Northcott survived this revelation and enjoyed his career without ever being held to account for his appalling breach of confidence.

In terms of keeping his indiscretions secret, Northcott's mistake was to tell Lloyd the details of the discussions in Cabinet. Unfortunately, Northcott seems to have not realised or had forgotten that Lloyd was not particularly bright or competent. Lloyd had no reservations in later using Northcott's information in a ham-fisted attempt to influence Hughes to have Cabinet rescind its decision to investigate the Security Service and Military Intelligence.[106] Such an attempt did not get past Knowles or Hughes.

Cabinet reacted to this politicking by making two decisions. The first was that Mawhood was to remain in Australia and that Bruce in London was to take action to see this was done. The second was that the Department of the Army was ordered to furnish a full report on how Sturdee's personal communication came to be despatched to the War Office contrary to the directions of the government.[107] By the end of August, Bruce had obtained the personal telegram that Sturdee had sent and passed part of it to Menzies. It read: 'I regard Mawhood totally unfitted for any employment in connection with Security Service Organisation or Army Intelligence in Australia.'[108]

Sturdee sent a telegram on 19 July, which implies there were at least two or more such telegrams sent, one before the Cabinet meeting of 18 July and one the day after. Sturdee was using a backchannel, an informal correspondence, using the War Office codes to speak directly to his fellow generals in London behind the back of his own government in Australia. If this is the case, then Australia's Chief of the General Staff had gone well beyond the bounds of propriety and deliberately disobeyed the direct order of his minister and his government. This was a direct attack by Australia's military leadership on the constitution their soldiers were fighting to maintain. In this situation one of two things should have happened.

The first, and by far the most honourable, should have been that Sturdee, having given his full and frank advice on Mawhood and the proposed investigation, should have resigned his commission when Cabinet rejected his advice. This action appears to have been well beyond him and this says a lot about Vernon Sturdee. Rather than take the honourable course, he chose to subvert the constitutional authority of the elected government of Australia, a government he was sworn to obey, protect and defend.

The second action that should have occurred is that, in the absence of resignations, the government should have sacked both Sturdee and Northcott on the spot and replaced them with men in whom they had complete confidence. The failure to take this action displays both the amateurish nature of Australia's administrative system of the time and the political weakness of the Menzies regime. The warring parties simply returned to their corners and prepared for the next round.

In anticipation of this, Bruce found himself on the end of a number of increasingly urgent telegrams from Menzies asking for information on Mawhood. On 22 July, Menzies finally got a reply containing a damning assessment of Mawhood by an unnamed informant, most likely from within the War Office. Mawhood was described as one of a number of officers who had been earmarked for security service work before the war and had been commissioned into the Territorial Army on its outbreak.

According to the information supplied by Bruce, Mawhood was appointed as the security officer for Eastern Command following his commissioning in 1939. Bruce's informant said he had shown himself 'a man of great keenness and energy, but rather heavy-footed and lacking in tact'. He was, the informant went on to say, not a man 'likely to go to the top of any organisation in which he may be serving.' Most damningly, it was reported to Bruce, Mawhood's 'superiors in the Security Service [MI5] were not particularly reluctant to release him for his Mission to Australia'.[109] Again, the contemporary record of Mawhood's mission in 1941 clearly shows that even in London it was accepted that he was working for MI5.

It was not all negative though. Bruce reported that his informant had said Mawhood had achieved a good report from his course in 'offensive security' and had discharged his 'limited responsibilities' satisfactorily.[110] All of this seems to show that Mawhood may have been blunt and tactless and, most importantly, ill-equipped to deal subtly with Australian politics, yet he was not necessarily bad at his job as a security intelligence officer.

It should also be borne in mind that in 1940, MI5, along with much of the British government, was in a state of turmoil and change. At MI5, the leadership had been removed by Churchill in early June and this opened up the prospect of quick advancement for all of the more experienced officers who would have been, as the head of Overseas Control Lieutenant Colonel Bertram Ede later admitted, more suitable to travel as MI5's representatives in Australia.[111] To get senior MI5 officers to leave London and the United Kingdom to travel to Australia, when serious job opportunities had opened up, was not almost impossible, it was very much impossible.[112] This made Mawhood the best candidate available to MI5 and the War Office at the time.

All of that said, the state of play in Australia—the naked ambitions, the political infighting, the personal and institutional animosities—would have made the task of getting agreement on the formation of an effective security service beyond even a Talleyrand.[113]

On 22 July, Bruce sealed the matter in his telegram to Menzies, and the War Cabinet at its meeting in Melbourne withdrew Minute (1171) and removed Mawhood from the role of investigator.[114] The General Staff had inflicted a humiliating defeat on its own government, an institution that Australia's military seemed to have regarded as just a collection of political frockcoats.[115]

The government now sought to save face and keep the investigation alive by appointing Alexander Duncan, the Commissioner of Police for Victoria, to do the job.[116] This appointment was more acceptable to the General Staff and, on 23 July, Northcott wrote to Spender confirming this.[117] This was a qualified acceptance, however. On 1 August, Sturdee notified Shedden that while Duncan was qualified to investigate the Security Service, the General Staff did not accept he was qualified to advise on military matters and, therefore, he was not qualified to investigate Military Intelligence. Just to make sure everyone understood the army's position, Sturdee estimated that Duncan only needed four days of visits, and could then conduct the rest of his inquiry from his Melbourne office.[118]

Happily for the General Staff, the premier of Victoria refused to release Duncan for more than a short time.[119] Even better for the General Staff, on 28 August Menzies resigned and was replaced by Fadden. The new administration happily accommodated the objections of the General Staff and excised Military Intelligence from the investigation. Mawhood was moved to the Attorney-General's Department where he could be protected by Knowles while he was made available to assist Duncan investigate the civilian Security Service.[120]

Despite the change in prime ministers, the fight continued behind the scenes and on 29 August, a day after Menzies was removed, a telegram was sent to Bruce, most likely by Menzies, telling him that 'I regret to say that this officer [Mawhood] appears to have been badly treated in Australia'.[121] Fadden, followed up on 1 September, telegraphing Bruce to thank the War Office for allowing Mawhood to stay in Australia and to let them know that the reports from Sturdee on Mawhood were 'quite unjustified and unfair'.[122] Sturdee's political masters were making it very clear in London that he had acted without authority. One can only imagine how all of this went down in Whitehall.

On 7 October 1941, the Fadden government finally collapsed and the ALP, led by Curtin, took over the leadership of Australia's governmental institutions. The new government had a lot to learn and a lot to do, and it had the additional burden of learning its job while running the country during a war.

In such circumstances, it would be entirely unreasonable to expect the new government to be in any position to address the needs of the security intelligence system as a priority.

Knowles, however, was ready to be entirely unreasonable. On 18 October, he wrote to his new minister, Attorney-General Evatt, describing the history of the attempt to form a civilian security service and remove Military Intelligence from involvement in civilian security intelligence matters. The 'bitter protests' of the General Staff were detailed, as was their opposition to Mawhood and the idea of a wide-ranging inquiry into the organisation and operations of Military Intelligence in Australia.[123]

All of this became moot on 8 December 1941, when the Japanese launched their long-expected assaults on Malaysia and Hong Kong, and unexpectedly on Pearl Harbor. Now it was impossible for the new government to take any action against the military establishment, assuming of course that they had ever intended to.

……… ……… ………

The story of John Mawhood is not one of an officer 'going beyond his brief' or suffering *folie de grandeur*; it was far more complex than any of that.[124] The Mawhood affair resulted from the convergence of two streams of circumstances. The first was the inability of the British authorities in mid-1940 to find a more suitable candidate for the job. The second was that whoever was selected was going to be plunged into a wider and faster-flowing political conflict in Australia, one that extended well beyond the history of Military Mission 104 and Mawhood.

As we have seen, Mawhood and his mission simply stumbled into a long-running bureaucratic war being fought over the control of Australia's security intelligence system. The result of this war would be the complete failure of Australian security, and the post-war humiliation of the Australian government and Australia, outcomes for which no politician, general or bureaucrat has been held to account.

CHAPTER 9

THE BATTLE OF THE REPORTS

The brawl that erupted over John Mawhood and his investigation was not waged over technical matters; it was a brawl over who would control the internal security intelligence system in Australia. The causes of this were manifold, but the leading one was the insularity of the professional military officer class that dominated the General Staff. The second-class status bestowed on this group by successive governments—which saw them as simply being facilitators for Australia's great part-time citizen army—bred resentment and defensiveness that ensured an attack on any one of them or any part of their organisation would be treated as an attack on them all.[1]

Behind this institutional problem lay a more sinister one: procedural corruption. This arose from the ad hoc and unconstitutional way in which security intelligence was administered and the military attitude of doing what was necessary to get the job done. This left the running of security intelligence matters in the hands of relatively junior officers who were completely unaccountable for their actions and who, lacking training and resources, leant heavily on their informal networks, particularly with police. The idea of allowing a British officer who reported to Sir George Knowles and the politicians to investigate Military Intelligence was far too dangerous to be countenanced. It is this that turned this brawl into a fight to the death.

Any investigation that risked uncovering the potential illegalities in Military Intelligence activities had to be stopped. The investigation by Alexander Duncan was never going to produce much of substance anyway. Firstly, his premier, who had insisted that Duncan's duties as the Commissioner of the Victoria Police came first and that Duncan could not be outside Victoria for an extended period, hamstrung Duncan. The General Staff added to this by imposing unworkable time limits on his access to Military Intelligence, ensuring that it was nothing more than a desktop audit, which could be easily ignored. On top of all of this, Knowles threw Mawhood into the investigation as a counterweight to Duncan.

The final factor invalidating the investigation was Duncan himself. He was an autocratic figure and a policeman first and foremost. As a result, it could easily be predicted that whatever the technical advice and recommendations of his final report, he would advocate that all of the powers and resources allocated to security intelligence should be vested by the Commonwealth in the state police commissioners.

As Duncan began his investigation, he only had the vaguest of terms of reference. There were no guidelines about intelligence at the strategic or operational levels, of how intelligence should be collected or by whom, how it should be reported and to whom, how it should be analysed, assessed and then integrated into the strategic picture being presented to the civilian and military leadership.

Despite the General Staff's victory, Longfield Lloyd, the newly appointed head of the CSS, ran a campaign against Duncan and his inquiry. There can be little doubt that Lloyd was acting in this as the proxy for the General Staff. By the end of September, Lloyd was delaying Duncan's investigations by raising concerns over his ability to authorise Duncan to see Cabinet documents and certain types of classified material. In a typically turgid and complex letter to Knowles, Lloyd asked for directions on this.[2] His disingenuous grounds for this were that he had not been 'officially' notified of Duncan's appointment and he was, as a result, unable to decide what documents Duncan could be shown.[3] Lloyd was playing a dangerous game. Knowles had little time for Lloyd; besides thinking Lloyd was not particularly capable, he suspected him of being an army sympathiser and stooge of the General Staff. It is almost certain that Knowles was waiting to find an opportunity to purge the CSS of Lloyd and the coterie of military and ex-military men whom Lloyd had recruited.

The direction Lloyd sought was soon provided in an abrupt memo Knowles shot back the same day. Knowles made it clear that Duncan had been commissioned by Cabinet to report on the CSS and that any document Duncan wished to see, including Cabinet minutes, was to be made available to him immediately.[4] It was petty squabbling over little points, and it would continue.

The report submitted by Duncan dutifully outlined how, from 1936, the services and the Defence Department had increasingly become concerned about Australia's security intelligence. Despite these concerns and the creation of numerous committees and working groups, nothing happened due to the internecine squabbling between the military and civilian departments. In fact, Duncan drew attention to this problem, particularly to the persistent uncooperative and hostile atmosphere he encountered from the CSS, its officials and the military, as being a significant factor in limiting the effectiveness of his inquiry and report.

This squabbling appears to have surprised Duncan, who commented in his report that since his arrival from Scotland he had not encountered such an atmosphere in Victoria, where the departments were all united in one aim and worked with 'the closest co-operation and accord for a common purpose'.[5] In contrast, he reported that while each of the squabbling services agreed that something needed to be done, they were not willing to surrender any of what they saw as their own 'preserves' in order to see it done.[6] This of course was the nub of the immediate problem. The nub of the entire problem was the weakness of the government.

In his final report, Duncan started by praising the enthusiasm and hard work of the officers of the individual services he had dealt with in Victoria, before damning them as being untrained and inexperienced.[7] The lack of experience and systemisation meant that the services were unable to conduct investigations efficiently. They were completely unable to match the volume of investigations undertaken by Victoria Police's Special Branch, which, by 1942, had supplied the CIB with over a thousand files on communists and their organisations.[8]

Interestingly, in his report Duncan listed the number of files supplied by Victoria Police on communists and their organisations, but did not mention a similar level of activity in relation to Nazis or fascists, although some matters arising from Japanese and Nazi activity are listed in Appendix B of his report.[9]

By comparison, he found the CIB and CSS lacked any appreciation of the seriousness of the investigations they were undertaking or even how to best conduct those investigations. He highlighted the CIB's lack of experience in investigations by describing how one suspect under surveillance was interrogated by a CIB investigator before she had demonstrated any suspicious activity, thereby warning her that she was a suspect and under surveillance.[10]

The biggest area of concern pre-war was the effective control of aliens in Australia and, as we have seen, this was very difficult in a country like Australia, which had such a large migrant population. The introduction of the *Aliens Registration Act 1939* and the declaration of war had made the job of tracking aliens easier, but the bulk of the work had fallen on state police forces and not the CSS. This work required 'permanently appointed and experienced investigators, with no interests outside their profession'.[11]

For Duncan, a professional policeman, the idea of any other agency undertaking investigative work was hard to accept. In this, he was no different to the Military Intelligence personnel who believed that police couldn't adequately examine military matters. This is the main flaw in Duncan's approach and in his report. The police attitude towards all investigations is that of the wielder of state power able, within the limitations of due process of law, to demand answers, and conduct searches and surveillance of suspects. This is not intelligence collection.

What Duncan's report does not address is the subject of what Mawhood would call 'offensive intelligence operations', like false flag operations, double agents and other entrapment activities, covert entry and searches, and allowing the continuation of illegal activity in order to develop a picture of just what the target individuals or organisations were really doing. Indeed, intelligence operations can also involve the enablement of such illegal activities and the subsequent use of coercion, including blackmail, and reward, including bribes and the supply of gifts or services, to those involved in order to obtain insight and information from them. All of these things are the tools of the HUMINT trade, and no police officers should ever be involved in such activities. Duncan's concept of intelligence was, thankfully, naive.

It is the agents of foreign powers—whether in Australia under the cover of personal, diplomatic or business activities, or when an Australian citizen has taken on the role of such an agent—who are the legitimate targets of such offensive intelligence operations. Citizens, even those misguided enough to involve themselves in illegal activity for political purposes, remain subject to the full protection of the law. The use of offensive intelligence against these wayward citizens is, as we will see later, fraught with danger.

One of the flawed approaches to security intelligence that Duncan singled out for early comment was the formation of Major R.F.B. Wake's Field Security Section (FSS) in Queensland. The FSS consisted of 50 men and Wake was using it, to Duncan's obvious chagrin, to neutralise the Queensland Police in their own jurisdiction. Wake's justification for doing this was that when it came to the Queensland Police, 'he had no confidence in them'.[12]

In reality, Wake's FSS was just another step in the accumulation of power by a man who concurrently held four Commonwealth offices concerned with security in Queensland. These positions included being the Director of Military Intelligence at 1st Military District in Brisbane, Inspector of the CIB in Queensland and Regional Director of the CSS in that state, as well as the head of the Peace Officer Guard, and he also controlled the FSS. Duncan completely ignored this dangerous accumulation of positions by a single individual who was operating without anything more than cursory oversight by senior officials. Rather, Duncan the policeman focused on the FSS's subversion of the position of the Queensland Police. Indeed, this was Duncan's main objection and he doesn't express any concern about the illegality of FSS actions, which included searching civilian premises and detaining Australian citizens. His concern arose from the fact that the Queensland Police were not being involved in the illegality.

The other organisations with roles in security intelligence were of course the state police forces, most of whom maintained a special branch capability to carry out investigations into the activities of subversive and disloyal elements in society. These special branches also investigated acts of sabotage or espionage and the leakage of information, but all of this was supposed to be state-focused and not in support of the Commonwealth.[13] This system led to invariable conflict, but also cooperation and even, particularly in New South Wales, a combined organisation, and it was this mixture of cooperation that would prove most problematic.

The most significant problem Duncan identified in relation to the cooperation between the Commonwealth security intelligence apparatus and state police forces was the lack of coordination of their work and the lack of effective oversight. From his perspective, this led to incompetent direction, confusion, duplication and the rapid multiplication of even more uncontrolled organisations. These organisations were assuming responsibility for security and then manoeuvring their superiors to fight off attempts by other departments to wrest any of this responsibility away from them. This resulted in the rivalries and feuds that utterly undermined Australia's wartime security. All of this was encouraged by the way in which politicians sought and bestowed favours on the bureaucracy and by their failure to implement a proper governance system to oversee Australia's largely dysfunctional and out-of-control security intelligence system.[14]

Duncan believed the organisation that should have been the centralising power within security intelligence was the CSS. Much to Director H.E. Jones' dismay, Duncan discounted the CIB entirely. The reasons he did this are entirely understandable. The majority of Commonwealth departments and the entire armed services held the CIB in contempt. Given this complete lack of confidence, something that MI5 would later comment upon in 1944 and 1945, Duncan could hardly proffer the CIB as the answer to the problem.[15] On top of this, Jones had refused to cooperate with Duncan in any way.[16] By contrast, Lloyd of the CSS was the 'most open and helpful person in the Attorney-General's Department and was anxious at all times to assist'.[17] It appears that Lloyd was better at influencing outcomes than the rather dull Jones. The result was that Duncan took great notice of what Lloyd had to say, and it appeared that Lloyd, as proxy for the General Staff, had a lot to say about Lieutenant Colonel Mawhood. Lloyd must have been pleased to find that Duncan had little time for Mawhood either.

The idea that anyone thought Mawhood and Duncan could work together on the inquiry and the final report is somewhat hard to fathom. For a start, Mawhood had been severely dealt with and his reputation was in tatters. On Duncan's side, he brought a policeman's arrogance to the job and a view that the only good investigators were police investigators. Duncan also seemed blissfully unaware that the government had accepted the argument that because he was not a military man, he could not understand military matters. Mawhood was a military man and his capacity to comment on military matters was harder to challenge, yet Duncan resented his continued role in the inquiry. It is unsurprising that Lloyd found it easy to influence Duncan in developing a more negative view of Mawhood.

The hostility between Mawhood and Duncan has often been put down to Mawhood's inability to work with others, but this is undermined by what happened in New Zealand where there were no such conflicts. The likelihood is that Duncan was reacting, probably quite correctly, to the idea that Mawhood was foisted on him to spy and report back to Knowles. Of course, it is always possible that the 'strong and silent' Duncan was antagonised by Mawhood's criticism of senior Australian officers, including Jones, for not communicating sufficiently with MI5 in the United Kingdom.[18] Whatever the real cause or causes, all we currently know is that Duncan had little time for Mawhood.

It is interesting that Mawhood criticised Jones for insufficient reporting to MI5 in the United Kingdom. This criticism raises the question of how Mawhood knew the extent of Jones' reporting, unless he had been briefed by someone within MI5. This is the likely explanation because it is impossible that he had access to Jones' message logs.

Duncan's unease about Mawhood's reliability was precipitated by his audit of Jones' message logs which found Jones had sent 42 messages to London in 1939 and 96 in 1940. For him, this was proof of frequent communication. In reality, that was a very low level of reporting and reflected the fact that Jones maintained the liaison activity as a one-man show. As for the absolute number of signals sent, that is a meaningless figure unless it is broken down into routine administrative checks, forwarding of assessments and actual operational reports. The evidence is that Jones sent very few operational reports and the extant MI5 files contain nothing other than his letters bemoaning his treatment by the Commonwealth government and a couple of general reports on the activities of the CIB.

Although Duncan admitted that his findings on the number of messages was 'quite a small matter', he used it to limit Mawhood's role to conducting investigations and interviews with the CSS, Military Intelligence and CIB in South Australia and Western Australia.[19] There is little doubt that Duncan actively sidelined Mawhood and that, other than producing a separate and dissenting report, Mawhood was now a spent force.

An interesting aside Duncan made about Mawhood in his report was that Mawhood claimed that one of his functions was to be posted overseas 'in an alien country, such as Iran, and cause disaffection'.[20] It was in Iran under Edmund Ironside that Mawhood did indeed act as an intelligence officer charged with overthrowing a government and reinstalling the shah. Whatever his failings, Mawhood was telling the truth about his expertise on Iran. This again raises the issue of just who Mawhood was: a man who was born and raised in India, who would thus have had language skills good enough to make him a brigade major in an Iranian brigade under Ironside. Intelligence agencies rarely overlook such individuals and the fact that Mawhood cannot be traced between 1925 and 1939 suggests they did not overlook him.

The results of the Duncan inquiry were exactly what one would expect from a police officer of the time. The first recommendation confirmed that there was a need to form a single security service. The second recommendation was that it should indeed be based in Canberra under the control of a director-general. The third recommendation was that the CIB, the RAN, RAAF and Army have representatives posted to the new organisation. The fourth was that it should consist of around twenty highly trained men with special qualifications, high standards of education and knowledge of foreign languages and cultures.[21] There were nine tasks for the new director-general, according to Duncan:

1. Demand the cooperation of state police forces,
2. Investigate suspects and make recommendations as a result,
3. Obtain desired personnel from any source whatsoever,
4. Make staff appointments,
5. Make direct reports to the Minister,
6. Have unrestricted powers of direction of all security matters,
7. Establish and maintain a centralised registry of records,
8. Establish and operate a school for the training of security personnel,
9. Direct methods of travel necessary to maintaining secrecy of his organisation.[22]

The first task Duncan listed is telling. He was recommending the formation of a single Commonwealth security organisation that would centralise records and functions but devolve its authority and responsibilities along with Commonwealth funding to the police commissioners of each state. It was classic Australian federal politics, and the model Duncan chose to base his recommendations on was that of the Commonwealth Auditor-General.[23]

This recommendation was bizarre even by the standards of 1941. The Commonwealth Auditor-General enjoyed a level of independence well beyond that of any other government agency. In 1940–42, the holder of the office could only be removed by an address from both houses of the

Commonwealth Parliament.[24] To put a security intelligence organisation, which is very much part of executive government, on a similar footing to an auditor who must be free to investigate executive government was not something that would work.

Unsurprisingly, the first response to Duncan's report came from Lloyd at CSS on 16 February 1942.[25] Lloyd wanted to make sure readers of the report appreciated that his CSS was already doing the work described in it and that this work had been disrupted by the decision to hold an inquiry in July of 1941.[26] As a good servant of the General Staff, Lloyd also made it clear that Duncan's report relied too much on the good offices of state police services and did not address the strategic nature of some of the CSS's work. Lloyd's real target, however, was not the policeman Duncan, it was the intelligence officer Mawhood.

Lloyd's enmity towards Mawhood is obvious in the way he described Mawhood as being 'evasive and also quite unwilling and, it seems unable to advise or assist' the Australian security authorities.[27] Additional evidence of Lloyd's antipathy towards Mawhood is that out of the 21 paragraphs in his response to Duncan's report, Mawhood is subjected to attack in six of them.[28]

Knowles was also concerned about Duncan's report, particularly with the recommendation that a director-general should have direct access to the minister, an idea previously pushed by Percy Spender. As a departmental secretary, Knowles was not going to undermine s. 25(2) of the Commonwealth Public Service Act, which made advising a minister the preserve of the permanent head of a department. A bureaucratic warrior like Knowles was never going to allow a subordinate official to usurp the prerogatives of the permanent heads.

Where Duncan was on stronger ground was in his recommendation that the position should be filled by someone trained and experienced in security matters, with an established reputation of being above personal, political or professional considerations. This person should also, according to Duncan, 'have a clear appreciation of the value of one of the most sacred assets of our democracy—the liberty of the subject—which must not be violated'.[29] This individual did not exist in the Australia of 1941–42 and the only way such an individual could have been found was for the Commonwealth to recruit a British intelligence officer.

It is therefore ironic that Duncan should then nominate William MacKay, the Commissioner of the NSW Police, to fill the position.[30] To propose one of the most procedurally corrupt police officers of the time is the stuff of farce. However, Duncan's recommendation is unsurprising because, just as the military have their club, so do police, and neither of these professions are connoisseurs of good farce.

Despite all that had happened, Mawhood had been retained in Australia under the auspices of the Attorney-General's Department to 'assist' Duncan. In fact, Mawhood had been privately tasked by William Hughes—who was being advised by Commander Long, the Director of Naval Intelligence, and most likely Knowles as well—to write his own report detailing where he did not agree with Duncan.[31] After being made aware of these secret instructions to Mawhood by Military Intelligence, who were illegally tapping Long's telephones, Duncan confronted Long.[32] Mawhood had already sent his dissenting report to Duncan on 10 November 1941, so Duncan had access to this before he completed the writing of his own report. Given this situation, it is unsurprising that Duncan was critical of him.

Mawhood's report started with Western Australia, where he interviewed Major R.M. Black, who had been the Officer-in-Charge of Military Intelligence (Ib) and had then been appointed the state director of the CSS as well. According to Mawhood, Black reported the only thing that had changed after this appointment was that he now wrote letters to himself.[33] Essentially, Black's work remained the same and consisted of identifying, registering and, where necessary, interning aliens, with most of the work done by the Police Special Branch.

Mawhood was critical of Black's lack of any 'offensive intelligence' activity, creating the likelihood that potential enemy agents were thus lying undiscovered. Yet Mawhood was also critical of the way in which a man of German descent, Henry Edward Myer, was interned on the basis of two conversations held two years earlier. For Mawhood, this sort of action seemed to be over the top. The problem, as Mawhood identified it, was that Black was a farmer and he had not been given any training in security or intelligence and 'could not be expected to supervise or operate this specialized and delicate work'.[34] Mawhood was right.

As to the CIB in Perth, Mawhood found the Inspector, Mr Adams, 'not personally impressive' and 'not held in high regard by the other services there'.[35] The only functions Adams seemed to carry out concerned the naturalisation and movement of aliens and the passing on of titbits of information to the services. Another problem observed in Perth was that while the CIB undertook responsibility for the security of government establishments, they had completely overlooked the necessity of guarding important civilian facilities, which were left entirely unprotected.

According to Mawhood, the RAN in Fremantle was running its own show following the ACNB's withdrawal from any involvement in the CSS. Consequently, the RAN had little interest in domestic security and fixed its focus firmly on operational intelligence matters. Lieutenant Commander James Rycroft, the Officer-in-Charge of Security at Fremantle, limited his dealings with Military Intelligence, the CIB and state police to obtaining vetting information on personnel prior to their appointment; and he refrained from handing over investigations into Australian and British citizens as he did not think the other agencies could effectively prosecute them.[36]

Mawhood reported that the RAAF in Western Australia was completely preoccupied with operational intelligence. There was nothing of a security intelligence nature managed by the RAAF in Western Australia.

In South Australia, Mawhood found the situation to be slightly different as Military Intelligence was separated from the CSS, and it had sufficient personnel and was less reliant on the police than in Western Australia. Other than that, he found the same limited appreciation of security intelligence work. He also found that no one had specialist training or experience of investigations or intelligence work and this resulted in very little of value having been accomplished.[37]

In South Australia, Mawhood reported that Professor A.L. Campbell, a lawyer and academic who was Chief Censor, supervised the CSS in the time he had available to him outside of his censorship duties. Campbell expressed the view to Mawhood that the CSS was 'superfluous' as it performed 'no new functions and makes no useful contribution to the security of South Australia.'[38]

Inspector Williams, who Mawhood found to be keen and energetic, but who admitted his own ignorance in how to conduct security intelligence work at higher levels, led the CIB in Adelaide. Mawhood noted that the Adelaide CIB often conducted its own investigations, but found that these frequently duplicated or crossed investigations being mounted by Military Intelligence or the state police. Mawhood also noted that in South Australia, as in Western Australia, government facilities were protected by Commonwealth peace officers, but important civilian facilities were left completely unprotected.[39]

Overall, Mawhood found one dividend of the White Australia Policy in that the identification, registration and control of aliens and their property was well under control in Australia, with each of the six agencies involved in security passing information freely to their counterparts in other states. Beyond this, Mawhood had found nothing else was happening. No enemy agents or suspected agents had been identified and no enemy intelligence activity had been detected. As Mawhood put it, 'either the western half of Australia ... has wholly escaped the attention of foreign agents, or they had carried out their work entirely undetected'.[40] Of course, as we now know, it was the first problem.

Following his investigation Mawhood made the following recommendations:

1. All matters pertaining to the security of the Commonwealth be centralised in one civilian organisation with its headquarters in Canberra and sub-departments in each state and territory.
2. All security records, as distinct from alien registration records, be handed over by all Commonwealth and state agencies to the new civilian security organisation.
3. That sections Ix and Ic of MI, where they are involved in security intelligence, be handed over to the new civilian organisation.
4. Registration and control of aliens to be handed over to state police forces who would then refer suspect individuals to the security service for investigation.
5. On receiving a referral from police, the security service would examine the case and make recommendations to the A-G.
6. The police would carry out executive actions such as arrest and prosecution of suspects.
7. All Commonwealth agencies, Security Service, CIB, Peace Officers, Army, Navy and Air Force, will report all security intelligence matters to the new civilian organisation for action.
8. Each state sub-department of the new organisation would have attached to it a small offensive intelligence section of trained personnel to prosecute the active collection of intelligence on targets of interest.
9. The Director General of the Security Service should be an Australian of outstanding ability with the freedom to select personnel who had high standards of education, sound knowledge of foreign countries and linguistic ability.

10. Attached to the Director General's office would be representatives of the three armed services to provide him with advice on service matters and to control the internal security of the armed services on his behalf.[41]

These recommendations predated those made by Duncan by almost two months, so either both men separately came to the same conclusions, or Duncan drew on Mawhood's insights.

This report was not the first prepared by Mawhood for the incoming Curtin government. An earlier one dated 18 October was written for Attorney-General H.V. Evatt and submitted via Knowles. This report contained observations on security intelligence in Australia and it was the more critical of the two reports Mawhood wrote at the time. It made plain to Evatt that Mawhood had been 'most unfavourably impressed and disturbed' by what he had seen of Military Intelligence in Australia, particularly the way the General Staff controlled it.[42] The major deficiencies identified by Mawhood were exactly what all of the other reports and discussions had identified: the lack of effective policy direction, insufficient and second-rate personnel, no effective training and the multiplicity of organisations involved in security and intelligence activity.

The most important problem Mawhood identified was the absence of any coherent government policy for the management of internal security and intelligence. No effort had been expended in investigating Australia's peacetime or wartime needs in this area. Policy reflected information gleaned from out-of-date publications supplied years earlier by the War Office. As a result, there was no agreement on what internal security and intelligence was and how it should be managed and conducted. It was because of this policy failure that the organisation for intelligence collection in Australia had grown and developed in a completely haphazard way.[43]

The second problem identified by Mawhood was the selection of personnel for Military Intelligence. All of the officers working within the area he had met seemed to have been selected on a haphazard basis with no thought given to their suitability for the work. According to Mawhood, this work required 'an alert and vigorous brain', something that he felt few working in Military Intelligence, CIB or the CSS demonstrated to any notable degree.

Mawhood criticised the lack of a systematic approach to the selection and training of officers for Military Intelligence duties in Australia. There was no training at all, as far as he could discern. None of the officers who filled roles in Military Intelligence had attended schools of instruction or had any formal education in intelligence. They seemed to depend on lecturing one another about their conception of their own jobs and this was entirely inadequate—'there is not an intelligence instructor in Australia who has had any practical experience in his subject since the last war'.[44]

All of this pointed to a lack of direction held by the military authorities, particularly men like Colonel J.A. Chapman, the current Director of Military Intelligence, who Mawhood described as not being up to the job because 'he has not the personality, intellect, education or training necessary for this important post'.[45] Language like this is probably what upset Duncan and perhaps many of the army officers Mawhood met.

The main reason for this state of affairs, Mawhood argued, was the 'Staff Corps Complex'.[46] This 'complex' arose from the way in which the Staff Corps of professional officers had controlled the army in peacetime and were now battling to keep that control during wartime. His observation that the expansion of the peacetime army to a wartime establishment had enabled mediocre officers to rise to levels they were unsuited for is sound. Yet, while this was true, Mawhood was letting Australia's governments off the hook by laying the entire blame at the feet of the Staff Corps.

The Staff Corps had suffered serious challenges maintaining itself and the army during the interwar period. Starved of resources and money, and confined to staff duties only, the corps saw many of its most capable members leave to pursue careers in civilian life. However, they were not alone in this opposition to Mawhood. The Militia, the part-time reservists, were also very much opposed to Mawhood and his recommendations.

A large number of Militia officers served in Military Intelligence, including Brigadier Bertrand Combes, who surrounded himself with 'henchmen', including Lieutenant Colonel Lloyd, Lieutenant Colonel C.A.K. Cohen, Lieutenant Colonel W.J.R. Scott and Lieutenant Colonel Powell.[47] R.F.B. Wake, as a later arrival in the army, was not really part of this group, but he was a useful adjunct operator for its purposes.

Scott was a notable personality among these henchmen; he had been heavily involved in the activities of right-wing groups during the interwar period. This was a man who is described in the *Australian Dictionary of Biography* as being 'arrogant and high handed in his relationships with other intelligence officers' and a 'focal point for interdepartmental wrangling'.[48] Scott was also the case officer running Harry Freame in security intelligence operations against the Japanese community, while he was himself publicly advocating Japan and things Japanese. He was also the officer appointed by Army HQ to keep Mawhood and Mission 104 under surveillance, when he was given command of the commando training centre at Wilson's Promontory in 1941.

Mawhood did not overlook Scott's history or the histories of those around him, suggesting 'close investigation into the antecedents of certain of the men named in this report would produce remarkable disclosures'.[49] To ram the point home, Mawhood advised Evatt and Knowles to bear in mind 'that these men, openly or under cover, were at one time active members of the New Guard'.[50] This may have been the biggest skeleton in the closet of Military Intelligence and the underlying reason why the attack on Mawhood was so savage.

Again, as in his later report for Duncan, Mawhood emphasised the failure of the security intelligence system in counterespionage. In support of this contention, he referred to the case of Major Hashida Sei, who—as an officer of the Japanese Department of Supply[51]—had visited Australia in 1941, presumably in preparation for the invasion of Malaya.[52] It was a little unfair to blame the security organisations for Hashida as his visit was notified and approved through the usual diplomatic channels and his intelligence gathering, although amateurish and disorganised, was only discovered by the Dutch on Java when they arrested him and searched his belongings.

He also mentioned the case of a Mr McHutchinson who had been found guilty of wearing a military uniform without authority and who was also found to have had secret documents in his possession.

There was no evidence presented that McHutchinson was attempting to steal the documents as part of an espionage operation or in order to sell them. In fact, it appears that McHutchinson might have just been one of those unfortunates who enjoy masquerading in military uniform and flaunting that they have access to secrets.

The problem that haunted all efforts to create a workable security intelligence service in Australia remained the unwillingness of the army to surrender what it erroneously believed to be the prerogatives of Military Intelligence to a civilian agency. The CSS headed by Lloyd had proven itself incapable of moving forward, just as the CIB had. Effectively, both organisations remained controlled by the Military Intelligence.

With the change of government on 7 October 1941, Knowles moved decisively to capture the support of his new ALP masters. To this end, he wrote two minutes for Evatt. The first of these, dated 18 October 1941, was a long and detailed briefing of the history of the Mawhood affair and the second, dated the same day, gave his recommendation, and the reasons for it, that neither Jones or Lloyd be appointed to head the new security service. In support of his minutes, Knowles also passed the report written by Mawhood, also dated 18 October 1941.[53] In this report, Mawhood recommended:

a) That all matters pertaining to Security (the Ib Sub-Section of MI) be handed over, as already agreed by the General Staff, to the new Security Service with a minimum of delay, and that their Secret Service Funds be discontinued forthwith.
b) That a director and deputy director of MI be drawn from experienced personnel now serving in the Middle East.
c) That personnel engaged on MI should attend the school mentioned later. For this purpose, it would also be advisable to bring back qualified Instructors from the Middle East to assist.[54]

He also recommended the appointment of a director-general as the sole authority for security in the Commonwealth and nominated the Director of Naval Intelligence, Commander Long, RAN, as the man to fill this position.[55] How the new Security Service would function, Mawhood left up to the new director-general and his staff who would need 'to hammer out each problem (including the general set-up), as it arises'.[56]

The final recommendation that Mawhood put forward was that an intelligence school be opened in Canberra for the centralised training of personnel for the new Security Service and for the armed services so that they would better understand their roles.[57]

None of it mattered, as the new government settled itself in and desperately tried to get control of a nation at war. All of this became even more difficult as the Japanese thrust southward sent panic through the population and the government itself. Behind the scenes, darker forces such as NSW Commissioner of Police MacKay were beginning their moves to take control of Australia's new security service.[58] MacKay was already a player in security intelligence through the MPIS in Sydney, which, by November 1941, had compiled 17,000 dossiers, 14,000 miscellaneous files and 130,000 index cards on NSW citizens.[59] MacKay was making his play to be the new Director-General of the Security Service.

Under Evatt, men of the calibre of MacKay and Wake would take control of Australia's security intelligence and introduce a whole new level of procedural corruption to a system that was already well out of control. Riding shotgun over all of this was the General Staff, where arrogance, self-interest and ignorance formed an unholy trinity that would protect the CSS and, later, the security service from effective oversight and accountability.

Whatever criticisms were directed at Mawhood, his analysis of the problems afflicting Australia's security intelligence system in 1941 and 1942 was insightful and, as we will see, correct. About the only errors he made in his analysis were his continued belief in the 'fifth column' threat and the existence of undetected enemy agents operating in Australia.[60] In fact, as all of the local Australian security intelligence officers, including Black in Western Australia and Campbell in Adelaide, told him, there were not and never would be any enemy agents in those states. Thus, as we will see, in the absence of a real threat to security, the temptation was to create one, and Australia's security intelligence system would soon fall for this.

All of this suggests that we should be careful of the critiques of Mawhood by officers who were violently opposed to him and, more importantly, his backers such as Knowles, and ministers in the Menzies government. The vitriol poured on him showed that the argument was not about Mawhood, but about the threat any investigation posed to the members of Military Intelligence and, by extension, to the Staff Corps.

Mawhood's recommendations for the Australian Security Service were eminently sensible. His recommendation for a single national security intelligence authority headed by a director-general answerable to the government of the day was exactly what was finally achieved in 1949 when ASIO was created. His recommendation for the careful selection of well-educated and ethical officers and personnel for the service was also finally adopted in 1949, as was his recommendation for professionally run, centralised training of all security intelligence personnel.[61] He was more farsighted than any of his contemporaries realised.

CHAPTER 10

THE WARTIME SECURITY SERVICE

By early 1942, it was patently obvious to everyone, including George Knowles and Rupert Long, that the Mawhood ploy to reorganise and civilianise the security intelligence system had failed. The General Staff had given ground, but only in a tactical retreat in the face of the arrival of John Curtin's ALP government and the submission of the Duncan Report. As the new government settled into place in late 1941 and early 1942, the national situation had changed dramatically as Japanese victories came one after another and the General Staff went to work on the new ministers, especially Frank Forde, the new Minister for the Army.

Despite everything that had happened, the state of Australia's security intelligence system was still dismal. Lloyd and his CSS remained small, ill-organised and inefficient. Military Intelligence was still trying to fill the role and the Attorney-General's Department had gone back to its corner for a rest. The delivery of Alexander Duncan's report, however, supported to some extent by John Mawhood's report, put the problems of security intelligence back on the table. It was now that NSW Police Commissioner William MacKay made his bid for the position of Director-General of the proposed security service.

MacKay's attempt began on 6 November 1941 when the premier of New South Wales, William McKell, forwarded a report from the NSW Police and

MPIS to the federal authorities, including Forde and Attorney General Doc Evatt. From this date until 10 March 1942, McKell forwarded twelve NSW Police reports to Curtin, almost one a week.[1] This was most definitely a campaign to raise MacKay's profile and get him the job, and it helped.

The report-writing campaign was not the only arrow in MacKay's quiver. He had gained the ear of his fellow policeman and Scotsman Duncan, who had already recommended him for the position. Just to ensure that the job was his, MacKay also met privately with Evatt and sent private letters to him with advice on how the new service should be run.

The campaign succeeded. The new Security Service was created on 9 March 1942 and, on 17 March 1942, following further consideration by Cabinet, Forde appointed MacKay as Director-General of the new Commonwealth Security Service.[2]

One of the first to congratulate MacKay on his appointment was Knowles, but if the note was heartfelt and sincere, it was not long before MacKay had alienated Knowles. The causes of this possibly lay in MacKay's pursuit of Duncan's plan for state police commissioners to act as the new service's enforcers, something neither Knowles nor the military would support. Another initiative that MacKay pushed, placing the headquarters in Sydney, met with a flat rejection from Knowles, who was a long and fervent supporter of Canberra as the national capital. MacKay had not impressed his new boss.

The new position of Director-General Security (DG-S) had direct access to the Attorney-General, and in the absence of the Attorney-General to the Minister of Defence, Forde.[3] It was decided that the location of the Security Service headquarters was to be Canberra and, as Forde made very clear to MacKay:

> lest you have misunderstood me on this point I make it quite clear in this letter that the headquarters of Security Service [sic] is not to perform merely a nominal role but is to be the nerve centre of your organisation; its eight principles are to be appointed at once; it is to absorb copies of all records; it is to supervise the work of the state branches . . . over whose workings it is to maintain a constant and real control[4]

Of all these directions given by the responsible minister, only one was obeyed: the Security Service headquarters was based in Canberra.

Of the more mundane aspects, the new organisation was to fall under the provisions of the Commonwealth Public Service Act, with some exemptions relating to gazetting and appeals to ensure secrecy and make sure salaries would be commensurate with those of the public service.[5] The new service had even made provision for liaison positions from MI5 and the FBI. It was also authorised to immediately establish a school in Canberra, but, sensibly, rejected the recommendation from MacKay that there be a school in each state.[6] Finally, Forde instructed MacKay not to concern himself with the departmental conference of 1 April, which had been held to 'clear up issues existing between Sir George Knowles and the services'.[7] There was little possibility that these issues between Knowles and MacKay—which the services saw as 'wide' and Forde hoped would be 'narrowed, if not completely bridged'—would be resolved.[8]

As DG-S, MacKay had a detailed list of responsibilities which included, as a start, the control through investigation, surveillance, prosecution and internment of all hostile, alien, subversive and pacifist individuals and classes of individuals or organisations.[9] This was so broad it was meaningless, and the inclusion of pacifists a highly dangerous sop to the bigotry of the General Staff.

Having provided these instructions to MacKay, Forde gave another set of vague directions on 19 June 1942, telling him he had to supervise security requirements; supervise the activities of disaffected persons; provide effective liaison to the armed services, the CIB, state police forces; and safeguard the armed forces and Commonwealth property from injury by sabotage, espionage and subversive action. Again, the direction was ludicrously broad and thus meaningless. It was the third set of broad instructions MacKay had received since 17 March and it tells us that despite the agreement on setting up the Security Service, the bureaucratic war was still raging behind the scenes.[10]

The army ramped up their attack by raising the difficulties of finding appropriate officers to fill the roles within the Security Service. One of the first requests MacKay made was to have Lieutenant Colonel C.A.K. Cohen appointed as both the Military Liaison Officer for the Security Service and as his deputy.[11] MacKay's bid to have Cohen appointed as his deputy failed but Cohen was approved for the position of Military Liaison Officer for the Security Service, effectively the gatekeeper between it and the armed services.[12] Lieutenant Colonel Lloyd, Lieutenant Colonel Wake and Major B. Tyrell were appointed as his three assistant directors.[13] By 3 July, Lieutenant Colonel Longfield Lloyd and Major Tyrell had been appointed directors,

Wake was appointed as Director (Fighting Services) and deputy directors of security were appointed to the states.[14]

The first course for security officers and operatives brought into the new service was conducted between 4 May and 17 June 1942 at Phillip House, Phillip Street, Sydney. This course consisted of 25 days of lectures covering everything from the definition of a war offence, delivered by a solicitor from the Crown Solicitor's Office, to methods of search, examination of scenes, the use of photography and the use of scientific aids in examining letters, typing, handwriting and fingerprints. These technical lectures were delivered by police officers Sergeant Jardine, Detective Rogers and Sergeant Ewing.

The entire emphasis was on forensic crime scene evaluation, not clandestine espionage. There was not a single presentation about tradecraft, how a real intelligence operative would work or anything about intelligence organisations or how they operated. What they did have on this course was a day dedicated to subversive associations, which were listed as Communism and the Jehovah's Witnesses.[15]

The fundamental flaw in Australia's security intelligence system continued to be the lack of centralised control. The deputy directors of security, the people in charge of the state offices of the Security Service, were bypassing the army chain of command, something the army did not like. The most likely offender was Lieutenant Colonel Wake in Brisbane, who was exercising his new powers in the Security Service. In a letter of 15 July 1942, the director of Military Intelligence, Colonel C.G. Roberts, made it clear to MacKay and Cohen that this practice was to cease.[16] The practice not only continued, it got worse.

Each deputy director held similar executive powers to MacKay, leaving them virtually autonomous.[17] Each deputy director corresponded directly with one another, thus cutting out the Canberra headquarters from the matters under discussion.[18] They even launched, justified and ran their own investigations without oversight from headquarters or the DG-S.[19] Not even their records were centralised.[20] The result of this autonomy was that, by tradition, the deputy directors of Military Intelligence, the CIB and now the Security Service were a law unto themselves.

The result was that politicians, including Commonwealth and even state ministers, communicated directly with deputy directors, bypassing headquarters, meaning the security intelligence system in Australia continued to be used for political purposes and 'imbued with political intrigue'.[21]

By the middle of July 1942, the unrestrained nature of the state deputy directors had raised the army's hackles enough for Colonel Roberts to write to MacKay and ask him to ensure that if a deputy director was writing to a command, in this case Headquarters, Allied Land Forces, they also provided copies to the headquarters of the Line of Communications as well.[22]

Another bone of contention was the Security Service's desire to stay out of the appeals process established for individuals who had been detained or interned by the army. The army was not happy with this and wanted the Security Service to 'co-operate with the Army in connection with appeals of internees' in order to 'obviate unnecessary movement of internees or guards'.[23]

One of the unforeseen problems that now made itself apparent was that the officers, non-commissioned officers (NCOs) and soldiers posted to the Security Service were unable to be promoted because, as a non-Army organisation, it had no establishment, the authorised list of funded positions for military personnel, and, for some reason, one could not be arranged. It was Wake who formally raised this issue with Lieutenant Colonel Little, the deputy director of Military Intelligence, in a letter dated 17 August 1942. Little bluntly noted in longhand on the bottom of this letter that there was no establishment and that he had informed Wake of this.[24]

To anyone uninitiated in army bureaucratic politics this manning issue may appear to be minor. However, what the army was doing, using the pretext of personnel management and lack of promotion opportunity, was removing all of its personnel from the Security Service, hoping to leave MacKay with an almost empty organisation. Military Intelligence was mounting a very potent attack on MacKay, one he would be unable to counter other than by complaining to Attorney-General Evatt.

As a result, in early September, the Chief of the General Staff ordered all officers, NCOs and other ranks, 163 in all, be transferred to Land Headquarters (LHQ) until the matter could be solved. The Security Service was given until 31 October to finalise the officers and other ranks they wished to keep, and the officers concerned would then be seconded to the service in civil appointments. The other ranks, including members of the FSS, were to be discharged from the army and taken up as civilian employees of the Security Service.[25]

One of the outcomes of this manning problem was the convening of a conference attended by the interested parties held in the Senate Chamber and chaired by Evatt, as the Attorney-General. Evatt had consistently expressed his opposition to the creation of a large security service.[26] Now, he revisited this and, during what seems to have been a meandering discussion led by him, announced the reduction of the Security Service's budget from £250,000 to £100,000, a massive cut of 60 per cent.[27] Evatt justified this by arguing that the army make the required manpower available for future operations of the Security Service, thus shifting the costs for the Security Service onto the army budget. How Evatt thought this would be acceptable to MacKay or the army is hard to grasp and can only be seen as a sign of a serious lack of foresight.

On 15 September another conference was held at LHQ in Melbourne. At this conference the Commander-in-Chief, General Blamey, stated he did not want army personnel subject to the direction of outside bodies like the Security Service. Now MacKay was caught between the extraordinary actions of his minister, Evatt, in destroying his budget, the army in withdrawing his newly trained—for what that was worth—workforce, and police services concurrently withdrawing their officers as a result of arguments over who paid for them. The outcome was obvious and at this conference MacKay announced he would not be seeking an extension of his appointment as Director-General and would be returning to his post as Commissioner of the NSW Police on 21 September 1942. There was no vote of thanks recorded in the minutes.[28]

On 23 September 1942, as MacKay returned to the safety of Sydney, Brigadier William Ballantyne Simpson was appointed as the DG-S by Evatt.[29] The charter for Simpson was basically that given to MacKay, but now Simpson would take on the job of managing internees, their detention, release and appeals. The General Staff had got what it wanted, including an army officer as the head of the Security Service.[30]

· · · · · · · · · · · · · ·

Simpson was born in Sydney on 12 June 1894 to a solicitor, William, and his wife Margaret. Young Simpson went to Fort Street High School, where he met Evatt for the first time. Like Evatt, Simpson studied law at the University of Sydney but interrupted his studies to join the 1st AIF in January 1916 as a driver in the 11th Field Company, Royal Australian Engineers. He returned to Sydney in 1918 and was discharged from the AIF. Simpson stayed in the militia and completed his law degree and was admitted as a barrister on 6 May 1920.

Following the war, Simpson became noted for representing insurance companies in cases where compensation was being claimed by drivers involved in accidents.[31] This type of work provided him with a good income, though his work was looked down upon by some of his more intellectual peers. He remained in the militia as a legal officer rising to the rank of lieutenant colonel by 1928. It was this position that finally saw Simpson posted into the 2nd AIF and sent to the Middle East as a temporary brigadier and deputy judge advocate general. On his return to Australia in 1941, Simpson remained in the AIF until he was selected by his old school mate, Evatt, to replace MacKay as Director-General of the Security Service.

Perhaps the most honest evaluation of Simpson was provided by Lieutenant Colonel E.A. Airy to MI5 in October 1944.[32] Airy, who thankfully avoided getting involved in the political infighting in Australia, described Simpson as fat, kindly and as having a great sense of humour. In fact, to Airy, he looked 'like a jolly, overgrown, bespectacled boy', who was at this time 48 years old.[33] Despite this, Airy found him to be 'clever, extremely quick witted and expresses himself (on almost any subject) most ably'.[34] Airy found that Simpson was firm and frank and able to stand up to Evatt, with whom he was personally acquainted; however, Airy also found him 'vain and personally very ambitious', and that he had been discharged from the army on Blamey's orders and refused permission to wear uniform, which had hurt him deeply.[35]

Like Justice Geoffrey Reed, another judge in Evatt's circle, Simpson hoped to become a High Court judge, and while Airy thought that Simpson 'was fundamentally honest (at any rate relatively speaking in Australia where political intrigue and corruption is rife)', he did not believe Simpson 'would hesitate to use very clever methods especially if it suited him personally'.[36] This description of Airy's could equally be applied to Simpson's old school chum, Evatt, whom Airy described as 'quite devoid of any scruples politically'.[37]

Simpson was Evatt's man, yet he was also acceptable to the General Staff where the job of smoothing out the relationships between the army and the Security Service offices in the various states was undertaken by Cohen over October and November 1942. By early December, there were no further issues concerning military personnel serving in the Security Service where, when on civil security duty they would wear civilian clothing and when not, they would wear uniform.[38] Apparently, the army was able to fix its establishment issues with Simpson and by 1 February 1943, the army contingent in the

Security Service had grown to 74 officers and 225 other ranks, a total of 299 who were providing administrative support and investigative personnel.[39]

By February 1943, Simpson—advised and assisted by Wake—settled into trying to control the service and its members. This led to a reorganisation of the service in May and June, which became more than just an adjustment, it was a great purge.

It began with the Brisbane office in June 1943, which Wake said was necessary because he was being tied up by 'minor queries' and he needed to divest himself of the day-to-day work 'in favour of matters of statewid [sic], interstate, Commonwealth or international significance', and counterespionage cases.[40] This Queensland reorganisation saw 77 people out of 214 lose their jobs—that is 36 per cent of all staff.[41] Removing such a large number of people cannot have been simply because they were not up to their jobs. The number of sackings suggests that the real reason was to remove anyone who had queried Wake, who did not appreciate his 'rude and hurtful tongue', or who had become concerned at what he was doing.[42]

A second objective behind the sackings in Brisbane, and then later in the other states, was to remove from the Security Service personnel that the Director-General deemed unsuitable or unnecessary. In Melbourne, 30 people lost their positions.[43] In Sydney, eighteen people were retired 'forthwith'.[44]

By the end of this reorganisation, the now slimline Security Service was effectively being run by Wake, behind the cover of Simpson, and this made complete sense. If Wake had angled for the top job, he would have been subject to far more oversight and the demands on his time for meeting with ministers and senior officials would have taken him away from what he needed to do. Thus, standing in Simpson's shadow and carrying out favours for Evatt ensured that Wake could survive any scandal and would not be as open to attack by jealous rivals than he would be if he took the top job.

As a consequence, Wake fostered the 'political intrigue' and 'corruption' that MI5 kept referring to.[45] A good example of this occurred in the lead-up to the 1944 Referendum on Post-War Reconstruction and Democratic Rights when Wake dedicated Security Service and CIB resources to assist Evatt's campaign in Northern New South Wales and Queensland.[46] Wake and his officers worked to identify and investigate anyone opposed to Evatt's position, and the Director-General of Security, Simpson, either didn't know about it or allowed it to happen.[47] All of this was just a continuation of the problems that

William Morris Hughes had created in 1915 when he established the CEB under George Steward and then used it to spy on his Cabinet colleagues, MPs and bureaucrats. Now, within Australia's wartime Security Service grew yet another and more extensive network of corruption and Wake, as the fireman, the person sent to quickly fix problems as they arose in the Security Service, helped create and foster this network.

In time, this network expanded to include Wake, Evatt, Reed, Simpson and a range of police officers, peace officers, military personnel, journalists and government officials. The most important thing about this network is that it provided major advantages to its membership. Simpson and Reed were lawyers desperate to get onto the bench, especially the High Court bench; although it would have been almost impossible to put men of their legal standing into any High Court judgeship, it did not stop them from wanting to get there.

For others, there was the assistance Wake and his friends could provide in helping their associates spy on their political opponents, especially those in their own parties. They also provided assistance in identifying bureaucrats opposed to government initiatives and who might be leaking information to the press or to the opposition in parliament.

While all of this reorganisation and reshuffling was happening, foreign spies were obtaining Australian and Allied secrets and using them to damage the war effort in the Pacific. This is where the real harm caused by Wake and his network occurred. Despite Wake's integral role, the central role really belongs to the politicians and officials who controlled the security intelligence apparatus and used it for their own ends. Their efforts to keep personal control of the system led them into dependence on men like Wake.

When the war with Japan came to an end in August 1945, the ambitious Simpson took the first judicial job that came his way, and, on 23 October 1945, he resigned as the DG-S to take up a position as the sole judge of the ACT Supreme Court. With Simpson's departure the superannuated Lloyd once again moved into the leadership of Australia's security intelligence system, supported by Wake and his cronies.[48]

Lloyd's return was no vote of confidence in him; in fact he was probably chosen by Evatt and others because he was ineffectual. Knowles was finally being prised out of the position of secretary of the Attorney-General's Department, with the pre-retirement sinecure of high commissioner to South Africa

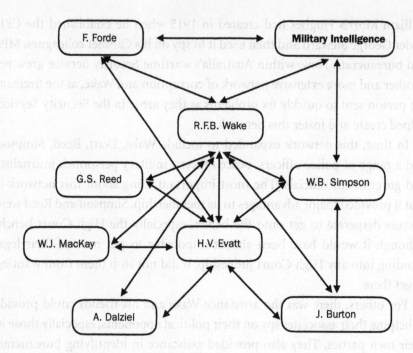

Figure 10.1: The Wake network, 1942–49

as a going-away present.[49] Knowles had little or no influence with Evatt, as the men despised one another, but being on the way out, Knowles probably didn't care or couldn't resist the return of Evatt's malleable drone, Lloyd.[50]

Australia's security intelligence situation was now out of control and its government and institutions were being penetrated by the clandestine agents of the CP-A and NKGB. The growing insecurity of the Australian government, its disinterest in protecting the national secrets of its allies and the growing success of the NKGB and the RIS in stealing these secrets was about to see Australia's political and government leadership faced with the realities of international power politics.

CHAPTER 11

THE SERPENT IN THE SACRISTY—R.F.B. WAKE

Robert Frederick Bird Wake was born to Robert William Charles Wake, an upholsterer, and Victoria Helena Wake (nee Young) on 27 December 1900 in Moonee Ponds, Victoria.[1] From this beginning, Wake grew up in the suburban setting of Moonee Ponds and does not seem to have made much of a mark until he was appointed on 27 November 1918 as a Naval Staff clerk, class V, at the Garden Island naval dockyard in Sydney.[2] In this position, Wake worked for Rupert Basil Michel Long, later Director of Naval Intelligence during World War II. Under the firm hand of the Navy, Wake appears to have been an effective employee.

In due course, Wake met and married Jessie Laurie Miller and settled at 41 Arthur Street, Kogarah, where they had a son, Grenville Robert, on 7 October 1924.[3] The next mention of Wake is his enlistment in the Australian Military Forces on 2 September 1931, in which he inefficiently served until his discharge on 31 October 1934, a rather eventful year for him. Interestingly, his enlistment form carries the first formal evidence of his capacity for lying, in that it notes his service in the British Expeditionary Force (BEF) for eight months in 1918.[4] This is a lie Wake would use again, and one that would get him into significant trouble with the Australian Army and its commanders.[5]

He was a man of limited intellectual scope, a distant father and a work-aholic who appears from the record to have been suffering from a significant inferiority complex. His long history in security intelligence work and his addiction to being in control sounds warning bells even now, and it did so at the time. He was not particularly trusted by his colleagues or by some of his more insightful superiors. His wartime boss, Brigadier William Simpson, described him as 'not everyone's love', going on to say that any deputy working for him would need to be thick-skinned in order to cope with Wake's 'rude and hurtful tongue'.[6] Interestingly, Simpson believed that any deputy bearing 'a little bit of the imprimatur of the old school tie' would cope better with Wake.[7] A clearer description of insecurity would be hard to find.

Others, such as the Director of Military Intelligence, Brigadier John Rogers, and his deputy, Colonel K.A. Wills, made clear their dislike of Wake, telling Simpson that 'neither John or I have any time for Wake at all, either as a man or as a Security Officer'.[8] Commander Long, the Director of Naval Intelligence, did not trust Wake at all.[9] Events would prove these critics right.

An incident in late 1933 provides early evidence of another of Wake's talents, that of getting his name into the newspapers. The story involved the ship's bell from a German raider, *Emden*, which was stolen from the doorway of the main official building on Garden Island on 8 August 1932 and later recovered from its burial place in The Domain by a party of police accompanied by intelligence officers, including Wake, then a senior clerical officer at Garden Island. Wake would later give evidence against a German immigrant, Charles Kaolmel, who admitted to receiving the bell but was convicted of the theft.[10]

The ACNB then presented the bell to the Australian War Memorial Museum for safekeeping. In events amounting to a French farce, the bell was again stolen on 28 April 1933 by no less than Charles Kaolmel, to the exquisite outrage of Australia's newspapers.[11] Fittingly, a party led by the intrepid journalists of the *Sydney Morning Herald* later recovered the bell from Melbourne, where it had been buried in Royal Park, and not, as most of Australia's newspapers had claimed, from Germany.[12]

The year 1934 was tumultuous for Wake as he was transferred from his position as a senior naval clerk to a position as a clerk in the CIB,[13] and was divorced by his wife who, on 13 September, obtained a decree nisi on the grounds of Wake's adultery with one Evelyn Woodiwiss, also known as Eve Wiss.[14] Given that the newspaper *Truth* covered the divorce proceedings

162

under the headline 'Careless wooers, Emden Bell–Finder Found Out', it is hard to believe that Wake was not humiliated. It is even harder to believe that the description of Wake as an 'intelligence officer in the Navy' who 'should have known a thing or two about covering up his tracks when he decided to have a love affair' didn't raise the ire of the ACNB.[15]

Wake was probably lucky that he had transferred to the CIB earlier in 1934 as the CIB may have been less inclined to accept him as a member of the organisation following his divorce and the coverage it received in the *Truth*. Yet all of this did nothing to damage Wake's prospects in the CIB. He fitted right in with H.E. Jones and Longfield Lloyd, and he would also be able to pursue his dalliances with other women.

The events of 1934 and 1935, and Wake's behaviour during this period, suggest that the later wartime allegations of underhandedness, corruption and an unnatural interest in other people's sex lives, including the use of prostitutes to entrap Australian and Allied military officers, may have more merit than previously thought.

The year 1934 also seems to have been tumultuous for the CIB led by Jones. Between 1931 and 1934 the CIB, as well as state authorities, especially in New South Wales, had faced the problem of growing militancy on both the left and right of politics. This militancy had created more fear than it warranted, a fear that was slowly drawing the army into greater involvement in civilian political affairs. This involvement included Military Intelligence conducting its own investigations of left-wing organisations and even drawing some less politically conscious officers into direct involvement with new right-wing organisations such as the New Guard in New South Wales and the White Army in Victoria.

The main advantage that the CIB had in dealing with these right-wing organisations was that other than voicing their disenchantment with government policies, they had no real agenda for revolution. Their loyalty to God, King and Country made them highly vulnerable to legitimate government authority exercised by the CIB.[16] The problem for the New Guard, and like bodies, is that they knew what they were against, but they had no idea of what they were for, other than God, King and Country. As a result, they were pathetically easy for the authorities to penetrate and spy upon, and in New South Wales, they faced William MacKay and the NSW Police Force, whose suppression of the New Guard was utterly ruthless and illegal.[17] The result was that on 23 December 1931, the NSW Legislative Assembly published MacKay's report detailing the entire New Guard establishment, including the names of all its office holders, general council members and commanders.[18] This report ensured the threat posed by the New Guard was exaggerated, thus providing a justification for future police action and reinforcing on the politicians the importance of a strong and effective police force.

This fractious political environment was simply a reflection of the fractiousness creeping through the everyday life of Australians afflicted by the economic downturn of the Depression. The motivation of the General Staff in involving itself in civilian affairs could have simply been a desire to protect the country from the internal security threat supposedly posed by the left, especially the communists, whose violent rhetoric and possible backing by the Soviet Union did nothing to alleviate the growth in unfounded fear. But it is also highly likely that the General Staff harboured real fears that many of their serving officers, both permanent and militia, were actively involved in the right-wing organisations, organisations like the New Guard that trumpeted its 50,000 members.

All of the writing about the New Guard needs to be taken with a pinch of salt because it suited all sides to make the New Guard appear more threatening than it actually was. In order to attract members and financial support, the leadership of the organisation needed to make it appear as strong and vital as they could get away with. The NSW Police needed to make it seem big and threatening so their victory appeared greater than perhaps it was. Those on the left needed to make it a focus of dread so that they too could attract members, supporters and money to combat it. Yet all of these claims and fears are undermined by the fact that an organisation of 50,000 tried-and-true members could only afford the rent on a small commercial office at Wingello House in Angel Place, Sydney.[19]

The best indicator of how threatened the Commonwealth felt is clearly shown at the end of 1934, when the CIB lost six of its investigating officers and inspectors. Their replacements included R.F.B. Wake, W.H. Barnwell, J.R. Magnusson, Herbert George Sturcke, Henry Scorer Bird and G.M.B. Longmore.[20] Other than Simpson's promotion to the Postmaster-General's Department, the reasons for this wholesale change in the CIB are not easy to identify. The loss of so many officers in such a short time indicates that all was not well within the CIB. Whatever the case, by May 1935, Wake was authorised as the Signing Officer for the Collector's Receipts Account and the Collector's Trust Account in the absence of Lloyd, who had been appointed to John Latham's mission to Japan and the Far East. The countersigning officer was another new boy, William Barnwell.[21] In a very short time, Wake had ensconced himself in the CIB and his star was rising.

The organisation that Wake had joined was small, around 30 people, and it had just gone through a turbulent time fending off the attempts of Military Intelligence to increase its hold on civilian security intelligence activity and dealing with the loss of a large number of its investigation staff. The Director of the CIB was still Jones, who operated an organisation with ambitions much greater than its resources could ever meet.

Wake established himself in the CIB very quickly and was soon demonstrating his capacity for accumulating more and more responsibilities. In less than a year, on 29 August 1935, Wake was promoted to the rank of inspector on a salary of £447 and sent off to Brisbane where he would proceed to build his legend.[22]

In Brisbane, Wake settled into the life of a senior officer. His duties covered the gamut of CIB responsibilities including fraud against the Commonwealth, theft and other petty crimes that called upon the CIB's time and resources.

The first public references to the now reconstructed Robert Wake was a dinner in honour of Mr Robert and Mrs Elizabeth Wake, his second wife, at the home of Mr and Mrs Harry Borradale in Auchenflower in April 1936. This rated a mention in the social pages, 'A Few Lines to Say', in Brisbane's *Courier-Mail* on 29 April 1936.[23] Elizabeth (Betty) Wake would now begin to be a feature of those and other social pages because of her taste in fashion and her charitable work.[24]

Wake began moving in the upper circles of Queensland society and he was cultivating his image in the newspapers, and not just those in Queensland. By September 1939, not only was he being quoted in relation to the activities of Italian criminal organisations, he also appeared in a puff piece in the *Sunday Mail* under the heading 'Our Own G-Men', a piece that extolled Inspector Wake as 'an impressive looking man', among other things.[25] Wake was even the subject of one of the caricaturist Ian Gall's cartoons for the *Sunday Mail*, something that would suggest a very close relationship between Wake and that newspaper. As an inspector in the CIB, this sort of publicity might have been okay, but for a security intelligence officer the creation of such a profile was less useful. Maintaining a public profile and providing journalists with stories would, however, become a much more important part of Wake's activities as he began manipulating Australia's newspapers to meet his own ends. This made him important to reporters always desperate to get a scoop on titbits, something that Wake's job gave him great access to.

One of his favourite journals appears to have been *Smith's Weekly*, which was able to publish juicy little items like this on the Jehovah's Witnesses: '£300 to £400 was drawn out of the Brisbane Bank by three members [Witnesses]. They re-banked the money in another bank under the name of a syndicate constituted by themselves'.[26] No other newspaper had these details, which are so precise that they could only have come from the CIB in Brisbane, and that meant Wake.

Smith's Weekly had a thing for the Jehovah's Witnesses, which it frankly admitted, and it was more than prepared to publish scurrilous articles condemning the Witnesses as 'fifth columnists' and traitors to Australia.[27] Wake's most likely contact at *Smith's* was Reginald Harris, a man who Wake would later look after when he enlisted in the AIF, by trying to find him a comfortable posting in Australia.[28]

Harris was among a bevy of tame reporters—including those at the *Sydney Morning Herald*, *Sunday Mail* and the *Daily Telegraph*. Wake was also friendly with Clive Ogilvie, later of Macquarie Broadcasting, and R. Fair of radio station 4BK through whom he seeded misinformation to undermine anyone he targeted.

Earlier in 1939, the threat of approaching war had reinvigorated Wake's interest in a part-time military career in the militia. He applied for a commission and was gazetted as a lieutenant in the Australian Military Forces on 9 March 1939.[29] By 7 September he was a temporary captain and by 7 December a temporary major, which was not bad going for a man with no military background. Importantly for our story, Wake was appointed to the Intelligence Corps on 1 November 1939, enabling him to assume an official role in Military Intelligence in Queensland, while remaining the inspector in charge of the CIB in Queensland.[30]

These concurrent postings suited both Wake and the General Staff. For Wake, it began the process of accumulating almost all military and civilian security intelligence functions in his own hands, while for the General Staff, it gave them someone senior within Sir George Knowles' department who they controlled. The dangers of this accumulation of power were not yet apparent to anyone; not the General Staff, not Knowles, not William Hughes or Jones. Perhaps, at this time, it was not even apparent to Wake. Yet this accumulation of power, something later MI5 visitors would consistently comment adversely upon, was the most obvious sign of the systemic failure in Australia's management of its internal security intelligence system.[31]

This underlines another of the secrets of Wake's success—his constant toadying up to and developing relationships with politicians, bureaucrats and others whom he perceived as powerful future supporters. An obvious example of this occurred with the assent of the Curtin opposition to the Treasury benches, which saw Wake immediately set about telegramming his congratulations to a bevy of new ministers, including J. Collins, S. Drakeford, F. Forde and E. Ward, all of whom replied.[32] Wake's son, Valdemar, who wrote a defence of his father's reputation called *No Ribbons or Medals*, highlights Wake's efforts in fostering such relationships.

Valdemar Wake makes play of the idea that Wake was an open-minded security officer willing to consider the ALP as legitimate. The reality was that his father was up to his old tricks—making himself very useful to his bosses and simply spreading his influence for his own gain. A more mundane consideration than Wake's political partisanship was the question of how he paid for the telegrams. In 1941 telegrams were not cheap and, given Wake was constantly being forced to repay the Security Service for the private use of Commonwealth telephones, it is highly likely that Wake used Commonwealth funds to pay for these messages of congratulations.

This might appear to the reader to be a minor historical oddity, but the reality was that whatever political party they came from, Australia's wartime leaders were more than willing to use the security intelligence system for their own ends, and H.V. Evatt was as procedurally corrupt in this way as William Morris Hughes.[33] Wake understood this, and he used it to his advantage. For all of his high moral claims, Evatt's handling of Australia's security intelligence would clearly demonstrate that MI5's evaluation of him as 'ambitious and quite devoid of any scruples politically' was pretty accurate.[34]

Although Wake seems to have been popular with many—particularly politicians for whom he did favours and those of his associates willing to become cronies—it is also obvious from the files that many people loathed him.[35] One man who quickly came to distrust Wake was Lieutenant Commander

Eric Feldt, the naval officer who created and commanded the ACNB's Coast-watch organisation.[36] Feldt initially had no axe to grind with Wake, having never worked with him. Feldt met Wake in Port Moresby in July 1940 when Wake had arrived with the aim, according to Feldt, of setting up an intelligence organisation.[37] Wake was 'dumbfounded' when he found out just how sophisticated the Navy's coastwatching organisation, codenamed FERDINAND, was. In fact, Feldt reported to Long that Wake actually said as much to him during the visit.[38] Feldt was to find out just how cunning Wake was.

What Wake was really up to was identifying how Feldt's coastwatching organisation actually worked. Once Wake had this information from his visit, he then worked with Military Intelligence to insist that Feldt took on the work of military censor in Papua and New Guinea in an attempt to bury Feldt in work, thus distracting him from running the coastwatch organisation. This would enable Military Intelligence to move on the Navy's coastwatch system. Later, in correspondence with Long on 19 October 1940, Feldt described to Long the army's attempt to load him up with censorship and described Wake as the 'worst double-crossing bastard I have ever had dealings with' if he was actually behind this.[39] Wake was indeed behind it.

This was the beginning of a long struggle between the ACNB and the General Staff for control of FERDINAND. Of course, the usual inter-service rivalry played its part, but so did serious operational and philosophical differences. Even something as simple as a unit reporting its daily status by radio to its headquarters was different in the navy and the army. In the navy, a unit did not report unless something had changed from the last report sent. This practice was designed to reduce radio traffic to a bare minimum in order to minimise the very real threat posed by enemy high frequency direction finding systems. This need also meant that naval radio messages were kept very short. The army required nil return, that is detailed reports specifying all subjects of interest and saying, if there was nothing new to report, 'nil'. To the navy a nil return report system was madness.

However, the real difference was philosophical and the codename, FERDINAND, chosen by Eric Feldt for the coastwatchers said it all.

Feldt chose the name Ferdinand from the book, *Ferdinand the Bull*, a children's story about a bull that would not fight in the bullring but chose to sit under the trees and watch the world go by. This codename was selected by Feldt to send a message to the army. That message was that FERDINAND would not undertake guerrilla warfare or sabotage missions, as these activities were ruinous to effective intelligence collection, which is why FERDINAND existed. They were ruinous, Feldt argued, because sabotage and guerrilla warfare operations were straight out of the *Boy's Own Annual* and all they would do was bring the full weight of the enemy down upon the guerrillas and saboteurs and this would end their effectiveness as intelligence gatherers. The history of special operations, including intelligence collection, in the Pacific between 1939 and 1945 shows he was right.[40]

Identifying where enemy bases and ports were, and reporting the movement of their vessels and aircraft, was vital to effective naval warfare and this was FERDINAND's only role.[41]

Although it is not part of our story, the battle between the navy and the army, which wanted FERDINAND to undertake guerrilla warfare and sabotage missions, continued almost to the end of the war. It only ended after the army, through the Allied Intelligence Bureau (AIB) gained control over FERDINAND in late 1944 and put FERDINAND personnel in extreme danger. The ACNB, which controlled the navy, simply recalled all naval personnel from detached duty with the AIB and army in Papua and New Guinea. Unfortunately, those members of FERDINAND who were army and RAAF officers were left in the AIB.

Wake's standing in the navy would never recover from his time there as a clerk and Rupert Long, the Director of Naval Intelligence, held firmly to the view that he was 'not a man of the integrity necessary' to work in security intelligence and not a man who could be trusted with secrets.[42] In fact, so concerned was Long about Wake's integrity that in 1941, after he was tipped off that Major General Northcott and General Sturdee had arranged for Wake to visit Singapore behind his back, Long signalled the British authorities there to ensure they did not introduce Wake to any SIGINT activity and that they told him as little as possible.[43]

Long frankly admitted that he did not trust Wake under oath at Justice Geoffrey Reed's inquiry into Wake in December 1943. When Long was asked by the examining counsel when he first formed the view that Wake was not to be trusted with sensitive information, he answered, 'five months after I first met him', which would have been in 1934 or 1935.[44]

All of this begs the question: if Wake was a man of little integrity, then how did he survive for so long? More than one historian has asked this.[45]

Some have attributed Wake's amazing survivability to the possibility that he blackmailed his superiors, especially Brigadier Simpson.[46] There are even stories of Long having a safebreaker released from prison in order to burgle the Brisbane office of the CIB and steal files on himself and Simpson from Wake's safe.[47]

The reality was more mundane and sadder. Wake was hard working and he was highly experienced in what passed for security intelligence at the time and, very importantly, he got things done. For many of his superiors, one of his more attractive characteristics was his ruthless determination to bring down a target.[48] He was not satisfied with simply investigating a suspect in order to exclude them; he was willing to use agent provocateurs and entrapment, if not outright lying, in order to get his man. For those whose moral and ethical frameworks were highly malleable, Wake was a very useful tool. Some of these men—including Sturdee, Northcott and members of the General Staff, especially the Commander-in-Chief, General Thomas Blamey—only turned on Wake after he used prostitutes to entrap fellow officers and, most embarrassingly, tried to entrap American officers using this technique. As General Blamey, who was also General MacArthur's ground force commander, found out, the Americans would not tolerate this behaviour from a country they simply regarded as the location of their forward operating base against Japan.

Wake also tried spying on the British, particularly their elements involved in Central Bureau; however, here he was up against MI6 professionals led by Captain Roy Kendall, RNR, and his countersurveillance officer, Third Officer Eve Walker, Women's Royal Naval Service (WRENS). Unlike the Americans, the British tolerated Wake's behaviour and Australian operations mounted against them and said nothing. The Americans were not, as Australia was about to discover, at all as tolerant or polite as the British.

One of the outcomes of the CIB's close association with Military Intelligence and state police forces was an unhealthy mixing of inexperience, authoritarianism, and procedural and other corruption. The CIB already had a reputation for corruption and inefficiency, while Military Intelligence was full of amateur militia officers playing at intelligence. These organisations were easy meat to experienced players in state police forces, particularly in New South Wales.

In Queensland, Wake had initially formed a reasonably close relationship with the state police, as shown by the cooperation between the CIB and police in the investigations into the Black Hand, the Italian mafia-style organisation that Wake claimed Queensland authorities had broken up by 1939. With the declaration of war, however, and Wake's move into military intelligence, the relationship soon began to sour as the Queensland police became suspicious of Wake's attempts to grow his own power at their expense. Eventually, this would lead to a complete breakdown in the relationship with the Queensland Police and Wake's CIB, Security Service and Military Intelligence establishment. This breakdown was so severe that the two groups expended considerable time and energy conducting spying operations and counter-spying operations on one another.[49]

The work of the CIB and Military Intelligence in Queensland, in cooperation with the Queensland Police, was focused on the activities of communists, fascists and Italians of any political hue. In pursuit of these enemies of the state, military officers and soldiers became involved in raiding and searching civilian premises, although no arrests were made. The Commonwealth had declared the CP-A and other communist organisations illegal on the quite reasonable grounds that the Soviet Union and the mendicant CP-A were the active allies of Nazi Germany. Targets of the raids included the CP-A headquarters in George Street, Brisbane, and the Anvil Bookshop, as well as private homes where it was suspected CP-A members had concealed banned or subversive literature. In June of 1940, the activities of Wake's men were making news, with reports that 100 police and Military Intelligence officers led by Major Wake were roaring around Brisbane in cars conducting raids.[50] This got Wake's name into the papers, even if the papers got his initials wrong.

As 1941 arrived, Wake had accumulated enough power in Queensland to be a real threat to civil liberty. He was concurrently the inspector-in-charge of the CIB, effectively the Director of Military Intelligence at Victoria Barracks, the superintending Officer-in-Charge of the Peace Guards and the man controlling security intelligence. On 1 June he would be promoted to the temporary rank of Lieutenant Colonel.[51] His networking in Queensland politics had proceeded apace and his standing had increased to the point where he could personally greet Queensland's premier, W. Forgan Smith, at the airport, which would be reported in newspapers.[52] More importantly, the fallout from the Mawhood affair had led to the establishment of a new Security Service under the direction of the somewhat ineffective Lloyd, a man who would never be able to control Wake.

As far as security intelligence was concerned, other than identifying and rounding up potential enemy aliens among the Italian farmers of Queensland's sugar fields, Wake's main activities appear to have been to provide the General Staff with intelligence on the ACNB's intelligence operations in Queensland and the islands to Australia's north, and to spy upon Military Mission 104 and its commander, Lieutenant Colonel John Mawhood, Roy Kendall's MI6 cell, the Queensland Police, the Americans and his fellow officers.

Although it is difficult to chart Wake's contribution to the attack on Mawhood, there is little doubt that he possessed the enthusiasm, ruthlessness, experience and professional capacity to undertake the kinds of actions that were required. This work involved the installation of telephone taps on Mawhood's office and, most likely, private lines, as well as Commander Long's telephones and, most likely, the telephones of anyone involved, including ministers and officials, particularly Knowles. His contemporaries within Military Intelligence at the time were civilians in uniform with no real experience in security intelligence. The only man with such experience was Wake who, as Long described, 'very definitely' had the ability to work as an intelligence officer.[53] It was this ability that made Wake effective as an intelligence officer and this, coupled with his ruthless ambition to get a job done legally or illegally, made him the fire brigade for his bosses within the CIB and, later, within the Security Service. If there was a problem, Wake would fix it, one way or another.

Long's high opinion of Wake as an intelligence officer did not extend to Wake's character as a man. As Long further testified, he found Wake had an 'instability in his character . . . a childish outlook . . . on the main principles which, I think, should guide people's lives'.[54] Effectively, if Wake were allowed freedom of action, his morality and ethics would make him very dangerous. As we will see, by the time Long was giving this testimony Wake had become very dangerous indeed, in fact so dangerous he had put the alliance with the United States at risk, alienated the British and was even threatening the reputation of many of the most senior members of the General Staff.

On 31 March 1941, the CSS began operations under the leadership of Lloyd, and Wake was soon appointed as the deputy director, Queensland, which meant he concurrently held the posts of head of Military Intelligence in Queensland, while also inspector-in-charge of the CIB and now the deputy director of the Security Service.[55] Wake now controlled all security intelligence and Commonwealth policing matters in Queensland. What he did not control, and despite his best efforts would never control, were the HUMINT activities of the ACNB's coastwatch organisation and, when it was formed, the SIGINT activities of Central Bureau.

It was now, with so much power concentrated in his hands and only loose supervision by Lloyd in Canberra, that Wake's ambitions overwhelmed his good sense. Wake already had a problem with Canberra, specifically with Knowles, who had become concerned about the FSS, which Wake had formed in his role as head of Military Intelligence in Queensland. Knowles did not specifically target Wake, probably because Wake was his employee, as he held posts in the CIB and CSS. Instead, Knowles went after the army more generally. This should not blind us to the fact that the FSS in Queensland was Wake's organisation, not the army's.

Knowles was antagonised by the activities of the FSS where, under Wake's direction, it was conducting searches of civilian premises and interfering in civilian internal security matters.[56] For Knowles, this was anathema and he wanted the military excluded from any involvement in civilian matters. As far as Knowles was concerned the activities of Wake's FSS were illegal and, worse, they were now drawing adverse comment.[57] Among them was criticism from the Queensland union movement where Mr M. O'Brien of the Australian Railways Union accused ALP members of the Legislative Assembly of being spies for Military Intelligence.[58] Despite Knowles' efforts, however, nothing happened, and no one appears to have shared his concerns. Perhaps everyone hoped that the formation of yet another Security Service on 31 March 1942 under the leadership of MacKay would fix the problems.

As part of his intelligence duties, Wake continued his work travelling widely around Queensland and interstate, particularly to Melbourne and Sydney fixing problems.[59] Wake was good at HUMINT, but he had to be kept on a tight rein.[60]

Among the cases that Wake assisted on was the investigation of a woman of German birth in March 1942. The person in question was Ella Horne, the widow of a British actor, who was an attractive woman who socialised with officers, and was therefore viewed by Military Intelligence as a security risk. The CSS was asked by MI5 to investigate Mrs Horne, and Lloyd asked Jones if Wake could be made available to the CSS.[61] At the time, Wake was the inspector-in-charge of the CIB in Queensland and head of Military Intelligence, Northern Command, but had not yet been brought into the CSS.[62]

Jones agreed to loan Wake to Lloyd but stipulated that Wake was to work in conjunction with the officers of the CIB in Sydney.[63] Wake arrived in Sydney and advised the CIB Inspector that the investigation was not being conducted by the CSS or CIB but by Military Intelligence. This is a perfect example of the way in which Wake could use his multiple offices to suit his own ends by moving the matter in hand around the jurisdictions to one where he held all the control.

Wake enlisted his old mate William Barnwell of the CIB to interview an 'informer' about Mrs Horne. He most likely did this in order to implicate the CIB in what he was about to do. Then, accompanied by Major Keefe, the Officer-in-Charge of MPIS, Wake interviewed Mrs Horne, thus blowing the entire operation against a suspected German spy.[64] Why Wake did this is unknown. Jones thought he had acted in this way to protect the army from another 'Mrs Freer' scandal in which a rich and beautiful British divorcee, Mabel Freer, who was having an affair with an Australian officer, Lieutenant R.E. Dewar, was forbidden to land in Australia after Military Intelligence had, at the instigation of Dewar's family, improperly provided the Immigration Department with the particulars of her private life and her affair with Dewar.[65]

Alexander Duncan, in his report, said Wake's actions unnecessarily disclosed the investigation and Knowles, most likely closest to the truth, called Wake's efforts 'blundering'. Knowles also identified that Wake had used his position as head of three different organisations to play one off against the other to suit his personal interests.[66]

At the same time that Wake was ruining the investigation into Mrs Horne, Australia was in a state of turmoil. The Japanese thrust south had seen them conquer Malaya, capture Singapore, destroy British and Allied naval power in South-East Asia and conquer most of the Philippines. The fear engendered by these Japanese successes was somewhat offset by the commitment of US troops to Australia in order to secure the country as a forward operating base for the coming offensives in the Pacific. For Australia's security intelligence organisations, this meant the arrival of the Americans and their security intelligence organisations, something that would complicate the lives of Wake and his superiors.

Among the US Army units that arrived in Australia in early 1942 was the Counterintelligence Corps (CIC), an organisation charged with protecting the security of US forces operating in foreign countries. At first, the CIC worked closely with Australia's Military Intelligence and, to a lesser extent, with the CSS and Security Service. As time went by though, relationships started to sour, particularly when the CIC began to realise that the Australians were mounting surveillance operations on US officers and units, and worse, were tapping their telephones and reading their mail. For the Americans, this behaviour was outrageous, and they were not slow in expressing their outrage.

In the meantime, life continued more or less as usual, but at a higher tempo due to the approach of Japanese forces in the islands. This resulted in action being undertaken against possible Japanese sympathisers, especially in relation to any Italians living in Australia. Queensland would see the highest number of internments in Australia as Wake and his organisations stripped farms of their farmers and cane fields of their cane workers, to such an extent that shortages of sugar now afflicted Australia. There were also complaints from the protecting powers—that is consulates of nations charged to watch German and Italian interests in Australia—that the wholesale arrests had left stock-in-trade of shops, livestock, growing crops and personal property unattended and thus open to theft and misappropriation.[67] When this was raised formally by Forde, Evatt didn't comment at all.[68]

Following the creation of the Security Service under MacKay, Wake was brought into yet another organisation to head its Queensland operations. By mid-1942, Wake was the security supremo of Queensland and the number one problem fixer across Australia for the CIB, Security Service and Military Intelligence. In these roles, Wake expanded his influence and made himself indispensable to MacKay and then, in September 1942, to Brigadier Simpson, MacKay's successor as Director-General of the Security Service. Wake also ingratiated himself with his two ministers, Evatt and Forde—men who understood favours.

The new Director-General, Brigadier Simpson, appears to have leaned heavily on Wake for his experience in security intelligence and for his ability to get things done. By mid-1943, Simpson, assisted by Wake, was carrying out the reorganisation of the Security Service. This reorganisation was about Simpson and Wake forming the Security Service into their organisation, an organisation where they could expect complete obedience from all of its members.

As all of this was happening, Wake's operational activities in surveilling Australian, British and US officers was leading to growing unrest at the various headquarters, and eventually Wake crossed a line that led to an explosion. That line was the use of prostitutes to entrap Australian and US officers into betraying secrets so that his organisation could show its value. The result was probably not what Wake expected.

There is no doubt that Wake used prostitutes to entrap fellow officers; furthermore, some Australian officials believed that some of these women were Wake's mistresses. The Director of Naval Intelligence, Commander Long, believed that Wake was using prostitutes. In his testimony at Justice Reed's inquiry, Long referred to an operation Wake had mentioned to him in which Wake intended to send a woman he had recruited to the American Red Cross Hostel in Mackay to sleep with various American officers to obtain secret information from them. Wake carried out this plan and used the services of a woman who signed one report she sent to him as 'G', and addressed Wake as 'Dear Chief' before signing off with 'Beerio'.[69] None of this was expressing a formal relationship of superior and subordinate.

In the report, G informs Dear Chief that she had 'already been in one car accident', and an attempted 'knifing party' in which she was injured. She also complains about 'sex-starved and drink-fuzzed G.I.'s'. Her aim is to get a job at the Red Cross, but she reports that it is difficult to gain admission to the various cliques in Mackay without a 'brass hat' to ease the way.[70] She suggests that perhaps the Chief might consider sending her further north, to Townsville or Cairns, where the Yanks had offered her employment as a driver. G reports on a 'tall Yank who came to see you re this district' and two men from 'A1', who are better types. She also mentions a Brouwer, 'a guy who is T. N. T., and that whoever had told Chief that Brouwer was woman shy is "nuts"'.[71] This man appears from the letter to be Muslim, maybe Indonesian, because the writer associates him with Mr H.H. Lennart of the Netherlands Indies Commission in Melbourne. Whoever he is, G 'would be happier, if he was with his ancestors, pronto'. G then compromises what appears to be her network by listing 'Bunny', 'Peggy', 'Robbie' and 'Silver', as well as Corporal Albert Klestadt.[72] All of this is in Wake's private collection of papers he collected during the inquiry, and supports all of Long's testimony.[73]

It did not take long for US commanders to complain directly to General Blamey, the Australian Commander-in-Chief and General MacArthur's ground force commander. These complaints were more significant than the incessant Australian complaining about Wake, because the Americans were livid and demanded action. The Australian Army now had no choice but to act because the future of its relations with the US Army were at stake and, more importantly, so was the future of Blamey as General MacArthur's ground force commander.

The first step was taken on 8 September 1943, when Brigadier E. Gorman interviewed Wake about the claims Wake had made about his experience and qualifications in a letter written and dated 10 April 1943. Wake admitted they were lies but justified them by claiming he was motivated by his ambition to serve overseas in the AIF.[74]

From here the problem was how to remove Wake, who they knew would fight, without creating a great fuss and scandal if the real reasons came out. The offence that was finally identified came out of the interviews that were being conducted when someone, it is not known who, alleged that Wake had worn medal ribbons from World War I that he was not entitled to. In the military, even today, this is something that is not tolerated and will lead to serious repercussions. It was decided to charge Wake with the wearing of these ribbons and, if this was proven, then with conduct unbecoming an officer. These allegations formed the substance of the inquiry.

The real problem for General Blamey and the army was that Wake's influence extended to members of the Commonwealth War Cabinet, particularly the Minister for the Army, Forde, and, very importantly, Attorney-General Evatt, as it was Evatt who would appoint the judicial officer to investigate the matter. More importantly, Evatt set the terms of reference for the inquiry.

Even in October and November 1943, as the date for the inquiry into his behaviour approached, Wake was travelling with Simpson and rearranging the Security Service to suit the requirements of both himself and Simpson.

The inquiry held before Justice Geoffrey Reed into Wake's fitness to hold the position of Deputy Director Security began on Friday, 17 December 1943. The inquiry would stretch out to the middle of 1944.[75]

The artifice of this inquiry is illustrated in the fact that it was tasked not with looking into his actual crimes, but instead was to focus on the issue of whether he wore medals he was not entitled to. Revealing that Military Intelligence and the Security Service were spying on US and Australian officers was an embarrassment that the Australian General Staff did not want to disclose. All Wake had to do was admit his military misdemeanours and Reed, with Simpson's subsequent support, would be able to ensure that Wake remained in his civilian positions. The worst that could happen is that Blamey would take administrative action against Wake, which he did.

Proving Wake had lied was easy. In his application for a commission in the 2nd AIF, dated 15 September 1939, Wake untruthfully claimed to have obtained a pass in the Public Service Entrance Examination.[76] On 10 April 1940, he then claimed that he had served in the British Army in 1918 under Sir Basil Thomson in security intelligence at the French ports. He also claimed to hold a pilot's licence and have 80 hours of solo flying under his belt.[77] In a letter to the Base Commandant in Brisbane in September 1939, he feigned knowledge of New Guinea, Solomon Islands and New Hebrides that he did not have and again declared that he was a pilot.[78] Luckily for Wake, Blamey does not seem to have been aware of this letter or of his enlistment papers from 1931, which show that his lying about having served in the British Army in 1918 was not, as he claimed, a one-off event produced by an over eagerness to serve his country overseas.[79]

If the Australian government had been interested in justice, the inquiry into Wake had a number of problems. The first problem was the limited scope of the inquiry. The second problem was the appointment of Justice Geoffrey Reed of the South Australian Supreme Court. Reed was an intelligence insider and an associate of Wake as a result of his position as the Chairman of the South Australian National Security Advisory Committee, a position that involved inquiring into security matters and a job he most definitely wanted to keep after he was elevated to the bench.[80] Evatt, most likely advised by Wake, would have understood that Reed was a man who could easily be persuaded to be a safe pair of hands.

The evidence for all of this is found in Wake's working file on the inquiry. This unofficial file is a jumble of official papers and it includes personal correspondence between Reed and Wake. One letter from Reed is addressed to 'My Dear Bob' and dated 21 July 1943, well before the inquiry was announced and Reed accepted appointment as the judicial officer heading it.[81] The letter is a reply to a telegram from Wake congratulating Reed on his elevation to the South Australian Supreme Court.[82] The letter is a warm, affectionate and rather open note between friends. Even in 1943, this constituted a clear conflict of interest for Reed, but no one, not the learned judge Reed or the esteemed jurist, Evatt, and certainly not Wake, appeared bothered by this.[83] One wonders how General Blamey would have reacted had he known.

One of the most important witnesses to appear before Reed was Wake's old boss, Commander Long. Long testified that Wake had ability as an intelligence operator but lacked the character to be left unsupervised. For Long, this was a problem because security intelligence was 'dirty work, very dirty, and it is only the very clean people who can come out of that dirt uncontaminated.'[84] Long went on:

> Any falling below the very highest [moral standards] is to me an indication that the person should be out of Security Service. It has such tremendous powers. It is playing around with people's private lives, that any weakness in anybody's character in the Security Service is a thing that must not be allowed to persist.[85]

This work, and the power it gives to security officers, corrupts, something Long emphasised, saying that the lesser powers of police was 'child's play compared with the opportunities a security officer would have' to blackmail and injure people.[86]

The concerns raised by Long were supported by the testimony of Colonel K.A. Wills, Deputy Director of Military Intelligence, who detailed how he had 'seen from my own experience—particularly in the early days of this war—how a dossier can be built up against a man who is completely innocent, and how it snowballs up and how dangerous it is against the personal liberty of the people'.[87] Wills backed up this assertion by detailing the case of Daniels, a German Jew, who had worked with him and who Wake accused of sexual perversion. Wake had made this accusation simply because when Daniels had been interviewed during his enlistment into the AIF, another man had been present in Daniel's room. The allegations made by Wake against Daniels arose when Wills had challenged the decision of Commander McFarlane, RAN, the Deputy Director Security in Queensland, and his assistant, Wake, not to use Daniels as an officer of the Security Service after they had literally begged Wills to make him available. The likelihood was that Daniels had rubbed Wake up the wrong way and Wake was simply getting rid of him by alleging falsehoods about his sexuality.

What annoyed Wills was that McFarlane and Wake had been given this information eighteen months before they decided that they did not want Daniels. This was one of the reasons Wills formed the view that Wake was overly interested in the sex lives of fellow officers, and that 'anybody engaged in Security work of any sort, who could down a man on that very scanty evidence, was not a very reliable man'.[88]

Wake survived the inquiry and he actually came out with his reputation, outside of the services anyway, undamaged. Reed, Simpson, Evatt and Forde were most responsible for saving Wake from the allegations against him.[89] Not only that, they also protected him from a subsequent attack by Blamey, when he attempted to force Simpson to sack Wake from the Security Service.[90] As the inquiry was completed and the file lost, Wake was readmitted to the inner sanctum of the Security Service as the DG-S's main advisor in the reorganisation of the Security Service, a reorganisation in which a lot of people lost their jobs on the spurious grounds of centralising all counter-espionage activity in Canberra under Wake's control, moving the state directors out of the picture and purging people from the service who Wake deemed didn't fit in.[91]

Despite his central role in advising the DG-S, Wake was a bad administrator and Simpson often wrote to him complaining of his maladministration, especially in relation to finance.[92] Wake's records, especially his financial records, were chaotic, complex and poorly assembled. One striking characteristic of Wake's financial paperwork is its bulk and the way in which personal and official matters are mixed.[93] To anyone familiar with accounting, his files scream financial irregularity and fraud.

Another warning flag was Wake's failure to take leave, which those naive in such matters put down to dedication.[94] In fact, getting into work first and leaving last and never taking recreational or other leave is one of the signs of someone involved in fraud. The dedication is required so that the fraudster can ensure no one else looks at or manages their affairs or responsibilities and thus discovers the fraud. Indeed, Wake's administrative oversights are so significant that either his almost complete autonomy in Queensland protected him, or Simpson, Evatt and others did.

One highly irregular administrative oversight committed by Wake was forgetting to return a 0.45 calibre automatic pistol loaned to him by Lieutenant Colonel W.H. Parker of the US Army on 2 October 1943.[95] Wake only returned the weapon after he received a letter from Major N.F. Marshall, Parker's Executive Officer, asking for the return of the weapon forthwith.[96] Marshall needed to account for the weapon as either stolen or in his unit's

Demonstration from Trades Hall coming down Edward Street from Adelaide Street in Brisbane, 1919. This was one of the demonstrations that directly led to the Red Flag Riot of 23 March 1919. *(State Library of Queensland)*

Alexander Mikhailovich Zuzenko with his wife Civa and daughter Ksenia, c. 1923. *(Courtesy of Ksenia Aleksandrovna Zuzenko and with the permission of Kevin Windle,* Undesirable, *Australian Scholarly Publishing, 2012)*

George Steward during his time as Chief Commissioner of the Victoria Police. *(Victoria Police Museum)*

George Pearce, an early advocate for an Australian national intelligence system. *(NLA)*

George Knowles, secretary of the Attorney General's Department and a long-time champion of a civilian security service. *(ags.gov.au)*

Prime Minister Billy Hughes, during his time in office from 1915 to 1923. *(NLA)*

H.E. Jones, sitting at centre in civilian clothes, in his role as head of the Commonwealth Investigation Service, 1930, outside Acton House in Canberra, which housed both the courthouse and the police station. *(ACT Heritage Library, Patricia Frei donation)*

A young Inspector William MacKay in his heyday, c. 1929, following his successful visit to the United States and United Kingdom. *(Sydney Living Museums)*

A policeman in the black coverall allegedly worn by the members of a secret section of the New Guard. *(Sydney Living Museums)*

William MacKay leading Francis de Groot away after his arrest on the Harbour Bridge, on 19 March 1932. *(Sydney Living Museums)*

The young General Pavel Fitin who, with no intelligence background at all, was appointed the head of the Foreign Section of the NKGB and went on to reform and reorganise it after the Stalinist purges of the 1930s.

E.E. Longfield Lloyd (left, holding speech) at the opening of the NSW Parliament in 1929. *(NLA)*

Victorian Police Commissioner Alexander Duncan working at his desk, c. 1945. *(NLA)*

Books on the history of Soviet Communism being inspected in the GPO, Sydney, in 1940. The Communist Party of Australia was distributing them to members, but the parcels were intercepted by the Censor in 1940. *(NAA, BC31325013)*

Father Ugo Modotti in 1946 at his desk in the Vatican. Modotti was victimised by Military Intelligence for providing spiritual support to Italian prisoners of war and internees and their families. *(Italian Historical Society)*

Commonwealth Investigation Service and police seizing the records and belongings of Jehovah's Witnesses in Sydney on 20 January 1941. *(Mitchell Library, State Library of NSW)*

Adela Pankhurst Walsh during her soapbox socialist period before she converted to the rightist Australia First Movement. *(NLA)*

Frank Forde, Minister for the Army under John Curtin and Ben Chifley. *(NLA)*

John Dedman, probably the most effective minister of the 1940s governments. *(NLA)*

Ben Chifley and H.V. Evatt speaking with British Prime Minister Clement Atlee in the garden of No. 10 Downing Street during the Dominion and British Leaders Conference of 1946. *(NAA, BC7815330)*

A photograph of Robert Frederick Bird Wake, taken in 1948 when Wake was at the peak of his influence. *(NAA, BC6759670)*

Feodor Nosov, TASS Representative and NKGB agent acting as the agent-runner in Sydney for the NKGB Residency. *(NAA, BC8763731)*

Flat 19, 16–18 Kings Cross Road, Sydney, home of TASS representative
Feodor Nosov and his wife Galina, both of whom were NKGB agents.

Vladimir Petrov during
his ASIO debriefing. He
is sitting in front of the
Governor Phillip Fountain,
in the Royal Botanic Gardens,
Sydney, which the NKGB
used as a contact point.
(NAA, BC7462029)

A Blue Streak missile being launched at Woomera Rocket Range, South Australia, in 1964. The British missile program at Woomera was a long-term target for the GRU. *(NAA, BC11460360)*

Ian and Margot Milner taking a holiday from their spying duties to relax at Lorne, Victoria, in 1941. *(Alexander Turnbull Library)*

Meredith Gardner, who broke into the GRU/NKGB codes and worked on them for over twenty years.

USSR

Ref. No.: 3/NBF/T179 (of 2/4/95?)

Issued :   31/1/1973

Copy No.: 50

REISSUE

"KLOD'S" REPORT ON MATERIAL SUPPLIED BY "BEN" FROM SYDNEY SECURITY
ORGANS' FILES, INCLUDING FILE ON MIKhEEV
(1945)

From: CANBERRA

To: MOSCOW

No.:   197   3rd July 945

To VIKTOR[i]. 8th Department[a].

"KLOD"[ii] has reported that "BEN"[iii] has been bringing a number of items
of operational material[MATERIALY][b] from the SYDNEY security organs for him to
see, in particular special files on the Soviet Legation and on TASS representative.
In "KLOD's" words, the former do not present any special interest, since the main
files on the Legation are in CANBERRA, whereas in SYDNEY material[b] is collected
only about journeys

[75 groups unrecoverable]

DISTRIBUTION: [Continued overleaf]

Facsimile of VENONA message referencing KLOD (Walter Seddon Clayton).
(National Security Agency)

Jack Skolnik, Melbourne businessman and leader of the Melbourne cell. *(ASIO)*

The Maroondah Lake Hotel secretly owned by Skolnik. He made his clandestine telephone calls from Gracedale, described as a cottage in ASIO's files. It was actually an entire wing of this hotel. *(State Library of Victoria)*

Scott's Hotel, Melbourne, identified by ASIO's Operation TOURIST as a meeting place for Soviet agents in the early 1950s. *(State Library of Victoria)*

A rare photograph of Solomon Kosky taken in 1954 during the Petrov affair. *(News Limited)*

The moment of truth: Vladimir Petrov, the NKGB Head of Station in Australia, defects by getting into an ASIO vehicle at Sydney Airport on 3 April 1954. His defection brought about the Royal Commission on Espionage. *(NAA, BC415719)*

Secured in the safe house, Evdokia Petrova and Vladimir Petrov sit for
photographs in 1954, flanking their handler, Ron Richards. *(NAA, BC7462044)*

David John Morris: engineer,
ardent communist and NKGB asset.
(NAA, BC30485606)

Walter Seddon Clayton attending the
Royal Commission on Espionage in
March 1955. *(ASIO)*

Operation Boomerang: Robert Wake (right) being surveilled in Martin Place, Sydney, on 21 July 1958. *(NAA, BC30030795)*

Justice Geoffrey Reed, first Director-General of ASIO and associate of Wake. *(NAA, BC1589285)*

Colonel Charles Spry (left) briefing General Douglas MacArthur (second from right) in New Guinea, 1942. Spry became the second Director-General of ASIO and ushered in a new era for the service. *(AWM)*

armoury. It is obvious that this matter was kept quiet because it would have reflected badly on Lieutenant Colonel Parker as well as Wake. It is also obvious that Wake deliberately stole the weapon in the hope the Americans would just write it off.

Wake was also reprimanded for consistently making private phone calls on official government telephones, something he kept being pulled up for by the accountants. At the time, making interstate telephone calls was an expensive hobby and making private calls on Commonwealth phones was, in well-run government organisations, viewed as a serious matter; so serious in fact that people were sacked for doing it. Wake was pulled up on this behaviour time and time again.[97]

The point of this extensive analysis of Wake's record and career is not to make him out to be the bad apple or to hold him up as the single cause of problems in Australia's security intelligence system, because he most certainly was not. His career clearly shows, however, how procedural corruption was employed to benefit individual security officers and their organisations, and how this was winked at by a succession of senior bureaucrats and government ministers of all persuasions.

Wake's career provides a clear example of why British observers from MI5 and MI6 held the views they did about the existence of widespread corruption and political chicanery in Australia. It also shows us why US officials would later treat Australia as a pariah state, lacking in moral and ethical strength and so completely unreliable that it could not be entrusted with any secret. If nothing else, the career of Wake serves to remind us of the dangers of poor oversight and flexible ethics in government and especially in the secret work of government.

At the very end of his legitimate intelligence career, before he began his illegitimate career working with the CP-A to destroy the leadership of ASIO in an attempt to get his old job back, it was Wake's penchant for fraud that brought him undone when his colleagues uncovered his use of agents so secret they were known solely to him. This is an old HUMINT problem, in which a corrupt agent-handler creates agents as a means of siphoning funds for their own use. What did Wake need this money for? Well, not his family, who seem to have been left in somewhat straitened circumstances. It is most likely that Wake used the money to pay for his many mistresses and the carousing that he and his cronies appear to have indulged themselves in.

Wake was never prosecuted for his frauds because, as always seemed to be the case with him, his employer—in this case ASIO—was too vulnerable to risk a scandal. Yet again, his actions were swept under yet another carpet allowing him and his later apologists to claim that nothing of substance was ever proved in a court of law. Wake worked in intelligence, however, where proof is not needed to reach the standard required in a court of law; in this arena, the standard is met when sufficient evidence exists for defensive measures to be taken to neutralise the threat that a person or organisation poses to the safety of the nation. The evidence shows that Wake posed such a threat and the hard proof of this lies in his later willingness to consort with his old enemies, the CP-A and its associates, to bring down his new enemies in the form of Charles Spry and a newly professionalised, if still struggling, ASIO.

By removing Wake and his cronies from ASIO, Spry finally broke the current of procedural corruption flowing into the new organisation. For this, we all should be thankful, and we should recognise that most of the allegations of misbehaviour thrown at ASIO relate not to ASIO, but to the organisations and individuals that Wake led or influenced from the shadows behind E.E. Longfield Lloyd, W. MacKay and W.B. Simpson. In that, Wake and his colleagues did damage to innocent people and innocent organisations and it is to this damage that we now turn our attention.

CHAPTER 12

DAGOES, WOGS AND POMMIES

The starting point in this part of our story is Dagoes. This term needs to be confronted fairly and squarely because, until recently, it was a term used openly and proudly by Australia's politicians, newspapers and teachers in the education system, although probably not in the Catholic system.[1] Its use was criticised by no less a visitor than H.G. Wells, who, at the 1939 Science Congress in Canberra, suggested that use of the words 'Dago' and 'Pommy' should be 'banished from the mouths of children, but also from the mouths of teachers'.[2] It first needed to be banished from the mouths of politicians like William Hughes, whose vitriolic attacks on Italian migrants in the late 1920s resulted in his condemnation by Prime Minister Bruce and his ministry.[3]

The attitude of Australians towards Italians is noteworthy given that the first two Italians, or descendants of Italians, to arrive in Australia were James Matra—after whom Matraville is named—and Antonio Ponto, who were among the 73 sailors that made up the crew of HMS *Endeavour*, and another, Giuseppe Tuzi, who was a prisoner in Phillip's First Fleet.[4] The first influx of Italians coming directly from Italy occurred during the gold rush periods and one, Raffaello Carboni, a political refugee from Urbino, played a significant role in the Eureka Stockade riot.[5] As a group, Italians were to become an important, if suspect, part of Australian society. To be fair, the use of the word

'Dago' was criticised by church leaders, as were other terms of racial abuse,[6] but pick up a newspaper from this time and you are likely to see the word Dago used to describe anyone with a swarthy complexion.

As we have already noted, the Italian community in Australia, particularly that in the North Queensland cane fields, had attracted the attention of both state police and the CIB as a result of the less-than-subtle activities of Italian crime organisations. These activities, which included murder, extortion, prostitution and loan sharking, all contributed to the existing prejudices against anyone who could easily be called a Dago.

As well as being poor and foreigners, the Italian immigrants added to their problems by speaking Italian, eating strange food and, worst of all, by being Catholic. Of course, in Australia between 1901 and 1950, there was no law against being Catholic, as long as you knew your place and stuck to being working class. This perception effectively persisted in middle-class Australia until the mid-1950s when the working-class Catholics who dominated the ALP campaigned to counter the communist penetration of that party. The campaign served to make Catholicism a little more palatable for many protestant Australians, who remembered the role of Dr Daniel Mannix, the Catholic Archbishop of Melbourne from 1917 to 1963, and the Catholic Church in criticising British policy in Ireland and in defeating the conscription referenda in 1916 and 1917. Even then, it took until the 1970s for the religious bigotry of many Australians to pass out of society, as death took those with entrenched attitudes and time produced new generations less addicted to heaven and more addicted to sex, drugs and rock and roll.

None of this mattered in 1939, when the activities of Italians around Australia were being subjected to greater scrutiny as the prospect of war grew from a possibility to a certainty. After the entry of Italy into the war in June 1940, the gloves came off when it came to Australia's Italian community; internment was now a real possibility. The saving grace was not some sort of human fellow feeling for the Italians concerned, although there is plenty of evidence that many Australians were perplexed by the actions of the authorities. Unfortunately, there is also plenty of evidence to suggest that the spiteful and ugly among us also revelled in their increased ability to hurt their Italian neighbours.

In Queensland, where military intelligence was part of Major Robert Wake's fiefdom, the Italian community was to suffer the heaviest burden when it came time to intern them as enemy aliens. Wake did not care about the damage excessive internment would do. Concern about what would happen to the families of the interned enemy aliens, or to their farms and the production of food, was not for him or for his minions. As a result, the internment of Italians came in waves, with the first occurring soon after the declaration of war.[7]

In all fairness, the action of the Australian government in interning Italians living in Australia was a reasonable step, particularly in light of the fifth column fear that was endemic throughout the Western world at the time. But there can be no doubt that in Queensland the authorities, led by Wake, were going after people who had previously escaped them rather than people who represented real threats to Australia's security. The evidence for this is that among the earliest targets were the suspect members of Italian criminal gangs such as the '30 notorious Black Hand terrorists on the North Queensland cane fields' who were interned.[8] One wonders how many of them were members of fascist organisations.

This first wave of internments does not look out of place until it is considered that few Germans had been interned since 3 September 1939, although 277 Germans and Austrians were interned after the Munich Crisis of 1938 and of these 170 were identified as Nazis.[9] By December 1939, after the war had been in progress for three months, 70 of the most obvious German and Australian Nazis had been interned.[10] By comparison, by 10 August 1940, two months after Italy entered the war, 1901 Italians, including many prominent citizens unconnected to the fascists, were interned.[11]

The difference between the two groups is that the Germans were more politically organised and assimilated as a community in the southern states, particularly South Australia and Victoria. They were also wealthier than the more recently arrived poor Italians.[12] This made them a little more influential than the Italian farmers and workers who flocked to Queensland's cane fields and workshops. Of course, there were practicalities that impacted as well. These included the lack of detention facilities large enough to house the internees and the issue of identifying who presented a risk and who did not. This invariably took time and resources Australia did not have.

There were other problems with internment. One was the unwillingness of the Australian government to spend more money than really necessary on the war. After all, the Germans were only killing Poles, and Norway was a bit of a sideshow. In May 1940 this changed, and the threat to Britain made the war effort urgent and large. It must not be forgotten that Italy waited until 10 June 1940, when the German victory over France and Britain was almost complete, to come into the war on Germany's side.

The other problem was, from a bureaucratic perspective, a little strange, and it was the variation in the way local and Commonwealth authorities approached internment. In Western Australia, South Australia and Victoria there was a more reasoned and less speedy approach to rounding up internees compared to New South Wales and, particularly, compared to Queensland, where all of the Commonwealth's security apparatus, the CIB and Military Intelligence, was led by Wake.

German aliens were now interned alongside the Italians. However, in June 1940, large-scale internment of Germans began.[13] The CIB and Military Intelligence, particularly in Queensland and New South Wales were also watching and reading the private correspondence of Italian residents, although it also has to be said they were reading the mail of anyone sending a letter overseas, and selectively reading the mail of nearly everybody in the country.[14]

The powers conferred on the military by the *National Security Act 1939* were draconian. Anyone whose loyalty was suspected could be interned. As with all of these kinds of knee-jerk laws, no one had thought the problems through. The first difficulty had already been encountered in Britain: internment of all enemy aliens created such a large number of internees that it cost a fortune to house, clothe, feed and care for them, and guarding and administering them cost even more.

In 1940, Australia could not even house the volunteers joining the armed services. In Melbourne, the volunteers for the RAAF were housed in the Melbourne Cricket Ground. In these circumstances, housing tens of thousands of Italians and others was impossible.[15] Not only that, but the removal of men alone would leave a large number of families completely destitute and deprive Australia of both skilled labour and experienced farmers. Wives and children were left defenceless in a hostile community, which frequently ostracised and assaulted them. Some suffered malnutrition, illness and, unsurprisingly, depression.[16]

As we have already noted above, Italians were first rounded up in June 1940, with the biggest sweeps taking place on the Queensland cane fields where men—farmers, labourers and professionals—were detained, and women and children left.[17] The basis for internment, although the law was very broad, was perfunctory and capricious. Being an Italian was almost all it took, although unproven and spiteful allegations by any good Australian would help get someone interned.

We can say that the internment of Italians was capricious because, as we have seen, the approach differed from state to state, with Victoria being more lenient in its approach and Western Australia less lenient with non-naturalised citizens, but more lenient with those who had become naturalised. It was Queensland where the hammer came down hardest.[18]

In South Australia, by comparison, the actions taken were both more effective and less burdensome on the bulk of the Italian community. The advantage in South Australia was that Alastair Wallace Sandford, universally known as Mic, was serving as a sergeant in Military Intelligence there. Sandford, a barrister, had enlisted as a private on 1 November 1939 in the Australian Army Intelligence Corps in Adelaide. His medical examination found he suffered from severe asthma, which required injections of adrenaline. He was rated as unfit for active service, a rating that did not prevent him from later serving in the Middle East or the Pacific.[19]

Mic Sandford is one of the most interesting men to have served in Australia's intelligence system at any time. He was born into privilege in Adelaide, the son of Sir James Wallace Sandford. He would go on to study literature and law at Balliol College, Oxford, where he became heavily involved in poetry groups. He also developed an interest in all things Italian and lived for a while in Italy, where he learned Italian, a language he learned to speak fluently. This language no doubt got him past his medical rating and into Military Intelligence. It also probably accounts for the speed of his promotion— within fifteen days he went from private to sergeant, a promotion made on 16 November 1939.[20]

What makes Sandford so interesting is that in 1939 he was an openly homosexual man whose soldiers would later nickname 'the Scarlet Pimpernel' after he arrived in the Middle East.[21] The name arose from his refined manners, his extrovert personality, his 'fancy ways and mode of dress' and his 'heady conversation, wild exaggerations and endless fund of stories'. Within hours Mic Sandford had won his soldiers over with his 'gift for making even the lowliest soldier feel that he mattered and his unique way of making a point'.[22] This facility, and his intelligence, would lead Sandford from being a sergeant in security intelligence in South Australia to being the senior Australian SIGINT officer at Central Bureau and, this writer suspects, the true father of Australia's post-war SIGINT organisation, the Defence Signals Bureau (DSB). It would also make him one of the most important influences in the creation of ASIO.

In South Australia in 1939, Sandford used his language skills and his famil-iarity with the local Italian community to identify Italian fascists. As well as interviewing suspected fascists, Sandford attended meetings addressed by Felice Rando, the Italian Consul, and reported on these and on conversations with his numerous Italian contacts.[23]

With the entry of Italy into the war in June 1940, the newly promoted Lieutenant Sandford used the intelligence he had collected to lead a raid on the Italian vice-consulate at 62 Currie Street. This raid seized all of the records of the consulate and the Fascio, the Italian Fascist organisation in South Australia, right back to its inception. In addition, Sandford raided the home of Pasquale Catanzaro, the secretary of the Fascio, in Port Pirie and discovered the Fascio's membership ledger.[24] This ledger contained the names of the 60 members. This benefitted the Italian community in South Australia because, unlike in other states, those involved were readily identi-fied, meaning that the majority of South Australia's Italian community was to be left alone during the war.[25]

Even in Queensland, the Italians who suffered most from this first round of internment were not fascists but community leaders and professional men of North Queensland.[26] This initial round of internments was eventually followed by a second wave in late 1941 and early 1942. These later rounds of internment were triggered by the hysteria that followed Japan's entry into the war. The justification was a concern that the region's Italian population would rush to aid Japanese landings in northern Australia.[27] There was also a vindictive character to many of these later internments as hard-working Italian farmers were arrested and interned because of the jealousy or xeno-phobia of their 'British' neighbours.[28]

In North Queensland, the Italian community faced not just a generally hostile community, they also faced Wake and his old colleague and now enemy, Commissioner C.J. Carroll of the Queensland Police, who was a keen advocate of not just rounding up all non-naturalised Italian men, but natu-ralised men as well, including those with sons serving in the armed services overseas.[29] Thankfully, these schemes were impossible.

In early 1942, the decision of the ALP government, when it came, was that the majority of fit enemy aliens between the ages of 18 and 45 would be conscripted for labour in central and western Queensland. The first group to be so conscripted were a thousand Italians living in northern Queensland.[30] Luckily for that community, and the reputation of Australia, the Director of Military Intelligence, Lieutenant Colonel C.G. Roberts, and the Deputy Chief of the General Staff, Major General Sydney Rowell, moderated this ridiculous idea.[31] Even so, the result was that the Minister for the Army, Frank Forde, ordered that 'as many as possible of the 7500 males should be immediately caught up for civilian auxiliary service (enemy nationals) or for military labour units (naturalised enemy aliens)'.[32]

The additional internments after Japan entered the war were of such magnitude that sugar production in North Queensland fell significantly. If the justification for this large-scale internment was the protection of Australia's war production, it would have been more sensible to round up those who were interning Italian farmers and cane growers.

Of course, Wake was proud of this campaign. Not only did it bolster the morale of his subordinates, it caught the eye of his superiors and it caught the imagination; however, he understood that interning farmers was not the same as finding a spy or a real fifth columnist. It was unfortunate for the security services that, other than the undetectable officers of the NKGB and their CP-A agents, there were no organised hostile spies in Australia and, other than the occasional aggressive unionist seeking higher wages and conditions, no saboteurs.

This did not deter Wake or the CSS. In the end, he would find someone who would fit the bill. If there was one thing that Wake understood, it was the old police saying that if you follow a driver for long enough they will break the law. The driver in our story is Father Ugo Modotti, a Jesuit priest who, for some reason, Military Intelligence and the security services decided was a bad man.

Father Ugo Modotti, of the Society of Jesus, arrived in Australia in 1938 at the invitation of the Archbishop of Melbourne, Daniel Mannix, to minister to the needs of Australia's growing Italian population.[33] Modotti had been born in Basiliano, Italy, in 1897 and trained as a priest at the Gregorian University in Rome. Modotti first began his religious work in Bangalore, India, serving as the principal of St Joseph's College. It was during this period that Modotti took his final vows and was ordained in Calcutta in 1926.[34]

Modotti had come to the attention of Military Intelligence because someone had decided that, in the words of the form drawn up on 11 June 1940 for his internment, he was 'regarded as a keen Fascist' who had 'been actively engaged in Fascist propaganda since his arrival from Italy in 1938'.[35] This evidence appears to have been nothing more than gossip, as the internment of Modotti was stopped dead by the intervention of Major R.S. Brown of the CIB and Archbishop Mannix.[36] This did not mean that Modotti was going to be left alone by Military Intelligence, however, who now wanted him confined to a small area.[37]

Circumstance conspired to bring Modotti into even greater conflict with Military Intelligence as they, assisted by the state police, rounded up Italian men for internment, leaving their families destitute. As a result, Modotti became heavily involved in providing food and other welfare for the families of interned Italians, who were, according to the bigotry of the day, all fascists. Thus, Modotti was a keen helper of fascists.

This situation was made even worse by the fact that with Australia and Italy now at war, the Japanese Consul-General, T. Hattori, became the custodian of Italy's consulate and the diplomatic representative on behalf of Italy in Australia.[38] As a result, Modotti, dealing with the needs of Italian internees and, later, prisoners of war (POWs), was in frequent direct contact with Hattori. Now Modotti was a Japanese spy, at least according to the imaginations of Military Intelligence.

The harassment of Modotti was a nonsense that eventually resulted in Archbishop Mannix taking it up with Minister for the Army, Brigadier Street. Street looked at Modotti's case and directed that no further action be taken. This served to protect Modotti until Street was gone.

By March of 1942, the harassment of Modotti by Military Intelligence and police officials had again become so severe Mannix wrote to the Minister for the Army, Forde, to complain about the travel restrictions placed on Modotti by the Victoria Police. These restrictions were so draconian, Modotti was prevented from leaving his district and he could not even visit the archbishop. Mannix had already shown one Australian government that he was not a man to be intimidated, and he made it clear to Forde that he was not just supportive of Modotti's work, he had ordered Modotti to continue, placing it and Modotti under his direct authority.[39] Again, this served to protect Modotti for a period of time, but again Military Intelligence began gradually increasing the pressure on him.

By early 1943, this pressure had increased to such an extent that Mannix was again called upon to intervene and this time he enlisted the aid of the Roman Catholic Chaplain General of the Australian Army, the Reverend Father Timothy McCarthy, who had served with the Director-General of Security, Brigadier Simpson, in the Middle East.[40] On 14 April 1943, McCarthy met personally with Simpson and strongly vouched for Modotti. The meeting led to Simpson writing on 15 April to his deputy director in Melbourne, S. Jackson, making him aware that Modotti was not popular with the Italian Fascist government and that he had been decorated by the Viceroy of India. However, Simpson spinelessly held back from calling off Jackson by ending his letter saying that he had passed these developments 'for your information and consideration when making a recommendation'.[41] However, Jackson was no fool and he read between the lines, replying on 17 April that 'on the strength of the information you have now given, I feel that Father Modotti's activities now be considered in a new atmosphere'.[42]

Yet, between 15 and 26 April something or someone modified Simpson's views. That someone may have been Wake in Brisbane, who had now become involved in the running of the Modotti case.

On 26 April, two plain clothes Security Service officials detained and 'very closely' questioned Mr Ramaswami, a returned Australian soldier who had served in the 2/2nd Pioneer Battalion, about his visits with Father Modotti. McCarthy claimed that Ramaswami had just been discharged from the army and was broke, so he visited Modotti to beg for money.[43]

This did not end the harassment of Modotti, as on 28 April Simpson was writing to McCarthy about the latter's new allegation that officers of the Security Service had forcibly detained 'Father Modotti's cooks just before lunch'. Simpson then went on, rather patronisingly, to tell McCarthy, whom he deliberately twice addresses as 'dear Tim', that his facts 'are very far from correct'.[44]

According to Simpson, the father and daughter involved had accompanied Security Service officials of their own free will so they could answer questions. The woman had been returned to Modotti's home by 10.50 a.m. and her father by 11.15 a.m.[45] As Simpson patronisingly put it to McCarthy, 'nobody went hungry'.[46] Apparently, for Simpson this was the crux of McCarthy's complaint.[47] In fact, it wasn't and it was Simpson's facts that were incorrect and not just by a little.

What actually happened is that two Security Service officials illegally forced their way into Manresa, the house of the Society of Jesus in Hawthorn, and spirited away a father and daughter called Mr and Miss Leoncelli, employees of the Society of Jesus.[48]

McCarthy was having none of Simpson's nonsense, and in a three-page reply on 7 May 1943, backed by a letter from Father J. Fitzgerald of the Jesuits, tells Simpson that far from being willing volunteers, the two had been forcibly detained and Miss Leoncelli was so upset upon her return she was unable to work for the rest of the day.[49] McCarthy then points out that the two had nothing to do with Modotti as they were the employees of the Society of Jesus, and Modotti was only a house guest.[50] McCarthy then asks Simpson if his Security Service officers were still conducting close surveillance of Modotti and intercepting and interrogating his visitors.[51]

In this letter of 7 May, McCarthy did not overlook Simpson's patronising and insulting language. McCarthy addressed his letter to 'My dear Bill',[52] and then went on to consistently refer to Simpson as 'dear Bill' throughout.

The sting was in the tail of McCarthy's letter, where he informs Simpson that he will be travelling to the Northern Territory on duty and, in his absence, has instructed Monsignor Lyons, the Vicar General of the Archdiocese of Melbourne, to ensure that if the Security Service detains Modotti while McCarthy is away, then he is to be accompanied during any subsequent detention by Chaplain Quinn of the 2nd AIF.[53] The Catholics were now circling their wagons around Modotti and not only that, they were telling Simpson that if he wanted a fight he was going to get one.[54]

This exchange demonstrates the level at which Simpson, Australia's new Director-General of Security, operated, and clearly demonstrates the vindictiveness and bloody-mindedness that permeated both Military Intelligence and the wartime Security Service. Not only did Simpson ride roughshod over a supposed friend, he did so rudely and stupidly, thus initiating a long, drawn-out fight with the Catholic Church in Australia. It was time to bring in Wake.

The action against Modotti was now ramped up in classic Wake style. First, old correspondence from known fascists in the files of *I 'Italiano*, the Italian newspaper in Brisbane,[55] whose mail had been intercepted since 1938 by the CIB, was dredged up and pored over. In one of the letters, from a Mr C. Albanese, a known fascist and editor of *I 'Italiano*, there was an attached copy of a letter to Father Modotti.[56] The inference was clear.

The next step was collecting all of the material that Modotti wrote, including church flyers, magazines and so on, in an attempt to find anything that could be interpreted as supportive of fascism. To top it all off, Wake and Simpson arranged with the Americans to use one of their CIC agents as an agent provocateur to entrap Modotti.

The agent provocateur was a US Army CIC staff sergeant called, Frank Collucci, codenamed GREEN, and he was briefed to entrap Modotti by pretending to be a US deserter. Collucci was to travel from either Brisbane or Sydney to Melbourne where he was to ingratiate himself into the community and then make confession, where he would tell Modotti that he was a deserter from the US Army.[57] Following on from this, it is assumed, the Security Service—armed with information obtained from a confessional—would move in and arrest Modotti. No wonder McCarthy had arranged for Chaplain Quinn to be made available.

The vileness of this operation not only lies in the use of an agent provocateur, but in the misuse of a sacrament to catch Modotti, a Catholic priest whose faith told him that his soul would be forfeit if he broke the seal of the confessional. Worse still, Wake planned this with the full knowledge and approval of Simpson who displayed no hesitation in setting up a priest.[58] Australia's Director-General of Security was actively complicit in arranging the entrapment of an innocent man.[59]

Collucci was to be assisted by Lieutenant William Etherington, who was codenamed ETHEL. Collucci was to be provided with falsified US Army identification papers and a cover story of having been drafted into the US Army in December 1942 and then shipped to Australia. This cover story involved Collucci becoming involved in a fight with a crew member en route to Australia and as a result being court-martialled, an event that, according to the cover story, made him even more disgruntled. As a result, he had deserted and come to Melbourne from Sydney. He was to attend the Catholic Church where Modotti presided and arrange to attend confession.[60]

The objective of this operation was not to secure the safety of Australia, its people or its forces overseas; it was to get Father Modotti. This behaviour caused no second thoughts, as is made clear by the plan: the sole objective was the arrest and internment of Modotti.

This operation came to nothing, as Modotti made no contact with Collucci. It is likely the local Italian community soon realised he was a Security

Service plant, as the community's mood towards Collucci suddenly changed. On 26 September 1943, the Americans terminated all action in the matter.[61] Unfortunately, the Security Service continued its harassment of Modotti, with Simpson continuing the surveillance operations against a man who was now the citizen of a friendly state following Italy's surrender. This extended to objecting to allowing Father McCarthy to nominate fathers Galanti and Modotti to minister to the spiritual needs of Italian POWs, instead asking that he, McCarthy, nominate a couple of Australians with a knowledge of Italian to carry out this work.[62]

Even this was not the end of the matter—both Military Intelligence and the Security Service continued to dog Modotti well after the war was over. In November 1944, Archbishop Mannix requested permission from Attorney-General Evatt for Modotti to travel to Italy to select priests to work in Australia.[63] Evatt immediately passed this letter to Simpson and the Security Service for urgent advice.[64] The Security Service were still intercepting and opening all mail to and from Italy and mail between Italian residents of Australia. From this they compiled as much scurrilous gossip on Modotti for the file as they could find. They then passed their information and concerns to MI5 in London, the only place Modotti could get a travel permit for Italy via official British military channels. They covered their actions by making a request for any details MI5 held so that if anything blew up, they had a legitimate excuse for what they had done.[65] The great Italian threat turned out to be unknown in London and Modotti was given his permit so he could visit the Vatican.

However, the Security Service got its man in the end. When Modotti tried to return to Australia he was banned as an undesirable alien. The depth of the illegality of this action can only be appreciated when it is realised that Ugo Modotti had applied for Australian citizenship prior to his departure for Italy, a fact known to the Security Service. The circumstantial evidence suggests that this application was deliberately delayed, most likely at the instigation of Simpson and the Security Service,[66] before finally being granted on 9 October 1945.[67] Modotti's naturalisation file was hidden away by changing his Italian first name, Ugo, to the anglicised Hugo. The Security Service had its final paltry victory. That the authorities allowed an Australian citizen to be banned from returning is a smear on the reputation of Australia, and one that was put there by an unholy alliance of Australia's

Military Intelligence and the Security Service, all under the supervision of Evatt, the friend of the downtrodden. At least Wake, unlike Simpson or Evatt, had no pretentions to serving justice. This travesty has still not been officially addressed.

Military Intelligence and the Security Service, all under the supervision of Evatt, the friend of the downtrodden. At least Waks, unlike Simpson or Evatt, had no pretentions to serving justice. This travesty has still not been officially addressed.

CHAPTER 13

JEHOVAH'S WITNESSES— THE ENEMY WITHIN?

If one thought the Catholics of the Italian variety had a tough time of it with Australia's wartime security intelligence organisations, then this chapter should put things in perspective. The religion that drew the greatest ire of the military, and thus Military Intelligence, was the Jehovah's Witnesses. The Witnesses first came to the attention of Australian authorities in 1936 following a request from the Colonial Secretary's Office in Fiji for information from Australia on the organisation.[1] This interest arose as a result of the Witnesses' success in proselytising among Fijians through their Watch Tower Bible and Tract Society. The Prime Minister's Department passed on this request to the Attorney-General's Department for action by the CIB.

The CIB completed its report on 17 November 1936 and forwarded it to Fiji via the Attorney-General's Department. The CIB found that the Watch Tower Bible and Tract Society was an American organisation incorporated in Pittsburgh and was run by 'Judge' J.F. Rutherford, President of the International Bible Society. In Australia, the organisation was based at 5 Beresford Road, Strathfield, New South Wales, under the management of an A. MacGillivray. The only complaints about the society in question had come from the Italian Consul-General who objected to a member of the society coming on board an Italian ship and trying to sell pamphlets written in Italian that were critical of the Italian government.[2]

The CIB decided, quite reasonably, that the Witnesses were just another American religious cult interested in making money; however, the Canadian government, which appears to have had a penchant for banning the Witnesses, had temporarily banned and suppressed them in 1918. The only other blip created by the Witnesses was Rutherford's visit to Australia in 1938. Having found out that Rutherford was about to arrive in Australia, and that it was alleged that he had a criminal conviction, the Attorney-General's Department requested information on him from the Office of the Commonwealth of Australia in New York.

The New York office could find little or no information on Rutherford. His so-called criminal convictions had been in the Federal Court, to which the New York Police had little or no access, and his standing as a judge was a matter for the state of Missouri. The Australian representative in the British Embassy in Washington similarly found the Federal Justice Department unable to assist with information on Rutherford.[3] There the matter rested until war broke out and the General Staff took an interest in the Witnesses.

The problem for the Witnesses was their pacifism, something generals dislike more than sloppy soldiers or the enemy. The pacifism of the Witnesses was seen as a threat to Australia's military preparedness for war and to the standing of the army in society.

The excuse for even more radical action against the Jehovah's Witnesses was provided to the English-speaking world by the Canadian government, which banned the religion again as an illegal organisation on 4 July 1940. This fact was duly reported in Australian newspapers on 6 July 1940.[4]

The attack on the Witnesses rapidly gained ground as their enemies in Military Intelligence, state governments, the newspapers and community spread the news of the Canadian government's ban. On 9 July, J.T. Fitzgerald, Secretary of the Department of the Army, referred to the Canadian action when he complained to Frederick Shedden that the Witnesses were 'spreading defeatist and seditious propaganda', which was 'very effective among the illiterate sections of the community, especially women'.[5] Other than aggressively promoting themselves and their religious pacificism in their literature and meetings, the Witnesses were not actually causing much trouble.[6]

The attack was not confined to the laity as the Director of Catholic Action in Sydney, the Reverend Dr Eris O'Brien, wrote to Commissioner MacKay complaining of the statements and actions of the 'Witnesses of Jehovah'

197

[sic] in refusing to cooperate patriotically in the war emergency.[7] O'Brien's concern was that their actions were causing worry among both Catholics and Protestants through their constant sowing of discord.[8] Of course, if one were sceptical, one would assume that O'Brien was perhaps taking an opportunity to, as Australians like to say, sink the boot in.

Catholic Action didn't need to worry, as MacKay's NSW MPIS was busy collecting information on the Witnesses already.

On 17 July 1940, a ten-page report by Sergeant E.R. Shaw and Constable L.W. Pratt of the MPIS detailing the history of 'these people' was finalised and submitted to their superiors for consideration.[9] This report detailed the problematic interactions between the Witnesses using their American 'hard sell' techniques and the more sardonic members of Australian society.[10] This, as well as other reports, were consolidated by MacKay and passed on to the Premier's Department on 19 July.

Between 12 July and the end of 1940, the Attorney-General's Department and the government were bombarded by demands for action to be taken against the Witnesses. The Department of the Army sent eleven letters supported by reports demanding the Witnesses be banned. Marginal notes on these files make it clear that the army was demanding its letters be answered.[11] One lone voice, that of the ALP Member of Parliament, Maurice Blackburn, attempted to stop the intolerance. Blackburn wrote to Prime Minister Menzies on 27 July 1940 asking him to adopt the British government's 'wonderful example of rendering heart-service to the principles which we in Australia are betraying', by not banning the Jehovah's Witnesses but rather coming to an accommodation with them for service to the nation in a manner acceptable to them.[12]

Blackburn's letter had no obvious effect, but it may have added a little to the concerns held in government about suppressing a religious group. Blackburn's concern and courage in defending the Witnesses goes some way to alleviating what is otherwise a very sordid tale of bigotry and intolerance.

Sir George Knowles and the Attorney-General's Department were not going to be hurried by the army, the press or state premiers because there was a substantial problem in section 116 of the Constitution which clearly laid out that 'the Commonwealth shall not make any law for ... prohibiting the free exercise of any religion'.[13] This meant that even though the Witnesses claimed they were not a religion, this was not necessarily how the High Court would view the matter and, as Knowles cannily identified, the Witnesses had substantial financial assets and support from its members that would result in protracted litigation.[14] Events would prove him right.

H.E. Jones provided the first CIB report to Knowles on 19 July, detailing the threat posed by the Witnesses. In it, Jones erroneously reports that in the United States, the Witnesses' new leader, Pastor Russell, and six followers were arrested under sedition and espionage laws and sentenced to twenty years' imprisonment. Actually Russell had died in 1916 and it was his successor, J.F. Franklin, and six others who were arrested and wrongly convicted of sedition on 21 June 1918. This action was overturned on appeal in which it was found that the Witnesses had been wrongly convicted. They were all released in March 1919.[15]

Another stupid error in this CIB report was the implication that, because they did not list branches in Germany and Italy in their literature, they were working in cahoots with the Nazis in Germany and the Fascists in Italy. The report writer makes the ludicrous assertion that it was 'significant that in the 39 countries named, no mention is made of Germany nor Italy in different countries but mentions none being established in Germany or Italy'.[16] Of course, the fact that the Witnesses were repressed in these countries, as well as in the Soviet Union, because of their insistence on theocratic government and refusal to swear oaths of loyalty was missed.[17] As intelligence work, this report was shameful.

The Witnesses played a role in their own misfortunes by alienating established religions and through their pointed refusal to acknowledge the authority of the state, and the political and bureaucratic leaderships as well. These attitudes made them especially vulnerable, as did their persistent door-knocking and missionary work. The Witnesses were easy targets for the bigotry of the newspapers, the Military, and broad sections of the Australian community, who now broke free of all the constraints of reason in a call for action from government that, if it had been accompanied by the burning of a Kingdom Hall and a private home or two as some advocated, would have amounted to a pogrom.[18]

This press campaign led by the Sydney *Truth* and *Smith's Weekly* is suspicious. We know Wake used these papers to influence public opinion and there can be no doubt that information damaging to the Witnesses was being fed to journalists at the *Daily Telegraph* in Sydney, *Smith's Weekly*, and the *Sydney Morning Herald*.[19]

Another group strongly connected with Military Intelligence was the Returned Sailors and Soldiers Imperial League of Australia, and it was a leading advocate for the immediate banning of any organisation that stopped its members taking the Oath of Allegiance.[20] In July 1940, the Witnesses did themselves no favour in holding a peaceful demonstration in Sydney, which gave MacKay's police the excuse to arrest 67 of them for carrying hoardings and for that good old police standby, offensive behaviour.[21] Now everybody piled in. Thomas Playford, premier of South Australia; Alex Mair, the premier of New South Wales; and Robert Cosgrove, the premier of Tasmania, were among those writing to Robert Menzies demanding that his government take action to declare the Witnesses unlawful.[22]

Thankfully, the Commonwealth, advised by its Solicitor-General Sir George Knowles, followed the dictates of the law. Knowles' assessment of the risks arising from banning the Witnesses limited the enthusiasm of Commonwealth ministers, but not state ministers, particularly premiers. However, it did enable the Commonwealth to sidestep taking action on state complaints.

In one case, referred by the premier of New South Wales, the attention of the Commonwealth was drawn to an open letter the Witnesses had addressed to the premier rebutting an attack he had launched on them under parliamentary privilege on 15 October. Knowles advised that the open letter simply rebutted the attack made by the premier and it did not constitute an attempt to influence public opinion in breach of section 42 of the National Security (General) Regulations, because it did not comment on matters directly related to the conduct of the war or the defence of Australia.[23] The matter was dropped.

In Queensland, Military Intelligence was very active in tracking the activities of the Witnesses and by November 1940 their efforts had established a list of 300 Jehovah's Witnesses, including 90 of alien origin. Not content with this, they also counted their cars, of which there were 45. On top of this, they were illegally searching the homes of Witnesses and reported that in one, the home of a Witness of German origin, they found ten county maps and an order for another fifteen. The explanation given by the Witness in question for this collection was, unsurprisingly, they were used for planning door-knocking activities.[24]

It is sobering to read through the documents prepared by the various officials in the war on the Witnesses. There is a seeming reluctance to proceed and some, like Knowles, were aware that any action put the Commonwealth at risk, yet the intense public and political pressure from the states added to the pressure for action by the army and intelligence and security organs it controlled, and it began to force the hand of a weak government.

In Brisbane, things were getting even worse. The FSS was not content with simply collecting information on the Witnesses; they moved to conducting operations to entrap Witnesses into breaches of the regulations. One of these entrapment operations undertaken by three FSS soldiers on 15 December 1940 involved inviting a group of Witnesses to the home of one of the soldiers to spread 'The Message'. The three people who turned up were a married woman, a young man and an eleven- or twelve-year-old boy. The resulting spreading of 'The Message' was so subversive the erstwhile soldiers reported that 'unless prompt action is taken against the collective activities of these people, as outlined under the heading subversive activities, much damage will be done to the War effort of this State'.[25] So, now there was a situation where soldiers were giving policy advice to government.

Action now started in New South Wales where CIB personnel and the NSW Police banned a convention of Witnesses planned to be held at Hargrave Park at Liverpool between 25 and 29 December 1940.[26] One man who was not convinced by all of this was William MacKay, who found the Witnesses to be quiet and lawful and not any particular threat. The banning of their convention was followed up on 8 January 1941 with a Commonwealth government announcement that four radio stations in South Australia owned by the Witnesses were to be closed down on the evening of 9 January.[27]

The justification for closing the four radio stations was that the navy had received a complaint that one of them—5KA in Adelaide—had sent a coded message to the enemy hidden within the jumbled words of a competition.[28] This message apparently was interpreted as detailing the departure of a troopship.[29] Although this ridiculous allegation is mentioned by a number of sources, there is nothing in the official files inspected indicating that any such intelligence report was generated. Indeed, there is not a single mention of this in any SIGINT file or log, suggesting it was a lie perpetrated to justify the illegal seizure of private property by the Commonwealth.

This action surprised many in government and the media.[30] It can only ever be conjecture as to why the government chose to close down the four radio stations, but the facts were that the Commonwealth Attorney-General,

William Hughes, was under real political pressure from the press, public and state premiers to suppress the Witnesses. Perhaps, and this is conjecture, the Minister for the Navy, the same William Hughes, planted a spurious story of coded messages being broadcast by a Witness-owned radio station with his tame coterie of journalists. Either that or the Australian government closed down four radio stations based on a single uncorroborated report of coded messages being sent. Even then the story does not stand up, because if the messages were encoded, who decoded them?

The idea that Hughes would manipulate the press to get himself out of a political problem is not discounted here. Any reader who has read this work up until now understands just how far Hughes would go to serve his own ends. A fact that further suggests the coded message story was a lie is that it was only run by two small regional papers: the *Maryborough Chronicle, Wide Bay and Burnett Advertiser* and the *Daily Advertiser* in Wagga Wagga. Such a story in the middle of a war would have been big news and every newspaper in Australia and overseas would have reported on it. The fact that no journal of record or major city papers touched it says it all. The story was a fabrication being perpetrated to enable the Commonwealth to illegally seize private property.

It is quite clear that this was an action squarely directed at the Witnesses for no other reason than that Hughes, the army and other powerful interests had set their sights on this annoying pacifist organisation. The Chief of the Naval Staff's power to order the closure of radio stations was the safest way of proceeding and offered the best opportunity of limiting the risk of a legal challenge based upon section 116 of the Constitution.[31] In this, the advice was completely wrong because the Witnesses, as Knowles had warned, possessed enough money to brief good lawyers.

The Watch Tower Bible and Trust Society, The International Bible Students Association, The Adelaide Company of Witnesses and the Consolidated Publishing Company—all organs of the Witnesses in Australia—were finally declared unlawful organisations on Friday 17 January 1941, although the issuing of the *Government Gazette* delayed the matter for a couple of days and a special proclamation had to be issued on Saturday 18 January.[32] As it would turn out, the decision to use the powers of the National Security (Subversive Associations) Regulations and the Defence powers was the right one.[33] When the case finally came before the High Court, the government was found to have committed unlawful trespass, but had not suppressed religious activity despite the closing of the stations being regarded as the 'most spectacular instance of government intervention in religious broadcasting' in Australian history.[34]

The Witnesses may have been pacifists, but that doesn't mean they were soft. They quickly and cleverly returned fire in a letter from a Mr F. Fitzgerald, dated 29 January 1941, requesting the Attorney-General of the Commonwealth order the return of his private property, to wit: furniture, bedding, tables, his wallet, a travelling wallet, a car cover and other items that were illegally seized when the Kingdom Hall at Sturt Street, Adelaide, was raided.[35] Fitzgerald was the chief representative of the Watch Tower Bible and Tract Society in South Australia and had been living with his wife on the Kingdom Hall premises when the Commonwealth authorities had taken it over and confiscated his private property. This letter was the start of a long, tedious campaign by the Witnesses to have these injustices addressed. How tedious this sort of campaign is can be attested by any public servant who has had to handle a stream of 'ministerials' on such a subject.[36]

The case of Fitzgerald's property dragged on until January 1942 when Knowles advised Dr Evatt, the Attorney-General succeeding Hughes, that as the property of the Fitzgeralds had been 'used by, or on behalf of, or in the interests of the banned organisations', it was forfeit to the Crown.[37] This was a stretch, and Knowles knew it. But, by this stage the Commonwealth was committed and Knowles, as the Commonwealth's lawyer, had to protect the interests of his client. Now he advised Evatt that, as the Attorney-General, he could direct that the property be returned to the Fitzgeralds but, putting his lawyer's hat on, he advised against this as it 'would, I think, be a sign of weakness on the part of the Commonwealth,' which should be avoided 'on the eve of the High Court proceedings'.[38] Knowles knew that the property was the personal property of the Fitzgeralds and that, whichever way the High Court case went, it would eventually be returned to them. They would be made to wait, however, until after the case was heard.

What the Witnesses called the Theocratic Embassy, a collection of buildings, in Strathfield, New South Wales, were not simply seized; guards were placed on them at a cost of £87 per week—a reason that underpinned the Commonwealth's decision not to adjourn the High Court case when the Witnesses suggested this.[39] This was not a trivial matter, as the CIB would find out in May 1943—the Witnesses owned at least 26 more premises including factories, timber mills, pig farms, printing presses and shops throughout New South Wales. This would, according to Acting Inspector D.A. Alexander in Sydney, require 'an army of guards'.[40]

Another problem that the military had not foreseen was that, having seized private property, they were now responsible for its upkeep and other costs, such as land rates. In planning the campaign against the Witnesses, no one had discussed the financial ramifications with Treasury and there was no money for roof repairs, repairs to fittings and the cost of general maintenance. As all sorts of governments learn, it is one thing to seize property from citizens and quite another to maintain it. If Inspector Alexander had a problem with supplying an army of guards, it was because he did not appreciate the additional costs of managing the properties concerned. The seizing of the property of the Jehovah's Witnesses was a thoughtless act of bureaucratic idiocy.

Yet, despite the impending decision of the High Court, the military, the CIB and the Security Service persisted in advising the government that the Witnesses be suppressed. They even concocted ways of getting around the court's decision by using Defence powers. The method used to attempt this subversion of the judgment was implemented by the army, which requisitioned the Witnesses' property at 7 Beresford Road, Strathfield, for purposes connected with the prosecution of the war—to wit, the housing of 5 Supply Personnel Company.[41] Both Military Intelligence and the NSW MPIS played a leading role in seizing this property, with a Captain Bray, Detective Sergeant Swasbrick and Constable Pratt calling on Mr MacGillivray at 11.40 a.m. on 8 May to serve the letters on him.[42]

On 4 July 1941, R.J.M. Newton of O'Connell Street, Sydney, launched the High Court action that would result in the rejection of the Government's case.[43] From this point onwards the two parties moved slowly towards an ultimate showdown before the full bench of the High Court. The slowness of this action was actually due to the Witnesses looking to win a bigger game than simply getting their property back. The bigger game was to force the Australian government into a position where it could never again victimise the Witnesses. As a result, the Witnesses conducted a quiet campaign to privately resolve the crisis. Of course, Military Intelligence, the CIB and the Security Service were all still trying to suppress the Witnesses, while wiser heads were looking for a way out of the mess.

The morass that Australia found itself in would quickly prove to have no discernible bottom. The cause of this was the reversal of the US Supreme Court's prior ruling that it was constitutional for the US government to coerce religious groups into swearing the oath of allegiance to the flag.[44] This was a significant development because Australia had relied on the Canadian, New Zealand and US precedents in taking action against the Witnesses. Britain avoided the problem by treating Witnesses as legitimate conscientious objectors. For the Australian government of the day, this meant that the highest judicial court of appeal, the House of Lords in London, would not be supportive of the Australian government case. Now the US Supreme Court had decided that compulsion of religious groups was unconstitutional, providing a legal precedent that the High Court of Australia and the House of Lords would look to in any judgment. The law was firming against the government's position.

In late 1941, the government changed and the ALP government of John Curtin took over the management of how the Commonwealth would deal with the Witnesses. It has to be said that Curtin's government behaved no better than its predecessors. It not only maintained the ban, but defended it and, in the case of the 1942 NSW Convention by the Witnesses, went well beyond anything that the Menzies government envisaged by ordering the military and police to use force to prevent Witnesses from assembling. The power to stop these assemblies had been provided by an amendment of the National Security (Subversive Associations) Regulations prohibiting any meetings or gatherings by members of a banned organisation. This amendment had been pushed through parliament and into law by the Attorney-General, Evatt, on 24 December 1941.

The approach of the ALP government to the NSW Convention was stern. Indeed, in a telephone call on 23 December, Evatt told Knowles the convention must be stopped and that the pending High Court proceedings did not justify police allowing any such meeting to take place.[45] On 27 December, Knowles ordered the Director of the CIB and the NSW Police Commissioner to disperse the convention by force if necessary. Luckily, MacKay chose not to exercise these powers and allowed the convention to continue. MacKay had made a point of visiting the area around Liverpool where many of the Witnesses were camped and as he later reported, having seen the 'types of men who were there', he 'concluded that there was no justification for stepping in and disturbing these people'.[46] MacKay simply placed them under surveillance in what was a good example of the better face of this very complex man. Evatt was very pleased it had passed off so peacefully.

A year later, and the whole farce had to be repeated as the Witnesses planned their next convention and the Commonwealth authorities again moved to stop it happening. Considerable police resources in both Sydney and Adelaide were committed to investigating the proposed convention. The Commonwealth Solicitor reviewed correspondence between the Witnesses organising it and found that it constituted a contravention of regulation 8A (4) (b), preventing people from meeting.

In this case the Commonwealth informed the Witnesses' legal representatives that the convention planned for 1942 could not be held under any circumstances until after the decision of the High Court was handed down.[47] On 11 September MacKay, now the Director-General of Security, sent a telegram to his deputies in all states and to all police commissioners telling them that under no circumstances were the Witnesses to be permitted to hold any conventions.[48]

The meetings in Sydney and Adelaide went ahead despite the efforts of the authorities to prevent them.[49]

On 14 June 1943, in a marvellous legal sleight of hand, the High Court of Australia assisted both sides by finding that the National Security (Subversive Associations) Regulations did not contravene section 116 of the Constitution and neither did the Order-in-Council, the legislative instrument issued by the Governor-General in Council constituting the executive orders to departments of state to take action. The Court also found that the direction the Attorney-General made subsequent to those regulations did not, as a result, contravene section 116 either. Thus, the Commonwealth had not unconstitutionally made laws that banned a religion; however, the High Court also found that regulation 6A was beyond the power conferred on the Commonwealth by the Constitution and the National Security Act and was therefore invalid. The court also found that the Order-in-Council and the direction of the Attorney-General were beyond the powers conferred by regulation.

After the judgment, the conflict between the Australian government and the Witnesses settled down. Despite the advice of Military Intelligence, the Security Service and the CIB, no further action was taken against the Witnesses, and the files stop at this time. The Australian government had learned that democratic government couldn't dispense with the rule of law, even in wartime. All that remained to be done was to work out the return of the confiscated property, and to put in place arrangements that the British had formalised at the beginning of the war that would allow Witnesses to claim exemption from military service and taking oaths on the basis of conscientious objection.

All of the actions taken in Australia against the Witnesses were illegal, and not just on the grounds that the High Court considered, but on the wider and more fundamental grounds of the Australian government's actions constituting a breach of section 161 of the Constitution, a breach the High Court managed to legally rationalise away. The actions of the Commonwealth of Australia in hounding and then suppressing the Witnesses was little short of a pogrom, in which the provisions of defence and security regulations were ruthlessly utilised by security intelligence officials, police forces and governments to hound a small group of annoying people. This pogrom thankfully did not include extrajudicial killings and the appalling abuses associated with that word, but it did involve the Commonwealth of Australia stealing private property including business premises, Kingdom Halls, radio stations and personal goods. The Commonwealth was very lucky the Witnesses did not aggressively seek recompense for the damage done to their reputations, their livelihoods and their freedoms. Their forbearance saved Australia from drawn-out humiliation and substantial financial losses.[50]

Australia was fortunate that all the Witnesses really wanted was to be left alone so they could worship God in their own way and knock on other people's doors at inconvenient times. Just how real the threat of financial losses was for the Commonwealth is shown by the advice provided to Knowles by W.J. Roberts of the Commonwealth Crown Solicitor's Office in Brisbane. In this letter, Roberts tells Knowles that:

> the Secretary might have regard to the amicable nature of the settlement which has so far been effected with the Witnesses and their forbearance to sue the Commonwealth for the many acts of trespass that were committed against their property and the property on individual members of the organisation subsequent to the 17th January 1941.[51]

It was good advice and it was advice that Knowles had already accepted as being true.

CHAPTER 14

SAD, MAD AND BAD— THE ABUSE OF THE AFM

The actions taken in the name of the people of Australia against the Jehovah's Witnesses demonstrates just how the power of the state can be misused by its secret servants when oversight of them is lax. The result is that they begin to seek better and more effective ways of dealing with individuals and organisations that they perceive as being a threat to the security of the nation. Their intentions can be seen as good; it is their actions that result in evil. As in almost all cases, the road to hell is always paved with good intentions.

Where the real evil creeps in though is in the selection of the threat. The focus on the Italian community and its Catholic priests reflects the religious bigotry prevalent during the period of our story. It also reflects the selection of what was thought to be a minority group in society, effectively an easy mark. As the security establishment soon found out, however, the Catholics were influential and powerful enough to fight back, and they did. The attack on the Jehovah's Witnesses, a religious group much smaller than Catholicism and far more despised by the wider society, also failed because what the Witnesses lacked in size, they made up for in financial muscle and clever politics.

What the security establishment really needed was a weak, marginalised and vulnerable group, a group of the sad, the mad and, if possible, the bad.

The group that the security services needed did indeed exist: it was called the Australia First Movement (AFM).

The AFM was not an appealing or pretty organisation, even in the 1930s when it was started. It was a small collection of right-wing individuals easily impressed with totalitarianism and intolerance, and wanting to enforce their world view on everyone else. Essentially, they were those people who make the most boring dinner companions—confused malcontents. They also happened to be right wing.

Like all right-wing malcontents, they were exasperated with the existing political system, exasperated with the available political doctrines and utterly sure of their own individual answers for the world's problems. They also faced the problem that no two of them could agree on whose ideas were better and so they moved in and out of one another's circles as the winds and currents of their political thinking flowed around the rocky ground of hard reality. They were the ultimate low-hanging fruit for any ruthless security organisation seeking to legitimise its existence and please its masters by finding threats to the security of the nation.

The individuals who formed the AFM in October 1941 had been members of a number of loosely associated groups, especially the Yabba Club in Sydney. What seemed to knit them together was that they all read *The Publicist*. This meant that, from 22 July 1936, when Military Intelligence, the CIB and the NSW Police began taking notice of the magazine, they had become persons of interest; although, initially, not too much interest.

The first thing noted by the CIB was that *The Publicist* was of questionable loyalty because it advocated Australia should have its own foreign policy, separate from that of Britain.[1] This information was important enough for the CIB in Sydney to take steps to identify the people behind the publication. A day after the Sydney CIB raised *The Publicist* as an issue, a CIB Inquiry Officer, William Barnwell, found *The Publicist*'s bookshop at 209A Elizabeth Street, Sydney. As a centre of revolutionary action, it was unimpressive. It was staffed by a young woman, Miss Allison, and an elderly gentleman, W.J. Miles.[2] The only stock in the shop consisted of copies of *The Publicist* and copies of Percy Stephensen's book *The Foundations of Culture in Australia*. In terms of its offerings, it was sparse.

Barnwell identified Forward Press as the printer of Stephensen's book and found that Gordon and Gotch had illegally distributed 2000 copies of the first edition of *The Publicist*, as it had not been registered at the Register General's Department in Sydney for transmission through the post. Barnwell had even obtained Stephensen's postal address and the details of Miles' accountancy practice.[3]

During 1937 and early 1938, surveillance of *The Publicist* appears to have been restricted to obtaining copies of the magazine and passing it around Commonwealth agencies for information purposes only. The anti-war, pro-fascist stances within the magazine attracted attention and some comment, but generally it appears not to have caused concern.

In April 1938, with the threat of war with Germany growing and the difficulties associated with Italian and Japanese aggression in Africa and China respectively, the CIB became more interested in the connections *The Publicist* had with Nazi Germany, Italy and Japan. These connections were that *The Publicist* advertised in the German-language weekly *Der Brucke* and the Italian weekly *Italo Australian*.[4] The CIB Inquiry Officer concerned, Barnwell again, even reported that a copy of *The Publicist* was found in the office of W. Ludendorff, leader of the Nazi Party in Sydney and, one suspects, prompted by these findings, Barnwell then engaged Miles in a discussion during which he 'happened to say to Miles' that he was interested in Germany's foreign policy. In response to this, Miles gave him a free copy of the May issue, so he could read Hitler's speech.[5]

Now things started to move down the usual investigative pathway with a collection of personal details on Miles and Stephensen all shared with the Governor of Fiji, who, as the British official responsible for the security of British colonies in the Pacific, received copies of all such reports. Stephensen was confirmed to be of alien extraction—his father being a Dane and his mother a French Swiss who had lived in Russia for a number of years. Stephensen's communist party connections at Oxford, where he was a Rhodes Scholar, and in Australia were also noted.[6] This flirtation with communism is unsurprising, as marginal figures like Stephensen are often found changing their authoritarian camps, as did Adela Pankhurst Walsh, another convert to the AFM.

Further work was done in identifying connections between *The Publicist*, *Der Brucke* and Ludendorff. These investigations uncovered that *The Publicist*'s relationship with Nazis in Australia extended beyond advertising to the exchanging of stories on Nazism and translations of Hitler's speeches into English.[7] By

October 1938, it is apparent that Barnwell had infiltrated the group and was being asked to contribute his view on whether there should be an Australia First Party, how it should be established and what its policies could be.[8]

After this report, interest in *The Publicist* and the groups involved diminished, although it was noted that a Captain Koehler, leader of the Deutsche Arbeiterpartei (German Workers Party) was a subscriber to *The Publicist*.[9]

The first politician to show any interest in *The Publicist* was the Minister for External Affairs, William Hughes, on 17 January 1939. Always on the lookout for a good target, Hughes wrote to H.E. Jones at the CIB asking if he could investigate the magazine. Hughes claimed to have received information that this paper was maintained by German propaganda funds.[10] Jones' reply is illuminating. He outlines what the CIB knew about *The Publicist* and its backers, particularly Stephensen. He then explains that, despite Stephensen's foreign extraction, virulent anti-English utterances and degree of mental instability, his real motivation was money.

Importantly, Jones plays down the idea that *The Publicist* was being funded by the German government or Nazi Party. All that was happening was that *The Publicist* was advertising itself in *Der Brucke*. Jones kept his options open though, telling Hughes that the CIB knew that the Nazi Austlands Organisation was actively seeking to influence pro-German opinion in Britain and Australia and that the CIB would continue its investigations. All in all, it was a fair and rational assessment of the information available in the file.[11]

The CIB and police continued to watch those associated with *The Publicist* and, while there were reports about connections with the Japanese consulate, there was no hard evidence and nothing showing any financial support flowing to *The Publicist* from the Germans, the Japanese or any other consulate for that matter. Nowhere in the files is there any suggestion that *The Publicist*, Yabba Club or the AFM ever received money from foreign interests, and the files show that the CIB and Military Intelligence monitored all cash transactions, including the opening and closing of bank accounts. What is obvious in the files is that these organisations were severely strapped for cash.[12]

The authorities did not restrict themselves to monitoring organisations; they also monitored the private financial activities of leading members, particularly Miles. In July 1940, William MacKay's MPIS in Sydney was supplying the CIB with details on Miles' financial situation. Miles was a well-off accountant with a personal worth of £80,000 in shares and cash. He was the person who underwrote the £4000 per month it cost to print and publish 1000 copies of *The Publicist*.[13] This means a cost of £4 per copy; that is, around $339 today. *The Publicist* was a very expensive publication. Captain B. Tyrell of Military Intelligence who had worked for the Bank of New South Wales as an accountant before being posted to full-time service seems to have extracted this information from the bank using the old boy network rather than a legal instrument.[14]

Although the CIB and MI authorities took an interest in Miles, Stephensen and their associates, and monitored *The Publicist* and various other groups, there was not a high level of concern about their behaviour. Of course, if one is inclined to see this as a right-wing conspiracy of tolerance within the CIB and Military Intelligence for fellow right-wingers, then at first glance you might be right. However, it was more likely the result of knowing them personally, as they all moved in the same social circles. This familiarity breeds contempt because the officials of the CIB and Military Intelligence would have run into people like Miles and Stephensen, if not the men themselves, and they would have found them noisy, ineffective and, as a result, essentially harmless.

Thus, the most likely explanation for the lack of official interest is, if we apply Ockham's razor to the problem, simply that Miles, Stephensen and their associates were, unlike the more disciplined and ideologically driven CP-A, slightly dotty, extremely boring but essentially harmless individuals incapable of organising a social outing let alone a coup d'état.

The evidence for this official lack of interest is the low level of correspondence about these people and their groups within the CIB. As late as March 1940, Robert Wake in Brisbane received a request from the Queensland Tourist Bureau for information on *The Publicist*.[15] Wake was obviously caught flatfooted and had no idea what *The Publicist* was about, so he wrote to his counterpart in Sydney, Inspector Mitchell, for advice and information. The reply Wake received from Mitchell gave a very brief description of the magazine and accurately described Miles as a crank.[16] No further action was taken at this time although the CIB continued to buy copies and keep an eye on the bookshop.

Nothing incriminating was picked up but despite this it did not take long for one of the CIB's inquiry officers—in the scheme of things a very junior official—to recommend that *The Publicist* be banned. This brought the magazine to the attention of Sir George Knowles who, after reading it, wrote to advise the Director of CIB that he saw no good reason to ban the magazine.[17] This is the last word on the issue at the higher levels of the CIB until late 1941, when the Inspector, CIB, Sydney, informed the Director that a public meeting was being organised by the AFM for Wednesday 12 November 1941, at Australian Hall in Elizabeth Street, Sydney.[18]

Although the CIB appears to have lost interest in the group behind *The Publicist* and the Yabba Club, Military Intelligence in Sydney had been running two penetration agents within the Yabba Club, one of whom was V.R. Alldis, run by Captain Tyrell, from the beginning of 1941 at least.[19] The reaction of Military Intelligence to their activities was, predictably, to recommend the suppression of the Yabba Club and the AFM, and the closing down of *The Publicist*.[20] This was not enough for Military Intelligence, which also recommended searching the offices and homes of all the members and associates of these organisations.[21] This was the usual lazy approach of Military Intelligence to any perceived threat.

Searching people's homes and offices in such circumstances was not being recommended as part of a rigorous investigation where the evidence of wrongdoing would be sufficiently strong for a judge or magistrate to issue a search warrant in order to find further evidence. The type of search proposed by Military Intelligence was of the fishing expedition sort, a search conducted in the hope that something incriminating could be found to justify further action. It is the approach of totalitarian secret police and, as noted by MI5, highly characteristic of Australia's security intelligence system during the war.[22]

The timing of the AFM's campaign to go public, November 1941, was going to prove extremely inauspicious for both them and for Australia's reputation as a liberal democracy. By November 1941, the Commonwealth was governed by the ALP which, despite all of its public pronouncements, was to prove as uninterested in civil rights as its predecessors had been. It should be noted though that its predecessor governments of Lyons, Menzies and Fadden did not face the crisis that would confront John Curtin and his ministers in December 1941.

Unlike Curtin's government, however, earlier governments cannot be accused of hypocrisy—claiming to be the defenders of freedom and the civil rights of the weak and vulnerable, while systematically allowing the abuse of vulnerable citizens.

The causes of this tendency within the new government were manifold. There was the problem of their inexperience as government ministers, and their overdependence on the advice of public servants and the military caste. Indeed, this latter problem was a big one because of the difficulties of the ALP's past relationships with the military, a caste upon whom the ALP government now utterly depended. Unsurprisingly, the new government needed to appease the military and unfortunately this involved being weak in the face of military demands.

One final and substantial factor that contributed to this abuse of the rights of citizens was the powerful drive to win at all costs that afflicts many politicians, and none as much as it seems to have affected the new Attorney-General, H.V. Evatt. In many ways, Evatt was a fitting successor to William Hughes. Neither man can be said to have contributed anything positive to Australia's development and, despite the glowing subsequent endorsements of Evatt's work in forming the United Nations, the hard truth is that he was reviled by much of the diplomatic corps. Even the NKGB Resident in Australia, Semen Ivanovich Makarov, in a message to General Pavel Mikhailovich Fitin of the NKGB, described Evatt's behaviour at one international conference as 'juvenile lecturing' and was critical of the way in which Evatt, seemingly without any insight, demanded other nations to spend money in Asia while not committing Australia to spend a penny.[23]

It should also not be forgotten that Evatt was no innocent and that he was more than willing to make clandestine and unconstitutional use of the security organisations he controlled to damage his friends and enemies, something even the NKGB knew.[24] Despite what Curtin may have hoped for, his new government was not going to be friendly to dissenting groups.

Another even more sordid influence that this author suspects may have existed at this time was the desire of Military Intelligence to achieve a big intelligence win before William MacKay took control of the new security service. Given that the subsequent actions against the AFM were all driven by Military Intelligence tends to add strength to such a suspicion. On top of this, in December 1941, the Japanese—whom some in the AFM so admired—were about to launch the most widespread and well-coordinated attack in human history, an attack that would bring them to the very shores of Australia. A new unfriendly government and fear were just what was needed to make the life of the AFM and its supporters miserable and that of the junior officials in Military Intelligence and the security organisations satisfying.

214

At first glance, early November 1941 looked like a good time to be launching a campaign promoting the idea that Australia should be adopting a more independent stance in international affairs. In the Middle East, Britain had suffered the reversals of Greece and Crete and the loss of the ground taken in the Western Desert earlier in 1941. The war in the Atlantic was going very badly and no one knew what the United States was going to do. In Russia, the Germans could see the Kremlin. It looked as if the end was coming and Britain would be defeated. Yet, in less than a month Winston Churchill would greet the news of the Japanese attack on Pearl Harbor with the words, 'We have won!'

The meeting held at Australian Hall on 12 November 1941 repositioned the AFM from being a small group attending the Yabba Club and reading and writing *The Publicist*, to a group organising a political movement. The speakers at this meeting were Stephensen, L.K. Cahill and Adela Pankhurst Walsh.[25] This drew the attention of the CIB for the first time since January of that year. It also drew the attention of MacKay's MPIS.[26]

The CIB investigators who attended the meeting were the old hands Jack Magnusson and William Barnwell. The meeting had 150 attendees, including a fair number of communists who, always blindly loyal to Moscow, were there to support the war by disrupting the meeting. Magnusson and Barnwell took pages of notes on what was said, including interjections of which there were many, particularly from the communists.[27] At the end of the meeting, the chairman acknowledged the communists' contribution saying, 'It is apparent that some representatives of international pressure groups have come along.' The *Sydney Telegraph* and *Mirror* reported the next day that the 'rowdy meeting' had ended 'in uproar'. If the authorities were worried about the AFM leading Australians astray, it appears they did not read the newspapers.[28]

The names of the leading lights of the AFM were now clearly identified as P.R. Stephensen, Chairman, W.F. Tinker, Treasurer, L.K. Cahill, Organiser, Adela Pankhurst Walsh, Organiser, Vera Parkinson, Marjorie Corby, Elaine Pope, G.T. Rice, Ian Mudie and Sheila Rice.[29] The outcome of the meeting was that the CIB authorised the Sydney office and Censor to take 'special action' against the AFM and its members.[30] No other action was taken by the CIB or the Attorney-General's Department.

The same cannot be said for Military Intelligence at Victoria Barracks in Sydney. Sometime after November 1941, it appears the CIB file was transferred across to the army and from there to MacKay's Security Service.[31] On 28 January 1942, MacKay contacted the Director of Military Intelligence to proffer the support of the Security Service for the limited action of imposing a restriction order on Stephensen.[32] The grounds for this were that the propaganda that Stephensen associated himself with was against the best interests of Australia and the Empire.[33]

The army wasted no time in taking action and Lieutenant General H.D. Wynter, the General Officer Commanding Eastern Command, signed off on the application for a Ministerial Order under the National Security (General) Regulations 25 and 26. Under this order, the army wanted Stephensen banned from associating with aliens and it also prevented him from changing his address without notifying police. It required him to submit all speeches and articles for censorship and he was banned from attending any meetings or activities where censorship had not already been performed. He was also to be ordered to immediately resign from all subversive organisations.[34]

Evidence was collected from people who knew Stephensen, including an informer who provided Military Intelligence with information that Stephensen frequently went to a secluded weekender, near Sutherland, to write. Military Intelligence was building its case.[35]

The premier of New South Wales, William McKell, was also getting worked up about the AFM. McKell passed twelve NSW Police reports to Curtin between 6 November 1941 and 10 March 1942.[36] It may be a tad cynical, but the extent of NSW Police reporting on the oddballs of the AFM cannot have harmed MacKay's job prospects.

On 17 February 1942, MacKay recommended to the Under-Secretary of the Chief Secretary's Office of New South Wales that the AFM be declared illegal.[37] MacKay was playing to Evatt by supplying him with copious reporting on the AFM and Evatt responded by writing to MacKay telling him to ensure that the NSW Police reports continued to be sent to him.[38] On MacKay taking up the position of Director-General of the new Commonwealth Security Service on 17 March 1942,[39] the AFM was caught between MacKay and Military Intelligence, who dearly wanted to deprive the newly appointed Director-General of Security an easy win. The army got the chance to move first as a result of a little bit of luck and an agent provocateur working on a completely different group in Perth.

The investigators working to entrap the group of Perth activists included members of Longfield Lloyd's CSS, Military Intelligence in Perth and the Western Australian Police Special Bureau, all of whom were part of Military Intelligence's network of influence. The operations in Perth were used by Military Intelligence to justify subsequent operations in Melbourne, Sydney and Brisbane, and this was highly problematic.[40]

On 9 March, two events occurred that enabled Military Intelligence's assault on the AFM and its associates. First, Evatt left Australia on an overseas visit and Forde was appointed to act in his stead in matters of national security. This placed all of the decision-making on security matters in the hands of a single minister. Second, on that day four sad individuals—Laurence Frederick Bullock, Nancy Rachel Krakouer, Edward Cunningham Quicke and Charles Leonard Albert Williams—whom we shall call the Bullock Group, were arrested in Perth and, under regulation 79 of the National Security (General) Regulations, charged with having 'conspired together to assist within the Commonwealth of Australia a public enemy, to wit, the armed forces of Japan contrary to section 86 of the Crimes Act'.[41]

These charges arose from what can only be described as an insane plan by four not very bright individuals to support a non-existent Japanese invasion of Western Australia by committing acts of sabotage.

The source of all the information used to bring these charges was an agent provocateur, a New Zealander named Frederick James Thomas who, using the covername Frederick Carl Hardt, had penetrated the group on the orders of Detective Sergeant G.R. Richards, Chief of the Western Australian Special Bureau, attached to Military Intelligence in that state.[42] Thomas appears at the time to have been a professional police spy who, under cross-examination, admitted he had previously joined the CP-A in Perth, also on the instructions of Richards.[43]

Thomas had a chequered past, which later came out under cross-examination. In court, Thomas admitted to prior minor criminal convictions for riding on trains in the eastern states. He also informed the court that he had been a member of the ALP in Sydney, the Left Book Club, the Committee for Medical Aid to Russia and the CP-A, and that he had been rejected by the army and the RAAF. This failure to enlist is what Thomas claimed motivated him to serve his country as a spy and informer.[44] How Thomas was actually recruited as a police spy was never precisely examined, but it will have involved him being caught in yet another misdemeanour by Sergeant Richards.

Given this, and supposing that Richards and the other officials involved were acting in good faith, there were considerable dangers associated in using a man like Thomas as an agent. Such agents are invariably unstable to begin with and Thomas displays all of the signs of such instability. His lifestyle, including the low-level criminal activity of riding trains, is itinerant and marginalised, and this most likely accounts for his rejection by the armed services. Flitting between left wing groups also suggests someone with a marked need for acceptance and recognition. Becoming a police informer and spy would provide an individual like Thomas with such recognition but, if Richards was any good as a policeman, only if Thomas produced the goods. In this case, 'the goods' was not providing information that could be used to rule people out of guilt, it was finding information that ruled them in and, unfortunately, when such information did not exist, then generating it as an agent provocateur became the easy option.

There is no doubt that Thomas acted as an agent provocateur and may even have been the person who actually initiated the plan. One hint that this may indeed have been the case is the speed with which the authorities responded to Thomas' reporting. Thomas passed his raw, uncorroborated intelligence—not evidence—to Richards on 8 March and the members of the Bullock Group were arrested on 9 March. Given there was no Japanese invasion fleet off Fremantle and the group had no weapons or explosives, there had been no urgency to act.

Most importantly, the speed with which the arrests took place meant there was no time for the information provided by Thomas to be properly considered by Richards, let alone more senior officers, and there was no corroborating evidence or time to collect any. The tight timeline strongly suggests the arrests were pre-planned and Thomas' reporting was part of this. Essentially, the Bullock Group was framed for ulterior motives held by the security officials involved.

In the minds of the police and security officials concerned, sacrificing a few right-wing lunatics was a small price to pay to provide Military Intelligence and police with a quick and spectacular win before MacKay became Director-General of Security. As Thomas' later testimony showed, his job was 'to uncover un-Australian activities'.[45]

The trigger for the arrests in Perth was therefore the report of a single individual of questionable reliability that, on Sunday 8 March 1942, Bullock, Williams, Quicke and Krakouer had conspired to assist the Imperial Japanese Army (IJA) invade Australia, if they happened to land in Perth.[46]

On 9 March, the evidence compiled by Lloyd's Security Service, Military Intelligence and the Police Special Bureau in Perth consisted of the statement of Thomas regarding the meeting on 8 March and, after searching Krakouer's flat, a single page of disjointed minutes dated Sunday 8 March 1942.[47] This very sketchy outline plan was for the four members of the Bullock Group to meet up with the invading Japanese who would intuitively understand their intentions and not arbitrarily bayonet them, as seemed to be their normal practice elsewhere.

According to the plan, the group was going to make an anonymous proclamation in an effort to gain new members at a fee of 10/-, to fund party activities. One member, No. 4, was to be responsible for contacting the Japanese if they landed in the south-west of Western Australia, No. 2, in the north, and Nos 1 and 5 in Perth.[48] Apparently No. 3, the future party secretary, was staying home during this invasion.[49]

The group, presumably assisted by the invading Japanese, were then going to 'liquidate ... politicians, Army? Police?' The presence of question marks against the words 'army' and 'police' seems to have indicated only some would be liquidated, while all the politicians would be. Maybe Thomas' police and Military Intelligence handlers were happy to have politicians on a death list, but a little squeamish having themselves on it as well. Yet it appears the group had second thoughts anyway as the heading 'liquidation' had been crossed out.[50]

This single page also listed vulnerable points, including the Bayswater subway, the Riversdale Bridge, the Fremantle Causeway, Perth Causeway and the bridge at Garret Road Bayswater. There is no plan of any action, just a list of vulnerable points. The poor old Jehovah's Witnesses were listed as nuisance value, so it would seem that Australia's right wing malcontents shared the same biases as Australia's security and government establishments.[51]

The paucity of the evidence and the obvious nature of this small group of oddballs were not missed in the subsequent judicial inquiry into this sordid affair by Justice Thomas Stuart Clyne. Of the Bullock Group, Clyne said, 'It is difficult to imagine what moved these puny conspirators to such ambitions and dangerous designs.'[52] It is difficult to imagine what they thought they were doing, if indeed they had thought it through at all. It appears Justice Clyne was being polite in implying that Bullock and the others were victims of an entrapment operation. Later in his report, Clyne finds that, based on the evidence, he was 'prepared to believe that Thomas was not a passive investigator'.[53]

The real judgment in the Perth case did not need to wait for Justice Clyne's findings. On 23 June 1943, in the Criminal Court of Western Australia, the jury found that Bullock and Williams were guilty as charged and Quicke and Krakouer not guilty.[54] Despite having been found innocent by a court of law, Quicke and Krakouer remained in detention awaiting the pleasure of Evatt or Forde, as advised by their officials.[55] The efforts of legal counsel, family, friends, colleagues and many concerned observers failed to move Evatt, Forde or even Prime Minister Curtin, who maintained the injustice as long as they held power.[56]

The conspiracy unearthed in Perth was utter nonsense and anyone with a modicum of intelligence would have recognised it as such, unless they had ulterior motives. In March 1942, it would prove to be manna from heaven for Military Intelligence. As a result of these arrests, military command in Perth telegrammed Melbourne and Sydney at 5.00 a.m. on 10 March 1942 and this led to immediate action being taken against the AFM in Victoria and New South Wales, even though no one in these organisations had any relationship with the Bullock Group in Perth.[57] The telegram itself was overblown in its allegations, claiming the four arrested in Perth

HAD IN THEIR POSSESSION MOST INCRIMINATING DOCUMENTS SHOWS INTENTION TO MAKE CONTACT WITH JAPANESE ARMY AT MOMENT OF INVASION. PLAN FOR SABOTAGE VULNERABLE POINTS THIS COMMAND PLAN FOR DEATH OF HEADS OF ARMY POLICE DEMOCRATIC POLITICIANS HIERARCAY [SIC] OF ALL DENOMINATIONS AND BUSINESSMEN. PROC-LAMATION WITH HEADING AUSTRALIA FIRST GOVERNMENT PREPARED FOR AUSTRALIA WIDE BROADCAST ON SIGNING OF ARMISTICE WITH JAPAN . . .[58]

In short, the telegram from Perth was a tissue of lies.[59] It was sent to eastern, southern and northern commands without any context or assessment of its reliability or seriousness. It was also factually wrong in stating that the individuals arrested in Perth were members of a group called Australia First. The only time this name appears is in the resulting proclamation, the writing of which involved Thomas. The extent of the contact between the Bullock

Group and AFM was nothing more than a couple of letters exchanged with Miles and Stephensen in Sydney and Cahill in Melbourne.

Of course, all of this could also have been a real case of panic within Australia's military and security establishments. After all, Singapore had fallen on 15 February 1942 and the Netherland East Indies surrendered to the IJA on 9 March.[60] On the other hand, we have a police officer, MacKay, stepping into the role of Director-General Security, a position the army wanted filled by one of its own. Although there is no evidence, the idea that the members of the AFM were arrested and interned to deprive MacKay of a quick win cannot, as we have already noted, be discounted.

In Melbourne, Major E. Hattam, the responsible Military Intelligence officer, was woken up at 5.20 a.m. and informed of the telegram. Hattam telephoned Sub-Inspector Birch and Major Brown. Brown arranged for A.E. Officer to accompany Birch and Hattam in searching the homes and premises of the AFM members in Melbourne.[61]

When Military Intelligence searched the homes of the Victorian AFM members it found a lot had changed. One leading member of the AFM, Leslie Kevin Cahill, was now Private Cahill, serving in the 20th Garrison Battalion. Hattam and party contented themselves by searching Cahill's previous address at 29 Station Street, Fairfield, where they found a Mrs Camille Bartram and seized two suitcases of books and papers relating to the AFM. The seized materials proved to be innocuous. There was no evidence to suggest the Victorian organisation was involved in subversive activities; however, Hattam did find a letter dated 27 July 1941 from Bullock in Perth to Cahill.[62]

The search party then went to the home of W.D. Cookes, the major shareholder and Managing Director of Ezywalkin Shoes, at 9 Heidelberg Road, Ivanhoe, just up the road from Fairfield. Cookes informed Hattam that he had donated £4500 to the Rationalist Organisation and that his old friend W.J. Miles was, unsurprisingly, in financial difficulty due to propping up *The Publicist*.[63] They then found and interviewed Alexander Rudd Mills and Able Seaman Max Knight, now a Writer in the RAN at Williamstown Dockyard who had severed all ties with the AFM upon enlisting. Hattam then interviewed a number of other members of the AFM, but took no further action against them.[64] At the end of all of this work, Hattam reported that the organisation in Victoria was not in any way engaged in subversive activity.[65] This report was forwarded to the Security Service in Canberra on 16 March 1942 by Lieutenant Colonel R.H. Weddell, Officer-in-Charge, Victoria State Branch.[66]

To his credit, Hattam arrested no one. He took statements, looked through their papers and books and took possession of those letters and papers that might have provided further information for his files. In Sydney, good old Emerald City, they went nuts.

On 10 March, a conference was called at Police HQ in Sydney by Lieutenant Colonel Reginald Powell, Officer-in-Charge of the Military Intelligence Section at Eastern Command.[67] Superintendent W.C. Watkins represented MacKay's MPIS, which included majors Tyrell and McGowan, Captain Newman from Military Intelligence, and Detective Sergeant Swasbrick and other NSW Police officers.[68] The purpose of the meeting was to consider the telegram received from Perth. Powell recommended immediate action in New South Wales to arrest the members of the AFM and detain its principals. The list of those to be arrested, sixteen in all, was tabled by Superintendent Watkins and Detective Sergeant Swasbrick.[69] They were all arrested on 10 March on the authority of Powell, who assumed full responsibility for the action.[70]

Powell's authorisation would later lead him to be singled out by Justice Clyne as being one of the main instigators of the arrests; however, Powell was not acting alone. The meeting he convened involved both military and NSW Police personnel and there was no way that Powell was acting without the authority of his superiors. Powell was just the front man in this whole disaster.[71]

The one government authority that was kept in the dark on the intended action against the AFM was the Attorney-General's Department. There was no way Military Intelligence was going to allow Knowles or MacKay to stop their operation or interfere with the prerogatives of the army in policing civil security. The timing of this whole affair, a Sunday, may just be luck, but the fact Evatt had handed over his responsibilities to the Minister for the Army and MacKay was just moving into his office as Director-General of Security does make it an awfully auspicious day for Military Intelligence.[72]

MacKay had nothing to do with this affair, which the circumstantial evidence suggests he saw as something other than the arrest of subversives. He would not have overlooked the timing of the events either. His subsequent coolness towards Military Intelligence, the army and the arrests makes it clear he was unhappy. This coolness, and the fact that he kept the Security Service completely clear of the business, suggests that MacKay saw the AFM affair as a looming disaster for all those involved. After all, MacKay was a very experienced policeman and he knew how to fit up a crook properly. The AFM had most definitely not been properly fitted up.

MacKay took his revenge in due course. He left the army and its allies to stew in their own juices and he purged the MPIS in Sydney of anyone who was not loyal to him. By August 1942, he was telling Evatt that the Security Service had nothing to do with the matters surrounding the AFM and neither had the Attorney-General's Department. Evatt was thus in the clear.

By the middle of 1942, despite the war, the government was facing a growing outcry from the relatives and friends of the victims and this outcry was being heard in parliaments and churches. The victims were also turning the tables on the government by refusing to accept a quiet release from detention. Instead they lodged appeals against their detention: they wanted their day in court and, as far as MacKay was concerned, they should have it. For him, it was simple: the army had created a mess and as 'they brought about the present position … they should alleviate it'.[73]

MacKay's letter to Evatt followed one from a desperate Frank Forde, Minister for the Army, which he sent on 31 July 1942. In this letter, Forde asked Evatt if the instructions he had given during Evatt's absence overseas requesting the appeals of the AFM detainees to be expedited had been implemented.[74] Forde's discomfort on this subject had arisen because of a complaint from Stephensen about his name being divulged during a parliamentary debate. Forde was at pains to point out to Evatt that he had not been the one who divulged Stephensen's name.[75]

It is painfully clear that Forde was more than uncomfortable with the whole AFM situation. To be fair to him though, he had rightly and clearly differentiated between the Bullock Group and the AFM. He also, he wrote to Evatt, 'gave instructions on several occasions … that the hearing of appeals to the appropriate Tribunal should be expedited'.[76] Forde asked Evatt to find out whether all of those wanting to appeal had been allowed to do so. He finished the letter by saying: 'I am anxious that there should be no unnecessary delay in hearing appeals.'[77]

The problem was that the delay in some of the appeals, particularly Stephensen's, was something Stephensen wanted. His ambition was to have his day in court with all of the publicity that this would entail so that he could put his case before the people of Australia and clear his name. William Hughes, who had done the naming of Stephensen in Parliament,[78] had no interest in protecting Stephensen's rights, or the rights of anyone, as he made clear when he told the House that calls for the protection of the detainees were just 'blithering about the Bill of Rights and habeas corpus and things of that kind', arguing, 'this is war; and the man who says he will betray us deserves death'.[79] Hughes was solely interested in the AFM as a means of striking at the Curtin government.

Stephensen may have been an unpleasant anti-Semitic bigot and an adherent of authoritarianism, but he did have a point, and some more sensitive souls, like Forde, knew this. In a letter to Evatt, Stephensen told him that 'A Labor government should be big-minded enough to admit that a mistake has been made …'[80] Unfortunately for Stephensen and the other AFM members involved, the Labor Party may have been big minded, but it was not stout hearted enough to admit it had just presided over a massive injustice.

The events of 10 March 1942 saw military personnel and members of the NSW Police Force illegally enter the homes and premises of sixteen Australian citizens, detain them and then kidnap them into detention for allegedly uttering disloyal sentiments. None of this action was covered by ministerial warrant or orders, as the application prepared on 9 January had not been presented to the minister. Every single act committed by the police and military was illegal.

On 13 March, three days after they had seized the persons and property of the sixteen, Eastern Command asked Army HQ to urgently present the application to the minister and get it signed. As the official historian Paul Hasluck puts it, Eastern Command asked that 'the execution of Ministerial warrants under regulation 26 of the National Security (General) Regulation be treated as one of extreme urgency.'[81] It was indeed a matter of extreme urgency because the minister did not know about the arrests in Perth, let alone those in Sydney. As a result, he had not formed the necessary view required by the regulation.[82] This was extrajudicial action by the organs of the Commonwealth against Australian citizens.

The Commonwealth authorities now simply circled the wagons. For Evatt and the Attorney-General's Department, their clear duty was to defend the Commonwealth and win the case at any cost and this included, when the day came to formally investigate this affair, Evatt drafting terms of reference for Justice Thomas Stuart Clyne's commission of inquiry to ensure Clyne could not do much damage. The terms of reference limited Clyne to inquire whether the detentions were 'justified', not whether they were 'legal'. So, right from the outset, Clyne's inquiry was hamstrung.

This legal sleight of hand allowed Clyne to take into consideration when making his findings that Military Intelligence was acting under the imperative of defending Australia from an impending Japanese invasion. This allowed Clyne to find the arrest and continued detention of some of the detainees 'reasonable in the circumstances'.[83] It was a very skimpy veil, but a veil nonetheless.

All of the other matters Clyne inquired into followed on from the first reference. Clyne's ability to investigate and make findings as to whether the detainees were given proper opportunity to appeal was reduced to simply checking that a procedure existed. As to whether the continued detentions were 'just and reasonable in the circumstances' was already answered with a yes if Clyne found the detentions were justified in the first place. Although Clyne found the initial and continued detentions were reasonable in the circumstances, he did find that the Commonwealth had overreached itself. As to compensation, Clyne's recommendations were laughable.[84]

What is most striking about Clyne's response to the terms of reference is that he accepted them. Thomas Stuart Clyne was an experienced judge and, one assumes, no one's fool. So, why did he accept such limited terms of reference? Was he suffering from the Denning effect? (Lord Denning, a UK judge, was so affronted by the idea that police and government authorities would exercise their powers so corruptly that they would deliberately send innocent people to gaol, he wrongly ruled against the appeal of the Birmingham Six.)[85] Maybe. Indeed, Clyne grasped at straws trying to justify the actions of the authorities as being reasonable in the strategic circumstances faced by Australia at the time. He even uses the words of Stephensen—a man previously assessed as a little mad by the CIB—'that the authorities were right to have arrested the AFM members at the time' to justify the actions of the authorities.

A more reliable insight into the mindset of the Curtin government is found in the immediate actions of an angry Forde who, belatedly, seemed to realise how dangerous Military Intelligence had become to civil liberty and he now began to impose civilian authority over it. Forde, and presumably

225

Curtin and the more sensible members of Cabinet, had had enough. On 2 April 1942, Forde held a conference of stakeholders in security intelligence at Victoria Barracks in Melbourne. As the Minister for the Army and the acting Attorney-General, Forde was in a strong position at this conference and he attempted to use it to rein in what he must have felt was a system out of control.

The impetus for Forde's action was a letter from MacKay written to him on 22 May 1942. In this letter MacKay, who seems to have been trying to have the Security Service made into a stand-alone agency outside the control of the Attorney-General's Department and the army, was complaining about Knowles interfering in the administration of the Security Service. Knowles had been a player in Canberra for too long to fall for MacKay's stratagems and had already moved to sideline MacKay, whom he had not wanted appointed to the position in the first place. Knowles' candidate for the job had been L.G.R. Thornber, the acting Second Secretary at the Attorney-General's Department.[86] With the loss of this battle, Knowles had ensured that MacKay was gazetted as the 'acting' Director-General on 21 May 1942, not as the Director-General as MacKay had expected and as the prime minister had promised the premier of New South Wales.

MacKay, now very unhappy with Knowles, wrote to Forde demanding that this matter be fixed in accordance with the undertakings he had been given. He also expressed the view that Evatt, with whom he had privately discussed his appointment before it was made, would be 'astounded' when he learned what Knowles had done.[87] MacKay requested Forde direct Knowles to stop interfering and to accept that the Security Service's relationship with the Attorney-General's Department was one of convenience to enable funding to be made via the vote of the department.[88]

MacKay was asking the impossible because, although Forde was the acting Attorney-General in Evatt's absence, this did not entitle him to make changes, simply to administer the department in the form he found it until Evatt returned. As a result, MacKay asked to meet with Curtin in order to put 'certain facts' that would result in the Security Service being placed under the control of another department, perhaps Defence or another department as the prime minister might direct.[89]

This was a typical MacKay ploy to remove threats to his power, and it had worked well in New South Wales. Unfortunately, in Canberra and more importantly in the immediate aftermath of the AFM affair, Forde was in no mood for petulant posturing from anyone within the security intelligence system. Forde's response was to call a conference on 2 April 1942 at Victoria Barracks in Melbourne and, to ensure he kept control, he served as the conference's chairman. The other attendees were Knowles, MacKay, the directors of the three service intelligence branches and a Mr Kevin of the Department of the Army. The decisions the conference made were then clearly detailed by Forde in a letter to MacKay dated 9 April 1942.[90]

The first thing Forde made clear to MacKay was that while he had direct access to the Minister for the Army in the absence of the Attorney-General, the Security Service would remain an intrinsic part of the Attorney-General's Department and that there was 'to be the fullest cooperation between yourself and the Permanent Head'.[91] This was unambiguous and although the army would slowly re-establish its influence over the Security Service, it did this despite the government's wishes and not in accord with them.

As to the headquarters of the Security Service, it was to be in Canberra, as Knowles had insisted. Forde also rejected the state-heavy structure put forward by MacKay and the idea that the records of the Security Service would be duplicated in Sydney and Melbourne. The full direction made by Forde to MacKay is worth reproducing:

> Lest you have misunderstood me on this point I make it quite clear in this letter that the headquarters of Security Service is not to perform merely a nominal role but is to be the nerve centre of your organisation. Its eight principals are to be appointed at once; it is to absorb copies of all records; it is to supervise the work of the State branches of Security Service over whose workings it is to maintain a constant and real control; it is to be at liberty at all times to send any of its experts into the field for the purpose of carrying out particular investigations.[92]

Forde then tells MacKay that he has personally and carefully gone through MacKay's intended structure for the service and amended it. The deputy directors of security in each state were to be Commonwealth officers, not state commissioners of police. Forde explicitly rejects MacKay's attempt, first mooted by Alexander Duncan, to integrate police commissioners into the system thereby effectively passing it over to state police forces to do with as they wished while the Commonwealth picked up the bill. Forde advises MacKay that he, as the relevant minister, will nominate and appoint the eight principals, the names of whom Forde was sending in a separate letter.[93]

Forde then goes on to direct that all files and records taken over or created by the Security Service are to be the property of the Security Service and that, as Minister of the Army, he will direct that Military Intelligence hand over all relevant files to the service. He then orders MacKay to establish links between the Security Service, the FBI and MI5 and that MacKay exchange liaison officers with these organisations.

In the penultimate paragraph, Forde tells MacKay that he wishes to discuss further minor matters with him, one of which is the 'scope of the powers to be delegated to you and the position of the state police in regard to summary prosecutions under certain National Security Regulations'. This is a clear reference to the summary arrests of the individuals associated with the AFM.

This letter to MacKay shows very clearly that Forde was not going to allow him to control the Security Service and that he was centralising it under the direct authority of the Attorney-General. Forde's handling of this matter was excellent. His clearness and determination to bring MacKay and the competing interests to heel, to subordinate them to serving the government of the day as was their duty is something he should be praised for. It was one of the few instances when a Commonwealth minister showed any gumption in dealing with the band of hysterics leading Australia's wartime security intelligence establishment. It also contained the plan for the running of the Security Service that would finally be implemented when ASIO was properly formed. All of it suggests that someone with an excellent grasp of Australia's security intelligence system had briefed Forde. That someone was most likely George Knowles.

All of this culminated on 31 March, when Knowles advised the War Cabinet that while the four individuals arrested in Perth on 9 March should be prosecuted on an ex officio indictment before the High Court, no action should be taken against any of the AFM members in Sydney or Victoria because, 'up to the present no evidence had been received by him implicating the 16 members of the Movement interned in Sydney' in any illegality.[94]

Knowles had struck a major blow against his bureaucratic enemies in the war over who should control the function of collecting intelligence on

Australian citizens. Military Intelligence and its supporters had excluded the Attorney-General's Department from any involvement in the AFM affair in an attempt to damage the new Director-General of the new Security Service. Their rush ensured it turned into a nightmare for the government and a stain on the nation.

However, you cannot keep a bureaucracy down for long and, as we have seen, the army moved against MacKay by withdrawing their personnel and using men like Longfield Lloyd and Robert Wake to further its control over MacKay's service. Eventually, with Evatt back and leading the Attorney-General's Department, the army would face no real resistance, as Evatt's capacity to focus on detail and to maintain interest in the administration of affairs was non-existent.[95]

By April 1943, the government had achieved some success in wrapping up the affair: there were now only three detainees—Stephensen, Cahill and a J. Kirtley—still in detention. Gordon Rice, Valentine Crowley and Edward Masey were restricted to moving to approved towns and also restricted from communicating with any internees, while the rest, including one Harley Matthews, were released and forbidden to meet with one another.[96]

The attitude of the army towards AFM victims remained bloody-minded and vindictive. Even in August 1943, when all of the actions taken were known to be illegal, the Chief of General Staff, Sir John Northcott, wrote to the secretary of the Department of the Army that:

> In my opinion, there is no reason why the Minister for the Army should be called upon to 'exonerate' Matthews or to recommend payment of compensation. Matthews was arrested and detained bona fide on evidence sufficient to satisfy responsible Army officers as to his connection with this movement and, at least up to the time of the transfer of administration to Security Service, no fresh facts were produced which might discredit that evidence . . .
>
> It is not known on what grounds the Attorney-General saw fit to order his release. But even if it could be shown now that, in the light of more recent and more complete information, the evidence against Matthews had no substance whatsoever and that a grave miscarriage of justice had occurred, it is still considered 'exoneration' and compensation would come more appropriately from the Attorney-General, who

discovered the fresh evidence and ordered his release, than from the Minister for the Army.[97]

This letter is proof of the arrogance of the General Staff in assuming that because a 'responsible Army officer' regarded evidence as sufficient to imprison a civilian, that was to be unquestioned. Northcott shows himself to be a small-minded, vindictive, barrack-room lawyer. This attitude also provides proof that the mindless way in which the General Staff ensured that Military Intelligence could freely victimise Father Ugo Modotti, the Jehovah's Witnesses and now members of Australia First, came right from the top. Northcott and the Australian Army are exposed as being utterly unfit to have any role in the management of Australia's civil security intelligence.

There was one thing that the government and the generals did agree on, and that was not paying compensation to those Australians who had suffered at the hands of the authorities. The case of Harley Matthews and his claim to compensation is worth looking at in this regard.

Matthews, an alleged AFM member, was arrested in the early hours of 10 March 1942 when police and Military Intelligence personnel entered and searched his home at Riverside Vineyard, Moorebank, New South Wales.[98] After stealing his documents and books, the police publicly humiliated Matthews by marching him through the streets in front of his neighbours before taking him to Liverpool Police Station and, from there, into internment.[99] Matthews was a returned soldier who had served his country by joining the 1st AIF on 4 April 1914, landed at Gallipoli on 25 April 1915, where he earned a mention in despatches, and served until 1918, when he was discharged as medically unfit.

After his arrest, he was released with restrictions on 12 September 1942, on the orders of the Attorney-General. This was far too late. He had been publicly humiliated as a traitor, both in parliament and in the press. Because of his internment, he lost his crop of grapes, which he believed sufficient to make 1200 gallons of wine.[100] He lost all of his stored wine and all of his vats and casks through neglect. Once released it was too late for him to prune and plough and, as he could not pay his mortgage, the Rural Bank took over his vineyard and put in a manager with no experience of vineyards. Matthews lost his business.[101]

Knowles informed the Department of the Army on 5 August that, 'as soon as the case of Mr Matthews came before him, the Attorney-General thought the case was not one for detention, and Mr Matthews was immediately released'. However, as Knowles passed on:

If compensation were awarded in this case, it would be a dangerous precedent and would, in the opinion of the Attorney-General, lead to the Commonwealth being liable to pay compensation in many hundreds of cases.

The Attorney-General cannot approve any payment in this case unless Cabinet approves. He thinks, however, that, later on, it may be wise to set up a War Claims Tribunal, but that it would be wise to do so now.[102]

This is the frankest admission by officials of the Australian government that hundreds of Australian citizens had had their reputations destroyed and, to put it in the legalese of the bureaucracy, their property and liberty subject to severe trespass to the person, trespass to chattels and trespass to their land at the hands of their own government.[103] In plain English, what was being admitted is that the Australian government illegally arrested Australian citizens and residents, destroyed their reputations by labelling them disloyal traitors and then allowed their property to be stolen or destroyed by others and the sole objective of the government was to ensure it never paid one penny of compensation to any of the victims, no matter how deserving.

Clyne found that in the case of Matthews, he should never have been detained and he awarded him the paltry sum of £700; however, this was over £200 higher than any other victim received.[104]

Clyne was scathing in his judgment of Military Intelligence in their treatment of Matthews, a man who, Clyne underlined, 'served with some distinction in the last war', and who Clyne believed remained 'a loyal subject of the King'. In Clyne's opinion, outlined in his report, Military Intelligence had 'committed a major blunder in procuring his [Matthews] arrest and recommending his detention'.[105]

As far as Northcott and the rest of the Australian General Staff were concerned, Matthews had deserved everything done to him.

Unfortunately for individuals like Matthews, the regime governing Australia between 1942 and 1946 ensured that none of the victims of the unbridled bigotry of Military Intelligence would get anything resembling adequate compensation. This was guaranteed by Evatt's appointment of none other than Justice William Ballantyne Simpson, the ex-Director-General Security and Evatt's old school chum, as the Commissioner to Make Recommendations in the Cases of Civilian Internees.[106] A better example of how to manage procedure in your own interests is hard to find, almost as hard as it was for Australia's security intelligence organisations to find a Soviet spy before 1949.

CHAPTER 15

RUSSIA'S INTELLIGENCE SERVICES AND THEIR WORK

When Alexander Zuzenko returned to Australia on 11 July 1922 using the alias of Norwegian Toni Tollagsen Tjorn, he found the CP-A completely ineffective and torn asunder by the personal and doctrinal disputes that had raged in the aftermath of the successful Bolshevik coup d'état of October 1917. When he left again on 22 September 1922, he had instilled some discipline that would serve the CP-A well in the near future. It would also help establish the CP-A's clandestine cell structure that would later enable the penetration of Australia's scientific, educational and governmental organisations. There can be no doubt that the foundations for the later successes of the Russian intelligence services (RIS) in Australia were laid down by Zuzenko between 1920 and 1922.

The extent of the CP-A's initial clandestine activity is not well documented, simply because it was clandestine, but also because Western security intelligence authorities, including Australia's, had not sufficient experience of how these organisations worked. SIGINT did, however, identify the work of the Second Comintern Conference of 1920, the one attended by Zuzenko, and the clandestine work authorised after it by Lenin. Britain, which initiated the Western intelligence attack on Bolshevik Russia, had a little luck with all of this in winning the services of an early Russian defector. Ernst Fetterlein, who had previously been a successful Tsarist cryptanalyst, led the Government Code and Cypher School's (GC&CS) SIGINT attack on the Soviet Union's diplomatic ciphers, which proved to be very susceptible compared with the unbreakable Tsarist diplomatic ciphers.[1]

Fetterlein made the major breakthrough in security intelligence against the Soviets during the Anglo–Soviet trade negotiations that began in London in May 1920. The information gleaned from this attack went beyond the Soviet's policy and attitudes towards Britain and the trade agreement itself into the clandestine work of the trade delegation in funding and developing secret networks within the Communist Party of Great Britain (CPGB).[2] Among this clandestine activity was the morbid operation to smuggle the Tsar's jewels into Britain for sale on the black market in London.[3]

The result of these SIGINT insights was that David Lloyd George successfully negotiated a trade agreement beneficial to Britain on 16 March 1921 secure in the knowledge that the Soviets were desperate to accomplish this outcome and, unlike his Foreign Secretary, Lord Curzon, he did not see any prospect of the stolen Tsarist jewels financing revolution in Britain.[4]

Despite Lloyd George's optimism and GC&CS's SIGINT, Britain's counter-intelligence authorities missed the clandestine work of the RIS's first London head of station, Nikolai Klimentovich Klishko, a communist activist who had previously been expelled from Britain for spying in 1919. Klishko returned to Britain as an interpreter on the trade delegation in 1920 and, under this cover, successfully established the spy ring headed by William Norman Ewer, codenamed TRILBY, the foreign editor of the *Daily Herald*.[5]

The methodology, or tradecraft, of the Bolshevik intelligence apparatus in penetrating foreign countries is clearly shown in the way Klishko was used to establish the TRILBY spy ring in Britain in 1920. Like Zuzenko, Klishko had lived in the United Kingdom for a time and so knew his way around the target country and, importantly, was known to communists there. The fact that Klishko had been deported from Britain was of no importance as long as he could gain entry and establish clandestine contact with trusted communist activists, who in this case included Ewer.[6]

The use of Klishko for such a mission provides an insight into early NKGB operations and it reflected the experience of Zuzenko in Australia, differing only in that Klishko's return to Britain under diplomatic cover was easy compared to Zuzenko's need to create a false identity.

Klishko was also lucky in that the British counterintelligence agencies lost him on more than one occasion. He was able to establish contact with the CP-GB and build the spy ring led by Ewer.[7] Both Ewer and his wife had been members of the London West Central Branch of the CP-GB, and both were rather extreme in their view of violent revolution as the only path to the workers' paradise.

The TRILBY network was well placed to undertake intelligence operations, as Ewer was not just the editor of the *Daily Herald* but also the agent of the Federated Press of America and could use his network of reporters to cover intelligence activity.

The result was that the TRILBY organisation was running intelligence operations in France and Belgium, among other places. In France, Ewer was passing $US1000 per month to George Slocombe, his *Daily Herald* reporter in Paris, to pay for documents being sold by someone inside the French Foreign Ministry. In Belgium, Rajani Palme Dutt, a Swedish-Indian surgeon, another reporter, was obtaining documents from someone within the Belgian Foreign Ministry in Brussels. The TRILBY network even extended to contacts with Indian and Japanese communists.[8]

Unfortunately for the Soviet Union, the tradecraft of the TRILBY organisation was extraordinarily amateurish. On 21 November 1924, Ewer placed an advertisement in the *Daily Herald* under the heading 'Secret Service' which informed interested readers that a 'Labour Group' was seeking 'information and details from anyone who has ever had any association with . . . any Secret Service department or operation'.[9] Of course, the only response Ewer got was from an MI5 agent called 'D'.[10]

At a meeting on 13 January 1925 at the Vodega Wine House in Bedford Street, Strand, Agent D met the less than mysterious QX, William Ewer himself, and arranged to work for the Labour Group. At a later meeting D passed over a military intelligence report, but Ewer was suspicious and dropped D very soon afterwards.[11] This event led to Sir Basil Thomson's counterespionage organisation and MI5 identifying the TRILBY organisation and its contact with Klishko and the Soviet Trade Delegation.

Between its creation sometime in 1920 and its demise in 1927, the TRILBY network penetrated the French Foreign Ministry, the Belgian Foreign Ministry and Scotland Yard's Special Branch. The penetration of the Belgian and French foreign ministries appears to have been managed respectively by Palme Dutt and George Slocombe. The value of the French material is

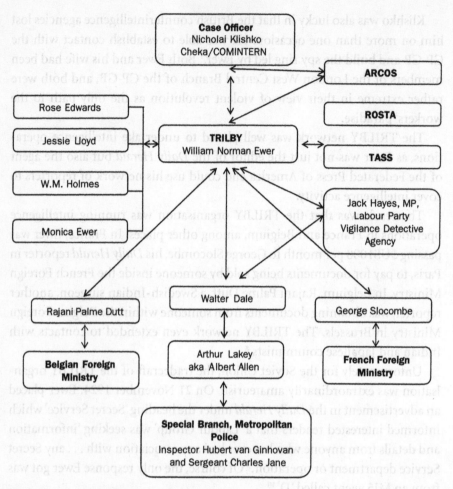

Figure 15.1: The TRILBY network, 1927

indicated by the monthly payment of $US1000 from Ewer to Slocombe, most likely for the payment of bribes to the source.

In Britain, the penetration of Scotland Yard's Special Branch was facilitated by Jack Hayes, an ex-policeman and the General Secretary of the National Union of Police and Prison Officers. He was also the owner of the Vigilance Detective Agency of Clapham Common where Joseph Paul, the father of Rose Edwards, Ewers' personal typist, also worked.[12]

The use of newly returned Bolsheviks such as Klishko and Zuzenko as agents in the countries where they had lived as political refugees would prove to be a short-term answer only. Co-opting local communists and their families into clandestine work would prove to be a much more effective way of establishing long-lived intelligence networks. Both were relatively easy ways of establishing intelligence collection networks, but neither would survive long if the counterespionage capabilities of the target country were even moderately effective.

The rather ill-thought-out advertisement that Ewer had placed in his own paper on 21 November 1924 led to the exposure of the entire TRILBY network and also revealed the involvement of the Soviet All-Russian Cooperative Society (ARCOS), the State News Agency, Rossiyskoye telegrafnoye agentstvo (ROSTA) and TASS News Agency. The outcome was that the British government raided the ARCOS offices and severed diplomatic relations with the Soviet Union.

For the Soviets, the positive side was that on 26 May 1928 Prime Minister Stanley Baldwin justified the ARCOS raid to the House of Commons by reading aloud four Soviet messages deciphered by GC&CS. The Soviets promptly adopted the unbreakable one-time pad system, where a page of a cipher book is only used to encrypt one message and then destroyed. This prevents a hostile SIGINT service from collecting sufficient amounts of the codes used to enable them to use a statistical brute force attack to break the code.

A subsequent referral by William Joynson-Hicks, the Home Secretary, and Austen Chamberlain, the Foreign Secretary, in the same debate to other intercepted Soviet messages is described in MI5's official history as 'an orgy of governmental indiscretion about secret intelligence for which there is no parallel in modern parliamentary history'.[13]

The importance of the TRILBY network's story to Australia is that the tradecraft uncovered in Britain, the use of police officers or ex-police officers, appears to be identical to that used in Australia by Zuzenko and, later, by the CP-A and NKGB. The evidence suggests Zuzenko planted the seeds of future success, even if Australia's communist organisation soon sundered after his departure.

The situation faced by communist activists in Australia was similar to that faced by their British counterparts, although the level of counterespionage expertise of the CIB and Military Intelligence was rudimentary to non-existent. As a result, the Australian archives are reasonably well provided with detailed information on the overt activities of the CP-A; meetings, publications, individuals and some aspects of the organisation are well documented.

But there is nothing about communist clandestine activity, although there is no doubt that clandestine operations on behalf of the RIS were being carried out.

A substantial move on the part of the RIS, this time the NKGB, was the arrival in Australia of TASS representative Vladimir Mikheev on 10 September 1942.[14] Mikheev was a representative of the London TASS News Agency, but moved to Australia to report from Sydney.[15] The establishment of the TASS Agency in Sydney provided the NKGB with a faster communications channel than would previously have been possible using strictly clandestine means, especially if operated under 'Moscow Rules', the operational rules used to avoid detection in a very dangerous environment.[16] It is likely that the arrival of a TASS representative in Sydney was part of an attempt to open an attack on Western Allied military and political intentions and activities.

The timing of this activity fits. From 22 June 1941 the Soviet Union was at war with Germany, which would have focused RIS intelligence interest towards Europe, the Mediterranean and the United States. With the Japanese decision to advance south against Britain, the United States and the Netherlands East Indies, the new Pacific and Asian theatre could not have failed to draw the RIS's gaze, as it posed a number of problems for Moscow.

The first of these problems was the diversion of US and British forces away from Europe, something Stalin and his regime were paranoid about, especially with the Germans having suffered no major reverses as yet. At the end of 1941, victory at Stalingrad was more than a year away and the Japanese had only recently made up their minds to go south, not north. Keeping an eye on the Allies in the Pacific now became a Russian priority.

Russia also needed to promote Soviet ambitions in Asia. US interest in China was a potential flashpoint between Moscow and Washington and, by mid- to late 1942, aggressive US action at Midway and, most importantly, Guadalcanal had stunned the Japanese and could not have failed to worry the Soviet government. The scene was now set for the possibility of swift US advances in the Pacific, leading to a direct US intrusion into Far Eastern areas of direct interest to the Soviet Union. There can be little doubt that slowing the US advance in the Pacific would have been attractive to Moscow. This objective could be achieved by stealing secrets in the United States, Canada, Britain and Australia and then feeding them to the Japanese.

Given the strategic situation in late 1941 and early 1942, the reactivation and re-tasking of existing agents towards military activity and the placement of faster communications via a TASS agency in Sydney would have taken until the middle of 1942 to arrange. The arrival of Mikheev in September 1942 fits such a scheme well.

Despite the desperate situation of the Soviet Union, the RIS also had its problems, one of which was that the GRU and NKGB were not as friendly as their codenames, NEIGHBOURS and NEAR NEIGHBOURS, would suggest. Like bureaucracies all over the world that work in the same field, they were already highly competitive but with the ascension of Lavrentiy Pavlovich Beria to the NKGB Main Directorate of State Security in September 1938, some 332 senior NKGB personnel and 275 of the 450 NKGB personnel overseas were purged. Of these, most were shot or imprisoned in the Gulag.[17] Beria then replaced these officials with his own men, one of whom was Vladimir Mikhaylovich Petrov, the Resident who would defect in Australia. This action embedded Beria in the position of head of the NKGB by destroying most of its capability overseas, but not all of it. It also allowed the recruitment of some very effective new blood, such as General Pavel Mikhailovich Fitin, codenamed VIKTOR, who would reorganise and lead the First Directorate, foreign, to become one of the most effective in the RIS.

At the same time, Beria, with Stalin's approval, liquidated the GRU leadership and most of their operatives overseas, leaving—according to the acting chief of the Western departments of the GRU—'the Red Army essentially without an intelligence arm'.[18] The GRU now came under Beria as part of a consolidated RIS. Beria next purged the Foreign Affairs Commissariat, thus freeing Stalin from the need to listen to experts.[19] All of this left Beria as the most powerful security and intelligence official in the Soviet Union.

There can be little doubt that an illegal NKGB or GRU residency was operational in Australia from the late 1920s and that it was little affected by the events of 1938–39 in Moscow and in RIS residencies around the world. Like many of the illegal networks, it simply continued operating and waiting until contact was re-established by Moscow Centre, which, in time, it was.[20] In the interim, the RIS illegal residency in Australia continued its work in directing the efforts of the CP-A towards establishing clandestine networks for future operations. There can be no doubt that it worked alongside the CP-A to identify young and promising communists, ensuring their membership of the CP-A was never compromised.

This was a sensitive area because, as a communist party, the CP-A was considered by the Politburo in Moscow to be a superior organ to both the NKGB and the GRU. This meant that the RIS residents had to tread carefully when interfering in the CP-A's internal affairs. Thus, directing the CP-A to quarantine one of its members away from open involvement in the CP-A and towards clandestine work for the RIS could be and often was successfully challenged by a local communist party. Despite this, the CP-A understood that part of its role in the great revolution was to provide the organs of the Soviet state with suitable clandestine workers who were then enrolled into the secret wing of the CP-A. Once inside the secret wing, they could be observed, checked and disciplined before being trained to undertake work on behalf of the CP-A itself, the NKGB or the GRU.

This may have been the process through which Franca Yakil'nilna Mitynen, codenamed SALLY, a notable Australian GRU operative, was recruited, trained and despatched to the wartime United States to undertake secret illegal operations. Mitynen was not an NKGB agent. It appears from the evidence available that Mitynen was being run as a deep cover illegal by the Soviet Naval GRU (N-GRU), whose amateurish efforts to infiltrate her into the United States seem, at first glance, to have utilised rather poor tradecraft.

However, the N-GRU were not completely amateurish as they were already running Jack Fahy, codename MAXWELL, the principal intelligence officer of the US Board of Economic Warfare, and Eugene Franklin Coleman, codenamed CARTER, at the Radio Corporation of America in Princeton, New Jersey.[21] Coleman ran a network similar to that run by Julius and Ethel Rosenberg, two United States citizens who the United States executed for espionage in 1953, who both operated in New Jersey where Julius worked for the United States Army Signal Corps engineering laboratories. Unlike the Rosenbergs, who were NKGB assets, Coleman was an N-GRU asset providing intelligence on radar-assisted bombsights and navigation.[22] So, although the N-GRU's tradecraft may have been poor and their communications security made even worse through the sending of very long messages, their efforts in penetrating high-value US targets appear to have been fairly successful.

Franca Mitynen was born in Sydney on 31 January 1914, the daughter of Russian émigré parents, James and Julie Mitynen.[23] The Mitynens had arrived in Australia on the *Kumano Maru* in May 1912 with their young son, Victor.[24] Their daughters Franca and Helene (Lena) were born in Sydney, making them Australians.[25] Victor developed the highest public profile as a cricketer in his schooldays and continued to play, until he and his wife Coral migrated to Russia with a delegation from the Friends of the Soviet Union on 8 March 1932. Both Franca and Lena were also noted in the newspapers for their sporting prowess, being listed as winners of events at the Parramatta Intermediate High School sports day.[26]

Franca's father, James, appears to have been employed as a fitter by NSW Railways at the Eveleigh workshop in 1918.[27] It also appears that despite his strong communist sympathies, James was willing to risk being a bit of a capitalist and in 1923, in association with a Mr L. Connolly, applied for a patent for an adjustable window hinge. There are no files suggesting they were successful.[28]

By March of 1926, James had returned to promoting socialism and was now secretary of the Sydney Branch of the Australasian Association for Economic Advancement of the USSR.[29] Franca's family appear to have been strong advocates of Russian socialism and her father had previously been fined for selling copies of *The Knowledge*, most likely Peter Simonoff's *Znanie I edinenie (Knowledge and Unity)*.[30] James appears to have inculcated his revolutionary fervour in his wife and children as, Franca aside, they all had returned to Russia by the early to mid-1930s.

As for Franca, from her late adolescence the future N-GRU agent seems to have adopted the characteristic low profile of the clandestine communist agent. Other than the press report about her sporting prowess at age fourteen, there is no further mention of her. She does not appear in the list of passengers departing Australia with her parents and sister on the *Kamo Maru* on 3 March 1934.[31] There is also no record of her marriage or death in any state or territory of Australia or of her ever departing Australia. The only mention of her after 1928 is on the outside of an empty folder, a local non-registry file held by ASIO, that contains information on the Friends of the Soviet Union delegation that her brother and sister-in-law accompanied to Europe in 1932 and nothing at all about her.[32]

The importance of Franca Mitynen, described as 'the Australian Woman', is that her story is hard evidence that dedicated members of the CP-A were connected to and recruited into the RIS between the wars. The fact that Mitynen was being illegally inserted into the United States in late 1942 means that she had to have been recruited, trained and qualified to undertake the mission well before 1942. Indeed, in a message sent from Moscow to

Washington on 10 June 1943, Captain I.A. Egorichev, the Washington N-GRU Resident, is rebuked by his superior in Moscow, Captain First Rank M.A. Vorontsov, for taking too long to insert Mitynen. Egorichev had been given eight months to arrange for Mitynen's reception in the United States. This puts the start date for this operation sometime in early November 1942.[33]

Mitynen's story is also important because it demonstrates the way in which the RIS operated through differing channels, which included the NKGB, the Red Army's GRU and the N-GRU working as independent agencies.

The N-GRU appears in late 1942 to have been the junior member of the RIS, and the message traffic concerning Mitynen clearly shows that it depended on the NKGB and the GRU for advice on conditions in the United States. The information for establishing Mitynen's legend, her cover identity in the United States, involved getting help from the NEIGHBOURS on how American citizens were identified. This led to discussions on birth certificates, drivers' licences and identity cards. The fact that the N-GRU's Moscow Centre was keen to have its Washington station collect advanced information on US governmental vetting procedures, including the need for 'three referees and the completion of a detailed questionnaire' detailing places of residence and personal particulars over a period of time, clearly demonstrates that Mitynen was being targeted at a US government department.[34]

The legend created for Mitynen drew on an identity from Seattle in Washington State. The identity was of someone who would have attended Ballard High School between the years 1926 and 1932, the period most suitable for Mitynen. Seattle was certainly the location of one of Mitynen's covernames and maybe even the covername Edna Margaret Patterson, as Patterson was a well-established name in Seattle at the time. In fact, there was a Dick and Edna Patterson living at 7119 34th Avenue, Seattle, an address in the catchment for Ballard High School. In the 1940 US census, the Pattersons had only one child, a daughter called Gay.[35] Gay's birth date was 1915, a year after that of Franca Mitynen.[36] If the Patterson's had lost a baby girl in 1914, then her name would be highly suitable for Mitynen. Although this is impossible to prove, the likelihood is that, following tradition, the Patterson's first daughter may have been named Edna after her mother and, following her early death, the name would understandably not have been used for Gay in 1915.

The N-GRU would have sent a ghoul to look for a covername in Seattle's public cemeteries. A ghoul was an operative working from the cover of a diplomatic mission or Soviet establishment whose job it was to search cemeteries for the names of dead babies and obtain their birth certificates, which were then used to construct a false identity. The ghoul would have sought the name of a female baby or infant with a birthdate close to that of Mitynen. This would enable them to obtain a real birth certificate with no complicating personal history attached to it for use in building the agent's legend, the falsified life history the agent would use. The choice of Seattle for this activity fits because it was a busy port frequently visited by Soviet vessels from which a search of the cemeteries could be conducted by the N-GRU without calling on the NEIGHBOURS, and it was remote from New York, where Mitynen would be operating as Edna Margaret Patterson.[37]

In addition to arranging Mitynen's arrival in the United States, Egorichev, the N-GRU Resident in Washington, had to provide advice on how Mitynen needed to dress and groom herself: everything from her stockings to her underwear, her toiletries, the grooming of her hair and quality of her clothes. It would even include buying American shoes for her, something which required Moscow to send her shoe size to Washington and for US dollars to be expended buying the shoes. All of this had to be arranged and coordinated, and it was.[38]

On 10 June 1943, Mitynen departed Moscow for the United States. Now Egorichev had to organise Mitynen's actual arrival and landing place. His choice was San Francisco because it was a big city close to Seattle, but easier to disappear in than somewhere like Portland or Seattle.[39] Mitynen was provided with US$900 by Moscow, and Vorontsov demanded to be assured that Egorichev changed this for used local currency to avoid the serial numbers of the Moscow-issued notes being tracked by the FBI. Vorontsov was also concerned to ensure that Egorichev had completed assembling the equipment that Mitynen needed for her clandestine work.[40] The N-GRU were not completely devoid of tradecraft.

Mitynen disembarked the *Sevastopol* in San Francisco on 13 August 1943, the same day as Ivan Alexeevich Sokolov, her contact in the United States, who was to operate under the cover of a clerk in the Soviet Naval Attaché's office in Washington, arrived elsewhere in the United States. Sokolov had been introduced to Mitynen in Moscow so she could recognise him when they made contact in the United States. It appears Sokolov's job was to escort Mitynen to a meeting with an agent codenamed JOHN somewhere on 8th

Avenue, New York.[41] On 14 August, Egorichev was able to signal Moscow that Mitynen had arrived and was feeling well and that she was to temporarily come under the control of someone else, presumably Sokolov or Grigorji Staphanovich Pasko, codenamed JIM, secretary to the Soviet Naval Attaché in Washington, on 15 August.[42] Pasko stayed with Mitynen until 9 September, presumably the day he and Sokolov handed her over to the clandestine cell run by JOHN in New York.[43]

During the course of the operation, N-GRU sent so many messages concerning her infiltration into the United States that it was completely compromised. All the N-GRU officers running this operation and Mitynen were subsequently compromised by VENONA. Mitynen—'the Australian Woman'—was one of the first RIS agents identified by the US Army's

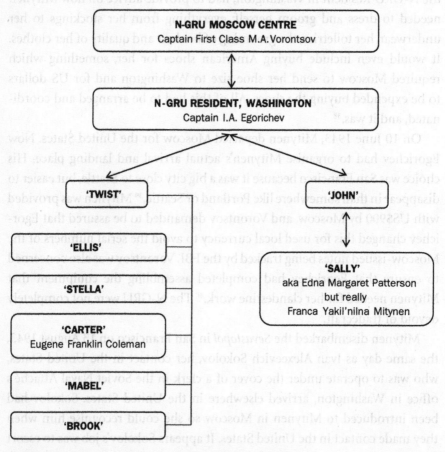

Figure 15.2: The N-GRU network, New York, 1943

SIGINT organisation at Arlington Hall when the attack on Soviet ciphers in 1943/44 was finally launched. Although there is no evidence provided, the VENONA team at the US National Security Agency later identified SALLY, most likely on the basis of information provided via the FBI who, by the mid-1950s, had identified SALLY as Edna Margaret Patterson and were now closing in on her. This most likely explains her successful exfiltration in 1956, presumably to a well-earned retirement in the Soviet Union. Other than CARTER, Eugene Franklin Coleman, none of the other clandestine agents run by TWIST or JOHN were ever publicly identified and neither were TWIST or JOHN.

... ...

Given the role SIGINT played in the uncovering of SALLY, this is perhaps a good point to explain something of what VENONA actually was. VENONA is the covername assigned to a SIGINT operation that attacked the Soviet Union's diplomatic cipher, and by association the RIS's ciphers. VENONA began from a very small bit of cleaning up when a young schoolteacher, Gene Grabeel, who had just joined the Signals Intelligence Service (SIS) at Arlington Hall was given the job of sorting out and collating all of the Soviet diplomatic raw take, the actual intercept forms filled in by the intercepting operators, into date–time order and then into categories of cipher type, possible call signs and transmission type.[44] This sort of work is extremely mundane and exhausting, but it forms the first step in breaking a code. Grabeel did a very good job.

By November 1943, Grabeel had made sufficient progress to enable more personnel to be assigned to the attack and allow Lieutenant Richard Hallock and Frank Lewis to get into the Soviet diplomatic cipher.[45] In November of the following year, the cryptologists Cecil Phillips, Genevieve Feinstein and Lucille Campbell finally broke into elements of the NKGB cipher. As the war wound down and more resources could be committed, one of the leading SIS cryptanalysts and linguists, Meredith Gardner, a man who had learned Japanese in three months, joined VENONA and provided the insights that were instrumental in breaking the underlying Soviet codes.[46] It was the product of this work, and of the attack on Comintern ciphers (codenamed MASK) by Britain's GC&CS, the British VENONA, that now began the erosion of the security of the RIS's signals traffic.

The importance of VENONA cannot be overstated, and neither can Gardner's contribution to it. He recognised that the VENONA decrypts were essential if the United States was to combat RIS espionage operations within its government and other institutions. It was his Special Report, No. 1, written for the senior officers of the Army Security Agency detailing what VENONA had already uncovered and discussing what it could potentially uncover, that led to the US Army opening up communications with the FBI. This was previously unheard of, and the SIGINT provided to the FBI allowed it to focus its HUMINT operations more effectively.[47] This cooperation enabled the FBI to identify SALLY as Edna Patterson.

The United States and Britain were now reading the most secret and most important of the Soviet Union's secrets, but slowly. The major error made in most writing about VENONA, or SIGINT for that matter, is that the code is broken, and all is beheld. That is not the case. Progress is slow as it relies heavily on other intelligence sources and new insights into the cryptology under attack. It is the slowness of this process and the danger that disclosure will lead to a complete change in the target's crypto systems that imposes the need for the severe security measures attached to all SIGINT. That meant that until Australia had an effective security intelligence organisation to protect SIGINT nothing of VENONA could be disclosed to Australian authorities.

What were the fatal flaws in the Soviet Union's code system? Well, first and foremost was the over confidence of the Soviet cryptologists and communicators in their own cleverness, a fault shared by their professional compatriots around the world. The second flaw was, as always, the humans who actually operate the system. The mistakes and laziness of these humans is what provides SIGINT organisations with their 'cribs', insights caused by operator errors in the sending of encoded messages. In the case of VENONA the crib was truly stupendous.

The cause of the crib was the German invasion of the Soviet Union in 1941. This event took the Soviet leadership—well, Stalin and his henchmen—completely by surprise and, as a result, the Soviet defence system was not ready for the attack. This included the small printing works that produced the one-time pads Soviet diplomats and the RIS used for coded communications. The printing works was already working at near full capacity when the war demanded an instant and massive increase in production of the pads. As a result—and facing Stalin's expectations of meeting demand targets or

246

else—the managers did what anyone in their position would have done: they simply reprinted copies of the same one-time pads and hoped no one would notice. Unfortunately for the Soviet Union, Richard Hallock and Frank Lewis noticed and the rest is history.

… … …

The story of Mitynen's infiltration into the United States clearly demonstrates the difficulties faced by an intelligence agency in running an illegal agent outside of diplomatic cover. From beginning to end, it took the N-GRU ten months to carry out the operation and this did not include preparing Mitynen or developing her legend. It also provides a very good example of how many people were involved in getting just one illegal into place. The time and resources required provides perspective on why illegal agents are so highly prized and why secrecy is so important.

At the time Mitynen was arriving in the United States, a signal was sent from the NKGB in Moscow on 21 August 1943 to the Soviet Legation in Canberra. This signal from VIKTOR, Lieutenant General P.M. Fitin at Moscow Centre, to EFIM, the NKGB Resident Semen Ivanovich Makarov, was issued on 16 June 1971, well after the events it described. It detailed the contact arrangements for an agent, MARAROVICH to be known in future as UNC44, with another agent in Sydney.[48] UNC44 came highly recommended, having done good work for 'another FLOOR', most likely the secret division of the NKGB.[49] The contact arrangements were for the agent, most likely Makarov, to approach UNC44 and tell him 'I knew Bobrov who studied at the Moscow Textile Institute . . '. The reply from UNC44 was to be 'I have a brother but he [two groups not recovered] did not study at the Textile Institute'. After this was given, the contact was to give UNC44 his covername.[50]

On the same day the Soviet Legation in Canberra also received a circular signal sent by Moscow Centre to residencies around the world with instructions for the setting up of illegal residencies. This signal emphasised the importance of selecting qualified local agents, referred to as FELLOW-COUNTRYMEN, who were not under suspicion of being communists by the authorities in their countries. As a result, the signal goes on, it was important that illegal residencies be totally independent of local communist organisations and that they should use commercial organisations as fronts that could build relationships into enterprises in the target country. Liaison should be

247

maintained with the FELLOWCOUNTRYMEN, so that they could channel intelligence to the residency via secret channels and provide an effective counterintelligence screen to protect the illegal residency.

In support of this activity, NKGB officers and workers, with the pre-approval of the ambassador or minister, were being encouraged to join sporting, cultural and social groups in the target country.[51] On 12 September, Fitin followed up this signal with another advising NKGB Residents that the dissolution of the Comintern (BIG HOUSE) now meant that FELLOW-COUNTRYMEN were completely off limits to residencies as Moscow wanted the Allies to be assured that the Comintern had indeed been dissolved. In order to ensure this, meetings with FELLOWCOUNTRYMEN were now forbidden unless they were 'special reliable undercover contacts' and, even then, the consent of Moscow Centre had to be obtained first. The rationale for this was that contact with the local FELLOWCOUNTRYMEN placed Moscow in a difficult position vis-a-vis its undertakings on the Comintern and placed NKGB agents at risk.[52]

On 3 December, the message about maintaining rigorous security of NKGB operations—VENONA 232–233—came right from the top, a signal to all Residents and workers from covername PETROV, who is believed to be none other than Beria, Minister of Internal Affairs of the Soviet Union and Generalissimo Stalin's chief enforcer. Beria's main concern was that there was too much talkativeness by the NKGB officers and staff in foreign residencies, which was allowing diplomatic officers, codenamed ENGINEERS in the signals, and non-NKGB personnel to become aware of NKGB operations. Added to this, Beria was unhappy about NKGB personnel not maintaining a strict need-to-know approach in relation to their operational activity.[53] The laxity that Beria was warning residencies about included NKGB personnel divulging their real names to other Soviet personnel, something utterly forbidden in the secret world. This signal would have sent shivers down spines in residencies all around the world.

As Moscow Centre was reorganising its residencies' work in target countries, arrangements were being made for the move of an NKGB asset codenamed PALM, Dr Boris Eliacheff, consul for the French Committee of National Liberation in San Francisco, from the United States to Sydney.[54] Eliacheff had been recruited as an NKGB source in late 1943, most likely as a paid informer, and it seems that Sydney was not his first choice as he wrangled with his NKGB handlers to get an appointment to 'the coast'.[55] Eliacheff was so keen to get to the coast that he asked to be put in touch with Vyshinskij, one of Stalin's senior associates and the deputy commissar for Foreign Affairs.

There is no record of whether Eliacheff ever got in touch with Vyshinskij, but the suspicion is that he did not as he then approached the Soviet Vice-Consul in San Francisco, Grigorij Markovich Khejflts, to write on his behalf to Alexander Efremovich Bogomolov, the Soviet Ambassador to the French Committee in Algiers, where Eliacheff would be arriving in January or February 1944.[56] Despite this toing and froing, on 29 August 1944 Fitin signalled Makarov in Canberra informing him that Eliacheff was arriving in Sydney. Fitin was adamant that Eliacheff be forbidden to become too close to Soviet diplomats in Australia.

The NKGB's new asset seems to have been playing a double game for twice the financial reward, always a risk with assets who are in it for the money. Fitin informed Makarov that the French intelligence service thought Eliacheff worked for them, but he actually worked for the NKGB. The truth though, and Eliacheff's laziness tends to support this, is that he was taking the payments from both sides and his salary as consul and doing just enough to keep the cash flowing. It took Eliacheff until November 1944 to finally arrive in Australia.[57] The contact procedure for Makarov and Eliacheff laid down by Fitin was that a week after his arrival in Sydney, Eliacheff would begin going out for a walk every Monday and Wednesday at 11 a.m. This walk would involve a stroll around the Governor Arthur Phillip statue in the Botanic Gardens for ten minutes.[58] He would carry in his hands a pale blue book in Russian, *Diplomatic Commentaries* by Philip Kudzirov, and this would mark him out for Makarov. The contact phrase for Makarov was 'Excuse me, I think you lived in Malyi Zlatoustinskij Pereulok'? The reply from Eliacheff was 'Quite right, evidently you know Aleksandr Aleksandrovich?' Once this contact had been established, Makarov was to signal Fitin immediately.[59]

The first inkling of Eliacheff's work for the NKGB in the VENONA signals came on 1 March 1945 when he passed a report on the UN's Relief and Rehabilitation Conference at Lapstone, New South Wales, during which Evatt lectured the assembled delegates on their duty to spend money in Asia. In his subsequent report to Fitin, Makarov labelled Evatt's behaviour as 'juvenile lecturing', demanding that other nations spend their money in Asia while not saying a word about what Australia was going to do.[60]

On 19 March, Makarov forwarded another report obtained from Eliacheff. This report detailed discussions between Eliacheff and Abbot Low Moffat of the US State Department's Division of South Eastern Affairs. Makarov does not appear to be too impressed, as he described the material to Fitin as being 'general chat'.[61] On 23 May, Makarov passed on another of Eliacheff's reports. This time the information related to the views of Archbishop Panico, the Apostolic Delegate of the Vatican in Australia.[62] Even at this distance in time, it is almost possible to hear both Makarov and Fitin groan as they read this dross.

Now Eliacheff began to really irritate his NKGB handlers by asking that they supply him with a technical encyclopaedia as a gift. In June 1945, Fitin advised Makarov that he believed that Eliacheff's request for the encyclo-paedia was an attempt to 'legalise his relations with us', to effectively have something to hold over the NKGB, most likely for the benefit of a French intelligence handler.[63] Fitin ordered Makarov not to agree to this and not to give Eliacheff any presents whatsoever. Later, Eliacheff requested permission via Makarov to visit the Soviet Union. Fitin replied in September 1945 by ordering Makarov to inform Eliacheff that 'we have not the slightest inten-tion of authorising PALM's entry into the USSR'.[64] By 19 September, Moscow Centre's patience with Eliacheff was exhausted. Fitin informed Makarov that Eliacheff's personality was now understood and that the information he was passing was of no interest and unsatisfying. Makarov was to cut back contact with Eliacheff to once every month or two.

The last report containing intelligence from Eliacheff was passed by Makarov to Fitin on 16 November 1945 and concerned low-level information on the problems Australia had encountered in deporting 140 Indonesians back into the hands of the authorities in the Netherlands East Indies. This had led to some ructions in the relationships with Britain, as most of these men had served the Allied cause working for MacArthur's Allied Intelligence Bureau. The British knew that the returning Indonesians would be harshly treated by the Dutch authorities in the Netherland East Indies, but Australia did not care.[65] Keeping Australia white was still more important, it would seem.

The problems with Eliacheff came to a head on 9 March 1946 when Makarov passed to Fitin the news that Eliacheff was being sent back to Paris by the French. Makarov believed that Eliacheff was attempting to escape from the clutches of the NKGB. This was not the bad news, however. The bad news was that Eliacheff's wife turned out to be Jeanne Germaine Chauby, a professional French intelligence operative who had been running a French intelligence network for several years.[66] Four days later, on 13 March, Fitin signalled Makarov ordering the termination of all contact with Eliacheff and the institution of special measures to protect Walter Seddon Clayton, codenamed KLOD, a New Zealander who ran the CP-A's clandestine and counterintelligence operations in Australia.[67] The question now was whether the double agent Eliacheff had betrayed his NKGB masters and whether the security of Clayton's organisation had been compromised.

The NKGB were right to be worried about the safety of Clayton's network because it had been built up over years and had attracted many of the impatient young smart set—intellectuals, academics and officials—to its ranks and from there, into clandestine work and treason. By 1946, like their FELLOW-COUNTRYMEN in Britain, Canada and the United States, Clayton's amateur spies had penetrated to the heart of their country's establishment and had been doing damage since around 1943.

CHAPTER 16

THE KLOD ORGANISATION—WALTER CLAYTON AND THE CP-A

W alter Seddon (Wally) Clayton was born in Ashburton, New Zealand, on 24 March 1906 to Thomas and Alice Clayton and was schooled at Opawa Primary School and Christ's College, both in Christchurch.[1] His family appears to have been prosperous, his father being a company manager.[2] Clayton began his working life as a shop assistant in sports stores in Christchurch until he left for Australia in 1931. It appears that he settled in Victoria and resided there from 1931 until 1939, when he moved to Sydney.[3] From police reporting it appears he was an overt member of the CP-A, holding the position of secretary of No. 2 Branch, and that he was employed as a full-time CP-A organiser.[4]

Within the CP-A Wally Clayton was seen as committed and humourless, something that many members found intimidating. However, he was more complex than he appeared. The reason for Clayton moving to Australia is unknown. It may have been that he was following the orders of the Comintern or even the NKGB, but it also could have been because he was in love with a singer, Hilda Mary Lane.

Hilda Lane was no stranger to socialism or communism, being the niece of William Lane, of the New Australia Colony in Paraguay. Hilda had been born in Paraguay in 1906, so was the product of the New Australia Movement's

252

utopian socialist experiment in that country. When the experiment imploded, the Lane family moved to New Zealand and it is there that Hilda and Walter may have met through their involvement in socialist or communist groups.[5] Hilda finally married Wally on 24 June 1931 at the Registrar's Office in Prahran, Victoria.

Somewhat oddly, for a man reputed to be a humourless fanatic, in 1931–32 Clayton wrote a musical comedy called *The Southern Star* set on a cattle station, most likely for Hilda to sing in.[6] It was never produced. Clayton then wrote a second play, a drama, called *The Beachcomber*, which he also registered for copyright.[7] It was not produced either. Wally Clayton remained with the CP-A.

In early 1939, Clayton was appointed to the NSW State Committee of the CP-A and charged with reorganising the finances of that body, which, at the time, appears to have been suffering the usual trials and tribulations of the amateur management and personality conflicts that abound in voluntary organisations. In New South Wales, Clayton continued his hard work and soon drew the attention of both the CIB and Military Intelligence, who referred him and his activities to the CSS for action in June 1941.[8]

The Clayton marriage produced no children and it ended with a separation in 1944 and divorce in 1945. Hilda later told her ASIO interviewers that she and Clayton hardly saw one another from 1939 because he was so busy with the CP-A. However, the real reason for the divorce was that Clayton was a drinker and a philanderer.

It appears Clayton's involvement with other women also led to problems with the Russians. This was discovered on 30 September 1960 when an ASIO listening device recorded Jessie Grant, a CP-A member and former comrade of Clayton's, reporting on him to the Executive of the CP-A. In her report, Grant outlined how in the 1940s the Russians had made it clear that Clayton had become 'quite unreliable and dangerous because of his addiction to drink and immoral involvement with women', particularly 'unpleasant happenings with one woman'. These things, Grant made clear, had led the Russians to rate him as 'quite unreliable and dangerous'.[9]

Our knowledge of what Clayton was really doing comes from VENONA, the SIGINT operation that broke into the NKGB codes. These clearly show that Clayton, codenamed KLOD, was running a number of clandestine agents, including a Commonwealth employee, A. Grundeman, codenamed VNUK.

Grundeman was a blind asset—that is, an agent working for the NKGB but not told that the NKGB were in fact his bosses.[10] The plan put by Lieutenant General Pavel Mikhailovich Fitin to the NKGB Resident, Semen Ivanovich Makarov, was to task Grundeman while keeping him under observation to establish his real intentions and willingness to carry out further work for the NKGB. From this, it can be readily accepted that Grundeman had already been identified and cleared for development by Clayton, as this was the usual process prior to an individual being offered up as an ATHLETE—an NKGB asset drawn from the CP-A.

Another well-established CP-A asset who was passed to NKGB control was NSW policeman Constable Alfred Thompson Hughes (codename BEN), who, along with at least two other unidentified officers, had probably been supplying the CP-A with counterintelligence on NSW Special Branch and the CIB for many years. Alfred Hughes reached the rank of sergeant in the NSW Police and, as a result, was well known to many of the players in counter-intelligence. His work investigating subversive organisations, including the CP-A, ensured that he was known to many within the ALP, trade unions and other left-wing organisations, and it explains the easy entrée he enjoyed in visiting Evatt's electoral and ministerial offices. If there was anything you could depend upon in Sydney at this time, it was favours for 'mates' and horse-trading across the lines.

For the NKGB, Hughes would have been important in 1944 and 1945 as he was an official of the Security Service. As a result, Makarov, most likely on Fitin's order, tasked Feodor Nosov, the TASS representative in Sydney, to indirectly raise with Clayton whether the NKGB could recruit Hughes. At the programmed 15 March meeting, Clayton did not object to Nosov's suggestion that Hughes be directly tasked by the NKGB, but he was uneasy about using him. Although the VENONA signal is corrupted, it appears that Clayton's main concern related to Hughes' malleable morality as, according to Nosov, his 'sole fear' was that Hughes was 'being used by the police' and that he had had 'insufficient preparation and tempering', which in 'certain circumstances' might lead him to make mistakes or compromise himself.[11] However, despite his lack of tempering, Alfred Hughes would completely expose the Security Service and H.V. Evatt's activities to Moscow Central.

The CP-A had also effectively penetrated Australia's scientific establishment at this time. The NKGB residency in Canberra took an interest in the

Association of Scientific Workers of Australia and, to a lesser extent, the Royal Australian Institute of Architects. The Association of Scientific Workers was a CP-A front organised by Dr Kathleen R. Makinson, a FELLOWCOUN-TRYMAN, referred to by the covername FRATERNAL, the label given to Communist parties within non-Communist countries. Most of the executive members were CP-A members and another CP-A member, Dr Hibbard, led the NSW organisation. As for the Royal Australian Institute of Architects, Henry Pynor was, according to the NKGB, a member of the CP-A and of interest following his visit to the Soviet Union in 1932;[12] however, Pynor died in 1946 and does not appear to have played much of a role.

A more useful NKGB asset was Francisca Bernie (aka Frances Bernie, Frances Gluck and Frances Garrett) nee Scott, codenamed SESTRA.[13] Bernie first came to the attention of the CIB in April 1943, when she was listed as an assistant secretary of the Eureka Youth League and then, in May 1944, identified as an assistant secretary in the CP-A.[14]

Frances Ada Scott had been born to an English couple from Oxford, Albert Sydney Scott and his wife Alma, at Sans Souci, Sydney, on 22 July 1922. She had an older brother, Harold, born in 1914.[15] Scott seems to have led a somewhat erratic life, attending nine public schools, three high schools, Sacred Heart Convent at Randwick and St Joseph's Convent at Naremburn—fourteen schools in less than twelve years.[16] There was something awry here.

It appears that Scott finally graduated from the convent in Naremburn directly to communism via the Eureka Youth League where, by age twenty, she had become a secretary. If nothing else, it appears she had found somewhere she fitted in and took her work in the League quite seriously. This commitment finally led to her leaving the Scott home and finding a room with a Mrs Smith in Ben Boyd Road, Neutral Bay.[17]

Frances's dysfunctional family life may explain her decision to adopt the name Bernie, becoming known as Miss Frances Ada Bernie rather than by her family name. It suggests that she may have been the product of an affair her mother had with another man. The circumstantial evidence for this is not just her incredibly disrupted school history. On 12 February 1945, Frances Bernie married a journalist and fellow traveller, Max Gluck, the son of a rabbi.[18] Gluck had been born in Vienna on 28 November 1913; he arrived in Australia on 31 May 1939 and took up work as a travelling salesman.[19] It is most likely they met through the CP-A and they were later married at the Congregational

Church in Gordon. Neither Frances or Max were Congregationalists and it is likely they chose this church because the clergyman was willing to marry them. However, the fact that there were only two other people present, to act as the legal witnesses, suggests that Frances's and Max's families would have nothing to do with the marriage. As a result, they had recourse to just two people, one being Mr P.E. McMaster, a solicitor who would later be Frances' legal counsel during the Royal Commission on Espionage, and the other a Mr A. Bernie, perhaps her real father.[20]

In May 1945, on the advice of the Department of the Interior, Max and Frances Gluck sought to change their names to Garrett, a request that was officially sanctioned by the authorities, including the Director-General of Security.[21]

As Frances advanced through the Eureka Youth League, she was recruited into the CP-A and became familiar with many of the notable Sydney communists of the time, including at least one secret communist, Constable Alfred Hughes. The circumstances of this meeting are well documented as Hughes included them in a MPIS report dated 26 July 1943 on the result of his investigations into the Eureka Youth League.[22] This report became a significant problem for Hughes, who had downplayed the influence of the CP-A on the league and did not identify Bernie as being a known communist. During subsequent investigations into Clayton and later, during the Royal Commission on Espionage, the information in Hughes' report was clearly identified as having been provided by a woman, and that woman was believed to be Frances Bernie. This became more problematic as Hughes never admitted having ever met Bernie or having known her.[23]

The importance of Frances Bernie lies in her clandestine career, which appears to have started soon after Hughes investigated her and the Eureka Youth League. In the latter half of 1943, she was so heavily involved in her party work that she became ill and had to step down for a while. This necessitated reporting her illness to the CP-A, and the official to whom she reported was Walter Seddon Clayton.[24] After this, and allegedly because of her health, Bernie dropped out of the CP-A, although she remained a financial member, and took a position at the Sydney Day Nursery. This action reflects the standard CP-A method of moving a member to clandestine work.

In November 1944, serendipitously, she saw an advertisement for a stenographer and typist in a federal parliamentarian's office and ended up employed by Alan Dalziel, the electorate officer and later private secretary to H.V. Evatt, the Foreign Minister.[25] She was not the first NKGB asset to join this office. Already working in Evatt's office was the blind NKGB asset Grundeman, who looked after the teletype machines and took the coded messages from them to be broken out, or decoded, so that Evatt could keep himself up to date. So now two NKGB assets had access to Australian and Allied secrets. Later, Bernie frankly admitted that she took secret messages from Evatt's office to Clayton, who copied them and passed them to Makarov via Nosov.

The significance of Bernie's role taking encrypted messages from the teletype directly to Clayton is that he would have been receiving similar messages from Grundeman as well. This provided a threefold benefit to the NKGB. First, they had access to secret and top-secret information being passed to Evatt's office in Sydney. Second, they could validate Bernie's value against Grundeman and vice versa. Third, they had in their hands both the encrypted message and the broken-out message, providing their SIGINT organisations with cribs of pure gold. The significance of this is not remarked upon in ASIO's files, but it would certainly have been discussed by the Y Board, the ruling body on all British SIGINT matters, in London and the equivalent committee in Washington and is part of the reason why the US reaction to the leaks from Australia was so severe.

The damage to the security of Australian government communications was extensive and, given the close cooperation of Britain in helping Australia in this area, the damage to Britain's communications security would also have been far-reaching. This damage significantly undermines the oft-put argument of CP-A apologists that the activities of the CP-A did not really hurt anyone. As we will see in the next chapter, the damage caused by the CP-A and its NKGB masters was far more extensive and dangerous than even this.

In 1954, during his debriefings, the former NKGB Resident Vladimir Petrov described the intelligence being supplied by Bernie as being 'very important' and that she may also have been 'very important' as an asset.[26] After the royal commission was over and some of the dust had settled, Bernie re-established contact with the CP-A and Alan Dalziel and was made a target by the Director-General of Security in operations HAWK and, later, PIGEON. These surveillance operations against the CP-A by Robert Wake continued up until the early 1960s. Despite the fact that he was targeted by ASIO in two operations, there was no hard evidence found of Dalziel having been a

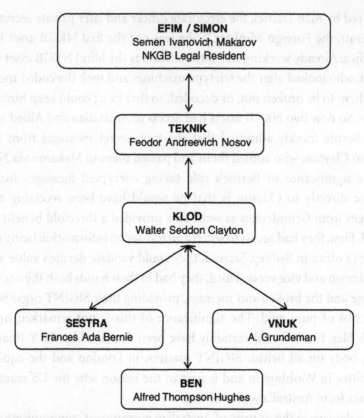

EFIM / SIMON
Semen Ivanovich Makarov
NKGB Legal Resident

TEKNIK
Feodor Andreevich Nosov

KLOD
Walter Seddon Clayton

SESTRA
Frances Ada Bernie

VNUK
A. Grundeman

BEN
Alfred Thompson Hughes

Figure 16.1: The NKGB network in Evatt's office, 1944–46

member of the CP-A, at least not of the declared CP-A. Despite this, his close associations with CP-A members, NKGB agents and Alfred Hughes, as well as his employment of Frances Bernie and Grundeman, raises serious questions.

In the late 1950s Bernie converted from communism to Christianity in the form of the extreme sect the Exclusive Brethren. As a result, at 11.30 a.m. on 16 November 1959, ASIO received a call from Bernie on the open line asking for Mr Gilmour or Mr Richards. When she was advised that neither were available, she left her home number and asked them to call her. On 17 November, J.M. Gilmour rang Bernie back and made an appointment for him and an unidentified ASIO officer to call and see her at home at 11.00 a.m.[27]

At the subsequent meeting, Bernie explained that because of her developing religious views she had decided to clear her conscience of all her work for Clayton and the CP-A. Her statement to Gilmour blew Clayton, Grundeman and Nosov and she described the continuing relationships she had with other members of the CP-A such as Lance Sharkey, Bill Wood and Ida Sherden, all of whom she had attempted to convert to the Brethren's version of Christianity.[28] This important information was the 'clincher' in proving at an intelligence level that Clayton was an NKGB spy.[29]

Although there is no commentary on Bernie's emotional or physical health in the files, the illnesses she suffered and the way she moved from one set of fervent beliefs to another suggests someone who is either highly strung or suffering emotional or psychiatric problems, or a mix of all of these. Emotional or psychological instability would explain the extraordinarily high number of schools she attended and her later rejection of Catholicism for communism, and later again her rejection of communism for religion in the form of the Exclusive Brethren, whose doctrines she approached in a manner described by Gilmour of ASIO as involving 'no half measures'.[30] For the NKGB and the CP-A, this made her an even bigger problem.

The group of spies, ATHLETES, that Bernie was recruited into were called the K 1943 Group within Moscow Centre. This suggests the KLOD network was only created in 1943. It consisted of Hughes, Grundeman, Bernie and someone at the Berlitz School of Languages in Sydney.[31] This was one of the groups run by Clayton, who appears to have been a very dedicated member of the CP-A.

All of these individuals were of high interest to the NKGB and the CP-A. The usual approach of the NKGB was to approach the CP-A via Wally Clayton and obtain a report on the suitability of the targeted individual as a clandestine operative. If Clayton provided a positive report, then a formal approach was made through him to the CP-A asking for permission to recruit an individual as an ATHLETE. Once this approval had been received, the CP-A, on behalf of the NKGB, would plant an informer on the individual who would observe and report on the individual's habits and character in minute detail. Once this was done, and the reporting was positive, the individual would be given small clandestine tasks to carry out. If all of this went well, then the final move into the secret world was orchestrated.

The move from open membership of the CP-A to clandestine membership was usually accomplished by the ATHLETE very publicly breaking with the CP-A and resigning. After this event, the ATHLETE would live a normal life with no contact with any of their old comrades or their previous life. They would wait until the agreed sign was provided before making contact with their clandestine superior and organisation.

When the NKGB looked at Bernie, they had Clayton task Alfred Hughes to carry out the clandestine investigation of her for Fitin. At the same time that this investigation of Bernie was being done, Fitin authorised Makarov to pay Clayton £50 'on the plausible pretext of compensating him for his personal efforts'.[32] This payment took Clayton aback. He may have realised that by paying him money, the NKGB were locking him into a very rigid relationship.[33] He would have been right.

This technique involved getting the ATHLETE, which, in the end is all that Clayton was, to a clandestine meeting in a room in which the NKGB would have planted cameras and recording devices. The meeting would follow normal practice and then the money would be handed over and all of this filmed and

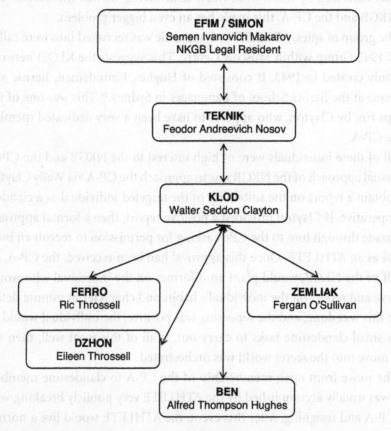

Figure 16.2: The KLOD network, 1940–49

recorded. This did two things: it was insurance cover for the relationship, as the payment could be used to blackmail or pressure Clayton should the need arise, and, more importantly, it established just who the bosses were. Wally Clayton would have been well aware that he was being pulled into line.

By June 1945, Fitin had increased the list of target organisations in Australia that Moscow Centre wanted penetrated. He directed Makarov to approach Clayton and establish whether the CP-A had sleepers in the ALP or Liberal Party and, if so, whether any of them would be useful in clandestine work.[34] Hughes was now earning his keep with the NKGB and was bringing Security Service files directly to Clayton, who forwarded the information to Makarov. On the one hand, according to Makarov, the information the Security Service had on the Soviet Legation was 'uninteresting', but the Australians were closely watching the movements of Vladimir Mikheev, the TASS representative. On the other hand, the information provided by Hughes to Clayton had allowed the latter to build up a very detailed picture of the Australian Security Service and other intelligence organisations, significantly reducing the threat from them.[35]

It was now that Clayton's limitations in intelligence work began to manifest themselves. The primary problem was that Hughes was literally stripping the Sydney office of the Security Service bare of its files. He was providing so much material Clayton could not process it and, significantly, he lacked the technical skills to oversee the photographing of the documents using specialist NKGB cameras. Makarov requested permission from Fitin to allow him to authorise Nosov to hand over such a camera to Hughes.[36] The idea was not well received in Moscow.

On 7 July, Makarov was told by Fitin that Moscow did not understand his request for direct liaison between Nosov and Hughes. Fitin pointedly told Makarov to address all such operational signals directly to him alone. The problem for Fitin was that Hughes was a CP-A asset working for Clayton, and for the NKGB to poach him would involve matters of high policy, possibly including permission from the Politburo, something even Fitin would be squeamish in obtaining.[37]

Clayton was left to run Hughes and, on 1 September, Makarov signalled Fitin that Clayton had now forwarded a detailed report from Hughes on Australia's security intelligence system, particularly the Security Service.

The information provided by Hughes described how, before the war, there was a counterintelligence department within the CIB and that during the war

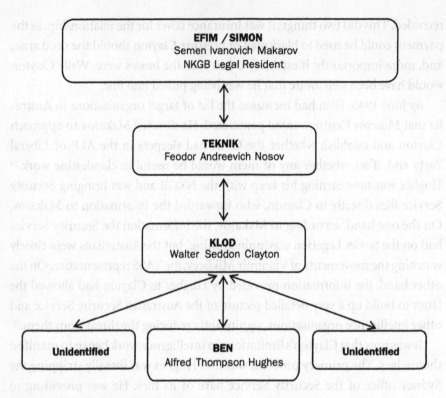

EFIM / SIMON
Semen Ivanovich Makarov
NKGB Legal Resident

TEKNIK
Feodor Andreevich Nosov

KLOD
Walter Seddon Clayton

Unidentified

BEN
Alfred Thompson Hughes

Unidentified

Figure 16.3: The NKGB counter-counterintelligence network, 1942–49

a new Security Service consisting of police and military personnel had been created under Evatt as Attorney-General. As a result of this, the influence of the military had been reduced and more rights and powers given to the police involved.

Hughes also reported that one of the sections of the new service had the dual tasks of investigating the CP-A and carrying out a counterespionage role. This was the section led by Robert Wake. The new service was, Hughes felt, more disciplined and had a better class of qualified permanent staff. Compared to the Security Service, Hughes reported the CIB was unimportant.

Hughes also described the internal organisation of the Security Service describing the five sections in New South Wales as follows:

1. Investigation of subversive activities of various organisations,
2. Investigation of anti-state activities of Germans ... Indonesians,
3. Chinese section,

4. Investigation of Italians, Greeks and people from the Balkans, and

5. Investigations with the Army, Navy and RAAF.

The investigation of the diplomatic and consular corps remained the province of the CIB.

The report by Hughes also detailed how investigators handled agents and how the identity of all such agents was only known to that investigator. These agents are both paid and unpaid, and the Security Service actively recruited agents from within any organisation it targeted for investigation.

Importantly, Hughes betrayed to the NKGB that the Security Service relied heavily on constant external surveillance of targets, but that it had no capability in internal surveillance using listening devices, cameras and so on.

Significantly, Hughes reported how Attorney-General Evatt maintained one 'special' officer in each state whose function was to conduct special operations ordered by Evatt. These special officers did not report their work for Evatt via the Security Service, but privately to his personal office. In New South Wales, Sergeant Wilke carried out Evatt's personal work.[38]

Hughes also outlined how at the end of the war the Director-General of Security, William Simpson, had prepared an order to disband the service but that this had been defeated in Cabinet by Evatt because Australia might still have need of it. Like many other organisations, however, the service was savagely cut back and Hughes had remained a member because of his expertise on left-wing organisations, particularly, and ironically, on the CP-A.[39]

One of the interesting insights we get from the reports that Hughes provided to the NKGB is the list of additional organisations that the Security Service under the ALP government was targeting. These organisations included the Political Research Society, Ltd, a reactionary organisation set up by the Liberal Party to combat left-wing organisations; the Australian Legion of Ex-Servicemen; and the Association of Greek Orthodox Christians.[40] Makarov told Fitin that these documents were of operational value, as they provided detailed information on political personalities in these organisations, which the NKGB and the CP-A could use.[41]

On 15 September, Fitin informed Makarov that Moscow Centre liked Hughes' report and wanted Makarov to thank Clayton for the success. Fitin emphasised to Makarov that he must ensure the line of contact between Hughes, Clayton and Nosov be carefully secured and not put at risk.[42] To this end, Nosov was to be released from all other tasks to presumably focus on this line but also, undoubtedly, to protect him from being detected as a result of other less important work.[43] These instructions from Moscow give us a good idea of just how important Clayton's network, and Hughes, had become.

Fitin's warning most likely also reflected the dismay of the RIS over a recent defection. The defector was Igor Sergeyevich Gouzenko, a GRU cipher clerk at the Soviet Embassy in Ottawa, and the ease with which he left the Embassy carrying highly sensitive RIS documents caused an uproar so great that Moscow Centre immediately authorised an assassination squad to kill or capture him. He walked out of the Embassy on 5 September 1945 with so many documents stuffed under his shirt that his wife said that if he hadn't held his stomach in, he would have looked pregnant.[44]

The extent of the damage caused by Gouzenko's defection soon became obvious. Although Gouzenko was GRU, his information extended right across the RIS, covering both tradecraft and operations. He also brought across information about RIS codes and communications systems.

In Australia, Makarov was now directed to provide a gift to Nosov that Makarov was to select himself. This no doubt occurred because of the success that Clayton's networks, particularly Hughes, were enjoying.[45] Despite this success, there was a major flaw in the NKGB system in Australia. The problem was that Clayton managed all of the NKGB's spy networks, other than one based in Melbourne. If Clayton were ever compromised, it would mean that nearly all of the CP-A networks would be at risk.

The problems of over-centralised networks and Gouzenko's defection were making Moscow Centre jumpy. This jumpiness was demonstrated by the reaction of Fitin to news that the First Minister, Nikolai Lifanov, had reported through the ENGINEERS line—diplomats—that the Canberra Legation had had a 'walk-in', someone who just walks into an embassy or legation and offers to serve as a spy.[46] Fitin was not happy to hear of this event via diplomatic channel and wanted an urgent explanation from Makarov.

The subsequent explanation was that a well-dressed man claiming to be Stuart Henry Moore of 59 Rawson Street, Haberfield, had met with the Second Secretary, Grigorij Stefanovich Paschenko, who had accepted documents from him. Although Paschenko had acted correctly, he had failed to obtain Moore's personal details and now Clayton was being tasked to check up on Moore. It was discovered that Moore was about to be discharged from the army and had made the acquaintance of a CP-A member, John Cecil Payne, who had sponsored him into the CP-A.[47] Moscow Centre quickly assessed Moore as being a Security Service plant and ordered all contact to be broken.[48] The speed with which Moore was identified as a plant is unsurprising, as the NKGB and CP-A had a number of agents working inside the classified registry of the Director of Military Intelligence at LHQ in Melbourne, and they had Hughes and at least two other agents working within the Security Service.

By 30 November 1945, the NKGB were sending messages to their residencies warning them of the surveillance techniques being used by counterespionage agencies around the world. Of particular interest were the shadowing techniques of US and British agencies, among others, and the double-surveillance method they had started using.

This method entailed using two groups; one group conducting surveillance in the usual way but being followed by a second group, so that if the target detected the first group, then the second stepped in to take over the surveillance. The presumption was that the target, having shaken the first group, would then become less vigilant. Moscow Centre and Fitin wanted residencies to consider this information and to report all suspicious behaviour they became aware of in terms of counterespionage activities concerning their operations.[49]

In late 1945, the clandestine network that Clayton had been building within the Department of External Affairs now began to produce material in greater volume. The group had been started with Ric Throssell. He was the son of the author and well-known CP-A activist Katharine Susannah Prichard, codenamed ACADEMICIAN. Prichard was a friend of Evatt, who tipped her off to the Security Service's surveillance against her son and herself.[50] Makarov was a little nonplussed that Throssell had been employed at External Affairs, given that Evatt and nearly everyone knew of his mother's communist predilections.[51] More importantly, Makarov seems to have accepted Clayton's evaluation of Throssell as not being very bright, as he passed this evaluation to Fitin in Moscow.[52]

Makarov was also suspicious that Throssell was an Australian coat-dragging operation. He tasked Clayton via Nosov to find out the 'real reason for Throssell's appointment'.[53] By 10 August 1945, however, information was beginning to flow from External Affairs, which was codenamed NOOK. Clayton handed Nosov photographs of a report by James Maloney, Australia's ambassador in Moscow. The report was probably 'The Soviet Trade Union Movement', which according to Makarov 'gives an exceptionally gloomy picture of working conditions in factories' and 'slanders Soviet workers'.[54] Eight days later, Fitin ordered Makarov to get Clayton to photograph the entire document.[55]

Clayton's initiative also caused problems for Makarov and Fitin within Moscow Centre when Clayton's unauthorised recruitment of two new members, Jim Hill and Ian Milner, as ATHLETES was questioned at a higher level, presumably by Beria or the Politburo. Fitin quickly made it plain to Makarov that he needed to exert more control over Clayton, and he must stop sending information of little value, especially by signal. Makarov was to tell Clayton he was starting to attract attention and he, Makarov, was to provide Fitin with biographical information on Hill and Milner. He was also explicitly told not to recruit any more agents without Moscow Centre's prior approval.[56]

In the middle of October, Makarov signalled Fitin for more NKGB personnel, in the form of a second TASS representative for Sydney. In particular, he suggested Nosov be brought into the work. His argument was that a second field operative would lighten the load on Clayton and, more importantly, allow the residency to exert more control over Clayton's networks. Makarov wanted to focus his efforts and the efforts of Clayton's cells on External Affairs, the Security Service and Australia's political parties.[57]

Fitin's reply on 20 October agreed with Makarov that Nosov should be brought into the clandestine work, and that Makarov was to focus all his efforts on External Affairs, political parties, intelligence and counter-intelligence organisations.[58] Moscow Centre was also going to replace another NKGB probationer, FED, Aleksej Ivanovich Osipov, who was working under the cover of a clerk at the legation.[59]

The security of the line, Hughes–Clayton–Nosov–Makarov, remained at the front of Fitin's mind and he emphasised that Makarov was not to put the line at risk by being too ambitious or moving too quickly.[60] The very next day, Makarov received another signal from Fitin outlining the precautionary measures to be put in place to protect the line. Makarov was to order Nosov not to receive any documents from Clayton until Moscow Centre had considered the matter and issued special orders cancelling this instruction. Meetings with Clayton were to be cut back to the minimum and Clayton was to be instructed to maintain contact only with Hughes at the Security Service and the network at External Affairs.

In this signal, we can see where the Soviet Union's interests lay. The intelligence coming out of the Security Service served to provide early warning of possible compromises of RIS operations both in Australia and the rest of the Anglo-Saxon world. It also provides insights into the changes in tradecraft of Western intelligence agencies as a result of the Gouzenko defection. As far as External Affairs was concerned, the value lay in the theft of Allied documents relating to Europe, the Atlantic and the United States. In 1945–46, this was pure gold for the Soviet Union.

Another protective mechanism put in place by Fitin was an order to Makarov to conduct counter-counterintelligence operations to ascertain whether Nosov or any NKGB operatives were being subjected to more intensive surveillance than previously seen. If these operations detected any such increase, Makarov was to temporarily break contact and cease all operations.[61] The Gouzenko defection and the approach by 'Stuart Moore' most likely triggered this action.

Despite Fitin's warnings to take it slowly, the External Affairs network now made the mistake that would bring them all undone. The members of the net had continued to plunder External Affairs and had provided secret British cables dealing with Argentina and Poland.[62] On 7 December, Clayton provided more documents dealing with Poland and Iceland.[63] Despite his own warnings about doing too much, in February 1946 Fitin ordered Makarov to get from Clayton the details of the scientific attaché at the Australian Embassy in Moscow, Professor Eric Ashby. This arose out of an earlier signal from Makarov on 8 January telling Moscow that Ashby had gone to Vladivostok when, as far as Fitin knew, he had not.[64] Fitin now wanted to know about Ashby and where he had actually been to in the Soviet Union. Why Fitin wanted to know about Ashby or what was done with this information is unknown, and presumably now resides in the file vaults of the Federal'naya sluzhba bezopasnosti Rossiyskoy Federatsii, the Federal Security Service of the Russian Federation (FSB).

The External Affairs net was now really getting into its stride and on 8 March it forwarded a report on an interview Evatt had with CP-A member and secretary of the Ironworkers Union, Ernest Thornton, to discuss his opinion of the Australian Ambassador in Moscow.[65] This was topped by the delivery on the same day of a signal—VENONA 101—about a document stolen by Milner (codename BUR).[66] This document was titled 'Security in the Western Mediterranean and the Eastern Atlantic' and had been written for Britain's Post Hostilities Planning Staff.[67] Milner had discovered its existence

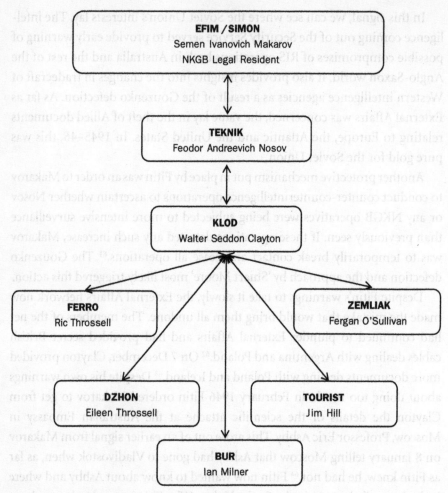

EFIM / SIMON
Semen Ivanovich Makarov
NKGB Legal Resident

TEKNIK
Feodor Andreevich Nosov

KLOD
Walter Seddon Clayton

FERRO
Ric Throssell

ZEMLIAK
Fergan O'Sullivan

DZHON
Eileen Throssell

TOURIST
Jim Hill

BUR
Ian Milner

Figure 16.4: The External Affairs network, 1944–47

and had wanted to get a copy of it for his masters. The problem had been that there was only one copy, and that was held by the fastidious Sir Frederick Shedden at Defence. This would turn from a coup to a disaster as it was the theft of this document that would incriminate Milner and lead to the unravelling of the network, a renewed focus on 'the Case', the investigation sparked by the compromise of ULTRA (highly secret SIGINT derived from high-level enemy coded messages) in 1944, the establishment of ASIO and, eventually, the Royal Commission on Espionage in 1954.

The antecedents of the Case lay in a signal from Mic Sandford at Central Bureau, the SIGINT organisation serving General MacArthur's South West

Pacific Area command and Australia. Central Bureau had detected classified Australian intelligence material being signalled in radio messages of the IJA in China and Japan. Sandford's recommendation to Stewart Menzies, the head of Britain's SIGINT organisation, and MI6, was that Central Bureau undertake a cryptanalytical attack on Soviet codes.[68] London's response was that as the Soviets used one-time pads their codes were unbreakable and Sandford and Central Bureau were to do nothing. The findings of the London authorities were that the breach had come from Nationalist Chinese liaison officers reporting to their government in Chungking (Chongqing).[69]

This appeared to be the end of the matter, although it seems Australia's Military Intelligence, particularly Central Bureau, still believed the Soviet Legation was stealing and passing Australian and Allied secrets to Moscow. It also seems that London was also worried, as they sent Group Captain Frederick William Winterbotham, the head of ULTRA security throughout the world, to deal with a number of extremely difficult breaches of ULTRA security in Australia in mid-1944. If Winterbotham was in Australia during the fighting in France, it was not for a holiday.[70]

While Winterbotham was in Australia an intercepted IJA message, No. MBJ 30028 of 25 November 1944, was identified as containing specific Australian military intelligence estimates and, dramatically, ULTRA. This, Sandford reported to his superior, produced 'a very considerable stir overseas'.[71] This incident led to London and Washington despatching their own SIGINT security detachments to Australia to communicate, receive, secure and distribute all SIGINT in accordance with the decisions of the Washington and London SIGINT authorities. The effect of this was to remove the management of all SIGINT away from both General MacArthur's headquarters and Australia.

The role of the RIS in compromising ULTRA and other allied SIGINT slowly came to light through the work of Meredith Gardner and the VENONA team in the US and the MASK operation in Britain. Corroboration of Soviet espionage then began to flow as the post-war security organisations in Western nations began focusing their attention on the RIS representatives and their contacts. In Australia, the interrogations of Frances Bernie provided information that tied Wally Clayton to the RIS and identified him as a receiver of stolen property. Her information also corroborated the information contained in Document G, which Vladimir Petrov stole from the NKGB Residency in the Soviet Legation in Canberra when he defected at Sydney

Airport on 3 April 1954 following a two-year long cultivation by ASIO.[72] The intelligence was no longer single source and it was growing.

· · · · · · · · ·

VENONA 101 is significant in another way in that it also contains a comment from Makarov on Clayton's welfare and state of mind following his 'great personal sorrow' on the 'death' of his wife. It would appear that Clayton was not willing to tell Makarov that Hilda had divorced him and this lie about his wife dying, when the NKGB finally uncovered it, would increase their concerns about Clayton's reliability.[73]

Fitin's anxiety about the security of the External Affairs–Clayton–Nosov–Makarov line persisted, and he now signalled Makarov to ensure that Clayton was advised to be more careful in his work. This was deemed necessary as Moscow Centre's residencies in Anglo-Saxon countries were being subjected to a campaign of surveillance and counterespionage operations. It was essential for Clayton to reduce his activity to merely studying CP-A members with a view to the NKGB developing them as assets. Under no circumstances was Clayton to continue receiving documents, as this was extremely dangerous.[74]

At the time that all of this was happening, Fitin was also aware there was a significant problem with the GRU residency at the Canberra Legation. What the exact problem was has never been revealed, but it involved a number of the officers and men of that residency being ordered home. All that is known is that the behaviour of the GRU Resident Victor Sergeevich Zajtsev, code-named SERGE, and his staff was the central issue.

Zajtsev was officially the Second Secretary at the legation. One of his GRU operatives, Georgij Mikhailovich Morozov codenamed ROK, was to be secretly observed and maximum care was to be taken to ensure he departed Australia.[75] His boss Zajtsev would follow, as would the doorkeeper at the legation, Petr Nikolayevich Terosikhorov, and the secretary to the minister, Antonina Semenovn Zolotukhina. The issue with these individuals was that they were seen as being too close to Australians, and Makarov had complained about them to Fitin. Zajtsev and Makarov had developed a stormy relationship and conflict between the two men had grown.[76] The situation appears to have been part of yet another purge, this one targeted against the GRU because of the Gouzenko defection.

Fitin's orders warning Makarov to be careful, to exercise increased security awareness and not take risks at this time appear to have fallen on deaf ears and these did not belong to Makarov. The deafest of those ears belonged to Wally Clayton and his CP-A networks, particularly Milner, who now stole the document 'Security in Western Mediterranean and the Eastern Atlantic'.[77] The theft of this paper, which would be discovered in 1948 when the VENONA operation read Makarov's signal, no. 123, of 19 March 1946, which contained the title of the document, would lead Australian and British security officials straight to Ian Milner.[78]

The risks being run by Clayton's networks were excessive, particularly in an environment where the intelligence agencies and governments in Western, particularly Anglo-Saxon, countries were beginning to become aware of the extent of Soviet theft of state secrets and technical information on military developments, technology, plans and strategies. In the aftermath of Gouzenko's defection it is indicative of the amateurism of the Clayton networks that Clayton had the highly classified 'Security in the Western Mediterranean and the Eastern Atlantic' in his car when he met Nosov in Canberra and that Nosov and other Russians took 35 minutes to photograph and return it to Clayton. The document was so big Makarov had to ask Fitin for advice on delivering it because it would require 'copious telegraphic correspondence' to send it to Moscow.[79] How it was eventually sent is unknown, but on 6 May, Fitin signalled Makarov that 'the BOSS', most likely Beria, had become acquainted with 'the report in question', so it is likely that it was passed by diplomatic courier.[80]

The importance of this episode is that it reinforced the RIS perspective that Australia provided the easiest window into the secrets of the West and that increasing operations in Australia would provide access to intelligence impossible to obtain in London or Washington. It was an affirmation of Alexander Zuzenko's arguments before Lenin and the Comintern back in the early 1920s.

On 1 April 1946, Beria signalled all NKGB Residents, informing them that Moscow Centre blamed 'complacency and self-satisfaction' for the Gouzenko defection.[81] There can be little doubt that this meant bad news for the GRU and any NKGB officers that Beria and other worthies in Moscow had in their sights. Zajtsev's problems did not arise from complacency or self-satisfaction, as none of his operations in Australia were ever compromised. Regardless, the recall occurred at the instigation of the GRU of the Red Army and finally, on

30 November 1946, Makarov was ordered to ensure the 'prompt return' of all the GRU officials mentioned to the Soviet Union.[82]

To add to Makarov's problems, it appears that someone at the legation was complaining to Moscow about him. Makarov became aware of this when Fitin sent a warning about his work habits, particularly his 'unpunctuality in coming to work', 'unwarranted absences' and 'trips out of Canberra'.[83] Makarov was also told that his habit of clumsily using information obtained from people within the legation against others was causing discontent and embarrassment. Fitin advised Makarov to take his advice and change his behaviour.[84] This appears to have been a friendly hint from Fitin, who would soon be handing over his 1st Directorate to Lieutenant General Petr Nikolae-vich Kubatkin.

By 1 August, the quality of the intelligence being obtained by Clayton from External Affairs resulted in Makarov's new boss, Kubatkin (codenamed EVGEN'EV), asking that Nosov work with Clayton to develop clandestine operations in Britain. Again, Zuzenko's idea of Australia being the weak link in the British Empire was being resurrected, even though questions about CP-A activity were now being asked in federal parliament.[85]

The clandestine operations of the NKGB in Australia continued to grow and a cipher clerk, Feodor Egorovich Gubanov, was sent out by the NKGB to take over the running of some of the CP-A agents working for Nosov and Clayton.[86] Makarov, who by now was tired and whose wife was sick, wanted to go home; however, Kubatkin would not spare him and he was kept at his post. Kubatkin was solicitous enough to ask about having Makarov's wife treated in Australia.[87]

Kubatkin didn't last long in his new posting[88] and he was replaced on 9 October 1946 by Lieutenant General Pyotr Vasileevich Fedotov, one of the officers who carried out the Katyn massacre of 22,000 Polish military officers, officials and other Poles deemed capable of leading Polish resistance to Moscow. Fedotov (codenamed IVANOV) announced his arrival by criticising his residencies around the world and by reiterating Moscow Centre's previous complaint about residencies recruiting and tasking new ATHLETES without getting Moscow Centre's approval.[89] As if this wasn't bad enough, Fedotov went on, these ATHLETES were then stealing documents and undertaking other 'important measures', often using 'unchecked or casual contacts'.[90] Again, Moscow forbade the recruitment of local communists into NKGB work.[91]

By this time in Australia the Security Service had fallen by the wayside and the old CIB had taken back the role of counterespionage. This entailed little more than changing the name and retaining the same people, resources, bad habits and criminality. There was no great increase in actual capability, and technical means such as the bugging of buildings and covert photography remained rudimentary. The CIB did possess capability in the forms of telephone taps and broad surveillance, however. The problem for Moscow Centre was assessing whether the increased surveillance they could see was the full extent of the counterintelligence effort directed against them. As a result, the safe course was to suspend all operations, and this was duly ordered.

To this end, Makarov ordered Nosov to provide Clayton with a procedure, including passwords, for re-establishing contact at a later date. Nosov was also to impress upon Clayton the need for increased care.[92]

By this stage, the RIS was under a sustained and successful attack by the US Army's SIS at Arlington Hall in Washington, which had been working on the Soviet diplomatic cipher since February 1943, exploiting the mound of Soviet messages that had been intercepted and then stored at the SIS.[93] By November 1943, the first break into the cipher was made and VENONA was expanded.[94]

The real breakthrough came in November 1944 when Phillips, Feinstein and Campbell got into the NKGB cipher. This work would then be supplemented considerably by the collateral intelligence gleaned from Gouzenko. By late 1945, US and British intelligence agencies would have been seeing the extent of the RIS penetration of government agencies in both countries and in Australia. Of course, Kim Philby, the MI6 officer and NKGB deep cover illegal, among others, was feeding this intelligence straight back to Moscow Centre, thus informing its concerns for Clayton and his networks.

In Australia the NKGB enjoyed several advantages. First, the new prime minister, Ben Chifley, was no friend of intelligence agencies and was loath to accept there was a problem. Second, the appallingly low levels of security across the Australian government meant that anything sent to Australia was either in a newspaper the next day or on Makarov's desk. Third, because of the poor security, no one in Australia outside of the Central Bureau SIGINT organisation, while it still existed, could be told about VENONA.

By 9 January 1947, the problems were now increasing for Makarov and the NKGB as Moscow Centre informed him that Nosov was blown. Of particular concern were the actions of Clayton and a woman, codenamed BITI, possibly one of Clayton's lovers, or even the woman concerned in the 'unpleasant happenings' that Jessie Grant later briefed the leadership of the CP-A about. On the other hand, BITI could have been Antonina Semenovna Zolotukhina, the secretary to the minister, who was being urgently recalled to Moscow.

On top of all of this, there was still the problem of the GRU. In January 1947, Zajtsev and the two other GRU officers were still at the legation when Makarov received news from Moscow Centre that the order for them to return to Moscow would soon arrive. Makarov was again ordered to ensure that Zajtsev was successfully despatched to Moscow.[95] It has all the hallmarks of a Beria play to take down Zajtsev, a senior GRU officer, as part of his plan to subject the GRU to his own control. In June 1947, Makarov was again ordered to investigate the GRU residency at the Canberra Legation in accordance with Moscow Centre's previous orders.[96]

This set of orders pitted Makarov against one of the GRU's outstanding officers, Viktor Sergevitch Zajtsev, and he had been through the wringer before. He had survived the 1938 purges before being sent to Japan in July 1940 to take control of the network run by Richard Sorge, codenamed RAMSEY. Sorge was a German journalist who was a GRU agent from around 1929. In Japan, Sorge began passing intelligence to the Soviet Union that warned of the impending German invasion in 1941. Sorge's warnings, like those of General Fitin, were arrogantly rejected by Stalin. However, Sorge's GRU controllers understood just how important his intelligence was and he was retained and closely supported.

The problem was that Sorge's network was sending its reports via radio to Vladivostok, thus exposing them to the Kempeitai, the IJA Military Police, which was responsible for all counterintelligence in Japan. Zajtsev was sent to take control of this undisciplined operation and keep it intact. He failed because by the time he arrived the Kempeitai, who were excellent at counter-intelligence operations, had most likely already identified all of Sorge's network and, following the German attack on the Soviet Union, they arrested every member of Sorge's network within 36 hours, a sure sign of a complete knowledge of the network.

One interesting sideline that arose from Zajtsev's experience in Japan was his subsequent refusal to use radio in his tradecraft. His clandestine radio, according to Petrov, remained dismantled under his desk in the Soviet Embassy. Another thing that has only recently become apparent is the network in Melbourne, which the circumstantial evidence suggests was a GRU network, did not use radio or telegrams to communicate. They used couriers, which kept them safe from VENONA. However, this is a story we will look at a little later.

This fits with the analysis of Desmond Ball and David Horner that Zajtsev was far too important a GRU officer to be in Canberra doing nothing. He was either setting up an illegal network or he was running an existing and successful illegal network.[97] As we will see below, it seems it was the latter. Indeed, it may have been the very success of this network that drew the jealous eyes of the NKGB onto him and created his problems at Moscow Centre.

The extent of Moscow Centre's knowledge about how much Nosov was compromised is hard to ascertain, but it was enough for them to assume that the CIB might attempt to entrap Nosov at legal meetings within the legation itself.[98] Fedotov even ordered Makarov to work out an 'action under threat' procedure for Nosov to use in an emergency and to warn the Soviet First Minister if he and his legation were under threat.[99] Whatever had happened to cause the panic in January, it had subsided by mid-1947 and, by early December 1947, Moscow Centre was asking Makarov to reopen links with Clayton via Nosov.[100]

From mid-1947 to mid-February 1948 there was a lot of signals traffic about Nosov and Clayton. By December, YUREV, an unidentified officer at Moscow Centre, probably Fedotov's deputy, sent a signal asking Makarov if he knew Clayton personally.[101] This signal also asked for the password and contact procedure that Nosov had been asked to set up with Clayton when the 'action under threat' suspension of operations had been instituted in January. The signal makes it clear that Nosov was to hand over contact with Clayton to a new 'comrade'. There was a new NKGB handler in Australia.

Now local problems intervened as it appears that Clayton had stopped attending locations where Nosov or other NKGB officers could carry out a brush contact, that is a meeting in which the parties recognise one another and perhaps quickly pass items by bumping into or brushing past one another in a crowd. By 17 February 1948, it appears some sort of contact had been re-established with Clayton as YUREV from Moscow Centre ordered Makarov to accompany Nosov to a meeting with Clayton on 19 February.[102] Makarov was to find out exactly what Clayton's position was and the state of his organisation, his ability to contact 'the group leaders' and their capacity to undertake clandestine work for the NKGB again.[103] It all seems a little rushed and disorganised and it is likely that some of the strain that Nosov and Makarov were showing at this time was due to the prompting they seem to have been subjected to from Moscow Centre.

Still, the work got done and by 26 March intelligence from Clayton's networks was flowing to Moscow; we know this because the Canberra residency, presumably Makarov, was being asked to clarify from whom and by what means Clayton had obtained information that Canberra had sent to Moscow.[104] A few days later, on 31 March, Fedotov was back behind his desk and was lecturing Makarov in a signal about lax security. Fedotov's concern was the use of the covernames and particulars of ATHLETES, clandestine NKGB agents drawn from the CP-A, in ciphered signals containing the intelligence they had collected. The two were now to be broken up, with the intelligence sent in one signal and the details of the agent concerned in another. This may be the first inkling we have of the NKGB gaining an insight into VENONA from their sources in Western intelligence, particularly Kim Philby at MI6 and Donald Maclean at the Foreign Office in London.

Despite his continuing concern about the security of the ATHLETES, Fedotov was impatient for the intelligence they were supplying, and he wanted Makarov and Clayton to recruit more of them. It appears from the signal traffic that Fedotov wanted the Clayton–Nosov–Makarov line up and running again and expanded. Among those Fedotov wanted to know about were TOURIST, Jim Hill at External Affairs; PROFESSOR, Frederick George Rose, at the Department of Territories; LEGGE, unidentified; PODRUGA, Doris Isobel Beeby, a journalist at the *Tribune*, and ARTISTE, Beeby's de facto husband, Herbert William Tattersall.[105] Now, for the first time, the NKGB and CP-A cells operating within the Commonwealth Scientific and Industrial Research Organisation (CSIRO) were being brought into the Clayton–Nosov–Makarov line with Wilbur Christiansen, codenamed MASTERCRAFTSMAN, being tasked to cooperate with Ric Throssell, codenamed FERRO.[106]

All of this activity was to be carried out by Makarov and Clayton using tradecraft of the highest order so as to ensure the security of the networks.[107] The creeping concern seen in the VENONA messages indicates that the NKGB were aware that they were leaking information about their operations in Australia and other Anglo-Saxon countries. It appears that by June 1948, the RIS and its masters finally realised or obtained information about the compromise of their diplomatic and intelligence ciphers because, with the exception of a very corrupted signal sent from London to Moscow on

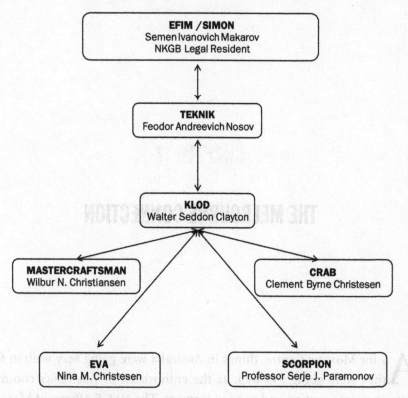

Figure 16.5: The CSIRO network, 1948

26 July 1948, no further readable signals were sent by any of the compromised circuits. VENONA was dead as an intelligence source on the NKGB, the GRU and all of the organs of the RIS. The only new insights now would be those obtained as more of the older ciphered material was broken out by VENONA and by hard counterintelligence operations on the ground.

In Australia, the government's security system had failed and the intensity of Washington's anger with Australia and Britain was reaching the point where they were even going to cut off Britain from classified US government information unless London cut off Australia from access to all British secrets or, preferably, forced Australia to take the breakdown of Australia's security seriously. Frankly, it was entirely reasonable for the Americans to be angry.

CHAPTER 17

THE MELBOURNE CONNECTION

As for Moscow Centre, things in Australia were going very well; in fact they were going too well, as the enthusiasm of Australia's communists overcame caution and good judgement. The NKGB officers at Moscow Centre were growing more and more concerned about the security of Clayton's tradecraft and the over-eagerness of the KLOD network, including its NKGB handlers in Australia. As American and British intelligence officials began to realise the extent and ruthlessness of the Soviet Union's policies and intelligence activities and as VENONA began to disclose the effectiveness of the penetration, new approaches to security intelligence were adopted and new technology used to monitor the Soviet Union's spies. The capability of Western counterintelligence agencies was growing as the threat posed by the RIS was gradually, and somewhat reluctantly, addressed.

In Australia, the government of Ben Chifley was coming under increasing pressure from Washington and London to replace its inept post-war security establishment with a more effective counterintelligence organisation. Moscow Centre's concern for its long-established and hard-to-maintain clandestine cells was becoming more justified. In Australia, the KLOD network and the Melbourne network, which appears to have been established as early as 1929, two years before Clayton immigrated from

278

New Zealand, were both now facing a greater threat, though not as great as Moscow Centre feared.

It is at this point that we need to examine the Melbourne cell, which appears to have been a long-term illegal operation of some significance.

The evidence that an illegal RIS residency was operating in Australia was first discovered in 1949 when Galina Nikolaevina Nosova, the wife of NKGB agent Feodor Nosov, made a mistake.[1] Galina was Nosov's communicator, charged with the laborious task of encoding and decoding messages. Her mistake was to do her encoding and decoding at home without playing loud music to prevent her vocalisations being overheard by a listening device, which, on 17 December, was exactly what happened.[2]

Galina was the victim of technological developments. Clandestine photography and listening devices, particularly the latter, had improved rapidly. The new technical spies used everything from the existing speakers on telephone handsets, fire alarms and public address systems as microphones, to cavity resonators, which produced no radiation, had no wires and used no power. Léon Theremin, the creator of the musical instrument that bears his name, designed and built a cavity resonator (later nicknamed 'The Thing') which was inserted into a wooden representation of the seal of the United States that the Soviet Young Pioneer Organization formally presented to the American ambassador in Moscow at the end of the war in Europe. The seal hung in the ambassador's residential study from 1945 until 1952.[3] It was not the first bug to be found there. In 1937, a dictaphone listening device was found in the ambassador's office and in 1944 a rare sweep of the embassy by the FBI found 120 listening devices. Even 'The Thing' was eventually found.[4]

In the West, the value of listening devices had been proven in Britain during World War II by MI19, a subsection of the Directorate of Military Intelligence responsible for the collection of intelligence from enemy prisoners of war. From early 1940 MI19 operated Trent Park, a large country house which it wired with listening devices connected to recorders from which teams of intelligence soldiers transcribed information in an adjoining facility. The first occupants were captured Luftwaffe pilots, whose private conversations provided sufficient intelligence to prove the system useful. Trent House was then used to house important prisoners, particularly generals and other senior officers, and extensive intelligence was collected, including evidence implicating the German army in the Holocaust.

The Nosovs were aware of this threat and should have been far more careful. Their flat, No. 19, 16–18 Kings Cross Road, Kings Cross, had been leased by TASS for some time and had already had one TASS occupant prior to the Nosovs. ASIO had had plenty of time to place a listening device in the wall. It was this bug that picked up Galina unwittingly and 'very quietly' verbalising a message about the secret division's longstanding Polish illegal.[5]

Galina's vocalisations provided three important clues. First, there was an illegal resident who had entered Australia twenty years before 1949, making his insertion around 1929. Second, the agent had entered Australia as a Polish refugee. Third, this agent was still active. It is from little pieces of intelligence like this that an intelligence picture is built and so it is from this small beginning that we are able to identify the Melbourne cell.

The timing of the illegal's insertion into Australia fits with what we know of the history of Soviet espionage at the time. In the late 1920s, finding itself treated as a pariah state, the Soviet government decided to rapidly expand its network of illegal residencies in foreign countries.[6] One of the initiatives, which was in itself a stroke of genius, was the setting up in Berlin in 1923 of WOSTWAG, the West-Osteuropaeische Warenaustausch Aktiengesellschaft, or West-East European Commodity Exchange Company, which dealt in furs, antlers, wool, pelts and bone glue. WOSTWAG established branches in Harbin, Hankou and Tientsin in China, and, as time passed, it also created subsidiary companies, including the Société Anonyme Français pour L'Importation de Legumes Secs in Paris, the Oriental Trading and Engineering Company in New York and, importantly for this story, the Far Eastern Trading Company in Tientsin in 1923 and, in London in 1936, The Far Eastern Fur Trading Company (FEFTC).[7]

When WOSTWAG was caught smuggling weapons to the Soviet Union in 1928 and wound up operations, its concessions, holdings and intelligence functions simply passed to its subsidiaries. In 1936, the FEFTC took over supporting the GRU illegal residencies. The beauty of this system was that all of these companies were real commercial companies involved in legitimate trade. The GRU's financial needs were met by the commercial profits of the legal businesses that only existed to provide cover for the GRU's intelligence activities. The vast majority of employees had no idea that their business was a GRU front. All aspects of the business, including the GRU activities, were run by the GRU operatives Uscher Zloczower and Rubin Glucksmann in

Britain, Europe and the United States, and Adam Purpiss in China.[8] Glucks-mann, whose real name was Reuben Gidoni, was a Jew born in Czernowitz, Romania, who claimed to be Austrian and held an Austrian passport but also utilised a Palestinian passport, which at the time was effectively a British passport. Glucksmann used his Palestinian passport to ease his travel in the British Empire, China and the United States.[9]

By 1939, the FEFTC had expanded WOSTWAG's original network in China to include company branches in Harbin, the regional headquarters for RIS operations in the Asia-Pacific region including all of the Americas, as well as Shanghai, and Ulan Bator in Mongolia.[10]

The FEFTC enabled GRU operatives to travel the world under the guise of fur traders and it enabled large sums of money, equipment and documenta-tion to be passed legitimately. And so, in Melbourne, three men involved in the fur trade start to become of interest to our story.

One of these men was Jack Skolnik. Skolnik, who changed his name from Isaac Shkdlnik, arrived in Melbourne on 4 August 1924 aboard the SS *Moncalieri* from Port Said, entering on a Palestinian passport.[11] Skolnik was born in Beltz, Romania, on 2 May 1904, before moving to Palestine to escape pogroms. According to Skolnik, in a letter he wrote to General Blamey in April 1940 offering himself as a spy, he had served as a British spy in Pales-tine during World War I under Sir Wyndham Deedes, a Turkish linguist and British Army staff officer. Skolnik claimed he spoke 'Arabic, English, German, Hebrew and Jewish' (perhaps he meant Yiddish), although he did not claim any capacity to speak Russian or Romanian.[12] Skolnik was inter-viewed by Military Intelligence and divulged the names of his fellow spies, an N. Belkind, the leader, Le Shanski, Aaronson and Fyne, an ex-Turkish army officer now supposedly living in Sydney. Their target was the German air squadrons in Palestine led by Captain Hellmuth Felmy and they operated by sending messages by courier to a village near the coast. From there, the messages were signalled to 'native vessels' lying offshore, which then passed the messages to Deedes.[13]

It all sounds a bit far-fetched, especially as Skolnik claimed that Belkind and Le Shanski had been hanged by the Turks and Aaronson killed in an aircraft crash, leaving Fyne and himself as the only survivors.[14] This story didn't leave many witnesses, and the choice of target—Captain Felmy and the German air squadron—was a little too obvious, as this officer was listed in the footnotes of the official Australian history of the war.[15] There is no record of the improbably named Fyne ever entering Australia—as a Turkish national, he most definitely would have left a trace.[16]

Skolnik settled in Melbourne where he opened a grocery and wine business at 635 Bridge Road, Richmond, and proceeded to build a large business empire involving hotels, nightclubs, brothels and other more legitimate businesses including wool and fur trading.[17] Skolnik also became a major patron of Australian soccer and ice hockey, and a major patron of the Jewish sporting club Hakoah.[18]

One of the businesses that Skolnik owned and operated from the shadows of proxies was the rather grand Maroondah Lake Hotel at Healesville. Skolnik used what he described as a cottage called Gracedale as his weekend retreat. In fact, Gracedale was one wing of the hotel and in it Skolnik had a telephone extension from the hotel switchboard installed for his own use.[19] ASIO had tapped the telephones at his office and home and found nothing of interest. However, when they uncovered his link to the Maroondah Lake Hotel and tapped its switchboard, they found what they were looking for. Legally, the evidence in the information from the intercepts is circumstantial at best, but, from an intelligence perspective it was solid gold.

....

Another member of the Melbourne cell was the successful furrier and fur trader Solomon Kosky, who was born in Vitebsk, Russia, on 3 June 1894, and arrived in Australia on 3 June 1912 from London aboard the SS *Ballarat*.[20] His early arrival means he could not be the secret division's Polish illegal. However, the care with which contact with Kosky was managed by the NKGB suggests he was an important and longstanding agent of the RIS. The question, though, is which part of the RIS Kosky was working for and whether Skolnik was part of this network as well.

What intelligence work Kosky actually did is unknown. By the time war came around again in 1939, Kosky, at 45, was too old to serve in the armed services or even in the bureaucracy, so he did the next best thing and applied for contracts to supply furs, skins and wool to the government. His business, innocently owned and operated by the Kosky family, operated from an impressive building in City Road, South Melbourne. For a long time, Solomon Kosky remained in the shadows, creating no interest among

Australia's security intelligence organisations, who were simply filing routine reports and requests dealing with applications for residence in Australia, use of motor vehicles and other simple matters.

The first indication that Kosky was more than a simple businessman came from an unexpected quarter, the Chinese consul, Mr L.M. (Martin) Wang, who had developed a personal dislike of Kosky and confidentially told D.A. Alexander, the Victorian Director of the CIS, that Kosky was the financial go-between the Soviet Legation in Canberra and the CP-A in Melbourne.[21] This was the first of many such allegations that Wang was to make and despite Alexander describing the allegation as being 'a matter of great interest', as usual under Lloyd, the CIS did nothing.[22]

The fact that the Chinese consul should make such an allegation was unexpected but given what we now know of the GRU's use of the fur and wool trade operated from Harbin and Shanghai in China, Mr Wang's allegations may have contained some substance. On 21 December 1948, Kosky again came to the attention of the CIS in Victoria when he was contacted by the Soviet wool buyer, T.G. Moskelev, a man who spoke more English than he let on and who appeared to be spying on the other Soviet officials involved in buying wool.[23] On top of this, Moskelev had dinner with Hirsch Munz, the Jewish academic and wool expert, at the Oriental Hotel on 15 December.[24]

The initial impression of the CIS watching Kosky was that he might have been approachable, that is someone who could be recruited to inform on the Soviets he was dealing with.[25] By February, the CIS were having doubts about this when Kosky was observed warning F.A. Krutikov, the commercial attaché at the Soviet Embassy and a suspected RIS operative, not to involve himself in a conversation with a CIS source.[26] Krutikov was most likely a GRU officer acting as Kosky's contact.

· · · · · · · · ·

At this point we can address an interesting anomaly in the VENONA record of RIS operations in Australia. The anomaly is that VENONA only compromised RIS activity in Sydney and Canberra, all controlled by the NKGB legal resident in Canberra. This is understandable, as the legal residency communicated with Moscow via encrypted telegrams, which were intercepted. In all of the VENONA record there is not one mention of the Melbourne cell or any of its activities, meaning it most likely communicated by courier. In fact, the activities of the Melbourne cell only became obvious after 1948, when Beria's NKGB were once again moving to take greater control of the GRU. Yet, Melbourne was the centre of the Australian government, particularly its defence establishment, and VENONA showed no evidence of RIS activity there.

There were only two reasons that there was no VENONA evidence of RIS activity in Melbourne: either there was none, or they were using couriers. The identification of the courier system in Melbourne took until 1952, when ASIO ran Operation TOURIST over two days, 3 and 4 September. This operation targeted three embassy officials, Nicolai Gregorievich Kovaliev, codenamed GRIGORIEV, the commercial attaché, Constantine Constantinovitch Didyk, employed in the commercial attaché's office, and Georgei Ivanovich Kharkovetz, the third secretary. The ASIO watchers believed that Didyk's body language was not that of a military man, which suggests the other two looked military, or GRU, and Kovaliev was most definitely the boss.[27]

The three arrived in Melbourne on 3 September 1952 and caught a taxi to Scott's Hotel at 444 Collins Street, where they arrived at 4.35 p.m. Ten minutes later, two of them, Didyk and Kharkovetz, went out visiting shops, most likely to divert the ASIO surveillance team, which they did. This allowed Kovaliev to slip out of the hotel unobserved later.[28] All three returned to the hotel and had dinner before heading to the San Moritz ice rink in Saint Kilda, the location for the Ice Hockey Lightning Premiership, a particular sporting interest of Jack Skolnik. However, the ice hockey game was scheduled for the next night.

They sat and watched the skating for around twenty minutes, from 8.15 to 8.35 p.m., before leaving and walked to the Palais Pictures on the Lower Esplanade in Saint Kilda. They stayed there until 11.10 p.m., after which they caught a taxi back to their hotel and presumably went to bed. Well at least the ASIO watchers did, as the surveillance stopped at 11.55 p.m.[29]

The following day, Didyk and Kharkovetz went out shopping at 9.35 a.m. before returning to the hotel. They then caught a taxi to Solomon Kosky's business. From there, accompanied by Kosky and Samuel Baum, the manager of the Fur Department of Myers, they went to lunch before going to the Myers Fur Salon where they talked business and examined furs until they returned to their hotel at around 3.45 p.m.

Kovaliev had left Scott's Hotel at 10.00 a.m. alone and carrying a bulky satchel. Working alone is significant because RIS couriers were, for obvious reasons, forbidden to do this. This behaviour marks Kovaliev out as a professional, perhaps the case officer of the Melbourne cell. The other significant behaviour that marked Kovaliev out was his countersurveillance tradecraft. He walked along Queens and Flinders streets carefully stopping at each crossing and then entered the New Theatre, where he remained for 30 minutes before leaving with his satchel and going to Coles in Swanson Street where he looked at, but did not buy, children's toys. This was not his first fleeting visit to the New Theatre. He had entered this venue on 19 May 1952 and left a satchel there indicating that the RIS were using it as a dead letter box, a clandestine and secure place for handlers and their agents to pick up and drop off materials.[30]

He then continued popping in and out of various stores, before booking three seats on Trans Australian Airlines Flight 535 back to Canberra for 7.40 p.m. that evening.[31] The ASIO watchers then lost him until he reappeared at Scott's Hotel that afternoon without the satchel.[32]

In January 1952, the new NKGB legal resident, Vladimir Petrov, had been warned not to contact Kosky without the direct approval of Moscow Centre. In June, he was ordered to use Kovaliev to establish official contact with Kosky. Petrov identified Kosky as an RIS agent of long standing, yet he used the word 'establish' rather than re-establish, suggesting Kosky was not an NKGB asset. This is further supported by Petrov's further orders to 'study' Kosky, that is to closely investigate Kosky by planting an agent on him to check he was safe to be used as an NKGB agent.[33] Kosky passed and was assigned the NKGB cover-name PRIYATEL (FRIEND).[34] According to Petrov, this was the first time that Kosky had been approached by any NKGB operative in Australia.[35]

It is interesting that Kosky, a man who had been a long-term RIS agent who had visited the Soviet Union and had a hands-off warning from Moscow, played it cool with Kovaliev. In fact, Kosky was so cool Kovaliev decided that Kosky was not worth pursuing as an agent. One wonders if Kosky was happy about being approached by the NKGB. This recruitment of Kosky coincided with the aftermath and reorganisation of the GRU following yet another purge by Beria, this time justified by the defection in Ottawa of the GRU cipher clerk, Igor Gouzenko. Kosky was right to be unhappy, because his recruitment by the NKGB led to his identification at the RCE.

....

However, neither Kosky nor Skolnik were Galina's Polish illegal. The man who best fits the bill is Hirsch Munz, born in Krynki, Grodno, Poland, on 21 April

285

1905.[36] Munz arrived in Australia on the *Morton Bay* on 15 December 1927, putting him close to Galina's twenty years.[37] Following his arrival in Melbourne, Munz settled down for four years working at the Gross Knitting Mills, where he earned £4 per week and supplemented his pay by teaching French and German, earning another £2 a week.[38] By August 1928, Munz had saved £20, and he unsuccessfully applied to bring his brother Icheskiel to Australia. He applied again in May 1929 and, as this resulted in a CIS investigation of the application, we have a typically casual anti-Semitic description of Munz as 'a superior type of Jew', one who was working hard, saving his money and putting himself through the University of Melbourne, where he eventually hoped to teach.[39] Icheskiel was duly approved.

By January 1933 Munz was in Adelaide working as a wool research officer at the Commonwealth Council for Scientific and Industrial Research and lecturing at the University of Adelaide where he was 'highly respected'.[40] The CIS reports describe him as fluent in English and capable of teaching French and German to native English speakers.[41] If Munz was a clandestine GRU operative, he had done very well indeed. Munz remained in Adelaide until 1936, when he left for the McMaster Animal and Health Laboratory at the University of Sydney.[42]

One hint of espionage about Hirsch Munz at this time was that, although he was a very successful academic, after his return from Sydney he owned and operated a tiny company, H. Munz Wool Trading Company, out of 473–481 Bourke Street, Melbourne. This firm was so small the CIS believed it was a front for other activities involving the Soviet Union. The CIS was probably right.[43]

The connection of Skolnik, Kosky and Munz with the fur trade, a marker of GRU tradecraft, suggests this group were a GRU, or Soviet Military Intelligence, illegal operating with support from the NKGB.

Munz's efforts to bring fellow Jews, especially his sister, Dora Sztejnsa-pir, and brother Joseph into Australia in the late 1930s, attracted attention from the authorities.[44] Then in September 1939, the Polish Consul-General in Sydney informed Major W.R. Scott of Military Intelligence in Sydney that Hirsch Munz should be interned immediately. However, having recommended this, the Consul-General refused to divulge his reasons for making the recommendation, leaving Scott at a bit of a loss.[45] The subsequent NSW Police investigation dismissed the possibility that Munz was pro-German in any way.[46] The Polish Consul-General knew that Munz was a communist, and perhaps even that he was a GRU officer.[47] On the basis of this, Military

Intelligence moved to have Munz interned, but stopped the action as there was nothing incriminating found.[48] On 12 January 1940, Military Intelligence were again investigating Munz, this time because he had applied for a position in the Censorship staff, reading letters in Yugoslavian, Czech, Hebrew and Yiddish, a perfect spot for an RIS operative collecting information on people writing home to eastern Europe.[49] It appears Munz did not get the position, but by mid-1942, Munz had managed to join the navy.[50]

Munz was appointed as a probationary paymaster-lieutenant, Royal Australian Navy Volunteer Reserve, in July 1942. The Paymaster Branch is the branch of the navy from which those naval officers involved in intelligence were placed.[51] The 37-year-old Munz was rated unfit for duty at sea and so joined Section B of the AIB on 13 September 1942. Essentially, Munz was working for Captain Roy Kendall, RNVR, the MI6 legal resident in Australia.[52] Munz served in this unit as the Research and Records Officer from 4 September 1942 until 3 August 1945.[53] In his confidential report on Munz, Kendall rated him as an 'outstanding Research and Records Officer', only deficient in leadership, and 'somewhat below standard in the social attributes normally associated with an Officer'.[54] If Munz was the illegal, the GRU must have been ecstatic.

... ...

In 1955 Skolnik employed a man called David John Morris and his firm, Industrial Plant Pty Ltd, to do a job for his wife at their house in Toorak—constructing and fitting a steel door on a room. Either Mrs Skolnik had a lot of jewels or someone at the Skolnik home wanted a secure space, possibly one that was also a Faraday cage.[55] Given Morris's expertise—he was a very highly qualified electrical engineer and physicist—a Faraday cage is a real possibility and, if this was being done, a mark of real sophistication in Skolnik's security arrangements. This work also provided an opportunity for Morris to meet and speak with Wally Clayton during the period leading up to and during the Royal Commission on Espionage (RCE) (often called the Petrov Royal Commission), a time when Clayton was hiding from the Australian authorities.[56] The work at Skolnik's Toorak home seems to have been just one facet of their relationship, and it stands out as Skolnik never provided his Toorak address in correspondence. He only ever used his business addresses for all business and personal correspondence.

... ...

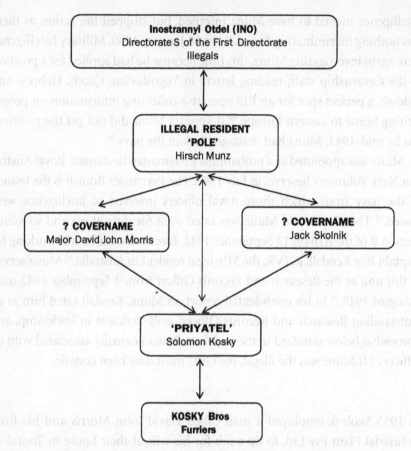

Figure 17.1: The Melbourne illegal cell, 1927–50

Note: Despite his high profile in the CP-A, Major David John Morris was part of this network.

David John Morris was born in Brisbane on 24 April 1910 to Leonard and Jessie Morris, prominent members of Brisbane's Baptist community. Morris's father was an educator and the Superintendent of the Central Technical College in Queensland. Morris had a normal middle-class education, attending Yeronga State School before Brisbane Grammar and then the University of Queensland, where he studied engineering. Somewhere along the way, Morris became a committed communist.

At university, Morris was recognised as brilliant and a little odd. He certainly made no secret of his utter commitment to communism and was a leading member of the Australian Communist Party Group at the University

288

of Queensland.[57] In 1931 Morris obtained a second class honours degree in engineering and went off to work before returning to the university in 1936 to do a degree in physics. Making full use of the Queensland government's generosity, he then travelled to the UK for free to undertake further studies at the General Electric Company, Birmingham.[58] While in Britain, Morris declared he was likely to visit France, Germany, Spain, Italy and the United States.[59] Officially, he said nothing about visiting the Soviet Union, but that was certainly his intention.[60]

Morris's plans to visit were stymied not by MI5 or the CIS but by the Soviets, who refused him a visa and would not be swayed by appeals from the CP-GB.[61] The refusal of the visa made Morris 'very indignant' and was noted as being 'interesting' by the CIS.[62] In 1939, it was out of the ordinary for the Soviets to refuse a visa to a sympathetic specialist like Morris unless he was involved in clandestine work or was being considered for such work. The RIS made a habit of refusing such people entry to the Soviet Union as it drew too much attention to them.

After his return to Australia, Morris sought work and, in December 1939, half-heartedly tried to join the militia but was rejected on the grounds that he was 'irresponsible', but more likely because he was still a prominent communist agitator at the University of Queensland.[63] Following this failure to enlist, Morris took part in a CP-A effort to spread communist-inspired propaganda among Australian troops in and around Brisbane. However, on 29 December 1941, Morris, because of his engineering talent, was appointed as an honorary lieutenant in the Australian Army and on 19 January 1942 was enlisted into the army.[64]

Morris was not good with troops and in August 1942 he was transferred to the AIF and then to the Mechanical Maintenance section of LHQ in October of that year. In March 1944 he was posted to the Military College of Science in Britain and the highly secret Tank Design Centre. Unexpectedly, on 8 March 1945, Morris was marched out of the Military College of Science and sent to fight in Europe. It would later be learned that the commanding officer of the Tank Design Centre, most likely on the advice of MI5, had banned Morris and rather than upsetting the already fragile relationship with Australia, the War Office sent him to Germany.[65] As a result, no one in Australia knew of his exclusion from the Tank Design Centre and in April 1945, Morris returned home.

Suspiciously, for a highly skilled and qualified engineer, Morris stayed on in the army although he did successfully apply for a position with the State Electricity Commission of Victoria earning £625 a year, a position he accepted in a letter of 22 March 1946. On 24 March, Morris withdrew his acceptance on the grounds that he was to fill a position in Britain for the army at a much higher salary.[66] The position he was heading off to fill in June 1946 was at the very establishment he had been banned from in 1945.

At the time Morris was heading back to Britain, the Australian army had finally had enough of Military Intelligence. The new Director of Military Intelligence was Colonel Charles Spry, an infantry officer who had long been a severe critic of the organisation. As director, he sacked the vast majority of his officers and instituted the security vetting of all personnel, military and civilian, in his directorate. As a result, Spry found undeclared CP-A members working in the organisation. At the same time, someone finally drew his attention to Morris, and Spry had him immediately recalled to Australia. His appointment as a serving officer was terminated on 11 December 1946. Morris now reapplied for the position he had turned down at the Electricity Commission and despite the position having been filled, the chief engineer began the process of creating a position to employ him.[67]

Morris's original army security clearance, if it could be called that, was provided by Robert Wake, who stated that 'there was no reason why he should not be in the army, but that he should not be placed on very secret jobs'.[68] This little bit of trivia was placed on the file by Wake for recording purposes, or to cover himself now that Morris had been identified as a security risk.

None of this stopped Morris. In April 1949, Morris was applying for a position on the Long-Range Weapons British Army Organisation, a high-value GRU target.[69] Later that month Lieutenant Colonel J. Wigglesworth, Superintendent of Design in the Mechanical Engineering Branch of LHQ, discovered that Morris had been appointed as the civilian Superintendent of Design (Mechanisation) of the army's Design Directorate, something he reported to his superiors. The senior intelligence officer at LHQ noted that this was 'very bad'.[70] He was not wrong, because at this time Morris was being studied by Valentin Matveevich Sadovntkov, the NKGB legal resident in Canberra.

We already know of David Morris's involvement with the Melbourne cell, particularly Jack Skolnik. However, other than his attempts to penetrate weapons design projects, we have little hard information on his intelligence activity. However, the fact that he was being studied by the NKGB in 1949 and the details of his subsequent history would suggest he was a useful intelligence operative, most likely for the GRU. The evidence for this comes from his career as a constructed martyr for the CP-A—Morris only applied for sensitive positions, knowing he would not get them. From the evidence of the files, it is also readily apparent he actively sabotaged some of his applications by withdrawing them or not turning up to the final interviews on spurious grounds, all the while telling his wife that ASIO had blocked his employment. Later comments made by a senior CP-A member, Ralph Siward Gibson, indicate this may have been a propaganda exercise to paint the Australian security services as having forced Morris to take his family overseas to the freedom of communism.[71]

The Morris family duly departed Australia for Beijing where, virtually imprisoned by the Chinese, Morris's wife became very disgruntled. In an effort to get her family home she came back to Australia and tried to get the CP-A to authorise David's return home. While she was in Australia, David Morris engineered the move of the family to Moscow, where he was treated as a very important person.

On their arrival in Moscow the Morris family, after a week in a hotel, was given a three-bedroom apartment, a rare gift that was highly prized in Moscow at this time. The apartment was supplied with a special telephone that connected with Valentine, the personal assistant to an unnamed member of the Politburo.[72]

This was exceptional treatment, indicating that David Morris was more than just another CP-A member seeking to live in the Soviet Union. Not only that, the Morris family were not subjected to NKGB visits and they had permission to mix with foreigners, including, for one son, having a teenage romance with the daughter of an American diplomat. As if this was not incriminating enough, the man with whom David Morris was most friendly, and the man appointed by Morris and his wife to oversee the family's affairs in Russia, was none other than Donald Duart Maclean of the Cambridge Five.[73]

· · · · · · · · ·

As we have noted above, when Vladimir Petrov stepped into an ASIO car at Sydney Airport on 3 April 1954, the NKGB's networks in Australia, including the Melbourne Cell, were completely compromised. The options Petrov's defection presented were clear. The Australian government could carry out arrests of suspects and then prosecute them in a court of law, something very difficult to do given the fragmentary and highly sensitive nature of clandestine intelligence. The other option was to use the defection to completely disrupt RIS operations by exposing these to the full glare of publicity and the best way of doing this was to launch a royal commission, the RCE.

The real purpose of the RCE, whatever the lawyers think, was not to put members of the CP-A on trial, it was to utterly disrupt the operations of the RIS in Australia by publicly exposing those individuals who had been identified as RIS assets and RIS agents or officers. It was about humiliation and forced reorganisation inducing chaos within the RIS, which it did for a time.

Despite the professionalism of the Melbourne cell, a number of its members, including Jack Skolnik, Solomon Kosky and David Morris, were swept up in the chaos when their names were found in an NKGB document listed by the RCE as Document G. The RCE did not recommend further action against any of the men named in Document G, although it did make adverse findings about their testimony. What betrayed them were their own lies at later ASIO interviews and their subsequent confusions and admissions.

When he testified at the RCE, Skolnik consistently denied that he knew of the whereabouts of Wally Clayton. But when David Morris was interviewed without notice by ASIO officers at his office on 21 March 1957, he admitted to having met Clayton, living under the covername Wally Thompson, during the work on Skolnik's safe room at his Toorak home in 1955, although he claimed that the two men did not speak to one another.[74] Morris also admitted that Skolnik knew who Clayton was and was quite familiar with him. Indeed, it appears that Clayton was hiding at Healesville, a town where Skolnik had close connections as the owner of the Maroondah Lake Hotel.

As if his admissions were not bad enough, immediately after his interview with ASIO in March 1957, Morris called Skolnik on his office telephone, which ASIO had tapped, and told him of the interview, the questions he had been asked and some of what he had said.[75] He didn't tell Skolnik of his admissions in relation to Clayton being at Skolnik's home in 1955.

All of this suggests that Jack Skolnik was more than a shady but successful businessman, sportsman and philanthropist. Skolnik was a player in the great game.

....

When we look back at the Melbourne cell, what we see is a network that operated so well that its members were not discovered until they were drawn into the growing control of the NKGB. While they remained isolated from the NKGB legal residency in Canberra, Australian authorities knew almost nothing about them, their work or their effectiveness, and the likelihood is that we will never know the full extent of what they did. They appear to have been part of the great GRU operation that started with WOSTWAG and passed down to the Far Eastern Fur Trading Company. As the American diplomat Herschel Johnson, who was charged with coordinating the counter-espionage effort of the United States with MI5 wrote to Guy Liddell of that organisation:

> the persons connected with these enterprises have acted with consummate Skill. Some of their actions may have appeared stupid but in reality on closer examination it is difficult to detect flaws in their method of operation'.[76]

Herschel Johnson could have been writing about the Melbourne cell.

CHAPTER 18

ARE WE IN HELL?
THE FRUITS OF INACTION

On 11 February 1946, Australia was faced with a real crisis. It was the position of the chiefs of staff of the armed services that Australia's future defence was dependent upon access to SIGINT derived from the United States and Britain and, as a result, Prime Minister Chifley approved the acceptance of an invitation from the British Government for an Australian delegation to attend a SIGINT conference in London.[1] The delegation was authorised, according to Secretary for Defence Co-Ordination Frederick Shedden, to officially discuss the proposals but not commit the Australian Government to anything. Australia was prepared to participate in a British Commonwealth SIGINT organisation operating under the broad direction of the United Kingdom.[2]

The impetus for this action was the desire of the chiefs of staff to maintain Australia's wartime SIGINT capability in a peacetime organisation. This desire was in line with Britain's to establish a British Commonwealth SIGINT organisation that, using facilities across the Commonwealth, would cover the entire world. In Australia, the push for a SIGINT organisation was accompanied by a concurrent push to establish a Joint Intelligence Bureau (JIB), staffed by military personnel and civilians.[3]

The Defence Committee had advised the government that, because of the differing needs of the services, it had not recommended the merging of individual service intelligence organisations; it believed a national level JIB was required for the analysis and assessment of strategic intelligence and that a national level SIGINT organisation was also required. If these organisations were to be established, to be fully effective they needed to receive intelligence from both Britain and the United States. As a result, they needed to be protected from hostile intelligence agencies and this required a national level defence security agency.[4]

The same need existed for the intended peacetime SIGINT organisation, but much more acutely, given the sensitivities surrounding SIGINT. The new British worldwide SIGINT organisation was being based in centres in the United Kingdom, Canada and Australia, with New Zealand's contribution being made through Australia's organisation.[5] With the addition of the United States, this arrangement became the 'Five Eyes' organisation beloved by modern conspiracy theorists.

The Australian SIGINT organisation, named the Defence Signals Bureau (DSB), was to be based in Melbourne, the then centre of the Commonwealth government, and created by merging British and Australian assets, including intercept sites and direction-finding stations in Asia. Each centre would undertake the collection of raw material and conduct traffic analysis, development and cryptographic attack, as well as translation and reporting on a basis agreed between the centre and London.[6] The resulting intelligence would then be distributed to the armed services, government departments and agencies on a need-to-know basis.[7]

All of this would be impossible without good security and the chiefs of staff advised the government that it was essential for the legislation to be tightened up so that the security service had effective legal powers to combat espionage. In the opinion of the chiefs, the sole law applying to peacetime security, Part VII of the Crimes Act, was insufficient, incomplete and out of date.[8] It would require a capital investment of £30,000 for the SIGINT organisation and involve annual costs in 1946–47 of £275,500 rising to £464,500, three quarters of which would be dedicated to the SIGINT organisation.[9]

These recommendations of the Defence Committee were submitted to the Ministerial Council of Defence on 9 April 1946, which failed to agree on taking them to the full Cabinet. The main objections, put by Dr Evatt, were that the proposals for a JIB and a national SIGINT organisation were 'contrary to established constitutional principles of Ministerial and Departmental control and responsibility'.[10] Other objections included the proposed machinery being 'neither effective nor economical', a rather laughable perspective coming from members of the Chifley Cabinet. Despite the objections, the committee approved the formation of a national level SIGINT organisation in principle.[11] While all of this was being debated and decided in Canberra, an old friend, Mic Sandford, slips back into the picture.

After his exploits in security intelligence in Adelaide, Sandford went on to serve as an intelligence officer attached to the British SIGINT system in the Middle East. It was here that he was introduced to ULTRA and to the work of Special Liaison Units (SLUs) and Special Liaison Officers (SLOs) whose task it was to receive, decode, disseminate and destroy all ULTRA signals. The codeword ULTRA was used to describe highly sensitive SIGINT derived from high-level German codes. It also covered high-level diplomatic traffic from other countries, such as Japan, whose codes were being read by Britain, the United States and the Soviet Union.

The importance of Japanese diplomatic traffic lay in the fact that the Japanese ambassador was the only source of intelligence on what Germany's political leadership was thinking or planning, because he was signalling the results of his discussions with Hitler, Goering, Goebbels and Himmler, as well as other senior leaders, back to Tokyo. All of these signals were being read by the United States and Britain, but the actual signals were intercepted in Australia.[12]

Sandford had been flown by Qantas via Calcutta to the Middle East. He arrived on 14 April 1941 and was officially posted to the SIGINT unit No. 2 Australian Special Wireless Section (ASWS) on 16 April 1941, which he finally joined at Chanea, on Crete, in late May, just in time to take part in the Battle of Crete and the withdrawal.[13]

Along with impressing the soldiers with his character and unconventional habits, Sandford caused a stir in the officers' mess by recommending they purchase curtains and tablecloths. The wine they served was not up to his standards so he went out and bought a barrel of the best Cretan wine he could find for 11,000 drachmas. It was his choice of dinner jacket, claret-coloured, that went too far, and his OC forbade him ever to wear it again.[14] This incident aside, Sandford's cryptographic skill, his dedication to his work, his courage and leadership on the retreat showed him to be a man worth following.[15]

From Crete, Sandford went with No. 4 ASWS to Lebanon and Syria before being seconded for duty with the British SIGINT organisation in the Middle East, most likely at 'M' at Heliopolis, and attached to British SIGINT units in the Western Desert.[16] It is during this time that Sandford most likely developed links with senior civilian and military officers from GC&CS and during which he was introduced to the full range of capabilities, including electro-mechanical attacks on Italian and German ciphers and codes. In mid-January 1941, No. 4 ASWS was warned to prepare for a move back home following Japanese strikes at Malaya, Hong Kong, Philippines and Pearl Harbor; Mic Sandford rejoined the unit.[17]

On arrival in Australia aboard the SS *Orcades*, Sandford was posted to G Branch of GHQ in Melbourne where he went to work establishing the Australian Army's SIGINT organisation.[18] On 2 April 1942, he was posted to Central Bureau as the officer commanding the Australian component, effectively, the second in command of the Combined US–UK–Australian unit.[19]

Sandford quickly became a force at Central Bureau and although Brigadier General Spencer Akin, US Army, formally commanded the unit, Akin left it up to his subordinates to run the technical operations. As a result, over a short period of time and supported by the MI6 Head of Station in Brisbane, Captain Roy Kendall, RNR, Sandford became the trusted link between GC&CS and Central Bureau.[20] Indeed, we know that Sandford was trained by Frederick Winterbotham in ULTRA security and dissemination techniques in London, home of the Y Board, the authority which controlled all SIGINT, and not at Bletchley Park, which was where SIGINT was produced.[21] This indicates that Sandford was an initiate of the SLU and SLO system for the communication, control and distribution of ULTRA.[22] Sandford was deeply inside the British system and trusted. As anyone who has worked in this area knows, once you are indoctrinated you become a member of all the organisations involved.

Among the activities Sandford became involved with was MI6's effort to protect ULTRA and Central Bureau from the depravations of Australia's dysfunctional and corrupt wartime Security Service, which in Brisbane was led by Robert Wake.[23]

The counterintelligence operations of the Brisbane MI6 station were the responsibility of Third Officer Eve Walker, WRNS.[24] Walker was well known in intelligence circles in Brisbane and northern Australia as the kind of person who got things done. If you needed a submarine, ship or aircraft and no one else could get you one, you talked to Third Officer Walker, who was described by a visiting MI5 officer, as being 'of the cloak and dagger type'.[25] She was also the officer who kept Wake bemused and away from Central Bureau and the MI6 station's operations in South-East Asia.[26] She also kept the Americans at bay from Kendall's operations in Asia and watched for any other intelligence activity by foreign services, including the RIS.

The relevance of all this is not simply that Sandford worked with MI6 to keep the Australian Security Service ignorant of Central Bureau's work, it is that it was Central Bureau that first discovered the leaks of secret information from Australia and that these leaks included SIGINT and even ULTRA material.

The problem of the leaking of secret information was not something that arose after the arrival of the Soviet Legation and its coterie of NKGB and GRU intelligence officers. The real problem was the Australian government's complete disregard for the security of its own secrets and the secrets of its allies. This disregard, as we have seen, went to the very top of Australia's government as evidenced by the leaking of British Cabinet secrets by Australia's prime minister, Robert Menzies, and his deputy, Arthur Fadden, in April 1941.[27]

Most of this caused little concern. The only people it upset were the British, and given their propensity for politeness, the Australian government does not seem to have been bothered by any concerns coming from London. All of this changed in early 1942, when US forces began to arrive in Australia. Once they were in Australia, the Americans were not impressed with what they found, and they would prove unforgiving about lax Australian security standards throughout the war. The least forgiving of the Americans would prove to be the US Navy, particularly their SIGINT detachment CAST, that had moved from Cavite on Luzon island in the Philippines to Melbourne via Corregidor and the Dutch East Indies.[28]

On arrival in Melbourne, the US Naval unit was renamed Fleet Radio Unit Melbourne (FRUMEL) and placed under the hard-driving Lieutenant Rudy Fabian. Among the first things Fabian did was have his sailors establish their intercept sites by taking tools from the Australian construction workers and building the facilities at Moorabbin to speed the work up. In the same no-nonsense way Fabian also began a process of driving out the Australian and British personnel working on Japanese diplomatic ciphers and cutting off ties with Central Bureau and the bulk of the Australian services, including to a lesser degree the RAN. From the very beginning, Fabian was highly critical of Australia's security standards.[29]

The critical attitude of the US authorities was not something that Australia could ignore. For one thing, the United States saw Australia as their forward base in the Pacific and not much else. Indeed, by June 1942, the Combined Chiefs of Staff in Washington made up of senior British and American officers had agreed that Australia, for HUMINT purposes, fell under the auspices of the US Office of Strategic Services (OSS), the forerunner of the CIA, and not Britain's Special Operations Executive (SOE).[30] This was a strong indication that US concern at poor security would carry increasing weight in Australia.

The first major breach of ULTRA affecting Australia occurred in June 1943, when the Australian Secretary of the Department of External Affairs, Colonel W.R. Hodgson, became aware of Australian-originated reporting relating to William Slater, Australia's first diplomatic representative to the Soviet Union, based in Kuybyshev.[31] Hodgson had not been indoctrinated and was not allowed to even know of the existence of ULTRA, let alone see it. This leak resulted from a Colonial Office official assuming one of Hodgson's officers in London was indoctrinated and then sharing ULTRA with that officer.[32]

By the end of July 1943, the panic caused by Hodgson's unauthorised access to ULTRA had subsided. He was indoctrinated for limited access and a sanitisation process was agreed to enable him to pass information to Evatt, his minister, after he threatened to take the matter directly to Evatt and Cabinet. This episode had hardly ended when Sandford at Central Bureau notified his superiors, and no doubt the Y Board in London, that there had been further and much more dangerous leaks of SIGINT and indeed ULTRA information.

On 29 July, Sandford passed a signal to 'C', the head of Y Board in London, that 'a fairly reliable source', a cover phrase denoting SIGINT, had shown that intelligence from inside Australia was being passed by the IJA from Harbin in China to GHQ in Tokyo.[33] Brigadier John Rogers, the Director of Military Intelligence, Sandford and Lieutenant Colonel R.A. Little believed the Soviet Legation in Canberra had somehow obtained the material and passed it to Moscow, from where the Japanese had obtained it or the Soviets had passed it to them.[34]

Although the Chinese were later identified as the source of some of the leaks, there is a possibility that some of the leaks were the work of the RIS, particularly the GRU, who we now know had penetrated the Australian Army.

That the GRU were not disinterested in Australia is amply demonstrated by the fact that the first legal GRU Resident in Australia was the highly experienced Victor Sergeevich Zajtsev, codenamed SERGE in VENONA traffic, who arrived in Australia on 16 March 1943, eighteen months after the arrest of Richard Sorge in Tokyo, to take up his cover duty as the Second Secretary. By 26 May, Zajtsev was travelling away from the legation in Canberra to address a public meeting in Sydney.[35] On 22 June, Zajtsev was addressing a dinner in Brisbane, given in his honour by the Australian–Soviet Friendship League of Queensland, at Lennon's Hotel; in December, he was in Perth attending a presentation by Jessie Street, proceeds from which went to the 'Sheepskin Appeal'. Later, he was able to travel freely around Canberra and environs.[36] Even as a Second Secretary, the freedom given to Zajtsev by the Soviet Minister made him very special and very trusted. In fact, a more sophisticated Security Service than that Australia possessed at the time would have marked Zajtsev's card as a spook.

Zajtsev was indeed a spook of some standing who had first come to attention following the collapse of the GRU's Sorge ring in Japan. Sorge's behaviour as an agent, and the behaviour of members of his cell, had caused growing concern in Moscow Centre and the GRU had sent Zajtsev there to take over control of Sorge from Helge Leonidovich Vutkevich, the GRU 'legal' in Tokyo.[37] But the Sorge ring was doomed already. Sorge had resorted to using a clandestine radio operated by his German assistant Max Klausen to send messages to Vladivostok. The Kempeitai, the highly efficient Japanese military police, soon detected their signals and closed in on the ring.

The evidence would suggest that the Kempeitai had long known of the Sorge ring and its activities. In a society as closed, hierarchical and conformist as that of Japan in the 1930s and 1940s, you could not operate a cell of around 40 people, many of whom were Japanese, and not be noticed. It does beggar belief that Sorge thought that the Kempeitai's efficient domestic 'block' reporting system would not pick up members of the network. This writer thinks that not only did the Kempeitai quickly identify the ring, but that it penetrated it using double agents.

Even if the domestic surveillance system had missed Sorge's network, it did not miss the radio transmissions. The SIGINT intercept and direction-finding system would soon have triangulated the position of the radio being used. There is even anecdotal evidence to suggest that the Kempeitai had broken the GRU codes being used by Sorge.[38] None of this failure was attributed by Moscow Centre to Zajtsev; however, the man he replaced, Vutkevich, was executed.

An interesting bit of evidence given by Vladimir Petrov in his testimony before the Royal Commission was that all communications with Moscow by the NKGB and GRU were via telegram through the Canberra Post Office and that a clandestine radio sent out for Zajtsev had lain dismantled under a table throughout Petrov's time at the embassy.[39] It would seem that Zajtsev did not repeat the mistakes of the Sorge ring.

There is little hard information available on Zajtsev, except what he told the Australian newspapers and what is known of his GRU career. In his public pronouncements, which need to be taken with a pinch of salt, he claimed to have been born in Moscow and to have attended Moscow University, where he studied economics and economic geography before joining the diplomatic service.[40] Perversely, given the need to keep the lies of your legend, your cover persona, as close to your truth as possible, he most likely was born in Moscow and did attend Moscow University.

In his diplomatic life, Zajtsev served as the Second Secretary at the Soviet Embassy in Tokyo until the destruction of the Sorge ring in October 1941.[41] After this, he was posted back to Moscow and, given that he was not shot but posted to Canberra as a Second Secretary, he seems to have done a good job in Tokyo.[42] In 1947, despite being sent home after his disagreements with the minister and the NKGB, Zajtsev remained a senior officer in the GRU and remained there when it returned to the control of the General Staff.[43] Again, this is not the career of a failure.

From its establishment in 1943, Zajtsev's GRU residency was actively targeting Australia's military and technical secrets, and the illegal RIS networks, some of which most surely were GRU.[44] In fact, we can be certain that the GRU were busy, as VENONA provides plenty of evidence that the NKGB took an interest in the problems of their NEIGHBOURS and would have been reporting if the five men of the Red Army GRU residency in Canberra were not conducting operations.

As for the illegal networks, as we have seen above, there can be little doubt that these were operational and that they may have been involved in transmitting Australian secrets to the Far Eastern Fur Trading Company, based in Harbin.[45]

The location of this company, Harbin, which was also the RIS HQ for operations in all of the Far East, including the Pacific, is important for our story. Harbin was also the major centre for Japanese intelligence operations against the Soviet Union and it is no surprise that it was on the IJA link between Harbin and Tokyo that Central Bureau intercepted Australian secret information being passed up to the IJA's GHQ.[46] This may have been the first indications of Zajtsev's illegal GRU operations in Australia.

Other points that seem to have been systematically overlooked by historians were that Zajtsev's career indicated he was an 'Easterner' and that the intelligence that was leaking was military intelligence, not political or economic intelligence. Zajtsev's operational experience, as far as we can ascertain, was in Japan, then Australia and within the GRU in Moscow. This provides a specific Eastern expertise, particularly in Japanese affairs, to his work, which would have made him the right Resident to run operations that could obtain intelligence of use to the Japanese. Zajtsev would have been well versed in working with and through Harbin and equally well versed in dealing with the Japanese. This would have meant he was highly capable of selecting the kind of intelligence here in Australia that would be of interest to them. All of this is very circumstantial, but an intelligence picture is bits and pieces of circumstantial evidence put together over time.

In Australia, the leaks had been detected by Central Bureau and, on 29 July 1943, Sandford passed this information directly to London after discussing it with the Deputy Director of Military Intelligence in Melbourne. The idea that the Soviets were deliberately passing ULTRA/ZYMOTIC to the Japanese is not, as already said, that far-fetched.[47] After all, the Soviet Union and Japan were not at war and Japan was a difficult neighbour for the Soviets. Keeping the Japanese focused on the Americans by passing them intelligence was eminently sensible. The Australian Army now attempted to use this allegation as leverage in obtaining permission for Australia to intercept and conduct a cryptanalytical attack on Soviet codes, something London and Washington had only just begun themselves and something they would not have wanted the Australians involved in.[48]

The reply, when it came sometime after 5 September 1943, made it clear that Australia was not going to be allowed to play in this game. The length of time it took for the reply to arrive, over five weeks, and only after multiple prompts from Sandford, said it all. London was stalling for time.[49]

The Y Board in London attempted to deflate Australian expectations by describing the Soviet use of one-time pads for diplomatic and RIS traffic. As a SIGINT operative, Sandford would have understood the implication of this information and the impossibility of ever breaking such a system cheaply and with the resources available in Australia. London then put forward the idea that perhaps the material had arrived in IJA hands via a fourth party, in this case, and not unreasonably, London nominated the Nationalist Chinese. With that information passed, London then asked Sandford to pass further specimens of the raw traffic for further investigation.[50] This clearly shows that London was very interested in this activity, but wanted no action taken that would lead to a change in Australian activity, something that would have alerted whoever was compromising Australia's security.

London also misdirected Australian attention onto the Chinese Nationalists by asking if the Australians had considered 'other Allied or neutral representatives' as the source of the leaks. This was an effective ploy as by this time GC&CS had utterly compromised Chinese Nationalist codes and ciphers.[51] Indeed, by 1943 several countries had broken the low-grade codes and ciphers used by the Chinese Nationalists including, in 1936, Japan.[52] In December 1944, Central Bureau finally officially identified the Nationalist Chinese military liaison officer network as being the IJA's source of some of the leaks, but by then there was hard evidence that the Soviet Legation in Canberra was stealing Australian secrets, and this was leaking or being leaked to the Japanese.[53]

On 2 December 1944, Central Bureau formally reported to the Director of Military Intelligence that further leaks had been identified. This information was obtained by the interception and breaking out of a signal from GHQ in Tokyo and it was among 'a number recently sighted in TOP SECRET material', namely SIGINT.[54] These leaks related to US operations on Leyte Island and the Camotes Sea and Allied assessments of Japanese air and ground strength in the Philippines.[55]

One of the sources for the information to the Japanese was D4, the Nationalist Chinese Liaison Officer in Sydney. D4 was just one of a number of Japanese sources and, vitally for our story, another source was clearly described by the Japanese as being the 'Soviet Minister in Canberra'. A paragraph further down, (b), the source is given as the 'Soviet Minister Canberra'.[56] Paragraph (c) was sourced to 'spy Reports—Swedish Military Attaché', most likely in Canada.

Despite the identification of the Chinese as being responsible for some of these leaks, the problem remains as to how Chinese liaison officers were getting access to Australian military secrets including ULTRA.

In early 1944, British concern over poor Chinese security had led to a blanket ban on their access to any information and, in the weeks prior to the invasion of Normandy on 6 June, all communications channels into and out of the Nationalist Chinese Embassy in London were cut off, outraging Generalissimo Chiang Kai-shek. In Australia, the military authorities had already taken steps to limit Chinese access in April 1943, ordering all commands and formations to 'ensure that no information is given to Chinese naval or military attachés that would be detrimental to the Allied cause'.[57] If this order was being enforced, then the Chinese were getting hold of secret information either because security was lax or they were conducting successful espionage operations.

In looking at the source of this information, some Australian historians have focused on which government department or which entity lost the information.[58] Although this is an understandable perspective given the files will always reflect the organisational imperative to escape blame, the question is not which organisation lost the information, but how did it arrive in Japanese hands?

What the circumstantial evidence indicates is that the early leaks, those of mid-1943, were most likely the work of Nationalist Chinese liaison officers and their insecure communications but, by 1944, the RIS networks were beginning to produce intelligence for Moscow Centre. The tasking of the existing GRU illegal networks moved from technology and industry to military matters and the NKGB and CP-A followed.

It is therefore likely that the CP-A network run by Walter Clayton on behalf of the NKGB, and perhaps the GRU cell in Melbourne, was providing military intelligence to Moscow via the Soviet Legation after mid-1944. As a result, this information was either being stolen by the Japanese from the Soviets or, as already described for realpolitik reasons, the Soviets were giving it to the Japanese in order to damage Australian and American progress in the Pacific. The evidence suggests that the Soviets were deliberately passing the material to the Japanese.[59]

Supporting the argument that the Japanese had penetrated the Soviet Consulate in Harbin was their success in recruiting a telegrapher at the consulate named Mikhailov, in 1936. This operation was carried out by Major

Yamamoto Hayashi. Mikhailov apparently provided the IJA with a wealth of information about Soviet communications procedures and intelligence activity, however, given the close surveillance of Soviet officials during this time, even this success is questionable. We know that when the RIS discovered Mikhailov was working for the Japanese they left him in play, to act as a conduit for disinformation. In turn, the Japanese quickly realised that Mikhailov was compromised and they left him in play in the hope of using a triple cross to deceive the Soviets. Of course, Mikhailov could have been an RIS trap from the very beginning.[60] This is the wilderness of mirrors and the only thing we can know for certain is that no one would have wanted to be in Mikhailov's shoes.

Whatever protestations the apologists of the CP-A and its coterie of fellow-travellers make, the hard reality is that the CP-A and its Soviet masters were more than happy to sacrifice Australian and American lives for their own benefit, or they were sloppy in protecting information they had stolen from their erstwhile allies. It's the old 'fools or crooks' conundrum.

This crisis in December 1944 goes back much further to the leaks of 1943 and perhaps even earlier. What gives this away in the files is that Group Captain Frederick Winterbotham was present in Australia in December 1944.[61] This was no accident. Winterbotham was the senior officer commanding the SLUs across the world. He was not in Australia and South-East Asia six months after the Normandy landings on a 'jolly'. Winterbotham was in Australia to work with Sandford to take control of SIGINT security in the South West Pacific Area (SWPA) away from Australia and General MacArthur, its Commander-in-Chief.

The importance of the information leakage was not lost on Australia's military commanders. Not only was Sandford working with the Y Board in London, he was being supported by General Blamey, the Commander-in-Chief of Australia's Military Forces, the Chief of the General Staff and the Director of Military Intelligence in dealing with this matter. By 25 January 1945, Assistant Director of Military Intelligence, Lieutenant Colonel Little, and Mic Sandford had identified the Nationalist Chinese as being responsible for the leaks of military information; they were also certain that the Soviet Legation was passing Australia's secrets as well.[62]

The most important voice in this issue was Winterbotham's, and his instructions were that no action was to be taken until there was more evidence.[63] The matter was, according to Sandford's reporting of Winterbotham's opinion, 'one of serious insecurity on a global scale' for which a 'special section has been set up to deal with precisely this type of leakage'.[64] Six days later, Sandford wrote to notify Lieutenant Colonel Little at Army HQ in Melbourne that Winterbotham was bringing to Australia 'a special section 5 man [*sic*] to deal with the problem'. Sandford re-emphasised Winterbotham's directive 'that no action whatever be taken until his arrival'.[65]

It would appear that there was no time to lose as now the intelligence leaking to the Japanese courtesy of the Soviet Minister in Canberra became a torrent, covering information ranging from the composition of the British fleet heading to the Pacific to the internal arguments of the Australian government on extending the graving dock at Garden Island in Sydney and not constructing docks at Darwin or Port Moresby.[66] Clayton's KLOD network was now getting into full stride in its efforts to bring about the revolution of the Australian proletariat by helping the IJA kill their sons on the battlefields of Asia.

That said, there were two parties to blame for this growing disaster. Those who had stolen and transmitted this intelligence—the Nationalist Chinese and the Soviets—and the Australian government, whose lax oversight of the nation's security intelligence permitted this to happen.[67] This laxness in security—abetted by a naive belief in open diplomacy and a world with no secrets and no self-interest, encouraged and practised by Dr John Burton, the newly appointed and very inexperienced Secretary of External Affairs, and Evatt—would eventually lead to Australia's ostracism from the halls of power in Washington.[68] Yet, it doesn't end with Burton or Evatt. Fault also lies with John Curtin's Cabinet, particularly his successor, the uninterested Ben Chifley. It would be Chifley's government that would eventually bear the full weight of American anger with Australia.[69]

The Australian Army and Defence Department, assisted by MI6 and the Y Board in London, had begun investigating the matter as soon as it arose in 1943. This investigation was the beginning of what would famously become known as 'the Case'. The problem for Australia, as the visiting MI5 officers later found, was that Australia's wartime Security Service was not a counter-intelligence agency.

It is easy from an Australian perspective to discount the judgements of the visiting MI5 officers as being biased against Australia. After all, they had an agenda, which was to convince the Australian government to form a proper counterespionage organisation within an Empire-wide security intelligence system capable of dealing with the extensive and hostile penetration operations of the RIS. The fact that the RIS only seems to have begun fretting about the security of its operatives from 10 April 1945, and then only in relation to poor communications procedures of residencies generally, is significant.[70] In fact, as we have already seen, with Alfred Hughes stealing the Security Service's files in Sydney and bringing them to Clayton to copy and then pass to the NKGB via Makarov, the NKGB had little to fear and the GRU even less.[71]

Up until now, the operational environment for the RIS in Australia could be aptly named the 'happy time'. The threat posed by Australia's security intelligence system was negligible and the men and women of the CP-A were eager, in fact far too eager, to bring socialist democracy to Australia by stealing Australian secrets for Moscow. In London, however, things were getting interesting as Moscow Centre began to appreciate the full ramifications of Gouzenko's defection in Canada. The most immediate action taken was the protection of Kim Philby, Donald Maclean and Guy Burgess.[72]

CHAPTER 19

A WAY BACK

In late 1944, Wing Commander Frederick Winterbotham had arrived in Australia to meet with Allied military commanders and senior Australian officials to discuss the security of ULTRA intelligence. Winterbotham's modest rank—he was a colonel equivalent—was a deception used by his organisation, which ran the Special Liaison Units (SLUs) and Special Liaison Officers (SLOs) who managed the receipt and distribution of all ULTRA materials on behalf of the British government. The modest ranks held by the SLOs, usually equivalent to the rank of major, was to hide their true function as the communication and control system for all ULTRA and other SIGINT traffic. The importance of the SLUs and SLOs was that all SIGINT communicated anywhere in the world was sent and received by an SLU or a SIGINT centre such as Arlington Hall in Washington, GC&CS in the United Kingdom and Central Bureau and FRUMEL in Australia.

The SLOs were officers who indoctrinated—another term for the special briefing—anyone, including senior commanders, needing to see ULTRA in order to carry out their duties. Indoctrination was more than a briefing; it was a signed undertaking that the individual would never divulge any information that they would learn from ULTRA. The final authority on whether that individual should be allowed to see ULTRA lay solely with the SLO overseeing and administering the indoctrination. In this, they had the full backing of Churchill and Roosevelt. Winterbotham was in Australia to deal with the urgent problem of SIGINT leaking to the Japanese.

Even before Winterbotham arrived, Australia's security intelligence system was being evaluated by MI5. This evaluation was carried out by Lieutenant Colonel E.A. Airy, the Security Liaison Officer in Ceylon on behalf of Sir David Petrie, the Director-General of Security in Britain. Airy, like Winterbotham, held only a mid-level rank, but the list of officials he interviewed suggests he carried more influence than his rank belied. Among those interviewed by Airy were Admiral Sir Guy Royle, Chief of Naval Staff, RAN; Lieutenant General Northcott, the Chief of General Staff; Air Vice Marshal Jones, Chief of the Air Staff; Dr Evatt, the Attorney-General; and Mr Forde, Minister for the Army.

It is highly suspicious that the Security Liaison Officer from Ceylon should be conducting a high-level visit to Australia to look at security intelligence and counterespionage at the exact time that Central Bureau, and thus MI6's station in Brisbane, were becoming aware of further leaks of sensitive intelligence from Australia to the Japanese. It is no accident that this was just two months before Winterbotham arrived.

In fact, the initial D intelligence leaks—supposedly due to poor Nationalist Chinese communications security—had been reported by an Australian entity on 29 August 1944, the month Airy arrived in Australia. It is highly likely that earlier indications of possible leaks of sensitive intelligence had been detected before this and perhaps, given Airy was from Ceylon, had even been detected by the IWIS, the Indian SIGINT authority monitoring Nationalist Chinese communications.

As well as meeting with senior Australian officers and government ministers, Airy had dinner with the acting British High Commissioner and the Canadian Military Attaché, Colonel Moore Cosgrave.[1] He also interviewed Colonel Wills, the acting Director of Military Intelligence; Lieutenant Colonel Irwin, US Army; Lieutenant General Lumsden, representing the British War Cabinet in Australia; and Brigadier Simpson, Director-General Security.[2] He also visited all state offices of the Security Service, other than Tasmania's, and he met clandestinely with Third Officer Eve Walker, the MI6 station deputy in Brisbane.[3]

Airy reported on the size and structure of Australia's Security Service and on its capabilities and personnel. He reported that from all he had seen of the Security Service it operated more like a 'secret police' than a counter-intelligence organisation, something he found surprising.[4] What he also discovered was that the Security Service had absolutely no capability whatsoever as an effective counterespionage organisation and that it could 'hardly be called an intelligence organisation'.[5]

The report was read by Petrie who commented that he had personally interviewed Airy to clarify the personal and political aspects of Australia's Security Service. His findings were that Airy's report confirmed what MI5 had been hearing about Brigadier Simpson, and the rest of the senior officers, what Petrie termed 'crabbing'.[6] He found that Australia's Security Service seemed more afflicted with personal rivalries, backbiting and jealousies than MI5.[7] Petrie's decision was that it was time for MI5 to establish direct, personal links with Australia's security services, no matter how bad they were.[8]

In the SIGINT world things were moving as well. Winterbotham's task was to look at the problem of the leakages, which, despite all of the earlier misdirection and messages to calm down, were being treated as urgent and dangerous by the Y Board in London.

On his way to Australia Winterbotham went through Italy to pick up an SLU and Squadron Leader S.F. Burley, RAF, as the SLO for the SWPA.[9] Once in Australia, Winterbotham found that the problem was real. Not only were the Chinese Nationalists stealing sensitive intelligence and sending it to Chungking, but the Russians were also stealing sensitive intelligence and sending it to Harbin via Moscow. Like Airy before him, Winterbotham discovered that Australia's Security Service was not fit for purpose and that the Australian government took little or no interest in protecting its own sensitive materials and was even more cavalier about the sensitive information of Allies.

The level of concern can be gauged from the way in which, by June 1945, only six months later, there were five RAF manned and commanded SLUs and one SLU Forward Section operating in and around Australia: one in Brisbane, attached to Central Bureau; two at Morotai, Netherlands East Indies; one at Lae, Papua New Guinea, supporting Australia's 1st Army; and one at RAAF HQ, NW Area. The SLU Forward Section was based at RAAF HQ.[10]

This allocation of SLU resources represented just over 13 per cent of all SLU resources in all commands around the world. This tells us two things. First, there was a major security problem in Australia. Second, Australia had effectively been deprived of the ability to control, communicate and disseminate

SIGINT as all such traffic was now managed by RAF SLUs on behalf of the Y Board in London.

As for the Americans, they had sent out their own version of the SLOs, Special Security Officers (SSO), to take control of SIGINT security, including distribution, away from the theatre commanders, including Douglas MacArthur. If we are looking for a starting point for the series of counter-espionage operations that were to become known as 'the Case', then the visits of Airy and Winterbotham during a period when real leaks of sensitive information to the Japanese were being detected is that beginning.

By mid-1945, Washington and London controlled all Allied SIGINT activity in the Pacific and Asia. The problem was what to do about Australia's Security Service, which had inadvertently been alerted to the problem and was now champing at the bit to find a spy, any spy, before the war ended.

This eagerness to find the spy did not please either London or Washington. The idea of taking any action without a careful appraisal of the opportunity to run a disinformation operation was silly. In addition, the opportunity to covertly monitor unsuspecting RIS operatives would have provided enormous insights. One, it would disclose what the RIS was and was not interested in, providing hard evidence, from an intelligence perspective, of their motives and policies. Two, it would expose their tradecraft and techniques for recording. Three, it would enable the identification of their officers, both legal and illegal, and their networks. In the intelligence world, this is striking gold. It was for this reason that London kept sending signals telling the Australian authorities to 'do nothing'.[11]

Unfortunately, while Lieutenant Colonel R.A. Little at GHQ, Military Intelligence Branch, and Mic Sandford at Central Bureau were highly professional, William Simpson and his Security Service were not. The other problem was that the Commander-in-Chief of Australia's Military Forces, Thomas Blamey, was after the Security Service, and thus Evatt and Simpson. Blamey had not forgotten Simpson's intervention in the inquiry into Robert Wake's behaviour in late 1943. Against Blamey's express recommendation, Evatt and Simpson had kept Wake in his positions as the Deputy Director Security in Brisbane and as the Chief Inspector of the CIB in Queensland.

Now, on 2 August 1944, Blamey returned to the attack and moved to withdraw all army personnel from the Security Service in the full knowledge this would gut it.[12] This assault, which was supported in Cabinet by Forde, was defeated in the War Cabinet by Evatt on 9 February 1945, although the War Cabinet were ambivalent about the need for a security service at all.[13] Evatt was not looking to Australia's needs in this, but to his own. What he had actually argued for was a small security service that he could use for his own political ends.

The ethical standards of the Security Service and its Director-General can be seen from his actions on 2 February 1945, when Simpson called the Assistant Director of Military Intelligence, Lieutenant Colonel Little, falsely claiming to have received information from London relating to the leakage of 'D Int', by the Nationalist Chinese.[14] The striking thing about this lie is its clumsiness as anyone who had thought about it would have quickly realised that Little would soon work out the truth. The truth was that Simpson had been inadvertently made aware of the leaks by the Director of Military Intelligence, Brigadier John Rogers, who showed him unsanitised ULTRA on the leaks.[15] Rogers was probably acting after a meeting on 17 January in which Blamey had told Simpson of the existence of ULTRA and that he, Blamey, was arranging for Simpson to have access to relevant ULTRA material.[16] There appeared to be no reason to lie to Little, yet Simpson did.

When considering what might have been behind this lie, we go back to the personalities within the Security Service, and inevitably come to Wake. For years he had been trying to penetrate the work of Central Bureau in Brisbane, as well as impose himself upon any other intelligence activity he could.[17] It is not hard to imagine that as soon as Simpson became aware of the matter, he would have communicated with Wake, who would have responded like a bull in a china shop and manipulated Simpson into seeking immediate access to all information using his position as Director-General Security. The problem was that the standing of the Australian government was not sufficient to play in this game, let alone try to dictate the rules.

Simpson's effort to intrude into the leaks matter was crushed by Blamey, who now demonstrated that while he might not be able to overcome Evatt in Cabinet, he could prevent Simpson from taking control of the investigation into the Case.[18] Blamey may have been losing the battle to withdraw the military component from Simpson's service, but he still controlled access to ULTRA via the Director of Military Intelligence and Central Bureau. The Commander-in-Chief now told Simpson that before he could see any SIGINT, he had to be indoctrinated by the SLO, Squadron Leader Burley. Blamey asked Simpson to meet with and assist Burley where he could. The meeting to indoctrinate Simpson was a further disaster for Australia's standing.

Burley turned up at Simpson's office in Canberra on 29 January to conduct the indoctrination.[19] During this meeting and the indoctrination Burley passed on the intelligence that the leakages were not Russian, but Chinese. Despite being assured by Burley that ULTRA was highly reliable, Simpson, not unreasonably, rejected the assurances. If the matter had stayed there, then the ramifications would have been less severe.

When Simpson was told by Burley that he could not pass ULTRA information to anyone else in any form whatsoever and that the ULTRA signal had to be immediately burned, Simpson, as Burley put it, 'got up on his hind legs' demanding to know how he could possibly use ULTRA if he was to be restricted in this way.[20] Simpson blustered and bluffed and told Burley that he would go and see the Prime Minister and General Blamey to discuss the matter more fully. To be fair, Simpson was probably concerned with how he was going to deal with Wake when he told him he could not see the SIGINT.

Burley reinforced with Simpson that he was not to take any action on the matter in hand without reference to the Chief of the General Staff. Simpson began to throw his weight around, flagging to Burley that he was a barrister and 'that he knew all the answers', and that he would be going to the prime minister. None of this posturing worked and, reluctantly, Simpson signed the indoctrination form, but not before he petulantly crossed out all reference to the British Official Secrets Act and US legislation on the document.[21] Unsurprisingly, in his report of the same day, Burley informed Blamey and his senior intelligence staff that 'I do not think Simpson is one who should handle or have access to the material'; in his opinion, Simpson was a man 'who would not hesitate to act first and ask after'.[22] Simpson's access to SIGINT was severely limited and, as a result of his actions on this day, Australia's post-war security services were unable to be told about VENONA, an outcome that caused major difficulties for Australia and ructions in the relationships with Britain and particularly with the United States.

After this indoctrination meeting, Simpson telephoned Little, and claimed he was under pressure from his minister, Evatt, to report on the progress of the investigation. Little bought off Simpson by telling him he would take the matter to the Chief of the General Staff and that, in the interim, Simpson's

Security Service was to take no action.[23] It appears that no one had any confidence that Simpson would do as he was told.

Things now started to speed up and Little contacted Sandford, telling him to signal London and request that a specialist MI6 officer who had already been 'promised', Australian-born Lieutenant Colonel Dick Ellis, be despatched urgently to Australia. Blamey was also brought into the matter and he ordered the Assistant Director of Military Intelligence to immediately set up a private meeting with Simpson in Canberra on 8 February, when Blamey would be there.[24] The idea of rushing Ellis to Australia was quickly dropped as cooler heads prevailed and it became apparent that the leaks could be blamed on the Chinese. The strategy that appears to have been put in place was a return to misdirection by broadcasting that the Chinese were the sole problem, while ramping up the cryptological attack on Soviet diplomatic traffic sent via the Canberra Post Office since the opening of the legation. All of this material was packaged up and sent to the United Kingdom on 12 February.[25]

A week later, on 19 February, Blamey supported the do-nothing position by telling Simpson in writing, as Simpson had demanded, that he was not to investigate the leakages of information via Chinese or Soviet channels until he was advised to do so. In an aside, Blamey stuck the knife in by telling Simpson that, in the meantime, he and his service could start taking steps to educate people working in government departments in 'security mindedness'.[26] As a bureaucratic put-down, this was severe.

The problems created by Simpson now rattled cages in London, if not Washington, and on 20 February a signal was received at Central Bureau from Winterbotham saying:

GRAVELY CONCERNED. GRATEFUL IF ROGERS WILL FIND EARLY OPPORTUNITY TO BRING TO NOTICE OF SIMPSON THAT NO ACTION MAY BE TAKEN ON THIS TYPE OF INFORMATION WHETHER SUPPLIED TO YOU FROM LONDON AND WASHINGTON OR PRODUCED BY C.B. WITHOUT FULL CONSULTATION WITH THE SIGINT BOARDS CONCERNED. THE MATTER OF ULTRA SECURITY IS GLOBAL.[27]

Essentially, if Simpson did not have the written permission of British and US authorities, he could take no action on the matter. At this point in time, everything goes dead on the Case. No doubt it was being aggressively pursued, but within the confines of the SIGINT world of Arlington Hall and GC&CS. The other message in this signal, that 'the matter of ULTRA security is global', was a clear threat that Washington and London were not going to allow the Australian government a say in the management of the matter. Australia's allies were losing patience.

By March 1946, the Australian government was demonstrating a growing level of indifference to security. The new Director-General, Longfield Lloyd, was off to Japan to waste his time as the Australian advisor to the British Commonwealth Member of the Allied Control Council there.[28] In his place as Director-General Security was his deputy, Major Rowland Browne, a long-time member of the CIB and, if MI6 is correct, an unimpressive man of small accomplishment.[29] The MI6 reporting to MI5 does show that Browne possessed one important strength for serving in the CIB in 1946: he was completely subservient to Evatt and the Department of External Affairs.[30]

If London and Washington thought Australia's government was taking serious notice of their concerns, this would have disabused them. It is no surprise that the reaction in Washington was outrage and that was now firmly directed at the Attlee Labour government in London. Now MI5 renewed its failed efforts to influence Australia to take action on security by creating a proper security intelligence organisation based on MI5.[31]

The efforts to influence Australia's government had begun in London in April 1945 when Evatt was approached to meet with Brigadier Oswald (Jasper) Harker, Deputy Director of MI5, to discuss Overseas Control. Then a meeting was held with another Australian visitor, Admiral Sir Louis Hamilton of the ACNB. By April 1946, a full year after the invitation to meet Evatt, MI5 was stepping up its interest as it had now embedded officers in the Security Intelligence Far East (SIFE) organisation at Singapore and, with Rowland Brown now the acting Director-General of Security in Australia, the MI5 officer Courtenay Young advised his Director-General, Petrie, to authorise the arranging of a liaison officer position for a representative of Australia's security organisation.

MI5 approached the problem through the auspices of the Admiralty and MI6 who were sending out Captain E. Hale, the Chief of Operational Intelligence Staff (COIS), British Pacific Fleet (BPF), to speak to the ACNB about naval intelligence in the region. Hale may have been representing the Admiralty, but he was also representing MI6, working under a charter from

Peter Dixon, the MI6 representative in Singapore, to investigate the security intelligence set-up in Australia.[32] Hale reported to Dixon and Young that the CIB was cordially disliked by other government departments and agencies. It was all pointless because, as MI5 learned in August 1946, the Australian Security Service was now effectively 'defunct'.[33] Despite this, there was some good news, as Colonel Charles C.F. Spry, DSO, had now been appointed as Director of Military Intelligence and in this position he would start weeding out all CP-A penetration agents, including the top secret registry.

One of the things that are often forgotten about Spry is that he was not an intelligence officer, but an infantry officer whose entire career had been in operations. In fact, he was one of the fiercest critics of Military Intelligence during his service and particularly during the war. It is highly likely that Spry was given the job of Director of Military Intelligence to clean the stable and get rid of all the deadwood that had accumulated within it and whose incompetence had so embarrassed the General Staff.[34]

At the same time, Australia's wartime SIGINT capability was being kept on life support as Sandford, supported by the Director of Military Intelligence, kept the remnants of Central Bureau together writing after-action reports and unit histories and managing the disposal of highly sensitive encryption and communications equipment. Having used SIGINT on the battlefield and in the conduct of their operational planning, none of the military services wanted to lose this capability.

The question was how it could be kept alive in the parsimonious military environment of the post-war rush to prosperity in 1946 and 1947. While the story of the creation of the Defence Signals Bureau (DSB) lies outside the purview of this work, the need to secure the DSB from HUMINT attack by the RIS and other hostile intelligence agencies does not. The decision to establish the Melbourne SIGINT centre along the lines of the London centre as part of an Australian, British, Canadian SIGINT system was approved by the British Commonwealth Signal Intelligence Conference held in London over February/March 1946 and accepted by the Australian chiefs of staff on 4 July 1946.[35]

The creation of the DSB formed part of a strategy that included the creation of a new analytical organisation, the Australian Joint Intelligence Committee (AJIC), which would oversee the setting of intelligence priorities and the subsequent analysis of collected intelligence. The initiative for the creation of the AJIC had come from the wartime Senior British Liaison Officer, Major General R. Dewing, and Vice Admiral Charles Daniel, in charge of Administration, British Pacific Fleet, who were attempting to overcome Australia's lack of a wartime joint planning organisation.[36] The problem with this initiative was that it was bitterly opposed by Blamey and Frederick Shedden, who was a great centraliser of all activity under his personal control.[37] Later, MI6 was more scathing of Shedden, describing him as the 'eminent grise of Australian politics' and the man who would have to be convinced if Australia was to have a proper security intelligence organisation.[38]

Of course, this was not a straightforward initiative and, outside of the bureaucratic wrangling endemic to the armed services, the major problem was the penetration of any such organisations by the CP-A and its affiliates.[39] The other problem though, as MI6 reported, was 'there is no security whatsoever in Australia on anything, including cipher communication' and this led Courtenay Young to warn Dick White, head of B Division at MI5, that the security of MI5's ciphers held by Lloyd and now Browne may now be at risk.

White told Courtenay Young to check the conditions under which they were being stored.[40] On 19 July 1946, Acting Minister for Defence Forde approved the formation of the AJIC and the DSB, but rejected the formation of a Defence security organisation, deferring to Evatt, who would investigate the existing legislation and system and report to the Defence Committee of Cabinet.[41] This agendum may have been put by Forde, but it was sponsored by the highly capable John Dedman, who concurrently held the positions of Minister for Defence, Minister for Post-War Reconstruction and Minister in Charge of the Council for Scientific and Industrial Research.[42]

This initiative of Evatt's, to review and report, is the usual political and bureaucratic method of killing off a proposal. There is no doubt that Evatt did not want the Australian government to create another security intelligence organisation that could effectively compete with the corrupt organisation he controlled via his department. As it was, the residual security intelligence function of the wartime Security Service was now back in the CIB, which Evatt ensured was subservient to him by putting men like Lloyd and Browne in charge of it. He also ensured that his friend Wake and his coterie of corrupt officers were successfully transferred into it.[43]

The work of Evatt in resisting the creation of a new security intelligence organisation should not be misinterpreted as some sort of crusade on behalf of the ordinary citizen's freedoms. The hard reality is that Evatt wished to maintain his own private intelligence service that would spy upon his political enemies and anyone who crossed him. The record suggests Evatt corruptly used Wake and other officers to spy upon members of the ALP, his Cabinet colleagues and public servants. This, and not any desire to protect civil rights, was the reason for Evatt's opposition to the creation of a Defence security organisation.[44] The last thing Evatt wanted was Blamey and Shedden having an organisation that would compete with his own.

The crux of the problem that was created by this conflict was that the CIB, which had taken back the counterespionage role and personnel from the now defunct Security Service, was compromised by the CP-A and was so incompetent that it was described by the Australian Director of Naval Intelligence as a 'combination of the notoriously ineffective prewar CIB and the wartime Security Service which was not much better'.[45] This organisation, led by Lloyd and Browne, could not protect the DSB or the proposed AJIC. In fact, the CIB was so irrelevant that, even at this late date, Australia was still considering the vetting of public servants who would be handling sensitive government secrets.[46]

For Britain, this was becoming a major issue because Australia was the only place that Britain could conduct atomic tests and experiments into rocketry. Both these activities were going to attract foreign, particularly Soviet, intelligence interest as effectively as an open jam jar attracts wasps; however, Britain had no choice. Rocket testing and atomic explosions could not be conducted on Salisbury Plain, but both could be conducted at Woomera in South Australia.

Because all of this weapons testing activity fell into the areas of research and development, it was the concern of the Ministry of Supply (MoS) and the security of the Blue Streak missile program, overseen by Lieutenant General J.F. Evetts, was the concern of the MoS's Security Section advised by MI5.[47] The MoS security officer being sent to Australia for this purpose was Lieutenant Colonel J.F.S. Rendell, and Browne was informed that Rendell would contact him directly or via the Director of Military Intelligence, Colonel Spry.[48] All of this was being done in an environment in which Dick White was advising all MI5 officers that 'when communicating with Australia . . . only give the bare minimum of facts necessary for enquiry' because 'the officers of the CIB in the states are not trained in security' and information given to the CIB 'is liable to leak out'.[49]

In December 1946, the needs of MI5 to conduct a sensitive investigation into an unknown individual in Australia brought counterespionage matters to a head. Courtenay Young of MI5 described the matter as 'rather too closely allied to dynamite to give to the CIB'.[50] Unfortunately, the name of the individual has been redacted in the MI5 file, so we do not know who or what the matter was about; however, the MI5 notes exchanged by senior officers provide insight into how the Australian security intelligence system was viewed in London.

Courtenay Young described the CIB as 'disorganised' and only capable of using 'flat-footed methods' in its operations.[51] A senior MI5 officer, A.J. Keller, believed that if the matter, which 'may also have a Russian interest', was disclosed to the Australians it would be 'blown'.[52] The new Director-General of MI5, Percy Sillitoe, thought the CIB 'in rather a bad state'.[53] As for passing them information on the undisclosed matter, it appears that MI5 was fully aware of the deficiencies in Australia's security intelligence system. It was at this time in 1948 that the VENONA program cracked Makarov's signal 123 of 19 March 1946 detailing for Moscow Clayton's theft of the British documents on post-war planning.[54]

We now return to this fateful event on 6 November 1945, when Ian Milner, an NKGB spy at External Affairs, wrote on behalf of the Acting Secretary of External Affairs to the Secretary of the Defence Post Hostilities Planning Committee (PHPC), requesting that two reports of the UK Post Hostilities Planning Committee's titled 'Security in the Western Mediterranean and the Eastern Atlantic' and 'Security of India and Security of the British Empire' be made available to the department's representative on the PHPC, none other than himself.[55] Milner committed two grievous errors. First, and contrary to the appeals from Moscow Centre, he was rushing to steal documents; second, he laid a paper trail that led directly back to his desk and himself.

In fact, Milner had already drawn adverse attention to himself in his handling of the documents and this attention came from the son-in-law of Brigadier Bertrand Combes, who would develop the plans for the AJIC and DSB. Combes' son-in-law worked at External Affairs and was greatly suspicious of Milner who he challenged over the documents. Milner couldn't produce the documents when asked for them but was able to 24 hours later.[56] This must have caused Makarov and Clayton a great deal of concern. It caused Sillitoe and Roger Hollis, MI5's leading expert on communist subversion, a great deal of joy, because it provided plausible cover for any intelligence interest in Milner.[57]

The history of Milner suggests that he was recruited by the NKGB in New Zealand because the Czech archives clearly show him as an operative from 1944, which is before he was recruited into the Australian Department of External Affairs.[58] Milner's recruitment may have been part of Moscow Centre's project to penetrate the United Kingdom using colonial recruits whose backgrounds would be far more difficult for MI5 and the security officers of government departments to properly vet. As a result, having been recruited to the Australian Department of External Affairs, Milner's membership of the CP-A came after he was recruited as an NKGB operative.

The Australian PHPC was an interesting body consisting of representatives of various government departments, including the armed services, Defence and External Affairs; however, its largest representation was from the CP-A, which had no fewer than three members attending its meetings. These CP-A representatives were Ian Milner, Ric Throssell and Jim Hill.[59] The later claims that Milner did not steal and copy these documents may have been based on this fact; however, the documentary evidence clearly shows that Milner took control of the documents in question from 15 November 1945 to 19 February 1946 and from 6 to 28 March 1946.[60] Neither Throssell nor Hill had official access to these documents for any period of time. Besides which, any claims that Milner was innocent died the day in 1996 that author Peter Hruby read Milner's personnel files at the Czechoslovak Ministry of the Interior.[61] These files disclosed that Milner had been an agent, No. 9006, from 1944 until 1951, when he defected to Czechoslovakia where he spied on his friends, colleagues and neighbours on behalf of the secret police.[62]

To give MI5 and MI6—ably supported by the Attlee government—their due, London tried manfully to solve this conundrum, even to the point where Britain's access to US secrets, including intelligence, technology and military, was being risked. The special relationship did not extend to allowing officials in London to inadvertently pass US government secrets to insecure officials in Australia. As a result of this, and due to the sensitivities created by the Mawhood affair, which still stank in Australia, and the need to protect VENONA, MI5 had to tread lightly in putting pressure on Australia.[63]

On 21 January 1948, Clement Attlee wrote to Ben Chifley asking him to meet with Sillitoe, telling Chifley that Sillitoe had his complete confidence. Attlee wanted Chifley to listen to Sillitoe who, Attlee went on, would verbally inform him of a most serious matter.[64]

Sillitoe arrived in Australia in early 1948 to meet with senior Australian officials and politicians, including Prime Minister Chifley, to try to convince them of the need for Australia to create a proper security intelligence organisation.[65] This visit, like all of the others before it, was unsuccessful. Sillitoe used a cover story—cover story A—in which the intelligence from VENONA was attributed to a HUMINT source identified as an ex-Soviet air force officer seconded to the political division just before the German invasion of 1941.[66] It is hard to say whether Chifley swallowed this story, but whatever he did swallow, he was not willing to launch an investigation of External Affairs while Evatt was overseas. As a result, Sillitoe had to await the return of Evatt and so he travelled to Malaya, intending to return to Australia in two weeks. Sillitoe became ill in Malaya, however, and Hollis was delegated the task of meeting with Chifley, Evatt and Dedman.[67]

Unsurprisingly, MI5 had worked out a number of contingencies in case cover story A was not believed. Sillitoe was provided with a second cover story to use with Chifley if cover story A didn't work. This cover story was MI5 reporting on the Soviet Ambassador to Australia Nikolai Lifanov who, under the influence of alcohol in the United Kingdom en route to Australia, boasted to Soviet officials in London that he had a number of informants in Australia, including one high up in the government, which made him master of the situation.[68] One member of his audience was a MI6 or MI5 informant, assessed as reliable, who reported his boasts to the British. These boasts, which were true, were then used by Sillitoe to needle Chifley. It worked and Sillitoe wrote to MI5 from New Zealand that 'C', the head of MI6, and Liddell at MI6 should be told 'that the second barrel was most useful'.[69]

Hollis later met with Chifley and, quite frankly, told him that the cover story was a fabrication disguising the real source.[70] Chifley accepted this without hesitation. The meeting with Chifley quickly identified that the leak was among departmental officials, as the document had never circulated among the political leadership. After this meeting, Hollis conducted some investigations of his own and quickly identified that Milner, a known Marxist, had held the documents for an extended period of time in his office in Canberra.[71] When Hollis passed this information to Chifley, Chifley replied that he had gotten rid of Milner by having him posted to Korea. It would appear that the Canberra grapevine had provided sufficient information on Milner to make everyone, including Chifley, nervous.

Sillitoe's evaluation of Chifley is worth mentioning because he later presented it to the United States Communications Intelligence Board (USCIB) in an attempt to mitigate Australia's attitude towards security problems. Chifley was, Sillitoe said, 'a politician', but a man who Sillitoe was firmly convinced could 'be trusted . . . [and] was as genuinely anti-communist as any one of us'.[72] Sillitoe also told the USCIB that 'the Australian people as a whole were pronouncedly anti-communist and the politicians were aware of this'. As for the Australian Cabinet, Sillitoe believed that Chifley 'was a very strong man who ruled his own house completely' and that any investigation would have to have his complete approval if it was to be vigorously pursued.[73] Despite his best efforts, Sillitoe's appeals to the USCIB were countered by Admirals Inglis and E.E. Stone, who were not inclined to be generous. The US Navy had a long memory.[74]

The failure of the Sillitoe mission led to the Chairman of the London Signals Intelligence Committee (LSIC), the head of MI6, writing to the chairman of the USCIB telling him that British Prime Minister Attlee, who had been indoctrinated into VENONA, was personally going to approach Chifley and inform him that VENONA was the source of the information that Sillitoe had provided to the Australian government during his visit.[75] Before going ahead, however, Attlee wanted US approval from the Secretary of State, George Marshall, and to ease this decision through the US administration, Sillitoe, with Foreign Secretary Ernest Bevin's support, was being sent to Washington.[76] On 8 May 1948, the Chairman of the USCIB replied approving the proposal.[77] On 14 May, a signal was sent from MI5 to the UK representative in Canberra asking whether Chifley, Evatt and Shedden would be available in mid-June to meet with Hollis.[78]

The problem facing MI5 was that the attitude of the Australian government was one of 'distrust and suspicion' caused not only by the mythology of Mawhood, but by the fact that the Australian officials and politicians knew that MI5 was not being frank about the source of their information.[79] It was this need to let the Australians know that VENONA was the source that was leading to the British government's efforts to convince Washington to allow it. The prospects of getting this approval looked slim and, working on the basis that Sillitoe's visit to Washington would not succeed, Harold Orme Garton Sargent, Permanent Head of the Foreign Office, wrote to the UK Ambassador, Sir Oliver Franks, to ask him to ensure that Sillitoe was personally introduced to Marshall.[80]

As it turned out, the meeting with the USCIB Chairman, while 'sticky', resulted in London getting provisional approval of 90 per cent of what was asked for; however, the US Navy, Australia's bête noire in Washington, imposed a delay.[81] A day prior to the meeting, a well-briefed Sillitoe met with Admiral T.B. Inglis and during this meeting 'it immediately became apparent what one was up against'.[82] What Sillitoe found he was up against was a 'deep American distrust of politicians in Australia' because, as Sillitoe suggested, they were 'Labour, they must therefore *ipso facto* be fellow travellers of the Communists'.[83]

On 2 June, the United States replied, agreeing to the British proposal but under the conditions that before Chifley be given the information he was to be indoctrinated and then given the bare minimum of information, and that he, as the prime minister, could be told the source was an intercepted Russian communication. Evatt and Dedman were not to be told anything.

The United States had no reservations about passing the names of the Australian suspects named in VENONA to Lloyd at the CIB, but he was not to be told the source and under no circumstances were the Australians to be told the United States was a participant in this affair. In return, the British were now required to keep the United States fully informed of all future developments in the Case.[84]

The reply to Sillitoe from London on 4 June pointed out the impracticality of the US demands. Evatt, Burton, Dedman and Shedden were responsible for the conduct of investigations within their departments and had to be told about the source. On top of this, the US demand that the United States not be mentioned as a participant meant that Attlee and British authorities would bear all of the Australian outrage at having vital information withheld from them. Sillitoe's response to instructions coming from London to hold firm made it clear that he was lucky to get anywhere with the Americans and that London's suggestions in relation to Burton, Evatt, Dedman and Shedden were unattainable, even if he did see Marshall.[85] Hollis was now to proceed to Australia and seek, diplomatically, to work around the problems in order to get the Australians to take action.

Finally, on 15 June, Sillitoe met with Secretary of State Marshall. As the Chairman of the US Joint Chiefs of Staff and the Combined Chiefs of Staff during the war, Marshall was very experienced in the sensitivities of managing the relationships between Britain, the Empire and the United States. Marshall agreed that Evatt and Dedman should be given the same information as Chifley, but he also supported the US position that no other Australian official should be given the information on the source. He also categorically rejected any linking of the United States to the matter.[86]

On 7 June, the report that Chifley had promised Hollis was finally sent to Attlee. Chifley did not waste words in expressing his concerns about the leaking of the documents. He told Attlee that he had brought Dedman and Evatt into the picture so that it could be properly investigated; however, he also made it clear that, in the absence of the full story, he and his government were at a significant disadvantage in dealing with the matter. Chifley hung onto the fact that the investigations had identified no culprit and, as he intimated, that as a result the leak could not be attributed to Australia.[87] It was here that the politician in Chifley showed through as he drew upon his statement to the House on 7 April that he could 'give a complete assurance that so far as the Commonwealth Investigation service and the state police forces can detect, no person whom Mr Attlee's description fits [a communist], is engaged in vital security work'.[88] Of course, this statement is true. Like all good political language, Chifley's statement hides the essential truth—that CP-A members were compromising vital security work every working day, and that the CIB and state police forces hadn't noticed this. In fact, the hard truth was that Australia's security intelligence organisations were incapable of finding communists anywhere other than at CP-A meetings.

On 17 June, Washington acted. A directive was sent to London banning all Australian access to US material classified above restricted. Up until this point, Australian military personnel and officials had been allowed to see US material classified to secret, although not top secret. This ban severely impacted the ability of Australia's representatives to work or liaise with US agencies and organisations. In fact, it made it impossible for Australians even to remain at their desks, if those desks were inside a US government building.

This ban affected Britain as well because Australian officers and officials were integrated into many of the British military, scientific and diplomatic missions working in the United States or with the United States on matters of mutual interest such as SIGINT, defence and nuclear power. For Britain, the effects of the US ban were twofold.

First, it disrupted the organisation of British representation in Washington and the United States as now the British faced the need to isolate or exclude all Australians from their missions and activities. The Americans were in no mood to be helpful with this, as their insistence that Britain could not tell Australia that the United States had imposed sanctions on it indicates. Washington had effectively forbidden Britain to tell Australia that it was persona non grata in Washington or to share details of the US SIGINT system's involvement in discovering the NKGB penetration of the Australian government.

The restrictions placed on the British raises the second of the effects of the ban on Australian official contact with or access to US government secrets. This effect was the impact on Britain's relations with Australia and the British Commonwealth more generally. The British were acutely aware that by forcing London to tell Australia the bad news and impose the US sanctions as if they were British sanctions, Britain became the bad cop at a time when it was desperately attempting to build worldwide military and intelligence systems using the framework of the Commonwealth. The impact of banning Australian access to US secrets was not going to help Britain win the support of the Australian government for such plans. This was politics being played hard.

Of course, the United States was well aware that if it was to counter the ruthless ambitions of Joseph Stalin and the Soviet Union, it too needed real estate around the world. As a result, a get out of jail card was left on the table and the friendly fellowship of the wartime alliance used to soften the blow on Britain. The US sanctions were now described by Major General Alexander Bolling, US Army, as temporary. Bolling still insisted the Australians were not to be told of the ban, something that it was shortly going to be impossible to manage.[89] The concern that most agitated the British was that the Australian government would wrongly associate the visit of Sillitoe to Washington with the imposition of the ban.[90]

In the face of the intransigence of the United States, the British reciprocated by insisting that General Bolling personally tell the Australian officers of their exclusion from US secrets rather than having the British do the dirty work of the United States. London now directed that British commanders in Washington refrain from any involvement in the matter.[91] Of course, this would have immediately told the Australians in Washington exactly who was behind the ban. In preparation for this, the British undoubtedly informally dropped hints to Major General John Chapman, the senior Australian Officer in Washington, as to what was really going on and left him free to do as he saw fit in the interests of Australia.[92] The effect of this was the complete cessation of the flow of US Army intelligence and technical information to Australia and the threat of a complete ban being imposed on Britain if London did not cut Australia off as well.[93]

Despite Bolling's friendly overtures, the ban was not temporary. It was reinforced by the newly formed US Army, Navy and Air Co-ordinating Committee (USANACC), which prohibited Australia from receiving any classified material of US origin without USANACC approval which, just to be bloody minded, was to be on a strict case-by-case basis.[94]

This was even more severe than the original set of sanctions because it affected all British intelligence and technical information being sent to Australia from London as it all contained US information. USANACC had now made it impossible for Britain to cooperate with Australia on any technical, intelligence or defence matter. Australia was to be excised from all British distribution lists.[95] Behind the ban was Admiral Inglis and the US Navy.[96] This was a big stick and it affected the standing of MI5 in London where there would be many disgruntled government departments who would now be unable to pursue their policy outcomes where Australia was involved. This was not just the Colonial Office or dominions; it extended across all of government, including defence and, vitally, nuclear research.

Now the carrot was produced by the USCIB, which Inglis chaired. The USCIB agreed with Britain's argument that Evatt and Dedman be briefed into VENONA and given the same information as Chifley.[97] Finally, the big guns were dusted off and Attlee was to be briefed to speak to Chifley when he arrived in London for the meeting of Commonwealth prime ministers in July. The hope was that Chifley would listen to Attlee, a fellow Labour man of similar political outlook. The Dominions Office prepared 'an infiltration telegram' that it intended to send to dominions prime ministers suggesting that the security precautions of all dominions should be aligned with those of the United Kingdom. This telegram was obviously intended to provoke dominion prime ministers to prepare themselves for the proposed discussions on security. It also prepared the way for the recommendation to the Dominions Conference in October that the security chiefs of all the dominions should hold a conference to discuss the security situation facing the British Commonwealth.[98]

The briefing prepared by MI5 for Attlee's discussion with Chifley was now drawn up. First, Attlee was to obtain from Chifley a promise that he would never disclose the source of the information he was about to receive. Once he had done this, Attlee could tell Chifley about the theft of the documents by Milner and that this intelligence came from the communications sent by the Russians from the Canberra Embassy. Attlee was also briefed to tell Chifley that this intelligence had been fully verified and was beyond question. Attlee was then to get Chifley's agreement for Hollis to return to Australia to assist with the investigation into the leaks and to safeguard VENONA.[99] All of this was seconded by MI6.

The pressure on Chifley was building exponentially with his government effectively banned from access to any technical, economic, military and intelligence information from Washington and London. Attlee, a fellow Labour leader, told him that Australia had a security problem and that if his government didn't fix it, then Australia was effectively out of the Western alliance in the very same way that South Africa was. On top of this, Sillitoe and MI5 were insisting that Australia's problem was the same as that afflicting Canada—meaning that the CP-A was undoubtedly involved.

As for the details, Sillitoe wanted Lloyd and the CIB brought into the Case, although Burton at External Affairs and Shedden at Defence had effectively sidelined the CIB. In addition, Sillitoe wanted Chifley's permission to send to Australia two officers from MI5's B Branch—Roger Hollis from B1, countersubversion, and Robert Hemblys Scales of B2, counterespionage. The selection of these two showed that the targets of MI5's activity were the subversive activities of the CP-A and the espionage activities of the NKGB.[100] In addition, Sillitoe, with the backing of Attlee, asked that these officers have direct access to Chifley while they were in Australia assisting the CIB. In the face of all this, Chifley agreed to the British requests.[101]

Having arrived in Australia, Hollis reported to Sillitoe on 2 August 1948 that he and Hemblys Scales had met with Chifley in Canberra and that Chifley had told them that Professor K.H. Bailey was now in charge of the investigation into the Case, something Hollis thought was excellent, if Bailey could devote enough time to it.[102]

Hemblys Scales and Hollis began their work on the Case and, on 4 August, interviewed the Secretary of External Affairs John Burton at his property outside Canberra. Hollis reported to Sillitoe that Burton appeared to have been an aspiring farmer with 600 acres and another 400 being added.[103] The description of Burton that Hollis provided to Sillitoe described him as 'a tough, practical and self-reliant type who is not afraid to take on big commitments'.[104] Burton, Hollis advised Sillitoe, appeared far tougher and more earthy than the description of him as 'Burton of External affairs' suggested.[105] One of the things Hollis appreciated about Burton was his honesty in revealing his dislike for Shedden; he told Hollis that he believed Shedden would try to pin the leak on External Affairs and that Shedden was using the whole affair to destroy Burton. He was no doubt partly correct in this belief.

... ...

John Wear Burton was born to Dr John Wear Burton, a Methodist missionary and future president-general of the Methodist Church in Australia, on 2 March 1915. He attended Newington College in Sydney before going to the University of Sydney, where he gained his degree. Burton joined the Commonwealth public service in 1937 and then, via a Commonwealth scholarship, attended the London School of Economics and obtained his doctorate in 1941.[106] On his return to Australia, he was posted to the Department of Labour and National Service where he did not get along with it and its staff did not get along with him.[107] His position, with him in it, was transferred to External Affairs, something that always indicates a very strong desire by the transferring department to rid itself of a highly undesirable official.[108]

Burton was reluctantly taken on at External Affairs by Hodgson, who most likely intended to pressure him to resign after his transfer so that the new position could be retained and refilled with a candidate of Hodgson's choosing.[109] Hodgson dealt with Burton by shipping him off to Evatt's office as the private secretary. Unfortunately, Evatt took a shine to Burton and Burton to him. Thus, is history made.

The problem in assessing John Burton's role in the affair of RIS penetration of his department is that it has become part of the partisan battle fought between the progressive left and the conservative right. This battle is somewhat trite, in the way of all such debates, and is of little interest to this work. However, that does not mean that the role of John Burton can be neglected.

In looking at the documentary evidence there is nothing that incriminates John Wear Burton as having ever knowingly worked as an agent of the RIS, either the NKGB or the GRU, or of the CP-A. Indeed, the most reliable files on Burton, those of MI5, contain many reports and file notes written by experienced senior officers such as Sir Percy Sillitoe, Dick White, Roger Hollis and Courtenay Young that discount the idea that Burton was ever an RIS asset let alone a CP-A operative.[110]

The main factor that damaged Burton was his inability to get along with his peers in Canberra, especially those he regarded as gnomes, men like Sir George Knowles and Sir Frederick Shedden, who appear to have regarded him, at best, as an ignorant young upstart. His boss at External Affairs, William Hodgson, couldn't stand him and, as we have seen above, didn't want him. Neither did Roland Wilson at Labour and National Service.[111] It was quite an effort for a young official to have accumulated such a long list of senior enemies so quickly.

The appointment of Burton to the position of Secretary of the Department of External Affairs at the age of 30 years by H.V. Evatt was particularly thoughtless. Evatt's penchant for cutting corners to win his point was facilitated by Burton who, if Paul Hasluck is to be believed, was even readier to pursue his objectives by whatever means necessary.[112] Perhaps this is why so many of his peers and superiors regarded him as 'crooked'.[113]

Yet, for all this, Burton was actually a reasonably good head of External Affairs. Evatt liked and, in his own way, respected him. One strength that is often overlooked is that he knew how to get around Evatt and encourage him to make the necessary decisions for the good of the department. He also knew how to counter Evatt's penchant for running Australia's foreign affairs from his private office.[114]

Burton was not an attractive target for recruitment to intelligence work. First of all, his tendency to do whatever it took—his willingness to be procedurally corrupt if it helped his cause—was a warning flag that he would have been a difficult man for the NKGB to control. It would have also made it difficult to judge what he would do if a 'pitch' was made to develop him and then convert him into a clandestine agent.[115] The second point in relation to Burton was that he was not going to add value. His department and his minister's office were penetrated by multiple agents and completely compromised already. No sensible intelligence officer, which Makarov was, would put all of this at risk by going after him.

Finally, it needs to be said that the appalling state of security at External Affairs existed prior to Burton's arrival. He inherited a mess created by

Hodgson that was exacerbated by the cavalier approach of Evatt.[116] It is often forgotten that when Milner and Hill were recruited into External Affairs, Burton was in Evatt's office, not the department. Burton was not an RIS asset.

This assessment is supported by his reaction to Hollis's interview at his property on 4 August. In his report to Sillitoe, Hollis emphasises how, once he was shown the brief, Burton's demeanour changed completely and he frankly admitted that if the information was true, then Milner was the culprit. The only thing Burton asked was to be given some time to examine his departmental records in order to trace the passage of the documents within the department. He requested to meet with Hollis and Hemblys Scales in his office at External Affairs in five days' time.[117]

At the 9 August meeting, Burton took Hollis through the department's documentary record and told him that the evidence now 'convinced him absolutely and definitely that the culprit was Milner'.[118] Hollis reported to Sillitoe that he had detected 'no indication of opportunism' or, to put it at its worst, 'crooked dealing' in Burton.[119] Hollis warned Sillitoe, however, that those in Australian government circles who knew Burton better, seemed to be 'so unanimous' in their opinion of his 'crookedness' that it needed to be borne in mind when dealing with him.[120]

More importantly for our story though was the later meeting between Bailey and Hollis during which Hollis confidentially briefed Bailey on the standing of the CIB with the armed services in Melbourne, who now refused to communicate any information to the CIB. It appears that this took Bailey by surprise and he admitted that he had not realised the situation was as bad as Hollis said. That Bailey would not have known is unsurprising as it is unlikely that Lloyd would have kept him honestly informed of the real situation. Bailey agreed with Hollis that the reorganisation of Australia's security intelligence system needed to be pursued; however, Bailey temporised and asked Hollis to postpone any further action for another week or so.[121] That said, Bailey agreed that Hemblys Scales and Hollis should go to Melbourne and hold further unofficial talks with Shedden, Spry and Brigadier Frederick Chilton, the Controller of Joint Intelligence in the Department of Defence.[122]

At this point, the MI5 strategy to move the Australian government towards creating a security intelligence organisation was making some headway. As Hollis reported, there was an increased awareness in Australia of the threat posed by the RIS and the CP-A. The challenge was to avoid the rebadging exercises that had previously been used to avoid the cost and disruption of actually creating what could become an effective security intelligence organisation. Hollis and Hemblys Scales were doubtful that the CIB had the 'knowledge, training and skills' to carry out the role.[123]

As MI5 work on the Case progressed, Hollis was writing a long letter to Sillitoe, describing how the political environment in Australia had changed. Chifley's government now faced growing political problems with the invalidation of the *Banking Act 1947* by the High Court, which destroyed their dreams of nationalising the banks. This, and the long drawn out industrial action by the communist-controlled Miners Federation that culminated in the 1949 coal strike, led to a decline in the energy of the Chifley government and an understandable lack of interest in security intelligence.

All of this impacted the work of Hollis and MI5 in Australia. The most immediate impact was that Bailey was not able to oversee and protect the reorganisation of security intelligence in Australia or the resumption of work on the Case.[124] On top of this, the changing political environment distracted the government which knew full well that reorganising security intelligence was not going to save the ALP from the advancing threat posed by the new Liberal Party of Robert Menzies.

Four days after Hollis's first long letter to Sillitoe, he sent another. In this letter he outlined the impact of the constitutional crisis surrounding the Australian government's attempts to nationalise the banks on Bailey's availability and that he now believed that Shedden, having lost his attempt to form a Defence security organisation, was willing to consider the formation of a new security intelligence organisation, even if it was within the CIB.[125] Indeed, following Chifley's conversations in London with Attlee and MI5, Lloyd and the CIB had been instructed to undertake the vetting of 150,000 government employees involved in secret work.

It was at this point that Australia's new SIGINT authority, the Defence Signals Bureau (DSB), created a bit of a stir when Hollis became aware that its Director, Lieutenant Commander T.E. Poulden of the Royal Navy, had made unauthorised inquiries about a CP-A member, Rupert Lockwood. Hollis immediately signalled Sillitoe, asking him to speak to C, the head of MI6, who was the Chairman of the London Signals Intelligence Committee (LSIC), previously called the Y Board. Hollis wanted Sillitoe to demand that C stop anyone making VENONA-linked inquires through the DSB and

Poulden.[126] On 30 August, C replied to Sillitoe that the LSIC had no idea why Poulden was making inquiries about Lockwood and that no information about Lockwood had been passed to Poulden.[127]

Meanwhile, in London, Sillitoe and White had given Bailey—who was in London to speak to legal experts about the likelihood of the House of Lords looking into Australia's constitutional banking crisis—the full treatment, with White showing Bailey around parts of B Division. Happily for MI5, they found Bailey receptive to their approaches.[128]

In Melbourne, Hollis and Hemblys Scales had been very busy. They had met with the Secretary of the Department of Defence, Frederick Shedden; the British officer commanding the Long Range Weapons Organisation in South Australia, General Evetts; the Chief of Naval Staff, Vice-Admiral J.A. Collins; the controller of Joint Intelligence in the Department of Defence, Brigadier Frederick Chilton; the directors of intelligence of the three services; and other 'lesser lights'.[129] All of the services and the Defence Department were now very conscious of the impact of the Case following their loss of access to all classified information from both the United States and the United Kingdom. This, according to Hollis, had produced 'a live and keen desire to get the security position put right'.[130] It was, Hollis went on, 'a most refreshing change from the lethargy of Canberra'.[131]

The lethargy of Canberra was, according to Hollis, a real problem and even Bailey, while very helpful and understanding, had actually done nothing practical. The meetings in Melbourne had dampened Hollis's expectations as the general view was that Bailey was not strong enough to deal with Evatt and 'Evatt will not favour the setting up of a real security service'.[132]

At the CIB, Lloyd added to the lethargy by catching the flu and taking to his bed, something he did often and with alacrity. Worse, Lloyd honestly believed that he and the CIB were on top of the Case and that they had a full working knowledge and understanding of RIS tradecraft. This was far from the truth, as Hollis frankly told Sillitoe that Lloyd 'demonstrably knows nothing of these matters and has almost no resources to deal with them', and that the CIB with its existing staff and Lloyd at its head had no possibility of ever becoming an effective counterespionage service.[133] What was more, Hollis found that Lloyd was reviled in Melbourne by the services and government departments, and that they held him personally responsible for the problems Australia now faced due to the breakdown of the government's security. They unanimously wanted Lloyd to go.[134]

332

They had a point. At the time that the CIB was being asked to conduct the security vetting of 150,000 public servants, a task well beyond its resources, Lloyd was talking to Hollis and others about the need for the CIB to vet the twenty million or so immigrants that Arthur Calwell wanted to bring to Australia. In what can only be regarded as an understatement, Hollis told Sillitoe that this would cause ructions with Calwell while adding nothing to the security position in Australia.[135]

In a separate meeting with Shedden, Hollis bluntly told him that when he left Australia, he would be seeing Chifley. He would tell him that they had identified some of the CP-A spies and others would be invariably identified in time. Damningly, Hollis told Shedden that he would be recommending the British government maintain its ban on sending sensitive information to Australia as Australia had no service capable of dealing with the RIS.[136] It was now apparent that the gentle prodding used to date could not hope to dispel the lethargy of Canberra, so Hollis had sharpened a stick.

It did not take long for Shedden to pass the word around that the horse was out of its stable. Now, Hollis adopted a more forceful approach based, as he explained to Sillitoe, on his assessment that Australia's political leadership, particularly Chifley and Evatt, were uninterested in security and little action could be expected from them until they were hurt. The best way to hurt Chifley and Evatt was to hurt the entire Australian government by stopping all Australian access to all British and American intelligence and technology. Hollis had seen how the American action had focused the minds of Australia's official class and he now advised that if the United Kingdom followed suit across all aspects of government, this presented the best opportunity for MI5 to get action taken on the creation of a new security intelligence service that could actually deal with the RIS.[137]

By 8 September, there was movement at the station and Shedden contacted Hollis to tell him that he had briefed his minister, Dedman. Shedden had been urged by Dedman to make the fullest use of Hollis and Hemblys Scales in order to put the security service on a satisfactory footing. Dedman was going to bring security up with Chifley.[138] On top of this, General Evetts had asked Hollis to brief N.K.S. Brodribb, the secretary of the Department of Supply, on the Case so that Brodribb could support the push for a security service by pointing out the impact of the ban on British and American technology transfer to Australia. While all of this was happening, Hemblys Scales was drawing up a blueprint of what an Australian security intelligence service should look like, and Director of Military Intelligence Spry was extending his reports on Russian diplomats and their activity to Hollis and to London.[139]

In his departure meeting with Chifley, Hollis briefed him on the progress in the Case and as he did so Chifley had, a little archly perhaps, pointed out that 'he supposed the Russians had spies in England too'.[140] Hollis jumped on this by pointing out that while this was true, Britain had the advantage of 'a scientific counter-espionage service' which enabled them to identify the Russian secret service members and thus work from the centre out, while the CIB floundered around trying to identify who, among the 30,000 CP-A members and supporters, actually posed a threat.[141] Chifley accepted Hollis's point and went on to say that he had already discussed reorganising security with the acting Attorney-General, John Beasley, and, despite the protestations of Bailey that they should wait for Evatt's return, Chifley proposed going ahead with the reorganisation in Evatt's absence.[142]

This was a major turning point, as Hollis was now in no doubt that Chifley was wide awake to the threat and to the failure of Australia's security estab-lishment, and was willing to exclude the disruptive Evatt from having further input into the matter.[143] By 29 September, the movement at the station had become a stampede when Canberra informed MI5 that Prime Minister Chifley, most likely advised by Dedman, intended to establish a new security organisation under his own control.[144]

Having made the decision, the Australian government now tested the waters in the United States when, in November, at the US-inspired trade negotiations, Dedman attempted to leverage a relaxation of the US ban. The US Ambassador in Canberra, Myron M. Cowan, flatly rejected the approach and told Dedman in no uncertain terms that the United States would pass nothing to Australia until the new security service was established under the authority and control of the prime minister.[145]

Adding to the Australian government's woes was the extension of the US ban by the British that Hollis had recommended. This extension now resulted in Australian scientists all over the United Kingdom being excluded from their places of work and the entire Australian scientific workforce from the Long Range Weapons Project at Salisbury in South Australia. This latter group, being well-organised Australian unionists, now created a fuss, which the government feared would lead to questions in parliament.

The Australian government would have been horrified to learn, as MI5 was just learning, that knowledge of the Case and Milner's role in it was widely known in Washington. One of MI5's representatives there was disconcerted to find out that not only were many American officials 'in the know', but so were a number of British officials working there.[146] This was very quickly brought to the notice of C by Sillitoe, and now investigations began to show that the FBI had come across Milner as an associate of individuals involved in one of their investigations into communists, the SPEED case.[147]

As if this was not bad enough, President Truman was personally urging Attlee to 'use every means at his government's disposal to impress upon the Australian government the acute necessity for accomplishing the various measures you describe in your letter'.[148] Truman then acceded to Attlee's request that Shedden should be fully briefed during a forthcoming visit to Washington. What had started as the detection of some secret Australian information in a routine IJA signal from Harbin to Tokyo had now become a landslide of pressure on the Chifley government to fix its security problems immediately.

On 24 February 1949, Chifley's decision to establish ASIO was communicated to MI5 from MANGO (the covername for Roger Hollis and Courtenay Young), the MI5 mission in Canberra.[149] Unfortunately, Evatt ensured that the new Director-General of Security and head of ASIO was his old mate Justice Geoffrey Sandford Reed of the Supreme Court of South Australia, and that his other mate, R.F.B. Wake, and his band of corrupt CIB investigators moved across to the new organisation. Once again, Australia faced the same old problem of a simple rebadging being presented as a new organisation without the procedural corruption and weaknesses of its predecessors.

CHAPTER 20

SUNLIGHT

In a massive piece of British understatement, the appointment of Justice Geoffrey Reed as the first Director-General of ASIO was described by Roger Hollis as 'not ideal'.[1] Hollis was not wrong. The creation of ASIO was not something anyone in the Chifley government really desired, except perhaps John Dedman, who held three ministries in the Chifley Cabinet and concurrently filled two other ministerial posts in 1946.

John Dedman was a strong and effective minister and a man who not only ran his ministries efficiently but also imposed unpopular policies and told prime ministers, including Ben Chifley, when they were wrong. The Ministry of Post-war Reconstruction was Ben Chifley's pet project and a subject close to his heart. The fact that Dedman held this portfolio under Chifley suggests Dedman was a man of capacity, and a man Chifley trusted. Dedman was indeed both of these things; he was one of those politicians seen frequently in the ALP who were highly capable, eminently sensible and hardworking but who, because they don't tick the right doctrinal boxes, are forgotten by the partisans of the party they represented.

In fact, Dedman stands out as a strong minister who was prepared to fight Chifley when he chose to, but was loyal enough to be well known as Chifley's 'indispensable henchman'.[2] Dedman was one of the more economically

336

literate members of Chifley's government and, like Chifley, a strong advocate for banking reform. He was also no fool and not a fan of H.V. Evatt and his ilk.

One of Dedman's characteristics was his austere political style, which, given his Scots birth, was unsurprisingly redolent of the harshness of the Kirk. He did not play the popularity stakes and was completely unperturbed by the constant lampooning of his management of wartime rationing in the press. It would be no surprise to find that Chifley's decision to create ASIO, something he was not personally comfortable with, was heavily influenced by Dedman. His support for the creation of ASIO would have been completely in line with his hard-nosed approach to, as he saw it, good policy formulation.

Adding to Dedman's willingness to support the formation of ASIO was the impact of the US and UK bans on technology transfers and access to information. After all, the scientists who now found themselves locked out of their offices and workplaces were his scientists. Of all the ministers in Chifley's cabinet, Dedman was the one most affected by the problem of insecurity.

During the war Dedman had been responsible for the development and growth of Australia's industrial and technological capabilities as the minister responsible for CSIR. Now, in 1946, he retained this responsibility and, as Minister for Defence, the newly created Defence technology programs including the Australian contribution to the British Ministry of Supply's (MoS) Long Range Weapons Project, Blue Streak, established at Salisbury and Woomera in South Australia. Dedman does not appear to have been a man who would have been happy at suffering the detrimental impact on his departments that was created by the US and British embargo, simply because his colleagues did not want a security service.

Hollis and Hemblys Scales identified the importance of the embargo to the Department of Supply, and to Dedman's departments in particular, and they sought permission to brief N.K.S. Brodribb, the Secretary of the Department of Supply, on the Case so that he could advise his minister, Bill Ashley, to support the establishment of a security service.[3]

Further evidence of Dedman's role bringing around his colleagues to accepting the need for a security service is that it was he who, in 1949, wound up the CSIR and rolled it into the new organisation, the CSIRO, run by an executive and not by a council. One of the major reasons he gave for this was improved internal security.[4]

The new CSIRO stopped all military research when its Fisherman's Bend laboratory in Melbourne was transferred to Defence, which also established a new metallurgy laboratory at Alexandria in Sydney's south and three new laboratories—High Speed Aerodynamics, Propulsion Research and Electronics Research—at Salisbury in South Australia. If Australia wanted to continue being part of this technological revolution and to stay part of the United Kingdom–United States Agreement SIGINT system, it had to establish ASIO, which Chifley did.

The year 1949 was thus a big year for Australia. The nation was trying to move into the front line of technological research and development, it was trying to industrialise, and it was trying to maintain its place as a trusted ally of Britain and the United States, sharing intelligence and technology. In December, there were more big changes when a resurgent Liberal-conservative alliance led by Robert Menzies was elected to govern. Ironically, it was Dedman's policy initiatives of rationing and wartime austerity and his post-war policy of banking reform that appear to have contributed most to the defeat. Adding to this was the fact that by 1949 the ALP had governed for just over eight years; it was a tired government with few new ideas or drive beyond that supplied by Chifley and Dedman.

ASIO was formed on 16 March 1949 under the leadership of Reed who had taken a year's leave of absence from his judicial duties in South Australia. There can be little doubt that the appointment of Reed was a compromise with Evatt in order to get the establishment of ASIO passed in Cabinet. Evatt, who believed that any new security intelligence organisation should only have twelve to fifteen investigators, finally agreed to the proposal and Reed was approached and appointed to the position of first Director-General.[5]

Reed's reasons for taking the post were less than altruistic. Even the Director-General of MI5 understood that Reed's real ambition was to gain an appointment as a High Court judge and that this is what he was mainly concerned about, particularly as the 1949 general election approached.[6] In February 1949, Reed had taken himself off to Canberra to meet with Professor Bailey; the Solicitor-General and Secretary of the Attorney-General's Department; Chifley; and the British representatives of MI5, Roger Hollis and Courtenay Young.[7] Also invited to these initial meetings was Robert Wake.[8] There can be little doubt that Wake was Evatt's representative at these meetings, and was reporting the details back to him.[9]

338

In his *Outline of the Foundation and Organisation of ASIO*, Reed fittingly starts with a lie on page one by claiming that the initiative for the founding of ASIO was instigated by Evatt, which, as anyone reading this work will know, is far from the truth.[10] Reed is more honest in using ASIO's original name, the Australian Security Service (ASS), a name which, understandably, was quickly changed to ASIO.[11] The new charter for ASIO, which followed the blueprint developed by Hemblys Scales, was prepared by Reed and signed off by Chifley on 16 March 1949.[12]

One of the first problems ASIO faced was the 'determined attempts' of the chairman of the Public Service Board to bring all ASIO personnel under the stultifying aegis of his board and its rules. More importantly though, the provisions of the legislation applying to public servants required the gazetting of vacancies and provisions for appeals against promotion decisions, and all of this was carried out in full public view. Effectively, all of this would expose to the outside world the structure and people working within the secret world of ASIO. It was more of the same old unthinking activity that had already blighted the CIB, the CSS and the Security Service. Luckily, these attempts were thwarted and ASIO personnel were employed under special contractual arrangements.

The mindset of Reed is on display in his *Outline* document in which he describes why basing ASIO in Canberra was impracticable and why the headquarters should be in Sydney. Essentially, Reed's argument was that Canberra was too small and that because the headquarters of the CP-A was in Sydney, ASIO's should be too.[13] This amply demonstrates the point made by Hollis to Chifley that the advantage MI5 had over the CIB was that it focused on the few dozen RIS operatives and did not try to monitor the tens of thousands of individuals attracted to or involved in communist groupings.[14] Reed, advised by Wake, was looking to deal with the mass of the CP-A's membership and associates, the vast majority of whom posed no real threat or usefulness to the RIS.

Reed's commentary illustrates his ignorance of effective counterespionage operations and it clearly shows that he was taking his advice from Wake, upon whom he entirely depended.[15] It is also likely that Wake recommended placing the headquarters in Sydney because he lived there and he understood that, as he was persona non grata in Melbourne, if the headquarters went there he would be subjected to close supervision by the armed services and other government departments who all wanted him out of ASIO. Placing the headquarters in

Sydney also ensured that Wake could sustain his nocturnal assignations with his female companions and have plenty of opportunity to develop non-existent agents whose payments were needed to fund his assignations.

On taking up his post, Reed made one of his first acts the appointment of three directors: Wake in Sydney; B.E. Tuck, a barrister and an associate from Adelaide, in Canberra; and H.C. Wright in Melbourne. Of the three, Wake enjoyed the greatest authority, being also responsible for Brisbane, his old stamping ground, Darwin and, projected, Port Moresby. Tuck was given Adelaide and Perth, and Wright, Melbourne and Hobart.[16] Reed's successor, Charles Spry, had no doubt that Wake was appointed at the direction of Evatt and that he was Evatt's man inside ASIO.[17] Where Spry was wrong was in supposing that Reed was innocent and would not have appointed Wake without pressure from Evatt.[18] Spry did not know about the relationship between Reed and Wake and Reed's continuing defence of Wake.[19]

This organisation reflected the old, ineffective Security Service and CIB set-ups. It also maintained the major weakness of these systems by vesting each state director with almost complete independence from headquarters. Wake could thus continue his activities just as he had done throughout the war. By the end of 1949, even Reed accepted that this organisation 'was not entirely satisfactory' as the Director-General could not control or even supervise the independent state offices.[20]

This situation was made even worse by the way in which personnel were recruited into ASIO. The recruitment process consisted of a personal invitation from someone inside ASIO to someone outside ASIO. It was the ultimate 'mate' system and it ensured that Wake populated his department with his cronies from the wartime Security Service and the CIB.[21]

The reorganisation, when Reed got it through, saw Wake take control of all B activities—B1 (Countersubversion) and B2 (Counterespionage)—while Tuck took on C activity—Protective Security—as it applied to the public service and Wright took C activity as it applied to the armed services and the Department of Supply.[22]

Wake remained, rightly, persona non grata with the armed services and government departments, who were mainly based in Melbourne. There was no shortage of gossip on his unreliability, unscrupulousness and corruption, and Young, the MI5 representative in Australia (Security Liaison Officer) and the custodian of VENONA, was well aware of the stories.[23]

Despite this, MI5 appears to have adopted the attitude that although Wake may have been a corrupt official, at least he was their corrupt official. Wake's low standing in the eyes of the military and government departments, however, began to impact the work on the Case, as Young found that he could not indoctrinate Wake into VENONA because of the likelihood that this action would generate a 'storm of protest from Melbourne'.[24] It was probably a good thing for MI5 that the Australian opposition to the indoctrination of Wake was so vociferous, as Britain had to get prior approval from the USCIB for the indoctrination of an Australian and the subsequent collaboration of Wake and the CP-A to damage ASIO and all who served in it would indeed have been embarrassing.[25]

One man who was outraged when he heard that Wake had been appointed to ASIO was the Director of Military Intelligence, Colonel Charles Spry, who did not hold back in telling Hollis exactly how unhappy he was and why. Spry regarded Wake as having a 'very dubious reputation' and he believed Wake was 'a bit crazy'.[26] As Spry later testified before the Royal Commissioner, Justice Hope, after Hollis had announced to the Melbourne meeting that Wake was being appointed as Reed's deputy he had confronted Hollis. All Hollis could say was that Wake 'was a good intelligence officer'. Spry testified that he told Hollis 'what would you know . . . you are only out here for three months'.[27] Spry was completely correct and Hollis completely wrong.

Added to this, ASIO also faced entrenched hostility from the CIB, which now fought a rather pathetic rearguard action under Longfield Lloyd. His tactics in this dispute were childish in the extreme and involved denying ASIO access to the CIB's files and then, when ordered to transfer them, transferring them in such a haphazard manner that effective cataloguing was made virtually impossible. All the time, this activity was supported by continuous moaning about ASIO in Canberra and Melbourne.[28] It was Australian bureaucratic politics at its worst, but Lloyd now took it much further when he had the CIB in Sydney raid the CP-A headquarters, Marx House, on 9 July 1949. The raid was at best a fishing expedition conducted under the auspices of section 10 of the *National Emergency (Coal Strike) Act 1949* and it did not involve ASIO. It is hard to work out what Lloyd hoped to achieve, other than to make mischief. The outcome, though, was that all of the documents the CIB seized were later passed to ASIO for examination.[29]

As all of this was happening, ASIO tried to pick up the pieces of the Case, with Young supplying sanitised prompts from the VENONA held in his safe to assist them.[30] Dick White, the new Director-General of Security in the United Kingdom, made an assessment of the situation during his 1949 visit, viewing it as a disaster that the band of novices at ASIO were having to confront a first-class RIS espionage case. He illustrated the problems using the CIB raid on Marx House on 8 July 1949 as an example, which he said the CP-A were fully aware of before it happened.[31] Even now, the Australian authorities had not yet understood that the entire old system and all of the people in it were compromised and that Alfred Hughes and his CP-A associates within the police and security system were still feeding the CP-A information.

While ASIO was attempting to progress the Case, at MI, Spry was imposing himself on his directorate. Spry understood that the entire existing system, including his own directorate, was penetrated by the CP-A. Among the first initiatives Spry instigated was the vetting of all military and civilian staff within the directorate.

While he was reorganising Military Intelligence, Spry was keeping a close eye on ASIO, the CIB and the CP-A, as well as mounting his own operations against suspected RIS personnel in Canberra. All of this he kept away from Reed, Wake and ASIO, although he kept MI6, MI5 and the LSIC, via DSB, informed. Although Spry had refused one of the positions within ASIO when it was formed, he had done this because he was not willing to serve under Reed if Wake was to be part of the organisation. This did not mean that Spry did not want to head ASIO.

By December 1949, the work on the Case was progressing satisfactorily and ASIO was beginning to utilise new techniques and new technology, including listening devices and telephone taps, the latter, for some odd reason, restricted to Sydney.[32] These new techniques and technology helped greatly and, as previously mentioned, one of the devices planted in Nosov's flat detected his wife Galina reading out the messages as she was encrypting and decrypting them for her husband.[33]

It did not go well every time, however, as a small incident on 8 December, during Operation SMILE, showed. This incident occurred when the technician drilled a hole for a listening device into the Nosov's flat from an adjoining room. After the drilling had been done and the device inserted, it was realised the device could be seen, as could the plaster dust on the floor.[34] The ASIO team, led by Ray Whitrod, gained entry to the Nosov's apartment through the good graces of the caretaker and cleaned up, but Whitrod believed Nosov would have known that someone had accessed his flat.[35] In fact, it was this sort of activity as well as the surveillance conducted against the Nosovs that began to tell on Galina, whose nervousness increased as time went by.

It was in December 1949 that the fates finally moved to bring about the real end of the old security intelligence system in Australia. The election of the new Liberal–Country Party coalition to government at the 10 December election meant the washing away of the ALP government and Evatt. This was the end of the second Chifley ministry and, although he did not know it, the end of Evatt's hold on power. Now Evatt would have to get along without the services of his special officers in the security system or the support of those seeking high judicial office.

The new government led by Robert Menzies was a different creature to that of Ben Chifley. There could be little doubt that among its first objectives on taking over the reins of power was the removal of the ALP's people in positions of power and influence. High on that list would have been those officials who had played roles in undermining Menzies in 1941; this included military officers, security officials and a range of others. However, it was not going to be a crude purge, just a delicate cutting of links with no waving goodbye.

As for ASIO, Menzies met with Reed on 3 January 1950, and was indoctrinated into the Case and the fragments of VENONA that Young was authorised to release to Australia. What Reed knew was that Ian Milner had been a successful RIS agent, as had Frances Bernie. He also would have reported on the Throssells and Jim Hill. After this, a program of briefing ministers was undertaken with the strangest briefing being given to Percy Spender, the new Minister for External Affairs, during which Wake, with no evidence whatsoever, impugned the reputation of Arthur Tange, a rising star in the Commonwealth bureaucracy, by telling Spender that his closeness to Hill made him highly suspect.[36]

The other matter that Wake discussed with Spender was the plan to post Hill to London in January 1950 in order for MI5 to interview him there. When Spender asked Young what he thought of this, Young answered that it would be easier to keep 'tags' on Hill in London and that having Hill isolated there during the time that ASIO was moving in on the spy network would enable his evidence to be taken as a comparative check against that of the suspects in Australia.[37] The subsequent events suggest there was more to this plan than MI5 was telling Australia.

The work that Reed was putting in was not sufficient to save him. By March, Menzies, after a little hesitation caused by how it would be perceived, had made it quite clear to Reed that his services were no longer required, and he could return to the bench of the South Australian Supreme Court. After this, Reed was a lame duck.

Reed was not the only casualty of the election of the Menzies government, as both Menzies and his deputy, Arthur Fadden, had scores to settle with Wake.[38] The only problem with moving on Wake was that he had been close to Fadden during the first Menzies ministry in 1941, and it is likely that his help to Fadden was similar to that he had provided to Evatt later on. Another problem that ASIO faced was the growing evidence of Wake's hard corruption, in particular Wake's frauds on the Commonwealth in creating fictitious confidential agents to whom substantial payments were made by Wake alone. Spry believed there were at least two such fictitious agents being run by Wake during Reed's term as Director-General, ASIO.[39] When he gave evidence before the Hope Royal Commission into Intelligence and Security in 1976, Spry explained that he had not had Wake prosecuted because it would have damaged Reed and ASIO as well.[40]

According to Young's reporting to MI5, on 12 January at a meeting in Melbourne between Menzies and Reed, Menzies offered Reed a further year as Director-General, ASIO.[41] Reed was not too happy with such a short-term appointment. What Reed did not know is that Chifley and Menzies had discussed 'the problem of the future director generalship of ASIO'. This discussion would have been frank and friendly as, personally, Menzies and Chifley got on very well and there can be little doubt that Chifley, no one's fool, would have pointed out the connections between Evatt, Reed and Wake.

As the meeting was coming up, however, Young and Wake both believed it was highly likely that Reed would retain the position.[42] They were both wrong. In addition to the advice he got from Chifley, Menzies, a member of the Melbourne establishment, would have been well advised by Spry and other mandarins in Melbourne on the state of play at ASIO, and he had most likely decided to terminate Reed as soon as he could do so without looking vindictive. The one-year extension he offered Reed is about the right amount of time for a sacking to look as if it is a gentle cutting of ties with no hard feelings.

One event of some significance that did occur just before Spry took over was the burning of Hill, in London. This operation, which Young raised as an aside when he met with Spender in January, was immediately put in place and arrangements were made to post Hill to Australia House on the Strand. The idea behind this plan was that in London Hill would be more vulnerable and less able to compare what he said with his CP-A colleagues than if he was interrogated in Australia. This doesn't ring true and it may be that MI6 and the USCIB were actually behind this operation, but were using MI5 to facilitate it and provide plausible denial. The idea that Jim Skardon, the senior MI5 officer who ran their surveillance sections, conducted an inept interrogation of Hill may be a misreading of what happened. From the events described, it strikes this author that Hill was deliberately burned.

This operation focused on one interview between Hill and Skardon on 6 June 1950, with three follow-up interviews ending on 13 June. The first interview involved Hill being brought into a room by his superior at Australia House in London to find himself being interrogated by Skardon, who had won some fame with an earlier interrogation of Klaus Fuchs, a German theoretical physicist and communist who escaped from Germany in 1939 and spied for the GRU. In 1949, Fuchs, codenamed REST and CHARLES, was identified from VENONA, interviewed by Skardon and, during the second interview, he admitted being a GRU agent. The information he provided implicated people in the United States who, in turn, implicated the Rosenbergs. They, unlike Fuchs, were executed.[43]

The interview with Skardon upset Hill, who seemed to be very nervous about the extent of Skardon's knowledge of his life.[44] Immediately Skardon let Hill go, Hill went out onto the Strand and made a telephone call to his wife from a public telephone box, which, amazingly, was tapped. Given that MI5's watchers would have a reasonable idea of how Hill would respond, it is likely that on that day a lot of public telephone boxes around Australia House were tapped, an easy task as they would all have gone to the same exchange.

As a result of this interview and the subsequent panicked telephone calls to all and sundry, MI5 would have been able to network the connections and map the extent of the CP-A and CP-GB cells operating in Britain. This looks more like the prime reason for interrogating Hill in London. After all, MI5's charter is about protecting the United Kingdom, not wasting its time and resources interrogating a minor player on behalf of Australia.

The immediate outcome of the Hill–Skardon interview was that Rupert Lockwood blew any semblance of cover he had left by desperately collecting money for a Qantas ticket to Sydney so he could warn Walter Clayton. Milner fled to Prague to spy on his friends and colleagues, and the wave of panic spread out, contaminating the CP-GB. All of this occurred while MI5 watched, listened and mapped.[45] Rather than being an inept interview, it is very possible that MI6 and the USCIB were throwing a pebble into the pond to startle the fowl into the air where they could be shot.

In support of this contention is the fact that Skardon's interrogation of Hill was planned and overseen by a veritable who's who of British intelligence including C, Stewart Menzies, Colonel Valentine Vivian, John Tiltman, all from MI6, and Sir Edward Travis from GC&CS, as well as the MI5 contingent and, one suspects, US representatives.[46] The only concern the planners of this action had was that it did not compromise VENONA. Hill was a disposable asset in this game.

How can we know this? Well, we can't, not for certain; however, if the Case had developed to the point where it was now not moving forward, and it had reached this point by June 1950, then this was a workable idea. It certainly appeals to this writer as a pretty good way of getting birds to fly so they can be shot.

With the demise of Reed as Director-General, things now started happening within ASIO that were long overdue. The first was that with Reed disarmed, Wake's enemies, and as we know, there were many of them, began circling and Young was sure that when the new Director-General arrived, 'Wake will either go or be pushed'. As a result, Young counselled Sillitoe that it would be 'most unwise' to indoctrinate Wake.[47] On 7 July 1950, Reed was informed by Bailey that his replacement was Colonel Charles Spry who would be taking up his post on 17 July 1950.[48]

When Spry took over at ASIO he later claimed that he did not want to move too quickly to reorganise it as he feared destroying what little morale it had built up. He very quickly addressed the political interference, however, and asked Menzies for permission to brief Chifley, now the leader of the Opposition. Menzies, Spry later testified, had no problems with this and told him that if he wanted to do it, then do it.[49] This was later extended to Evatt when he took over from Chifley.

The other change Spry implemented was the extension of the telephone tapping capability from Sydney to Canberra and Melbourne. For some unknown reason, this capability had been restricted.[50] In seeking this extension, Spry spoke to Menzies and made it clear that he was going to forbid ASIO monitoring the telephones of ministers, politicians and senior public servants, something the official record makes clear was a common practice under the previous security organisations, including the time Reed led ASIO.[51]

The other actions taken by Spry included Operation SALTMINES, which destroyed the independence of the state directors by centralising all records, specialist teams and support personnel at headquarters.[52] With this done, Spry then moved to remove unwanted personnel, starting with Wake who was confronted by Spry with the evidence of his fraudulent agents and told to resign. This he did on 4 September 1950. He had survived Reed by just two months.

Spry then went after the rest of the organisation by moving headquarters to Melbourne, something he knew would weed it of the unwanted cronies of Wake. Now, having somewhat cleaned house, Spry began formalising recruitment, targeting university students with good arts and law degrees. Finally, Australia's security intelligence system was climbing back into the light. Now, although the Case had lost momentum, ASIO would start getting wins, one of the first of which was obtaining a copy of the Twentieth Party Congress in Moscow before any other intelligence agency. This coup was possible because the Soviet official who collected it from the embassy in Canberra took it to a betting shop and left it there.[53] Now ASIO and Australia were almost ready to manage a major defection, which was just as well, as Vladimir Mikhaylovich Petrov and his wife Evdokia were about to arrive in Australia.

Sunlight

CONCLUSION

The history of Australia's security intelligence system in the first half of the twentieth century is not particularly uplifting. Despite this, we should take heed of it, for we will always learn more from our mistakes than we ever will from our successes. On this basis, modern Australia should have a security intelligence organisation in ASIO that is highly professional and competent, because as this work clearly shows, we made many mistakes along the way. The story we have followed tells us that, despite all of the criticisms, ASIO is a security intelligence organisation far and above anything that went before. It also tells us that, however much we may regret the necessity, a well-resourced, well-led and highly professional security intelligence organisation is an absolute necessity for the protection of the nation Australians are building.

The story of the development of Australia's security intelligence establishment begins, as it should, with the need identified by the Australian government of 1901 to meet its undertakings to pass and enforce the Immigration Restriction Act that had been demanded by the people and political parties in Australia, in return for the formation of a Commonwealth of Australia. The enforcement of the White Australia policy required a security system and this required intelligence to be collected. All of this was put together by Atlee Hunt and his departments, who then ran the system until the policy was dismantled.

The reality that our security intelligence system arose from what is now a detested and embarrassing desire to keep the nation ethnically pure should not lead us into the trap of unjustly condemning the people who developed and ran the security intelligence system of those early days. Australia then

348

was a liberal democracy which had voted for ethnic exclusivity. Hunt and his fellow public servants were simply enforcing the dictates of their democratically elected governments, as was their duty.

Of course, the benefit to Australia of the work put in by Hunt, Piesse and other early officials is that it gave the country the framework that enabled the construction of a working security system. The problem was that this framework only worked against readily identified groups whose skin colour or political activity easily marked them out. What Hunt's system did not equip the nation with was the organisational culture, skills and knowledge that would enable it to detect and counter the espionage of foreign intelligence organisations and their agents.

What it also failed to do was to ensure that the necessary checks and balances were put in place to ensure that someone was watching someone who was watching the watchers, so as to ensure that the abuse of power that comes so easily to those charged with protecting the nation from subversion and espionage did not easily occur.

The initial signs of abuse came out of the bitter political struggle over conscription in 1916 and 1917, when the first security intelligence organisation was unconstitutionally formed and manipulated by no less a person than Australia's own prime minister, William Morris Hughes, the Little Digger—an accurate description, as no smaller man has ever served in the post.

The procedural corruption that this work has highlighted really began with the use to which Hughes put the CEB of George Steward and the willingness of Steward to carry out Hughes' bidding. Both of these men began a tradition that was not erased until Charles Spry cleaned out ASIO in the early to mid-1950s. Yet, is it not fickle that we overlook Hughes and Steward and pillory Spry? This work hopefully serves to correct this oversight.

With the destruction of the intelligence initiatives put in place by Hunt, Piesse, Senator George Pearce and William Watt in 1922, the story of Australia's security intelligence descends into one of lethargy and lazy investigations conducted by a small organisation with no resources and no political standing. At the same time, the threats posed by foreign espionage and political subversion, which were beginning to arise due to dedicated agents like Alexander Zuzenko, were growing apace. The CP-A and all of its associates then picked up the baton from Zuzenko and passed it from hand to hand until it was placed in the highly competent grasp of Walter Seddon Clayton.

Alongside this work, another unrecognised threat was developing as skilled and deep-cover illegal residents were brought into Australia to begin their operations on behalf of the RIS. Among these operatives were the Melbourne cell of Solomon Kosky, Jack Skolnik, Hirsch Munz and David Morris, and their wool and fur businesses. All along, our security intelligence organisations focused on the loud and obvious purveyors of revolution, not the actual agents of it, who remained silently in the shadows.

Other easily identified groups drew attention with their language, food and habits. Among these were Italians, Eastern Europeans and the Irish, especially the Catholics and, even worse, Jehovah's Witnesses. Alongside all of these groups were the truly subversive members and followers of the CP-A and its affiliate organisations. These were the groups that became the targets of Australia's disorganised and badly led security establishment and it is telling that there was more injury inflicted on the Jehovah's Witnesses and the Australia First Movement than was ever inflicted on communists and their fellow travellers. From 1939, we see the full danger presented by an unprofessional security intelligence establishment—the intrusion of the military into civil life.

Thankfully, the soldiers never got the control they demanded as their malign influence on our wartime security intelligence led to some of the most egregious abuses in the history of the Commonwealth, abuses that were recognised at the time by other bureaucrats and politicians possessed of better moral and ethical compasses. Men like Sir George Knowles, John Dedman and, after a rocky start, Franke Forde. There was even the occasional voice, such as Maurice Blackman's, protesting about injustice.

The battle between these forces led to bureaucratic infighting in defence of departmental and organisational status that was nothing short of scandalous. Within this turmoil ran the steady current of procedural corruption first created by Hughes and Steward, fostered by the weakness of men like H.E. Jones and E.E. Longfield Lloyd, and further strengthened by the morally weak, like R.F.B. Wake and his cronies. This situation progressed, finding new players in William MacKay and William Ballantyne Simpson, and political figures like H.V. Evatt and, for a short time, Forde. They all stand responsible for the abuses carried out by Australia's security intelligence system in our name.

While Australia's government fought its internal battles, the RIS and its associates in the CP-A built extensive clandestine networks within Australia's government, its scientific and educational institutions and our cultural groupings in order to destroy all of them. It was not until ASIO came under Charles Spry's leadership that the necessary order, professionalism and focus were created to enable the few professional intelligence officers—the spies working from foreign embassies and organisations—to be placed at the heart of our security intelligence effort and the mass of individuals exhibiting temporary or permanent attachment to subversion ignored. By watching the spies, we finally identified the traitors within the mass of disgruntled.

To learn this, we had to outrage our friends until, finally, we faced the reality that if we were to be taken seriously as a nation, we needed to protect not only our own secrets, but also those of our friends. Finally, in 1949—but more so in 1951 when the last of the corrupt officials were swept away—ASIO, Australia's first effective security intelligence organisation, was formed and set on its course. For this, we can thank Sir George Knowles, Sir Charles Spry, John Dedman, Ben Chifley and perhaps even Frank Forde, who redeemed himself by arguing for a better system. We should not forget to also thank Sir Percy Sillitoe, Sir Richard (Dick) White, Sir Roger Hollis, Robert Hemblys Scales and Courtenay Young of MI5. We should also thank John Charles Mawhood as well.

351

ACKNOWLEDGEMENTS

Acknowledgements are a poor way for an author to thank the people who have contributed to the book just written. There are people who influenced the writing, such as Raymond Chandler, Niall Ferguson, Shelby Foote, David S. Landes and George Orwell, all of whom I cannot thank enough for their greater skill. There are those, like Professor David Horner, who gave worthwhile advice and those, such as Kevin Windle, who graciously assisted in making the book a little bit better. There are the people in the National Archives of Australia and the National Archives in London without whom I could not have researched as well as I did. Then there are Allen & Unwin's staff, my publisher Elizabeth Weiss and editor Angela Handley, who chiselled, sanded and carried the book to finality. Lastly, there are those who suffered the longest in listening to my enthusiasms—my good friends and my family, especially Frances, my wife. I acknowledge you all for your inspiration, your support and especially your patience.

ABBREVIATIONS

ACNB	Australian Commonwealth Naval Board
ADB	*Australian Dictionary of Biography*
AFM	Australia First Movement (extremely boring dinner companions)
AIB	Allied Intelligence Bureau
AIC	Australian Intelligence Corps
AIF	Australian Imperial Force
AJIC	Australian Joint Intelligence Committee
ASIO	Australian Security Intelligence Organisation
ASWS	Australian Special Wireless Section—SIGINT unit
AWM	Australian War Memorial
CCEB	Central Counter Espionage Bureau (British domestic HUMINT)
CEB	Counter Espionage Bureau (Australian domestic HUMINT)
CGS	Chief of the General Staff—Australia
CIB	Commonwealth Investigation Bureau
CIC	Counterintelligence Corps—US Army
CIGS	Chief of the Imperial General Staff—Britain
CNS	Chief of the Naval Staff
CP-A	Communist Party of Australia
CP-GB	Communist Party of Great Britain
CSS	Commonwealth Security Service
DCGS	Deputy Chief of the General Staff
DDMI	Deputy Director of Military Intelligence
DD-S	Deputy Director of Security
DG-S	Director-General of the Security Service (Australia after 1942)
DMI	Director of Military Intelligence
DNI	Director of Naval Intelligence
DSB	Defence Signals Bureau (SIGINT)
FBI	Federal Bureau of Investigation (US civilian domestic HUMINT)
FRUMEL	Fleet Radio Unit Melbourne (US Navy SIGINT)
FSS	Field Security Section (Queensland)
GC&CS	Government Code and Cypher School (UK SIGINT)
GHQ	General Headquarters
GRU	Glavnoye Razvedyvatel'noye Upravleniye, the main military intelligence directorate of the general staff of the Soviet Army (HUMINT and SIGINT)
HUMINT	human intelligence
IJA	Imperial Japanese Army

IJN	Imperial Japanese Navy
JIB	Joint Intelligence Bureau—Australia
LHQ	Land Headquarters
LSIC	London Signals Intelligence Committee
M	British SIGINT centre at Heliopolis in Egypt
MI	Military Intelligence
MI5	Security Service Britain (Domestic)
MI6	British Secret Intelligence Service (Overseas HUMINT)
MPIS	Military and Police Intelligence Section (New South Wales)
NAA	National Archives of Australia
N-GRU	Naval GRU
NKGB	Soviet civilian HUMINT, Narodnyy Komissariat Gosudarstvennoy Bezopasnosti (People's Commissariat for State Security)
NKVD	Main Directorate of State Security
NZSIB	New Zealand Security Intelligence Bureau
OC	Officer Commanding
OP-20-G	SIGINT Staff (US Navy SIGINT)
OSS	Office of Strategic Services—US external HUMINT and sabotage organisation
RAAF	Royal Australian Air Force
RAF	Royal Air Force
RAN	Royal Australian Navy
RIS	Russian intelligence services
RN	Royal Navy
RNR	Royal Naval Reserve
RWA	Russian Workers Association
SIB	Special Intelligence Bureau
SIGINT	signals intelligence
SIS	Signals Intelligence Service (US Army SIGINT)
SLO	special liaison officer—commander of the SLU and the indoctrination officer for the supported organisation or headquarters
SLU	Special Liaison Unit—the organisation responsible for all aspects of SIGINT security, including communications
SMH	*The Sydney Morning Herald*
SOE	Special Operations Executive—British sabotage organisation
UK	United Kingdom
US	United States
USANACC	United States Army, Navy and Air Co-ordinating Committee
USCIB	United States Communications Intelligence Board
Y Board	SIGINT authority for traffic analysis and lower level SIGINT

GLOSSARY

. . .	in quotes from VENONA signals this represents gaps in the intercepted text
action under threat	RIS emergency procedure for extracting compromised operatives
agent	individual on the payroll of an intelligence agency
asset	individual spying for an intelligence officer or agent
ATHLETE	RIS penetration agent recruited from local communist parties
BIG HOUSE	Communist International (Comintern)
blind asset	individual who does not know who they are spying for
blown	the uncovering of a clandestine identity or activity
brush contact	a contact by two operatives quickly passing one another in a crowded place in which items may or may not be passed
coat dragging	operation designed to draw intelligence attention
crib	mistake or oversight allowing insights into a code
ENGINEERS	Soviet diplomatic staff
false flag operation	operation disguised as that of another nation
FELLOWCOUNTRYMEN	Communist Party members
fit up	plant false evidence to bring about a conviction
FRATERNAL	Communist Party of a non-Soviet country
front	activity or organisation used to hide clandestine work
ghoul	RIS operative who finds names of dead babies for fake identities
illegal resident	the representative of an RIS agency, either NKGB or GRU, not working under diplomatic cover, often under deep cover in the country on which the resident is spying
jolly	official travel undertaken for private reasons
Kempeitai	Japanese Military Police
legal resident	the representative of an RIS agency, either NKGB or GRU, working under diplomatic cover
legend	false identity constructed for a clandestine agent
line	the line of control of an agent from Moscow Centre through the residency to the agent
Moscow Centre	Moscow headquarters of NKGB and GRU respectively
Moscow Rules	rigorous tradecraft used in hostile environments
NEIGHBOURS	RIS cover term for other RIS agencies

NOOK	Department of External Affairs in Australia or a foreign ministry elsewhere
probationer	junior NKGB officer still in the developmental stage
Resident	the senior representative of an RIS agency in a country
spook	a spy or intelligence officer
take	raw signals taken down in SIGINT operations
tradecraft	behaviours used to disguise clandestine action
ULTRA	codeword designating SIGINT derived from high-level code breaking
walk-in	an individual who walks into an embassy or mission offering to serve as an intelligence agent
Witnesses	Jehovah's Witnesses

NOTES

Introduction: Security Intelligence in Australia, 1901–50

1   Transcript of evidence by Rupert Basil Michel Long, 21 December 1943, BC1134482, NAA, A7359, BOX 4/MS200/23, f 70 and 83.
2   Transcript of evidence by Commander Long, BC1134482, NAA.
3   Transcript of evidence by Commander Long, BC1134482, NAA.
4   P. Hasluck, *The Government and the People, 1942–1945*, Vol. 2, AWM, Canberra, 1970, pp. 718–42.
5   Transcript, 19–20 December 1922, of interrogation of Alexander Suzenko aka Toni Tollagsen by captains Miller and Liddell of MI5, BC43659, NAA: A1, 1924/30649, A.M. Soosenko—Undesirable (Alias Tuzenko—alias Matulishenko).
6   K. Windle, *Undesirable*, Australian Scholarly Publishing, North Melbourne, 2012, p. 15.
7   Windle, *Undesirable*, pp. 15–16.
8   Windle, *Undesirable*, p. 92.

Chapter 1: Keeping Australia White

1   Letter, Foreign Office to Japanese Minister resident in London, Baron Hyashi, 8 February 1902, BC2001, NAA: A1, 1904/7830, *Correspondence Immigration Act 1901*. This letter firmly established the grounds upon which Japan objected to Australia's laws as having nothing to do with the 'modification of the laws by which a certain part of the Japanese population was excluded Australia and NZ', but the language used 'classed them for the purpose of the proposed legislation with others to whom they bore no real similarity' thus inflicting on the Japanese nation 'an insult which was not deserved'.
2   *Daily News*, 20 September 1935, p. 5, and *SMH*, 15 March 1877, p. 9.
3   Classified advertisement in educational section, *SMH*, 17 January 1891, p. 13.
4   *SMH*, 22 March 1892, p. 7.
5   *Daily News*, 20 September 1935, p. 5.
6   C. Cunneen, 'Steward, Charles Thomas', *ADB*.
7   Year Book Australia, 1908, p. 145.
8   Year Book Australia, 1908, pp. 145 and 147.
9   Year Book Australia, 1908, pp. 145 and 147.
10   Year Book Australia, 1908, p. 906.
11   Year Book Australia, 1908, p. 905.
12   Year Book Australia, 1908, p. 906.
13   Year Book Australia, 1908, p. 905.

14   Letter, Attlee Hunt to Barton, 10 January 1902, BC2001, NAA.

15   See J. Fahey, *Australia's First Spies*, Allen & Unwin, Sydney, 2018, pp. 51–62.

16   See Fahey, *Australia's First Spies*, p. 54.

17   N.S. Pixley, 'Presidential address: Pearlers of North Australia', https://espace.library.uq.edu.au/view/UQ:209190, accessed 30 December 2018.

18   Letters, Atlee Hunt and 'Ted' Foxall, 22 and 26 April 1910, Papers of Atlee Hunt, NLA, MS52/24,25,26/1287–1336, folder 28.

19   See Fahey, *Australia's First Spies*, pp. 51–62.

20   Letters, Atlee Hunt and 'Ted' Foxall, 3 and 8 December 1908, Papers of Atlee Hunt, NLA, folder 28.

21   Letter, A. Hunt to T. Foxall, 3 December 1908, Papers of Atlee Hunt, NLA, folder 28.

22   Letter, A. Hunt to T. Foxall, 3 December 1908, Papers of Atlee Hunt, NLA, folder 28.

23   Letter, T. Foxall to A. Hunt, 11 December 1908, Papers of Atlee Hunt, NLA, folder 28.

24   See Fahey, *Australia's First Spies*, pp. 1–8.

25   Papers of Atlee Hunt, NLA, MS52/7/611–634, folder 12.

26   Papers of Atlee Hunt, NLA, MS52/8/635–716, folder 13.

27   Undated letter, James Johnston to Honourable Batchelor, MHR, and letter, 22 May 1909, Atlee Hunt to James Johnston, BC5367, NAA, A1, 1909/12239, Japanese Near Port Stephens. Reports of Australian Intelligence Corps.

28   Undated letter, James Johnston to Honourable Batchelor, MHR, and letter, 22 May 1909, Atlee Hunt to James Johnston, BC5367, NAA.

29   Formation of Australian Intelligence Corps, BC324142, NAA: MP84/1, 1849/2/13.

30   Draft minute, CGS, 20 May 1909, BC331612, NAA: MP84/1, 1877/5/5.

31   Minute on Army Administration, 16 June 1909, p. 3, BC694183, NAA: A5954, 1203/6.

32   See Fahey, *Australia's First Spies*, pp. 15–16.

33   Marginal notes, 6 December 1907, on front page detail the need for a meeting of the full Promotions Board to deal with the claims of passed over officers and the outcome, the promotion of McCay, BC324142, NAA: MP84/1, 1849/2/13.

34   Lecture, Lieutenant Colonel McCay, Troops in War, BC4039793, NAA: A1194, 15.19/5612, Lectures Delivered by Officers During School of Instruction for Australian Intelligence Corps.

35   Annual Report, OC, NSW AIC, 11 February 1911, p. 3, BC331919, NAA: MP84/1, 1902/7/47A, Reports by Commandant on Works and Training etc of the Australian Intelligence Corps.

36   Re visit of German De Haaz [*sic*] to Island and Darwin, see BC12184, NAA, A1, 1911/19743.

37   Re visit of German De Haaz, BC12184, NAA.

38   C. Andrew, *The Defence of the Realm*, Allen Lane, London, 2009, p. 44.

39   Karl Paul Gustav Hentschel—Naturalization Certificate, BC15655, NAA: A1, 1913/9176.

40   Andrew, *The Defence of the Realm*, p. 44.

41   Andrew, *The Defence of the Realm*, p. 44.

42   Letter, John Fearnley to Senator George Pearce, 17 May 1909, BC331612, NAA; MP84/1, 1877/5/5.

43   Memoirs of Malcolm Lindsay Shepherd, BC4994275, NAA, A1632, 1, Part 2.

44   Hunt served Barton in both roles, 1901–03; Alfred Deakin, 1903–04, 1905–08, 1909–10; John 'Chris' Watson, 1904; George Reid, 1904–05; Andrew Fisher, 1908–09, 1910–13. In the role of departmental head of External Affairs and Home Affairs and Territories, he served Joseph Cook, 1913–14, Andrew Fisher, 1914–15, and then William Hughes, 1916–21.

Chapter 2: War, Security, Political Subterfuge and Corruption

1   *War Precautions Act 1914*, s. 4, www.legislation.gov.au/Details/C1914A00010, accessed 1 January 2019.
2   *War Precautions Act 1914*, s. 4, accessed 1 January 2019.
3   Memorandum (No. 471-M), Overseas Sub-Committee of the Committee of Imperial Defence, CAB 38/25/38, Postal Censorship, NA, UK.
4   Memorandum (No. 471-M), CAB 38/25/38, NA, UK.
5   Memorandum (No. 471-M), p. 1, CAB 38/25/38, NA, UK.
6   Memorandum (No. 471-M), p. 3, CAB 38/25/38, NA, UK.
7   E. Scott, *Australia During the War*, Angus & Robertson, Sydney, 1936, p. 60.
8   Intelligence Summary for week ending 21 November 1914, BC4384184, NAA, BP4/2, DISTRICT 1, 1st Military District (Queensland) Censor's Intelligence Reports.
9   Memorandum (No. 471-M), CAB 38/25/38, NA, UK.
10   Scott, *Australia During the War*, pp. 98–100.
11   Letter, George Steward to Secretary, Prime Minister's, 9 August 1914, BC32089, NAA: A1, 1914/24363, Permission to Germans to Leave Commonwealth—Arrest of German and Austrian Reservists, and BC338073, NAA: BP230/12 1, Austrian Officers and Reservists to be kept under surveillance.
12   Letter, Atlee Hunt, External Affairs to Secretary, Prime Minister's, 7 August 1914, BC32089, NAA.
13   Letter, John T. Bray, American Consul-General, to Prime Minister Joseph Cook, 5 August 1914, BC32089 NAA.
14   Letter, US Consul-General to Prime Minister Cook, 5 August 1914, and memo Atlee Hunt to Cook, 7 August 1914, BC32089, NAA.
15   Letter, Atlee Hunt to P&O Shipping, 18 August 1914, BC33022, NAA: A1, 1915/10455, Coloured Crews of Detained German and Austrian Ships.
16   Letter, Sly and Russell, Solicitors and Notaries Public, to the Collector of Customs, Sydney, 19 August 1914, BC33022, NAA.
17   BC33022, NAA.
18   Scott, *Australia During the War*, pp. 112–36.
19   Scott, *Australia During the War*, p. 111.
20   Letter, George Steward to Prime Minister W. Hughes, 26 November 1915, BC275070, NAA: A3932, SC298, Commonwealth Police.
21   The Governor-General's involvement in this communications link was completely innocent. The problem the British government had was that Britain's ciphers and codes could only be held by appointed British officials. In foreign countries these were the members of the accredited British diplomatic mission. Australia, as a dominion, had no British diplomatic mission and thus no official who could hold the codes and ciphers. The Governor-General, as the King's representative, came closest to this and thus, handled all encoded messages between London and Melbourne.
22   Letter, George Steward to Hughes, 14 January 1916, BC275070, NAA.
23   Cunneen, 'Steward, Charles Thomas', *ADB*.
24   Letter, Steward to Secretary, Prime Minister's, 14 January 1916, BC275070, NAA.
25   Letter, Steward to Secretary, Prime Minister's, 14 January 1916, BC275070, NAA.
26   Letter, Steward to Hughes, 14 January 1916, BC275070, NAA.
27   Letter, Hughes to Steward, 14 January 1916, BC275070, NAA. The CEB was often referred to as the Special Intelligence Bureau (SIB). To avoid confusion, Steward's organisation will be referred to as the CEB and the Special Investigation Bureau formed within the Attorney-General's Department in early 1919 will be referred to as the SIB.

28   Circular letter from Hughes, 14 January 1916, BC275070, NAA.

29   Letter, Steward to J.H. Starling, 17 January 1916, BC275070, NAA.

30   Note, Atlee Hunt to Prime Minister's, 18 January 1916, BC275070, NAA.

31   Minute, Garran to Attorney-General, 11 February 1916, BC1110736, NAA: A432, 1955/4429, Commonwealth Police—Establishment of CIB.

32   E. Childers, *The Riddle of the Sands*, Penguin Classics, Harmondsworth, 2011. Ironically, Childers, an extremely patriotic British imperialist who became an Irish nationalist extremist, was executed by the Irish Free State in 1922.

33   Novar Papers, MS696, Series 4, Items 901, 902 and 903, quoted in J.T. McPhee, 'Spinning the Secrets of State: The History and Politics of Intelligence Politicisation in Australia', PhD thesis (unpublished), RMIT University, June 2015, p. 147.

34   Letter, Steward to Hughes, 2 February 1917, BC275070, NAA.

35   Letter, Steward to Hughes, 2 February 1917, BC275070, NAA.

36   Letter, Steward to Hughes, 2 February 1917, BC275070, NAA.

37   Letter, Steward to Hughes, 12 February 1917, BC275070, NAA.

38   Memo, Prime Minister's to Steward, 24 February 1917, BC275070, NAA.

39   Circular No. 1, 1 February 1916, BC246073, NAA: CP46/2 24, Commonwealth Counter Espionage Bureau.

40   Circular No. 1, BC246073, NAA.

41   Letter, Garran to Attorney-General, 11 February 1916, BC1110736, NAA.

42   Marginal note on Garran letter, 11 February 1916, BC1110736, NAA.

43   Undated memo, A432, 1955/4429, Commonwealth Police—Establishment of CIS, BC1110736, p. 118, NAA.

44   Letters, Steward to Secretary, Attorney-General's, 4 September 1917, BC1110736, NAA.

45   For some unexplained reason a number of writers have erroneously described John Latham as having been the head of the RAN's security intelligence and even Naval Intelligence. Latham was an Honorary legal officer who appears to have joined the RANVR for professional reasons and seems to have marked time in an intelligence role until something better came along. By April 1918 it had, and Latham was accompanying Prime Minister Hughes to the Imperial War Conference. Telegram, Prime Minister, 1 May 1918, BC258026, NAA: CP359/3, 1, Personal Papers of Prime Minister Hughes. In 1925, Latham, probably realising that the RAN's cachet had slipped, transferred to the army. For examples of this, see F. Cain, *The Australian Security Intelligence Organisation*, Frank Cass, Abingdon, 2005, p. 3, and D. Ball and D.M. Horner, *Breaking the Codes*, Allen & Unwin, Sydney, 1998, p. 12.

46   Letter, Secretary, Prime Minister's to Steward, 22 September 1917, BC275070, NAA.

47   R. Lamont, 'Thring, Walter Hugh Charles Samuel', *ADB*.

48   Letter, Governor-General's Office to Secretary, Prime Minister's, 23 August 1917, BC275070, NAA.

49   By 14 April 1919 Ainsworth had become the official representative in Queensland of Harold Edward Jones, Director of the Special Intelligence Bureau (SIB). Letters and minutes, from 18 November 1915 to 29 April 1919, Bolshevism, Sedition and Disloyalty, BC237172, NAA: A3932, SC294.

50   Undated minute, p. 1, BC1110736, NAA.

51   Letter, Acting Secretary, Department of Defence to Secretary, Prime Minister's, 8 February 1918, BC275070, NAA.

52   Conferences, Intelligence Arrangements of Commonwealth Departments—Police Co-Operation, BC48075, NAA: A2, 1918/877.

53   Memo, Secretary, Prime Minister's to the Acting Secretary, Defence, 12 February 1918, BC48075, NAA.

54 Letter, Premier Western Australia to the Acting Prime Minister, 11 December 1918, BC39551, NAA: A1, 1921/2322, Duties Performed by Western Australian Police for Commonwealth Departments—Question of Payment.
55 Letter, Secretary of Home and Territories to Secretary, Prime Minister's, 18 January 1919, BC39551, NAA.
56 Report, James Mitchell, Inspector-General of Police, 4 February 1918, BC275070, NAA.
57 Letter, W.A. Holman to Prime Minister, 6 February 1918, BC275070, NAA.
58 Letter, Chief of General Staff—Australia to All Military Districts, 25 February 1918, BC65724, NAA, A400, 1, Commonwealth Investigation Service Historical—Miscellaneous Matters from Queensland.
59 Memo with marginal notes by William Watt, 6 November 1918, BC275070, NAA.
60 Letter, Governor-General's Office to Secretary, Prime Minister's, 14 January 1916. BC275070, NAA.
61 Undated minute, pp. 2–3, BC1110736, NAA.
62 In order to keep the text simple, the various iterations of the SIB, CIS and CIB will be referred to as the CIB throughout.
63 Undated minute, p. 2, BC1110736, NAA.
64 Telegrams from Hughes, 28 February and 7 March 1919, p. 1, BC1110736, NAA.
65 Undated minute, p. 1, BC1110736, NAA.
66 Undated minute, p. 1, BC1110736, NAA, and J. Templeton, 'Jones, Harold Edward', *ADB*.
67 Letter, Pearce to Watt, 24 January 1919, BC1110736, NAA, and BC275070, NAA.
68 Letter, Steward to Acting Prime Minister, 12 February 1919, and reply, Acting Prime Minister to Steward, 12 February 1919, BC1110736, NAA.
69 BC275070, NAA.
70 Letter, Pearce to Watt, 24 January 1919, BC1110736, NAA.
71 Undated notes on the Justification for a SIB in Attorney-General's Department, pp. 1–3, BC1110736, NAA, and BC48075, NAA.
72 Undated notes on the Justification for SIB, pp. 1–3, BC1110736, NAA.
73 Undated notes on the Justification for SIB, p. 2, BC1110736, NAA.
74 Templeton, 'Jones, Harold Edward (1878–1965)', ADB.
75 Templeton, 'Jones, Harold Edward (1878–1965)', ADB.
76 Minute, Sir George Knowles to Attorney-General, 18 October 1941, p. 3, BC1110955, NAA, A432, 1955/0432, A.M. Duncan—Report on Security Service.
77 Templeton, 'Jones, Harold Edward', ADB.
78 List of Positions of SIB, BC1110736, NAA.
79 Minute for Executive Council, 30 May 1919, BC275070, NAA.
80 Budget calculations, SIB, 1919–1920, BC1110736, NAA.
81 Minute Paper for the Executive Council, 30 May 1919, BC275070, NAA.
82 Duty statement, undated but possibly 1 July 1921, Jones, BC775888, NAA: A367, C17200, Lieutenant Colonel Jones.
83 Memo, Secretary Attorney-General's, 30 November 1922, BC1110955, NAA.
84 Very Secret note, 15 August 1919, BC275070, NAA, and memo, Secretary Attorney-General's, 30 November 1922, BC1110955, NAA.

Chapter 3: Utopia and Its Agents

1 W.M. Hughes, 'The Case for Labor', *Daily Telegraph*, 8 August 1908, p. 4.
2 See 'Strife at the Barrier', *Evening News*, 14 January 1909, p. 5, and 'Broken Hill Trouble', *Singleton Argus*, 16 January 1909, p. 3.

3   Socialistic Demonstration, *Maitland Daily News*, 9 February 1910, p. 5.

4   'Workers Procession', *Bendigo Advertiser*, 9 February 1910, p. 5.

5   Website, Pozieres, The Battle of the Somme, 1916, www.awmlondon.gov.au/battles/pozieres, accessed 25 December 2019.

6   The activities of Paul Bolo, also known as Bolo Pasha, in secretly meeting with the German Ambassador to the United States, in 1916 to obtain $US1,683,500 to enable him to buy French newspapers in order to promote a pacifist and defeatist editorial policy seriously damaged the standing of pacifists who would subsequently be accused of Boloism, that is using the propaganda of defeatism and pacificism to support an enemy. Report by Mr Basil Thomson of New Scotland Yard, 24 November 1917, CAB 24/34/9, NA, UK. The French executed Bolo for treason on 17 April 1918.

7   R. Fitzgerald, '*Red Ted*', University of Queensland Press, St Lucia, 2002, p. 96.

8   Kaiser Wilhelm II quoted in Weekly Report on Germany XLI by Intelligence Bureau; Department of Information, 7 March 1918, CAB 24/44/51, NA, UK.

9   V. Mitrokhin and C. Andrew, *The Mitrokhin Archive*, Allen Lane, Penguin Press, London, 1999, p. 34.

10   Mitrokhin and Andrew, *The Mitrokhin Archive*, p. 33.

11   Mitrokhin and Andrew, *The Mitrokhin Archive*, p. 32.

12   CAB 24/4/23, NA, UK.

13   Cabinet minutes, 14 November 1918, CAB 24/8/23, NA, UK. Lord Burnham, Harry Levy-Lawson, 1st Viscount Burnham was the owner of the *Daily Telegraph* and a Liberal MP before taking his father's seat in the House of Lords. Riddell was the managing director of the *News of the World* and the owner of a number of other papers. He was also a close personal friend of David Lloyd George. Riddell played a major role on behalf of newspaper proprietors in ameliorating the D Notice regime imposed during the war. See N.J. Wilkinson, *Secrecy and the Media*, Routledge, London, 2009, pp. 103–20.

14   Political Intelligence report, June 1918, CAB 24/54/30 and Monthly Review of Revolutionary Movements in British Dominions Overseas and Foreign Countries, Intelligence Department, Home Office, July 1920, CAB 24/111/4, NA, UK. By 1920, the Intelligence division of the Home Office, the department that oversaw MI5, took responsibility for the *Monthly Report* from the Foreign Office, most likely because it now covered the activities of revolutionary movements in British dominions as well as foreign countries. The *Monthly Report* was classified SECRET and it became strictly prohibited to send it by post, registered or not.

15   Report, Office of the Administrator, Northern Territory detailing concern over the activity of the unions on the government jetty in Darwin, 4 August 1921, BC99425, NAA: A467, SF42/321, Communism and Anti-War Movement.

16   Political Intelligence Department, FO, memo on Switzerland as a Bolshevik Centre, 2 November 1918, BC237172, NAA, A3932, SC294, Bolshevism, Sedition and Disloyalty.

17   Report of letter, Professor William T. Goode to R. Ross published in *The Socialist*, 8 November 1922, BC99425, NAA. Goode was active in the CP-A and wrote a book on Russia, *Splendid Order, Wonderful Organisation and Good Conditions for Everybody*, Andrade's, Melbourne, 1920. See D.W. Lovell and K. Windle, *Our Unswerving Loyalty*, ANU Press, Canberra, 2008, p. 92.

18   Re IWW, see *Cumberland Argus and Fruitgrowers Advocate*, 22 October 1919, p. 1, accessed 30 August 2014; Text of letter, Arnold Holmes to Noel Villers, 18 May 1919, BC237172, NAA.

19   Memo for CGS and Deputy Chief Censor, 17 December 1918, BC237172, NAA, and cutting from *The Argus*, 13 September 1920, Repatriation of Russians, BC43185, NAA:

A1, 1923/8359. Peter Simonoff was an Australian resident working as a miner at Broken Hill who was appointed by Maxim Litvinov, the Soviet Ambassador at large to Britain and its Empire, as the Soviet Consul-General to Australia. In earlier press reporting, the *Brisbane Courier* of 30 January 1918 reported Simonoff had only recently read about his appointment in the newspapers, but he was aware of a cable from Petrograd to London removing Mr M. D'Abaza and making him Consul-General in Australia. See http://trove. nla.gov.au/ndp/del/article/20209124, accessed 31 August 2014.

20   Letter, Inspector, Sydney to Director, CIB, 11 August 1922, and Order for Deportation, 25 March 1919, BC449358, NAA: SP43/2 N59/21/962 Alexander Michael Zuzenko. Alexander Michael Zuzenko, aka Margan, Mamon, Mammon and Toni Tollagsen Tjorn (Swedish Passport Number 30397) was a COMINTERN agent tasked with mobilising socialist and Russian émigrés in Australia into a Bolshevik group. He was originally deported from Australia following the Brisbane Red Flag incident in March 1919 but re-entered using the name Margin in 1922. His task was to bring the warring factions of communists and socialists together.

21   Memo, Deputy Chief Censor, 17 December 1918, BC237172.

22   Weekly report No. 24, 26 August 1918, BC395800, NAA: B741, V/71, Subside Melbourne Weekly reports 1918–1919.

23   Report, Constable 31, H.L. Foote, on Domain Meetings, 8 September 1918, the same day, BC1173011, NAA, A9650, Folder 1, Attorney-General's File, Commonwealth Police Force Reports.

24   United States, Library of Congress, http://id.loc.gov/rwo/agents/nb2013012495.html, accessed 6 January 2019.

25   Windle, *Undesirable*, pp. 6–9.

26   Windle, *Undesirable*, pp. 10, 84, 192, 197, 224 and 247. Peters, Zakovsky and Zuzenko were all Latvians and Zakovsky, like Zuzenko, was a sailor.

27   Letter, Collector of Customs Brisbane to Secretary, External Affairs, 22 May 1903, BC5058145, NAA: J3116, 93, Alien Immigration—Correspondence Relating to a Deserter R. Jensen [Danish] the Gulf of Bothnia at Brisbane.

28   Report of Interrogation of Mr Toni Tollagsen Tjorn, aka Suzenko, by Captain Miller and Captain Liddell 19 December 1922, p. 10, BC43659, NAA.

29   BC9066713, NAA, BP4/3, RUSSIAN SOOSENKO AM.

30   Report of Interrogation of Mr Toni Tollagsen Tjorn, aka Suzenko, by Captain Miller and Captain Liddell 19 December 1922, p. 10, BC43659, NAA. The official record suggests that Zuzenko entered Australia in 1911, see letter Attorney-General's to Secretary Home and Territories Department, 25 August 1922, BC43659, NAA. This date appears to have been derived from Zuzenko's formal application for resident alien status at Innisfail in 1911 and letter H. Jones to Inspector Lloyd, 3 August 1922, discloses Margan as one of Zuzenko's aliases. See BC9066713, NAA. Also, see Soosenko, Alexander Michael—Russian Nationality—Alien Registration Certificate No. 36 issued 3 November 1916 at Mourilyan [QLD], BC449358, NAA: SP43/2, N59/21/962, Alexander Michael Zuzenko [Box 7].

31   Windle, *Undesirable*, pp. 19, 75.

32   Windle, *Undesirable*, p. 99.

33   Windle, *Undesirable*, pp. 91–3 and 97–9.

34   Windle, *Undesirable*, p. 98.

35   Windle, *Undesirable*, pp. 99–100.

36   John Reed quoted in Windle, *Undesirable*, p. 102. Freeman was arrested near Cloncurry in January 1919 and, as an American citizen, deported to the United States. Unfortunately, the United States Government refused to admit him, leaving him aboard the ship for

four trips across the Pacific as each government refused to let him disembark. Australia finally deported him to Germany, his place of birth, in 1919. In late 1920, like Zuzenko, Freeman clandestinely returned to Australia to unite the warring communist factions. He failed and returned to the Soviet Union where he died of injuries sustained in a railway accident there in July 1921: F. Farrell, 'Freeman, Paul', *ADB*.

37 Windle, *Undesirable*, p. 93.

38 Windle, *Undesirable*, pp. 127–43.

39 Letter, OC, RCMP, Southern Saskatchewan, BC449358, NAA.

40 Letter, OC, RCMP, Southern Saskatchewan, BC449358, NAA.

41 Letter, OC, RCMP, Southern Saskatchewan, BC449358, NAA.

42 Letter, OC, RCMP, Southern Saskatchewan, BC449358, NAA.

43 Letter, OC, RCMP, Southern Saskatchewan and letter H. Jones to Lloyd detailing cover-name MARGAN, 3 August 1922, BC449358, NAA.

44 Letter, Commandant, 1st Military District to Commissioner, Queensland Police, 2 April 1919, BC335787, NAA: BP4/1, 66/4/3660, Files on Russians, Russian Association. This lists a Michael Rosenberg of Abes House, Merivale Street, South Brisbane, arrested for offences related to Red Flag incident of 23 March 1919. May be the same Michael Rosenberg who attempted to return to Australia with Zuzenko.

45 Letter, Inspector Mackishan, CIB, to Collector of Customs, Brisbane, 3 December 1924, BC3066606, NAA: J2773, 713/1929, Shipboard Registration of Aliens. Toni Tollagsen Tjorn was arrested in Melbourne on 9 August 1922 and arraigned before the Police Court on charges of being a prohibited migrant and an accredited agent of the Soviet Government. *Barrier Miner*, 31 August 1922, p. 1.

46 United States, Library of Congress, http://id.loc.gov/rwo/agents/nb2013012495.html, accessed 6 January 2019.

47 Memo, Captain C. Wood for Secretary, Defence re Agent 77, 28 July 1919, BC237172, NAA. Also referenced in letter Commander 1st Military District to CGS, 27 August 1919, BC335787, NAA.

48 Memo, Captain Wood re Agent 77, 28 July 1919, BC237172, NAA, and BC335787, NAA.

49 Memo, Captain C. Wood, 28 July 1919 BC237172, NAA.

50 Memo, Re: Inquiry Officers, 14 January 1918, BC1173011, NAA.

51 R. Evans, *The Red Flag Riots*, University of Queensland Press, St Lucia, 1988, p. 8. Like many overly romantic socialist thinkers of the late twentieth century, Raymond Evans portrays the activities of the RWA and its adherents as a struggle for equality, fraternity and liberty. The suggestion (p. 4) that the Red Flag Riots were an organised suppression of a 'small civil liberties protest march' by Bolsheviks and their supporters is disingenuous.

52 Report, Sergeant A.M. Short, Commonwealth Police Force, Brisbane to Commissioner, Sydney, 24 March 1919, BC76534, NAA: A456, W26/241/45, Unrest in Queensland—Bolshevism, and BC335787, NAA.

53 Cuttings, *Daily Mail*, 11 April 1919, BC335787, NAA. These reported that a returned soldier, Thomas Drane, was charged with firing a revolver at Queensland Police Detective O'Driscoll with intent to cause grievous bodily harm on 24 March and another returned soldier, James Mills, was charged with going armed in public in such a manner as to cause fear on 25 March. Yet another returned soldier, Thomas Cunningham, was also charged. The result of this incident was seven mounted police officers and their horses were injured with two suffering gunshot wounds. Notably, the Queensland State Secretary of the Returned Sailors and Soldiers Imperial League, W.A. Fisher, was prosecuted and fined for having conducted a procession without a permit in Queen Street. The Queensland Traffic Branch, which had not been consulted about the parade, undertook the prosecution.

54   Report, Richard James, 25 March 1919, BC335787, NAA. Amusingly, James reports the
      Chief Commissioner of the Queensland Police was among the several police officers
      injured when a bayonet wielded by one of his officers accidentally stabbed him.
55   Report, Richard James, 25 March 1919, BC335787, NAA.
56   Report, Richard James, 25 March 1919, BC335787, NAA.
57   Report, Richard James, 25 March 1919, BC335787, NAA.
58   R.K. Debo, 'Lloyd George and the Copenhagen Conference of 1919–1920: The initiation
      of Anglo-Soviet Negotiations', *The Historical Journal*, 1981, 24(2): 429–41.
59   Letter, Representative of Russian Soviet Government to Minister for Home and Territories
      with list of 817 persons, men, women and children, who wished to return to Russia,
      7 March 1921, and letter, Winston Churchill to Governor-General of Australia, 7 May 1921,
      BC43185, NAA, Repatriation of Russians, Agreement Between Imperial Government and
      Soviet Government. All of this came to nothing as the Soviet Government actually did
      not want the overseas Russians to return, because among them would be people working
      against the Bolsheviks and, besides, they would not pay the fares.
60   Cutting, *The Argus*, 13 September 1920, BC43185, NAA. Like Litvinov in Britain,
      Simonoff was not given official recognition and was additionally banned from giving
      lectures on Bolshevism in Australia. As a result, he was arrested and imprisoned for six
      months, leading to the Soviet government accusing Australia of persecuting Russians.
      MHR for the Barrier (Broken Hill).
61   Letter, Peter Simonoff to Secretary Home and Territories, 17 July 1920, BC43185, NAA.
62   Memo, to Secretary, Prime Minister's and Secretary, Home and Territories, 27 July 1920,
      BC43185, NAA.
63   Undated draft of reply to Peter Simonoff, BC43185, NAA.
64   Undated draft of reply to Peter Simonoff, BC43185, NAA.
65   *Soviet Russia*, Vol. 1, No. 1, Sydney 7 April 1920, in BC76552, NAA: A456, W26/241/84.
66   Cutting, 'Unrest in Queensland—Bolshevism, Sinn Fein', *The Sun*, 19 April 1920,
      BC76552, NAA. In the file, someone has circled the letters 'un' in the word 'unprejudiced'
      used in the editorial. Perhaps a sense of humour existed in MI. Lloyd would later be given
      the nickname 'Linger Longer' by MI because of his perceived slowness and weakness. See
      Transcript of Evidence, Sir Charles Spry, 27 February 1976, BC4751094, NAA: A8913,
      3/1/13, Private Hearings (Non-official Evidence). Also, D. Sadleir, 'Lloyd, Eric Edwin
      Longfield', *ADB*.
67   Letter, Lloyd to DMI, 21 April 1920, BC76552, NAA.
68   Letter, Lloyd to DMI, 21 April 1920, BC76552, NAA.
69   Letter, Lloyd to DMI, 21 April 1920, BC76552, NAA.
70   Letter, Lloyd to DMI, 21 April 1920, BC76552, NAA.
71   Minute, Attorney-General's, 30 April 1920, BC76552, NAA.
72   See www.comlaw.gov.au/Details/C2004C07843, accessed 20 December 2015. The War
      Precautions Act was repealed on 2 December 1920. This was the Act and regulations
      that Lloyd was attempting to use to suppress Soviet Russia. Minute, Attorney-General's,
      30 April 1920, BC76552, NAA.
73   Minute, Attorney-General's, 30 April 1920, BC76552, NAA.
74   Letter, Major-General Lee to Secretary, Defence, 31 March 1919, BC237172, NAA.
75   Letter, Major-General Lee to Secretary, Defence, 31 March 1919, BC237172, NAA.
76   Letter, Major-General Lee to Secretary, Defence, 31 March 1919, BC237172, NAA.
77   Letter, Major-General Lee to Secretary, Defence, 31 March 1919, BC237172, NAA.
78   J. Schrantz, *The Reverend's Revenge*, Infinity Publishing Co, West Conshohocken, PA,
      2005, p. 214.

79   Schrantz, *The Reverend's Revenge*, p. 214.
80   Community of Drum, 'The story of Fr James Coyle', https://web.archive.org/web/20101010181724/http://www.drum.ie/about/fr-james-coyle.
81   Memo, Secretary, Attorney-General's to Secretary, Prime Minister's, 4 October 1920, BC237172, NAA.
82   Intelligence report by Captain Jones and Detective H.W. Sainsbury, 13 January 1916, BC109644, NAA: B741, V/3426, Adele Pankhurst—Anti Conscription Fellowship.
83   Letter, 14 January 1916, BC1096445, NAA.
84   Report of comments by Comrade Cain, Yarra Bank, 19 March 1916, Memo, District Paymaster to Cain, 29 March 1916, Statutory Declaration, 7 April 1916, Memo, A/Commandant, 3rd Military District to Secretary, Defence, 9 May 1916, BC1096445, NAA.
85   Report of comments, Yarra Bank, 10 September 1916, BC1096445, NAA.
86   Intelligence Diary Reference, 23 March 1916, BC1096445, NAA.
87   Letter, E. Bateman to General Williams, 10 January 1916, BC1096445, NAA.
88   'Three Weeks. Briefest Summary of Sensational Attacks Upon Free Speech and Right of Assemblage', *The Socialist*, 14 January 1916, p. 2.
89   Intelligence report by Captain Jones and Detective H.W. Sainsbury, 17 January 1916, BC1096445, NAA, and 'Socialist Hall Searched by Military Officers and Detective and Fred Holland's Home Invaded', *The Socialist*, 21 January 1916, p. 2, and the *National Advocate*, 14 June 1916.
90   *National Advocate*, 14 June 1916.
91   *The Socialist*, 14 March 1919, p. 2.
92   Solicitor-General's Opinion, 26 November 1919, pp. 1–3, BC237172, NAA.
93   Solicitor-General's Opinion, 26 November 1919, p. 4, BC237172, NAA.
94   'Malicious and Seditious Libel Alleged Against Newspaper', *Brisbane Courier*, 11 December 1919, p. 2, *The Herald*, 11 December 1919, p. 10 and many others.
95   'Printers of "Republic" Exonerated', *Geelong Advertiser*, 31 March 1920.
96   Minute attached to Instruction to abolish Commonwealth Police, 25 February 1919, NAA, BC1110736, minute.
97   Letter, Commissioner of Commonwealth Police to Sir Robert Garran, 23 January 1918, BC1173011, NAA.
98   Letter, Secretary, Defence to Secretary, PM's, BC237172, NAA.
99   BC237172, NAA. Just pick a spot and jump in. The file is full of this sort of stuff.
100 Letter, Vancouver Branch of British Empire League to Hughes, 16 February 1921, BC237172, NAA.
101 Letter, Vancouver Branch of British Empire League to Hughes, 16 February 1921, BC237172, NAA.

Chapter 4: Unwanted and Unloved—Security intelligence, 1919–39

1   See BC275070, NAA, in toto and particularly the letter, 23 August 1917, George Steward to Secretary, Prime Minister's. Also, letter, 4 February 1918, James Mitchell, NSW Inspector General of Police to Prime Minister with covering letter, W. Holman, Premier of New South Wales, 6 February 1918, complaining of the multitude of Commonwealth agencies requesting investigative support from NSW Police. See also BC48075, NAA, for coordinating conference 1918 to address Commonwealth use of state police. Also, BC39551, NAA.
2   Memo, Secretary, Attorney-General's, 11 January 1923, BC209208, NAA: A433, 1942/2/2815, Aliens, Registration of, also Appointment of Officers Investigation Branch under Immigration Act.

3   Letter, Director, CIB, to Secretary, Interior, 16 November 1934, BC209208, NAA.

4   B. Swanton and G. Hannigan, *Police Source Book 2*, Australian Institute of Criminology, Canberra, 1985, p. 386 and R. Evans, 'Murderous coppers: Police, Industrial Disputes and the 1929 Rothbury Shootings', *History Australia*, 2012, 9(1): 176–200.

5   Evans, 'Murderous coppers', p. 176.

6   F. Cain, 'MacKay, William John', *ADB*.

7   William John MacKay, Law and Order in the Pioneering Days of NSW', www.australianpolice.com.au/nsw-police-history-index/police-commissioners-of-nsw/william-john-MacKay/, accessed 20 December 2015.

8   'William John MacKay, Law and Order in the Pioneering Days of NSW'.

9   'William John MacKay, Law and Order in the Pioneering Days of NSW'.

10   'William John MacKay, Law and Order in the Pioneering Days of NSW'.

11   A. Moore, 'Policing enemies of the state: The New South Wales Police and the New Guard', in M. Finnane (ed.), *Policing in Australia*, University of NSW Press, Sydney, 1987, p. 134.

12   Evans, 'Murderous coppers', p. 176.

13   R. Evans, 'William John MacKay and the NSW Police Force, 1910–1948: A study of police power', PhD thesis, Monash University, 2005, pp. 127–31, and R. Evans, '"A menace to this realm": The New Guard and the New South Wales Police, 1931–32', *History Australia*, 2008, 5(3): 76.1–76.20.

14   See V. Kelly, *Man of the People*, Alpha, Sydney, 1971, pp. 56–7 and Cain, 'MacKay, William John', *ADB*.

15   Evans, 'William John MacKay and the NSW Police Force', p. 131.

16   Evans, 'Murderous coppers', p. 176, and Evans, 'William John MacKay and the NSW Police Force', pp. 112–13.

17   The source of this tale was the writer and journalist Vince Kelly, a very close friend and associate of MacKay. Evans describes Kelly's description of MacKay's actions at Rothbury as being 'farcically inaccurate'. See Evans, 'William John MacKay and the NSW Police Force', p. 128. Evans' assessment of MacKay's odd behaviour in not refuting the untrue allegations that he was at Rothbury when the riot occurred, and his boasting about his involvement in the notorious case of the Glasgow Police falsifying evidence to prosecute a German Jew, Oscar Slater, for the murder of Marion Gilchrist in December 1908, as being evidence of a desire to be seen as a hard and ruthless man at the centre of great events has merit.

18   Evans, 'William John MacKay and the NSW Police Force', pp. 137–8.

19   Evans, 'A menace to this realm', and Evans, 'Murderous coppers'.

20   Evans, 'Murderous coppers', p. 184.

21   Evans, 'A menace to this realm', pp. 76–7.

22   The New Guard and 'The Association', BC65290, NAA: A367, C94121. This file provides extensive information on the organisation.

23   Evans, 'A menace to this realm', pp. 76–7.

24   Evans, 'A menace to this realm', pp. 76–7.

25   The public unease was not due to any widespread support for the New Guard but because of the violence of MacKay's non-bourgeois coppers.

26   Report, 11 May 1932, Lloyd to Director, CIB, BC65290, NAA. The famous photograph of the costume purportedly worn by the 'inner "Fascist" group' was found in the home of one of the suspects arrested as a result of this supposed attack.

27   Letter, Lloyd to Jones, 11 May 1932, BC65290, NAA. J.J. Garden, although an ardent unionist, went straight to MacKay, the killer of miners, following the assault and, appropriately, was later jailed for corruption. See Evans, 'A menace to this realm', p. 76.15.

28 Evans, 'A menace to this realm', pp. 76.13–76.14.
29 See Evans, 'Murderous coppers', pp. 184–9.
30 Cain, 'MacKay, William John', *ADB*.

Chapter 5: Persons of Interest, 1919–39

1 'A Brief Overview of the Work of the Security Section of the Commonwealth Investigation Branch', by Jones, 31 December 1943, p. 1, KV4/453, NA, UK.
2 'A Brief Overview', p. 1, KV4/453, NA, UK.
3 'A Brief Overview', p. 1, KV4/453, NA, UK.
4 'A Brief Overview', p. 1, KV4/453, NA, UK.
5 'A Brief Overview', p. 3, KV4/453, NA, UK.
6 'A Brief Overview', p. 2, KV4/453, NA, UK.
7 'A Brief Overview', KV4/453, NA, UK.
8 'A Brief Overview', p. 2, KV4/453, NA, UK.
9 '"Black Hand"' 'Gang Mentioned', *Daily Standard*, 3 July 1934.
10 H.G. Liddell and R. Scott, *A Greek–English Lexicon*, accessed 30 December 2019.
11 'Bomb Outrage at Ingham', *The Telegraph*, 23 May 1935, p. 11.
12 'Black Hand in Q'Land', *Truth*, Sydney, 16 June 1935, p. 24, and 'Black Hand Terrorists in Ingham', *The Courier-Mail*, Brisbane, 15 December 1939, p. 7.
13 Report, Lloyd to Director, CIB, 7 January 1931, BC1368165, NAA, A6122, 2715, Camorra, Black Hand, Mano Nero Society Vol. 1.
14 BC1368165, NAA.
15 'Federal Govt.'s Benign Blessing on Bomb Terrorists', *Truth*, Brisbane, 13 June 1937, p. 23.
16 'State Authorities uncover Widespread Subversive Movement', *The Telegraph*, 17 September 1939, p. 9.
17 'No Black Hand in Queensland', *The Sun*, 17 December 1939, p. 10.
18 'Black Hand Terrorists in Ingham', *The Courier-Mail*, p. 7, and 'Federal Govt.'s Benign Blessing on Bomb Terrorists', *Truth*, p. 23.
19 'A Brief Overview', p. 2, KV4/453, NA, UK.
20 'A Brief Overview', p. 3, KV4/453, NA, UK.
21 'A Brief Overview', p. 3, KV4/453, NA, UK.
22 'A Brief Overview', p. 3, KV4/453, NA, UK.
23 B. Winter, *The Most Dangerous Man in Australia*, Glass House Books, Brisbane, 2010, p. 15, and G. Cresciani, 'A not so brutal friendship: Italian responses to National Socialism in Australia', Migrazioni Italiane in Australia, Centro Altreitalie, Edizioni della Fondazione Giovanni Agnelli, Milano, 1984, p. 9.
24 Winter, *The Most Dangerous Man in Australia*, p. 12, and BC9902448, NAA: MP1103/2, PWN1132, Prisoner of War/Internee: Brundahl, Lars Gustave.
25 Winter, *The Most Dangerous Man in Australia*, p. 12.
26 Winter, *The Most Dangerous Man in Australia*, p. 14.
27 Winter, *The Most Dangerous Man in Australia*, p. 15.
28 'Demonstrators Fined', *SMH*, 8 February 1939, p. 10.
29 Winter, *The Most Dangerous Man in Australia*, p. 15, and Cresciani, 'A not so brutal friendship', p. 9.
30 Winter, *The Most Dangerous Man in Australia*, p. 14, and J. Perkins, 'Becker, Johannes Heinrich', *ADB*.
31 'A Brief Overview', p. 3, KV4/453, NA, UK.
32 'A Brief Overview', p. 4, KV4/453, NA, UK.

33 Hasluck, *The Government and the People*, Vol. 2, p. 719.
34 Hasluck, *The Government and the People*, Vol. 2, p. 720.
35 Report of Commissioner, His Honour Mr Justice Clyne, 5 September 1945, p. 4, BC65666, NAA: A374, 1, Inquiry into Matters Relating to the Detention of Certain Members of the 'AFM' Group.
36 See Fahey, *Australia's First Spies*, pp. 26–32.
37 'Relations of Australia & Japan', p. 83, BC148060, NAA.
38 K. Kotani, *Japanese Intelligence in World War II*, Osprey Publishing, Oxford, 2009, pp. 98–107.
39 BC416253, NAA: B197, 1877/5/15, Legislation for protection against espionage [Major Asada suspected Japanese spy].
40 See Fahey, *Australia's First Spies*, pp. 63–74.
41 Letter, Director, CIB, to Secretary, Interior, 16 November 1934, BC209208, NAA.
42 Letter, Dr John A. Holt, 28 November 1938, BC775888, NAA, Lieutenant Colonel Jones.

Chapter 6: What? Again? 1939 and war

1 Telegram, 13 December 1939, CAB 66/1/27.
2 Hasluck, *The Government and the People*, Vol. 1, pp. 216–29.
3 Minutes of War Cabinet Meeting, 25 October 1939, BC689081, NAA: A5954 803/1.
4 Minutes of War Cabinet Meeting, Canberra, 30 November 1939, BC689081, NAA.
5 Record of Decisions of Full Cabinet, Canberra, 28 November 1939, BC689081, NAA.
6 Undated minute, BC1110736, NAA. The concerns of the Attorney-General's Department ran back to 1914–19 when Sir Robert Garran and his assistant, George Knowles, had tried to limit the influence of the military in civilian security intelligence and close down the CEB led by Steward.
7 Letter, B.S. Stevens, Premier of New South Wales, to Joseph Lyons, Prime Minister, 8 February 1939, BC161618, NAA: A664, 479/401/299, Liaison between Police and Naval and Military Authorities re Intelligence Suggested by Commissioner NSW Police.
8 Minute: Liaison Between Police Authorities and Intelligence Branch, Defence, 12 May 1939, BC161618, NAA.
9 A467, SF43/1, Investigations into Australian Activities—Jehovah's Witnesses—Watchtower Bible and Tract Society, Judge Rutherford—Activities in Australia Part 1, BC99427, NAA.
10 See Fahey, *Australia's First Spies*, pp. 123–35.
11 'A Brief Overview', p. 4, KV4/453, NA, UK.
12 War Cabinet Agendum 148/1940, 25 June 1940, by Robert Menzies, Minister for Defence Co-Ordination, BC170613, NAA: A816, 31/301/21, Establishment of Local Security Officers Force.
13 War Cabinet Agendum 148/1940, 25 June 1940, and Cabinet Agenda Item submitted by Attorney-General, W.M. Hughes, 7 December 1940, BC170613, NAA.
14 War Cabinet Agendum 148/1940, BC170613, NAA.
15 War Cabinet Agendum 148/1940 and Cabinet Agenda Item submitted by Attorney-General, W.M. Hughes, 7 December 1940, BC170613, NAA.
16 War Cabinet Agendum 148/1940, 25 June 1940, BC170613, NAA.
17 War Cabinet Agendum 148/1940, BC170613, NAA.
18 War Cabinet Agendum 148/1940, BC170613, NAA.
19 War Cabinet Agendum 148/1940, BC170613, NAA.
20 War Cabinet Agendum 148/1940, BC170613, NAA.
21 War Cabinet Agendum 148/1940, BC170613, NAA.

22   War Cabinet Agendum 148/1940, BC170613, NAA.
23   War Cabinet Agendum 148/1940, BC170613, NAA.
24   War Cabinet Agendum 148/1940, BC170613, NAA.
25   Telegram, Menzies to Bruce, 1 July 1940, BC91491, NAA: A461, BZ6/1/1 Part 1, Security Service Part 1.
26   Letter, Assembled Police Commissioners to Prime Minister, 12 September 1940, BC170613, NAA.
27   Letter, Forgan Smith to Secretary, Defence Co-ordinator, 10 June 1940, BC170613, NAA.
28   Letter, Forgan Smith to Secretary, Defence Co-ordinator, 10 June 1940, BC170613, NAA.
29   Letter, Forgan Smith to Secretary, Defence Co-ordinator, 10 June 1940, BC170613, NAA.
30   Summary of Replies Received from States in Relation to Draft Regulations, BC170613, NAA.
31   Letter, State Police Commissioners to Prime Minister and Minister for Defence Co-ordination, 12 September 1940, p. 1, BC170613, NAA.
32   Letter, Assembled Police Commissioners to Prime Minister, 12 September 1940, BC170613, NAA.
33   Letter, Assembled Police Commissioners to Prime Minister, 12 September 1940, BC170613, NAA.
34   Letter, Assembled Police Commissioners to Prime Minister, 12 September 1940, BC170613, NAA.
35   Letter, Assembled Police Commissioners to Prime Minister, 12 September 1940, BC170613, NAA.
36   War Cabinet Minute, 18 February 1941, BC170613, NAA.

Chapter 7: 1940—The fifth column panic

1   Telegram, 13 December 1939, CAB 66/1/27, NA, UK.
2   Second Interim Report of the Leakage of Information Committee, 30 December 1939, CAB 67/3/55, NA, UK.
3   War Cabinet 32 (39) Conclusions, 30 September 1939, CAB 65/1/32, NA, UK.
4   Second Interim Report, 30 December 1939, CAB 67/3/55, NA, UK.
5   F.H. Hinsley and C.A.G. Simkins, *British Intelligence in the Second World War*, Vol. 4, *Security and Counter-Intelligence*, Cambridge University Press, New York, 1990, p. 33.
6   Hinsley and Simkins, *Security and Counter-Intelligence*, p. 34.
7   Second Interim Report of the Leakage of Information Committee, 30 December 1939, CAB 67/3/55.
8   Hinsley and Simkins, *Security and Counter-Intelligence*, p. 35.
9   War Cabinet Conclusions, 4 January 1940, CAB 65/5/3.
10   Even at this time the response was measured as there were 45,000 Australian residents of German or Italian birth alone and then there were the far more easily identified Japanese. In September 1942, there were 1029 Germans, 3651 Italians, mainly from Queensland, and 1036 Japanese. By September 1944, there were 1380 individuals in internment including 704 Germans, 135 Italians and 480 Japanese. Internees could appeal against their detention and there was a significant public outcry among Anglo-Saxon-Celtic Australians about government imprisoning their non-British neighbours: Hasluck, *The Government and the People*, Vol. 1, p. 594.
11   Hinsley and Simkins, *Security and Counter-Intelligence*, p. 32, fn.
12   Hinsley and Simkins, *Security and Counter-Intelligence*, p. 32.
13   Hinsley and Simkins, *Security and Counter-Intelligence*, p. 9.

14   Hinsley and Simkins, *Security and Counter-Intelligence*, pp. 9–10.

15   Hinsley and Simkins, *Security and Counter-Intelligence*, pp. 11–12 and 41.

16   Hinsley and Simkins, *Security and Counter-Intelligence*, p. 41.

17   Hinsley and Simkins, *Security and Counter-Intelligence*, p. 41.

18   Hinsley and Simkins, *Security and Counter-Intelligence*, pp. 11–12 and 41–3.

19   Hinsley and Simkins, *Security and Counter-Intelligence*, p. 65, and War Cabinet 144, 28 May 1940, CAB 65/7/39, NA, UK.

20   C. Andrew, *Secret Service*, Heinemann, London, 1985, p. 478.

21   Home Defence (Security) Executive—Special Operations Executive—memo by the Lord President of the Council, 19 July 1940, CAB 66/10/1, NA, UK.

22   Hinsley and Simkins, *Security and Counter-Intelligence*, p. 65.

23   A. Cave Brown, *The Secret Servant*, Sphere Books, London, 1987, pp. 232–57.

24   Hinsley and Simkins, *Security and Counter-Intelligence*, p. 57.

25   Hinsley and Simkins, *Security and Counter-Intelligence*, pp. 67–9.

26   Andrew, *Secret Service*, p. 478.

27   Hinsley and Simkins, *Security and Counter-Intelligence*, p. 69.

28   Hinsley and Simkins, *Security and Counter-Intelligence*, p. 69.

29   The Commonwealth government did not have the same constitutional power over state police forces that the government of the United Kingdom had.

30   Cablegram, Prime Minister to Secretary of State for the Dominions, 4 March 1941, with copies to Acting Prime Minister and Defence Co-ordination, BC206047, NAA: A1608, G39/2/1, War 1939—Special Operations Executive. Christopher Andrew calls Ironside's claim of people building aerodromes 'extraordinary'. See Andrew, *Secret Service*, p. 478.

31   Seventh Report—*Australian Intelligence/Security Services 1900–1950* by Jacqueline Templeton, p. 169, BC4727814, NAA: A8908, 7A, Royal Commission on Intelligence and Security, Vol. 1.

32   Memo by Attorney-General, 9 July 1940, BC1110955, NAA.

33   Letter, Percy Spender to Prime Minister, 10 June 1941, BC217054, NAA, AA198/132, 1, World War 2—The Security Service. BC950483, NAA: A5954, 849/A, Brief Historical Note on a Security Intelligence Organisation, Internal Security—Establishment of a Security Service.

34   Letter, Percy Spender to Prime Minister, 10 June 1941, BC217054, NAA. In this letter, the influence of Lieutenant Colonel John Mawhood is readily seen in Spender's recommendations to Menzies on the widening of the CSS's activities.

35   Minute, Knowles to Attorney-General, 18 October 1941, BC1110955, NAA.

36   Secret Report for the Minister, 10 November 1941, p. 3, BC1110955, NAA.

37   Military Board Memorandum to All Commands and Formations, 3 March 1941, AA1981/132, World War 2—The Security Service, BC217054, NAA.

38   Military Board Memorandum to All Commands and Formations, 3 March 1941, BC217054, NAA.

39   Letter, Colonel K.A. McKenzie to Secretary, Army, 14 May 1941, BC217054, NAA.

40   Cablegram, Menzies to Fadden, 26 April 1941, BC257498, NAA: CP290/9, 13, Personal Papers of Prime Minister Menzies.

41   Cables Regarding War Situation, NAA, BC257498, telegram M.84, Menzies to Fadden, 26 April 1941 and M.86, Menzies to Fadden, 26 April 1941, and 'Military Advice to Government', *SMH*, 23 April 1941, p. 11.

42   See Fahey, *Australia's First Spies*, pp. 123–35.

Chapter 8: The Mawhood Mystery

1   Sir William Birdwood was commander of the ANZAC Corps during the time that John Mawhood was transferred to the Indian Army as an officer cadet; Long service medals from the collection formed by John Tamplin, www.dnw.co.uk/auction-archive/special-collections/lot.php?specialcollection_id=57&lot_id=67264. The above details were obtained by Thacker's Indian Directory of 1902 by the auction house, Dix Noonan Webb of Mayfair, conducting a provenance check on John Mawhood senior's medal. He was awarded the medal on 10 February 1899. The name of the family home in Ascot Vale is incorrectly spelled 'Kirlee' in John Mawhood's enlistment documentation. See BC8030333, NAA: B2455 Mawhood, John Charles. For arrival in Australia, see the Public Record Office Victoria, Unassisted Passenger Lists, 1852–1923.

2   BC6044592, NAA, MT1487/1 Mawhood J.C., Mawhood J.C., Lieutenant Guides Cavalry, and BC8030333, NAA.

3   J.W. Mawhood and his family left Australia for British Columbia after his son Ron married a Canadian girl. Mawhood senior and his wife then returned to the United Kingdom. Information supplied by Richard Mawhood, 28 December 2015.

4   BC6044592, and BC8030333, NAA. Information on education from Richard Mawhood and Dookie College records. This explains why he enlisted in the AIF at Shepperton and not in Ascot Vale.

5   This was not a slow promotion in such a unit. Provosts do not suffer casualties as front-line units do, let alone the horrendous casualties of the infantry. The result was slow promotion.

6   BC8030333, NAA.

7   Letter, OIC, Army Department, Government of India to OIC, Base Records, Australian Army, 9 January 1922, BC8030333, NAA.

8   B199A Form, J.C. Mawhood, NA UK and information from Richard Mawhood, 31 December 2015.

9   Notes on reply, Section of Medal Distribution Form, 20 December 1921, BC8030333, NAA.

10 Memo, A.R. Nankervis, Secretary, Navy to William Hughes, then Minister of Navy, copy to Shedden, 6 August 1941, BC648984, NAA: A5954, 427/3. This may have some significance for our story as Sir Edmund Ironside played a significant role in the events in Persia at this time. It was a small army and Ironside would have known Mawhood.

11 Memo, A.R. Nankervis to Minister of Navy, 6 August 1941, BC648984, NAA.

12 Reza Shah Pahlavi, the first Shah of Iran of the Pahlavi Dynasty, had been a battalion commander in the Persian Cossack Brigade before being promoted by Major General Ironside to command the entire brigade. It was this brigade that, in February 1921, marched under British direction to capture Tehran and make the Mayor of Tehran, Seyyed Zia'eddin Tabatabaee, prime minister with Reza Khan his defence minister. Over the next two years, this government fought a war of suppression against its opponents, including the Bolsheviks, before Reza Khan made himself Shah in 1925.

13 Memo, A.R. Nankervis to Minister of Navy, 6 August 1941, BC648984, NAA, and Public Record Office Victoria, Unassisted Passenger Lists, 1852–1923, which records Mawhood as being a lieutenant not a major.

14 Email, Richard Mawhood, 2 January 2016.

15 Email, Richard Mawhood, 2 January 2016.

16 *London Gazette*, 20 April 1923, Issue 32816, p. 2894.

17 *London Gazette*, 29 August 1939, Issue 34660, p. 5928.

18 *London Gazette*, 29 August 1939, Issue 34660, p. 5928.

19 *London Gazette*, 9 September 1939, Issue 34676, p. 6182.
20 Venn and Avison were promoted to substantive captain and then to temporary majors in the Intelligence Corps on 19 December 1940, a month after Mawhood was promoted to the same rank. See *London Gazette*, Supplement 35017, p. 7105, and *London Gazette*, 22 November 1940, Issue 35000, p. 6750. On 12 July 1943, Mawhood is listed as being appointed an honorary lieutenant colonel on ceasing his employment in the army and in 1945, Avison is listed as having been appointed an honorary lieutenant colonel upon relinquishing his commission. On 28 March 1948, Venn is listed as being reinstated as a lieutenant colonel against his publicised rank of captain. On 22 April 1949, Mawhood is last mentioned as having exceeded the age limit and as being retired with the rank of honorary lieutenant colonel. Whoever they were, this group of officers had been well looked after, even if they may not have performed as expected in some cases.
21 Andrew, *The Defence of the Realm*, p. 219.
22 In the British documentary record KV4/45, on p. 3 of letter, H. Jones to Sir David Petrie, 31 December 1941, someone has written the letter 'D' next to Mawhood's name and a question mark next to Jones' comments on Mawhood's status as an MI5 officer having been confirmed to him by MI5.
23 Airy Report, 1944, p. 9, KV4/453, NA, UK.
24 File note by Sir David Petrie, 1 November 1944, p. 5, KV4/453, Vol. 1, NA, UK.
25 Report on the Operations of Overseas Control in Connection with the Establishment of DSOs, Australia, Part XIII, KV4/18, NA, UK and Andrew, *The Defence of the Realm*, p. 125.
26 Undated copy of undated telegram. CIGS to CGS attached at Annex A to letter Vernon Sturdee to Minister, 30 September 1940, BC648984, NAA, and telegram No. 39 Secretary of State for Dominion Affairs to Prime Minister via High Commissioner, 22 January 1941, BC206047, NAA.
27 By the end of June 1940 when the signal was sent, the CIGS was Sir John Dill and not Sir Edmund Ironside. However, this signal and the personal and disorganised nature of the arrangements surrounding Military Mission 104 reflected more of Ironside's methods of administration than it did those of Sir John Dill.
28 F. Spencer Chapman, *The Jungle is Neutral*, The Reprint Society, London, 1950, p. 21.
29 'Social and Personal', *SMH*, 27 November 1940, p. 7.
30 Spencer Chapman, *The Jungle is Neutral*, p. 19.
31 In strict military terms, Calvert was the senior officer on Military Mission 104. He was a professional soldier in the Royal Engineers who had graduated Cambridge with a degree in mechanical engineering. Calvert had been posted to Hong Kong in 1936 and had gained considerable experience of the Far East and the Japanese. He was proficient in Cantonese and he had closely observed Japanese military operations against Shanghai and Nanking from December 1937 until January 1938, when he was taken prisoner by the Japanese and subjected to interrogation as a spy. See Spencer Chapman, *The Jungle is Neutral*, p. 20.
32 Spencer Chapman, *The Jungle is Neutral*, p. 19.
33 Spencer Chapman, *The Jungle is Neutral*, p. 19 and BC648984, NAA.
34 https://legalopinions.ags.gov.au/opinionauthor/knowles-george-shaw, accessed 18 March 2019.
35 E.G. Whitlam, 'Knowles, Sir George Shaw', *ADB*, and https://legalopinions.ags.gov.au/opinionauthor/knowles-george-shaw.
36 https://legalopinions.ags.gov.au/opinionauthor/knowles-george-shaw.
37 https://legalopinions.ags.gov.au/opinionauthor/knowles-george-shaw.
38 Whitlam, 'Knowles, Sir George Shaw', *ADB*, and https://legalopinions.ags.gov.au/opinion author/knowles-george-shaw.

39   Minute, Knowles to the Attorney-General, 12 November 1941, BC1110955, NAA.
40   Minute, Knowles to the Attorney-General, 12 November 1941, BC1110955, NAA.
41   Minute, Knowles to the Attorney-General, 18 October 1941, BC1110955, NAA.
42   *Hansard*, 11 November 1941, in BC1110955, NAA.
43   VENONA 324–325, 1 September 1945.
44   Minute, Sir George Knowles to Attorney-General, 9 March 1942, p. 2, BC1110955, NAA.
45   Minute, Sir George Knowles to Attorney-General, 9 March 1942, BC1110955, NAA.
46   Minute, Vernon Sturdee to Minister, 30 September 1940, BC648984, NAA and Minute Sir George Knowles to the Attorney-General, 9 March 1942, p. 1, BC1110955, NAA.
47   White and Knowles would have frequently crossed paths in their official roles as chairman of the Commonwealth Public Service Board, responsible for moving government departments to Canberra, and Knowles, a strong advocate for Canberra, and as deputy Commonwealth solicitor-general, handling the legal side of this. See BC228711, NAA: A8510, 190/ and Opinion by George Knowles, 11 January 1924, BC3139189, NAA: A2863, 1920/22, Commonwealth Institute of Science and Industry.
48   Minute, Sir George Knowles to Attorney-General, 9 March 1942, BC1110955, NAA.
49   R. Menzies, *Afternoon Light*, Cassell, Australia, Melbourne, 1967, p. 18, and minute, Sir George Knowles to the Attorney-General, 9 March 1942, p. 2, BC1110955, NAA.
50   Menzies, *Afternoon Light*, p. 18, and minute, Sir George Knowles to the Attorney-General, 9 March 1942, p. 2, BC1110955, NAA.
51   Minute, Lieutenant General V. Sturdee to Minister, 30 September 1940, p. 1, BC648984, NAA.
52   Minute, Minister for the Army, 2 October 1940, BC648984, NAA.
53   M.L. Wharton, 'The Development of Security Intelligence in NZ, 1945–1957', MA thesis, Massey University, Manawatu, NZ, 2012, p. 14.
54   Wharton, 'The Development of Security Intelligence in NZ', p. 14.
55   Minute, Sir George Knowles to Attorney-General, 9 March 1942, BC1110955, NAA and Aaron Fox, 'A formidable responsibility': The rise and fall of the New Zealand Security Intelligence Bureau 1940–1945', *Security and Surveillance History Series, 2018/1*, p. 4.
56   Fox, 'A formidable responsibility', p. 14.
57   Fox, 'A formidable responsibility', p. 17.
58   Telegram, Prime Minister, New Zealand, to Prime Minister, 26 November 1940, War 1939 Special Operations Executive, BC206047, NAA.
59   Telegram, Prime Minister, New Zealand, to Secretary, Army, 26 November 1940, BC648984, NAA.
60   Telegram, Prime Minister, New Zealand, to Secretary, Prime Minister's, 20 December 1940, and timed at 3.15 p.m. BC648984, NAA.
61   Telegram, Prime Minister, New Zealand, to Prime Minister, 20 December 1940, BC206047, NAA.
62   Telegram, Prime Minister, New Zealand, to Prime Minister, 20 December 1940, BC206047, NAA.
63   Qantas Schedule, 11 January 1941, p. 2 and Cablegram to Administrator Darwin, 21 January 1940, informing him the Prime Minister and his party would be arriving on 25 January 1940, BC257486, NAA: CP290/9, 1, Personal Papers of Prime Minister Menzies.
64   Minute, Major General Northcott to Minister, Defence Co-ordination, 6 January 1941, with marginal notes by Menzies, 21 January 1941, BC648984, NAA.
65   The remarkable behaviour of Australia's generals is well covered by David Horner in his book *Crisis of Command*, Australian National University Press, Canberra, 1978, and by numerous other sources in the British, Australian and US archives.

66   Cable No. 39, 22 January 1941, BC648984, NAA.
67   Cable No. 39, 22 January 1941, BC648984, NAA.
68   Cable, Secretary of State for the Dominions to UK High Commissioner in Australia and Prime Minister, 27 January 1941, BC648984, NAA.
69   Memo, Secretary of State for the Dominions to UK High Commissioner, Australia, 31 January 1941, BC648984, NAA.
70   BC648984, NAA.
71   Memo, Secretary, Army to Secretary, Defence Co-ordination, 11 February 1941, letter, Secretary, Army to Secretary, Defence Co-ordination, 22 April 1941 and cable, Prime Minister of New Zealand to Prime Minister, 8 May 1941, BC648984, NAA.
72   Letter, 22 April 1941, and cable, Prime Minister to Prime Minister, 8 May 1941, BC648984, NAA.
73   Letter, 22 April 1941, and cable, Prime Minister to Prime Minister, 8 May 1941, BC648984, NAA.
74   Cable to Secretary of State for Dominion Affairs, 28 April 1941, and cable, Acting Prime Minister of New Zealand to Prime Minister, Australia, 8 May 1941, BC648984, NAA.
75   Memo A.F. to Minister for the Army, 20 May 1941, BC648984, NAA.
76   Report on Proposed Formation and Training Special Assault Troops (Para-Military Troops), 6 June 1941, p. 3, BC648984, NAA.
77   Report on Special Assault Troops, pp. 1–2, BC648984, NAA.
78   Report on Special Assault Troops, p. 3, BC648984, NAA.
79   Report on Special Assault Troops, p. 3, BC648984, NAA.
80   Minute by Director-General Petrie, 8 November 1944, KV4/453, Vol 1, NA, UK.
81   Airy Report, 1944, KV 4/453, Vol. 1, NA, UK.
82   Memo, Minister for the Army to the Prime Minister, 10 June 1941, BC648984, NAA.
83   Memo, George Knowles to Acting Attorney-General on Mawhood, 17 April 1942, BC648984, NAA.
84   Memo, George Knowles to Acting Attorney-General on Mawhood, 17 April 1942, BC648984, NAA.
85   Memo, George Knowles to Acting Attorney-General on Mawhood, 17 April 1942, BC648984, NAA.
86   War Cabinet minute (1171), Agendum No. 238/1941, 4 July 1941, BC648984, NAA.
87   War Cabinet minute (1171), Agendum No. 238/1941, 4 July 1941, BC648984, NAA.
88   Menzies, *Afternoon Light,* p. 109.
89   Memo for Mawhood, Shedden, 8 July 1941, BC648984, NAA. Shedden, called 'Pocket Hankey' behind his back (a reference to his oft-stated pride on having learned his job under Maurice Hankey, Britain's first Cabinet Secretary), held the dual positions as Secretary to the Cabinet and Secretary of the Department of Defence Co-ordination throughout the war. Shedden was a notorious seeker and holder of power and influence, a micromanager and retentively finicky.
90   Letter, Mawhood to Shedden, 8 July 1941, BC648984, NAA.
91   Letter, Mawhood to Shedden, 8 July 1941, BC648984, NAA.
92   Memo, Shedden to Minister for the Army, 9 July 1941, BC648984, NAA.
93   Letter, Mawhood to Shedden, 11 July 1941, BC648984, NAA.
94   Letter, Mawhood to Shedden, 11 July 1941, BC648984, NAA.
95   Letter, Mawhood to Shedden, 11 July 1941, BC648984, NAA.
96   Minute, Secretary, Defence Co-ordination to Prime Minister, 11 July 1941, BC648984, NAA.
97   Cablegram, Menzies to High Commissioner London, 11 July 1941, BC648984, NAA.

98   Cablegram, Menzies to High Commissioner, London, 12 July 1941, BC648984, NAA.
99   Letter, Shedden to Spender, 12 July 1941, BC648984, NAA.
100 Letter, Shedden to Spender, 12 July 1941, BC648984, NAA.
101 Letter, Shedden to Spender, 12 July 1941, BC648984, NAA.
102 Signal, War Office, TROOPERS 78053, 14 July 1941, BC648984, NAA.
103 Airy Report, 1944, KV 4/453, Vol. 1, NA, UK.
104 Letter, F. Forde to Evatt, 5 March 1942, and personal letter, Jones to Sir David Petrie, 31 December 1943, KV 4/453, Vol. 1, NA, UK
105 Draft War Cabinet minute, Sydney, 18 July 1941 (1227) Lieutenant Colonel Mawhood, BC648984, NAA.
106 Draft War Cabinet minute, Sydney, 18 July 1941 (1227), BC648984, NAA. The actions of Lloyd in this affair and his involvement in the Harry Freame affair place him in a bad light. At best, he appears vacuous and completely out of his depth, even in wartime Australia.
107 Draft War Cabinet minute, Sydney, 18 July 1941 (1227) Lieutenant-Colonel Mawhood, BC648984, NAA.
108 Cable No. 22, Bruce to Prime Minister, 30 August 1941, BC1110955, NAA.
109 Cable, Bruce to Menzies, 21 July 1941, BC648984, NAA.
110 Cable, Bruce to Menzies, 21 July 1941, BC648984, NAA.
111 Memorandum, Bertram Ede to Director-General, 26 January 1944, KV4/453, Vol. 1, NA, UK.
112 It does not pay to be away from head office, 'the coalface', when a promotions round is on.
113 Charles Maurice de Talleyrand-Périgord was a diplomat and foreign minister to Louis XVI of France, Napoleon I, Louis XVIII and Louis-Philippe I. He was a master of cynical diplomacy and fixed objective.
114 War Cabinet minute (1137), Lieutenant Colonel Mawhood, 22 July 1941, BC648984, NAA.
115 Australia's generals were not alone in holding their political masters in contempt. In Britain, the CIGS, General Alan Brooke, firmly believed that Churchill and other politicians, contemptuously called 'frockcoats', were ignorant and weak and that if they were the best democracy could provide, then perhaps it was time to dispense with it. See, Field Marshall Lord Alanbrooke, *War Diaries 1939–1945*, A. Danchev and D. Todman (eds), Phoenix Press, 2002, entry for 10 July 1941, p. 171 and fn. p. 171.
116 War Cabinet minute (1137), Lieutenant Colonel Mawhood, 22 July 1941, BC648984, NAA.
117 Letter, Northcott to Minister, 23 July 1941, BC648984, NAA.
118 Letter, CGS to Secretary, Defence Co-ordination, 1 August 1941, BC648984, NAA.
119 Letter, Premier of Victoria to Prime Minister, received 15 August 1941, BC648984, NAA.
120 Minute, Secretary, Defence Co-ordination, 3 September 1941, BC648984, NAA.
121 Cable, unsigned but most likely Menzies to Bruce, 29 August 1941, with copies to Fadden and Spender and, later on 3 September, to Shedden, BC206047, NAA.
122 Cable, Fadden to Bruce, 1 September 1941, BC206047, NAA.
123 Minute, George Knowles to Evatt, 18 October 1941, p. 3, BC1110955, NAA.
124 D.M. Horner, 'Australia and Allied Strategy in the Pacific 1941–1946', Vol. I, PhD thesis, Australian National University, 1980, p. 219 and fn. p. 219.

Chapter 9: The Battle of the Reports

1   See J. Mawhood, Secret Report for the Minister via the Solicitor-General, 18 October 1941, Minute by Sir George Knowles for Evatt, 18 October 1941, in BC1110955, NAA. Also, G. Long, *To Benghazi*, AWM, Canberra, 1961, p. 11, and Horner, *Crisis of Command*, among others.

2   Minute, to Evatt, 18 October 1941, BC1110955, NAA. Knowles described Lloyd's writing style as 'too convoluted' and 'involved in the extreme'. Having read some of Lloyd's letters, and this letter to Knowles, one has to agree entirely.

3   Letter, Lloyd to Secretary, Attorney-General's, 30 September 1941, BC1110955, NAA.

4   Memo, George Knowles to Lloyd, 30 September 1941, BC1110955, NAA.

5   Duncan Report, 7 January 1942, p. 1, BC1110955, NAA.

6   Duncan Report, p. 1, BC1110955, NAA.

7   Duncan Report, p. 1, BC1110955, NAA, p. 1.

8   Duncan Report, p. 1, BC1110955, NAA, p. 2.

9   Duncan Report, p. 2, BC1110955, NAA.

10   Duncan Report, p. 2, BC1110955, NAA. Some care needs to be taken with Duncan's observations on the CIB as its Director, Jones, refused to cooperate with him. A similar caution needs to be exercised with his comments on Mawhood as Duncan appears to have resented Mawhood being imposed on him.

11   Duncan Report, p. 3, BC1110955, NAA.

12   Duncan Report, p. 3, BC1110955, NAA.

13   Duncan Report, p. 3, BC1110955, NAA.

14   Duncan Report, p. 16, BC1110955, NAA.

15   Duncan Report, p. 17, BC1110955, NAA, and for the MI5 view, KV4/453, Vol. 1.

16   Duncan Report, p. 17, BC1110955, NAA.

17   Duncan Report, p. 17, BC1110955, NAA.

18   R. Haldane, 'Duncan, Alexander Mitchell', ADB, and Duncan Report, p. 17, BC648984, NAA.

19   Duncan Report, p. 18, BC1110955, NAA.

20   Duncan Report, p. 17, BC648984, NAA.

21   Duncan Report, p. 18, BC1110955, NAA.

22   Duncan Report, pp. 18–19 and Appendix E, BC1110955, NAA.

23   Duncan Report, p. 18, BC1110955, NAA.

24   Memo, Knowles to the Attorney-General, 9 March 1942, BC1110955, NAA.

25   Memo on report by A.M. Duncan, 16 February 1942, BC1110955, NAA.

26   That he so obviously makes this point suggests he had seen a copy of Mawhood's private and confidential report to the Attorney-General sent via the Solicitor-General in October 1941.

27   Memo by Lloyd on report by A.M. Duncan, 16 February 1942, p. 1, BC1110955, NAA.

28   Memo by Lloyd on report by A.M. Duncan, BC1110955, NAA.

29   Covering letter for Duncan Report to Evatt, 7 January 1942, BC1110955, NAA.

30   Duncan Report, p. 18, BC1110955.

31   Briefing for the Attorney-General by George Knowles, 9 March 1942, p. 3, BC1110955, NAA.

32   Winter, The Intrigue Master, p. 109.

33   Secret Report for the Minister, 10 November 1941, p. 1, BC1110955, NAA.

34   Secret Report for the Minister, 10 November 1941, p. 2, BC1110955, NAA.

35   Secret Report for the Minister, 10 November 1941, p. 2, BC1110955, NAA.

36   Observations by Lieutenant Colonel Mawhood, 10 November 1941, p. 2, BC1110955, NAA.

37   Observations by Lieutenant Colonel Mawhood, 10 November 1941, p. 2, BC1110955, NAA.

38   Observations by Lieutenant Colonel Mawhood, 10 November 1941, p. 3, BC1110955, NAA.

39 Observations by Lieutenant Colonel Mawhood, 10 November 1941, p. 3, BC1110955, NAA.
40 Report by John Mawhood, 10 November 1941, p. 4, BC1110955, NAA.
41 Secret Report for the Minister, 10 November 1941, p. 5, BC1110955, NAA.
42 Secret Report for the Minister, 10 November 1941, p. 1, BC1110955, NAA.
43 Secret Report for the Minister, 10 November 1941, p. 1, BC1110955, NAA.
44 Secret Report for the Minister, 10 November 1941, p. 2, BC1110955, NAA.
45 Secret Report for the Minister, 10 November 1941, p. 2, BC1110955, NAA.
46 Report for the Minister via the Solicitor-General, 18 October 1941, p. 2, BC1110955, NAA.
47 The Cohen mentioned here is the same one that provided Gavin Long with the alleged disparaging remarks Sturdee made about Mawhood.
48 A. Moore, 'Scott, William John', ADB. Scott somehow managed to wrangle being appointed Commander of Gull Force, a job for which he was entirely unsuited and in which he performed abysmally. See L.G. Wigmore, The Japanese Thrust, AWM, Canberra, 1957, Chapter 19: 'Loss of Ambon'.
49 Secret Report for the Minister, 10 November 1941, p. 2, BC1110955, NAA.
50 Report for the Minister via the Solicitor-General, 18 October 1941, p. 2, BC1110955, NAA.
51 Teleprinter message, Department of Defence Co-ordination to secretaries, Army and External Affairs, 14 January 1941, BC170437, NAA: A816, 25/301/176, Major Hashida—visit to Australia.
52 M. Tsuji, Singapore, trans. Margaret E. Lake, New York: St Martin's Press, 1960, pp. 29–31, 41–52.
53 BC1110955, NAA.
54 Report for the Minister via the Solicitor-General, 18 October 1941, p. 4, BC1110955, NAA. Mawhood claims here he had recommended this to Vernon Sturdee in December 1940.
55 Report for the Minister via the Solicitor-General, 18 October 1941, p. 5, BC1110955, NAA. Mawhood reports he had sounded out Long who had agreed he would be willing to relinquish his naval rank and serve in the position as a civilian.
56 Report for the Minister via the Solicitor-General, 18 October 1941, p. 2, BC1110955, NAA. Mawhood claims here he had recommended this to Vernon Sturdee in December 1940. If he discussed these recommendations with Sturdee, it would explain the strength of the reaction to him.
57 Report for the Minister via the Solicitor-General, 18 October 1941, p. 2, BC1110955, NAA.
58 Letter, MacKay to Evatt, 17 November 1941, BC1110955, NAA.
59 Letter, MacKay to Evatt, 17 November 1941, BC1110955, NAA.
60 Reports by John Mawhood to A.M. Duncan, 10 November 1941, p. 4, BC1110955, NAA.
61 Reports by John Mawhood, 18 October 1941 and 10 November 1941, BC1110955, NAA.

Chapter 10: The Wartime Security Service

1 BC821583, NAA, A8911, 130, Australia First Movement - Miscellaneous.
2 Letter, Frank Forde to W.J. MacKay, 9 April 1942, BC217054, NAA, AA1981/132, 1, World War 2—The Security Service.
3 Letter, Frank Forde to W.J. MacKay, 9 April 1942, BC217054, NAA.
4 Letter, Frank Forde to W.J. MacKay, 9 April 1942, BC217054, NAA.
5 Letter, Frank Forde to W.J. MacKay, 9 April 1942, BC217054, NAA.

6   Letter, Frank Forde to W.J. MacKay, 9 April 1942, BC217054, NAA.
7   Letter, Frank Forde to W.J. MacKay, 9 April 1942, BC217054, NAA.
8   Letter, Frank Forde to W.J. MacKay, 9 April 1942, BC217054, NAA.
9   Letter, Frank Forde to W.J. MacKay, 17 March 1942, BC217054, NAA.
10 Letter, Frank Forde to W.J. MacKay, 19 June 1942, BC217054, NAA.
11 Letter, DG-S to CGS, 20 April 1942, BC217054, NAA.
12 Minute, Director of Military Intelligence to CGS, 22 April 1942, BC217054, NAA.
13 Minute, Secretary, Army to CGS, 21 April 1942, BC217054, NAA.
14 Minute, 6 May 1942, BC217054, NAA.
15 Training of Security Officers and Operatives, May 42, BC217054, NAA.
16 Letter, DMI to DG-SS, 15 July 1942, BC217054, NAA.
17 Templeton, Seventh Report, p. 166, BC795990, NAA.
18 Letter, DD-S Melbourne to Wake, 5 March 1943, B1134482, NAA.
19 Templeton, Seventh Report, p. 166, BC795990, NAA.
20 Airy Report, 1944, p. 5, KV4/453, NA, UK.
21 Airy Report, 1944, p. 5, KV4/453, Vol. 1, NA, UK.
22 Letter, DMI to DG-S, 15 July 1942, BC217054, NAA.
23 Letter, D-CGS to Secretary, Army, Functions of Army and Security Service, 4 August 1942, BC217054, NAA.
24 Teleprinter message to Mr Brennen from Mr Sinclair, 11 September 1942, and letter, Wake to DDMI, 17 August 1942, and notations by Lieutenant Colonel Little, 23 August 1942, BC217054, NAA.
25 Signal, SM16645, 3 September 1942, BC217054, NAA.
26 Letter, Evatt to Forde, 24 August 1942, BC217054, NAA.
27 Signal SM16645, 3 September 1942, BC217054, NAA.
28 Minutes of a Meeting Held at Victoria Barracks, Melbourne on 15 September 1942, BC217054, NAA.
29 Memorandum from DG-S, 25 September 1942, BC217054, NAA.
30 Memorandum from H.V. Evatt, Attorney-General, 28 September 1942, BC217054, NAA.
31 Report by E.A. Airy, Security Liaison Officer, Ceylon, on his Visit to the Security Service of the Commonwealth of Australia, 15 August 1944–48 October 1944, 18 October 1944, KV4/453, NA, UK.
32 Airy Report, 1944, p. 5, KV4/453, Vol. 1, NA, UK.
33 Airy Report, 1944, p. 5, KV4/453, Vol. 1, NA, UK.
34 Airy Report, 1944, p. 5, KV4/453, Vol. 1, NA, UK.
35 Airy Report, 1944, p. 5, KV4/453, Vol. 1, NA, UK.
36 Airy Report, 18 October 1944, KV4/453, Vol. 1, NA, UK.
37 Airy Report, 18 October 1944, KV4/453, Vol. 1, NA, UK.
38 Employment of Army Personnel by Security Service, 5 December 1942, BC217054, NAA.
39 Signal SM2273, 1 February 1943, BC217054, NAA.
40 Staff Instruction No. 30, 30 June 1943, BC272808, NAA, A373, 7831, Security Service Reorganisation.
41 Letter, Jenkins to Director-General, 13 November 1943, BC272808, NAA.
42 Letter, Simpson to Brigadier Rogers, DMI, 21 May 1943, folio 584, BC1134482, NAA.
43 Letter, DD-S, Melbourne, to DG-S, 3 December 1943, BC272808, NAA.
44 Direction, Sydney Office, undated, 1943, BC272808, NAA.
45 File note by B. Ede, 5 November 1944, note by David Petrie, 8 November 1944, Airy Report, 1944, KV4/453, Vol. 1, NA, UK.
46 Airy Report, 1944, p. 5, KV4/453, Vol. 1, NA, UK.

47 Note to Director-General from JCGK, 10 August 1944, BC30944654, NAA, A7359/84, BOX 10/17 Part 2, unnumbered.

48 Telegram, Lloyd to Sir David Petrie, 29 October 1945, KV4/453, NA, UK.

49 Cabinet Agendum 1135, 8 April 1946, BC227921, NAA, A2703, 1946–1946, Minutes of the Full Cabinet Meeting, 17 January–19 December 1946, Chifley Ministry.

50 Lloyd was so memorable to Lieutenant Colonel Airy that when he was asked to describe Lloyd for Sir David Petrie, the best he could do was to say he had met with him, but had forgotten what he did or even what he looked like. File note to D.G., 12 November 1945, KV4/453, NA, UK.

Chapter 11: The Serpent in the Sacristy—R.F.B. Wake

1 V.R. Wake, *No Ribbons or Medals*, Jacobyte Books, Adelaide, 2005, p. 24.

2 BC1010436, NAA, MP729/8, 41/431/136, Re Lieutenant R.F.B. Wake (Retired List).

3 *SMH*, 8 November 1924, p. 16, BC1010436, NAA.

4 BC9321799, NAA, B4747, Wake, Robert Frederick Bird. Wake had a number of other files relating to his military service—BC378141, NAA, B1535, 736/15/335, Application for a Commission R.F.B. Wake, BC1010436, NAA, BC9094137, NAA, J1795, 6/522, Wake, Robert Frederick Bird—Military Officer's Record of Service and BC12147809, NAA, J1795, 2/255, Wake, Robert Frederick Bird, Military Officer's Service Record. For an officer of his rank and position, this is a red flag suggesting unofficial manipulation of his files.

5 There is no doubt Wake lied on official forms. On his militia enlistment form he told outright lies about serving with the British in World War I, despite being far too young to have done so. He lied on his enlistment application for the 2nd AIF, see BC1010436, NAA. In addition, Wake claimed to have served under Basil Thomson, from whom he had learned the methods of Scotland Yard and the French Sûreté Nationale. He also lied about being a licensed pilot with 80 hours of solo flying.

6 Letter, Simpson to Brigadier Rogers, DMI, 21 May 1943, folio 584, BC1134482, NAA.

7 Letter, Simpson to Brigadier Rogers, DMI, 21 May 1943, folio 584, BC1134482, NAA.

8 Letter, Colonel K.A. Wills to Simpson, 24 May 1943, folio 583, BC1134482, NAA.

9 B. Winter, *The Intrigue Master*, Boolarong Press, Brisbane, 1995, p. 8.

10 'Emden Bell', *SMH*, 6 December 1933, p. 13. See *The Sun*, 2 September 1932, p. 9, and *The Herald*, 2 February 1932, for examples of the coverage.

11 'Ship's Bell from SMS *Emden*: HMAS *Sydney* (I)', www.awm.gov.au/Collection/RELAWM12275/, accessed 26 December 2019. See *Daily Telegraph*, 29 April 1933, p. 1, and a multitude of other publications all eager to accuse the Germans of having committed an outrage. At least the *Daily Telegraph* reported that the bell was probably stolen for its metal.

12 *SMH*, 2 January 1934, p. 1.

13 BC1829155, NAA, A6119, 2216, Wake, Robert Frederick Bird. Wake was appointed on 12 March 1934 and took up his appointment on 9 April at a salary of £327 per annum.

14 Divorce Court, *The Propeller*, 13 September 1934, p. 3.

15 *Truth*, Sydney, 16 September 1934, p. 14. The divorce was granted despite the fact that Wake had been separated from his wife for around two years because of earlier difficulties in the marriage. Perhaps Eve Wiss was not Wake's first adulterous affair.

16 The New Guard and 'The Association', BC65290, NAA, A367, C94121.

17 Evans, 'A menace to this realm'.

18 New Guard Movement, Legislative Assembly New South Wales, 23 December 1931, BC4727772, NAA, A12393, 7/99, Para-Military Groups. The accepted history, including

Jacqueline Templeton's history of intelligence reporting for the Royal Commission on Intelligence and Security, see BC795990, NAA, is wrong in its evaluation of the size and effectiveness of the New Guard and has been taken in by the myth of the non-existent 'Old Guard'. See Richard Evans for the definitive destruction of the Old Guard myth.

19   Letterhead of New Guard, 28 January 1932, BC65290, NAA.
20   Aliens, Registration of, BC209208, NAA.
21   Letter, Lloyd to Director CIB, 22 May 1935, BC764264, NAA, A367, C23512 Part 1, Longfield, Lloyd, E.E.
22   Folio 57, BC1829155, NAA.
23   Mr and Mrs Robert Wake (Melbourne) attendance at dinner in their honour, 'A Few Lines to Say', *The Courier-Mail*, Brisbane, 29 April 1936, p. 22. The Wakes were going to be neighbours having moved into 26 Mary Street, Auchenflower. See BC12147809, NAA.
24   'Women's Realm', *Sunday Mail*, Brisbane, 19 July 1936, p. 17. This appears to be the first of these stories and notes. Elizabeth Wake (nee Burns) was a native of Edinburgh, Scotland. See letter, Elizabeth Wake to Robert Menzies, 10 July 1951, in ASIO file BC1829155, NAA.
25   'Our Own G-Men', *Sunday Mail*, Brisbane, 10 September 1939, p. 6.
26   'And That's That! Exit Jehovah's Witnesses', *Smith's Weekly*, Sydney, 25 January 1941, p. 3.
27   'And That's That! Exit Jehovah's Witnesses', *Smith's Weekly*, Sydney, 25 January 1941, p. 3.
28   Letter, NX84863, Private R. Harris, to Lieutenant Colonel R. Wake (Bob), 29 March 1943, BC1134482, NAA.
29   BC378141, NAA.
30   BC12147809, NAA.
31   Airy Report, 1944, p. 5, KV4/453, NA, UK.
32   Wake, *No Ribbons or Medals*, pp. 142–3.
33   File note by B. Ede, 5 November 1944, note by David Petrie, 8 November 1944, Airy Report, 1944, KV4/453, NA, UK.
34   File note by B. Ede, 5 November 1944, note by David Petrie, 8 November 1944, Airy Report, 1944, KV4/453, NA, UK.
35   Airy Report, 1944, p. 5, KV4/453, NA, UK. MI5 were quite aware of Wake's close connections with Labor ministers and his willingness to accept directions from Evatt and other ministers to undertake unconstitutional investigations of political opponents, including those in the ALP. Also see letter from Captain B. Tyrell to Director-General, 29 December 1942, BC65399, NAA, A373, 3149, Security Service—Victorian Branch, BC65399, NAA. Details the destructive effect of Wake on the morale of staff in Victoria.
36   E. Feldt, *The Coastwatchers*, Oxford University Press, Melbourne, 1946.
37   Letter, Feldt to Cocky [Long], 2 August 1940, BC508663, NAA, B3476, 49C, Commander E Feldt, Reports.
38   Letter, Feldt to Cocky [Long], 2 August 1940, BC508663, NAA.
39   Note, 19 October, on letter Feldt to Cocky [Long], 18 October 1940, NAA, BC508663.
40   Feldt, *The Coastwatchers*, pp. 95–6.
41   Feldt, *The Coastwatchers*, pp. 95–6.
42   Testimony Commander Long, Judicial Inquiry into R.F.B. Wake, folio 290, BC1134482, NAA.
43   Testimony Commander Long, folio 290, BC1134482, NAA.
44   Testimony Commander Long, folio 290, BC1134482, NAA.
45   Ball and Horner, *Breaking the Codes*, pp. 43, 300, and Winter, *The Intrigue Master*, p. 178.
46   Ball and Horner, *Breaking the Codes*, p. 43. These claims are drawn from an uncorroborated interview in Templeton's history for the Hope Royal Commission. See p. 209, fn. 43 BC795990, NAA.

47 Winter, *The Intrigue Master*, p. 178. There is no source given for this information.

48 In January 1942, Wake harassed *The Telegraph* through the Censor because CIB investigators could not find an Adam Corbett who had a letter of his published by the paper. Wake deemed the letter to be 'discouraging of the war effort'. See letter, R. Wake to State Publicity Censor, Brisbane, 22 January 1942, BC337326, NAA, BP361/1, 12/1/11 PART 2, Commonwealth Investigation Bureau and Security Service Correspondence. The writer had, unsurprisingly, given a false address. The matter was hardly earth-shattering, but Wake wanted a scalp and used the Censor to try, unsuccessfully, to find Corbett. This small episode shows Wake's willingness to use the full weight of government against someone expressing a petty complaint in a letter; it clearly shows his ruthless unreasonableness.

49 An example of Wake's methods is shown in an undated letter from 'Peter', BC1134482, NAA. This letter to 'Dear Colonel' (Wake) tells him that the Com's (Queensland Police Commissioner's) 'verdict is against your man' travelling with 'two unauthorized females in the car' and advising Wake to speak to Bill Power, probably William Joseph Power, MLA, Queensland Minister for Public Works, Housing and Local Government, for political support if needed. 'Peter' is none too happy, as the answers Wake's man gave to the investigating police showed he had been tipped off as to the line of inquiry, and now a 'heresy hunt' was on. This matter appears to involve one of Wake's peace officers, William Hall Robinson, who forfeited his bail on a driving matter in January 1947. See letter, Deputy Superintending Peace Officer, R.F.B. Wake to Commissioner Queensland Police, 5 March 1947, BC1134482, NAA.

50 'Startling Results from Raids', *The Sun*, 17 June 1940, p. 3, 'No Arrests in Brisbane', *Daily News*, 17 June 1940, p. 2, and *Cairns Post*, 17 June 1942, p. 6.

51 'Major Wake Promoted to Lt. Colonel', *The Telegraph*, 15 August 1941, p. 3.

52 'Inspector Wake Speaking to Premier at Airport', *The Telegraph*, 6 May 1941, p. 11.

53 Transcript of Evidence by Commander Long, 21 December 1943, folio 294, BC1134482, NAA.

54 Folio 294, BC1134482, NAA.

55 Minute Sir George Knowles for Attorney-General, 12 November 1941, BC1110955, NAA.

56 Minute Sir George Knowles for Attorney-General, 12 November 1941, BC1110955, NAA.

57 Minute Sir George Knowles for Attorney-General, 12 November 1941, BC1110955, NAA.

58 'MLA Spies Union Protest', *The Courier-Mail*, 29 November 1941, p. 3.

59 Social notices show Inspector Wake staying at the Criterion Hotel for the night. *Evening News*, 20 March 1941, p. 6.

60 Transcript of Evidence by Commander Long, 21 December 1943, folio 294, BC1134482, NAA.

61 Memo by Jones, 7 March 1942, p. 3, BC1110955, NAA.

62 Minute Sir George Knowles to Attorney-General, 9 March 1942, p. 7, BC1110955, NAA.

63 Minute Sir George Knowles to Attorney-General, 9 March 1942, and memo by Jones, 7 March 1942, pp. 3, 8, BC1110955, NAA.

64 Minute Sir George Knowles to Attorney-General, 9 March 1942, p. 8, BC1110955, NAA, BC73138, NAA, A432, 1943/1139, The Freer Case, and BC72470, NAA, A432, 1936/1360, Mabel Magdalene Freer. Exclusion from Australia.

65 Memo by Jones, 7 March 1942, p. 3, BC1110955, NAA.

66 Minute Sir George Knowles to Attorney-General, 9 March 1942, and memo by Jones, 7 March 1942, p. 3, BC1110955, NAA.

67 Letter, Frank Forde to H.V. Evatt, 18 August 1942, BC217054, NAA.

68 Letter, Frank Forde to H.V. Evatt, 18 August 1942, and reply from Evatt, 24 August 1942, BC217054, NAA.

69   Letter, G to The Chief, 21 June 1943, BC1134482, NAA.
70   Letter, G to The Chief, 21 June 1943, BC1134482, NAA.
71   Letter, G to The Chief, 21 June 1943, BC1134482, NAA.
72   Letter, G to The Chief, 21 June 1943, BC1134482, NAA.
73   See Wake's private collection of papers in BC1134482, NAA.
74   Minute by Brigadier E. Gorman, 8 September 1943, MP729/8, 41/431/136, Re Lieutenant R.F.B. Wake, BC1010436, NAA.
75   BC1134482, NAA.
76   Application for a Commission in the 2nd AIF, 15 September 1939, BC1010436, NAA.
77   Letter, General Blamey to Minister for the Army, 5 October 1943, BC1010436, NAA.
78   Lieutenant R.F. Wake to Base Commandant, 20 September 1939, BC1134482, NAA.
79   Attestation Form, 2 September 1931, BC9321799, NAA.
80   Letter, Geoffrey Reed to Robert Wake, 21 July 1943, folio 391, BC1134482, NAA.
81   Letter, Geoffrey Reed to Robert Wake, 21 July 1943, folio 391, BC1134482, NAA.
82   Telegram Wake to Reed, 19 July 1943, folio 390, BC1134482, NAA.
83   This would not be the only time that Justice Reed placed himself in a position where a conflict of interest could be alleged against him. In 1959, Reed sat as a Royal Commissioner of the Royal Commission established by the South Australian Government into the safety of the conviction of Rupert Max Stuart, an Aboriginal man charged with the murder of a nine-year-old girl, Mary Olive Hattam, near Ceduna, South Australia. The astonishing thing about this was that Reed had been the judge in the original case against Stuart and had condemned him to hang. See Hon. Justice M. Kirby, 'Keynote address: The lessons of the Stuart Case', Elder Hall, University of Adelaide, 1 April 2006.
84   Testimony of Commander Long, folio 292, BC1134482, NAA.
85   Testimony of Commander Long, folio 280, BC1134482, NAA.
86   Testimony of Commander Long, folio 280, BC1134482, NAA.
87   Testimony of Commander Long, folio 272, BC1134482, NAA.
88   Testimony of Commander Long, folio 272, BC1134482, NAA.
89   Letter, Forde to Evatt, 6 October 1943, and letter, Simpson to Evatt, 21 October 1943, BC1134482, NAA.
90   Letter, Blamey to Forde, 5 October 1943, BC1134482, NAA.
91   Direction Melbourne Office, 29 November 1943, BC272808, NAA.
92   Letter, Director-General to My Dear Hereward, 26 February 1943, BC1134482, NAA.
93   BC1134482, NAA.
94   Letter, Simpson to Wake, 3 March 1945, BC1866560, NAA, A7359/84, Box 10/17 Part 1. This letter had become necessary because if Wake did not take his leave, a certificate saying he could not be spared would have to have been raised by the Permanent Head of the Attorney-General's Department, Sir George Knowles. Neither Simpson nor Wake would have been keen to let Knowles start looking at their records.
95   Letter, Major Marshall to Colonel Wake, 11 October 1943, BC1866560, NAA.
96   Letter, Major Marshall to Colonel Wake, 11 October 1943, BC1866560, NAA.
97   BC1134482, NAA.

Chapter 12: Dagoes, Wogs and Pommies

1   'Consul's Reply to Mr. Hughes, "Childish, Vulgar and Discourteous"', *Daily Standard*, 30 March 1928, p. 1.
2   'Terms "Pommies and Dagoes"', *The Telegraph*, 17 January 1939, p. 9.
3   'Angry Words at Conference', *The Argus*, 31 March 1928, p. 33.

4   A. Frost, *The Precarious Life of James Mario Matra*, The Miegunyah Press, Carlton, 1995, p. 1. Matra's family were Corsican, which in 1746, when Matra was born in New York, was part of Genoa, Italy. Matra was a British subject. Also, Museums Victoria, 'Origins: Immigration history from Italy to Victoria', https://origins.museumsvictoria.com.au/countries/italy.

5   J. Lorch, 'Carboni, Raffaello', *ADB*.

6   'Racial Prejudice', *SMH*, 5 December 1935, p. 5, and 28 October 1947, p. 7.

7   'Nazis Being Rounded Up, Close Watch On Italians', *The Advertiser*, 4 June 1940, p. 12.

8   'Tighter Hand on Aliens', *Daily Telegraph*, 7 June 1940, p. 4.

9   K. Saunders, '"Inspired by patriotic hysteria?"': Internment policy towards enemy aliens in Australia during the Second World War', in Panikos Panyani (ed.), *Minorities in Wartime*, Bloomsbury, London, 2016, p. 299.

10   Saunders, '"Inspired by patriotic hysteria?"', p. 299.

11   G. Cresciani, 'The bogey of the Italian Fifth Column: Internment and the making of Italo-Australia', in R. Bosworth and R. Ugolinini (eds), *War, Internment and Mass Migration*, Gruppo Editoriale Internazionale, 1992, p. 20.

12   Cresciani, 'A not so brutal friendship', p. 16.

13   'Police Swoop on Aliens', *Daily Advertiser*, 7 June 1940, p. 4.

14   See Italian Activities in Sydney, BC12054874, NAA, CP00/0/1, 3, Intelligence—Italian Central File.

15   Minute DCGS to Secretary, Army, Report, 27 January 1942, BC65354, NAA, A373, 1681, Internment Policy, and Report, DMI to DCGS, 22 March 1942, BC65341, NAA.

16   G. Rando, 'Italo-Australians during the Second World War: Some perceptions of internment', *Studi d'Italianistica nell'Africa Australe*, 2005, 18(1): 20–51.

17   'Troops Stationed on Cane Fields', *The Herald*, 11 June 1940, p. 7.

18   Rando, 'Italo-Australians during the Second World War', p. 6.

19   BC6389615, NAA, B883, SX11231, Sandford AW, record of service.

20   BC6389615, NAA.

21   G.S. Ballard, *On ULTRA Active Service*, Spectrum Publications, Richmond, 1991, p. 71.

22   Ballard, On *ULTRA Active Service*, p. 71.

23   D. O'Connor, 'Viva il Duce: The influence of fascism on Italians in South Australia in the 1920s and 1930s', *Journal of the Historical Society of South Australia*, 1993, 21: 20–2.

24   Membership ledger from the South Australian Fascio seized by Sandford in June 1940, BC2015386, NAA, AP501/2, Sandford.

25   O'Connor, 'Viva il Duce', p. 22.

26   Menghetti, D., 'Their country, not mine: The internments', Lecture to the Second Australian Conference on Italian Culture and Italy Today, Frederick May Foundation, University of Sydney, 6 August 1982, p. 2.

27   Internment of Enemy Aliens—Representation by Organisations and Communities, BC65344, NAA, A373, 1272.

28   Letter, Mrs P.E. Pettit, Peacock Siding, Ingham, to Department of Information, 6 June 1944, BC337326, NAA, BP361/1, 12/1/11 PART 2, CIB and Security Service Correspondence. Mrs Pettit wanted something done about Mr W. Preveteria and A. La Rosa of Stone River because the 'Italians are trying to be Boss up this way'.

29   Representations by Mr. C.J. Carroll, Commissioner of Police, Queensland, and supporting letter by the D-G Security, W.J. MacKay, undated but March 1942, BC65354, NAA.

30   Minute, DCGS to Secretary, Army, 5 March 1942, BC65354, NAA.

31   Minute, DMI, C.G. Roberts to DCGS, 22 March 1942, and Minute DCGS, Sydney Rowell to Secretary, Army, 5 March 1942, BC65354, NAA.

32   War Cabinet Addendum 161/1942, 28 March 1942, BC65354, NAA.

33   B. Niall, *Mannix*, Text Publishing, Melbourne, 2015, p. 247.

34   C. Elkner, *Enemy Aliens*, Connor Court, Bacchus Marsh, 2005, p. 61.

35   Particulars of Person for Internment signed by Lieutenant General J.L. Whitlam, 11 June 1940, BC781312, NAA, A367, C62490, Modotti, Reverend Hugo.

36   Report by E.H., Captain Ib, Southern Command, date 24 June 1940, BC781312, NAA.

37   Report by E.H., Captain Ib, BC781312, NAA.

38   Copy of letter T. Hattori to Father Modotti, 6 October 1941, and letter Archbishop Daniel Mannix, 26 March 1942, p. 2, BC781312, NAA.

39   Copy of letter T. Hattori to Father Modotti, 6 October 1941, and letter Archbishop Daniel Mannix, 26 March 1942, p. 2, BC781312, NAA.

40   Memo on comments by Father McCarthy, 13 April 1943 and letter D-G Security to D-DS, 15 April 1943, BC781312, NAA.

41   Letter, DG-S to DD-S, Melbourne, 15 April 1943, BC781312, NAA.

42   Letter, DD-S, Melbourne to DG-S, 17 April 1943, BC781312, NAA.

43   Letter, Chaplin-General McCarthy to DD-S, 28 April 1943, BC781312, NAA.

44   Letter, DG-S to Chaplin-General McCarthy, 7 May 1943, BC781312, NAA.

45   Letter, Brigadier Simpson to Chaplain-General McCarthy, 28 April 1943, BC781312, NAA.

46   Letter, Brigadier Simpson to Chaplain-General McCarthy, 28 April 1943, BC781312, NAA. Simpson's claims do not accord with those provided by Father J. Fitzgerald and Mr and Miss Leoncelli in a letter, 30 April 1943, also in BC781312.

47   Letter, Brigadier Simpson to Chaplain-General McCarthy, 28 April 1943, BC781312, NAA. Simpson's claims do not accord with those provided by Father J. Fitzgerald and Mr and Miss Leoncelli in a letter, 30 April 1943, also in BC781312.

48   Letter, Father J. Fitzgerald, SJ, to Father McCarthy, 30 April 1943 and Letter Chaplain-General McCarthy to Brigadier Simpson, 7 May 1943, BC781312, NAA.

49   Letter, Chaplain-General McCarthy to Brigadier Simpson, 7 May 1943, BC781312, NAA.

50   Letter, Chaplain-General McCarthy to Brigadier Simpson, 7 May 1943, BC781312, NAA.

51   Letter, Chaplain-General McCarthy to Brigadier Simpson, 7 May 1943, BC781312, NAA.

52   Letter, Chaplin-General McCarthy to DD-S, 28 April 1943, BC781312, NAA.

53   Letter, Chaplain-General McCarthy to Brigadier Simpson, 7 May 1943, BC781312, NAA.

54   Letter, Chaplain-General McCarthy to Brigadier Simpson, 7 May 1943, BC781312, NAA.

55   A. Tosco, 'Features of early ethnic Italo-Australian newspapers: A case study of L'Italo-Australiao (1885)', *Italian Historical Society Journal*, 2005, 13(1–2): 10.

56   Letter, C. Albanese to Rev. Father Modotti, 26 October 1938, BC781312, NAA.

57   Letter, Lieutenant Colonel Wake to Director-General Security, 15 July 1943, BC781312, NAA.

58   Letter, Lieutenant Colonel Wake to DD-S, 15 July 1943, BC781312, NAA.

59   Letter, D-DS to DG Security, 8 July 1943, BC781312, NAA.

60   Unsigned memo to DG-S, 15 July 1943, BC1134482, NAA. See report of GREEN and Agent report attached to letter Lieutenant James W. McColl, Counterintelligence Corps, US Army to Colonel Wake, 26 September 1943, BC781312, NAA.

61   Minute James W. McColl, 26 September 1943, BC781312, NAA.

62   Note of conversation, 13 July 1944, BC781312, NAA.

63   Letter Archbishop Mannix to H.V. Evatt, Attorney-General, 23 November 1944, BC781312, NAA.

64   Letter Archbishop Mannix to H.V. Evatt, Attorney-General, 23 November 1944, BC781312, NAA.

65   Letter, DG-S to Sir D. Petrie, DG, MI5, 22 February 1945, BC781312, NAA.

66   Letter J.D.L. Hood to Archbishop Mannix, 5 January 1945, BC781312, NAA.

67   See A714, 34/13063, Surname-Modotti; Given Names: Hugh, NAA BC31755983, and A. Cappello, 'A brief survey of the Italian Catholic in Australia until the Second World War: An Italian problem', in A. Paganoni, *The Pastoral Care of Italians in Australia*, Connor Court Publishing, Ballan, 2007, p. 36.

Chapter 13: Jehovah's Witnesses—The enemy within?

1   Letter, Colonial Secretary's Office, Suva, to Prime Minister, Australia, 22 October 1936, BC99427, NAA.

2   CIB report on The Watch Tower Bible and Tract Society, 17 November 1936, BC99427, NAA.

3   Report, C.V. Kellaway, Acting Official Secretary to Attorney-General's Department, 6 May 1938, BC99427, NAA.

4   'Jehovah's Witnesses Banned in Canada', *The Advertiser*, 6 July 1940, p. 12.

5   Letter, Secretary, Army to Secretary, Defence Co-ordination, 9 July 1940, BC99427, NAA.

6   Letter, Secretary, Army to Secretary, Defence Co-ordination, 9 July 1940, BC99427, NAA.

7   Report to Metropolitan Superintendent Police Station No. 4 Sydney, 18 July 1940, BC99427, NAA.

8   Report to Metropolitan Superintendent Police Station No. 4 Sydney, 18 July 1940, BC99427, NAA.

9   MPIS report on The Activities of the International Bible Students Association for Inspector Keefe, 17 July 1940, BC99427, NAA.

10 MPIS report for Inspector Keefe, 17 July 1940, BC99427, NAA.

11 Letters, 9, 12, 24 July, 5, 14 August, 3, 6, 14, 25 September, 3, 5, October, 13 November and one undated, BC99427, NAA, also army letters, 8 September 1940, and letter, 24 October, stating MI has been active against the Witnesses and has been looking into their ownership of radio stations, BC99448, NAA, A467, SF43/26, Investigation into Jehovah's Witnesses Control of Wireless Stations.

12 Letter M. Blackburn to Mr Menzies, 27 July 1940, BC99427.

13 Copy of letter, Knowles to Prime Minister's, 2 December 1940, and subsequently reproduced as a letter, Menzies to Premier of New South Wales, 8 December 1940, BC99427, NAA.

14 Copy of letter, Knowles to Prime Minister's, 2 December 1940, and subsequently reproduced as a letter, Menzies to Premier of New South Wales, 8 December 1940, BC99427, NAA.

15 Report, Jones to Knowles, 19 July 1940, BC99427, NAA.

16 Report, Jones to Knowles, 19 July 1940, BC99427, NAA.

17 Report, Jones to Knowles, 19 July 1940, BC99427, NAA.

18 For those who doubt this, go to the NLA Trove website, digital newspapers, and search 'Jehovah's Witnesses' between 1939 and 1945. See cutting, 'Jehovah's Dealt with by Govt.', *Truth*, 21 July 1940, 'These Specimens Won't Even Fight for their Country', *Truth*, 13 July 1940, *Smith's Weekly*, 25 January 1941, and *Truth*, 13 July 1943, for some examples of the vulgarity of the reporting.

19 BC1134482, NAA.

20 Letter, L.A. Robb to Prime Minister, 27 July 1940, BC99427, NAA.

21 Cutting, 'Sequel to City Parade, Jehovah's Witnesses, 67 in court', *SMH*, 30 July 1940, BC99427, NAA.

22   BC99427, NAA.

23   BC99427, NAA.

24   Opinion provided by Crown Solicitor to Secretary, Attorney-General's, 29 November 1940, and MI report, 4 November 1940, BC99427, NAA.

25   Copy of report prepared by J.P. Bergin, H. McAuliffe and R.P. Harrison, Privates, Field Security Police, 16 December 1940, BC99427, NAA.

26   'Witnesses of Jehovah Convention Banned', *SMH*, 24 December 1940, p. 7.

27   'Radio Stations Close Down', *Canberra Times*, 9 January 1941, BC99448, NAA.

28   'Serious Allegations Made by Navy', *Maryborough Chronicle, Wide Bay and Burnett Advertiser*, 10 January 1941, p. 5, and 'Closure of Broadcasting Station', *Daily Advertiser*, Wagga Wagga, 11 January 1941, p. 2.

29   B. Griffen-Foley, *Changing Stations*, UNSW Press, 2009, p. 178.

30   'Federal Ban on Sect', *SMH*, 17 January 1941, p. 7.

31   'Radio Ban, Why Ministry Acted, Mr Hughes's Explanation', *SMH*, 10 January 1940, p. 9.

32   'Federal Ban on Sect, Cabinet Acts, The Jehovah's Witnesses, Radio Investigation', *SMH*, 17 January 1941, p. 7, and 'Now Declared Illegal, Ban on Jehovah's Witnesses', *The Age*, 18 January 1941, p. 22. See also memo for Cabinet, 7 February 1941, BC99444, NAA, A467, SF43/19, Investigations into Australian Activities—Jehovah's Witnesses—Postmaster-General's Cabinet minute.

33   'Station to Re-Open, Federal Control', *The Argus*, 27 January 1941, p. 4. Order Under Regulation 6A, 17 January 1941, BC99461, NAA, A467, SF43/39, Investigations into Jehovah's Witnesses. These were 7 Beresford Road, Strathfield, New South Wales; 22A George Street, East Melbourne; Ann Street, Brisbane; 33 Sturt Street, Adelaide; 15 Catherine Street, Subiaco, and 403 Elizabeth Street, Hobart.

34   Griffen-Foley, B., *Changing Stations*, p. 177.

35   Letter, F. Fitzgerald to Attorney-General, 29 March 1941, BC99460, NAA, A467, SF43/38, F. Fitzgerald—Request for Return of Private Property.

36   A ministerial is a letter directed to a minister which must be replied to and which the department must investigate, draft a reply letter and provide a brief for the minister detailing why the minister should sign the draft letter of reply, creating a lot of very pointless work.

37   Memo, Knowles to Attorney-General, 3 January 1942, BC99460, NAA.

38   Memo, Knowles to Attorney-General, 3 January 1942, BC99460, NAA.

39   Memo to the Attorney-General Knowles, 24 April 1942, BC99461, NAA.

40   Memo to the Director, CIB, D.A. Alexander, 17 May 1943, BC99461, NAA.

41   Copy of letter GOC, Eastern Command, to Mr A. MacGillivray, 7 May 1942, BC99438, NAA, A467, SF43/13, Investigation into Jehovah's Witnesses, 7 Beresford Road, Strathfield.

42   Report, D.A. Alexander to Director, CIB, 9 May 1942, BC99438, NAA.

43   Statement of Claim, High Court of Australia, 4 September 1941, BC99461, NAA.

44   Cutting, 'Supreme Court Ends Compulsion of Flag Salute', *New York Times*, 15 June 1943, BC99461, NAA.

45   Notes, Knowles telephone conversation with Evatt, 23 December 1941, BC99462, NAA, A467, SF43/40.

46   Letter, W. MacKay to Commonwealth Crown Solicitor, 30 December 1941, BC100789, NAA, A472, W5107, Jehovah's Witnesses, Christmas Convention, Banning of, Instructions to Police.

47   Telegram, Knowles to H.G. Alderman, 10 September 1942, BC99462, NAA.

48   Telegram, D-G, Security to Knowles, 11 September 1942, BC99462, NAA.

49   Telegram, Knowles to NSW Police Commissioner, 27 December 1941, BC99462, NAA.

50   Deed of Release and Indemnity between Phillip David Morgan Rees and Commonwealth of Australia, 14 July 1943, BC99448, NAA.
51   Letter, W.J. Roberts, Crown Solicitor's Office, Brisbane, to Crown Solicitor, 12 October 1943, BC99448, NAA.

Chapter 14: Sad, Mad and Bad—The abuse of the AFM

1   Letter, D.R.B. Mitchell to Director, CIB, 22 July 1936, BC821583, NAA, A8911, 130.
2   BC821583, NAA.
3   Letter, Inquiry Officer W.H. Barnwell to Inspector, Sydney, 23 July 1936, and letter, Mitchell to Director, CIB 23 July 1936, BC821583, NAA.
4   Letter, Barnwell to Inspector, Sydney, 23 July 1936, and letter, Mitchell to Director, CIB, 23 July 1936, BC821583, NAA.
5   Letter, Barnwell to Inspector, Sydney, 23 July 1936, and letter Mitchell to Director, CIB, 23 July 1936, BC821583, NAA.
6   Letter, Barnwell to Inspector, Sydney, 14 June 1938, BC821583, NAA.
7   Letter, Barnwell to Inspector, Sydney, 14 June 1938, BC821583, NAA.
8   Letter, Barnwell to Inspector, Sydney, 10 October 1938, BC821583, NAA.
9   Letter, Barnwell to Inspector, Sydney, 1 November 1938, BC821583, NAA.
10   Letter, Minister for External Affairs to Director, CIB, 17 January 1938, BC821583, NAA.
11   Report, Director, CIB to Minister for External Affairs, 18 January 1939, BC821583, NAA.
12   Handwritten file note to Director, 5 September 1940, BC821583, NAA.
13   Letter, Inspector D. Mitchell, CIB to Attorney-General, 15 July 1940, BC821583, NAA.
14   Letter, Acting Inspector F.G. Galleghan to Director, CIB, 4 September 1940, BC821583, NAA.
15   Letter, C.B. Christesen to Officer-in-Charge, CIB, Brisbane, 6 March 1940, BC821583, NAA.
16   Letter, Wake to Inspector, CIB, Sydney, 7 March 1940, and reply Mitchell to Inspector, CIB, Brisbane, 12 March 1940, BC821583, NAA.
17   Letter, Secretary, Attorney-General's to Director, CIB, 30 October 1940, BC821583, NAA.
18   Report of Speeches, 12 November 1940, BC821583, NAA.
19   Report by V.R. Alldis, 20 January 1941, BC821583, NAA.
20   ISGS report, *The Publicist*, January 1941, BC821583, NAA.
21   ISGS report, *The Publicist*, January 1941, BC821583, NAA.
22   KV 4/453, Vols 1 and 2, NA, UK.
23   VENONA 77 and 78, 1 March 1945.
24   VENONA 324–325, 1 September 1945, A report on Australia's Security Intelligence System by BEN, Alfred Hughes.
25   Letter, Acting Inspector D.A. Alexander, CIB, Sydney, to Director, CIB, 31 October 1941, BC821583, NAA. Amusingly, the flyer advertising this meeting, which is appended to this letter, was 'one of many' left at the Imperial Services Club, the club for officers and ex-officers of the armed services in Sydney.
26   Letter, W.J. McKell Premier of New South Wales to John Curtin, Prime Minister, 26 November 1941, and MIPS report, 21 November 1941, BC274835, NAA, A1608, S39/2/3/, AFM. Part 1.
27   Report of Meeting Held at Australian Hall, Elizabeth, Sydney, on 5 November 1941 at 8 p.m. launching a series of meetings of The AFM, 5 November 1941, and letter, W. Barnwell to Inspector, CIB, Sydney, 6 November 1941, BC821583, NAA.
28   Cuttings 'Rally Ends in Uproar', *The Telegraph*, and 'Woman Speaker at Rowdy Meeting', *The Mirror*, both 13 November 1941, BC821583, NAA.

29 Brief on AFM, 6 November 1941, BC821583, NAA.
30 Letter, Acting Inspector, Sydney, to Director, CIB, 6 November 1941, BC821583, NAA.
31 BC821583, NAA. After a letter to the Director, CIB, 21 November 1941, an Army Central Registry File Cover dealing with the Seditious utterances of M.G. and R.H. Thiele is found in this file. After this, with the exception of a Military Intelligence report, 12 March 1942, all the correspondence is internal Security Service.
32 Letter, Director, Security Service to DMI, 28 January 1942, BC821583, NAA.
33 Letter, Director, Security Service to DMI, 28 January 1942, BC821583, NAA.
34 Application for Ministerial Order, 14 January 1942, B821583 NAA.
35 Letter, B. Tyrell, OIC, State Branch to Director, Security Service, 19 February 1942, and Statement of Mr P.L. Robbins to Director, Security Service, 11 February 1942, BC821583, NAA.
36 BC821583, NAA.
37 Letter, W.J. MacKay, Commissioner of Police to Under-Secretary, Chief Secretary's, 23 February 1942, BC274835, NAA.
38 Letter, Sir George Knowles to Secretary, Prime Minister's, 13 February 1942, BC274835, NAA.
39 Letter, Frank Forde to W.J. MacKay, 9 April 1942, BC217054, NAA.
40 Letter, Security Service, Perth, to Director, Security Service, Canberra, 13 March 1942, BC821578, NAA, A8911, 129. This letter calls the work done by the agent provocateur F.J. Thomas 'extraordinarily courageous and clever'.
41 Hasluck, *The Government and the People*, Vol. 2, p. 729.
42 Hasluck, *The Government and the People*, Vol. 2, p. 728, and 'Conspiracy Trial' 'Decoy Questioned', *West Australian*, 6 June 1942, p. 6 and 'Conspiracy Trial' 'Severe Cross Examination of Principal Crown Witnesses', *Kalgoorlie Miner*, 6 June 1942.
43 'Work for Police' 'Man's Story in Plot Case', *SMH*, 9 May 1942.
44 'Work for Police' 'Man's Story in Plot Case', *SMH*, 9 May 1942.
45 'Work for Police' 'Man's Story in Plot Case', *SMH*, 9 May 1942.
46 'Work for Police' 'Man's Story in Plot Case', *SMH*, 9 May 1942.
47 Inquiry into Matters Relating to the Detention of Certain Members of the 'AFM' Group, report of Commissioner (His Honour Mr Justice Clyne), 12 September 1945, BC274835, NAA.
48 Minutes of Meeting, 8 March 1942, BC821583, NAA.
49 Minutes of Meeting, 8 March 1942, BC821583, NAA.
50 Minutes of Meeting, 8 March 1942, BC821583, NAA.
51 Minutes of Meeting, 8 March 1942, BC821583, NAA.
52 Clyne Report, 12 September 1945 p. 7, BC274835, NAA.
53 Clyne Report, 12 September 1945 p. 9, BC274835, NAA.
54 'Conspiracy Case. Gaol Sentences', *West Australian*, 30 June 1942, p. 4.
55 'Conspiracy Case. Gaol Sentences', *West Australian*, 30 June 1942, p. 4.
56 There is a substantial level of hypocrisy surrounding these injustices. See BC734697, NAA, A432, 1945/875 PART 3, Part File. Evatt was never afraid to appoint men with safe hands to conduct his inquiries, Geoffrey Reed for Wake and Simpson for internees.
57 Letter, D-DS Sydney to D-G, Security, 22 September 1943, BC65442, NAA, A373, 4522B, Percy Reginald Stephensen.
58 Extract, Security Report No. 32, 12 March 1942, BC821583, NAA.
59 Minutes of Meeting, 8 March 1942, BC821583, NAA.
60 Sir Frederick Shedden later commented on the panic that affected the Curtin government at this time, even suggesting that there was talk of evacuating the government and its

departments to Wagga Wagga, away from the coast. There is some tantalising evidence of this in BC274835, NAA, Clyne Report, 12 September 1945, pp. 90 and 125.

61   Report on Activities of AFM Major Hattam to GSO (MI), Southern Command, 12 March 1942, p. 1, BC821583, NAA.

62   Hattam Report, p. 1, BC821583, NAA.

63   W.J. Miles was in fact dead by this time, Hattam Report, p. 2, BC821583, NAA.

64   Hattam Report, p. 1, BC821583, NAA.

65   Hattam Report, p. 3, BC821583, NAA.

66   Letter, R.H. Weddell, Victoria to Canberra, 16 March 1942, BC821583, NAA.

67   Reginald Powell was a militia officer and company director of Mosman whose file lists him as an expert in advertising, BC5601022, NAA, B884, N60119, Powell, Reginald, N60119.

68   Clyne Report, p. 7, BC274835, NAA.

69   Clyne Report, p. 7, BC274835, NAA.

70   Clyne Report, p. 7, BC274835, NAA.

71   Clyne Report, p. 7, BC274835, NAA. As the fallout from this action spread, the army moved Lieutenant Colonel Powell. See BC1134482, NAA, private letter, 31 May 1943, NX16460, Sergeant Michael Eugene Kartzoff to Lieutenant Colonel R. Wake. Kartzoff, who appears to have been an inquiry officer for MI in Sydney, mentions that Reg Powell was 'now being hounded out of the Service'. In his file, Powell appears to have been quickly transferred to HQ 2 Australian Corps on 9 April 1942.

72   Hasluck, *The Government and the People*, Vol. 2, p. 729.

73   Letter, W. MacKay, Director-General of Security to Attorney-General, 18 August 1942, BC821583, NAA.

74   Letter, Frank Forde, Minister for the Army to the Attorney-General, 31 July 1942, BC821583, NAA.

75   Letter, Frank Forde, BC821583, NAA.

76   Letter, Frank Forde, BC821583, NAA.

77   Letter, Frank Forde, BC821583, NAA.

78   *Hansard*, House of Representatives, Friday, 27 March 1942, p. 1, Mr William Morris Hughes.

79   *Hansard*, House of Representatives, 27 March 1942, p. 1, Mr William Morris Hughes. The more one listens to William Hughes, the worse he seems.

80   Letter, Percy Stephensen to Dr Evatt, 24 June 1934, BC821583, NAA.

81   Hasluck, *The Government and the People*, Vol. 2, p. 729.

82   Commonwealth of Australia, Statutory Rules 1939, No. 87, National Security (General) Regulations, Regulation 26, (1), (a), (b) and (c).

83   Clyne Report, p. 1, BC274835, NAA.

84   Clyne Report, pp. 1, 20, BC274835, NAA.

85   Evans, 'William John MacKay and the New South Wales Police Force', p. 209.

86   Minute, Knowles to Attorney-General, 9 March 1942, p. 14, BC1110955, NAA.

87   Letter, Director-General of Security to Minister for the Army, 22 May 1942, BC1110955, NAA. MacKay had an extensive private correspondence with Evatt in 1941 and 1942 prior to his appointment as D-G. See Letters, MacKay to Evatt, 12 January 1941, 30 December 1941, A472, W5107, Jehovah's Witnesses—Christmas Convention, BC100789, NAA, and two letters MacKay to Evatt, 17 November 1941, BC1110955, NAA.

88   Letter, D-G Security to Minister for the Army, 22 May 1942, BC1110955, NAA.

89   Letter, D-G Security to Minister for the Army, 22 May 1942, BC1110955, NAA.

90   Letter, Forde to MacKay, 9 April 1942, BC1110955, NAA.

91 Letter, Forde to MacKay, 9 April 1942, BC1110955, NAA.
92 Letter, Army Minister to D-G Security, 9 April 1942, p. 1, BC1110955, NAA.
93 Letter, Forde to MacKay, 9 April 1942, BC1110955, NAA.
94 War Cabinet minute (2067), 31 March 1942, BC674385, NAA.
95 J. Killen, *Killen*, Methuen Haynes, 1985, p. 19, and Hasluck, *Diplomatic Witness*, pp. 30–2.
96 Letter, D-G Security to M. Blackburn, MHR, 9 April 1943, A373, 4522B, Percy Stephensen, BC65442, NAA.
97 Minute, CGS to Secretary, Army, 4 August 1943, BC392061, NAA, MP742/1, 175/1/81, AFM—Harley Matthews.
98 Harley Matthews ex Australia First Internee, BC65437, NAA, A373, 4190.
99 BC65437, NAA.
100 BC65437, NAA.
101 BC65437, NAA.
102 Minute, Knowles to Secretary, Army, 3 November 1943, BC392061, NAA.
103 Clyne Report, BC274835, NAA.
104 BC5393481, NAA, A2700, 935, Australia First Inquiry—Report of Commissioner.
105 Clyne Report, p. 13, BC274835, NAA.
106 Civilian Internees, BC333541, NAA, A472, W29728 PART 1, Civilian Internees, BC396448, NAA, A472, W29728 PART 2, and Civilian Internees, BC734697, NAA.

Chapter 15: Russia's Intelligence Services and Their Work

1 Andrew, *The Defence of the Realm*, pp. 143–4.
2 Andrew, *The Defence of the Realm*, p. 144.
3 Andrew, *The Defence of the Realm*, p. 144.
4 Andrew, *The Defence of the Realm*, p. 145.
5 Andrew, *The Defence of the Realm*, p. 145.
6 Ewer, William Norman, Vol. 4, KV2/1016, NA, UK. William Ewer was not a working-class lad by any stretch of the imagination. Ironically, he had attended Cambridge University after going up from the Merchant Tailor's School in London and was the product of the upper-middle class and an intellectual.
7 Précis of Information, Folio 59p, 16 October 1925, KV 2/1016, Vol. 4, NA, UK.
8 Folio 5730a, undated, p. 1, KV 2/1016, Vol. 4, NA, UK.
9 Folio 5730a, undated, p. 1, KV 2/1016, Vol. 4, NA, UK.
10 Folio 5730a, undated, p. 1, KV 2/1016, Vol. 4, NA, UK.
11 Folio 5730a, undated, p. 2, KV 2/1016, Vol. 4, NA, UK.
12 Folio 5730a, undated, p. 3, KV2/1016, Vol. 4, NA, UK. Jack Hayes was never prosecuted because in 1923 he had been elected to parliament as the Labour Party member for Edge Hill and by 1924 was the Parliamentary Private Secretary to the Pensions Minister, Frederick Roberts and was later promoted to Vice-Chamberlain of the Household. Prosecuting Hayes was not a possibility at the time.
13 Andrew, *The Defence of the Realm*, p. 153.
14 BC3437986, NAA, PP246/4, RUSSIAN/MIKHEEV V, MIKHEEV, Vlademir.
15 'Russians Can Take Austerity', *Daily Telegraph*, 20 September 1942, p. 5.
16 Slang term made famous by John le Carré. It denotes the rigorous level of clandestine tradecraft required of HUMINT intelligence personnel when operating in an extremely hostile environment.
17 Kotkin, *Stalin 1929–1941*, pp. 588–90.
18 Kotkin, *Stalin 1929–1941*, p. 589.

19 Kotkin, *Stalin 1929–1941*, pp. 623–6.

20 Kotkin, *Stalin 1929–1941*, p. 589.

21 J.H. Haynes, H. Klehr and A. Vassiliev, *Spies*, Yale University Press, New Haven, CT, 2009, pp. 253–7, and S.T. Usdin, *Engineering Communism*, Yale University Press, New Haven, CT, 2005, p. 88.

22 Haynes, Klehr and Vassiliev, *Spies*, pp. 253–7, and Usdin, *Engineering Communism*, p. 88.

23 Birth Registration Number 1385/1914, https://familyhistory.bdm.nsw.gov.au/lifelink/familyhistory/search/result?4, accessed 12 June 2019.

24 Letter, H. Jones to Secretary, External Affairs, 1 April 1932, Franca Yakilnilin Mitynen—Miscellaneous Papers, BC4025406, NAA, A6119, 2853.

25 Letter, H. Jones to Secretary, External Affairs, 1 April 1932, BC4025406, NAA.

26 *Cumberland Argus and Fruitgrowers Advocate*, 31 August 1928, p. 20, and *Daily Telegraph*, 1 February 1928, p. 13.

27 *Government Gazette of New South Wales*, Sydney, 27 June 1918, No. 80 (Supplement), p. 2898.

28 Commonwealth Patents Applications Received, *Daily Commercial News and Shipping List*, Sydney, 5 December 1923, p. 11.

29 'Australasian Association for Economic Advancement of the USSR', *Workers' Weekly*, 29 July 1927, p. 4.

30 Bolshevism Russian Society in Brisbane, *The Sun*, 31 January 1919, p. 8.

31 'Sailing Today on the Kamo Maru', *Daily Telegraph*, 3 March 1934, p. 13.

32 BC4025406, NAA.

33 VENONA 1006, 10 June 1943.

34 VENONA 2505–2512, 31 December 1942.

35 Ancestry.com, 'Gay Trick in the 1940 Census', www.ancestry.com/1940-census/usa/Washington/Gay-Trick_285v6h.

36 Tombstone of Gay Shelton Patterson Trick, Acacia Memorial Park and Funeral Home, King County, Washington, USA, www.findagrave.com/memorial/85310237/gay-shelton-trick, accessed 13 June 2019. The Patterson family is well represented here with an Edna May Patterson also listed with date of death 1948. There is also a Margaret M. Sullivan Patterson date of death 1958 at Calvary Cemetery.

37 VENONA 1006, 10 June 1943. In this signal, Vorontsov in Moscow berates Egorichev in Washington for, among other things, using the NEIGHBOURS when 'you have so many people of your own'.

38 VENONA 2505–2512, 1040–1041, 13 May 1943 and 863, 17 May 1943. SALLY's shoe size was 36 (size 4).

39 VENONA 2505–2512.

40 VENONA 1006.

41 VENONA 1600, 12 July 1943, and 1902, 8 August (no year given).

42 VENONA 1348, 19 June 1943, and 1983, 14 August 1943.

43 VENONA 2124, 27 August 1943.

44 R.L. Benson, *The Venona Story*, Center for Cryptologic History, NSA, Fort Mead, MD, p. 2.

45 Benson, *The Venona Story*, p. 7.

46 Benson, *The Venona Story*, p. 2.

47 'Meredith Gardner', www.nsa.gov/About-Us/Current-Leadership/Article-View/Article/1622408/meredith-gardner/, accessed 15 February 2020.

48 VENONA 124, Moscow to Canberra, 21 August 1943, and 213, Moscow to Canberra, 30 August 1944.

49 VENONA 124.

50   VENONA 124. The signal uses 'you' in detailing the contact procedure for UNC44 and then goes on to provide instructions on other operations being overseen by the NKGB residency in Canberra. Thus, the signal must be to Makarov, the Resident.

51   VENONA 126, 21 August 1943.

52   VENONA 142, 12 September 1943.

53   Need-to-know is a policy that restricts access to those with a proven need to see information for their work. See VENONA 232–233, 3 December 1943.

54   VENONA 448, 31 October 1943, and 563, 31 December 1943.

55   VENONA 538, 31 December 1943, 1, 2 January 1944, and 212, 29 August 1944.

56   VENONA 1, 2 January 1944.

57   'French to Fight in Pacific', *The Sun*, 18 November 1944, p. 3.

58   VENONA 212, 29 August 1944.

59   VENONA 212, 29 August 1944.

60   VENONA 77 and 78, 1 March 1945.

61   VENONA 101, 19 March 1945.

62   VENONA 162–163, 23 May 1945.

63   VENONA 113, 13 June 1945.

64   VENONA 186, 7 September 1945.

65   VENONA 450, 14 November 1945.

66   VENONA 102, 9 March 1946.

67   VENONA 55, 13 March 1946.

Chapter 16: The KLOD Organisation—Walter Clayton and the CP-A

1   Cablegram High Commission, Wellington, 3 April 1957, BC8334740, NAA, A6119, 955, Clayton, W.S., Vol. 3, Part 2.

2   Personal Particulars, BC12234352, NAA, A6119, 953, Clayton, Walter Seddon, Vol. 1, Part 3.

3   Clayton was still an employee of the CP-A in 1959. See Non-Gratis Report, John Richard Kelly, 16 March 1959, BC1327922, NAA, A6119, 1597, Clayton, Walter Seddon, Vol. 9.

4   Personal particulars, BC12234352, NAA.

5   www.migrationheritage.nsw.gov.au/exhibition/objectsthroughtime/1893-the-new-australia-colony-collection/index.html, accessed 15 June 2019.

6   *The Southern Star*, Author Walter Seddon Clayton, Address Melbourne, BC3503440, NAA, A1336, 22357 and for a description of Clayton, ASIO Memo, Walter Seddon Clayton, 19 December 1955, p. 2, BC12234352, NAA, A6119, 953, Clayton, Walter Seddon (TS).

7   *The Beachcomber*, Author Walter Seddon Clayton, Address Melbourne, BC9598122, NAA, A1336, 2656.

8   Report to Director Security Service from Eastern Command, 23 June 1941, BC821420, NAA, A8911, 46, Communist Party of Australia, Activities.

9   Non-Gratis Report, controlled by Special Services Section, 2–4 October 1960, f. 62, BC1327922, NAA.

10   VENONA 213, 30 August 1944.

11   VENONA 96, 17 March 1945. Care needs to be exercised with this signal as the relevant parts are corrupted and specific details are missing; however, there is no mistaking the tone of concern over Hughes' morality.

12   VENONA 129, 25 April 1945 and www.builtheritage.com.au/dua_pynor.html, accessed 14 June 2019.

13 Frances Ada Scott had a multitude of names, but mostly innocently. Her parents' name was Scott, which she later chose to abandon in favour of Bernie, the name of an A. Bernie, one of the two witnesses at her wedding and perhaps her real father. The name Bernie has been misspelt Birney, Burney and Burny in Australian files and NKGB signals. The correct spelling is Bernie. As for her married name, Gluck, both her husband and she changed their name by deed poll to Garrett.

14 Briefing note, 28 September 1949, BC12095329, NAA, A6119, 794, Frances Ada Gluck (aka Garrett, aka Bernie) nee Scott, Vol. 1.

15 Briefing note, 7 July 1949, BC12095329, NAA.

16 Letter, McMaster, Holland & Co., Solicitors, 21 October 1954, BC12095341, NAA, A6119, 799, Frances Ada Gluck (aka Garrett, aka Bernie) nee Scott, Vol. 6.

17 Statement by Frances Ada Garrett, pp. 3–4, BC12095341, NAA. It appears that when Frances became ill, she stated that she returned to her parents' house to recuperate. The use of the plural would suggest this was the Scott's home.

18 Reports to Sergeant Campbell from Alfred T. Hughes and A.L. Walsh, 30 April 1943 and 14 October 1943, BC12095329, NAA.

19 Letter, Deputy Director, Security Service, New South Wales to Director-General of Security, June 1945, BC12095329, NAA.

20 Report by R. Gamble, ASIO, 7 July 1949, BC12095329, NAA. The report makes it clear that the wedding was a small affair and it does not mention the Scotts as being present.

21 Letter, Frances Garrett (Gluck) to Director-General of Security, 25 May 1945, BC12095329, NAA.

22 Report for Sergeant Campbell, 26 July 1943, BC12095341, NAA.

23 Compare statements 11 March 1955 in which Hughes admits knowing Frances Scott and telephone exchanges with ASIO officers denying such, BC12095341, NAA. Also, Security Service Report, International Youth Committee, for Sergeant Campbell signed by A.T. Hughes, 14 October 1943, BC12095329, NAA.

24 Statement by Frances Garrett, pp. 3–4, BC12095341, NAA.

25 Statement by Frances Garrett, pp. 4–5, BC12095341, NAA

26 Extract of debriefing of V. Petrov, 6 April 1954, BC12095341, NAA.

27 Report by J.M. Gilmour, 17 November 1959, BC12095329, NAA.

28 Report by J.M. Gilmour, 17 November 1959, BC12095329, NAA.

29 Marginal notes on report by J.M. Gilmour, 17 November 1959, BC12095329, NAA.

30 Report on Frances Ada Garrett nee Burnie by J.M. Gilmour, 17 November 1959, BC12095329, NAA.

31 Extracts from debrief of V. Petrov, 6 April 1954, BC12095341, NAA.

32 VENONA 141, 5 May 1945.

33 VENONA 141, 5 May 1945.

34 VENONA 121, 1 July 1945.

35 VENONA 197, 3 July 1945.

36 VENONA 198, 3 July 1945.

37 VENONA 127, 7 July 1945.

38 VENONA 324–325, 1 September 1945.

39 VENONA 324–325, 1 September 1945.

40 VENONA 324–325, 1 September 1945.

41 VENONA 324–325, 1 September 1945.

42 VENONA 193, 15 September 1945.

43 VENONA 193, 15 September 1945.

44 Mitrokhin and Andrew, *The Mitrokhin Archive*, pp. 80–3.

45 VENONA 200, 20 September 1945.
46 VENONA 245, 28 October 1945.
47 VENONA 413, 414 and 420, 31 October 1945.
48 VENONA 431, 8 November 1945. There is no record of service for a Stuart Henry Moore in the Australian Army in the National Archives of Australia. The only record for a Stuart Henry Moore is for a man who retired from the RAN as a chief petty officer in 1925.
49 VENONA 266, 30 November 1945.
50 VENONA 363, 30 September 1945.
51 VENONA 363, 30 September 1945.
52 VENONA 363, 30 September 1945.
53 VENONA 363, 30 September 1945.
54 VENONA 268, 10 August 1945.
55 VENONA 155, 18 August 1945.
56 VENONA 215, 6 October 1945.
57 VENONA 390, 15 October 1945.
58 VENONA 235, 20 October 1945.
59 VENONA 235, 20 October 1945.
60 VENONA 235, 20 October 1945.
61 VENONA 236, 21 October 1945.
62 VENONA 431, 8 November 1945.
63 VENONA 473, 7 December 1945.
64 VENONA 1, 8 January 1946, and 43, 16 February 1946, and 44, 17 February 1946.
65 VENONA 100, 8 March 1946.
66 VENONA 101, 8 March 1946.
67 VENONA 123, 19 March 1946.
68 See Fahey, *Australia's First Spies*, p. 252.
69 See Fahey, *Australia's First Spies*, p. 253.
70 See Fahey, *Australia's First Spies*, pp. 256–7.
71 See Fahey, *Australia's First Spies*, p. 257.
72 Horner, *The Spy Catchers*, Allen & Unwin, Sydney, 2014, p. 340.
73 VENONA 101, 8 March 1946.
74 VENONA 55, 13 March 1946.
75 VENONA 56, 13 March 1946.
76 VENONA 65, 22 March 1946.
77 VENONA 123, 19 March 1946.
78 Benson, *The Venona Story*, p. 2.
79 VENONA 123, 19 March 1946.
80 VENONA 215, 6 May 1946.
81 VENONA 76, 1 April 1946.
82 VENONA 265, 30 November 1946.
83 VENONA 121, 30 May 1946.
84 VENONA 121, 30 May 1946.
85 VENONA 162, 1 August 1946.
86 VENONA 185, 1 September 1946.
87 VENONA 186, 5 September 1946.
88 Pavel Mikhailovich Fitin was a professional intelligence officer who barely escaped execution for insisting that Hitler was about to launch Operation Barbarossa. In fact, the launch of the attack on 22 June 1944 is what saved his life. He was then left to run 1st Directorate until mid-1946, when he was removed and demoted. He was subsequently

sacked after Beria fell in 1953, and was denied his pension. Spitefully, he was banned from working until 1959. See VENONA 220, 9 October 1946. Kubatkin fared worse than Fitin and was arrested on 23 July 1949 and condemned to twenty years in the Gulag. This didn't suit Stalin, and he was condemned to death on 27 October 1950.

89   VENONA 220, 9 October 1946.
90   VENONA 220, 9 October 1946.
91   VENONA 220, 9 October 1946.
92   VENONA 243, 24 October 1946.
93   Benson, *The Venona Story*, pp. 1–3.
94   Benson, *The Venona Story*, p. 7.
95   VENONA 12, 18 January 1947.
96   VENONA 265, 30 November 1946, and 132, 7 June 1947.
97   Ball and Horner, *Breaking the Codes*, pp. 144–5.
98   VENONA 7–8, 9 January 1947.
99   VENONA 7–8, 9 January 1947.
100 VENONA 246, 9 December 1947.
101 VENONA 246, 9 December 1947. This change, although temporary, meant the 1st Directorate had four different bosses between August 1946 and February 1948. This cannot have done much for the smooth running of the directorate. The absence of Fedotov may have been due to the forced abdication of King Michael of Romania and the communist takeover of that country in December 1947 and the similar seizure of power in the Czechoslovakian coup d'état of February 1948.
102 VENONA 22, 17 February 1948.
103 VENONA 34, 8 March 1948.
104 VENONA 47, 26 March 1948. This signal is a very small fragment.
105 VENONA 92, 16 May 1948, and Horner, *The Spy Catchers*, p. 300.
106 VENONA 104, 5 June 1948.
107 VENONA 63, 15 April 1948.

Chapter 17: The Melbourne Connection

1   Debrief of V. Petrov, Spool 217, 13 April 1954, A6119, 1247/REFERENCE COPY, NOSOV, Feodor Andreevich, folio 32, BC1116109, NAA.
2   Log, 17 December 1949, A6119, 1248/REFERENCE COPY, NOSOV, Feodor Andreevich, folio 32, BC1116109, NAA.
3   Linux Security Solutions, Hacking Exposed Linux, p. 298, https://archive.org/details/hackingexposedli00hatc_0/page/298, accessed 2 January 2020.
4   C. Andrew, *The Secret World*, Allen Lane, London, 2018, pp. 593, 662.
5   Log, 17 December 1949, folio 32, BC1116109, NAA.
6   Mitrokhin and Andrew, *The Mitrokhin Archive*, p. 50.
7   Debrief of General Walter Germanovich Krivitsky, January–February 1940 and letter from H.V. Johnson, American Embassy, London, to Guy Liddell, MI5, 7 June 1938, KV2/1655, NA, UK.
8   Letter, H. Johnson to Guy Liddell, 7 June 1938, KV2/1655, NA, UK.
9   KV2/1655, NA, UK and Committee on Un-American Activities, US House of Representatives (not the Senate committee of Senator Joseph McCarthy), *The Shameful Years*, US Government Printing Office, Washington, 1952, p. 20.
10 Letter from N.D. Borum, American Embassy, London, to Sir Vernon Kell, MI5, 29 September 1938, and identifying Purpiss and Glucksmann as GRU operatives, letter to L.W. Clayton,

Home Office, 18 May 1940 from Watt, and letter to H.V. Johnson, 7 June 1940, KV2/1655, NA, UK. Glucksmann was killed in 1940 when a ship transporting enemy internees, the *Arandora Star*, was sunk by the German U-boat ace, Gunter Prien on 2 July 1940, Report on WOSTWAG and its Associated Companies, p. 8, KV2/1655, NA, UK.

11   Incoming Passenger List for MONCALIERI arriving Melbourne, 4 August 1924, A907, 1924/8/40, BC9571815, NAA.

12   Letter, Jack Skolnik to General Thomas Blamey,1 April 1940, BC12085117, NAA.

13   Report to D-G Security, 13 January 1943, BC12085117, NAA.

14   Report to D-G Security, 13 January 1943, BC12085117, NAA.

15   F.M. Cutlack, *The Australian Flying Corps in the Western and Eastern Theatres of War 1914–1918*, Angus & Robertson, Sydney, 1933, p. 65.

16   Cutlack, *The Australian Flying Corps*, p. 65.

17   BC12085117, NAA, A6119, 251/REFERENCE COPY, SKOLNIK, Jack, Vol. 1.

18   Letter, DD-S, Victoria to DG-S, 19 March 1942, and Letter to Regional Director, Victoria BC12085117, NAA.

19   Transcripts of intercepts in BC12085117, NAA.

20   Application for Passport, folio 29, 8 January 1945, BC8334724, NAA, A6119, 925/REFERENCE COPY, Solomon KOSKY, Vol. 1.

21   Letter, DD, CIS, Melbourne to Director CIS, 17 December 1948, BC994003, NAA.

22   Letter, DD, CIS, Melbourne to Director CIS, 17 December 1948, BC994003, NAA.

23   Letter, DD, CIS, Melbourne to Director CIS, 21 December 1948, BC994003, NAA.

24   Letter, DD, CIS, Melbourne to Director CIS, 21 December 1948, BC994003, NAA.

25   Letter, D-CIS to DD, CIS, Melbourne, 30 December 1948, BC994003, NAA.

26   Letter, DD, CIS, Melbourne to Director CIS, 2 February 1949, BC994003, NAA.

27   Operation TOURIST, Senior Field Officer Report, 9 September 1952, BC994003, NAA.

28   Operation TOURIST Report, 9 September 1952, BC994003, NAA.

29   Operation TOURIST Report, 9 September 1952, BC994003, NAA.

30   Memo to Headquarters ASIO, from Regional director, Victoria, 11 September 1952, BC994003, NAA.

31   Surveillance Report, 5 September 1952, BC994003, NAA.

32   Operation TOURIST Report, 9 September 1952, BC994003, NAA.

33   Solomon Kosky, Briefing Note, Petrov Interrogation, 20 May 1954, pp. 1–2, BC8334724, NAA, A6119, 925/REFERENCE COPY, Solomon KOSKY, Vol. 1.

34   Solomon Kosky, Briefing Note, Petrov Interrogation, 20 May 1954, p. 1, and notes at folio 127, BC8334724, NAA.

35   Debriefing notes, V. Petrov, 12 September 1954, p. 4, BC1116110, NAA, A6119, 1247/REFERENCE COPY, NOSOV, Feodor Andreevich, Vol. 2.

36   Briefing Paper, 21 December 1948, BC994003, NAA.

37   Briefing Paper from D.A. Alexander to Director, 21 December 1948, BC994003, NAA and Statutory Declaration by Hirsch Munz, 16 December 1932, BC1123987, NAA, A1, 1933/792, Hirsch MUNZ—Naturalization.

38   Report by Inspector R. Browne, 6 January 1933, BC1123987, NAA. Icheskiel was admitted to Australia and, interestingly, between 1927 and 1929 both Hirsch and Icheskiel applied for the admission of one Alfred Lipshut, who is described in the files as being both Polish and Palestinian. See A261, 1927/1693, BC8163080, NAA, A261, 1928/877, BC8161278, NAA and BC8161673, NAA, A261, 1929/645. It also appears that Icheskiel enlisted in the Australian Army. See BC5577847, NAA, B884, N191638, MUNZ Isac.

39   Report by Inspector R. Browne, 6 January 1933, BC1123987, NAA.

40   BC1123987, NAA, A1, 1933/792, Hirsch MUNZ—Naturalization.

41 Report on Application for Naturalization by Hirsch Munz, 11 January 1933, BC1123987, NAA.
42 Letter from Deputy Director, Victoria to Director CIS, 21 December 1948, BC994003, NAA, A6119, 925, Solomon Kosky, Vol. 1.
43 Letter from Deputy Director, Victoria to Director CIS, 21 December 1948, BC994003, NAA.
44 Letter, Inspector D.R.B. Mitchell to Munz, 2 June 1938 and letter, R.S. Browne to Inspector-in-Charge, 7 December 1938, BC1118736, NAA, A6119/79, 1304/REFERENCE COPY, MUNZ, Hirsch.
45 Letter, Major Scott to Military Intelligence, Army HQ, 17 September 1939, BC1118736, NAA.
46 Report, Constable A.G. Clark to Inspector Keefe, 8 September 1939, BC1118736, NAA.
47 Undated note by B. Tyrell, f. 39, BC1118736, NAA.
48 Letter, Major Scott to Police HQ, Sydney, Army HQ, 12 October 1939, BC1118736, NAA.
49 Letter, Military Intelligence, Eastern Command to Police HQ, 12 January 1939, BC1118736, NAA.
50 MUNZ H, MUNZ HIRSCH RANVR Record of Mobilised Service, BC5332357, NAA, A6769.
51 MUNZ H, RANVR Officers Personnel Record, BC30926355, NAA, A3978.
52 BC5332357, NAA, A6769, MUNZ H.
53 BC30926355, NAA, A3978.
54 Supersession of Commanding Officer of SI(A)BC30926355, NAA.
55 Telephone intercept, 15 March 1957, of call F.R. Smith and David Morris, BC4358172, NAA. Faraday cages prevent electronic eavesdropping by blocking electromagnetic fields and are used to protect electronic equipment, which emit radiation. For example, data on a television or computer screen used outside a Faraday cage can be intercepted and read in a vehicle across the street.
56 Report of interview with David John Morris on 21 March 1957, dated 12 August 1957, BC4358172, NAA.
57 Report Inspector Wake to D-CIS, 20 October 1936 and Summary, Folio 2, BC4358173, NAA, A6119, 61, MORRIS, David John, Vol. 1.
58 Letter, Sir Vernon Kell, MI5 to Colonel Jones, Canberra, 25 January 1937, BC4358173, NAA.
59 Application for Passport, 27 October 1936, BC4358173, NAA.
60 Letter, Wake to D-CIS, 17 November 1936, BC4358173, NAA.
61 Letter, Sir Vernon Kell, MI5 to Colonel Jones, Canberra, 6 March 1939, BC4358173, NAA.
62 Letter, D-CIS to Inspector in Charge, Brisbane, 2 May 1937, BC4358173, NAA.
63 Personal Particulars, David John Morris, folio 61, BC4358173, NAA.
64 Particulars of Soldier, folio 49, BC4358173, NAA, and Statement of R.A. Nairn, 30 March 1955, BC4358172, NAA, A6119, 263, MORRIS, David John, Vol. 2.
65 Particulars of Soldier, folio 49, BC4358173, NAA.
66 Memorandum, Chief Engineer, State Electricity Commission of Victoria, 17 October 1946, BC4358173, NAA.
67 Memorandum, Chief Engineer, State Electricity Commission of Victoria, 17 October 1946, BC4358173, NAA.
68 Memo for Record Purposes by R. Wake, 23 August 1946. BC4358173, NAA.
69 Letter, DD-CIS, Victoria to D-CIS, 5 April 1949, BC4358173, NAA.
70 Memo, J. Wigglesworth to DMGO, 30 April 1949, BC4358173, NAA.
71 Evaluation report, Tasmania, Political, 24 June 1959, BC30485603, NAA, A6119, 5794, MORRIS, David John, Vol. 3.

72   Transcript of telephone intercept, 31 August 1970, BC14306175, NAA, A6119, 7062, MORRIS, Bernice Merle (nee McCoy), Vol. 1.

73   Transcript of telephone intercept, 31 August 1970, BC14306175, NAA.

74   Operation Pigeon, Interview of David John Morris, 12 August 1957, BC4358172, NAA, A6119, 263, MORRIS, David John, Vol. 2. The ASIO interviewer formed the view from Morris's behaviour that he had been warned that the interview was to be conducted. If so, there was a leak inside ASIO. ASIO did not obtain the work documentation from Morris's firm showing exactly what it was that Industrial Plant Propriety Ltd built for Mrs Skolnik. Apparently, all the work was for her, not her husband. Another element of note is that Jack Skolnik always used his business address of 67 Queens Road, Melbourne, as his address for all official purposes including giving this as his residential address in Evidence at the RCE on 1 November 1954. BC12085116, NAA, A6119, 252/ REFERENCE COPY, SKOLNIK, Jack, Vol. 2. It was as if Heyington Place was off limits, compartmentalised outside of his professional life.

75   File note of telephone intercept, 21 March 1957, BC4358172, NAA.

76   Letter, H. Johnson, American Embassy, London, to Guy Liddell, MI5, 16 July 1938, KV2/1902, NA, UK.

Chapter 18: Are We in Hell? The fruits of inaction

1   Minute by the Chiefs of Staff at Meeting Held on 4 July 1946, KV5/454, Vol. 2, NA, UK.

2   Brief for the Delegation, KV 5/454, Vol. 2, NA, UK.

3   Cabinet Agendum, Joint Intelligence Organisation—Post War, KV 5/454, Vol. 2, NA, UK.

4   Cabinet Agendum 1213, Joint Intelligence Organisation—Post War, 19 July 1946, KV 5/454, Vol. 2, NA, UK.

5   Cabinet Agendum, 19 July 1946, p. 3, KV 5/454, Vol. 2, NA, UK.

6   Cabinet Agendum, 19 July 1946, p. 3, KV 5/454, Vol. 2, NA, UK.

7   Cabinet Agendum, 19 July 1946, p. 3, KV 5/454, Vol. 2, NA, UK.

8   Cabinet Agendum, 19 July 1946, p. 4, KV 5/454, Vol. 2, NA, UK.

9   Cabinet Agendum, 19 July 1946, p. 6, KV 5/454, Vol. 2, NA, UK.

10   Cabinet Agendum, 19 July 1946, p. 6, KV 5/454, Vol. 2, NA, UK.

11   Cabinet Agendum, 19 July 1946, p. 10, KV 5/454, Vol. 2, NA, UK.

12   See Fahey, Australia's First Spies, pp. 231–46.

13   BC6389615, NAA, and Ballard, On ULTRA Active Service, pp. 71–3.

14   Ballard, On ULTRA Active Service, pp. 71–2.

15   Ballard, On ULTRA Active Service, p. 72.

16   D. Alvarez, Allied and Axis Signals Intelligence in World War II, Frank Cass, London, 1999, p. 97, and Ballard, On ULTRA Active Service, p. 136.

17   Ballard, On ULTRA Active Service, p. 136.

18   BC6389615, NAA.

19   BC6389615, NAA.

20   Japan's rapid destruction of British power in Asia and the Pacific was not unwelcomed in Washington. Up until the defeat of Germany in Europe, Britain's only leverage in Washington on matters affecting the Pacific and Asia was intelligence. The result of this was that MI6 invested assets and resources in countering US influence in South-East Asia generally and Roy Kendall in Brisbane ran this work. Commander A.E.N. Merry in Melbourne and other MI6 personnel performed other, unidentified, work; however, the relationship between MI6 and the US authorities was one of ensuring the self-interests of their governments were protected first.

21 F.W. Winterbotham, *The ULTRA Secret*, Harper and Row, London, 1974, p. 172.
22 The SLO was the senior officer commanding and SLU the unit to which all SIGINT and ULTRA intelligence was sent. Most SLU personnel for British Commonwealth forces, including Australia, were RAF.
23 Airy Report, 1944, p. 5, KV4/453, Vol. 1, NA, UK. Airy reported to the Director-General of MI5 that there was no cooperation between MI6 and the Australian Security Service, and that Brigadier William Simpson did not understand MI6's role. He also reported that Kendall and Walker were extremely distrustful of the Security Service and especially, 'with some reason', distrustful of Wake. The relationship between Roy Kendall and Mic Sandford was professionally very close. They shared the same house as living quarters in Brisbane and Kendall would not have missed the relationship between Sandford and Sandford's soldier-servant (Batman), as well as his association with the artist Donald Friend among others.
24 Airy Report, 1944, p. 5, KV4/453, NA, UK.
25 Airy Report, 1944, p. 5, KV4/453, NA, UK.
26 Airy Report, 1944, p. 5, KV4/453, Vol. 1, NA, UK.
27 Telegram 38/89, W104, 26 April 1941, BC257498, NAA.
28 S.A. Maneki, *The Quiet Heroes of the Southwest Pacific Theater*, Center for Cryptologic History, NSA, Fort Meade, MD, 2007, p. 55.
29 Memorandum, Fabian to McCollum, 29 January 1943, A1/27, 5500/1 FRUMEL (Fleet Radio Unit, Melbourne, Australia) SECURITY, NAI6230486, Declassification Authority 003012, National Archives, College Park, MD.
30 JSC 86/1, Agreement between OSS and SOE, 26 August 1942, A7-2, CINCPAC FILES 1943, Censorship, declassification No. NND745002, National Archives, College Park, MD.
31 BC3023506, NAA, A6923, 37/401/425, Special Intelligence Section, GCS Branch SIGINT.
32 Letter, Consul Hubert Graves to Lieutenant Colonel Little, 10 June 1943, BC3023506, NAA,
33 Signal CXG 613, Sandford to 'C' as Chairman of 'Y' Board and Director of GC&CS, 29 July 1943, HW 52/93, NA, UK.
34 Signal CXG 613, 29 July 1943, HW 52/93, NA, UK.
35 'To Celebrate Soviet Treaty', *Daily Telegraph*, 25 May 1943, p. 4.
36 Personal, *The Courier-Mail*, 18 June 1943, p. 4, Special Advertisements, *West Australian*, 14 December 1943, p. 2 and 'The Soviet Comes to Canberra', *The Herald*, 22 April 1944, p. 9.
37 Massachusetts Institute of Technology, AFSOR 70-1139 TR, *Biographical Index of Soviet Intelligence Personnel, Appendix C, Soviet Clandestine Communication Nets*, Behavioural Science Division, Air Force Office of Scientific Research, SRLB, P.C-115.
38 R. Deacon, *A History of the Japanese Secret Service*, Frederick Muller, Wimbledon, 1982, pp. 202–8.
39 'Communications All Through Usual Telegraph Channels', *The Age*, 6 July 1954, p. 5.
40 'Soviet Legation Emphasises Family Ties', *The Mercury*, 8 May 1944, p. 3.
41 A. Best, *British Intelligence and the Japanese Challenge in Asia, 1914–1941*, Palgrave-Macmillan, Basingstoke, 2002, p. 179.
42 Massachusetts Institute of Technology, *Biographical Index*, P.C-115. The assessment in this document suggests that Yury V. Zajtsev, a senior officer in the Agitprop Section of the Central Committee in January 1966 who had been expelled from the United States on 8 July 1962, was his son. See Foreign Affairs Note, *Expulsion of Soviet Officials Worldwide*, 1986, US Department of State, Washington, DC, January 1987. If so, it appears that Victor Zajtsev had a successful career in the GRU.
43 'Migrant Work Claimed as Cover to Intelligence Officers', *The Telegraph*, 2 July 1954, p. 2.

44 VENONA 131 and 132, 7 June 1947 as an example.
45 KV2/1655, Far Eastern Fur Trading Company, NA, UK.
46 Signal CXG 613, 29 July 1943, HW 52/93, NA, UK.
47 In discussing SIGINT product only SIGINT produced in the UK, under London's control, was termed ULTRA. That produced in Delhi was SIRDAR; Melbourne, Brisbane and Washington was ZYMOTIC; Soviet SIGINT was ARSENIC; and that from the Middle East theatre, SWELL. See Minute, Sandford for DMI, 29 October 1943, BC3023487, NAA, A6923, SI/10, Australian Military Forces DMI Central Bureau. This differentiation was dropped in November 1943 and ULTRA became the standard codeword. Minute, Sandford to DMI, 21 November 1943, BC3023487, NAA.
48 Signal CXG 613, 29 July 1943, HW 52/93, NA, UK.
49 Signal 655, to Chairman 'Y' Board, undated, referencing Sandford signal, 5 September 1943, National Archives, HW 52/93, NA, UK.
50 Signal SJ 195, undated, but references a signal Sandford sent on 5 September 1943 to Brisbane, HW 52/93.
51 Letter, A. Sandford to DMI, 2 April 1945, BC3023441, NAA, and Best, *British Intelligence*, p. 171.
52 Kotani, *Japanese Intelligence in World War II*, pp. 20–1.
53 See Fahey, *Australia's First Spies*, pp. 247–62.
54 Resume of Significant and Interesting Items SWPA, 13 December 1944, p. 2, BC3023441, NAA.
55 Raw 'Take' of IJA General Broadcast from GHQ, Tokyo 11 November 1944 and Resume of Significant and Interesting Items SWPA, 13 December 1944, p. 2, BC3023441, NAA.
56 Resume of Significant and Interesting Items SWPA, 13 December 1944, p. 2, BC3023441, NAA.
57 Signal, MIS 568, 2 April 1943, BC3023441, NAA.
58 Ball and Horner, *Breaking the Codes*, pp. 82–5.
59 www.cia.gov/library/center-for-the-study-of-intelligence/csi-publications/books-and-monographs/venona-soviet-espionage-and-the-american-response-1939-1957/preface.htm, accessed 10 July 2019.
60 Kotani, *Japanese Intelligence in World War II*, pp. 36–7.
61 Letter, Sandford to Little, 19 December 1944, BC3023441, NAA.
62 Letter, Sandford to DMI, 25 January 1945, BC3023441, NAA.
63 Letter, Sandford to DDMI, Lieutenant Colonel R.A. Little, 19 December 1944, BC3023441, NAA.
64 Letter, Sandford to DDMI, 19 December 1944, BC3023441, NAA.
65 Letter, Sandford to DDMI, Lieutenant Colonel R.A. Little, 25 December 1944, BC3023441, NAA.
66 Raw 'Take' of signal Tokyo to Palau, 10, 19 November, 16, 24, 26, 27, 29 December 1944, BC3023441, NAA.
67 Ball and Horner, *Breaking the Codes*, p. 86.
68 Ball and Horner, *Breaking the Codes*, pp. 152–3.
69 See Cabinet Minutes September 1939—February 1940, Minutes 14 February 1940, BC689088, NAA, A5954, 803/2 and BC640278, NAA, A5954, 429/15, Internal Security Leakages of Military Information December 1944 to January 1945. The laxity extended from the governments of Lyons to Chifley.
70 VENONA 68, Moscow to All Residencies (including Canberra), 10 April 1945.
71 VENONA 197 and 198, 3 July 1945.
72 VENONA 47, Moscow to London, 18 September 1945.

Chapter 19: A Way Back

1 Airy Report, 1944, p. 5, KV4/453, Vol. 1, NA, UK.
2 Airy Report, 1944, KV4/453, Vol. 1, NA, UK.
3 Airy Report, 1944, KV4/453, Vol. 1, NA, UK.
4 Airy Report, 1944, p. 6, KV4/453, Vol. 1, NA, UK.
5 Airy Report, 1944, p. 5, KV4/453, Vol. 1, NA, UK.
6 Minute 5, D. Petrie, 8 November 1944, KV4/453, NA, UK.
7 Minute 5, D. Petrie, 8 November 1944, KV4/453, NA, UK.
8 Minute 5, D. Petrie, 8 November 1944, KV4/453, NA, UK.
9 Winterbotham, *The Ultra Secret*, pp. 168–76.
10 GC&CS Signal, SW 43, 26 March 1945, BC3023487, NAA. SLUs and their personnel were centrally administered by the Y Board through its own administrative system—they only operated within a command or theatre and were not commanded, controlled or seconded in any way to the local commanders. Effectively, they were outside the authority of all Allied commanders at all levels.
11 Letter, Sandford to Little, 2 February 1945, BC3023441, NAA.
12 War Cabinet Agendum 24/1945, Submission by H.V. Evatt, Attorney-General, Military Personnel Attached to Commonwealth Security Service, 8 January 1945, BC7564965, NAA, A2671, 24/1945, War Cabinet Agendum No 24/1945.
13 Supplement No. 1, War Cabinet Agendum 24/1945, BC7564965, NAA.
14 File note in Little's hand, re 'D' Intelligence and the DG Security, 2 February 1945, BC3023441, NAA.
15 File note in Little's hand, re 'D' Intelligence and the DG Security, 2 February 1945, and note in Little's hand on p. 2 of letter, Sandford to Little, 2 February 1945, BC3023441, NAA.
16 Letter, General Blamey to DG Security, 25 January 1945, BC3023441, NAA.
17 For examples of this see Fahey, *Australia's First Spies*, pp. 177–80. Wake's attempts to impose himself upon the coastwatch organisation, FERDINAND, commanded by Eric Feldt on behalf of the ACNB, was particularly egregious.
18 Letter, Blamey to DG Security, 25 January 1945, BC3023441, NAA.
19 Minute, Burley to Winterbotham, Blamey, 1 February 1945, BC3023441, NAA.
20 Minute, Burley to Winterbotham, Blamey, 1 February 1945, BC3023441, NAA.
21 Minute, Burley to Winterbotham, Blamey, 1 February 1945, BC3023441, NAA.
22 Minute, Burley to Winterbotham, Blamey, 1 February 1945, BC3023441, NAA.
23 File note in Little's hand, re 'D' Intelligence and the DG Security, 2 February 1945, BC3023441, NAA.
24 File note by Little, 2 February 1945, BC3023441, NAA.
25 Note by Little on letter from Sandford to Little, 5 February 1945, BC3023441, NAA.
26 Letter, Blamey to D-G Security, 19 February 1945, BC3023441, NAA.
27 BC3023441, NAA.
28 This can justifiably be regarded as a waste of time if you consider the Allied Control Council had to deal with the US government's plans and then those of the new shogun, General MacArthur. Frankly, this writer cannot think of a more pointless job.
29 Letter, Courtenay Young to Dick White, 24 August 1946, KV4/454, NA, UK.
30 Letter, Courtenay Young to Dick White, 24 August 1946, KV4/454, NA, UK.
31 Draft letter, 5 April 1946, to Rowland Browne from David Petrie, KV4/453, NA, UK.
32 Letter, Courtenay Young to Dick White, 24 August 1946, KV4/454, NA, UK.
33 Letter, Lieutenant Colonel Jackson in Australia to Commander Guernsey, Intelligence Division, SACSEA, mentioned in file note, 23 August 1946, KV4/453, NA, UK.

34 Transcript of Evidence, Sir Charles Spry, 27 February 1976, p. 610, Hope Royal Commission into Intelligence and Security, BC4751094, NAA.

35 Minute by the Chiefs of Staff at Meeting held on 4 July 1946, KV4/454, NA, UK. Eric Nave, Royal Navy, attended as part of the Australian delegation despite the fact he was a British officer not an Australian one. Mic Sandford was most likely the main Australian representative as he travelled to the United Kingdom on special duty on 16 February 1946 and returned on 28 April 1946. See BC6389615, NAA. There is little doubt in this writer's mind that Sandford, Australia's most senior SIGINT officer, was the father of the DSB.

36 Letter, Major General R. Dewing to General John Kennedy, 2 June 1944, WO106/4847, NA, UK.

37 Letter, Major General R. Dewing to General John Kennedy, 2 June 1944, WO106/4847, NA, UK.

38 Letter, Courtenay Young to Dick White, 24 August 1946, KV4/454, NA, UK.

39 Signal, High Commissioner for Canada in Australia, 27 May 1947, KV4/454, NA, UK.

40 Letter, Courtenay Young to Dick White, 24 August 1946, KV4/454, NA, UK.

41 Cabinet Agendum 1213, 19 July 1946, p. 11, KV4/454, NA, UK.

42 Transcript of Evidence, Sir Charles Spry, 27 February 1976, p. 610, BC4751094, NAA.

43 Evatt's role in undermining the creation of an effective security intelligence organisation is well documented in the files in the National Archives of Australia. See BC4725226, NAA, A12389, A13 PART 1, The Circumstances Leading to the Foundation of ASIO, BC1067010, NAA, A6122, 1428, Circumstances Leading to the Establishment of ASIO, and BC227921, NAA.

44 See letter, Roger Hollis to Guy Liddell at MI5, 13 March 1948, KV4/450, NA, UK. Hollis frankly describes how Evatt dominates Lloyd, who is 'desperately weak', and the CIB, the personnel of which are of a pretty poor calibre, and how there is, consequently, a serious risk that the CIB is being and will be used for political work that Hollis adamantly tells Liddell 'we don't want to be involved'.

45 Minute DNI, W.E. Parry, to the DMI, Assistant Chief of the Air Staff (Intelligence), DG Security service and Director JIB, 17 October 1946, and signal from High Commissioner for Canada in Australia, 27 May 1947, KV4/454, NA, UK.

46 Signal Dominions Office, 17 April 1947, KV4/454, NA, UK.

47 Letter, Percy Sillitoe to Sir John Stephenson, 7 March 1947, KV4/454, NA, UK.

48 Letter, Courtenay Young to Rowland Browne, 6 January 1947, KV4/454, NA, UK.

49 B Division Instruction from D.G. White, January 1947, KV4/454, NA, UK.

50 Minute B.3b, by Courtenay Young, 4 December 1946, KV4/454, NA, UK.

51 Minute B.3, by A.J. Keller, 13 December 1946, KV4/454, NA, UK.

52 Minute B.3b, by Courtenay Young, 4 December 1946, KV4/454, NA, UK.

53 Letter, Sillitoe to Sir John Stephenson, 7 March 1947, KV4/454, NA, UK.

54 Benson, *The Venona Story*, p. 2.

55 A6991, AS3/1, section 6, Missing Documents: Secret Defence Information, BC42862, NAA.

56 Transcript of Evidence, Sir Charles Spry, 27 February 1976, p. 613, BC4751094, NAA.

57 Transcript of Evidence, Sir Charles Spry, 27 February 1976, p. 613, BC4751094, NAA.

58 P. Hruby, *Dangerous Dreamers*, iUniverse, Bloomington, NY, 2010, p. 5.

59 Folio 13, BC424862, NAA.

60 Letter, Shedden to Burton, 7 April 1948, BC424862, NAA.

61 Hruby, *Dangerous Dreamers*, p. 7.

62 Hruby, *Dangerous Dreamers*, pp. 3–46.

63 Letter, Courtenay Young to D. White, 24 August 1946, KV4/454, NA, UK, and letter, Sillitoe to C, Sir Stewart Menzies, 8 March 1948, KV4/450, NA, UK. All the way through the whole affair of 'the Case', MI6 sat in the background pushing MI5 to force Australia towards establishing an effective security organisation.

64 Letter, Attlee to Chifley, 21 January 1948, KV4/450, NA, UK.

65 Undated and unsent minute referencing 'the reports which Chifley promised', KV4/451, NA, UK.

66 Draft Material for the Purpose of Sir Percy Sillitoe's Visit to Australia, 15 January 1948, and Cover Story B, undated, KV4/450, NA, UK.

67 Brief Account of Meeting of Sir Percy Sillitoe with USCIB, 2 June 1948, p. 1, KV4/451, NA, UK.

68 Signal, London to Melbourne, 17 February 1948, Signal to Hollis, 3 March 1948, letter Guy Liddell to C, 3 March 1948, and signal to Melbourne, 4 March 1948, KV4/450, NA, UK.

69 Letter, from Sillitoe, 25 February 1948, precis 8 March 1948, KV4/450, NA, UK.

70 Extract from Reports Volunteered by Defector X, 15 January 1948, and Cover Story B, undated, KV4/450, NA, UK.

71 Brief Account of Meeting of Sir Percy Sillitoe with USCIB, 2 June 1948, p. 1, KV4/451, NA, UK.

72 Brief Account of Meeting of Sir Percy Sillitoe with USCIB, 2 June 1948, p. 2, KV4/451, NA, UK.

73 Brief Account of Meeting of Sir Percy Sillitoe with USCIB, 2 June 1948, p. 2, KV4/451, NA, UK.

74 Minute, Hollis, 22 June 1948, KV4/451, NA, UK. In this minute Hollis makes it very clear that the US suspicions of Australian security had originated during the war. The concerns of the US Navy's OP-20-G, Rudy Fabian and FRUMEL had come home to roost.

75 Undated signal from Chairman LSIC to Chairman USCIB, KV4/451, NA, UK.

76 Undated signal from Chairman LSIC to Chairman USCIB, KV4/451, NA, UK.

77 Signal, SLO Washington to Chairman, LSIC, DTG 081548z/5/48, KV4/451, NA, UK.

78 Signal 293 to UKREP Canberra, 14 May 1948, KV4/451, NA, UK.

79 Letter, Percy Sillitoe to UK High Commissioner in Canberra, 25 May 1948, KV4/451, NA, UK.

80 Letter, Sir Harold Orme Sergeant to Sir Oliver Franks, 26 May 1948, KV4/451, NA, UK.

81 Signal, Washington for Liddell, 1 June 1948, KV4/451, NA, UK.

82 Undated draft note by Sillitoe, KV4/451, NA, UK.

83 Undated draft note by Sillitoe, KV4/451, NA, UK.

84 Signal, DG to Liddell, 2 June 1948, KV4/451, NA, UK.

85 Signal, DS/138, 5 June 1948, KV4/451, NA, UK.

86 Signal, Washington to Liddell, 15 June 1948, KV4/451, NA, UK.

87 Letter, Chifley to Attlee, 7 June 1948, KV4/451, NA, UK.

88 Letter, Chifley to Prime Minister Attlee, 7 June 1948, KV4/451, NA, UK.

89 Minute, Hollis, 22 June 1948, KV4/451, NA, UK.

90 Minute, Hollis, 22 June 1948, KV4/451, NA, UK.

91 Signal, War Office to Army Staff, Washington, 24 June 1948, KV4/451, NA, UK.

92 Signal, War Office to Army Staff, Washington, 24 June 1948, KV4/451, NA, UK.

93 Signal, Army Staff, Washington to War Office, 23 June 1948, KV4/451, NA, UK.

94 Signal, General Morgan to VCIGS, SF/53/24/4, KV4/451, NA, UK.

95 Signal 13151GI, FARELF to War Office, DTG 051400GH, July 48, KV4/451, NA, UK.

96   Letter, Dick White to Roger Hollis, 25 June 1948, KV4/451, NA, UK.
97   Signal, Washington for Director, DTG 191937z/6/48, KV4/451, NA, UK.
98   Minute, Hollis, 8 June 1948, KV4/451, NA, UK.
99   Draft Brief, 5 July 1948, KV4/451, NA, UK.
100 Andrew, *Defence of the Realm*, p. 370.
101 Brief for DG's Meeting Talk with Mr Chifley, 12 July 1948, and B1 Minute, Hollis, 13 July 1948, KV4/451, NA, UK.
102 Signal, Hollis Canberra to DG, 2 August 1948, KV4/451, NA, UK.
103 Letter, Hollis to Sillitoe, 11 August 1948, KV4/451, NA, UK.
104 Letter, Hollis to Sillitoe, 11 August 1948, KV4/451, NA, UK.
105 Letter, Hollis to Sillitoe, 11 August 1948, KV4/451, NA, UK.
106 http://nla.gov.au/nla.obj-340342029/findingaid, accessed 27 July 2019.
107 Hasluck, *Diplomatic Witness*, p. 15.
108 Hasluck, *Diplomatic Witness*, p. 15.
109 Hasluck, *Diplomatic Witness*, p. 15.
110 'Missionary's Son is Now Man of the Hour', *The Argus*, 28 March 1951, p. 6.
111 Hasluck, *Diplomatic Witness*, p. 15.
112 Hasluck, *Diplomatic Witness*, pp. 35–6.
113 Letter, Hollis to Sillitoe, 11 August 1948, KV4/451, NA, UK.
114 Hasluck, *Diplomatic Witness*, pp. 15–16.
115 In the development of an individual from being a friendly contact to an agent, the 'pitch' is the act that locks the individual into clandestine work. The danger lies in how the individual reacts. See US Department of Defence, *Hostile Intelligence Threat—US Technology*, DoD 5200.1-PH-2, November 1988.
116 Hasluck, *Diplomatic Witness*, pp. 5–8, 30–2.
117 Letter, Hollis to Sillitoe, 11 August 1948, KV4/451, NA, UK.
118 Letter, Hollis to Sillitoe, 11 August 1948, KV4/451, NA, UK.
119 Letter, Hollis to Sillitoe, 11 August 1948, KV4/451, NA, UK.
120 Letter, Hollis to Sillitoe, 11 August 1948, KV4/451, NA, UK.
121 Letter, Hollis to Sillitoe, 11 August 1948, KV4/451, NA, UK.
122 Letter, Hollis to Sillitoe, 11 August 1948, KV4/451, NA, UK.
123 Letter, Hollis to Sillitoe, 11 August 1948, KV4/451, NA, UK.
124 Letter, Hollis to Sillitoe, 11 August 1948, KV4/451, NA, UK.
125 Letter, Hollis to Sillitoe, 15 August 1948, KV4/451, NA, UK.
126 Signal, Hollis to DG, 26 August 1948, KV4/451, NA, UK.
127 Letter, C to Sillitoe, 30 August 1948, KV4/451, NA, UK.
128 Signal, DG to Hollis, 2 September 1948, KV4/451, NA, UK.
129 Letter, Hollis to Sillitoe, 28 August 1948, KV4/451, NA, UK.
130 Letter, Hollis to Sillitoe, 28 August 1948, KV4/451, NA, UK.
131 Letter, Hollis to Sillitoe, 28 August 1948, KV4/451, NA, UK.
132 Letter, Hollis to Sillitoe, 28 August 1948, KV4/451, NA, UK.
133 Letter, Hollis to Sillitoe, 28 August 1948, KV4/451, NA, UK.
134 Letter, Hollis to Sillitoe, 28 August 1948, KV4/451, NA, UK.
135 Letter, Hollis to Sillitoe, 8 September 1948, KV4/451, NA, UK.
136 Letter, Hollis to Sillitoe, 28 August 1948, KV4/451, NA, UK.
137 Letter, Hollis to Sillitoe, 28 August 1948, KV4/451, NA, UK.
138 Letter, Hollis to Sillitoe, 9 September 1948, KV4/451, NA, UK.
139 Letter, Hollis to Sillitoe, 8 September 1948, KV4/451, NA, UK.
140 Letter, Hollis to Sillitoe, 17 September 1948, KV4/451, NA, UK.

141 Letter, Hollis to Sillitoe, 17 September 1948, KV4/451, NA, UK.
142 Letter, Hollis to Sillitoe, 17 September 1948, KV4/451, NA, UK.
143 Letter, Hollis to Sillitoe, 17 September 1948, KV4/451, NA, UK.
144 Minute by Hollis for Sillitoe, 29 September 1948, KV4/451, NA, UK.
145 Letter, Hemblys Scales to Sillitoe, 11 November 1948, KV4/451, NA, UK.
146 Signal, Washington to DB, 7 January 1949, KV4/451, NA, UK.
147 Letter, Sillitoe to C, 1 January 1949, KV4/451, NA, UK.
148 Letter, President Truman to Attlee, 2 February 1949, KV4/451, NA, UK.
149 Signal, MANGO to DB, 24 February 1949, KV4/451, NA, UK.

Chapter 20: Sunlight

1   Letter, Hollis to Sillitoe, 23 February 1949, KV4/451, NA, UK.
2   A. Spaull, 'Dedman, John Johnstone', *ADB*.
3   Letter, Hollis to Sillitoe, 8 September 1948, KV4/451, NA, UK.
4   Spaull, 'Dedman, John Johnstone', *ADB*.
5   BC4725226, NAA.
6   Report on Visit to Australia, 4 January 1951, p.4, KV4/452, NA, UK.
7   A12389, The Circumstances Leading to the Establishment of ASIO—Documents 1–24, BC4725226, NAA.
8   BC4725226, NAA.
9   Transcript of Evidence Sir Charles Spry, 27 February 1976, p. 610, BC4751094, NAA.
10 BC4725226, NAA.
11 BC4725226, NAA.
12 BC4725226, NAA.
13 BC4725226, NAA.
14 Letter, Hollis to Sillitoe, 17 September 1948, KV4/451, NA, UK.
15 Report on Visit to Australia, 4 January 1951, p. 4, KV4/452, NA, UK.
16 Reed, *Outline*, 30 January 1950, pp. 11–12, BC4725226, NAA.
17 Transcript of Evidence, Sir Charles Spry, 27 February 1976, p. 610, BC4751094, NAA.
18 Transcript of Evidence, Sir Charles Spry, 27 February 1976, p. 610, BC4751094, NAA.
19 Report on Visit to Australia, 4 January 1951, p. 4, KV4/452, NA, UK.
20 BC4725226, NAA.
21 BC4725226, NAA.
22 BC4725226, NAA.
23 Letter, Courtenay Young to Sillitoe, 4 July 1949, KV4/451, NA, UK.
24 Letter, Courtenay Young to Sillitoe, 4 July 1949, KV4/451, NA, UK, and Horner, *The Spy Catchers*, p. 106.
25 Extract from Note following DB's Discussions in Australia, 31 January 1950, KV4/452, NA, UK.
26 Transcript of Evidence, Sir Charles Spry, 27 February 1976, BC4751094, NAA.
27 Transcript of Evidence, Sir Charles Spry, 27 February 1976, p. 610, BC4751094, NAA.
28 Reed, *Outline*, 30 January 1950, p. 27, BC4725226, NAA.
29 Folio 160, BC4725226, NAA.
30 Report on Visit to Australia, 4 January 1951, p. 5, KV4/452, NA, UK.
31 Report on Visit to Australia, 4 January 1951, p. 5, KV4/452, NA, UK.
32 Folio 18, BC1067010, NAA.
33 Briefing Paper, 21 December 1948, BC994003, NAA.
34 Horner, *The Spy Catchers*, p. 132.

35 Horner, *The Spy Catchers*, p. 132.

36 Letter, Courtenay Young to Sillitoe, 6 January 1950, KV4/452, NA, UK, and Horner, *The Spy Catchers*, p. 134. The story in the official history is entirely within the character of Wake and not the character of Young who was alert to the need not to become involved in the petty political games played in Australia. The MI5 file, KV4/452, clearly shows Young said nothing other than as a British representative, it was not his place to comment. Behaviour like this is why observers like Spry thought Wake slightly crazy.

37 Letter, Courtenay Young to Sillitoe, 6 January 1950, KV4/452, NA, UK.

38 Transcript of Evidence, Sir Charles Spry, 27 February 1976, p. 610, BC4751094, NAA.

39 Transcript of Evidence, Sir Charles Spry, 27 February 1976, p. 616, BC4751094, NAA.

40 Transcript of Evidence, Sir Charles Spry, 27 February 1976, p. 616, BC4751094, NAA. If Spry had been less concerned about Reed and taken action against Wake it might have led to Reed's removal from the Supreme Court of South Australia.

41 Letter, Courtenay Young to Sillitoe, 12 January 1950, KV4/452, NA, UK. At this meeting Menzies was not indoctrinated into SIGINT. That was done later that week by the Minister for Defence; however, Reed was told to treat Menzies as if he had been indoctrinated on the source for the Case and provide him a full briefing. See letter, Sillitoe to C, 6 February 1950, KV4/452, NA, UK.

42 Letter, Courtenay Young to Sillitoe, 9 January 1950, KV4/452, NA, UK.

43 Andrew, *The Defence of the Realm*, pp. 378–88.

44 Horner, *The Spy Catchers*, p. 142.

45 Horner, *The Spy Catchers*, p. 142.

46 Minute B2c, A.S. Martin, 26 April 1950, KV4/452, NA, UK.

47 Extract from letter, Courtenay Young to Sillitoe, 6 March 1950, KV4/452, NA, UK.

48 Signal 314, 7 July 1950, SLO, Australia, Courtenay Young for DG, KV4/452, NA, UK.

49 Transcript of Evidence, Sir Charles Spry, 27 February 1976, p. 619, BC4751094, NAA.

50 Folio 18, BC1067019, NAA.

51 Folio 18, BC1067019, NAA.

52 Folio 20, BC1067019, NAA.

53 Transcript of Evidence, Sir Charles Spry, 27 February 1976, p. 618, BC4751094, NAA.

BIBLIOGRAPHY

Records

NAA

AAAAA

A1, 1904/7830, BC2001.
A1, 1909, 12239, BC5367.
A1, 1911/19743, BC12184.
A1, 1913/9176, BC15655.
A1, 1914/24363, BC32089.
A1, 1915/10455, BC33022.
A1, 1921/2322, BC39551.
A1, 1923/8359, BC43185.
A1, 1924/30649, BC43659.
A1, 1933/792, BC1123987, Munz.
A2, 1918/877, BC48075.
A367, C94121, BC65290.
A367, C62490, BC781312.
A367, C23512 Part 1, BC764264.
A367, C172000, BC775888.
A373, 1272, BC65344.
A373, 1681, BC65354.
A373, 3149, BC65399.
A373, 4522B, BC65442.
A373, 7831, BC272808.
A374, 1, BC65666.
A400, 1, BC65724.
A432, 1936/1360, BC72470.
A432, 1943/1139, BC73138.
A432, 1945/875 PART 3, BC734697.
A432, 1955/4429, BC1110736.
A432, 1955/4432, BC1110955.
A433, 1942/2/2815, BC209208.
A456, W26/241/45, BC76534.
A456, W26/241/84, BC76552.
A461, BZ6/1/1 Part 1, BC91491.
A467, SF42/321, BC99425.
A467, SF43/1, NAA BC99427.

A467, SF43/26, BC99448.
A467, SF43/19, BC99444.
A467, SF43/39, BC99461.
A467, SF43/13, BC99438.
A467, SF43/38, BC99460.
A467, SF43/40, BC99462.
A664, 479/401/299, BC161618.
A472, W5107, BC100789.
A472, W29728 PART 1, BC333541.
A472, W29728 PART 2, BC396448.
A816, 25/301/76, BC170437.
A816, 31/301/21, BC170613.
A1194, 15.19/5612, BC4039793.
A1136, 2656, BC9598122.
A1336, 22357, BC3503440.
A1608, G39/2/1, BC206047.
A1608, S39/2/3/, BC274835.
A1632, 1, Part 2, BC4994275.
A2671, 24/1945, BC7564965.
A2700, 935, BC5393481.
A2703, 1946–1946, BC227921.
A2863, 1920/22, BC228711.
A3932, SC294, BC237172.
A3932, SC298, BC275070.
A3978, MUNZ H, BC30926355.
A5954, 427/3, BC648984.
A5954, 429/15, BC640278.
A5954, 803/1, BC689081.
A5954, 803/2, BC689088.
A5954, 849/A, BC950483.
A5954, 1203/6, BC694183.
A6119, 794, BC12095329.
A6119, 799, BC12095341.
A6119, 925, BC994003.
A6119, 953, BC12234352.

A6119, 955, BC8334740.
A6119, 1248/REFERENCE COPY, BC1116109.
A6119, 1597, BC1327922.
A6119, 2216, BC1829155.
A6119, 2217, BC1829162.
A6119, 2853, BC4025406.
A6122, 1428, BC1067010.
A6122, 2715, BC1368165.
A6769. MUNZ, H, BC5332357.
A6923, 37/401/425, BC3023506.
A6923, SI/10, BC3023487.
A7359, BOX 4/MS200/23, BC1134482.
A7359/84, BOX 10/17 Part 1, BC1866560.
A7359/84, BOX 10/17 Part 2, BC30944654.
A8510, 190/1, BC3139189.
A8908, 7A, BC4727814.
A8908, 7A, BC795990.
A8911, 46, BC821420.
A8911, 129, BC821578.
A8911, 130, BC821583.
A8913, 3/1/13, BC4751094.
A9650, Folder 1, BC1173011.
A12389, A13 PART 1, BC4725226.
A12393, 7/99, BC4727772.
AA1981/132, 1, BC217054.
Ap501/2, BC2015386, NAA.
AWM62, 97/3/74, BC3476135.
AWM62, 97/3/75, BC3476138.
B741, V/71, BC395800.
B741, V/3426, BC109644.
B883, SX11231, Sandford AW, BC6389615.
B884, N60119, Powell, Reginald, N60119, BC5601022.
B884, V350815, BC6261368, Milner.
B1535, 736/15/335, BC378141.
B197, 1877/5/15, BC416253.
B2455, BC8030333.
B3476, 49C, Commander E Feldt, Reports, BC508663.
B4747, Wake, Robert, BC9321799.
BP4/1, 66/4/3660, BC335787.
BP4/2, DISTRICT 1, BC4384184.
BP4/3, RUSSIAN SOOSENKO AM, BC9066713.
BP230/12 1, BC338073.
BP361/1, 12/1/11 PART 2, BC337326.
CP000/0/1/3, BC12054874.
CP46/2 24, BC246073.
CP290/9, 1, BC257486.

CP290/9, 13, BC257498.
CP359/3, 1, Personal Papers of Prime Minister Hughes, BC258026.
J1795, 2/255, Wake, Robert, BC12147809.
J1795, 6/522, Wake, Robert, BC9094137.
J2773, 713/1929, BC3066606.
J3116, 93, BC5058145.
MP84/1, 1849/2/13, BC324142.
MP84/1, 1877/5/5, BC331612.
MP84/1, 1902/7/47A, BC331919.
MP472/1, 1/18/2935, BC378656.
MP472/1, 1/19/7747, BC374729.
MP729/8, 41/431/136, BC1010436.
MP742/1, 175/1/81, BC392061.
MP1103/2, PWN1132, BC9902448.
MT1487/1, BC6044592.
PP246/4, RUSSIAN/MIKHEEV V, MIKHEEV, BC3437986.
SP43/2, N59/21/962, BC449358.

UK OFFICIAL RECORDS
The London Gazette
CAB 24/4/23
CAB 24/8/23
CAB 24/34/9
CAB 24/44/51
CAB 24/54/30
CAB 24/111/4
CAB 38/19/59
CAB 38/25/38
CAB 38/25/38
CAB 65/1/32
CAB 65/7/39
CAB 66/1/27
CAB 66/10/1
CAB 67/3/55
CAB 67/3/55
HW 52/93
KV2/1016, Ewer, William Norman, Vol. 4
KV2/1655, Far Eastern Fur Trading Company
KV4/18
KV4/450
KV4/451
KV4/452
KV4/453, Vol. 1
KV4/453, Vol. 2
KV4/454
KV 5/454, Vol. 2
WO106/4847

US OFFICIAL RECORDS

A1/27, 5500/1 FRUMEL (Fleet Radio Unit, Melbourne, Australia) SECURITY, NAI6230486A1, 1904/1037, BC2001, Declassification Authority 003012, National Archives, College Park, MD

JSC 86/1, Agreement between OSS and SOE, 26 August 1942, A7-2, CINCPAC FILES 1943, Censorship, declassification No. NND745002, National Archives, College Park, MD

Massachusetts Institute of Technology, AFSOR 70-1139 TR, *Biographical Index of Soviet Intelligence Personnel*, Appendix C, Soviet Clandestine Communication Nets, Behavioral Science Division, Air Force Office of Scientific Research, SRLB

United States, Library of Congress, http://id.loc.gov/rwo/agents/nb2013012495.html, accessed 6 January 2019

United States, Library of Congress, http://id.loc.gov/rwo/agents/nb2013012495.html, accessed 6 January 2019

VENONA documents, www.nsa.gov/news-features/declassified-documents/venona/

Official publications

AUSTRALIA

Commonwealth of Australia, Statutory Rules 1939, No. 87, National Security (General) Regulations, Regulation 26, (1), (a), (b) and (c)

Commonwealth of Australia, *Crimes Act 1914*, www.legislation.gov.au/Details/C2020C00012, accessed 15 February 2020

Cutlack, F.M., *The Australian Flying Corps in the Western and Eastern Theatres of War 1914–1918*, Vol. VIII, *Official History of Australia in the War of 1914–1918*, Angus & Robertson, Sydney, 1933

Dookie College records

Fitz-Gibbon B. and M. Gizycki, M., *A History of Last Resort Lending and Other Support for Troubled Financial Institutions in Australia*, Research Discussion Paper, 2001–17, Reserve Bank of Australia, Sydney, October 2001

Government Gazette of New South Wales

Hasluck, P., *The Government and the People, 1939–1941*, Vol. 1, Series 4—Civil, *Australia in the War of 1939–1945*, AWM, Canberra, 1965

Hasluck, P., *The Government and the People, 1942–1945*, Vol. 2, Series 4—Civil, *Australia in the War of 1939–1945*, AWM, Canberra, 1970

Horner, D.M., *The Spy Catchers*, Vol. 1, *The Official History of ASIO 1949–1963*, Allen & Unwin, Sydney, 2014

Long, G., *To Benghazi*, Vol. 1, Series 1—Army, *Australia in the War of 1939–1945*, AWM, Canberra, 1961

Scott, E., *Australia During the War*, Vol. XI, *Official History of Australia in the War of 1914–1918*, Angus & Robertson, Sydney, 1936

Wigmore, L.G., *The Japanese Thrust*, Series 1—Army, Vol. 4, *Australia in the War of 1939–1945*, AWM, Canberra, 1957

Year Book Australia, No. 1, 1908

Year Book, Australia, 1939

OFFICIAL AUSTRALIAN ONLINE

www.australianpolice.com.au/nsw-police-history-index/police-commissioners-of-nsw/william-john-MacKay/, accessed 20 December 2015

www.awm.gov.au/encyclopedia/prime_ministers/menzies/, accessed 24 December 2015

Birth Registration Number 1385/1914, https://familyhistory.bdm.nsw.gov.au/lifelink/family history/search/result?4, accessed 12 June 2019
www.comlaw.gov.au/Details/C2004C07843, accessed 20 December 2015
https://legalopinions.ags.gov.au/opinionauthor/knowles-george-shaw, accessed 18 March 2019
www.naa.gov.au/collection/snapshots/internment-camps/introduction.aspx, accessed 3 March 2019
http://prov.vic.gov.au, Index to Inward Passenger Lists to Victoria 1852–1923, accessed 3 January 2019
http://search-cloudfront.records.nsw.gov.au/agencies/1222, accessed 20 December 2015
War Precautions Act 1914, Section 4, https://www.legislation.gov.au/Details/C1914A00010, accessed 1 January 2019

UNITED KINGDOM
Andrew, C., *The Defence of the Realm: The Authorized History of MI5*, Allen Lane, London, 2009
Hinsley, F.H. and Simkins, C.A.G., *British Intelligence in the Second World War*, Vol. 4, *Security and Counter-Intelligence*, Cambridge University Press, New York, 1990
The London Gazette

US
Benson, R.L., *The Venona Story*, Center for Cryptologic History, National Security Agency, Fort Meade, MD, 2012
Committee on Un-American Activities, US House of Representatives, *The Shameful Years: Thirty years of Soviet espionage in the United States*, United States Government Printing Office, Washington, 1952
Maneki, S.A., *The Quiet Heroes of the Southwest Pacific Theater: An oral history of the men and women of CBB and FRUMEL*, Center for Cryptologic History, NSA, Fort Meade, MD, 2007

OFFICIAL US ONLINE
www.cia.gov/library/center-for-the-study-of-intelligence/csi-publications/books-and-monographs/venona-soviet-espionage-and-the-american-response-1939–1957/preface.htm, accessed 10 July 2019
www.nsa.gov/Portals/70/documents/news-features/declassified-documents/venona/dated/1942/31dec_naval_gru.pdf, accessed 12 June 2019

Newspapers and periodicals
The Advertiser, Adelaide
The Age, Melbourne
The Argus, Melbourne
Bendigo Advertiser
Brisbane Courier
Cairns Post
Canberra Times
The Courier-Mail, Brisbane
Cumberland Argus and Fruitgrowers Advocate
Daily Advertiser, Wagga Wagga
Daily Commercial News and Shipping List, Sydney
Daily News, Perth
Daily Standard, Brisbane

Daily Telegraph, Sydney
Evening News, Rockhampton
Evening News, Sydney
Geelong Advertiser
The Herald, Melbourne
Kalgoorlie Miner
Maitland Daily News
Maryborough Chronicle, Wide Bay and Burnett Advertiser
The Mercury, Hobart
Morning Bulletin, Rockhampton
National Advocate, Bathurst
Northern Herald
The Propeller, Hurstville
The Publicist
Singleton Argus
Smith's Weekly, Sydney
The Socialist, Melbourne
South Australian Register, Adelaide
Soviet Russia
The Sun, Sydney
Sunday Mail, Brisbane
Sydney Morning Herald
The Telegraph, Brisbane
West Australian
Truth, Brisbane
Truth, Sydney
The Workers' Weekly, Sydney

Personal interviews/correspondence

Richard Mawhood, 28 December 2015
Richard Mawhood, 2 January 2016

Personal papers

Novar Papers, MS696, Series 4, Items 901, 902 and 903, quoted in J.T. McPhee, 'Spinning the
    Secrets of State: The History and Politics of Intelligence Politicisation in Australia', PhD
    thesis (unpublished), RMIT University, June 2015, p. 147
Papers of Atlee Hunt, NLA MS52/24,25,26/1287–1336, Folder 28
Papers of Atlee Hunt, NLA MS52/7/611–634, Folder 12
Papers of Atlee Hunt, NLA, MS52/8/635–716, Folder 13

Australian Dictionary of Biography

National Centre of Biography, Australian National University, *ADB* entries:
Anderson, J. and Serle, G., 'Watt, William Alexander (1871–1946)', http://adb.anu.edu.au/
    biography/watt-william-alexander-9011/text15869, accessed 27 July 2019
Beddie, B., 'Pearce, Sir George Foster (1870–1952)', http://adb.anu.edu.au/biography/pearce-
    sir-george-foster-7996, accessed 24 January 2014

Bolton, G.C., 'Evatt, Herbert Vere (Bert) (1894–1965)', http://adb.anu.edu.au/biography/evatt-herbert-vere-bert-10131, accessed 27 July 2019

Cain, F., 'MacKay, William John (1885–1948)', http://adb.anu.edu.au/biography/mackay-william-john-7381, accessed 27 July 2019

Cunneen, C., 'Steward, Charles Thomas (1865–1920)', http://adb.anu.edu.au/biography/steward-sir-george-charles-thomas-8657/text15137, accessed 24 February 2020

Farrell, F., 'Freeman, Paul (1884–1921)', http://adb.anu.edu.au/biography/freeman-paul-6245, accessed 24 February 2020

Gill, J.C.H., 'Feldt, Eric Augustas (1899–1968)', http://adb.anu.edu.au/biography/feldt-eric-augustas-10163, accessed 27 July 2019

Haldane, R., 'Duncan, Alexander Mitchell (1888–1965)', http://adb.anu.edu.au/biography/duncan-alexander-mitchell-10062, accessed 1 January 2016

Heenan, T., 'Milner, Ian Frank (1911–1991)', http://adb.anu.edu.au/biography/milner-ian-frank-16424, accessed 27 July 2019

Lamont, R., 'Thring, Walter Hugh Charles Samuel (1873–1949)', http://adb.anu.edu.au/biography/thring-walter-hugh-charles-samuel-8804, accessed 23 June 2014

Lorch, J., 'Carboni, Raffaello (1817–1875)', http://adb.anu.edu.au/biography/carboni-raffaello-3163, accessed 27 July 2019

Meaney, N.K., 'Piesse, Edmund Leolin (1880–1947)', http://adb.anu.edu.au/biography/piesse-edmund-leolin-8046, accessed 27 July 2019

Moore, A., 'Scott, William John (1888–1956)', http://adb.anu.edu.au/biography/scott-william-john-8373, accessed 27 July 2019

Parker, R.S., 'Garran, Sir Robert Randolph (1867–1957)', http://adb.anu.edu.au/biography/garran-sir-robert-randolph-410, accessed 27 July 2019

Perkins, J., 'Becker, Johannes Heinrich (1898–1961)', http://adb.anu.edu.au/biography/becker-johannes-heinrich-9467, accessed 27 July 2019

Sadleir, D., 'Lloyd, Eric Edwin Longfield (1890–1957)', http://adb.anu.edu.au/biography/lloyd-eric-edwin-longfield-10840, accessed 27 July 2019

Spaull, A., 'Dedman, John Johnstone (1896–1973)', http://adb.anu.edu.au/biography/dedman-john-johnstone-303, accessed 14 July 2019

Stevenson, R., 'Reed, Sir Geoffrey Sandford (1892–1970)', http://adb.anu.edu.au/biography/reed-sir-geoffrey-sandford-11495, accessed 27 July 2019

Templeton, J., 'Jones, Harold Edward (1878–1965)', http://adb.anu.edu.au/biography/jones-harold-edward-6873, accessed 27 July 2019

Whitlam, E.G., 'Knowles, Sir George Shaw (1882–1947)', http://adb.anu.edu.au/biography/knowles-sir-george-shaw-6987, accessed 27 July 2019

Winter, B., 'Long, Rupert Basil Michel (1899–1960)', http://adb.anu.edu.au/biography/long-rupert-basil-michel-10858, accessed 27 July 2019

Books

Alanbrooke, Field Marshall Lord, *War Diaries 1939–1945*, A. Danchev and D. Todman (eds), Phoenix Press, London, 2002

Alvarez, D., *Allied and Axis Signals Intelligence in World War II*, Frank Cass, London, 1999

Andrew, C., *Secret Service: The making of the British Intelligence Community*, Heinemann, London, 1985

Ball, D. and Horner, D.M., *Breaking the Codes: Australia's KGB network*, Allen & Unwin, Sydney, 1998

Ballard, G.S., *On ULTRA Active Service: The story of Australia's Signals Intelligence Operations during World War II*, Spectrum Publications, Richmond, 1991

Best, A., *British Intelligence and the Japanese Challenge in Asia, 1914–1941*, Palgrave-Macmillan, Basingstoke, 2002

Booker, M., *The Great Professional: A study of W.M. Hughes*, McGraw Hill, Sydney, 1980

Burgmann, M. et al., *Dirty Secrets: Our ASIO files*, University of New South Wales Press, Sydney, 2014

Cain, F., *The Australian Security Intelligence Organisation: An unofficial history*, Frank Cass, Abingdon, 2005

Cappello, A., 'A brief survey of the Italian Catholic in Australia until the Second World War: An Italian problem', in A. Paganoni (ed.), *The Pastoral Care of Italians in Australia: Memory and prophecy*, Connor Court Publishing, Ballan, 2007

Casey, Lord, *Personal Experience: 1939–1946*, Constable, London, 1962

Cave Brown, A., *The Secret Servant: The life of Sir Stewart Menzies, Churchill's Spymaster*, Sphere Books, London, 1987

Childers, E., *The Riddle of the Sands*, Penguin Classics, Harmondsworth, 2011

Cresciani, G., 'The bogey of the Italian Fifth Column: Internment and the making of Italo-Australia', in R. Bosworth and R. Ugolinini (eds), *War, Internment and Mass Migration: The Italo-Australian experience 1940–1990*, Gruppo Editoriale Internazionale, Rome, 1992

Deacon, R., *A History of the Japanese Secret Service*, Frederick Muller, Wimbledon, 1982

Edwards, J., *John Curtin's War: The coming of war in the Pacific and reinventing Australia*, Penguin-Viking, Ringwood, 2017

Elkner, C., *Enemy Aliens*, Connor Court, Bacchus Marsh, 2005

Evans, R., *The Red Flag Riots: A study of intolerance*, University of Queensland Press, St Lucia, 1988

Fahey, J., *Australia's First Spies: The remarkable story of Australia's intelligence operations, 1901–1945*, Allen & Unwin, Sydney, 2018

Feldt, E., *The Coastwatchers*, Oxford University Press, Melbourne, 1946

Fitzgerald, R., 'Red Ted': The life of E.G. Theodore*, University of Queensland Press, St Lucia, 2002

Fitzhardinge, L.F., *William Morris Hughes: A political biography*, Vol. 1, *That Fiery Particle, 1862–1914*, Angus & Robertson, Sydney, 1964

Frost, A., *The Precarious Life of James Mario Matra*, Miegunyah Press, Carlton, 1995

Griffen-Foley, B., *Changing Stations: The story of Australian commercial radio*, UNSW Press, Sydney, 2009

Hasluck, P., *The Change of Politics*, Text Publishing Company, Melbourne, 1997

Hasluck, P., *Diplomatic Witness*, Melbourne University Press, Melbourne, 1980

Haynes, J.H., Klehr, H. and Vassiliev, A., *Spies: The rise and fall of the KGB in America*, Yale University Press, New Haven, CT, 2009

Hayward, J., *Double Agent Snow: The true story of Arthur Owens, Hitler's chief spy in England*, Simon & Schuster, London, 2013

Henderson, A., *Joseph Lyons: The People's Prime Minister*, NewSouth Publishing, Sydney, 2011

Hinsley, F.H. and Simkins, C.A.G., *British Intelligence in the Second World War*, Vol. 4, *Security and Counter-Intelligence*, Cambridge University Press, Cambridge, 1990

Horne, A., *To Lose a Battle: France 1940*, Penguin, London, 1969

Horner, D.M., *Crisis of Command: Australian generalship and the Japanese threat, 1941–1943*, Australian National University Press, Canberra, 1978

Hruby, P., *Dangerous Dreamers: The Australian anti-democratic Left and Czechoslovak agents*, iUniverse, Bloomington, NY, 2010

Kelly, V., *Man of the People: From boilermaker to Governor-General—A biography of Sir William McKell*, Alpha, Sydney, 1971

Killen, J., *Killen: Inside Australian politics*, Methuen Haynes, North Ryde, 1985

Kotani, K., *Japanese Intelligence in World War II*, Osprey Publishing, Oxford, 2009

Lodge, B., *Lavarack: Rival general*, Allen & Unwin, Sydney, 1998

Lovell, D.W. and Windle, K., *Our Unswerving Loyalty: A documentary survey of relations between the Communist Party of Australia and Moscow, 1920–1940*, ANU Press, Canberra, 2008

Maro, Publius Vergilius, *The Aeneid*, Book 6, Translated by Fairclough, H.R. and Goold, G.P., Loeb Classical Library, Harvard University Press, Cambridge, MA, 1999

Martin, A.W., *Robert Menzies: A life*, Vol. 1, *1894–1943*, Melbourne University Press, Melbourne, 1993

Menzies, R., *Afternoon Light: Some memories of men and events*, Cassell, Melbourne, 1967

Middlebrook, M. and Everitt, C., *The Bomber Command War Diaries: An operational reference book, 1939–1945*, Midland Publishing, East Shilton, Leicester, 1996

Mitrokhin, V. and Andrew, C., *The Mitrokhin Archive: The KGB in Europe and the West*, Allen Lane, Penguin Press, London, 1999

Moore, A., 'Policing enemies of the state: The New South Wales Police and the New Guard', in M. Finnane (ed.), *Policing in Australia: Historical perspectives*, University of NSW Press, Sydney, 1987

Niall, B., *Mannix*, Text Publishing, Melbourne, 2015

Saunders, K., '"Inspired by patriotic hysteria?": Internment policy towards enemy aliens in Australia during the Second World War', in Panikos Panyani (ed.), *Minorities in Wartime*, Bloomsbury, London, 2016

Schrantz, J., *The Reverend's Revenge*, Infinity Publishing Co, West Conshohocken, PA, 2005

Spencer Chapman, F., *The Jungle is Neutral*, The Reprint Society, London, 1950

Swanton, B. and Hannigan, G., *Police Source Book 2*, Australian Institute of Criminology, Canberra, 1985

Tsuji, M., *Singapore: The Japanese version*, trans Margaret E. Lake, St Martin's Press, New York, 1960

Usdin, S.T., *Engineering Communism: How two Americans spied for Stalin and founded the Soviet Silicon Valley*, Yale University Press, New Haven, CT, 2005

Wake, V.R., *No Ribbons or Medals*, Jacobyte Books, Adelaide, 2005

Wilkinson, N.J., *Secrecy and the Media: The official history of the United Kingdom's D-Notice*, Routledge, London, 2009

Windle, K., *Undesirable: Captain Zuzenko and the Workers of Australia and the World*, Australian Scholarly Publishing, North Melbourne, 2012

Winter, B., *The Most Dangerous Man in Australia*, Glass House Books, Brisbane, 2010

Winter, B., *The Intrigue Master: Commander Long and Naval Intelligence in Australia, 1913–1945*, Boolarong Press, Brisbane, 1995

Winterbotham, F.W., *The Ultra Secret*, Harper and Row, London, 1974

Articles and lectures

Cresciani, G., 'A not so brutal friendship: Italian responses to National Socialism in Australia', Migrazioni Italiane in Australia, Centro Altreitalie, Edizioni della Fondazione Giovanni Agnelli, Milano, 1984

Debo, R.K., 'Lloyd George and the Copenhagen Conference of 1919–1920: The initiation of Anglo-Soviet Negotiations', *The Historical Journal*, 1981, 24(2): 429–41

Evans, R., 'Murderous coppers: Police, industrial disputes and the 1929 Rothbury shootings', *History Australia*, 2012, 9(1): 176–200

Evans, R., '"A menace to this realm": The New Guard and the New South Wales Police, 1931–32', *History Australia*, 2008, 5(3): 76.1–76.20

Fox, Aaron, 'A formidable responsibility': The rise and fall of the New Zealand Security Intelligence Bureau 1940–1945, *Security and Surveillance History Series, 2018/1*, www.wgtn.ac.nz/__data/assets/pdf_file/0010/1675927/2018-1-A-Formidable-Responsibility-The-Rise-and-Fall-of-the-New-Zealand-Security-Intelligence-Bureau-1940-1945--Aaron-Fox,-2018.pdf, accessed 26 December 2019

Kirby, Hon. Justice M., 'Keynote address: The lessons of the Stuart Case', Elder Hall, University of Adelaide, 1 April 2006

Menghetti, D., 'Their country, not mine: The internments', Lecture to the Second Australian Conference on Italian Culture and Italy Today, Frederick May Foundation, University of Sydney, 6 August 1982

O'Connor, D., 'Viva il Duce: The influence of fascism on Italians in South Australia in the 1920s and 1930s', *Journal of the Historical Society of South Australia*, 1993, 21: 5–24

Pixley, N.S., 'Presidential address: Pearlers of North Australia—the romantic story of the diving fleets', Royal Historical Society of Queensland, 1972, https://espace.library.uq.edu.au/data/UQ_209190/s00855804_1971_1972_9_3_9.pdf, accessed 30 December 2018

Rando, G., 'Italo-Australians during the Second World War: Some perceptions of internment', *Studi d'Italianistica nell'Africa Australe*, 2005, 18(1): 20–51

Tosco, A., 'Features of early ethnic Italo-Australian newspapers: A case study of L'Italo-Australiao (1885)', *Italian Historical Society Journal*, 2005, 13(1–2): 9–25

Unpublished theses

Evans, R., 'William John MacKay and the NSW Police Force, 1910–1948: A study of police power', PhD thesis, Monash University, 2005

Fahey, J., 'Britain 1939–1945: The economic cost of strategic bombing', PhD thesis, University of Sydney, 2004

Horner, D.M., 'Australia and Allied Strategy in the Pacific 1941–1946', Vol. I, PhD thesis, Australian National University, 1980

Wharton, M.L., 'The Development of Security Intelligence in NZ, 1945–1957', MA thesis, Massey University, Manawatu, NZ, 2012

Other online sources

Ancestry.com, 'Gay Trick in the 1940 Census', www.ancestry.com/1940-census/usa/Washington/Gay-Trick_285v6h, accessed 13 June 2019

Community of Drum, 'The story of Fr James Coyle', https://web.archive.org/web/20101010181724/http://www.drum.ie/about/fr-james-coyle, accessed 7 January 2019

Long service medals from the collection formed by John Tamplin, www.dnw.co.uk/auction-archive/special-collections/lot.php?specialcollection_id=57&lot_id=67264, accessed 26 December 2015

Museums Victoria, 'Origins: Immigration history from Italy to Victoria', https://origins.museumsvictoria.com.au/countries/italy, accessed 23 February 2020

INDEX

Notes: All articles, ranks, titles and honorifics are ignored in filing.
Page numbers in *italics* refer to figures.

420

ULTRA 268–9, 296–7, 299, 308, 312–13
United Kingdom
  bans Australian access to classified material
    334
  enemy aliens in 98, 103
  forced to impose US sanctions 325–6
  government indiscretion with secret
    intelligence 237
  intelligence operations in Germany 102–3
  Leakage of Information Committee 97
  machinations over intelligence 94
  moves to counter Soviet propaganda 45
  opposes White Australia Policy 6
  overestimates German intelligence 96
  pushes for Commonwealth signals
    intelligence organisation 294
  Security Executive 101–2
  severs diplomatic ties with Russia 237
  Special Operations Executive 102–3, 122,
    124–5, 299
  suppresses Easter Rising 40
  War Office 113
  weapons testing in Australia 318
  see also Government Code and Cypher
    School (UK); MI5; MI6
United States 241–5, 324–6, 334
United States Army 174–7, 193, 246, 273,
    298, 311
United States Army, Navy and Air
    Co-ordinating Committee 326
United States Communications Intelligence
    Board 322, 326, 341
United States National Security Agency 245
United States Navy 298–9, 322–3, 326
  see also Fleet Radio Unit, Melbourne
United States Office of Strategic Services 299
United States Supreme Court 205
Urquhart, Frederic 53
USSR see Soviet Union

Vancouver 50–1
Vanuatu see New Hebrides
Venn, Lieutenant Colonel H.W.S. 112
VENONA
  access to jeopardised by Simpson 313
  breaks first Russian cipher 273
  ceases as an intelligence source 277
  Chifley informed of 322
  discloses effectiveness of Russian
    penetration 278
  Hollis sent to safeguard 327
  importance of Gardner's contribution 246
  Menzies indoctrinated into 343
  N-GRU officers compromised by 244–5

names of suspects passed on to CIB 323
  no mention of Melbourne cell in 283–4
  origin of 245
  provides intelligence on Clayton 253–4
  reads Eliacheff's report 249
  reads Makarov's signal to Moscow 271,
    319
  slow progress of 246
  uncovers NKGB interest in GRU 301
  uncovers role of RIS in compromising
    ULTRA 269
  Young declines to indoctrinate Wake into
    341
VENONA 101 270
Ventura (ship) 22
Victoria Police 60–1, 136, 190
Vitali, Commander 83
Vivian, Colonel Valentine 346
Vorontsov, Captain M.A. 242, 244
Vutkevich, Helge Leonidovich 300–1

Wade, Charles 40
Wake, Elizabeth 'Betty' 165
Wake, Lieutenant Colonel Robert Frederick
    Bird
  abuses position 158, 181, 350
  accumulates power 171
  accuses applicant of perversity 179
  allegations of underhandedness 163
  asked for information on The Publicist 212
  association with Combes 147
  attempts to penetrate Central Bureau 312
  attends early meetings of ASIO 338
  campaign to round up Italians 188–9
  character of 162, 170, 172
  checks status of Italians 78–9
  as CIB's inspector in Brisbane 78, 165–6,
    171–3
  collaborates with CP-A 181–2, 341
  conducts raids in Brisbane 171
  as deputy director of Security Service 172,
    175
  as a director of ASIO 340
  as director of Security Service 153–4, 297
  divorces 162–3
  early life 161
  ensconces himself in CIB 164–5
  entraps fellow officers 170, 176
  Eric Feldt on 168
  as Evatt's man in ASIO 338
  extra-legal activities of 116
  fails to return gun 180–1
  forms Field Security Section 138, 173
  fraud committed by 181–2, 344, 347

435